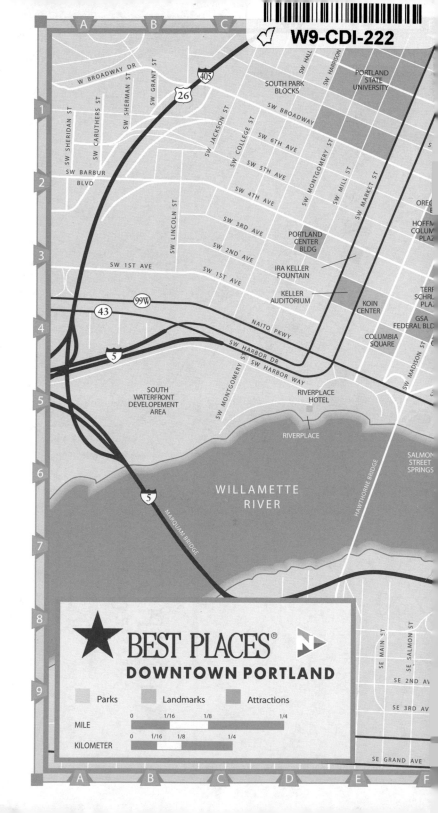

W9-CDI-222

BEST PLACES®
DOWNTOWN PORTLAND

Parks   Landmarks   Attractions

MILE
0   1/16   1/8   1/4

KILOMETER
0   1/16   1/8   1/4

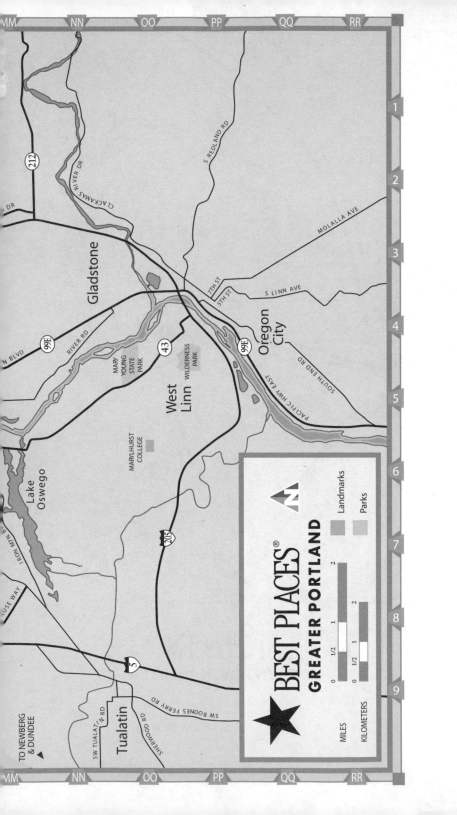

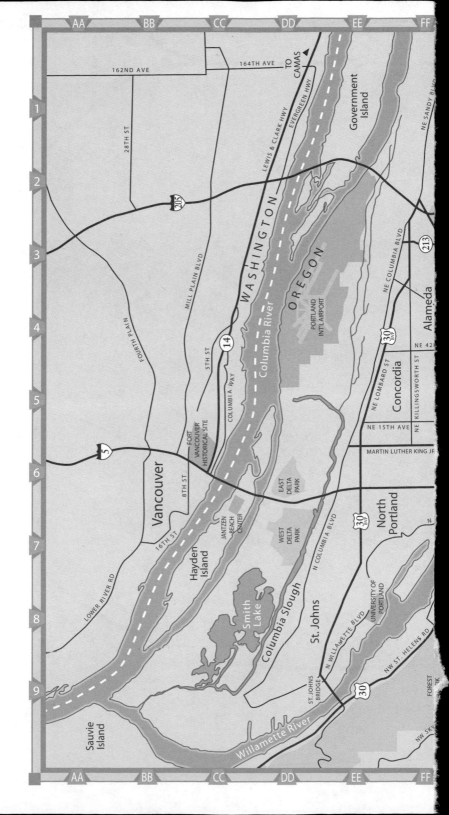

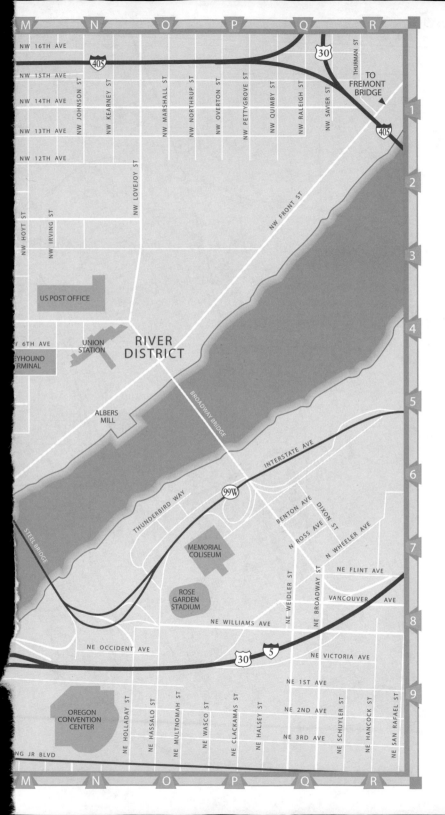

Praise for Best Places® Guidebooks

"Best Places *are the best regional restaurant and guide books in America.*"
—THE SEATTLE TIMES

"Best Places *covers must-see portions of the West Coast . . . with style and authority. In-the-know locals offer thorough info on restaurants, lodgings, and the sights.*"
—NATIONAL GEOGRAPHIC TRAVELER

"*. . . travelers swear by the recommendations in the* Best Places *guidebooks . . .*"
—SUNSET MAGAZINE

"*Known for their frank yet chatty tone . . .*"
—PUBLISHERS WEEKLY

"*For travel collections covering the Northwest, the* Best Places *series takes precedence over all similar guides.*"
—BOOKLIST

"*The best guide to Seattle is the locally published* Best Places Seattle *. . .*"
—JONATHAN RABAN, MONEY MAGAZINE

"*Whether you're a Seattleite facing the winter doldrums or a visitor wondering what to see next, guidance is close at hand in* Best Places Seattle."
—SUNSET MAGAZINE

"Best Places Seattle *remains one of the best, most straightforward urban guidebooks in the country.*"
—THE SEATTLE TIMES

"*This tome* [Best Places Seattle] *is one of the best practical guides to any city in North America.*"
—TRAVEL BOOKS WORLDWIDE

"*Visitors to Washington, Oregon, and British Columbia would do well to pick up* Best Places Northwest *for an exhaustive review of food and lodging in the region . . . An indispensable glove-compartment companion.*"
—TRAVEL AND LEISURE

TRUST THE LOCALS

The original insider's guides, written by local experts

COMPLETELY INDEPENDENT
- No advertisers
- No sponsors

EVERY PLACE STAR-RATED & RECOMMENDED

★★★★   The very best in the city

★★★   Distinguished; many outstanding features

★★   Excellent; some wonderful qualities

★   A good place

MONEY-BACK GUARANTEE
We're so sure you'll be satisfied, we guarantee it!

HELPFUL ICONS
Watch for these quick-reference symbols throughout the book:

 FAMILY FUN

 GOOD VALUE

 ROMANTIC

 EDITORS' CHOICE

BEST PLACES®

PORTLAND

The Locals' Guide to the Best Restaurants,
Lodgings, Sights, Shopping, and More!

Edited by
JOHN GOTTBERG

EDITION

SASQUATCH BOOKS
SEATTLE

Printed in the United States of America
Published by Sasquatch Books
Distributed by Publishers Group West

Sixth edition
12 11 10 09 08 07 06   6 5 4 3 2

ISBN: 1-57061-400-8
ISSN: 1095-9742

Cover illustration/photograph: Rick Schafer
Cover design: Nancy Gellos
Interior maps: GreenEye Design
Interior composition: Bill Quinby

SPECIAL SALES

Best Places guidebooks are available at special discounts on bulk purchases for corporate, club, or organization sales promotions, premiums, and gifts. Special editions, including personalized covers, excerpts of existing guides, and corporate imprints, can be created in large quantities for specific needs. For more information, contact your local bookseller or Special Sales, Best Places Guidebooks, 119 S Main Street, Suite 400, Seattle, Washington 98104, 800/775-0817.

SASQUATCH BOOKS
119 South Main Street, Suite 400
Seattle, WA 98104
(206) 467-4300
www.sasquatchbooks.com
custserv@sasquatchbooks.com

CONTENTS

Contributors and Acknowledgments

Portland is an urban center that national publications have designated the most livable big city in the United States. There is no shortage of great restaurants, stunning parks, unique attractions, fine hotels, and transportation options—not to mention an intriguing and growing arts scene. The question was not what to include in *Best Places Portland*. It was more difficult to keep the volume to a manageable size. This book could not have been produced without these people, our major contributors:

Nanine Alexander is a writer for the *Oregonian*.

Gail Dana is a freelance writer whose work regularly appears in the *Portland Tribune*, the *Business Journal, Yoga Northwest Magazine, Animal Fair,* and other local and national magazines and literary journals.

Guitarist and lead singer for the rock band Nordic, **Elizabeth Dye** also designs clothing and contributes articles to *Willamette Week* and *Portland* magazine.

Kathryn Kurtz is a freelance food and travel writer who writes regularly for the *Oregonian*. She leads small culinary groups to Thailand and Vietnam and teaches English to refugees.

Nancy Levenson is a writer at Curiosity, a creative agency in Portland. She also writes about spas, shopping, and nightlife for Citysearch.com, and is a contributor to *Best Places to Kiss in the Northwest*.

Christina Melander is a freelance food writer in Portland.

Terry Richard is a reporter for the Travel section of the *Oregonian*, where he specializes in outdoor recreation and regional travel destinations.

Julianne Shepherd is arts editrix of the *Portland Mercury* and a regular contributor to *Hit It or Quit It, Punk Planet, Alternative Press,* and more. She is currently writing a book about spirituality as expressed in album liner notes.

Special thanks are due Deborah Hall Wakefield and Gretchen Heilshorn of the Portland Oregon Visitor Association. Thanks also to Kim Carlson and Carrie Floyd, editors of previous editions of this book; Wm. Steve Humphrey of the *Portland Mercury*, Byron Beck and Caryn Brooks of *Willamette Week*, Michaela Lowthian of the *Portland Tribune*, David Sarasohn of the *Oregonian,* Jim Dixon of RealGoodFood.com, Bud Clark, John Harrington, Thomas Lauderdale, Julie Mikalson, and especially to Paige Powell and Bette Sinclair.

At Sasquatch Books, the driving forces behind this publication were managing editor Heidi Schuessler, Cassandra Mitchell, Terence Maikels, Suzanne DeGalan, and Kurt Stephan. Thanks also for the contributions of copy editor Julie Van Pelt, proofreader Amy Smith Bell, and designer Bill Quinby.

About Best Places® Guidebooks

People trust us. Best Places guidebooks, which have been published continuously since 1975, represent one of the most respected regional travel series in the country. Our reviewers know their territory and seek out the very best a city or region has to offer. We are able to provide tough, candid reports about places that have rested too long on their laurels, and to delight in new places that deserve recognition. We describe the true strengths, foibles, and unique characteristics of each establishment listed.

Best Places Portland is written by and for locals, and is therefore coveted by travelers. It's written for people who live here and who enjoy exploring the city's bounty and its out-of-the-way places of high character and individualism. It is these very characteristics that make Best Places Portland ideal for tourists, too. The best places in and around the city are the ones that denizens favor: independently owned establishments of good value, touched with local history, run by lively individuals, and graced with natural beauty. With this 6th edition of Best Places Portland, travelers will find the information they need: where to go and when, what to order, which rooms to request (and which to avoid), where the best music, art, nightlife, shopping, and other attractions are, and how to find the city's hidden secrets.

We're so sure you'll be satisfied with our guide, we guarantee it.

NOTE: *The reviews in this edition are based on information available at press time and are subject to change. Readers are advised that places listed in previous editions may have closed or changed management, or may no longer be recommended by this series. The editors welcome information conveyed by users of this book. Feedback is welcome via email: bestplaces@SasquatchBooks.com.*

How to Use This Book

This book is divided into twelve chapters covering a wide range of establishments, destinations, and activities in and around Portland. All evaluations are based on reports from local and traveling inspectors. Final judgments are made by the editors. **EVERY PLACE FEATURED IN THIS BOOK IS RECOMMENDED.**

STAR RATINGS *(for Top 200 Restaurants and Lodgings only)* Restaurants and lodgings are rated on a scale of one to four stars (with half stars in between), based on uniqueness, loyalty of local clientele, performance measured against the establishment's goals, excellence of cooking, cleanliness, value, and professionalism of service. Reviews are listed alphabetically, and every place is recommended.

BEST PLACES® STAR RATINGS

Any travel guide that rates establishments is inherently subjective—and Best Places is no exception. We rely on our professional experience, yes, but also on a gut feeling. And, occasionally, we even give in to a soft spot for a favorite neighborhood hangout. Our star-rating system is not simply a checklist; it's judgmental, critical, sometimes fickle, and highly personal.

For each new edition, we send local food and travel experts out to review restaurants and lodgings, and then to rate them on a scale of one to four, based on uniqueness, loyalty of local clientele, performance measured against the establishment's goals, excellence of cooking, cleanliness, value, and professionalism of service. That doesn't mean a one-star establishment isn't worth dining or sleeping at—far from it. When we say that all the places listed in our books are recommended, we mean it. That one-star pizza joint may be just the ticket for the end of a whirlwind day of shopping with the kids. But if you're planning something more special, the star ratings can help you choose an eatery or hotel that will wow your new clients or be a stunning, romantic place to celebrate an anniversary or impress a first date.

We award four-star ratings sparingly, reserving them for what we consider truly the best. And once an establishment has earned our highest rating, everyone's expectations seem to rise. Readers often write us letters specifically to point out the faults in four-star establishments. With changes in chefs, management, styles, and trends, it's always easier to get knocked off the pedestal than to ascend it. Three-star establishments, on the other hand, seem to generate healthy praise. They exhibit outstanding qualities, and we get lots of love letters about them. The difference between two and three stars can sometimes be a very fine line. Two-star establishments are doing a good, solid job and gaining attention, while one-star places are often dependable spots that have been around forever.

The restaurants and lodgings described in *Best Places Portland* have earned their stars from hard work and good service (and good food). They're proud to be included in this book—look for our Best Places sticker in their windows. And we're proud to honor them in this, the sixth edition of *Best Places Portland*.

★★★★ The very best in the region

★★★ Distinguished; many outstanding features

★★ Excellent; some wonderful qualities

★ A good place

UNRATED New or undergoing major changes

(For more on how we rate places, see the Best Places Star Ratings box on the previous page.)

PRICE RANGE *(for Top 200 Restaurants and Lodgings only)* Prices for restaurants are based primarily on dinner for two, including dessert, tax, and tip (no alcohol). Prices for lodgings are based on peak season rates for one night's lodging for two people (i.e., double occupancy). Peak season is typically Memorial Day to Labor Day; off-season rates vary but can sometimes be significantly less. Call ahead to verify, as all prices are subject to change.

$$$$ Very expensive (more than $125 for dinner for two; more than $250 for one night's lodging for two)

$$$ Expensive (between $85 and $125 for dinner for two; between $150 and $250 for one night's lodging for two)

$$ Moderate (between $35 and $85 for dinner for two; between $85 and $150 for one night's lodging for two)

$ Inexpensive (less than $35 for dinner for two; less than $85 for one night's lodging for two)

RESERVATIONS *(for Top 200 Restaurants only)* We used one of the following terms for our reservations policy: reservations required, reservations recommended, no reservations. "No reservations" means either reservations are not necessary or are not accepted.

PARKING We've indicated a variety of options for parking in the facts lines at the end of each review.

ADDRESSES AND PHONE NUMBERS Every attempt has been made to provide accurate information on an establishment's location and phone number, but it's always a good idea to call ahead and confirm. For establishments with two or more locations, we try to provide information on the original or most recommended branches.

CHECKS AND CREDIT CARDS Many establishments that accept checks also require a major credit card for identification. Note that some places accept only local checks. Credit cards are abbreviated in this book as follows: American Express (AE); Carte Blanche (CB); Diners Club (DC); Discover (DIS); Enroute (E); Japanese credit card (JCB); MasterCard (MC); Visa (V).

EMAIL AND WEB SITE ADDRESSES Website or email addresses for establishments have been included where available. Please note that the Web is a fluid and evolving medium, and that Web pages are often "under construction"—or, as with all time-sensitive information, may no longer be valid.

MAP INDICATORS The letter-and-number codes appearing at the end of most listings refer to coordinates on the fold-out map included in the front of the book. Single letters (for example, F7) refer to the downtown Portland map; double letters (FF7) refer to the Greater Portland map on the flip side. If an establishment does not have a map code listed, its location falls beyond the boundaries of these maps (for example, Oregon Wine Country locations).

HELPFUL ICONS Watch for these quick-reference symbols throughout the book:

 FAMILY FUN Family-oriented places that are great for kids—fun, easy, not too expensive, and accustomed to dealing with young ones.

 GOOD VALUE While not necessarily cheap, these places offer you the best value for your dollars—a good deal within the context of the city.

 ROMANTIC These spots offer candlelight, atmosphere, intimacy, or other romantic qualities—kisses and proposals are encouraged!

 EDITORS' CHOICE These are places that are unique and special to the city, such as a restaurant owned by a beloved local chef or a tourist attraction recognized around the globe.

 Appears after listings for establishments that have wheelchair-accessible facilities.

INDEXES In addition to a general index at the back of the book, there are five specialized indexes: restaurants are indexed by star-rating, features, and location at the beginning of the Restaurants chapter, and nightspots are indexed by features and location at the beginning of the Nightlife chapter.

PLANNING A TRIP

PLANNING A TRIP

How to Get Here

BY PLANE

The good news is that **PORTLAND INTERNATIONAL AIRPORT**, or **PDX** (7000 NE Airport Wy; 503/460-4234 or 877/739-4636; www.portlandairportpdx.com; map: DD4), is served by most major U.S. airlines and some foreign carriers, with excellent connections from points around the Pacific Northwest and beyond. The bad news is that the airport is forever in a state of expansion, which can mean difficult parking, unexpected gate changes, and long walks from the terminal to baggage claim. Allow at least 30 minutes—more during rush hours—to get between the airport and downtown.

The Tri-Met (503/238-7433; www.trimet.org) **MAX RED LINE**, an extension of eastside light-rail service, takes 38 minutes to make the trip between Pioneer Courthouse Square and Tri-Met's terminal near baggage claim at PDX. Cost is $1.55. There are several intermediate bus-transfer stations for visitors staying on Portland's east side.

All major **CAR RENTAL** companies operate from the airport. **TAXIS** and **SHUTTLES** are readily available on the lower deck; after picking up your baggage, cross the first roadway, which is reserved for passenger pickup, and proceed to the commercial roadway. Expect to pay about $25 for the trip downtown.

PARKING (503/288-PARK or 800/PDX-INFO) at PDX comes in three flavors, and where you park probably depends on how long you'll be there. The Economy Lot ($48 per week and served by a free shuttle) is a good bet for extended parking. Close to the terminal, the Long-Term Lot ($12 per day) is designed for parking over a one- to three-day period; the Parking Garage, or short-term parking ($1.50 per half hour), is best for quick trips. Call ahead for space availability.

BY BUS

Near Union Station, just north of Old Town, is the **GREYHOUND** station (550 NW 6th Ave, River District; 503/243-2357 or 800/231-2222; www.greyhound.com; map:M4) with a complete schedule of buses each day. Both the train station and the bus station are within walking distance of the downtown core known as "Fareless Square," where you can ride MAX trains or Tri-Met buses for free, and where you can catch MAX and Tri-Met into downtown and beyond, to most suburbs in the metropolitan area.

BY TRAIN

Amtrak (503/273-4866 recorded arrival and departure times; 800/872-7245 reservations; www.amtrak.com) operates out of the lovely Union Station (800 NW 6th Ave, River District; map: N4), just north of downtown Portland (look for "Go By Train" written in neon on the tower). With its prominent clock tower, great curving entrance, and muscular features, this romantic structure memorializes the bygone era of the great railways. Trains come from and head for points north, east, and south daily.

BY CAR

Most drivers come into Portland via either **INTERSTATE 5**, which runs north–south between Canada and Mexico, or **INTERSTATE 84**, which extends west into Portland through the Columbia Gorge. US Highway 26 links Portland to the Oregon Coast via Hillsboro (west) and to central Oregon via Mount Hood (east).

Interstate 205 is a 36-mile, semibeltway route through Portland's east side that loops off I-5 between Tualatin (12 miles south of downtown) and north Vancouver, Washington (16 miles north). It passes near Lake Oswego, West Linn, Oregon City, and Milwaukie, among other towns. **INTERSTATE 405** is a 3-mile-long alternative route to I-5 that skirts the western edge of downtown. Rush hours in Portland can mean standstill traffic on all highways, but if you arrive midday (after 9am but before 3pm) or after 7pm, you should have clear sailing into town.

When to Visit

Portland is in bloom—culturally speaking—year-round. When to visit is strictly a matter of preference, but there are a few constants that can make planning a trip a little bit easier.

WEATHER

Unless you plain don't mind getting soaked—and many natives own neither slicker nor umbrella—bring something water-resistant no matter what the season. Portland skies are ever changing. The common denominator is precipitation, but all the rain does pay off: Portland boasts close proximity to fabulous skiing on Mount Hood, lush year-round parks, and a temperate clime that makes it OK to have hot chocolate or ice cream pretty much any time of year.

Outside of snow on the nearby mountains, frozen, fluffy white flakes are generally not welcomed. Childrens' peals of "No school!" may seem premature when only a trace of snow is visible, but they know that the City of Roses is a city that closes when snow falls. Still, snow rarely lasts long on city streets (not because plows remove it, but because it simply melts), so enjoy the dusted evergreens while you can. If you visit in winter, be prepared for bus delays and traffic snarls on those rare occasions when snow falls.

Portland's true summer runs from July to early October, so sun worshippers should time their trips accordingly. Bring the shades and—gasp!—sunscreen. Allergy sufferers will find May and June the toughest going for sensitive eyes and noses, but they can still enjoy the fulsome beauty of Bridgetown's gardens. Early spring is redolent with its magnolia, cherry, and plum blossoms; June's end sees the full explosion of Portland's famous International Rose Test Garden.

Average temperature and precipitation by month

Month	Daily Max. (degrees F)	Daily Min. (degrees F)	Monthly Precipitation (inches)
January	45.4	33.7	5.35
February	51	36.1	3.85
March	56	38.6	3.56
April	60.6	41.3	2.39
May	67.1	47	2.06
June	74	52.9	1.48
July	79.9	56.5	0.63
August	80.3	56.9	1.09
September	74.6	52	1.75
October	64	44.9	2.67
November	52.6	39.5	5.34
December	45.6	34.8	6.13

Source: U.S. National Oceanic and Atmospheric Administration

TIME

Portland is on Pacific Standard Time (PST), which is 3 hours behind New York City, 2 hours behind Chicago, 1 hour behind Denver, 1 hour ahead of Anchorage, and 2 hours ahead of Honolulu. Portland is 17 hours behind Tokyo and 8 hours behind London. Daylight saving time begins in early April and ends in late October.

WHAT TO BRING

The Portland fashion aesthetic is ever evolving, but most locals aren't too picky (much to the dismay of some bigger-city transplants). Rule of thumb for tourists: dress for comfort, with good walking shoes a must. Men may want to pack a jacket for dinner, but it won't be required anywhere; women, as usual, have more choices: dresses, skirts, or pants are all fine, and you should know that many people—though not everyone—will be wearing jeans, T-shirts, and Nikes (or the equivalent) no matter what day of the week it is (or what line of work they're in). If you want to draw attention, dress Miami Beach; to blend, think fleece and cotton.

Essentials for all seasons include a water-resistant shell; comfortable, water-resistant shoes; sunglasses (rain or shine); lip balm; and a mind toward layering. Summer days are often cool in the mornings and evenings, so pack a jacket, even in August.

General Costs

Visitors are often surprised to find that Oregon has no sales tax (hence higher income and property taxes than many states), making it a shoppers' paradise . . . and ensuring that there's always a tax revolt in the works. Portland's economy is driven by a broad base of services and industry. Manufacturing includes machinery, electronics, metals, transportation equipment, and lumber and wood products, and there are some 1,000 high-tech companies in the metro area, the largest of which is Intel. Among other large companies in the Portland area, a few internationally known names stand out, including Nike, Columbia Sportswear, and Tektronix.

The residential real-estate market in Portland has been stratospheric for years, but if you're planning only a visit, you might find some good deals on bedrooms. It's a buyer's market in the luxury hotel trade in downtown Portland, at least until the demand catches up to the supply. In the past few years a number of new downtown hotels, large and small, have opened for business, and now there are too many to fill on a regular basis. Inquire about special rates and packages; you might find a bargain, or at least a set of amenities (maybe a shopper's package or a romance package) that will make your hotel stay memorable.

Prices at Portland restaurants may be above the national average, but for visitors who are used to eating out in San Francisco or Seattle (Portland's closest big-city neighbors), dining in the City of Roses may seem like a bargain.

Average costs for lodging and food

DOUBLE ROOM

Inexpensive	**$40–$75**
Moderate	**$75–$120**
Expensive	**$120 and up**

LUNCH FOR ONE (INCLUDING BEVERAGE AND TIP)

Inexpensive	**$6–$10**
Moderate	**$11–$18**
Expensive	**$19 and up**

BEVERAGES

12-ounce house coffee	**$1.30**
Pint of microbrew	**$3.75**
Glass of wine	**$5–$8**

OTHER COMMON ITEMS

Movie ticket	**$7.50**
Taxi	**$2.50 pickup; $1.80 per mile**
Rock show (local acts)	**$3–$10**
Admission to Oregon Zoo	**$5–$8**

PORTLAND ON THE PAGE

The best way to experience Portland is to get out, get wet (if necessary), and see it for yourself. You can read about the city's bridges, its roses, its parks, shops, and restaurants, but until you actually "do" Portland, your impressions will be borrowed ones.

Still, the tone for many of our meanderings has been set or enhanced by literature. Frances Mayes's *Under the Tuscan Sun* (for Italy) and John Berendt's *Midnight in the Garden of Good and Evil* (for Savannah, Georgia) are particular favorites: both paint unforgettable pictures of their geographical settings.

What follows is a short Portland reading list. For more ideas, visit any of the bookstores listed in the Shopping chapter; many have sections that feature the works of local authors.

Ramona the Pest lives in northeast Portland, as her author, Beverly Cleary, once did. The Ramona books are surefire hits with kids (and their grown-ups); *Ramona Quimby, Age 8* is an all-time favorite. To see a tribute to Cleary, check out the statues of Ramona, Henry Huggins, and Ribsy in Grant Park (between the tennis courts and NE 33rd Ave, Hollywood).

Author and chef extraordinaire James Beard grew up in Portland during the early 20th century. His book *Delights and Prejudices* contains lavish passages about Portland markets, the city's social life, a summer trip to the Oregon Coast on the train, and other aspects of life in Portland a century ago. *The Solace of Food: A Life of James Beard*, by Robert Clark, affords a broader view of Beard's world than Beard himself could offer.

Tips for Special Travelers

FAMILIES WITH CHILDREN

If you think your child has ingested something toxic, call the **POISON CENTER** (503/494-8968 or 800/222-1222). To report child abuse, call the **CHILD ABUSE HOTLINE** (503/238-7555). For other emergencies, dial 911. **LEGACY EMANUEL HOSPITAL AND HEALTH CENTER** (2801 N Gantenbein Ave, North Portland; 503/413-4840; map:FF6) has an excellent children's facility; **LEGACY GOOD SAMARITAN HOSPITAL AND MEDICAL CENTER** is close to the downtown center (1015 NW 22nd Ave; 503/413-7711; map:GG7) in Northwest Portland. Another close-in hospital is the **PROVIDENCE ST. VINCENT HOSPITAL** (9205 SW Barnes Rd, West Slope; 503/216-1234; map:HH9), and the **PORTLAND CLINIC** (800 SW 13th Ave; 503/221-0161; map:I1) is in the heart of downtown.

Most major hotels can arrange for babysitters if notified in advance. The **NORTHWEST NANNIES INSTITUTE** (503/245-5288) places course graduates for live-in or daily care throughout the metro area. **CARE GIVERS PLACEMENT AGENCY** (503/244-6370) also matches families with daily or overnight nannies. **METRO**

If Oregon has a modern literary classic, it is Ken Kesey's *Sometimes a Great Notion*. Though Kesey lived near Eugene and this book is set in a coastal logging town, the novel is instructive in understanding the Oregon mind-set. So, too, is Tim Egan's *The Good Rain*; Egan, a correspondent for the *New York Times*, presents an insightful region-by-region view of his home turf, including a chapter on Portland. Hometown novelist Chuck Palahniuk (*The Fight Club*) takes a close look at the city's seamier side in his 2003 memoir, *Strangers and Refugees: A Walk in Portland, Oregon*.

Beloved poet William Stafford taught for years at Lewis and Clark College and contributed much to the literary life of his adopted city until his death in 1993. *The Way It Is: New and Selected Poems* is an invaluable collection of his work. Another poet, Pulitzer Prize–winner Gary Snyder, once taught at Reed College; the flavor of the region comes through in many of his works, such as *Mountains and Rivers Without End*.

A book that's worth seeking out is *The Portland Bridge Book*, by Sharon Wood Wortman. With complete descriptions of Portland's many bridges, this Oregon Historical Society volume is a treasure for visitors and residents alike. William J. Hawkins III and William F. Winnigham's *Classic Houses of Portland, Oregon: 1850–1950*, published by Timber Press, tells stories of many local manses and comes complete with black-and-white photos. *One City's Wilderness: Portland's Forest Park*, by Marcy Cottrell Houle, includes an excellent map of the 5,000-acre park, plus trail descriptions. *Wild in the City: A Guide to Portland's Natural Areas*, edited by Mike Houck and M. J. Cody, is a must-have blueprint for the urban naturalist.

CHILD CARE RESOURCE AND REFERRAL (503/253-5000) offers free information on day-care services in the tricounty area.

Many young families move to Portland with the idea that it is a great place to raise children—and they're right. Not surprisingly, there is plenty to do here for children of all ages. The new **CHILDREN'S MUSEUM** (4015 SW Canyon Rd; 503/823-2227; map:HH7), opposite the zoo in Washington Park, is a local philanthropic success story. Check out the climbing structure and the waterworks. Both the **OREGON ZOO** (4001 SW Canyon Rd, Washington Park; 503/226-1561; map:HH7) and **OMSI**, the **OREGON MUSEUM OF SCIENCE AND INDUSTRY** (1945 SE Water Ave, Southeast; 503/797-4000; map:HH6), are top-notch family standbys.

For an up-to-date overview of possibilities, pick up a copy of *Portland Parent* magazine (503/638-1049; www.parenthoodweb.com), *Portland Family* magazine (503/255-3286; www.portlandfamily.com), and Bravo Publications's annual *Family Resource Guide* (503/675-1380; www.bravofamily.com). These free publications have activity calendars and can be found at coffee shops and newsstands. When copies are scarce, try Finnegan's Toys and Gifts (922 SW Yamhill St, Downtown; 503/221-0306; map:H2) or Rich's Cigar Store (820 SW Alder St, Downtown; 503/228-1700; map:I3).

For a copy of the **OFFICIAL OREGON KIDS TRAVEL GUIDE AND EXPLORER PASSPORT**, call the state tourism commission (800/547-7842; www.travel oregon.com) or visit the Web site. The guide features youngsters sharing their favorite activities, and the passport lets young travelers collect stickers from designated Oregon attractions.

Watch for this icon throughout the book; it indicates places and activities that are great for families.

SENIORS

In Multnomah County, the **AGING SERVICES DEPARTMENT** operates a **SENIOR HELPLINE** (503/988-3646), which assists seniors with information about health services, low-income housing, recreation, transportation, legal services, volunteer programs, and other matters. Washington County also has an **AGING SERVICES DEPARTMENT** (503/640-3489); its counterpart in Clackamas County is **AGING AND DISABILITY SERVICES** (503/655-8640).

SENIORS ALA CART TRANSPORTATION SERVICES (503/591-9161) operates what is essentially a senior-citizen taxi. The pickup charge is higher than a standard taxi, but the cost per mile is lower, making it an economical option for longer excursions. Senior citizens and people with disabilities receive free transportation when participating in activities sponsored by the **PORTLAND CITY PARKS PROGRAM FOR DISABLED CITIZENS AND SENIOR LEISURE** (503/823-4328).

PEOPLE WITH DISABILITIES

Public transportation in Portland, on Tri-Met buses and MAX trains, is wheelchair accessible. Press the blue button outside the MAX doors for ramp access. The doors will remain shut longer than the doors for foot traffic, but don't panic—the beeping sound means that the ramp is being lowered.

INDEPENDENT LIVING RESOURCES (503/232-7411) assists people of various disabilities. The **ARC OF MULTNOMAH COUNTY** (503/223-7279) offers services for people with developmental disabilities, including in-home and center-based respite care. Call well in advance to take advantage of this service. **TRIPS INC. SPECIAL ADVENTURES** (800/686-1013; www.tripsinc.com) has provided chaperoned excursions for people with developmental disabilities since 1991. Many of these Trips Inc. adventures are out-of-state, but check with the office for in-state camping and rodeo offerings.

To contact people who are deaf or hearing- or speech-impaired, call the **OREGON TELECOMMUNICATIONS RELAY SERVICE** (800/735-1232 or TTY 800/735-2900).

WOMEN

Portland is a relatively tranquil place, but as in most cities, women travelers should take extra safety precautions at night. The **WOMEN'S CRISIS LINE** number is 503/235-5333. For health and reproductive services, call **PLANNED PARENTHOOD** (503/775-0861 or 503/288-8826).

PET OWNERS

Portland is an exceedingly dog-friendly city. There's even a free 32-page monthly newspaper, *Dog Nose News* (www.dognosenews.com), dedicated to dog lovers (with full event listings) and available at coffee shops around the city. Many leading hotels allow pets, including the **5TH AVENUE SUITES** (506 SW Washington St, Downtown; 503/221-0001; map:H4) and the **HOTEL VINTAGE PLAZA** (422 SW Broadway, Downtown; 503/228-1212; map:I4).

The **DOVE LEWIS EMERGENCY ANIMAL HOSPITAL** has trained staff on call 24 hours (1984 NW Pettygrove St, Northwest; 503/228-7281, www.dovelewis.org; map:GG7).

A handful of city parks allow dogs to run off leash: **CHIMNEY PARK** (16 unfenced acres at 9360 N Columbia Blvd, Saint Johns; map:DD7); **GABRIEL PARK** (fenced, 1.5-acre off-leash portion at SW 45th Ave, near SW Vermont St, Multnomah Village; open May–Oct; Map:JJ8); **EAST DELTA PARK** (5 fenced acres on N Union Ct off I-5, exit 307, North Portland, open May–Oct; map:DD6); and **WEST DELTA PARK** (3 open acres on N Expo Rd, North Portland, near the entrance to Portland International Raceway; map:DD7). There are plans to open more dog areas and parks in the future.

GAYS AND LESBIANS

Portland is in all things low-key, but its gay scene is growing. The **PORTLAND OREGON VISITORS ASSOCIATION** (877/678-5263) publishes its *GLBT Portland Guide* as a resource for gay, lesbian, bisexual, and transgendered visitors, and includes a link on its website (www.pova.com). Visitors can also pick up a copy of the widely available tabloid newspaper, *Just Out* (503/236-1252; www.justout.com), a free weekly source for gay news, arts, and community events.

For a complete rundown of gay-friendly businesses, pick up a copy of *Portland's Gay & Lesbian Community Yellow Pages*. The free directory is published annually and can be found at most coffee shops and the like. To scope out the city before arriving, visit its website (www.pdxgayyellowpages.com). The **GAY RESOURCE CONNECTION** operates a hotline (800/777-2437) and will provide referrals for both services and activities.

FOREIGN VISITORS

Oregon has long had a relationship with Japan, its neighbor across the Pacific, and Portland continues to fuse its down-to-earth sensibilities with a cosmopolitan flavor. Some tour companies will track down a translator if they know in advance which language is needed, or inquire through the **PORTLAND OREGON VISITORS ASSOCIATION** (800/962-3700).

Exchange currency at any main bank branch, at the **AMERICAN EXPRESS TRAVEL AGENCY** (1100 SW 6th Ave, Downtown; 503/226-2961; map:H4), or at **TRAVELEX AMERICA** (503/281-3045), located at Portland International Airport across from the United Airlines ticket counter. Money can also be swapped at the Thomas Cook counter inside **POWELL'S TRAVEL STORE** in Pioneer Courthouse Square. Ask about commission charges, or call 800/CURRENCY.

For general visa information, contact the **U.S. CITIZENSHIP AND IMMIGRATION SERVICES** (511 NW Broadway, Downtown; 503/326-3409 or 800/375-5283; map:L4). Oregon is home to a number of foreign consulates, some large, some small, and most of them in Portland. Visitors from around the globe can contact their local consulates.

9

BARBADOS, 10202 SE 32nd Ave, Ste 601, Milwaukie; 503/659-0283

BELGIUM, 2812 NW Imperial Terr, Hillside; 503/228-0465

CYPRUS, 1130 SW Morrison St, Ste 510, Downtown; 503/248-0500

CZECH REPUBLIC, 10260 SW Greenburg Rd, Ste 560, Tigard; 503/293-9545

DENMARK, 888 SW 5th Ave, Downtown; 503/802-2131

FINLAND, 2730 SW Cedar Hills Blvd, Beaverton; 503/526-0391

FRANCE, PO Box 751, Portland 97201; 503/725-5298

GERMANY, 200 SW Market St, Ste 1695, Downtown; 503/222-0490

ITALY, 4507-A SE Milwaukie Blvd, Brooklyn; 503/287-2578

JAPAN, 1300 SW 5th Ave, Ste 2700, Downtown; 503/221-1811

KOREA, 805 SW Broadway, Ste 1900, Downtown; 503/224-5560

MALAYSIA, 7497 SW Aloma Wy, Ste 6, Garden Home; 503/246-0707

MEXICO, 1234 SW Morrison St, Downtown; 503/274-1442

NETHERLANDS, 520 SW Yamhill St, Ste 600, Downtown; 503/222-7957

NORWAY, 4380 SW Macadam Ave, Ste 120, John's Landing; 503/228-8828

PANAMA, 829 N Russell St, Albina; 503/284-1189

SWEDEN, 111 SW 5th Ave, Ste 2900, Downtown; 503/227-0634

THAILAND, 121 SW Salmon St, Ste 1430, Downtown; 503/221-0440

UNITED KINGDOM, 520 SW Yamhill St, Downtown; 503/227-5669

WEB INFORMATION

The best general-interest websites include those for the **PORTLAND OREGON VISITORS ASSOCIATION** (www.pova.com) and the **PORTLAND CHAMBER OF COMMERCE** (www.pdxchamber.com). The **CITY'S OWN WEBSITE** (www.portland online.com) has links to a variety of urban requirements. For information on **LOCAL MICROBREWERIES**, see www.oregonbeer.com; for **LOCAL WINERIES**, head to www .oregonwine.com; and for a **LOCAL FOODIES' CALENDAR**, go to the website for *Northwest Palate Magazine* (www.nwpalate.com). For *The Oregonian*'s calendar of events, go to www.oregonlive.com; and for *Willamette Week*'s calendar of events, see www.wweek .com. Finally, to check **CURRENT WEATHER CONDITIONS**, visit www.channel6000 .com/weather.

LAY OF THE CITY

LAY OF THE CITY

Orientation

The mighty **COLUMBIA RIVER** and the oft-bridged **WILLAMETTE RIVER** set the blueprint for Portland. In fact, natural landmarks eliminate the need for a compass, at least when skies are clear. Mount Hood marks the east like a glistening guardian and the verdant green West Hills mark, appropriately, the west. To the north, visible from many parts of the city, is Washington's volcanic Mount St. Helens, whose top from this perspective appears flat.

The Willamette (pronounced "wil-LAM-it") enters town from the south, cleaving Portland's west side from its east. Burnside Street separates north from south. The light-rail, known as MAX, runs basically east–west. Each quarter of town has its own flavor, and new cultural environments are always emerging.

PIONEER COURTHOUSE SQUARE, Portland's public red-bricked plaza, marks central downtown and contains the city's visitors center. Most of the bricks are engraved with names of donors to what some call Portland's living room. Portlanders gather here for lunch, for people watching (the Square attracts many young alternative folk), and for various events. SW Broadway, which skirts the west side of the Square, is downtown's aorta, and many of the major city hotels are located either on this thoroughfare or within a couple of blocks east or west.

The Square, shadowed on the east by its namesake 1860s courthouse, is only six blocks from the banks of the Willamette, where **GOV. TOM MCCALL WATERFRONT PARK** stretches riverside for more than a mile. Extending north from the new RiverPlace development to the Steel Bridge, and passing beneath three other bridges en route, the grassy strip replaced a four-lane expressway. Beneath the west end of the Burnside Bridge, it passes Portland's **SATURDAY MARKET**, which is as busy on Sunday as it is the day before. There's plenty to see and hear and smell as artisans hawk their wares and steamy ethnic foods make mouths water.

PGE PARK (formerly Civic Stadium), home of minor-league baseball and college football, is about 12 blocks west of Pioneer Courthouse Square, a five-minute MAX ride. The **ROSE GARDEN** (aka the Rose Quarter), home of the Portland Trail Blazers pro basketball team and a major concert venue, is a 15-minute MAX ride to the east. The ultra-modern **OREGON CONVENTION CENTER**, its twin towers a city landmark, is but a couple of blocks' walk from the Rose Garden.

Across Burnside Street from PGE Park is Portland's trendy **NORTHWEST NEIGH-BORHOOD**. Though divided by the I-405 corridor, shoppers along NW 23rd Avenue ("Nob Hill") and gallery-goers in the **PEARL DISTRICT** (between 9th and 15th Aves) find getting around as easy as A-B-C, 1-2-3. The north–south avenues march westward in numerical order, and the east–west streets (Burnside through Wilson; Ankeny is south of Burnside) are helpfully named in alphabetical order.

The top of the neighborhood, at the end of NW Thurman Street, marks the beginning of 5,000-acre **FOREST PARK**, which cloaks much of the West Hills. Forest Park's 23-mile Wildwood Trail extends south to **WASHINGTON PARK**, climbing the hills immediately west of downtown (beginning just 1 mile from Broadway). It includes several of Portland's best-known visitor attractions, including the Oregon Zoo and the International Rose Test Garden.

On the east side of the river, Grand Avenue northbound and Martin Luther King Jr. Boulevard southbound are speedy through streets that parallel I-5. With few exceptions, however, eastside neighborhoods have an east–west orientation, perhaps reflecting a sprawl from downtown toward Mount Hood. The eastside business focus is still the **LLOYD CENTER** (south of Broadway between NE 9th and 15th Aves), built in 1960 as the nation's first indoor shopping mall. The Irvington and Alameda districts, beyond the Lloyd Center, are known for their many gracious and well-kept older homes.

Elsewhere in **NORTHEAST PORTLAND**, a recent economic upswing has come both from external gentrification and community-based business development. In the residential Northeast neighborhoods, pedestrians will have the best luck exploring NE Alberta and Fremont Streets, as well as Broadway. **SOUTHEAST PORTLAND** is the city's hippest area, sort of like what Berkeley is to San Francisco. Sections of SE Hawthorne and Belmont Streets, the Laurelhurst district near 28th and Burnside, and the Clinton Street neighborhood at SE 25th Avenue, are good bets for food-and-wine aficionados, bargain-hunting moviegoers, thrift-store devotees, and shoppers of all persuasions. **MOUNT TABOR PARK** marks the eastern edge of the hip Southeast. A view of downtown from the top and the endless staircases that mark the back entrance make this a popular spot for runners and relaxers alike.

A couple of quirky neighborhoods worth noting are south of the downtown core. The adjacent Sellwood and Westmoreland districts, with great dining and antiquing, are along SE Milwaukie Avenue, south of Bybee Boulevard, and along SE 13th Avenue. The Multnomah Village neighborhood winds along SW Capitol Highway at SW 35th Avenue.

Beyond Portland's urban boundaries, surburbs, and bedroom communities spread in all directions. Directly south—up the north-flowing Willamette River via Highway 43 (SW Macadam Ave) through the Johns Landing neighborhood—are the towns of Lake Oswego (7 miles), West Linn (12 miles), and Oregon City (13 miles). Moving west around the clock face are Tualatin (12 miles) at 7 o'clock, Tigard (9 miles) at 8 o'clock, and Beaverton (8 miles), home to the Nike empire, at 9 o'clock. Hillsboro (15 miles) is at 10 o'clock.

Milwaukie (6 miles) and Clackamas (10 miles) are to the southeast, at around 5 o'clock. Gresham (12 miles) and Troutdale (14 miles) are due east, at 3 o'clock. And due north, spreading along the opposite bank of the Columbia River from about 11 to 2, is the burgeoning Washington city of Vancouver.

Visitor Information

People have been moving to Portland at such a clip that sometimes it seems as if there's been another homesteading act. A good place to start, for both visitors and new Oregonians, is the **VISITOR INFORMATION AND SERVICES CENTER**, located on the lower west side of Pioneer Courthouse Square (701 SW 6th Ave at Morrison

St, Downtown; 503/275-8355 or 877/678-5263; www.pova.com; map:H3). It's open daily (Mon–Fri 8:30am–4:30pm, Sat 10am–4pm, Sun 10am–2pm). Here shelves are well stocked with brochures in English; ask about foreign-language guides to the area. Inside the center, visitors can surf the website and purchase discounted tickets to events happening that day. The main office of the parent Portland Oregon Visitors Association (POVA) is nearby on the 23rd floor of 1000 SW Broadway (800/962-3700). If you're planning a convention, you might want to look into the Oregon Convention Center (take their virtual tour at www.oregoncc.org).

Maintained in cooperation with the *Oregonian* newspaper, www.oregonlive .com lets surfers stay up-to-date with local news stories and arts coverage. The CitySearch website (www.portland.citysearch.com) offers food and music reviews. Find out more about the City of Portland—everything from which parks have dog runs to how city government is run—at www.portlandonline.com. Finally, the Portland Chamber of Commerce (221 NW 2nd Ave, Downtown; 503/228-9411; www .portlandalliance.com) can answer questions about doing business in Portland.

For statewide tourism information, contact the Oregon State Tourism Division (800/547-7842).

Getting Around

BY BUS OR MAX

Tri-Met (503/238-7433; www.trimet.org) operates both the city bus system and the sleek Metropolitan Area Express (MAX) trains; tickets for the two systems are interchangeable. All vehicles are wheelchair accessible. Almost all the bus lines run through the Portland Transit Mall (SW 5th and 6th Aves, Downtown); MAX lines also cross through downtown, extending east to Gresham and west to Hillsboro. Construction on a new MAX loop through downtown, from Union Station to Portland State University, is proposed to begin in 2005, and there are plans to extend new lines to suburban Milwaukie and along I-205 in East Portland.

Buses run north across Burnside all the way to the Tri-Met North Terminal, just past the Greyhound station and across the street from Union Station. The terminal is the first stop on the transit mall and serves as a pit stop for bus drivers, providing a place to park their buses while they take a break and wait to complete their schedule.

Travelers in the downtown area can ride buses or MAX for free anywhere in the 330-block **FARELESS SQUARE**. The square extends from I-405 on the south and west to NW Irving Street on the north; to the east, it crosses the Willamette River to the Rose Quarter and the Lloyd Center.

Fares outside the square are $1.25 for travel in two zones (from downtown to residential areas within the metropolitan area) and $1.55 for three zones (necessary for travel from downtown to most parts of Tigard, Beaverton, Gresham, Milwaukie, Lake Oswego, and the airport). Youth tickets are 95 cents per ride, and as many as three children age 6 and younger can ride free with a fare-paying customer. All-day tickets are $4; a special three-day visitors pass is $10. Honored citizens—those 65 and older or disabled—can catch a bus for 60 cents per ride or pay $14 for a monthly pass. Tickets can be purchased on the bus (exact change only) or at MAX stops. **TRI-MET'S CUSTOMER ASSISTANCE OFFICE** is in the middle of Pioneer Courthouse Square, in the center of downtown. Open weekdays 9am–5pm, this is the place for face-to-face route information or ticket purchases. MAX trains run on the honor system; that is, MAX drivers never check fares. However, Tri-Met inspectors do randomly request proof of fare payment on buses and MAX, and passengers who haven't paid are fined or cited in district court.

The **MAX LIGHT-RAIL SYSTEM** extended its reach to 38 miles with the opening of its Portland Airport extension in September 2001—the West Coast's only "train-to-plane" service. Airport travelers may board the Red Line downtown or transfer at several stations en route.

The new 5.8-mile Yellow Line, between downtown and North Portland's Multnomah County Expo Center, is set to open in September 2004. The route, mainly along North Interstate Avenue, will add nine new stops.

MAX's original Blue Line starts from Hillsboro in the west and winds through Beaverton, making its first Portland stop at the Oregon Zoo. From there it stops in the Goose Hollow neighborhood at SW Salmon Street and 18th Avenue, passes through downtown and Old Town, crosses the Steel Bridge, and continues on the east side, swinging by the Oregon Convention Center and the Lloyd Center before making its way along I-84, then east beside Burnside Street, to Gresham.

Glass-covered stations along the way maintain schedule information and ticket machines. The comfortable trains run every 15 minutes most hours of the day—more frequently during rush hour—every day of the week. Trains are generally spacious during non-rush-hour times, but they get packed (although not quite Tokyo-style) during the morning and evening commute.

Of the 20 stops between downtown and Hillsboro, 9 have parking lots with room for a total of 3,700 vehicles. Hang on to your transfer and check out the public art at these stations. Architects, artists, and engineers collaborated to create individual identities for each station. Art brochures are available on MAX trains and buses.

You can take your bike on the bus or train. All Tri-Met buses and MAX trains are outfitted with bike racks; a good-for-life bike pass costs $5.

BY STREETCAR AND TROLLEY

Since summer 2001, the **PORTLAND STREETCAR** (www.portlandstreetcar.org) has been whisking travelers 4.8 miles from Portland State University, through the downtown core, into the Pearl District and up to NW 23rd Avenue at Northrup Street. Book lovers appreciate the stop smack in front of Powell's City of Books, but there are plenty of other intriguing stops along the way. Streetcars run seven days a week (Mon–Thurs 5:30am–11:30pm, Fri 5:30am–1am, Sat 7:30am–1am, Sun 7:30am–10:30pm). Cars arrive every 14 minutes during peak hours (Mon–Fri 7am–8pm, Sat 11am–6pm), and every 20 to 25 minutes during other periods. Fares are the same as Tri-Met's—in other words, free within Fareless Square, $1.25 (for adults) beyond NW Irving Street.

Another option is the oak-paneled and brass-belled **VINTAGE TROLLEY**. Four of these circa-1900-style vehicles follow the MAX line from the Lloyd Center to

PORTLAND'S BRIDGES

Portland has its great art museum. It has its history museum, its interactive science museum, its children's and maritime and forestry museums. But the biggest museum of all right is in front of your nose: this city has the most remarkable collection of full-scale moveable bridges—all of them in daily use—that you'll see anywhere.

This open-air museum includes 10 highway bridges that span the Willamette River within the city; two more south to Oregon City, and another two crossing the Columbia River between Portland and Vancouver, Washington. There are also railroad bridges.

The collection features all three basic bridge types (arch, suspension, and truss), all three movable span types (swing, vertical lift, and bascule or seesaw), bridges that are close to one another (eight within 3 miles of one another), and midtown bridges with short and safe pedestrian approaches.

From north to south, Portland's highway bridges are the St. Johns (built in 1931), Fremont (1973), Broadway (1913), Steel (1912), Burnside (1926), Morrison (1958), Hawthorne (1910), Marquam (1966), Ross Island (1926), and Sellwood (1925).

The Willamette Valley's only suspension bridge, the **ST. JOHNS BRIDGE** (6.6 miles north of Burnside) is rumored to have been a model for the Golden Gate, built in San Francisco six years later. When this impressive, cathedral-like bridge opened to great fanfare, byplanes flew beneath its twin towers en route to the long-defunct Swan Island airport. Today the city landmark welcomes marine traffic traveling upriver to Portland.

The **FREMONT BRIDGE** (1.3 miles north of Burnside) is the world's longest (1,255 feet) tied–arch bridge—which means it has no in-water pier supports in the main channel. The 902-foot midspan of this three-span bridge was built off-site and assembled on Swan Island, a mile downstream. Engineers from around the world watched as its 6,000 tons were raised 175 feet above the river at a rate of 7 feet per hour.

The **BROADWAY BRIDGE** (0.7 mile north) was the world's longest double-leaf drawbridge when it opened and is still considered the single outstanding example of the Rall-type bascule span: its hinged lift-span leaves glide backward and upward on wheels along steel tracks.

The **STEEL BRIDGE** (0.3 mile north) is the only vertical-lift bridge in the world with twin decks capable of independent movement. The lower rail deck, normally kept in raised position, moves independently of the upper deck, which carries cars, pedestrians, bicycles, and the MAX light rail. It is Portland's shortest bridge at 211 feet.

The city-center **BURNSIDE BRIDGE** is best known locally as the site of the Saturday Market, which operates weekends (except January and February) under its west end. Above its west end is the revered "Made in Oregon" neon sign; until 1998, it advertised White Stag sportswear. A double-leaf bascule drawbridge like the Broadway and Morrison Bridges, the Burnside replaced an earlier (1894) truss bridge.

The **MORRISON BRIDGE** (0.4 mile south of Burnside) opened in 1958 to replace Portland's first river bridge, an 1887 toll bridge that charged 15 cents for a horse, buggy and driver. With its concrete and steel pile foundations, open–grating steel deck and double-leaf trunnion bascule, this minimalist bridge was considered cutting-edge modern architecture five decades ago.

The **HAWTHORNE BRIDGE** (0.7 mile south) predates (by two years) the Steel Bridge as the world's oldest vertical-lift bridge still in full operation. (Designer John Waddell's original was built in Chicago in 1894.) Its open steel gratings, which "sing" as vehicles cross, replaced a wooden deck in 1945.

Closing the last gap in the Mexico-to-Canada interstate freeway system when it opened in 1966, the **MARQUAM BRIDGE** (1.1 miles south) is a double-deck canti-lever truss. It was designed for "simplicity and economy of design," its engineers told a public disenchanted with its utilitarian, "Erector Set" appearance. Unlike other Portland bridges, the Marquam does not allow pedestrian access.

Pedestrians have always used the **ROSS ISLAND BRIDGE** (2.6 miles south), the first downtown bridge built without streetcar tracks. Today, this cantilever-truss span— designed by Gustav Lindenthal, who also created New York's Queensboro Bridge—is Portland's most heavily traveled nonfreeway bridge, serving the city's sprawling south-east neighborhoods. It is named for three midriver islands (just south of the bridge) where bald eagles and great blue herons nest.

For 40 years before construction of the **SELLWOOD BRIDGE** (4.1 miles south), Portlanders depended upon the Spokane Street Ferry to take them across the Wil-lamette River to the Oaks Amusement Park. The narrow (two-lane) Sellwood, a four-span continuous deck truss design, was Portland's first fixed-span vehicle bridge.

Of Portland's other bridges, two are contemporary spans on I-205: the sleek **ABER-NETHY BRIDGE** (1970) near Oregon City and the 600-foot **GLENN L. JACKSON MEMORIAL BRIDGE** (1982) across the Columbia River, named for Oregon's longtime State Highway Commission chairman. The **INTERSTATE BRIDGE** on I-5 between Portland and Vancouver replaced an interstate ferry when it was built in 1917; its second (southbound) span didn't open until 1958.

More interesting is the **OREGON CITY BRIDGE** (1922). The only Portland-area span designed by Conde McCullough, famed for his Oregon Coast bridges, this 745-foot arch bridge features fluted Art Deco main piers and hammered inset panels. Just north, on the Clackamas River, McCullough's McLoughlin Bridge has been rated the most beautiful steel bridge of its kind in the U.S.

—John Gottberg

the downtown turnaround at SW 11th Avenue and back. Top speed is 35 miles an hour, and (best of all!) rides are free. The round-trip takes about 40 minutes, and trolleys run about a half hour apart: 10am–6pm weekends, 9:30am–3pm weekdays, May–December. (Trolleys operate weekends only in March and April and take January and February off.)

BY CAR

Although Portland is relatively easy to navigate using mass transit, you may want a car for driving to wineries or to the Columbia River Gorge or Oregon City. Most major **RENTAL CAR** companies have offices at the airport; some have locations throughout the metro area. Here are some downtown agents: **AVIS** (330 SW Washington St; 503/227-0220); **DOLLAR** (132 NW Broadway; 503/228-3540); **ENTERPRISE** (445 SW Pine St; 503/275-5359); **HERTZ** (1605 SW Naito Pkwy; 503/223-1234); **THRIFTY** (632 SW Pine St; 503/227-6587). If you're a AAA member, you can pick up free maps and route advice at **AAA OREGON** (600 SW Market Ave, Downtown; 503/222-6734; map:E2); if not, try the **VISITOR INFORMATION AND SERVICES CENTER** at Pioneer Courthouse Square (503/275-8355; map:H3).

The best bet for **PARKING** downtown is in one of the six **SMART-PARK** garages; many merchants will validate your parking ticket for one or two hours of free parking with a minimum purchase of $25. You can find these garages at SW First Avenue and Jefferson Street; SW Fourth Avenue and Yamhill Street; SW Third Avenue and Alder Street; SW Tenth Avenue and Yamhill Street; SW Naito Parkway and Davis Street; and under O'Bryant Square, at SW Park Avenue and Stark Street. Of course, many other parking garages exist downtown, but their rates are usually higher for short-term usage. In most of downtown Portland and north to Union Station, solar-powered **SMARTMETERS** have replaced traditional parking meters for street parking. A single meter collects payment (by coin or credit/debit card) for multiple parking spaces, typically one side of a block, returning a stick-on receipt that is fastened to the inner car window. Rates vary, but are reasonable compared with other major cities.

Driving in Portland is not difficult once you figure out the woven pattern of one-way streets downtown (although beware of the tangle beneath the Morrison Bridge's west entrance). A warning about crossing town: The drawbridges open frequently for Willamette River traffic. Always expect a delay so you won't be surprised when there is one.

BY TAXI

Portland is not New York City, and cabbies are not used to being flagged down on the street. You'll have better luck finding a phone and calling for one. Your options include Broadway Cab (503/227-1234), Green Cab (503/234-1414), Portland Taxi (503/256-5400), Radio Cab (503/227-1212), and Sassy's Cab (503/656-7065). At press time, all five companies charged identical pickup and per-mile rates, so let cab availability be your guide. If you're headed to the airport, expect to pay about $25.

BY BICYCLE

Bicycling magazine has ranked Portland as the number-one city in the United States for two-wheelers. New bike lanes are still being added to the city streets, and even the police operate a cadre of bike patrollers. Most of Portland is flat enough that it can be enjoyed by bike, so feel free to go for it, even if you aren't an ironman or ironwoman.

The **YELLOW BIKES** are Portland's noted on-again, off-again experiment with bike sharing. The solid yellow cycles can (sometimes) be found unlocked against buildings or trees. Take one for a spin around town, then leave it in a moderately visible spot. The bikes last as long as the honor system prevails.

For bike-centric maps of the city, visit the **BICYCLE TRANSPORTATION ALLI-ANCE** (717 SW 12th Ave, Downtown; 503/226-0676; map:I2). The BTA is a great source for bike advocacy and up-to-date cycling information.

Essentials

BANKS

The usual major West Coast suspects can be found downtown. Most offer money exchange services but will cash personal checks only for account holders. Call for branch locations and hours: **BANK OF AMERICA** (503/279-3445), **BANK OF THE WEST** (503/225-1766), **KEY BANK** (503/323-6767), **US BANK** (503/872-2657), **WASHINGTON MUTUAL** (503/238-3100), and **WELLS FARGO** (503/886-3340).

BUSINESS, COPY, AND MESSENGER SERVICES

For high-quality business copy services, **CLEAN COPY** (1704 SW Broadway, Downtown; 503/221-1876; map:D1) features offset printing, color laser copies, and photocopying, and has desktop publishing services, plus free parking and delivery to the nearby Portland State University campus. **KINKO'S COPIES** (locations throughout the metro area: downtown at 1503 SW Park Ave; 503/223-2056; map:E1; and 221 SW Alder St; 503/224-6550; map:H5) is usually helpful and friendly—even at 3am—although these shops do high-volume business, and small jobs sometimes don't get the attention they deserve. You can rent Macintosh computers or PCs by the hour here, or check your e-mail at an online rate of 20 cents per minute. Color laser copiers and fax service are also available.

LAZERQUICK COPIES (1134 SW 5th Ave, Downtown; 503/228-6306; map:F3) offers more than 30 locations throughout the Portland metro area. This is a home-grown company that began its modest operations in a small Tigard house. Today, in addition to its offset printing and high-speed copying services—and a savings of 3 cents per copy over Kinko's in the do-it-yourself department—Lazerquick provides a host of computer and digital imaging solutions. All branches have scanners and rent Macs and PC-platform workstations.

At the **LADD CARRIAGE HOUSE** (1331 SW Broadway, Downtown; 503/222-1313; map:F3), once a livery stable, personalized secretarial services are the specialty. Word processing, tape transcription, and mailing services are available at an hourly rate. A pleasant conference room and 16 offices can be rented by the hour

PLACES OF WORSHIP

Like any major city, Portland has sanctuaries for people of all faiths. Many long-established churches are grouped downtown, which allows these historical structures to be easily visited in a pleasant walking tour.

Start at the oldest, an 1883 Carpenter Gothic edifice known only as **THE OLD CHURCH** (1422 SW 11th Ave; 503/222-2031; www.oldchurch.org). Saved from the wrecker's ball in 1970 and no longer used for regular services, the church is the site of meetings, performances, weddings, and other events.

Two blocks east on the South Park Blocks, the **SIXTH CHURCH OF CHRIST, SCIENTIST** (1331 SW Park Ave; 503/227-6024) features elaborate Byzantine/Art Deco exterior brickwork typical of the Depression era (1932) in which it was built. Next door, a castle-like stone tower rises above **ST. JAMES LUTHERAN CHURCH** (1315 SW Park Ave; 503/227-2439; www.stjameslutheranportland.org). The Gothic Revival structure dates from 1910, although its 1891 Pioneer Chapel is contained within the church.

Across the Park Blocks is the **FIRST CHRISTIAN CHURCH** (1315 SW Broadway Ave; 503/228-9211; www.firstchristianpdx.com), on this site since 1890. (The current structure dates from 1922.) This church has a brick exterior embellished with glazed terra cotta, a semicircular brick stairway, Doric portico columns, and a collection of Povey stained-glass windows. Just north, next to the Portland Center for the Performing Arts, is the **FIRST CONGREGATIONAL CHURCH** (1137 SW Broadway; 503/228-7219). Built in 1889–95, it is an impressive Venetian Gothic building modeled after Boston's Old South Church. It has a dramatic 175-foot latticed bell tower and is often used for literary arts lectures.

or the day. An answering service and mailbox rental are available for most any length of time.

PRONTO MESSENGER SERVICE (503/239-7666) is a Portland favorite, especially for crosstown deliveries. ("I'll Pronto it over to you" is a frequently heard phrase in business conversations.) For farther deliveries, try **TRANSERV PACKAGE EXPRESS** (503/241-0484).

COMPUTER RENTALS AND REPAIRS

BIT-BY-BIT (16295 SW 85th Ave, Tigard; 503/443-3833; www.bit-by-bit.com; map:NN9) is a well-established, nationwide rental service that will rent you an IBM-compatible PC and even deliver and set it up for you anywhere in the Portland metro area. They also lease laptops and some Macintoshes, as well as peripheral equipment. Twenty-four-hour service is available. For repairs, the **COMPUTER STORE** (700 NE Multnomah St, Irvington; 503/238-1200; map:GG6) and **COMTEK**

Four other important churches are on the west side of downtown. **FIRST UNITED METHODIST CHURCH** (SW 18th Ave and Jefferson St; 503/228-3195; www.fumcpdx.org) adjoins the UMC Center, which serves the Oregon-Idaho region. One of the largest U.S. Unitarian Universalist congregations makes its home at **FIRST UNITARIAN CHURCH** (1011 SW 12th Ave at Main St; 503/228-6389, www.firstunitarianportland.org), built in 1924. **FIRST BAPTIST CHURCH** (909 SW 11th Ave; 503/228-7465, www.fbc-portland.org), known as the White Temple, was built in 1892–94. **FIRST PRESBYTERIAN CHURCH** (1200 SW Alder St; 503/228-7331, www.fpcpdx.org) was built in 1890.

Outside of Downtown, classical concerts are sometimes performed at the **ST. PHILIP NERI CATHOLIC CHURCH** (SE 18th Ave and SE Division St; 503/231-4955). **ST. MARY'S CATHEDRAL** (1716 NW Davis St; 503/228-4397) is in the Nob Hill area, just a few blocks from the massive **TEMPLE BETH ISRAEL** (1972 NW Flanders St; 503/222-1069). This reform congregation was founded in 1858, the temple built in 1926–28.

On the east side, near Laurelhurst, the immense **HOLY TRINITY GREEK ORTHODOX CHURCH** (3131 NE Glisan St; 503/234-0468; www.goholytrinity.org) hosts a lavish festival each October. Covering a full city block, **ALL SAINTS EPIS-COPAL CHURCH** (4033 SE Woodstock Blvd; 503/777-3829) is a Southeast Portland landmark. At the **DHARMA RAIN ZEN CENTER** (2539 SE Madison St; 503/239-4846; www.dharma-rain.org), disciples of Soto Zen meditate and study Buddhist teachings. **MASJID AL-HIJRAH** (7007 NE Martin Luther King Jr Blvd; 503/281-7691) is Portland's Muslim center.

—*John Gottberg*

(1135 SW Alder St, Downtown; 503/227-4328; map:J2) are two of many places to take ailing PCs or Macs.

DRY CLEANERS, TAILORS, AND LAUNDROMATS
Many hotels offer dry cleaning and laundry services, or they can direct you to the closest place that does. One of the most convenient dry cleaners in the downtown area is **BEE TAILORS AND CLEANERS** (939 SW 10th Ave; 503/227-1144; map:G2), open weekdays and Saturday mornings. Bee offers curbside service; just honk. Or try **LEVINE'S**, with several branches downtown and the main location at 2086 W Burnside Street (503/223-7221; map:GG6). Near the Oregon Convention Center, **NEW CHINA LAUNDRY AND DRY CLEANERS** (105 NE 8th Ave, Downtown; 503/239-4100; map:GG6) offers delivery service. Many self-service laundries are tucked into neighborhood commercial centers or located in strip malls, so you can do your errands while your clothes wash.

GROCERY STORES

Grocery shoppers in Portland have many choices: FRED MEYER (aka "Freddy's"), the most central of which is just off Burnside Street near PGE Park (100 NW 20th Ave, Downtown; 503/273-2004; map:GG7), has for many years been the local favorite. Others prefer the upscale feel of ZUPAN'S (3301 SE Belmont St, Belmont; 503/239-3720; map:HH5; 2340 W Burnside St, Northwest; 503/497-1088; map: HH7; and other locations), the quasi–health food offerings at NATURE'S (3535 NE 15th Ave, Fremont; 503/288-3414; map:FF5; and other locations), or the variety of QFC (7525 SW Barnes Rd, West Haven; 503/203-0027; map:HH9; and other locations).

HOSPITAL AND MEDICAL/DENTAL SERVICES

Several hospitals provide physician referrals, including ADVENTIST MEDICAL CENTER (10123 SE Market St, Russellville; 503/256-4000; map:GG2) and EAST-MORELAND HOSPITAL (2900 SE Steele St, Eastmoreland; 503/234-0411; map: HH4). PROVIDENCE PORTLAND MEDICAL CENTER (4805 NE Glisan St, Laurelhurst; 503/215-1111; map:GG4) and PROVIDENCE ST. VINCENT MEDICAL CENTER (9205 SW Barnes Rd, West Hills; 503/216-1234; map:HH9) share a referral line (503/216-6595). LEGACY HEALTH SYSTEM, whose local facilities include both EMANUEL HOSPITAL AND HEALTH CENTER (2801 N Gantenbein Ave, North Portland; 503/413-2200; map:FF5) and GOOD SAMARITAN HOS-PITAL AND MEDICAL CENTER (1015 NW 22nd Ave, Northwest; 503/413-7711; map:FF6) also have one physician referral line (503/335-3500). The MULTNOMAH DENTAL SOCIETY (503/513-5010) provides emergency and routine referral service at no charge.

LEGAL SERVICES

The OREGON STATE BAR LAWYER REFERRAL SERVICE (5200 SW Meadows Rd, Lake Oswego; 503/684-3763; map:LL8) has offered referrals since 1971. Expect to pay $35 for an initial office consultation, after which you'll be charged the firm's normal hourly rates. A reduced-fee program is available.

PETS AND STRAY ANIMALS

If you see a stray or any animal in need of help, or if you've lost your furry travel companion, call MULTNOMAH COUNTY ANIMAL CONTROL (503/988-7387) or the nonprofit OREGON HUMANE SOCIETY (503/285-7722). For emergency medical care for your pet, call the highly respected DOVE LEWIS EMERGENCY ANIMAL HOSPITAL (1984 NW Pettygrove St; 503/228-7281; map:GG7), with a Nob Hill clinic and two branches, Eastside and Aloha (Beaverton area).

PHARMACIES

National giant RITE AID has numerous locations in Portland, including downtown (622 SW Alder St; 503/226-6791; map:I3); call 800/748-3243 to find the one nearest you. Ditto WALGREENS (800/925-4733), which has 24-hour prescription service at three stores. Nearest downtown is its Belmont store (940 SE 39th Ave; 503/238-6053; map:HH5). Several grocery stores (Fred Meyer, Safeway) contain pharmacies also. For downtown-area delivery, go to CENTRAL DRUG CO. (538 SW

4th Ave; 503/226-2222; map:H5); for deliveries in Northwest Portland, go to **NOB HILL PHARMACY** (2100 NW Glisan St; 503/227-1489; map:GG7).

PHOTOGRAPHY EQUIPMENT AND SERVICES

Film can be dropped off for developing at most major grocery stores, but for special treatment, helpful staff, and custom orders, head for **SHUTTERBUG** (501 SW Broadway at Washington St, Downtown; 503/227-3456; map:I3), where all color film development is done on-site. **WOLF CAMERA** (several locations including 900 SW 4th Ave, Downtown; 503/224-6776; map H3) is also reliable. For a full selection of the newest photography equipment, **CAMERA WORLD** (400 SW 6th Ave, Downtown; 503/205-5900; map:I4) is the spot.

POLICE AND SAFETY

In serious, life-threatening emergencies, dial 911. In nonemergency situations, dial 503/823-4636 for **PORTLAND POLICE INFORMATION**, or 503/823-3333 to make a report. Unlike those of many American cities, Portland's downtown is active by night as well as by day, at almost any hour, so it is generally safe for walking; but if you're out after dark, let common sense be your guide: know your destination. Another common-sense tip: Don't leave your valuables in the car, anytime.

POST OFFICES

Three full-service post offices are located in the downtown core. Across the street from Pioneer Courthouse Square, **PIONEER STATION** (520 SW Morrison St; map: H3) is open Monday through Friday from 8am to 5pm; **UNIVERSITY STATION** (1505 SW 6th Ave; map:E2) is just blocks from Portland State University and is open Monday through Friday from 7am to 6pm and Saturday from 10am to 3pm. For the best choice of stamps, visit the **MAIN OFFICE** at 715 NW Hoyt St (map:M4), open Monday through Friday from 7am to 6:30pm and Saturday from 8:30am to 5pm. Call 800/275-8777 to locate additional branches.

PUBLIC REST ROOMS

The most centrally located public rest rooms downtown are those in **PIONEER COURTHOUSE SQUARE** (701 SW 6th Ave; map:H3), near the Tri-Met office. The lobby opens at 8:30am and closes at 5pm weekdays and is open during the afternoon on weekends (hours vary). Farther south, there are public rest rooms in the **CLAY STREET PARKING GARAGE** (map:E3) between SW Third and Fourth Avenues. Restrooms are also available at **PIONEER PLACE** and in **MAJOR DEPARTMENT STORES** such as Meier and Frank and Nordstrom.

SALONS

There are many reputable hair salons in Portland, and sometimes the best stylists are hiding out in small neighborhood salons; ask a local with a great cut for a suggestion. Or check out one of these larger salons, listed for each quadrant of the city: in Northeast, **GARY LUCKEY HAIR DESIGN** (4016 NE Fremont St; 503/281-7831; map:FF5); in Southwest, **ROBERT'S OF PORTLAND** (5131 SW Macadam Ave; 503/222-4301; map:JJ6); in Southeast, **LA BELLE VIE** (Clackamas Town Center, 12000 SE 82nd Ave; 503/652-1618; map:KK3); and in Northwest, **APHRODITE** (1100 NW Glisan St; 503/223-7331; map:GG6).

HIGHER EDUCATION

Portland is a young city, so it makes sense that it's an educational hub. With a dozen four-year schools and numerous additional junior colleges and technical schools, its institutions of higher learning offer something to everyone.

PORTLAND STATE UNIVERSITY, Oregon's urban university, straddles the south end of downtown's South Park Blocks (724 SW Harrison St; 503/725-3000; www.pdx. edu; map:E1). It was established as a four-year college in 1955. Perhaps its most unmistakable structure is the Millar Library (SW 9th Ave and Harrison St), its convex glass facade overlooking the Park Blocks and built around a venerable copper beech tree. Other notable sites are Science 2 (SW 10th Ave and Montgomery St), which displays a variety of animal skeletons; Lincoln Hall (SW Park Ave and Mill St), the first campus building, now a performing-arts center; and The Urban Center Plaza (SW Montgomery St and 6th Ave), which houses a nationally renowned public-affairs school.

In north Portland, the **UNIVERSITY OF PORTLAND** (5000 N Willamette Blvd; 503/943-7911; www.up.edu; map:EE8) was founded in 1901 by the Roman Catholic archbishop of Oregon, and remains a Catholic university. Architect Pietro Belluschi, better known for the Portland Art Museum (1932), designed the handsome Chapel of Christ the Teacher in 1986, more than a half-century later, at the south end of the campus quadrangle beside the Willamette River bluffs. Imposing Waldschmidt Hall (1891) is the oldest campus building. West of the Chapel is the 1952 Merle Starr Observatory, home of a 20-inch reflector telescope. UP's women's soccer team, a national collegiate power, plays home matches at 5,000-seat Merlo Field (N Willamette Blvd and Hodges Ave).

Nationally renowned for its academic rigor and free-thinking student body, **REED COLLEGE** is located in the Eastmoreland area of southeast Portland (3203 SE Wood-

Local Resources

BOOKSTORES

POWELL'S CITY OF BOOKS (NW 10th Ave and W Burnside St, Downtown; 503/228-4651; map:J2) is the nation's largest independent bookseller, and despite a labor-union controversy, the store remains a Portland favorite. Occupying an entire block, Powell's has color-coded rooms and free maps to the store to help bookworms find their way around. Specialty satellite stores buttress the million-plus volumes. The major chains have made their way into Portland in recent years—most with an in-house coffee shop. **BORDERS** (503/220-5911; map:G5) is conveniently located on the light-rail line at SW Third Avenue and Morrison Street. **BARNES & NOBLE** has several Portland-area stores, including one near the Lloyd Center at 1231 NE Broadway (503/335-0201; map:GG6). There are dozens of others; see listings in the Shopping section of this book.

stock Blvd; 503/771-1112; www.reed.edu; map:II5). Founded in 1908 by a pioneer estate, the campus straddles a stretch of Crystal Springs Creek preserved as a wildlife refuge. At the Cooley Art Gallery in the Hauser Memorial Library (just east of Eliot Cir off SE Woodstock Blvd), major touring exhibitions share gallery space with a permanent collection of 19th and 20th-century American and European masters. Chamber Music Northwest plays a regular concert schedule at Kaul Auditorium (off SE Botsford Dr).

LEWIS AND CLARK COLLEGE, founded in 1867, is Portland's oldest; a liberal arts school known for its international programs, it is located off SW Terwilliger Boulevard in the Riverdale area (0615 SW Palatine Hill Rd; 503/768-7000; www.lclark.edu; map:JJ6). A visitor highlight is its interfaith Agnes Flanagan Chapel (1968), designed by architect Paul Thiry. Northwest Coast Indian influence evident in the circular building carries through the Native American spiritual sculptures on its approach bridge. Adjacent is the acclaimed Northwestern School of Law, founded in 1884, merged with Lewis and Clark in 1965.

Specialized four-year institutions include **OREGON HEALTH SCIENCES UNIVERSITY** (3181 SW Sam Jackson Park Rd; 503/494-8311; www.ohsu.edu; map:HH6); **OREGON GRADUATE INSTITUTE OF SCIENCE AND TECHNOLOGY** (20000 NW Walker Rd, Beaverton; 503/748-1121); **PACIFIC NORTHWEST COLLEGE OF ART** (1241 NW Johnson St; 503/226-4391; www.pnca.edu); and **OREGON COLLEGE OF ART AND CRAFT** (8245 SW Barnes Rd; 503/297-5544; www.ocac.edu). Nearby are **PACIFIC UNIVERSITY** (2043 College Wy, Forest Grove; 503/357-6151; www.pacificu.edu) and **MARYLHURST UNIVERSITY** (17600 SW Pacific Hwy, Lake Oswego; 503/636-8141; www.marylhurst.edu; map:NN5).

BROADCAST MEDIA

KBOO RADIO is a true labor of love for each of its hundreds of volunteers. The station has been on the air since 1975, and visitors will find it a great way to tap into Portland's vibrant eclectic communities. Tune into Iranian music, local newshounds, ditties from Holland, or local hip-hop megastars. Pick up a schedule at the station (20 SE 8th Ave, Buckman; 503/231-8032; map:GG5) and listen your way to Portland's epicenter. The city does, of course, offer standard radio and TV fare. Headbangers and those fond of honky-tonks will soon find their homes on the dial; cable-access scholars and soap-opera junkies can get comfy on the couch. Here's a basic rundown:

Radio Stations

NEWS	750 AM	KXL
COUNTRY	970 AM	KUPL
TALK	1150 AM	KKGT
TALK, NEWS, SPORTS	1190 AM	KEX
BUSINESS	1410 AM	KBNP

JAZZ	89.1 FM	KMHD
ECLECTIC	90.7 FM	KBOO
NATIONAL PUBLIC RADIO	91.5 FM	KOPB
CLASSIC ROCK	92.3 FM	KGON
NEW/ALTERNATIVE ROCK	94.7 FM	KNRK
DANCE/ROCK	95.5 FM	KXJM
OLDIES	97.1 FM	KKSN
COUNTRY	99.5 FM	KWJJ
TOP 40	100.3 FM	KKRZ
NEW/ALTERNATIVE ROCK	101.1 FM	KUFO
ADULT CONTEMPORARY	103.3 FM	KKCW
ADULT CONTEMPORARY	105.1 FM	KRSK
SMOOTH JAZZ	106.7 FM	KKJZ

Television Stations

ABC	2	KATU
CBS	6	KOIN
NBC	8	KGW
PBS	10	KOPB
UPN	12	KPTV
FOX	49	KPDX

Newspapers and Periodicals

The lone daily in Portland, the *Oregonian* (503/221-8327), has been published since 1850 and reigns as the king of print journalism in the city. Call the newspaper's telephone information service, **INSIDE LINE** (503/225-5555), to hear everything from lottery results to movie schedules. The newspaper doesn't maintain its own website, but you can glean much of what's in the *Oregonian* from www.oregonlive.com. The useful arts-and-entertainment section, *A&E*, appears on Fridays.

The *Oregonian* is joined on Tuesdays and Fridays by the news feature–oriented *Portland Tribune* (503/226-6397; www.portlandtribune.com), available free from racks throughout the city. The *Tribune* has been honored as the nation's best non-daily newspaper with a circulation exceeding 10,000. *Cue* is its Friday calendar section.

Willamette Week (503/243-2122; www.wweek.com) is Portland's alternative newsweekly. Thought provoking, irreverent, and often controversial, it covers politics, the arts, and civic matters, appears on Wednesdays, and is distributed free.

The *Portland Mercury* (503/294-0840; www.portlandmercury.com) is a *very* alternative weekly aimed at a more 18-to-35-aged crowd; appearing each Thursday, it also offers alternative arts and limited news coverage. *Just Out* (503/236-1252; www.justout.com), Portland's free gay and lesbian newspaper, is published on the first and third Friday of each month.

Portland business people are devotees of the *Daily Journal of Commerce* (503/226-1311; www.djc-or.com) and the weekly *Business Journal of Portland* (503/274-8733; www.bizjournals.com/portland).

The *Columbian* (503/224-0654; www.columbian.com) is the daily paper in Vancouver, Washington. Many of Portland's other suburbs have newspapers of their own. They include the *Beaverton Valley Times* (weekly), *Canby Herald* (biweekly), Forest Grove *News-Times* (weekly), Gresham *Outlook* (biweekly), *Hillsboro Argus* (biweekly), *Lake Oswego Review* (weekly), the *Newberg Graphic* (biweekly), the *Sandy Post*, (weekly), the *Tigard Times/Tualatin Times* (weekly), and *West Linn Tidings* (weekly).

Portland Magazine (503/558-5259; www.portland-magazine.com) is a handsome glossy that is published quarterly. Feature articles focus on home and lifestyle. It's available at newsstands for $3.95.

PUBLIC LIBRARIES

The **MULTNOMAH COUNTY LIBRARY** has 15 branches throughout the city, with film, tape, and book borrowing plus other services. The library sponsors a variety of films, lectures, and programs for children. Portlanders are exceedingly proud of their **CENTRAL LIBRARY** (801 SW 10th Ave; 503/248-5123; map:H1), which was completely remodeled in the mid-1990s; in 1998 voters also approved funds for upgrading many branch libraries. Cardholders are entitled to one hour of Internet access per day; visitors can obtain a 24-hour card for Internet use. Clackamas County has 10 city libraries and 3 county libraries. Call individual branches for hours and events. The **BEAVERTON CITY LIBRARY** (12375 SW 5th Ave, Beaverton; 503/644-2197; map:II9), Washington County's biggest, is available for use by citizens in Washington, Multnomah, or Clackamas Counties and is open seven days a week. Although Washington County's 11 libraries are individual, nonbranch entities, they all share databases.

INTERNET ACCESS

The branches of the Multnomah County Library all have Internet access (see above). Another place to get online is at the **VISITOR INFORMATION AND SERVICES CENTER** (Pioneer Courthouse Square; 503/275-8355; map:H3). Or you can pay 20 cents per minute of Internet time at any Kinko's outlet; see Business, Copy, and Messenger Services, in this chapter, for further information.

Important Telephone Numbers

EMERGENCY: POLICE, FIRE, AMBULANCE	911
DIRECTORY ASSISTANCE	411
AAA (Automobile Association of America) OREGON	503/222-6734
AIDS HOTLINE	503/223-AIDS
ALCOHOL AND DRUG HELPLINE	503/244-1312
ALCOHOLICS ANONYMOUS	503/223-8569
AMERICAN RED CROSS	503/284-1234
ANIMAL CONTROL	503/988-7387
AUTO IMPOUND	503/823-0044
BETTER BUSINESS BUREAU	503/226-3981

BIRTH AND DEATH RECORDS (Oregon vital records)   503/731-4095
BLOOD DONATION (Red Cross)   503/284-4040
CHAMBER OF COMMERCE   503/228-9411
CHILD ABUSE HOTLINE (Multnomah County)   503/731-3100
CITY OF PORTLAND (general information)   503/823-4000
COAST GUARD   503/240-9310
CONSUMER COMPLAINTS   503/229-5576
ENVIRONMENTAL PROTECTION AGENCY   503/326-3250
FEDERAL BUREAU OF INFORMATION (FBI)   503/224-4181
HEALTH INFORMATION AND REFERRAL   503/248-3816
HUMANE SOCIETY (lost pets)   503/285-7722
IMMIGRATION AND CITIZENSHIP (information)   800/375-5283
INTERNAL REVENUE SERVICE   800/829-1040
MARRIAGE LICENSES   503/988-5027
OREGON DEPARTMENT OF REVENUE   800/356-4222
OREGON STATE TOURISM   800/547-7842
PARKS AND RECREATION INFORMATION   503/823-PLAY
PASSPORTS   503/988-4508
PERMIT CENTER INFORMATION   503/823-7310
PLANNED PARENTHOOD   503/775-0861; 503/288-8826
POISON CONTROL CENTER   503/494-8968; 800/222-1222
POLICE (NONEMEREGENCY)   503/823-3333
POSTAL SERVICE INFORMATION   800/ASK-USPS
POWER OUTAGES (24 hours)   503/464-7777; 800/544-1795
RECYCLING INFORMATION   503/823-7202
ROAD CONDITIONS   503/588-2941; 800/977-6368
STATE PATROL (Mon–Fri)   503/731-3020
SUICIDE AND MENTAL HEALTH CRISIS   503/215-7082
TICKETMASTER   503/224-4400
TIME, TEMPERATURE, AND WEATHER (750 AM KXL)   503/243-7575
TRI-MET   503/238-RIDE
VISITOR INFORMATION   503/275-8355
VOTER INFORMATION   503/988-3720
WOMEN'S CRISIS LINE (sexual assault, domestic violence) 503/235-5333

RESTAURANTS

RESTAURANTS

Restaurants by Star Rating

★★★★
Castagna
Genoa
The Heathman Restaurant and Bar
Paley's Place

★★★⯪
Higgins
The Joel Palmer House
Morton's of Chicago: The Steak-
    house
Wildwood

★★★
Andina
BeWon
Bluehour
Caprial's Bistro
El Gaucho
Fratelli
Giorgio's
Lucy's Table
Nick's Italian Cafe
Pho Van
Restaurant Murata
Saucebox
Sin Ju
Taqueria Nueve
Typhoon!
Veritable Quandary
Winterborne

★★⯪
Assaggio
Bijou Café
Bugatti's Ristorante Italiano
Café Castagna
Caffe Mingo
Dragonfish Asian Café
Fernando's Hideaway
Fife

Gino's Restaurant and Bar
Hudson's Bar & Grill
Il Piatto
Justa Pasta
Lemongrass Thai
Mother's Bistro & Bar
Navarre
¡Oba!
Park Kitchen
Portland City Grill
Red Hills Provincial Dining
Red Star Tavern & Roast House
The Ringside
Rivers Restaurant
Ruth's Chris Steak House
Serratto
Sungari Pearl
Sungari Restaurant
Tabla
3 Doors Down
Tina's

★★
Acadia
Alba Osteria
Basta's Trattoria
Bernie's Southern Bistro
Besaw's
Bombay Cricket Club
Bread and Ink Café
Caffe Allora
Cañita
Clarke's
Colosso
Crowsenberg's Half & Half
Daily Café
Dining Room
Dundee Bistro
Esparza's Tex-Mex Café
Fa Fa Gourmet

The Farm Café
Gotham Building Coffee Shop
Green Onion
Hall Street Bar & Grill
Harborside
Henry's Café
Holden's
Il Fornaio
Jake's Famous Crawfish
Jake's Grill
Jo Bar and Rotisserie
John Street Café
Ken's Artisan Bakery & Café
Ken's Place
Khun Pic's Bahn Thai
La Calaca Comelona
Lauro Kitchen
Le Bistro Montage
Le Bouchon
Le Happy
London Grill
Lucère
Marco's Café and Espresso Bar
McCormick & Schmick's Seafood
    Restaurant
McCormick's Fish House and Bar
Nicholas' Restaurant
Pambiche
Papa Haydn
Pazzo Ristorante
Piazza Italia
Plainfield's Mayur
Portland Steak and Chophouse
Rheinlander and Gustav's Bier Stube
Ringside East
Saburo's
Saigon Kitchen
Sala
Salvador Molly's
750 ml
Southpark Seafood Grill and Wine
    Bar
Swagat
Syun Izakaya
Tartine
Thai Orchid

Three Square Grill
Tucci
Vat and Tonsure
Wild Abandon
Ya Hala
Zell's: An American Café

★★☆

Al-Amir
Aura
Beaches Restaurant & Bar
Black Rabbit Restaurant and Bar
Byways Café
Café Dacx
Campbell's Bar-B-Q
Cha! Cha! Cha! Mexican Taqueria
Corbett Fish House
DaVinci's Ristorante Italiano
Delta Café
Elephant's Delicatessen
Fong Chong
Fujin
Grand Central Bakery and Café
Grolla
Hands On Café
Hiro Sushi
Horn of Africa
India House
J+M Café
Little Wing Café
Malanga
Manzana Rotisserie Grill
Marrakesh
Milo's City Café
Mint
Obi
Original Pancake House
Paragon Restaurant & Bar
Perry's on Fremont
Pizzicato Gourmet Pizza
Riccardo's Restaurant
Sammy's Restaurant and Bar
Savory Bistro
Sayler's Old Country Kitchen
Seasons & Regions
Second Story Bistro

Sweet Basil Thai
Tin Shed Garden Café
Todai Restaurant
Tokyo Restaurant
Tuscany Grill

★

Abou Karim
Alameda Café
Alexis
Baan Thai
Bacchus
Beau Thai
Brasserie Montmartre
Burgerville
Bush Garden
Cactus Ya Ya
Cadillac Café
Café du Berry
Caldera
Chez José
Chez Machin
Clay's Smokehouse Grill
Cool Runnings
Dahlia Café
Dan and Louis' Oyster Bar
Dots Café
Fat City Café
Foothill Broiler
Fusion

Giant Drive-In
Good Dog/Bad Dog
Hoda's Middle Eastern Cuisine
Hunan
Little Italy's Trattoria
Jam on Hawthorne
Jarra's Ethiopian Restaurant
Koji Osakaya
Kornblatt's Delicatessen
La Cruda
La Prima Trattoria
Legin
Madame Butterfly
Misohapi
Noho's Hawaiian Cafe
Old Wives' Tales
Pastini Pastaria
Pho Thanh Thao
The Purple Parlor
Rose's Deli & Bakery
San Felipe Taqueria
Stickers Asian Cafe
Tara Thai Northwest
Taste of Asia
Touché
Umenoki
Vista Spring Cafe
Wu's Open Kitchen
Yam Yam's Southern Style Barbecue
Yuki Japanese Restaurant

Restaurants by Neighborhood

ALAMEDA/BEAUMONT (FREMONT)
Acadia
Alameda Café
Cool Runnings
Dining Room
Fife
Malanga
Perry's on Fremont
Savory Bistro
Winterborne

ALBERTA
Bernie's Southern Bistro

Tin Shed Garden Café

ALBINA
Mint

BEAVERTON
Bush Garden
Hall Street Bar & Grill
McCormick's Fish House and Bar
Pho Van
Sayler's Old Country Kitchen
Swagat
Taste of Asia
Typhoon!
Wu's Open Kitchen

BELMONT
Genoa
Hoda's Middle Eastern Cuisine
Khun Pic's Bahn Thai
La Calaca Comelona
Salvador Molly's
Wild Abandon

BROOKLYN
Sala

BUCKMAN
Il Piatto
J+M Café
Lemongrass Thai
Old Wives' Tales
Zell's: An American Café

BURLINGAME
Chez José
Original Pancake House

CHINATOWN
Fong Chong

CLINTON
Dots Café
Henry's Café
La Cruda
Little Italy's Cucina
Noho's Hawaiian Café

DOWNTOWN
Aura
Baan Thai
Brasserie Montmartre
Bush Garden
Cha! Cha! Cha! Mexican Taqueria
Crowsenberg's Half & Half
Dragonfish Asian Café
Elephant's Delicatessen
El Gaucho
Fernando's Hideaway
Good Dog/Bad Dog
Green Onion
The Heathman Restaurant and Bar
Higgins
Hunan

India House
Jake's Famous Crawfish
Jake's Grill
Koji Osakaya
London Grill
Madame Butterfly
McCormick & Schmick's Seafood
    Restaurant
Morton's of Chicago: The Steak-
    house
Mother's Bistro & Bar
Pazzoria
Pazzo Ristorante
Pizzicato Gourmet Pizza
Portland City Grill
Portland Steak and Chophouse
Red Star Tavern & Roast House
Restaurant Murata
Ruth's Chris Steak House
Saucebox
Southpark Seafood Grill and Wine
    Bar
Sungari Restaurant
Todai Restaurant
Typhoon!
Vat and Tonsure
Veritable Quandary

GLENDOVEER
Ringside East

GRESHAM
Typhoon!

HAWTHORNE
Bombay Cricket Club
Bread and Ink Café
Café Castagna
Castagna
Chez Machin
Fujin
Grand Central Bakery and Café
Jam on Hawthorne
Jarra's Ethiopian Restaurant
Ken's Place
3 Doors Down

33

HILLSBORO
Syun Izakaya
Tokyo Restaurant

HILLSDALE
Alba Osteria
Salvador Molly's
Seasons & Regions
Three Square Grill

HOLLYWOOD
Rheinlander and Gustav's Bier Stube

INNER SOUTHEAST
Daily Café
The Farm Café
Le Bistro Montage
Nicholas' Restaurant

IRVINGTON/LLOYD CENTER
Burgerville
Cadillac Café
Cha! Cha! Cha! Mexican Taqueria
Chez José
Colosso
Grand Central Bakery and Café
Koji Osakaya
Milo's City Café
Misohapi
Pastini Pastaria
Saigon Kitchen
Sweet Basil Thai
Yuki Japanese Restaurant

JOHN'S LANDING/SW MACADAM
Café du Berry
Corbett Fish House
Koji Osakaya
Rivers Restaurant
Taste of Asia

LAKE OSWEGO
Clarke's
Giant Drive-In
Hiro Sushi
Riccardo's Restaurant
Tucci

LAURELHURST
Esparza's Tex-Mex Café
Navarre
Pambiche
Tabla
Taqueria Nueve

MILWAUKIE
DaVinci's Ristorante Italiano

MOUNT TABOR
Caldera
Ya Hala

MULTNOMAH VILLAGE
Fat City Café
Grand Central Bakery and Café
Marco's Café and Espresso Bar

NORTHEAST
Dahlia Café
Grolla
Horn of Africa
Yam Yam's Southern Style Barbecue

NORTH PORTLAND/SAINT JOHNS
Gotham Building Coffee Shop
John Street Café
Pho Thanh Thao
The Purple Parlor

NORTHWEST
Basta's Trattoria
Beau Thai
Besaw's
BeWon
Café Dacx
Caffe Mingo
Elephant's Delicatessen
Foothill Broiler
Il Fornaio
Jo Bar and Rotisserie
Justa Pasta
Ken's Artisan Bakery & Café
Koji Osakaya
Kornblatt's Delicatessen
Le Happy
Lucy's Table

Marrakesh
Misohapi
Paley's Place
Papa Haydn
Pastini Pastaria
The Ringside
Rose's Deli & Bakery
Sammy's Restaurant and Bar
Serratto
Swagat
Tara Thai Northwest
Thai Orchid
Tuscany Grill
Typhoon!
Umenoki
Wildwood

OLD TOWN
Abou Karim
Al-Amir
Alexis
Bijou Café
Cañita
Dan and Louis' Oyster Bar
Obi
Second Story Bistro

OREGON CITY
Bugatti's Ristorante Italiano

PEARL DISTRICT
Andina
Bluehour
Byways Café
Caffe Allora
Cha! Cha! Cha! Mexican Taqueria
Daily Café
Fratelli
Giorgio's
Holden's
Le Bouchon
Little Wing Café
Manzana Rotisserie Grill
¡Oba!
Paragon Restaurant & Bar
Park Kitchen
Pho Van

Piazza Italia
750 ml
Sin Ju
Sungari Pearl
Touché

PORTLAND HEIGHTS
Plainfield's Mayur
Vista Spring Café

RALEIGH HILLS
La Prima Trattoria

RIVERPLACE
Harborside
Lucère

SELLWOOD
Assaggio
Gino's Restaurant and Bar

SOUTHEAST
Campbell's Bar-B-Q
Clay's Smokehouse Grill
Fusion
Lauro Kitchen
Legin
Pho Van
Saigon Kitchen
Sayler's Old Country Kitchen

SWAN ISLAND
Misohapi

TIGARD
Wu's Open Kitchen

TROUTDALE
Black Rabbit Restaurant and Bar

TUALATIN
Bush Garden

VANCOUVER, WA
Bacchus
Beaches Restaurant & Bar
Burgerville
Cactus Ya Ya
Fa Fa Gourmet
Hudson's Bar & Grill

Little Italy's Trattoria
Pasta Cucina

WEST LINN
Bugatti's Ristorante Italiano

WESTMORELAND
Caprial's Bistro
Papa Haydn
Saburo's
San Felipe Taqueria
Stickers Asian Café

Tartine

WEST SLOPE
Hands On Café

WINE COUNTRY
Dundee Bistro
The Joel Palmer House
Nick's Italian Cafe
Red Hills Provincial Dining
Tina's

Restaurants by Food and Other Features

WOODSTOCK
Delta Café

AMERICAN
Alameda Café
Bacchus
Beaches Restaurant & Bar
Besaw's
Black Rabbit Restaurant and Bar
Byways Café
Cadillac Café
Café Castagna
Caldera
Caprial's Bistro
Dahlia Café
Daily Café
Dining Room
Dots Café
Fat City Café
Fife
Foothill Broiler
Gotham Building Coffee Shop
Hall Street Bar & Grill
Jake's Grill
Jo Bar and Rotisserie
John Street Café
Ken's Place
London Grill
Manzana Rotisserie Grill
Mother's Bistro & Bar
Paragon Restaurant & Bar
Perry's on Fremont

Portland City Grill
Portland Steak and Chophouse
Red Star Tavern & Roast House
Rivers Restaurant
Sammy's Restaurant and Bar
Sayler's Old Country Kitchen
Three Square Grill
Vat and Tonsure
Zell's: An American Café

BAKERIES
Grand Central Bakery and Café
Il Fornaio
Ken's Artisan Bakery & Café
Pazzoria
Rose's Deli & Bakery

BENTO
Dragonfish Asian Café
Hiro Sushi
Tokyo Restaurant
Umenoki

BARBECUE
Campbell's Bar-B-Q
Clay's Smokehouse Grill
Yam Yam's Southern Style Barbecue

BREAKFAST
Alameda Café
Besaw's
Bijou Café
Black Rabbit Restaurant and Bar

Bread and Ink Café
Byways Café
Cadillac Café
Caffe Allora
Café du Berry
Cool Runnings
Crowsenberg's Half & Half
Dahlia Café
Daily Café
Dragonfish Asian Café
The Farm Café
Fat City Café
Foothill Broiler
Fusion
Gotham Building Coffee Shop
Grand Central Bakery and Café
The Heathman Restaurant and Bar
Henry's Café
Hudson's Bar & Grill
J+M Café
Jake's Grill
Jam on Hawthorne
John Street Café
Ken's Artisan Bakery & Café
Kornblatt's Delicatessen
La Cruda
La Prima Trattoria
London Grill
Lucère
Marco's Café and Espresso Bar
Milo's City Café
Mother's Bistro & Bar
Old Wives' Tales
Original Pancake House
Park Kitchen
Pazzo Ristorante
Portland Steak and Chophouse
The Purple Parlor
Red Star Tavern & Roast House
Rivers Restaurant
Rose's Deli & Bakery
Seasons & Regions
Second Story Bistro
Tin Shed Garden Café
Typhoon! (Downtown)
Wild Abandon

Zell's: An American Café

BRUNCH

Besaw's
Bread and Ink Café
Daily Café
Grolla
Hands On Café
Il Fornaio
Jo Bar and Rotisserie
London Grill
Papa Haydn
Park Kitchen
Red Star Tavern & Roast House
Sammy's Restaurant and Bar
Savory Bistro
Three Square Grill
Tucci
Veritable Quandary
Wild Abandon

BURGERS

Alameda Café
Aura
Beaches Restaurant & Bar
Bijou Café
Bread and Ink Café
Burgerville
Byways Café
Café Castagna
Daily Café
Dots Café
Fat City Café
Foothill Broiler
Giant Drive-In
Higgins
Holden's
Jo Bar and Rotisserie
London Grill
Laslow's Northwest
Lauro Kitchen
Lucère
Manzana Rotisserie Grill
Marco's Café and Espresso Bar
Mother's Bistro & Bar
Paragon Restaurant & Bar
Perry's on Fremont

Portland Steak and Chophouse
Red Star Tavern & Roast House
The Ringside
Ringside East
Savory Bistro
Sayler's Old Country Kitchen
Three Square Grill
Vista Spring Café
Wildwood
Zell's: An American Café

CAJUN/CREOLE
Acadia
Delta Café
Le Bistro Montage
Perry's on Fremont

CAMBODIAN
Taste of Asia

CARIBBEAN
Cool Runnings
Mint
¡Oba!
Salvador Molly's

CHINESE
Fa Fa Gourmet
Fong Chong
Fujin
Hunan
Legin
Stickers Asian Café
Sungari Pearl
Sungari Restaurant
Taste of Asia
Wu's Open Kitchen

COCKTAIL LOUNGE
Andina
Aura
Basta's
Black Rabbit Restaurant and Bar
Bluehour
Bush Garden
Dahlia Café
Dragonfish Asian Café
El Gaucho

Fernando's Hideaway
Gino's Restaurant and Bar
Hall Street Bar & Grill
Harborside
The Heathman Restaurant and Bar
Hudson's Bar & Grill
Jake's Famous Crawfish
Jake's Grill
Lucère
Mint
Morton's of Chicago: The Steak-
  house
Mother's Bistro & Bar
¡Oba!
Pazzo Ristorante
Portland Steak and Chophouse
Rhinelander and Gustav's Bier Stube
The Ringside
Ringside East
Rivers Restaurant
Ruth's Chris Steak House
Sammy's Restaurant and Bar
Sungari Pearl
Typhoon! (Downtown)
Veritable Quandary
Wild Abandon
Wildwood

COFFEEHOUSES
Caffe Allora
Crowsenberg's Half & Half
Gotham Building Coffee Shop
Henry's Café
Jam on Hawthorne
Ken's Artisan Bakery & Café
Marco's Café and Espresso Bar
Pazzoria
Riccardo's Restaurant

CONTINENTAL
Brasserie Montmartre
Castagna
Clarke's
London Grill
Rivers Restaurant
Second Story Bistro

CREPES
Chez Machin
Le Happy

CUBAN
Cañita
Malanga
Pambiche

DELICATESSEN
Elephant's Delicatessen
Kornblatt's Delicatessen
Rose's Deli & Bakery

DESSERTS (EXCEPTIONAL)
Bluehour
Bread and Ink Café
Bugatti's Ristorante Italiano
Castagna
Fernando's Hideaway
Genoa
Hands On Café
The Heathman Restaurant and Bar
Higgins
Ken's Place
Le Happy
Marco's Café and Espresso Bar
Paley's Place
Pambiche
Papa Haydn
Wildwood

DIM SUM
Dragonfish Asian Café
Fong Chong
Legin

EAST AFRICAN/ETHIOPIAN
Horn of Africa
Jarra's Ethiopian Restaurant

ECLECTIC
Aura
Caldera
Colosso
Hands On Café
Holden's
Marco's Café and Espresso Bar
Mother's Bistro & Bar

Old Wives' Tales
Savory Bistro
750 ml
Wild Abandon

FAMILY
Alameda Café
Alexis
Bread and Ink Café
Burgerville
Caffe Mingo
Chez José
Clay's Smokehouse Grill
Dan and Louis' Oyster Bar
Dining Room
Fat City Café
Foothill Broiler
Giant Drive-In
Gino's Restaurant and Bar
Grand Central Bakery and Café
Il Fornaio
Justa Pasta
Ken's Artisan Bakery & Café
Koji Osakaya
Legin
Little Italy's Trattoria
Little Wing Café
Manzana Rotisserie Grill
Marco's Café and Espresso Bar
Mother's Bistro & Bar
Old Wives' Tales
Original Pancake House
Pastini Pastaria
Perry's on Fremont
Piazza Italia
Pizzicato Gourmet Pizza
Rheinlander and Gustav's Bier Stube
Rose's Deli & Bakery
Salvador Molly's
San Felipe Taqueria
Sayler's Old Country Kitchen
Second Story Bistro
Swagat
Sweet Basil Thai
Three Square Grill
Tin Shed Garden Café
Todai Restaurant

Vista Spring Café
Ya Hala
Yam Yam's Southern Style Barbecue
Wu's Open Kitchen
Zell's: An American Café

FIREPLACE
The Heathman Restaurant and Bar
Hudson's Bar & Grill
Il Fornaio
Jake's Famous Crawfish
The Joel Palmer House
Lucère
¡Oba!
Paragon Restaurant & Bar
Plainfield's Mayur
Red Hills Provincial Dining
The Ringside
Sayler's Old Country Kitchen
Tina's

FRENCH
Café du Berry
Chez Machin
The Heathman Restaurant and Bar
Le Bouchon
Second Story Bistro
Tartine
Winterborne

FUSION
Fusion
Grolla
3 Doors Down

GERMAN
Rheinlander and Gustav's Bier Stube

GOOD VALUE
Basta's Trattoria
Beau Thai
Besaw's
Burgerville
Caldera
Cha!Cha!Cha! Mexican Taqueria
Chez José
Chez Machin
Colosso

Corbett Fish House
Crowsenberg's Half & Half
Fa Fa Gourmet
Fife
Fujin
Gino's Restaurant and Bar
Henry's Café
Hoda's Middle Eastern Cuisine
Horn of Africa
Justa Pasta
Ken's Place
Koji Osakaya
Le Bouchon
Legin
Lucy's Table
Manzana Rotisserie Grill
Misohapi
Nicholas' Restaurant
Original Pancake House
Pambiche
Pho Thanh Thao
San Felipe Taqueria
Savory Bistro
Stickers Asian Café
Swagat
Taqueria Nueve
Tin Shed Garden Café
Ya Hala
Zinc Bistrot

GOURMET TAKEOUT
Elephant's Delicatessen
Ken's Place
Seasons & Regions

GREEK
Alexis
Foothill Broiler
Lauro Kitchen
Sammy's Restaurant and Bar

HAWAIIAN
Noho's Hawaiian Café

HISTORIC BUILDING
Al-Amir
Caldera
Dan and Louis' Oyster Bar

Gotham Building Coffee Shop
Jake's Famous Crawfish
Jake's Grill
The Joel Palmer House
Marco's Café and Espresso Bar
Nick's Italian Cafe
Plainfield's Mayur
The Purple Parlor
Red Hills Provincial Dining
Touché

HOT DOGS
Good Dog/Bad Dog

INDIAN
Bombay Cricket Club
India House
Plainfield's Mayur
Swagat

ITALIAN
Alba Osteria
Assaggio
Basta's
Bugatti's Ristorante Italiano
Caffe Allora
Caffe Mingo
DaVinci's Ristorante Italiano
Fratelli
Gino's Restaurant and Bar
Giorgio's
Il Fornaio
Il Piatto
Justa Pasta
La Prima Trattoria
Little Italy's Cucina
Little Italy's Trattoria
Nick's Italian Cafe
Pasta Cucina
Pastini Pastaria
Pazzo Ristorante
Piazza Italia
Pizzicato Gourmet Pizza
Riccardo's Restaurant
Sala
Serratto
Tucci
Tuscany Grill

JAPANESE
Bush Garden
Koji Osakaya
Madame Butterfly
Restaurant Murata
Saburo's
Sin Ju
Syun Izakaya
Todai Restaurant
Tokyo Restaurant
Umenoki
Yuki Japanese Restaurant

JEWISH
Kornblatt's Delicatessen
Mother's Bistro & Bar
Rose's Deli & Bakery

KOREAN
BeWon
Noho's Hawaiian Café

LAOTIAN
Saucebox
Tara Thai Northwest

LATE NIGHT
Aura
Bacchus
Brasserie Montmartre
Dots Café
El Gaucho
Holden's
La Cruda
Le Bistro Montage
Le Happy
Madame Butterfly
Pazzo Ristorante
Saucebox
Touché
Wild Abandon

LATIN AMERICAN
Andina
¡Oba!
Salvador Molly's
Taqueria Nueve

MEDITERRANEAN

Abou Karim
Café Dacx
Grolla
Lauro Kitchen
Lucy's Table
750 ml
Southpark Seafood Grill and Wine Bar
Tabla
3 Doors Down
Touché

MEXICAN

Café Dacx
Cha! Cha! Cha! Mexican Taqueria
Esparza's Tex-Mex Café
La Calaca Comelona
La Cruda
San Felipe Taqueria

MIDDLE EASTERN

Al-Amir
Abou Karim
Hoda's Middle Eastern Cuisine
Nicholas' Restaurant
Ya Hala

MILK SHAKES

Bijou Café
Burgerville
Byways Café
Fat City Café
Foothill Broiler
Giant Drive-In
Mother's Bistro & Bar
Sayler's Old Country Kitchen
Vista Spring Café

MOROCCAN

Lauro Kitchen
Marrakesh

NORTHWEST

Bluehour
Caprial's Bistro
Castagna
Dundee Bistro

The Farm Café
Hands On Café
The Heathman Restaurant and Bar
Higgins
Hudson's Bar & Grill
The Joel Palmer House
Lucère
Lucy's Table
Paley's Place
Park Kitchen
Tina's
Veritable Quandary
Wildwood

ONION RINGS

Burgerville
Byways Café
Hudson's Bar & Grill
Portland Steak and Chophouse
Red Hills Provincial Dining
The Ringside
Ringside East
Ruth's Chris Steak House
Salvador Molly's
Wildwood

OUTDOOR DINING

Alameda Café
Basta's
Beaches Restaurant & Bar
Black Rabbit Restaurant and Bar
Bugatti's Ristorante Italiano
Café du Berry
Caldera
Castagna
Chez José
Chez Machin
Hall Street Bar & Grill
Hands On Café
Harborside
Henry's Café
Il Fornaio
The Joel Palmer House
Khun Pic's Bahn Thai
La Cruda
Little Wing Café
Malanga

Noho's Hawaiian Café
Paley's Place
Pambiche
Perry's on Fremont
Riccardo's Restaurant
Salvador Molly's
Sammy's Restaurant and Bar
Savory Bistro
Tin Shed Garden Café
Tucci
Typhoon! (Northwest)
Veritable Quandary
Wild Abandon
Wildwood

OYSTERS
Aura
Bread and Ink Café
Corbett Fish House
Dahlia Café
Dan and Louis' Oyster Bar
El Gaucho
Jake's Famous Crawfish
Jo Bar and Rotisserie
Harborside
Le Bistro Montage
McCormick & Schmick's Seafood
    Restaurant
McCormick's Fish House and Bar
Red Hills Provincial Dining
Seasons & Regions

PAN-ASIAN
Dragonfish Asian Café
Misohapi
Saucebox
Stickers Asian Café

PERSIAN (IRANIAN)
Green Onion

PERUVIAN
Andina

PIZZA
Beaches Restaurant & Bar
Bugatti's Ristorante Italiano
Café Castagna

DaVinci's Ristorante Italiano
La Prima Trattoria
Little Italy's Trattoria
Nicholas' Restaurant
Pizzicato Gourmet Pizza
Touché
Vista Spring Café

PRIVATE ROOMS
Black Rabbit Restaurant and Bar
Bush Garden
Caprial's Bistro
Serratto

ROMANTIC
Acadia
Assaggio
Bluehour
Castagna
El Gaucho
The Farm Café
Fernando's Hideaway
Fratelli
Genoa
Giorgio's
The Heathman Restaurant and Bar
Henry's Café
Higgins
Hudson's Bar & Grill
Il Piatto
Le Happy
Lucy's Table
Marrakesh
Mint
¡Oba!
Paley's Place
Papa Haydn
Pho Van
Piazza Italia
Portland City Grill
Red Hills Provincial Dining
Rivers Restaurant
Saucebox
Serratto
750 ml
Tabla
Tuscany Grill

43

Wild Abandon
Wildwood
Winterborne

SEAFOOD

Acadia
Aura
Café Dacx
Corbett Fish House
Dan and Louis' Oyster Bar
The Farm Café
Fong Chong
Harborside
Jake's Famous Crawfish
Jake's Grill
Le Bistro Montage
Legin
McCormick & Schmick's Seafood
  Restaurant
McCormick's Fish House and Bar
Mint
¡Oba!
Perry's on Fremont
Rivers Restaurant
Sala
Sammy's Restaurant and Bar
Saucebox
Seasons & Regions
Southpark Seafood Grill and Wine
  Bar
Todai Restaurant
Typhoon!
Winterborne
Wu's Open Kitchen

SOUP/SALAD/SANDWICH

Alameda Café
Bijou Café
Bread and Ink Café
Byways Café
Cadillac Café
Caffe Allora
Crowsenberg's Half & Half
Dahlia Café
Daily Café
Dots Café
The Farm Café

Fat City Café
Foothill Broiler
Gotham Building Coffee Shop
Grand Central Bakery and Café
Hands On Café
Henry's Café
Holden's
J+M Café
John Street Café
Kornblatt's Delicatessen
Little Wing Café
Manzana Rotisserie Grill
Marco's Café and Espresso Bar
Milo's City Café
Mother's Bistro & Bar
Rose's Deli & Bakery
Savory Bistro
Three Square Grill
Tin Shed Garden Café
Vista Spring Café
Zell's: An American Café

SOUTHERN/SOUL FOOD

Bernie's Southern Bistro
Delta Café
Le Bistro Montage
Three Square Grill
Yam Yam's Southern Style Barbecue

SOUTHWESTERN

Cactus Ya Ya
Chez José
La Cruda
San Felipe Taqueria
Taqueria Nueve

SPANISH

Fernando's Hideaway
Lauro Kitchen

STEAK HOUSES

El Gaucho
Jake's Grill
Morton's of Chicago: The Steak-
  house
Portland Steak and Chophouse
The Ringside
Ringside East

Ruth's Chris Steak House
Sayler's Old Country Kitchen

SUSHI
Bush Garden
Dragonfish Asian Café
Hiro Sushi
Koji Osakaya
Madame Butterfly
Obi
Portland City Grill
Restaurant Murata
Saburo's
Sin Ju
Syun Izakaya
Todai Restaurant
Tokyo Restaurant
Umenoki
Yuki Restaurant Restaurant

TAPAS
Colosso
Fernando's Hideaway
Navarre
Tabla

THAI
Baan Thai
Beau Thai
Khun Pic's Bahn Thai
Lemongrass Thai
Misohapi
Stickers Asian Café
Sweet Basil Thai
Tara Thai Northwest
Thai Orchid
Thanh Thao
Typhoon!

UNIQUELY PORTLAND
Alexis
Bijou Café
Black Rabbit Restaurant and Bar
Bluehour
Brasserie Montmartre
Burgerville
Byways Café
Caprial's Bistro

Daily Café
Dots Café
Elephant's Delicatessen
Esparza's Tex-Mex Café
The Farm Café
Genoa
Gotham Building Coffee Shop
Hands On Café
Higgins
J+M Café
Jake's Famous Crawfish
John Street Café
London Grill
McCormick & Schmick's Seafood
     Restaurant
Mother's Bistro & Bar
Original Pancake House
Paley's Place
The Ringside
Typhoon!
Vat and Tonsure
Veritable Quandary
Wildwood

VEGETARIAN/VEGAN
Bombay Bicycle Club
Byways Café
Café Dacx
Caprial's Bistro
Chez Machin
Dahlia Café
Dots Café
The Farm Café
Fratelli
Higgins
Horn of Africa
Jarra's Ethiopian Restaurant
Khun Pic's Bahn Thai
Misohapi
Nicholas' Restaurant
Old Wives' Tales
The Purple Parlor
Tin Shed Garden Café

VIETNAMESE
Misohapi
Pho Thanh Thao
Pho Van
Saigon Kitchen
Savory Bistro
Taste of Asia

VIEW
Bacchus
Beaches Restaurant & Bar
Lucère
Harborside
Portland City Grill
Rivers Restaurant

WINE BAR
Alba Osteria
Assaggio
Caffe Allora
Dundee Bistro
Grolla
Ken's Artisan Bakery & Café
Lucy's Table
Navarre
Paley's Place
Riccardo's Restaurant
Savory Bistro
Serratto
750 ml
Southpark Seafood Grill and
    Wine Bar
Tabla
Tina's

TOP 200 RESTAURANTS

Abou Karim / ★

221 SW PINE ST, OLD TOWN; 503/223-5058 Though the menu offers all the traditional chicken and lamb dishes that typify Mediterranean cuisine, those in the know choose the meze platter: a groaning board loaded with enough garlicky hummus, mint-scented tabbouleh, dolmas, silky baba ghanouj, and falafel to serve four hungry guests from a half-dozen food groups. Add a savory kebab or two, a steaming bowl of spicy lentil soup, and a dish of rice, and what started as a light snack becomes a substantial meal that's anything but square. Speaking of squares, save room for a block of sticky-sweet and crackling baklava. **COME HERE FOR BIG PORTIONS AND GOOD LEBANESE COFFEE.** *$$; AE, MC, V; checks OK; lunch Mon–Fri, dinner every day; full bar; reservations recommended; map:J6*

Acadia / ★★

1303 NE FREMONT ST, ALAMEDA; 503/249-5001 Acadia stakes its singular identity by taking Northwest products and blending them with distinctive seafood imported from the Louisiana Gulf Coast. The food is a marriage of Cajun and Creole. Acadia's dishes are not as robustly flavorful as what you'd find in the French Quarter, but they're not as fatty either. The Taste of New Orleans is an instant star, pairing crawfish étouffée with a delicacy not commonly found in these parts: soft-shell crab with a tempura-like batter. The corn flour used in catfish Belle Chasse also gets high marks, as do the seductive mashed potatoes that accompany this fish platter. The plump juiciness of Gulf shrimp and crawfish outshine even the strong flavors found in gumbo, étouffée, and a crawfish–corn bread dressing featured in Sunday chicken. Classy touches—warm bread served with silver tongs, attractive place settings replete with heavy cutlery and Spiegelau crystal—complete the winsome experience, along with tiptop service in the candlelight-bathed dining room. **COME HERE FOR A RARE TASTE OF THE BAYOU.** *$$; AE, DC, DIS, MC, V; no checks; lunch Wed, dinner Mon–Sat; full bar; reservations recommended; www.creolapdx.com; map:FF5* &

The Alameda Café / ★

4641 NE FREMONT ST, BEAUMONT; 503/284-5314 This low-key neighborhood bistro has a pleasant, all-day/everyday quality. The small dining room and scattering of outdoor tables receive a regular weekend crowd that clamors for the hale and hearty breakfasts, including cinnamon-dusted baguette French toast and the best—maybe only—apple-bacon-blue cheese omelet within the city limits, the Klickitat. Lunches feature a sturdy, stick-to-your-ribs club sandwich and garlicky Caesar salad. For dinner, options are all-American, with a streak of French-by-way-of-Santa Fe. Entrées range from a simple Alameda Burger (say yes to the superb fries) to the more elaborate grilled salmon or halibut, paired with unique citrus-seasoned butters: chipotle-orange, lemon-ginger, or grapefruit-basil. Crayons and plenty of butcher paper on the tables are a nice touch for the child in everyone. **COME HERE FOR FAMILY-FRIENDLY DINING.** *$–$$; MC, V; local checks OK; breakfast, lunch, dinner every day; beer and wine; no reservations; map:FF4* &

THE LIFE OF JAMES BEARD

James Beard (1903–1985) is widely acknowledged as the "father of American gastronomy," the leader in the 20th-century movement to recognize cuisine as art, not just something for survival. Few are aware, though, that Beard was a native of Portland or that he maintained lifelong ties with the city of his birth.

Beard's father, John, worked at Portland's Customs House, still a landmark building in the North Park Blocks. His English mother, Elizabeth, ran a boardinghouse and enthusiastically cooked for her renters. The family summered on the Oregon Coast at Gearhart, just north of Seaside, where they fished, gathered shellfish and wild berries, and feasted on their harvest.

James Beard briefly attended Reed College but left Portland in 1923 hoping to become an actor. Despite four years of voice and theater study abroad, however, his career in show business never blossomed, and in 1935 he began a catering business to supplement his meager acting income. Two years later, Beard opened a small New York gourmet shop called Hors d'Oeuvres, Inc., and refocused his career goals. His 1940 cookbook, *Hors d'Oeuvre & Canapés*, was the first major cookbook devoted to cocktail food and helped to overturn the notion that "small bites" could not be substantial cuisine. His second cookbook, *Cook It Outdoors* (1942), did the same for outdoor cooking.

After a World War II stint with the United Seamen's Service, Beard returned to the East Coast, where he immersed himself in the culinary arts. Between 1945 and 1955,

Al-Amir / ★★

223 SW STARK ST, OLD TOWN; 503/274-0010 Housed in the historic Bishop's House—an 1879 Gothic confection that is one of Portland's most charming architectural oddities—Al-Amir is the elder statesman of local Middle Eastern restaurants. Stepping into the somber, stained-glass chamber is an immersive experience, as you're greeted by spicy scents of Lebanese cooking and by soft-spoken and gracious servers. Ambience, gentility, and attention to detail set the place apart—care is taken with every dish from a simple *ful mudammas* (marinated fava-bean salad) to the elaborately seasoned and prepared *kharouf muhammar* (roasted lamb with a cucumber-yogurt sauce). Take your refreshment from the intriguing selection of Lebanese beers and wines, or have a cup of the house tea—an intoxicating mixture of black tea, mint, anise, and cardamom. **COME HERE FOR A GRACIOUS MIDEAST DINING EXPERIENCE.** *$$; AE, MC, V; no checks; lunch Mon–Fri, dinner every day; full bar; reservations recommended; www.alamirportland.com; map:I5* &

Alba Osteria / ★★

6440 SW CAPITOL HWY, HILLSDALE; 503/977-3045 You don't have to vacation in Italy's Piedmont region—with its nebbiolo grapes and white truffles—to appreciate Alba Osteria's menu. But after eating your way down the teasingly short list of he wrote five more cookbooks, co-authored two others, became a regular on NBC television's first cooking show (in 1946), and ran a Nantucket restaurant. He established the James Beard Cooking School in New York in 1955 and added a second school in Seaside, Oregon, soon thereafter. He wrote 10 more cookbooks between 1959 and 1983 and traveled tirelessly, teaching and lecturing about good, fresh, well-prepared food wherever he went.

Today, nearly two decades after his death, James Beard's name remains synonymous with wholesome American cuisine. His legacy of integrity and culinary excellence is perpetuated by the James Beard Foundation, championed by chef Julia Child, among others. Based in Beard's renovated brownstone in New York City's Greenwich Village, the foundation honors the country's finest chefs, provides scholarships and workshops to train new chefs, and welcomes visitors to its library and archives.

The first Monday in May, the James Beard Foundation stages the American culinary industry's biggest party—its annual awards banquet, honoring chefs, restaurants, food journalists, and cookbook authors. Portland chefs are regularly nominated in the "Best Chef: Northwest/Hawaii" category. First-place winners have included Cory Schreiber of **WILDWOOD** (1998), Philippe Boulot of **THE HEATHMAN** (2001), and Greg Higgins of **HIGGINS** (2002). Vitaly Paley of **PALEY'S PLACE** (2003) has been a finalist for the award, and Caprial Pence of **CAPRIAL'S BISTRO** has been honored for her television cooking series.

—*John Gottberg*

handmade pastas, don't be surprised if you become possessed of a forceful desire to visit the land that spawned the exquisite recipes. The trio of pastas—not one with tomato sauce—could make an Atkins devotee forsake his diet, if only for a night. Tajarin, the most basic, is a tangle of egg noodles accented by Parmigiano cheese, morels, and porcini. The wispy lightness of the chive-thin strands comes as a delicious surprise; the mushrooms contribute earthiness. Maltagliate (wide, flat noodles with torn edges) mingle with firm asparagus nubs, bits of prosciutto, and Parmigiano. Entrées also veer from the cadre of usual suspects. Finanziera is a rich and silky mélange of sweetbreads, chicken livers, and mushrooms. Tender roasted duck breast is served in rosy, half-inch slices with fingerling potatoes and glazed carrots. Knowledgeable servers and a charming *enoteca*, or wine bar, increase Alba's appeal. **COME HERE FOR AUTHENTIC, OUT-OF-THE-ORDINARY PASTAS.** *$$–$$$; AE, DIS, MC, V; checks OK; lunch Wed–Fri, dinner Tues–Sun; full bar; reservations recommended; map:JJ7* &

Alexis / ★

215 W BURNSIDE ST, OLD TOWN; 503/224-8577 This boisterous Portland institution—replete with blue-and-white-checked tablecloths and waiters yelling "Opa!"—is one of only a handful of Greek restaurants in town. The longstanding family operation makes every diner feel like a cousin: the welcome is warmer than the flaming *saganaki* (kasseri cheese doused with ouzo and set ablaze). On their journey toward substantial, fork-tender moussaka and lamb souvlaki, diners are slowed by plump grape-leaf packets, terrific calamari with tzatziki, and little pillows of phyllo and feta known as *tiropetes*. Baskets of warm, addictive house bread come with the meal, loaves of which are available to take home, along with other specialties. Consider Alexis if you have a large group: the staff will rearrange tables at a moment's notice and dish up the $13.95-per-person family-style dinner option. **COME HERE FOR GREEK STANDARDS AND A FESTIVE ATMOSPHERE.** *$$; AE, DC, MC, V; no checks; lunch Mon–Fri, dinner Mon–Sat (belly dancers Fri–Sat); full bar; reservations for 10 or more; map:K6* &

Andina / ★★★

1314 NW GLISAN ST, PEARL DISTRICT; 503/228-9535 This Pearl District newcomer serves *Novo* (New) Peruvian cuisine. Open since mid-2003, Andina's open kitchen showcases the talents of French-trained, Lima-born chef Emmanuel Piqueras Villarán. You might start with *ensalada Machu Pichu*, a quinoa-and-vegetable salad with avocado and duck confit, or with *anticuchos*, marinated beef skewered with grilled yucca and served with *salsa criolla*. For the main course, consider *pachamanca del Inca*, a traditional hunter's meal of venison and pheasant baked in a clay pot, or *bonito con nopal*, sautéed albacore tuna marinated in a sauce of passion fruit, bell pepper, and lime and served on a cactus leaf. Photos of Peruvian life and a museum-quality art collection—fabric art, Spanish colonial pieces, pre-Incan woodcraft—provide the perfect setting, as does a skylit atrium with wrought-iron railing that overlooks a small courtyard. Don't leave without trying Peru's signature drink, *pisco*, a white-grape brandy. Enjoy it with dinner or sip it in the spacious bar, where you're likely to find Latin Americans cheering a TV *futbol* (soccer) match. **COME HERE FOR NOVO PERUVIAN CUISINE AND A PISCO SOUR.** *$$–$$$; AE, DIS, MC, V; local checks OK; lunch Mon–Fri, dinner Mon–Sat, brunch Sun; full bar; reservations recommended; www.andinarestaurant.com; map:M1* &

Assaggio / ★★⯪

7742 SE 13TH AVE, SELLWOOD; 503/232-6151 Assaggio takes pasta very seriously—and it's taught Portlanders to take it seriously as well. Its name means "sampling" or "tasting," and that's what the booming neighborhood trattoria encourages diners to do. The house specialty, Assaggio di Pasta, is a sampling of three separate pastas chosen by the chef and served family-style to the entire table. These might be penne (with Italian sausage, or prosciutto and leeks), fusilli (with duck and red-wine sauce, or wild mushrooms and butternut squash), the ever-popular spaghetti alla puttanesca, or some Neapolitan noodle you've never met. You might want to start with the nifty bruschetta, the crimini mushrooms, or the smoked-trout mousse, but don't fill up too early This intimate trattoria, with its

50

low lighting and classical decor, is not just a pastaria. The delectable dinner entrées, which change monthly, also include the likes of *borsette al carni* (pasta purses filled with rabbit and veal, topped with shaved pilota cheese) and *pesce al forno* (fresh fish baked with prosciutto, served with sautéed spinach, red pepper, fennel, and creamy yellow polenta). In the adjoining *enoteca* (wine bar), you can dine while imbibing one of 10 fine Italian wines offered by the glass. **COME HERE FOR GREAT PASTA IN AN INTIMATE ATMOSPHERE.** *$$; AE, DIS, MC, V; checks OK; dinner Tues–Sat; beer and wine; reservations recommended; www.assaggiorestaurant.com; map:KK5* &

Aura / ★★☆

1022 W BURNSIDE ST, DOWNTOWN; 503/597-2872 There's a certain aura about Aura, and we're not just talking food. A wall-size set of three multimedia panels projects an ever-changing light show of high-tech art, evolving from an early-evening aurora borealis to a fiery late-night inferno when the dance floor heats up. It's good that the built-in entertainment starts slowly, because dinner deserves your attention. Chef Chad Leighton has created a playful menu strong in seafood and influenced by a broad range of world cuisines. You might opt for his orange-jicama salad to start, or peppercorn-crusted seared tuna Nicoise with wasabi sour cream and an olive tapenade. A sweet potato–vanilla bean purée is a remarkable accompaniment to Jamaican skirt steak. Or, if you've got company, consider one of Aura's "tier" meals, feeding two to four. The Blue Tier includes a crab-and-shrimp cocktail, oysters on the half shell, a smoked-mussel sushi risotto, shrimp tempura sticks, and a lime-tequila ceviche. For the late-night dance crowd, a small-bite menu—available till 2am weekends—features miniburgers (jerked chicken, salmon, portabella) and skewers (Yucatan tuna, Vietnamese chicken, Caribbean conch). **COME HERE FOR THE LIGHT SHOW.** *$$; AE, DIS, MC, V; no checks; dinner Wed–Sun; full bar; reservations recommended; www.auraportland.com; map:K2* &

Baan Thai / ★

1924 SW BROADWAY, DOWNTOWN; 503/224-5155 With its gold-and-purple paint job, standing-room-only lunch rushes, and warrenlike floor plan, this popular Thai cafe near Portland State University has the appearance of a well-loved hangout serving up wholesome rice and noodle dishes to famished college kids. And while it's true the menu offers such standards as chicken satay and phad thai, you'll be rewarded for venturing into less-trodden territory. Crispy catfish stir-fried with basil and lemon leaf is multitextured and complex in flavor, while a trout salad with julienned fruit provides surprising refreshment after a bout with the spicy rice and noodle dishes. (Diners may request any of several levels of hotness—but don't get too brave.) *Plar kung*, a grilled prawn salad, is a gorgeous spread of mesclun greens, diced cucumbers, chopped scallions, mint, and cilantro, tossed with a handful of crisp shrimp barely charred at the edges and dressed in a spicy, lime-scented vinaigrette. And don't miss the Volcano Chicken, a house specialty that involves a whole game hen, spicy barbecue sauce, and dancing live flames. **COME HERE FOR ADVENTUROUS THAI CUISINE.** *$$; AE, DIS, MC, V; no checks; lunch, dinner Mon–Sat; beer and wine; no reservations; map:D1* &

51

Basta's Trattoria / ★★

410 NW 21ST AVE, NORTHWEST; 503/274-1572 Basta's continues doing what it has done well since it opened: serving well-priced and mostly reliable Italian fare. The jewel-toned interior has been enhanced by a slick lounge with midcentury-modern furniture. While there are many superlative Italian restaurants in Portland, Basta's should not be overlooked. The emphasis is on Tuscan specialties—look for occasional Porcetta Toscona nights, when a whole stuffed suckling pig is sliced tableside—but chef Marco Frattorilli does not neglect the rest of his native Italy. From super-simple penne with plum tomato sauce and mozzarella to Uncle Vittorio's Ragout with delicious braised baby back rib meat, pastas do not disappoint. Basta's crunchy Caesar salad, *arancini* (saffron rice fritters), and an especially nice slow-cooked lamb shank in an herby tomato sauce studded with pancetta are clear standouts. **COME HERE FOR THE MOD COCKTAIL LOUNGE.** *$$; AE, MC, V; no checks; lunch Tues–Fri, dinner every day; full bar; reservations recommended; www.bastastrattoria.com; map:HH7* &

Beau Thai / ★

730 NW 21ST AVE, NORTHWEST; 503/223-2182 Going strong for a decade, this neighborhood spot is a stalwart member of Portland's legion of commendable Thai restaurants. It may not be innovative and refined, but it's certainly above average and easy on the wallet. The plant-filled interior is welcoming and tasteful, the service friendly and efficient. The bountiful menu offers about 100 choices, from tom yum soup to an omelet-like seafood dish. Portions are as large as the menu; an order of phad thai—filled with lots of egg bits, shredded chicken or firm, fried tofu, and topped with raw bean sprouts and a peanut sauce that's not jarringly sweet—easily passes the litmus test. Appetizers such as chicken satay and salad rolls pair well with Asian lagers to make a nice start on dinner. Indicate the desired level of spiciness when you place your order—anyone who likes it hot won't be disappointed by four-star treatment. **COME HERE FOR DEPENDABLE THAI STANDARDS.** *$; AE, DIS, MC, V; no checks; lunch, dinner Mon–Sat; beer and wine; reservations for 5 or more; map:GG7* &

Bernie's Southern Bistro / ★★

2904 NE ALBERTA ST, ALBERTA; 503/282-9864 Instead of dishing up dyed-in-the-wool Southern classics, Bernie's tweaks soul-food recipes to suit Northwest palates and to take advantage of local bounty. While the seafood étouffée may lack heat, the moist buttermilk-fried chicken—a skinless, boneless breast and thigh—is a smart update that doesn't trade flavor for less fat. From blackened catfish in bourbon-brown-butter sauce to chicken-fried steak with creamy gravy and mashed potatoes, you'll find the smash hits of Southern cooking here, along with such nontraditional renditions as roasted vegetable gumbo and pecan-crusted salmon with a dried cherry-port cream sauce. Salads that change with the seasons—house-pickled beets with wilted greens in winter, strawberries and cucumbers in a raspberry-mint vinaigrette in spring—are especially appealing. Deep-fried appetizers, including featherweight hush puppies and fried dill pickles, are a worthy indulgence. **COME HERE**

FOR THE HOUSE-MADE CORN BREAD AND HONEY BUTTER. *$$; AE, DIS, MC, V; no checks; dinner Tues–Sat; full bar; reservations recommended; map:FF5* &

Besaw's / ★★

2301 NW SAVIER ST, NORTHWEST; 503/228-2619 Nothing seems to shake the powerful loyalty and affections of Besaw's customers—whom the restaurant repays with free coffee as they wait in line outside. Besaw's has been here since the turn of the last century, and it has aged beautifully; everything seems polished, from the mirror above the bar to the gracious service. The cafe is currently operating on a high level of imagination. The core menu may run to Mother's meat loaf and roast chicken, but nightly specials expand to include dishes like habañero-glazed pork chop and bronzed scallops. At weekend brunch, when enthusiasm burns hottest, hearty servings of farmer's hash or French toast might be bolstered by hand-lettered specials such as poached eggs on crab cakes over yakisoba noodles with Thai curry hollandaise or grilled salmon Benedict with rosemary-garlic potatoes. In the best tradition of the neighborhood cafe, Besaw's serves three squares a day in a bright, high-ceilinged dining room that beckons the neighbors—as well as others from well beyond the reaches of Nob Hill—to come back for repeat performances. **COME HERE FOR FARMER'S HASH AT WEEKEND BRUNCH.** *$–$$; DIS, MC, V; checks OK; breakfast Tues–Fri, lunch, dinner Tues–Sat, brunch Sat–Sun; full bar; dinner reservations recommended; www.besaws.com; map:GG7* &

BeWon Korean Restaurant / ★★★

1203 NW 23RD AVE, NORTHWEST; 503/464-9222 BeWon is one of those rare restaurants that sticks to its guns, dictating what people want rather than the other way around. By virtue of meticulous cookery and presentation, and servers' contagious verve and patient explanations, BeWon has quickly carved out a gleaming reputation. There are two routes to take: the prix-fixe path of *han jung shik*, an eight-course extravaganza that approximates a traditional Korean meal for an unbelievably affordable $24.95; or a dinner constructed of à la carte orders. Try both. *Han jung shik* is a stimulating meal that takes diners on a memorable tour of the five flavors of Asian cooking (salt, sweet, sour, hot, and bitter). À la carte ordering allows sampling of not-to-be-missed dishes that aren't in the prix-fixe menu. Main courses, such as broiled mackerel caked in sea salt and sliced pork in a red-pepper barbecue sauce, are satisfying, but they take a backseat to the vivid parade of accompanying side dishes. Teensy saucers hold the likes of dried cod, kimchee, small pancakes chunked with vegetables and crab, delicious flank-steak strips, and dried kelp flakes sprinkled with sugar. The restaurant has gained a legion of new Korean food lovers; try it once, and you may soon BeWon. **COME HERE FOR TRADITIONAL KOREAN CUISINE AND INTRIGUING RICE WINES.** *$$; AE, DIS, MC, V; no checks; lunch Mon–Sat, dinner every day; beer and wine; reservations recommended; map:GG7* &

Bijou Café / ★★½

132 SW 3RD AVE, OLD TOWN; 503/222-3187 Twenty-five years old, the handsome Bijou Café long ago attained breakfast-landmark status in Portland, and the remodeling of neither the restaurant nor the surrounding neighborhood has changed its position. Lunch, with its one-third-pound Painted Hills beef burger, phenomenal milk shakes, soba noodle salad, and seasonal specials ranging from an avocado-grapefruit salad to steamed fish with red curry sauce and basmati rice, can pack quite a full house. But the real crush still happens before noon, especially on the weekend, when the lines stretch out the door for grilled cinnamon bread, terrific scrambled eggs, and as many as three kinds of pancakes. The tofu scramble is the best in town, the spicy French toast is made with thick brioche, and salmon hash has a reverent following. Be prepared to wait for a table during peak hours and brace yourself for service that is not exactly accommodating. Microbrews and local wines are available, and since the breakfast menu is served all day, you can pick just the right vintage to go with a blueberry pancake. **COME HERE FOR BREAKFAST IN A CLASSIC ATMOSPHERE.** *$–$$; MC, V; local checks only; breakfast every day, lunch Mon–Fri; beer and wine; no reservations; map:J5* &

Black Rabbit Restaurant and Bar / ★★☆

2126 SW HALSEY ST (EDGEFIELD), TROUTDALE; 503/492-3086 One thing that strikes a guest immediately at Edgefield, the estate home of Black Rabbit and a smattering of smaller, less formal eateries and watering holes, is that everyone seems to be having a good time. One reason may be that there's something for everyone to like on these 38 acres. That's true of Black Rabbit, too: not only is there the large, pleasant dining room hung with Edgefield's ubiquitous and eclectic art, but there's also a bar serving light meals and, outside, a New Orleans–style courtyard for elegant and romantic supping on a summer evening. What the menu lacks in surprises it makes up for in successes. Variations on the meat-and-potato theme result in beef tenderloin with garlic mashed potatoes, grilled pork chops encrusted with herbs, and sautéed prawns with poblano chiles and lime juice. When the food matches the Columbia Gorge-ous setting, when the wind carries to your nose the scent of herbs from the nearby estate gardens, and when there's a bed-and-breakfast room upstairs reserved in your name, Edgefield's Black Rabbit is a great place to spend an evening. **COME HERE FOR THE ENTIRE EDGEFIELD EXPERIENCE.** *$$–$$$; AE, DIS, MC, V; local checks only; breakfast, lunch, dinner every day; full bar; reservations recommended; www.mcmenamins.com* &

Bluehour / ★★★

250 NW 13TH AVE, PEARL DISTRICT; 503/226-3394 Love it or shun it, everyone's got an opinion about Bluehour, including those who have never stepped inside the cavernous, million-dollar restaurant. Some complain it's too chic for its own good; but baby, Portland's not a lumberjack town anymore. Co-owner Bruce Carey has done oodles to elevate the culinary standard in Stumptown. With its menu fueled by the passion and prowess of chef Kenny Giambalvo, Bluehour continues this legacy handily. The cosmopolitan interior is part of the fun and reward of laying down your bills, but Giambalvo validates the outlay with seriously well-crafted food. His signature gnocchi are velvety, cheesy cushions with a salty kick and hint of black truffle. Made-to-order risotto—touting an ever-changing list of accents that can include cuttlefish braised in squid ink or woody wild mushrooms—takes longer to prepare than most appetizers, but the first bite assuages the wait. Seared sea scallops cosseted by strips of bacon are a heady, reliable treat. Intriguing ingredients unexpectedly pop up all over the menu. Watercress and a sweet-onion salad lend perkiness to grilled hanger steak; grapefruit and leeks accompany excellent seared foie gras. Even desserts, such as chocolate caramel tart spiked with *fleur de sel*, take a walk on the wildish side. **COME HERE FOR THE GLAMOUR.** *$$$; AE, DC, MC, V; checks OK; dinner Tues–Sat; full bar; reservations recommended; www.bluehouronline.com; map:L1* &

Bombay Cricket Club Restaurant / ★★

1925 SE HAWTHORNE BLVD, HAWTHORNE; 503/231-0740 This lively little restaurant on Hawthorne serves familiar and darn-good Indian food—curries, vindaloo, tandoori, biryani—plus a small selection of Middle Eastern dishes. All the while, the TV at the tiny bar broadcasts recorded cricket matches. If cricket is not your thing, never mind; once you've tasted your first mango margarita and dipped a samosa into the tangy tamarind chutney, you'll find yourself distracted by the potential of such intriguing flavors. Don't miss chewy naan stuffed with onions and spices, succulent tandoori chicken with basmati rice, and garlicky-hot fish vindaloo. Spicy curries include lamb, chicken, and vegetarian options. The only disappointment is that the condiments that usually accompany an Indian meal—mango chutney, yogurt raita, and dhal—must be ordered separately. The dozen-or-so tables are often packed, and service can be slow; but if you don't make a reservation well in advance, you can expect to wait in line. **COME HERE FOR THE AWESOME NAAN.** *$$; AE, DIS, MC, V; no checks; dinner every day; full bar; reservations recommended; map:HH5* &

Brasserie Montmartre / ★

626 SW PARK AVE, DOWNTOWN; 503/224-5552 The dress code is casual, but aided by a snazzy black-and-white-tiled floor, clubby upholstery, and grand chandeliers, the Brasserie Montmartre evokes bohemian glamour worthy of its namesake in Paris. The swank factor is upped when you sip on a K. Rae's martini and nibble plump, hot-and-sweet prawns. Most entrées are very moderately priced, and while they're a bit passé, they are well executed. Tender chicken breast is stuffed with chèvre, crabmeat, and spinach and sliced into rounds for a classic presentation. Service is swift and professional. Jazz musicians, from Everything's Jake to the Gordon Lee Trio, play nightly on an enclosed stage at a volume that permits conversation. And as one of only a few places for after-midnight dining, Brasserie does brisk trade well into the night. Until 1am weekdays and 3am weekends, you can find everything from veal with mushrooms, to eggs Benedict, to Beluga caviar. **COME HERE FOR OLD-SCHOOL AMBIENCE AND EXTENDED DINING HOURS.** *$$; AE, DC, DIS, MC, V; no checks; lunch, dinner every day, brunch Sat–Sun; full bar; reservations recommended; www.brasseriemontmarte.com; map:I3* &

Bread and Ink Café / ★★

3610 NE HAWTHORNE BLVD, HAWTHORNE; 503/239-4756 There's more to the beloved Bread and Ink than its blintzes. This homey, light-filled bistro in the heart of the funky Hawthorne District serves a marvelous Jamaican jerk-chicken sandwich, grilled black-bean cakes, and panfried oysters with chipotle-lime aioli for lunch. At dinner, you can't go wrong with the chèvre, arugula, and hazelnut salad, risotto primavera, or pork tenderloin in fresh rosemary, garlic, and white wine. Regulars rave about the oversize hamburger, with house-made condiments to do it justice, and the impressive baked desserts, including a legendary cassata. Intriguing framed line drawings on the walls, crayons by request, and huge windows onto Hawthorne are more reasons the place has become a neighborhood landmark. But the biggest is the hallowed blintzes. Enjoy these delicately crisped squares of dough, enfolding a lemony ricotta, with Bread and Ink's raspberry jam. **COME HERE FOR THE BLINTZES.** *$$; AE, DIS, MC, V; checks OK; breakfast, lunch, dinner Mon–Sat, brunch Sun; beer and wine; no reservations; map:HH5* &

Bugatti's Ristorante Italiano / ★★★

18740 WILLAMETTE DR, WEST LINN; 503/636-9555 / 334 WARNER MILNE RD, OREGON CITY; 503/722-8222 Lydia Bugatti and John Cress's endearing Italian restaurant in West Linn features fine Italian wines at affordable prices, a friendly, attentive staff, and seasonal foods with a menu that changes every few weeks. Anytime, watch for rigatoni carbonara and spaghetti frutti di mare. Regulars also love the pasta della casa: fettucine with cremini mushrooms and artichoke hearts in a creamy tomato sauce. On the entrée side, you might find a grilled chicken risotto or veal with shallots and grilled asparagus. There's a nice olive oil spiked with garlic for dipping the crusty rustic bread, but save room for dazzling desserts, such as the cloudlike tiramisu or the melt-in-your-mouth cannoli. The well-dressed yet simple dining room is quite large, but reservations are a good idea; it's a popular place. Those who can't get in can console themselves with a spot at Bugatti's Caffe and Pizzeria in downtown West Linn (1885 Blankenship Rd; 503/557-8686; map: PP5). The new Oregon City restaurant, strong in pastas and pizza, fills a void in that town's dining scene. **COME HERE FOR THE PASTA DELLA CASA.** *$$; MC, V; local checks only; dinner every day; beer and wine; reservations recommended; map: OO5; map:QQ3* &

Burgerville / ★

307 E MILL PLAIN BLVD, VANCOUVER (AND BRANCHES); 360-693-8801 Halibut fish and chips with Walla Walla sweet onion rings, a fresh strawberry-banana yogurt smoothie, and a 2 percent decaf latte—this sounds like a bistro order, not something spoken into a box at a drive-through. But locally owned Burgerville, a four-decade-old regional fast-food chain with 39 outlets in Washington and Oregon, caters to time-crunched appetites with good, fresh food. Local ingredients are made to order: dissect the Pepper Bacon Tillamook Cheeseburger, for instance, to discover Northwest ground chuck, Tillamook cheddar, local bacon, Portland pickles, lettuce, and tomato on a bun baked nearby. Nothing ever sees a freezer or travels far by truck, and that includes black-bean garden burgers with sweet-potato fries. Nine outlets are in Portland; check out the centrally located Rose Quarter shop (1135 NE Martin Luther King Blvd, near Lloyd Center; 503/235-6858; map:GG6). **COME HERE FOR QUICK BURGERS AND MILK SHAKES.** *$; MC, V; checks OK; lunch, dinner every day; no alcohol; no reservations; www.burgerville .com; map:CC6* &

Bush Garden / ★

900 SW MORRISON ST, DOWNTOWN (AND BRANCHES); 503/226-7181 There's something of a Dr. No quality to downtown Portland's most established Japanese restaurant. Pass a foyer decorated with trickling stone fountains into the dining area, where a sushi bar is backed by a lair of rice-paper booths lined with bamboo and tatami mats. All the regular raw-fish offerings are here, with seasoned chefs willing to entertain special requests when possible. You'll also get sukiyaki and a *shabu shabu* tabletop, and unexpected offerings such as scallop *batayaki*. Live music nights with DJs and bands had begun to turn the once-sedate restaurant into a raucous hipster joint, but edicts from management have created a quieter karaoke scene. Although the new rules make dining more pleasant, the lounge's swanky leather swivel chairs and geode-jeweled tabletops look strangely neglected. Bush Garden has branches in Tualatin (8290 SW Nyberg Rd; 503/691-9777; map:OO9) and Beaverton (at the Uwajimaya supermarket; map:II9). **COME HERE TO DINE IN A PRIVATE TATAMI ROOM.** *$$; AE, DC, DIS, MC, V; no checks; lunch Mon–Fri, dinner every day; full bar (Downtown), beer and wine (Tualatin), no alcohol (Beaverton); reservations recommended; map:I2* &

Byways Café / ★★

1212 NW GLISAN ST, PEARL DISTRICT; 503/221-0011 The American road trip sets the theme of what was once known as Shakers, where hundreds of salt and pepper shakers lined the walls. State plates and pendants now fill the room and a Viewfinder graces every table. Although owners have come and gone, this place has stayed true to form with a simple, wholesome menu of no-frills diner food in lumberjack-size portions. Breakfast customers load up on griddlecakes, omelets, Scottish oatmeal, or Meg's Vegetarian Hash. The lunch menu includes burgers (with a very popular ground-turkey version), soups, onion rings, and fries. In the grilled Reuben, corned beef—cooked on the premises and used in the best-selling morning hash—towers between slices of rye bread slathered with house-made horseradish sauce. That's just one example of the generous serving sizes, which you should keep in mind when you order fries: a half order easily feeds two. Save room for a milk shake, served the old-fashioned way in a tall glass with extra in a tin vessel on the side. **COME HERE FOR A TURKEY BURGER AND A MILK SHAKE.** *$; no credit cards; checks OK; breakfast Tues–Sun, lunch Tues–Sat; no reservations; www.bywayscafe.com; map:M2* &

Cadillac Café / ★

1801 NE BROADWAY, IRVINGTON; 503/287-4750 The neon sign, pink paint job, and glass-encased vintage Caddy in the dining room may make you feel like you're breakfasting in a car dealership, but fans of the Cadillac Café aren't bothered by such trifles. Since moving east a few blocks to new, glitzier digs, this breakfast joint remains as solidly popular as ever—particularly with the Bloody Mary and mimosa crowd. Custard-topped French toast is festooned with seasonal fruit and nut additions, while the oversize omelets and creamy Benedicts satisfy those savory cravings. The decor and menu are fun-loving, verging on goofy: be prepared to repeat phrases like "Bunkhouse Vittles" when ordering your food. The CC's most salient feature is the legendary weekend wait for a table—upwards of 45 minutes on a Saturday morning. But hundreds of hungry Portlanders can't be wrong. **COME HERE FOR THE PHENOMENAL FRENCH TOAST.** *$; AE, MC, V; no checks; breakfast, lunch every day; no alcohol; no reservations; map:GG5* &

Café Dacx / ★★☆

1937 NW 23RD PL, NORTHWEST; 503/274-4004 In a humble bungalow at the very end of shop- and restaurant-studded NW 23rd, Café Dacx serves a fresh and healthy breed of pescatarian cuisine. Mediterranean and Mexican touches flicker in the entrées, which may include spicy fish tacos for lunch (served open-faced with plenty of black beans and brown rice) and Athenian prawns for dinner (sautéed in a cream sauce fortified with feta cheese and tomatoes). The halibut entrée, which wraps the fish in a pumpkin-seed crust and covers it in a tangy, spicy tomatillo sauce, is Dacx at its best. Vegetarians will find many inventive choices, notably a tempeh-and-rice phyllo square baked spanikopita-style and served with a tomato-mint relish. An assortment of small salads and starter plates—grilled goat cheese, hummus, and baba ghanouj—take the edge off while you're waiting for dinner. And while you wait, take note of the artwork on the walls; it changes frequently and is available for sale. **COME HERE FOR UNIQUE SEAFOOD AND VEGETARIAN DISHES.** *$$; DIS, MC, V; no checks; lunch Wed–Fri, dinner Tues–Sat; beer and wine; reservations recommended; map:GG7* &

Café du Berry / ★

6439 SW MACADAM AVE, CORBETT; 503/244-5551 Good news: breakfasts at Café du Berry are sublime, especially the house specialty, French toast served with a sprinkling of berries. The toast arrives like an edible cloud on a plate—light, sweet, and delicious—and is served alongside a heap of well-cooked hash browns. Order a side of the country sausage, a glass of fresh-squeezed orange juice, and a steaming cup of coffee, and you've got a dream breakfast that may just take you right through the lunch hour. Country French-style lunches and dinners are simple and reasonably priced, and tend toward bistro fare—*Salad nicoise* or roast beef on a baguette at midday; chicken Dijon, pork au normande, salmon in a raspberry vinaigrette sauce, or roast rack of lamb in the evening. Choose a table in the upstairs dining room and watch the world go by on busy Macadam Avenue. **COME HERE TO ENJOY SUMMER BREAKFAST IN THE OUTDOOR COURTYARD.** *$$; AE, DIS, MC, V; no checks; breakfast, lunch every day, dinner Wed–Sat; beer and wine; reservations recommended; map:JJ6*

Caffe Allora / ★★

504 NW 9TH AVE, PEARL DISTRICT; 503/445-4612 It's uncanny how sitting at one of Allora's tiny tables can instantly transport you to Italy. You taste the heady vapor of strong espresso in the air. You smell the fresh, pungent aromas of oak, olive leaves, and chopped garlic. You take note of the handsome young men chattering on cell phones outside and the insouciant servers grinning and shrugging as they shuffle plates and glasses, and the fantasy is complete. Allora is both espresso bar and *enoteca*, paying equal tribute to caffe and vino. Traditional small plates like the *bresaola* (thinly sliced cured beef, arugula, and shaved parmesan) and *proscuitto melone* are handsomely prepared and presented as light accompaniments to that glass of pinot grigio: the wine list is packed with romantic choices. Panini and bruschetta are available with a variety of pungent fillings—chunked tuna, speck, sautéed peppers, sliced pear, fresh mozzarella. A narrow chalkboard advertises daily specials of zuppa and pasta. If you're just there for coffee, order it in one of the cute, sherbet-tinted demitasse cups piled atop the espresso machine. Viva Italia. **COME HERE FOR TRUE ITALIAN AMBIENCE.** *$$; MC, V; no checks; breakfast, lunch, dinner Mon–Sat; beer and wine; dinner reservations recommended; map:M3* &

Caffe Mingo / ★★☆

807 NW 21ST AVE, NORTHWEST; 503/226-4646 Caffe Mingo is what so many places aspire to: always packed, buzzing with good humor, and absolutely confident in its ability to produce splendid, uncomplicated meals. The dishes that made this tiny trattoria an immediate smash when it opened in the mid-1990s are still drawing crowds that spill out the door. Diners eagerly wait in line for spiedini with prawns and croutons, Gorgonzola and walnut raviolini, and juicy chicken breast with fluffy gnocchi. One bite of the signature penne in red wine–espresso sauce (how Portland!) and you know you'll be back for more. Seasonal salads—such as beets with green beans and wax beans in nutty garlic-almond dressing—are one-of-a-kind beauties. The menu has grown more ambitious over time, pushing the prices up a bit (you can spend $100 on the reserve wine list), but not sky-high. A seat at the counter gets you a close-up view of the kitchen's preparations, perhaps inspiring some homemade Italian fare of your own, while a seat in front lets you watch people ogling your table. **COME HERE FOR PENNE WITH BRAISED BEEF IN RED WINE–ESPRESSO SAUCE.** *$$; AE, DC, DIS, MC, V; no checks; dinner every day; beer and wine; reservations recommended; map:GG7* &

Caldera / ★

6031 SE STARK ST, MOUNT TABOR; 503/233-8242 Housed in the 1910 Graham Pharmacy building high on the shoulder of Mount Tabor, you'd never guess that serene and homey Caldera rests on a slumbering volcano. A beautiful varnished bar (left over from the apothecary days) gives the small dining room a seasoned gravitas, while ample patio seating lets large parties dine in the flickering light of tiki torches. The menu is a mix of home cooking's greatest hits, with a few echoes of exotic locales thrown in. Ingredients as daring as papaya-rubbed pork (in the Caribbean salad) feel right at home alongside the stick-to-your-ribs simplicity of beef stroganoff—a savory platter of wide fluttery egg noodles, strips of stewed beef, and mushroom gravy. Such pasta dishes as shrimp linguini, lasagna, and cheese manicotti provide sustenance without a lot of fanfare. The affordable prices make the comfort food here that much more comforting. **COME HERE FOR AN ERUPTION OF SOLID HOME COOKING.** *$–$$; AE, MC, V; no checks; dinner Tues–Sun; full bar; reservations recommended; map:HH4* &

Campbell's Bar-B-Q / ★☆

8701 SE POWELL BLVD, SOUTHEAST; 503/777-9795 People who come into this little house along Powell Boulevard and inhale deeply get more of a barbecue hit in one breath than some places provide in a rack of ribs. The dining area is quaint, the servers are cheerful and efficient, and side dishes (especially potato salad and corn bread) are inviting. But what packs the place is an exuberant vision of barbecue. Pork and beef ribs, slathered with one or all of four sauces (including a smoky brown-sugar sauce), are messy and satisfying. There are plenty of other options too, including smoked turkey, barbecued chicken, brisket of beef, and link sausage. Campbell's sauce has more zip to it than you can generally find up here in the Northwest; as they might say in the heart of barbecue country, this is right good Q. A space is available for parties, though some people claim any meal here is a party; and the party is never over until they've run out of peach cobbler and sweet-potato pie. **COME HERE FOR MARVELOUSLY SLOPPY BARBECUE.** *$–$$; AE, DIS, MC, V; no checks; lunch, dinner Tues–Sun; no alcohol; no reservations; map:II3* &

Cañita / ★★

503 W BURNSIDE ST, OLD TOWN; 503/274-4050 Don't come to Cañita looking for Pambiche (see review). From its location in a grimy nightclub-and-mission zone to its long list of fried snacks, John Connell Maribona and Hada Salinas's second Cuban restaurant, tucked away in a quiet eastside neighborhood, has a very different vibe from Pambiche. Instead of reaching for a fancier setting and more elegant fare, this husband-and-wife duo took the low road. They chose what some might consider an undesirable locale and plumped the menu with croquetas, frituras, and empanadas. Painting their building the colors of flamenco dancers' skirts, they instantly gave new life to the corner of Fifth and Burnside. You can make a great meal of appetizers—pumpkin or black-eyed-pea frituras, beef or codfish empanadas—and clever salads such as marinated beet or avocado and pineapple. The starters come with hot sauce, banana sauce, and a thin, sweet ketchup that partners well with menu items. Entrées include *vaca frita* (fried cow), a smoky mélange of shredded beef, onion, and garlic, and the more complex *bacalao a la Vizcaina*, morsels of salt cod in *sofrito*—a stew with achiote seeds, olive oil, garlic, bell pepper, onion, and potatoes. **COME HERE FOR FULL-BODIED CUBAN STREET FOOD.** *$–$$; MC, V; no checks; lunch, dinner Tues–Sat; full bar; reservations recommended; map:K5* &

Caprial's Bistro / ★★★

7015 SE MILWAUKIE AVE, WESTMORELAND; 503/236-6457 Open kitchens permit a close-up peek at the fairly chaotic business of readying meals at breakneck pace: a chance to glimpse chefs tending to four pans with one hand while creating spunky garnishes with the other. At Caprial's, the best spot in the house may be at the end of the kitchen counter, where you get to witness a cook's occasional meltdown and hear waiters cursing when they deliver salmon and duck to the couple who ordered vegetarian tamales. (You won't see that on any of foodie celeb Caprial Pence's public TV shows.) But those who choose to sit away from the fray won't entirely miss out on drama: there's plenty in the intriguing regional American dishes produced by Pence and Co. Only four or five entrées are offered nightly, but they explode with flavor and include embellished sides that get as much love as the main dish. Pork loin chop, marinated and glazed in a maple-spiked pork stock reduction to extract robust flavor, is served with fried cheddar-bacon grits and sautéed chard. Never had hazelnut-thyme gnocchi? You'll find them here alongside duck and stewed cabbage. Appetizers are even more attention grabbing;

prawns sautéed sticky-sweet in a garlic-chile glaze, served with noodles and chopped cashews, is a lip-tingling starter. Caprial's specialty cocktails (try the bourbon-based Brown Sugar), though a steep $9 apiece, elevate the restaurant's fun factor. **COME HERE FOR THE SPIRITED ATMOSPHERE.** *$$$; AE, MC, V; checks OK; lunch, dinner Tues–Sat; full bar; reservations recommended; www.caprial.com; map:JJ5* &

Castagna / ★★★★
Café Castagna / ★★☆

1752 SE HAWTHORNE BLVD, HAWTHORNE; 503/231-7373 / 1758 SE HAWTHORNE BLVD, HAWTHORNE; 503/231-9959 As impeccable as Castagna's entrées are, crafting a meal from several starters can be even more seductive. This approach allows you to sample more of Castagna's pristine cooking, such as irresistible duck confit agnolotti (stuffed crescent-shaped pasta), white bean soup, and the delightful appetizer dubbed Trio: an ever-changing mix that might include fried parsnip curls, magenta beets, and delicately perfumed chickpeas. One of the most striking first courses is also the simplest: butter lettuce leaves stacked to resemble a whole head of the stuff and drizzled with an herby vinaigrette. Everything looks beautiful on the plate, nothing more so than the towering haystack of down-market french fries next to a grilled New York steak reclining in porcini butter. The restaurant's monochromatic minimalism and austerity, emphasized by too-bright lighting, makes an ideal backdrop to the exquisite plates and striking floral arrangements. **COME HERE FOR SOPHISTICATED, FORWARD-THINKING CUISINE.**

While Castagna is for those *dolce vita* nights, its more relaxed next-door offspring, Café Castagna, offers affordable, everyday indulgences. There's nothing quotidian about the achingly crisp gem of a Caesar salad or the robust cheeseburger; each simple dish is executed with enviable prowess. Arancini, fried risotto dumplings with oozing centers, crepe-thin pizzas, and brownie sundaes are menu highlights. **COME HERE FOR COMFORT FOOD SEVERAL STEPS UP FROM MACARONI AND CHEESE.** *$$$; $$; AE, MC, V; checks OK; dinner Wed–Sat (Castagna), every day (Café Castagna); full bar; reservations recommended (Castagna); map:HH5* &

Cha! Cha! Cha! Mexican Taqueria / ★★☆

1208 NW GLISAN ST, PEARL DISTRICT (AND BRANCHES); 503/221-2111 Three pizza joints and a Subway later, the Pearl District finally got a taqueria. Judging by noon and evening crowds, the neighborhood is thrilled by its arrival. The cheery, exclamatory sign over the door beckons hungry Pearl denizens into the narrow space painted bright maize. Simple tables perch wherever there's room—in front of the massive windows, near the door that never seems to close properly, lining the hallway that leads back to the busy kitchen. Cha! Cha! Cha!'s casual style—orders are taken at the counter—is no-frills, but the restaurant is neat and clean, and the service gracious. The mile-long menu offers about a dozen tacos, 15 burritos, quesadillas, nachos, and tostadas, as well as tortas (French-bread sandwiches) and specialty plates. Best of all, everything is doled out in heaping portions. Look for the Cha Plate—a light, fragrant stew of ground beef, carrots, fat raisins, olives, potatoes, onions and tomatoes—served with pinto beans, rice, sour cream, pico de gallo, guacamole, and corn tortillas for a paltry $5.50. There are branches downtown (1986 SW 6th Ave; 503/294-0677; map:D2) and in Irvington (2635 NE Broadway; 503/288-1045; map:GG5). **COME HERE FOR BARGAIN TAQUERIA FARE A STEP ABOVE THE NORM.** *$; AE, MC, V; no checks; lunch, dinner every day; no alcohol; no reservations; map:M2* &

Chez José / ★

2220 BROADWAY, IRVINGTON; 503/280-9888 / 8502 SW TERWILLIGER BLVD, BURLINGAME; 503/244-0007 The larger, flashier Northeast outpost of this local Southwestern favorite has a bar and a slightly bigger menu, but most dishes appear in both places, to general satisfaction. *Cacahuate* (chicken breast with spicy peanut sauce), grilled shrimp with chipotle honey dip, and the weird but truly addictive squash enchiladas span both sides of the Willamette, as do the blackboard specials; corn and black beans come with every entrée. Sometimes a bowl of the rich black-bean soup with a dollop of sour cream is all you need. Chez José East has a lot more seating, a booming bar, and garden tables outside when it's not raining. There's a kids' menu, too. The original Chez José attracts students (and elders!) from the Lewis and Clark College area. **COME HERE FOR HAPPY HOUR, WHEN KIDS EAT FREE.** *$; MC, V; no checks; lunch Mon–Sat, dinner every day; full bar; reservations recommended; map:GG5; map:KK7* &

Chez Machin / ★

3553 SE HAWTHORNE BLVD, HAWTHORNE; 503/736-9381 *Quelle surprise!* This little piece of the Left Bank, a heartbeat for Portland's small French community, has found a home in Hawthorne. A crêperie that doubles as a bistro, Chez Machin transports diners to Paris with its sidewalk seating, recorded jazz, and fine list of French wines by the glass and bottle. You can dive into a bowl of vegetarian French onion soup or a classic salade niçoise any time, but keep an appetite for a couple of crepes, savory (*galettes*) and sweet (*crêpes sucres*). There are dozens. Savory buckwheat crepes (none priced over $8.25) are stuffed with a combination of meat, cheese, and vegetables; the best are finished with a delicious Dijon crème fraîche. A dozen sweet thin crepes (which top out at $5.25) come with fruit, jam, chocolate, custard, and other yummy confections. A few entrées, including coq au vin and boeuf bourguignonne, are served after 5pm. Check the list of blackboard specials and head for the rear-garden seating if weather permits. **COME HERE FOR THE EXQUISITE CREPES.** *$; AE, MC, V; no checks; lunch, dinner every day; beer and wine; no reservations; map:HH5* &

Clarke's / ★★

455 2ND ST, LAKE OSWEGO; 503/636-2667 Transplanting himself from downtown Portland, where he produced an alluring menu before Toulouse decided it really wanted to be a bar, British-born Jonathan Clarke has scored a solid hit in a place where upscale dining has been a sometime thing. Even allowing for its location in a strip mall, Clarke's is a serious, skillful restaurant, and its proprietor has a sure sense of what to do with dishes such as Muscovy duck, goat-cheese soufflé, and fresh fish. Notably, he has shrewd ideas about gravlax, sweetbreads, and roast Cornish game hen. Presentations are particularly interesting (we like the ravioli of smoked-salmon mousse in caviar sauce), fitting into the grace and soft lighting of the restaurant (if you don't look out the window). At lunchtime the place is more casual but no less popular. Expect interesting twists on sandwiches (the Greek wrap is like a gyro in a tortilla) and pasta (including the stoneground pasta carbonara), as well as soup and salad. **COME HERE FOR THE LOBSTER AND SHRIMP RISOTTO.** *$$; AE, DIS, MC, V; checks OK; lunch Tues–Fri, dinner Tues–Sat; full bar; reservations recommended; self parking; www.clarkes.citysearch.com; map:MM6* &

Clay's Smokehouse Grill / ★

2932 SE DIVISION ST, SOUTHEAST; 503/235-4755 There are two schools of thought on barbecue: if it has sauce, it's not real barbecue; or, if it *doesn't* have sauce, it's not real barbecue. Clay's falls into the more-sauce-is-better category—especially when it comes to the brisket sandwich, a mouth-watering heap of hickory-smoked beef, onions, melted cheddar cheese, and sweet-and-tangy Smokehouse barbecue sauce. All sandwiches and barbecue come with home fries drizzled with garlicky sour cream and an unusual, zingy coleslaw enlivened with ginger and chile. Clay's in-house smoker comes into contact with almost everything on the menu, from the salmon gracing the spinach salad to the barbecued quarter chicken served with hot links. Smoky and casual, this is the kind of place that is comfortable for kids and grandparents, as well as bikers. **COME HERE FOR THE BRISKET.** *$; AE, DIS, MC, V; no checks; lunch, dinner Tues–Sun; beer and wine; reservations recommended; map:II5* &

Colosso / ★★

1932 NE BROADWAY, IRVINGTON; 503/288-3333 Patrons of Colosso know that sharing an assortment of tapas, a bottle of sherry, and a stirring conversation with a tableful of friends is a rich way to spend an evening without becoming poor in the process. In two low-lit, bronze-painted dining rooms, owner Julie Colosso and her staff cook up a dozen tapas and half as many entrées, plus a couple of salads. Look for garlicky, piquant prawns in olive oil and sautéed mushrooms with sherry and lemon thyme, mounded on a thick slice of grilled bread. The Painted Hills flank steak with port-wine sauce and olive-infused celery-root purée and the seared ahi with chipotle sauce are flat-out bargains at $12 each. The menu changes twice yearly (with the two seasons in Portland, Colosso jokes), and there's a long list of creative cocktails and nonalcoholic drinks made with such tantalizing ingredients as fresh grapefruit juice and coconut milk. If you munch on the addictive nuts—spicy-sweet roasted pistachios, almonds, walnuts, and filberts—drinks such as Ginger Lynn (bourbon, ginger ale, and lemon) or the wild Zirkpatrick (black pepper–infused tequila, Cointreau, and lime and pomegranate juices) will go down even faster. **COME HERE FOR THE HIPSTER VIBE AND INVENTIVE COCKTAILS.** *$$; MC, V; no checks; dinner every day; full bar; no reservations; map:GG5* &

Cool Runnings / ★

4110 NE FREMONT ST, BEAUMONT; 503/282-2118 Bob Marley still croons reggae tunes at the city's favorite Jamaican cafe as chef/owner Calhoun Ferris stirs the pot of chicken-and-andouille sausage gumbo in the kitchen. Colorful folk art leaps from bright yellow walls, overlooking a handful of tables where fresh flowers bloom from Red Stripe beer bottles. Cool Runnings gives Northeast Portland a taste of the tropics, from crawfish frittata to ripe plantains sautéed in Appleton's rum, from red beans and rice to classic Jamaican jerk chicken. Everything is made from scratch: even the blackened 'gator and curried goat. Best of all is that gumbo, finished with onions, peppers, and okra, served with rice and corn bread. **COME HERE FOR THE GUMBO.** *$; AE, MC, V; no checks; breakfast Wed–Sat, lunch, dinner Mon–Sat, brunch Sun; beer and wine; no reservations; map:FF4* &

Corbett Fish House / ★★☆

5901 SW CORBETT AVE, JOHNS LANDING; 503/246-4434 All smiles, long braids swinging and knee socks pulled high, the waitresses at Corbett Fish House seem like they, along with the restaurant's recipes, were plucked from the Midwest. They deliver imperial pints in a flash and tell you truthfully that the Pilsner Urquell isn't running well on a given night. Inspired by Heartland fish-fry joints, the Fish House menu stars five fried-fish platters ranging from chile-fried catfish to coveted walleye, a lake perch seldom found at West Coast restaurants. Rather than overcooking seafood in heavy batter, Corbett uses light breading and flash-fries fish, rendering a delicate flavor and nongreasy texture. Your best bets are walleye and halibut, in regular and jumbo sizes with wasabi-spiked coleslaw and the World's Greatest Fries (long, lean, and crispy, they certainly come close). Also recommended: the fried-oyster poor boy. **COME HERE FOR THE FRIED WALLEYE PLATTER.** *$–$$; AE, DIS, MC, V; no checks; lunch, dinner every day; beer and wine; reservations for 8 or more; www.corbettfishhouse.com; map:II6* &

Crowsenberg's Half & Half / ★★

923 SW OAK ST, DOWNTOWN; 503/222-4495 Half cafe, half sundry shop, Crowsenberg's Half & Half quickly became a Portland fixture upon opening in 2000. It's a place that possesses originality and spunk in spades. The quirky, campy charm of the teensy cafe—with its array of Japanese candy and out-moded trinkets for sale—would be reason enough to visit. But in the kitchen, there is Robin Rosenberg, master of the sandwich. Her selection changes daily, pairing prime deli meats with roasted vegetables, quality cheeses, and house-made mayon-naise on great bread. There's always a vegan option and interesting grain-salad side dishes. The muffuletta, turkey-with-cranberry, and tofu-salad sandwiches are not to be missed. For breakfast, there's house-made granola with whole almonds, hazel-nuts, and smooth green pepitas; toast doused with cinnamon or Nutella and sliced bananas; and tempting doughnuts. Stumptown coffee, friendly counter banter, and a superb magazine selection (*Black Book, BOMB, New Yorker*) make a meal com-plete. **COME HERE FOR GREAT SANDWICHES AND HIGH CAMP.** *$; no credit cards; checks OK; breakfast, lunch every day; no alcohol; no reservations; map:J3* &

Dahlia Café / ★

3000 NE KILLINGSWORTH ST, NORTHEAST; 503/287-4427 This isn't an outpost of Chef Tom Douglas's noted Seattle restaurant of the same name, but a spacious and inviting deli-café, located where the vegan-oriented Counter Culture once operated, on gentrifying Killingsworth Street. The Dahlia still caters to vegans with many of its dishes, but this neighborhood center has become a three-meal, seven-day outpost of solid home-style cooking. Big wrap-around corner windows and a Rockola jukebox set the scene. You can get breakfast anytime, from a smoked-salmon scramble to a breakfast burrito. Soups and salads come start at about 11am each morning, while dinners feature the likes of pan-fried oysters, chipotle-prawn linguine and chicken-fried steak. Vegetarians can enjoy such meals as pesto couscous with tempeh or the Basque: roasted portobello mushrooms, spinach, eggplant, oven-dried tomatoes, and Havarti cheese on sourdough. A small adjoining bar mixes unusual cocktails like the Purple Suitor: Absolut Citron, Cointreau, Chambord, and lime juice. **COME HERE TO TAP INTO THE NORTHEAST PORTLAND COMMUNITY SCENE.** *$; AE, MC, V; no checks; breakfast, lunch, dinner every day; full bar; no reservations. map: FF5* &

Daily Café / ★★

902 NW 13TH AVE, PEARL DISTRICT; 503/242-1916 / 1100 SE GRAND AVE (REJUVENATION HOUSE PARTS), INNER SOUTHEAST; 503/234-8189 It's hard to say which is the best meal at the Daily Café. Is it the multicourse, bargain-basement Sunday brunch with its appetizer-size blintzes, colorful scrambles, and hedonistic French toast? Would it be the supremely fresh dishes such as blue-cheese-and-leek soufflé and porter-braised venison offered at dinnertime? Or even lunch, when the Daily does brisk trade in firm quiches, melty panini, and chocolate-apricot macaroons? No matter what the time of day, the Daily turns out creative, seasonal treats in a hip, tasteful setting without pretension. Dinner in particular presents some intriguing plates. A half-pound burger, made with Sauvie Island beef, gets a blanket of maple-glazed ham and comes off as inspired. Even a basic salad of organic greens is something special, thanks to a zingy Meyer lemon vinaigrette. Goat-cheese pizzetta, topped with olives and caramelized onions and paired with a glass of syrah, makes an ideal light meal . . . and leaves room for chocolate pot-de-crème with beignets. The Daily's original location inside Rejuvenation House Parts offers the same great breakfast and lunch, but no dinner or Sunday brunch. **COME HERE FOR THE $12 THREE-COURSE, PRIX-FIXE SUNDAY BRUNCH.** *$–$$; MC, V; no checks; breakfast, lunch every day (Pearl District and Inner Southeast), dinner Wed–Sat, brunch Sun (Pearl District); beer and wine (Pearl District), no alcohol (Inner Southeast); reservations for 6 or more (Pearl District); map:N1; map:F9* &

Dan and Louis' Oyster Bar / ★

208 SW ANKENY ST, OLD TOWN; 503/227-5906 Tourists who visited Portland before the advent of the automobile came to this Old Town establishment for seafood. Now diners come for an alternative to the preciousness of early 21st-century restaurant cuisine. Just about everything is deep-fried or stewed, although a few grilled items peep through. Among the place's charms are value ($9.95 for the classic oyster fry, served with a hunk of sourdough and a haystack of iceberg lettuce sprinkled with tiny pink shrimp) and its coffee and pie (the marionberry is wonderful). Its shortcomings are efficient but unexciting preparations and friendly but not especially swift service. The decor is family friendly, with a lot to look at, from plates on the walls to maritime bric-a-brac everywhere; you get the feeling the Wachsmuth family has held their restaurant together through thick and thin for almost a century, serving up oyster stew every single day. **COME HERE FOR (WHAT ELSE?) THE OYSTERS.** *$–$$; AE, DC, DIS, JCB, MC, V; local checks only; lunch,*

THE PINOT NOIR GRAPE

It is remarkable that the rapid quarter-century growth of the Oregon wine industry is inextricably linked to a temperamental grape among the most difficult to produce.

Pinot noir is found throughout the world under different names, but its reputation was established in France's Burgundy region. The long, narrow stretch of hills southeast of Paris was for centuries the only area to consistently produce high-quality pinot noir wines. Now Oregon has challenged that supremacy.

Not surprisingly, the two districts share similar characteristics. Vineyards are planted on gently sloping east-facing hills, providing long sun exposure with minimal afternoon heat. (Oregon's most successful vineyards are on the west side of the Willamette River.) Soil is high in calcium carbonate, allowing good drainage and rapid ripening.

Pruning begins in February and continues until harvest in September and October, by which time weather reports are monitored hourly. Grapes are harvested by hand, with each cluster individually inspected; they are destemmed directly into fermenters where they spend about a month, after which the wine is transferred to oak barrels for aging.

Yet production of these grapes is rife with problems. The pinot noir plant, as opposed to other grape varieties, is a fragile vine susceptible to spring frosts, and its leaf cover is often inadequate to protect the fruit from predatory birds. An insect known as the sharpshooter leafhopper spreads Pierce's disease, which can destroy a vineyard in three years. Plants more than 10 years old are subject to leaf-roll virus.

Tender, thin-skinned pinot grapes must be picked promptly at maturity or they rapidly desiccate. High in amino acids, the grapes ferment so quickly that they can "boil" out of control from the container. The grapes also are prone to acetification, or "turning

dinner every day; beer and wine; reservations recommended; danandlouis@integrity
.com; map:J6

DaVinci's Ristorante Italiano / ★★☆

12615 SE MCLOUGHLIN BLVD, MILWAUKIE; 503/659-3547 This place is a major secret that the residents of Milwaukie obviously want to keep to themselves. Patrick Conner brings his San Francisco cooking experience to bear on a substantial menu with three dozen pasta plates, multiple veal dishes, cioppino, and pizza to go—and he manages it all with prices that don't shock the suburban market. Elegance and suave service are not the hallmark here, but solid, skillful Italian cuisine (check out the scaloppine with mushrooms or artichoke hearts) brings in local crowds and some well-informed westsiders. One way to capture Conner's broad menu is to order the $25, five-course dinner, which includes an antipasto, soup or pasta, entrée (grilled prawns, rockfish piccata, or chicken marsala), salad, dessert, and espresso. Another is to sign on for his annual culinary tour of Italy: each year, patrons join him on a seven-month "tour" of the cuisine of 15 distinct regions, with two weeks vinegar," causing the wine to lose its color, aroma, and flavor.

Today, progressive Oregon winemakers are eschewing traditional "knowledge"—chemical sprays, artificial fertilizers—in favor of a more holistic, sustainable approach to grape farming. And it seems to be working.

"We look at the vineyard as a small ecosystem," says Sokol Blosser winemaker Russ Rosner. "We encourage microbial activity in the soil and wildflowers in the buffer zones around the vines. These encourage beneficial insects and birds. The vineyard looks more beautiful, but the key is that sustainably grown grapes are healthier and make better wine. Our approach protects the environment and increases wine quality."

The pinot noir grape is prone to genetic mutation. Offspring will bear fruit that is nothing like the parent vine's—not only in physical appearance, but in flavor and productivity level. This is both a curse and a godsend. There are at least 200, perhaps thousands, of pinot noir clones. (By comparison, cabernet sauvignon has about a dozen.)

With so many clones—and vineyards love to experiment with them—pinot noir has a wide range of characteristics. Varietals' aroma and/or flavor can range from fruit (cherry, strawberry) to floral (violet, rose petal), spice (peppermint, cinnamon) to herbal (rhubarb, oregano). Processing may inject new aroma and flavor: terroir (mushroom, leather), oak (vanilla, coconut, smoke), bottle age (cedar, cigar box).

If you're unfamiliar with Oregon pinot noirs, ask the sommelier or wine steward at any fine-dining restaurant to make a recommendation in your price range.

—John Gottberg

devoted to each. **COME HERE TO TRY A WIDE RANGE OF ITALIAN FOODS.** *$$; AE, MC, V; no checks; dinner Tues–Sun; full bar; reservations recommended; www.davincisitaliano.com; map:LL5* &

Delta Café / ★★

4607 SE WOODSTOCK BLVD, WOODSTOCK; 503/771-3101 Just up the boulevard from Reed College is this hip hangout, decorated with ropes of Mardi Gras beads in the windows and Klimt reproductions on the walls and serving steaming plates of Southern cooking on Formica-topped tables. The menu is pure Elvis, with some Cajun/Creole influence: fried chicken, blackened catfish, jambalaya, pork ribs, collard greens, corn bread, succotash, and apple-cheddar pie for dessert. No grits, but if it's comfort food you're after, you can get a substantial portion of mac-n-cheese for $3.50. No matter what you get, you'll find it difficult to spend $15 for dinner. And if your thirst matches your appetite, you can wash it all down with a fresh-squeezed lemonade spiked with Jack Daniels. The Delta's major drawback has been a long, long wait for a table, but a new expansion should help. If you still must wait, head down the block to the super-cool Lutz Tavern for a beer; the friendly folks at the Delta will call when your table is ready. **COME HERE FOR A 40-OUNCE PABST BLUE**

RIBBON SERVED IN A CHAMPAGNE BUCKET. *$; no credit cards; checks OK; lunch Sat–Sun, dinner every day; full bar; no reservations; map:JJ4* &

Dining Room / ★★

3449 NE FREMONT ST, ALAMEDA; 503/288-5500 Mike Siegel, former chef and partner in the now-closed Compass World Bistro, opened the Dining Room in late 2002 to serve what he considers true American cuisine: the time-honored recipes immigrants brought from their native countries. Those warm-in-the-belly dishes we've come to call comfort food also satisfy our craving for nostalgia. The menu is mostly meat and potatoes, with a couple of hearty pastas and salads thrown in; but these common foursquare meals are distinguished at the Dining Room by prime ingredients. Siegel relies upon hormone-free Oregon Country Beef and naturally raised lamb, and he uses local, organic produce as much as possible. The simplest selections, like tender-sweet pot roast with firm potato kugel, are the best. Ravioli—bulging with chèvre, feta, and pecorino Romano—is completely satisfying, complemented by a tangy sauce of red pepper, tomato, and cream. Like the food, the atmosphere is homey and unfussy. The patina of dark-wood surfaces gleams in sleepy candlelight as soaring ceilings lend grandeur; a handsome partition divides dining area from bar without severing the two. **COME HERE FOR HOME COOKING WHEN YOU DON'T FEEL LIKE DOING THE COOKING.** *$$; AE, DIS, MC, V; checks OK; lunch Tues–Fri, dinner Tues–Sun, brunch Sat–Sun; full bar; reservations recommended; map:FF5* &

Dots Café / ★

2521 SE CLINTON ST, CLINTON; 503/235-0203 Dots is Dots is Dots. As long as Portland has a hipster intelligentsia, it will have Dots. A dark box of a nouveau diner, Dots is adored for its cheap, proven, veggie-friendly menu and its established cool. Velvet wallpaper, offbeat ephemera, and an ever-hopping bar provide the vibe, and it's all backed by a dependable menu. Looking for a quick, inexpensive lunch or dinner? Dig into a Ms. Bunny's Gardenburger with cream cheese and alfalfa sprouts or a gooey grilled cheese with soup. Want a bite after a night of carousing? Count on Dots to serve food long after other restaurants have been put to bed. Pay close attention to the fries, honored as an entire menu category here: cheese fries, bacon-cheddar fries, fries with spicy tofu sauce. Portions are very generous; a small plate will feed several. Check the white board for daily specials, including tried-and-true desserts like devil's food cake. **COME HERE TO EXPERIENCE A TRUE-BLUE PORTLAND HIPSTER HANGOUT.** *$; no credit cards; checks OK; lunch, dinner every day; full bar; no reservations; map:II5* &

Dragonfish Asian Café / ★★☆

909 SW PARK AVE (PARAMOUNT HOTEL), DOWNTOWN; 503/243-5991 From the moment you spot the pachinko machines in the bamboo lounge, you know this isn't the hotel restaurant of your father's memory! In fact, this pan-Asian dining room—which has a near-identical twin in Seattle's Paramount Hotel—may even challenge you. Featuring the cuisines of Japan, China, Korea, Vietnam, Thailand, and the Philippines, it operates on the principle that the more people you bring, the more small plates you can share. Launch into the evening with one of the intriguing cocktails, like an electric blowfish (Long Island iced tea with Midori) or a sake drop (Absolut Citron, tequila, sake, and lime juice), then test the many-dishes theory. Good bets are wok-seared sugar snaps and shiitakes, calamari katsu, *pancit guisado* rice noodles, and coconut curry chicken. If the fresh sheet offers *zensai*—seared tuna poke, tossed with ginger, sesame seeds, chile oil, and avocado—jump for it. Ditto the honey-lime sushi rolls with crab and avocado. As this is a hotel cafe, Dragonfish also serves breakfast (try the Chinese sausage and scallion scramble), and from noon to 4pm weekends there's a unique dim sum lunch. **COME HERE TO TRY SOMETHING NEW.** *$$; AE, CB, DC, DIS, JCB, MC, V; checks OK; breakfast, lunch, dinner every day; full bar; reservations recommended; valet parking; www.dragonfishcafe.com; map:H2* &

Elephant's Delicatessen / ★★⯪

13 NW 23RD PL (UPTOWN SHOPPING CENTER), NORTHWEST; 503/299-6304 The city's premier, full-course take-out deli, with a few tables and chairs outside, is to adults what a toy store is to kids: pure, unadulterated temptation. Showing remarkable longevity and renewable creativity, Elephant's tempts shoppers with a constant favorite, tomato-orange soup, and seasonal specialties such as summer strawberry cake. Meals or snacks are easily assembled from flame-roasted sweet corn and peppers, Toscano salami sandwiches with garlic parsley spread, Carolina-pulled pork, and curry-roasted shrimp. Crusty sourdough loaves, cream-frosted chocolate-buttermilk cake and thick sugar cookies justify every calorie. Surrounding the displays are retail food items such as mustards and jams, a small but impressive wine selection, and the best new cookbooks. Its sister Flying Elephant Deli (801 SW Park Ave, Downtown; 503/546-3166; map:H2) caters to the business and movie crowd with a smaller selection of the same fine fare and a few tables and chairs. **COME HERE FOR TOMATO-ORANGE SOUP AND SOURDOUGH BREAD.** *$$; AE, MC, V; checks OK; breakfast, lunch, dinner every day; beer and wine; www.elephantsdeli.com; map:HH7* &

El Gaucho / ★★★

319 SW BROADWAY (BENSON HOTEL), DOWNTOWN; 503/227-8794 Expect schmoozing, cigars, martinis, and broker conferences at this upper-crust steakhouse, which caters to local and visiting celebrities and to politicos with campaign chests. Couples seeking shadowy romance come for the moody, elegant sophistication interrupted only by an open kitchen, and they don't protest some of the highest prices in town. A menu complete with American steak-house traditions (and no bold ethnic moves) opens with oysters Rockefeller, shrimp Louis, and Caesar salad tossed tableside. Steaks include the signature roquefort baseball cut—a 16-ounce, 4-inch round of tender, 28-day dry-aged New York Angus—and chateaubriand for two. Formally clad waiters presenting shish-kebab torches spread light into the dark booths and across the center tables, adding an element of performance to what would otherwise be a private, clubby dining room. A lobster tail–beef fillet combo will set you back nearly $100; noncarnivores order fish broiled with lemon butter and sea scallops on linguine. All meals come with baked potatoes, sautéed spinach, and garlic bread. Bananas Foster and cherries jubilee are flambéed dessert classics. A first-class international wine list is heavy on reds. As this is one of the few

Portland restaurants serving a full menu until the morning hours, it's becoming the city headquarters of visiting NBA teams, providing other diners with eye candy of a different kind. **COME HERE TO PEOPLE WATCH.** *$$$$; AE, DC, MC, V; checks OK; lunch Mon–Fri, dinner every day; full bar; reservations recommended; valet parking; www.elgaucho.com; map:J3* ♿

Esparza's Tex-Mex Café / ★★

2725 SE ANKENY ST, LAURELHURST; 503/234-7909 People may wonder how a Tex-Mex restaurant has become a landmark in Portland—but the surprise doesn't survive the first visit, nor certainly the first smoked beef-brisket taco. By then, new visitors have already been seduced by this eatery straight outta San Antone—replete with stellar jukebox, Mexican marionettes creepily dangling from the ceiling, and an exhaustive array of tequilas. Servers will help you choose the right tequila to match the Cowboy Tacos—hearty buggers filled with thick slabs of smoked sirloin, barbecue sauce, guacamole, and pico de gallo—or the Uvalde, a smoked-lamb enchilada. True to Texas form, portions are meaty and as big as the great outdoors. If you can manage an appetizer, go for *nopalitos*, a tasty cactus dish. Augmented by daily specials, the menu has quite a reach, running the gamut from red snapper (smothered with sautéed peppers and tomatoes) to smoked pork loin (stuffed with spiced buffalo). Unusual meats—ostrich in enchiladas, calves' brain in tacos—also crop up. Watch the blackboard, and the satisfied faces of other diners, to catch Joe Esparza's latest inspiration. And don't leave without trying a big-and-bold margarita. **COME HERE FOR BORDER KITSCH AND VARIETY MEATS.** *$$; AE, DC, DIS, MC, V; no checks; lunch, dinner Tues–Sat; full bar; reservations recommended; map:HH5* ♿

The Farm Café / ★★

10 SE 7TH AVE, BUCKMAN; 503/736-3276 The Farm is a petite, decidedly urban Victorian cottage set back—not by a pasture, but by a parking lot—from bustling E Burnside. The house's moody interior has been restored beautifully to an old-Portland gloss, dressed up with salvage from the neighboring Viscount Ballroom. A glowing red "FARM" sign is a lodestar for diners seeking an enlightened breed of regional cooking. The emphasis on fresh Northwest produce (almost all ingredients are supplied by area growers) makes for a light and lovely menu. Entrées are evenly divided between seafood and vegetarian, with a breaded tofu cycling as a frequent special. A popular favorite is the grilled citrus halibut—a compact halibut steak marinated in lemon and lime juices and lightly browned, served with yellow saffron rice and asparagus. Although dessert listings are limited, a molten chocolate soufflé and a mascarpone cheesecake will make you forget you needed options. **COME HERE FOR STRAIGHT-FROM-THE-FARM PRODUCE.** *$$; MC, V; checks OK; breakfast, lunch, dinner every day; beer and wine; reservations recommended; map:HH6* ♿

Fat City Café / ★

7820 SW CAPITOL HWY, MULTNOMAH VILLAGE; 503/245-5457 Diners in general are fading bits of American culinary history, and this particular one has its own place in Portland's past: it's where Mayor Bud Clark (a regular even now, years after he left office) fired his police chief back in 1987. Inside is the classic narrow layout of booths and a counter, with walls covered in street and traffic signs. The menu is exactly what you'd expect. For breakfast, there are monster stacks of pancakes, eggs every which way, and legendary hash browns; for lunch, substantial burgers, great sandwiches, and marvelous milk shakes. The name has less to do with any geographic location than with how you're going to feel after you've eaten here. There's no such thing as a small meal at the Fat City, so you might want to opt for a spot at the counter and have the benefit of gravity to help you out of your seat. **COME HERE TO FILL UP YOUR TANK.** *$; DIS, MC, V; no checks; breakfast, lunch, dinner every day; full bar after 5pm; no reservations; map:JJ7* &

Fernando's Hideaway / ★★☆

824 SW 1ST AVE, DOWNTOWN; 503/248-4709 Picture a dimly lit cellar and the strains of flamenco guitar drifting through a maze of stone walls alive with fine paintings. That's where you think you are when you visit Fernando's. The restaurant drips with a seedy, lived-in sensuality that confirms it as the most romantic and seductive of Portland's Spanish eateries. Its roaring bar is a first-rate singles scene, and the upstairs area hosts salsa dancing (free lessons Thurs–Sat) and flamenco exhibitions. In keeping with the scene, many folks come to sup on the extensive menu of Andalusian-style tapas. Favorites are the *gambas pil pil*, prawns sautéed in a hot chile garlic oil; *tarta de congrejo*, crab cakes with lobster sauce; *pechuga de pato*, seared duck breast with spaghetti squash; *tortilla Española*, a potato-and-egg pie; and *pulpo a la gallega*, marinated octopus with picante sauce. Chef Benny Somera's deft touch in the kitchen has lifted the entrées to a level worthy of the ambience. Sequester yourselves in a rear booth for an authentic paella, or opt for the marvelous *chuleta de ternera*, a grilled veal chop topped with a dried-cherry-and-red-wine sauce. Desserts are impressive—a Catalan crème brûlée flavored with cinnamon and lemon, for instance—and the long list of Spanish wines is one of the finest in the country. **COME HERE FOR A TASTE OF SPAIN.** *$$–$$$; AE, MC, V; checks OK; lunch Mon–Fri, dinner every day; full bar; reservations recommended; www.fernandosportland.com; map:G5* &

Fife / ★★☆

4440 NE FREMONT ST, BEAUMONT; 971/222-3433 When it opened in the waning days of 2002, Fife brought a blast of something edgy and delicious to the residential Beaumont neighborhood. The cooking and the vibe are at once sophisticated and accessible, qualifying Fife as both a neighborhood joint (with the reasonable price points to match) and a popular destination. The spacious, square dining room, warmly cast in the color of red-dirt fields, feels even larger thanks to a ceiling that reaches for the sky. Chef/owner Marco Shaw, who formerly manned the saucepans at Tuscany Grill (see review), uses fresh, top-grade ingredients to craft dishes that you might find at grandma's table. Fewer meals could be humbler than chicken cooked in a cast-iron pan, but Shaw's generous breast-and-thigh serving is insanely juicy and deep with flavor from accompanying mushroom sauce. Delicate roasted quails, sweet and tender in a shallot-garlic confit, are served with simple wild rice. Market-driven fish selections such as Alaskan cod and Pacific sea bass are consistent standouts, and the spot-on crab cakes, made with

Chesapeake Bay blue crab, can make a Marylander weep for joy. **COME HERE FOR REVVED-UP AMERICAN CLASSICS.** *$$; MC, V; no checks; dinner Tues–Sat; full bar; reservations recommended; www.fiferestaurant.com; map:FF4* ⅃

Fong Chong / ★★☆

301 NW 4TH AVE, CHINATOWN; 503/223-0287 Chinese women in black pants, white shirts, and red scarves shuffle behind trolleys stacked with Portland's best dim sum, announcing, "*Hum bao, shiu mai,*" as they roll past. This Chinatown favorite is a scene right from Hong Kong, including the bilingual menu of bite-size dim sum (little snacks). Diners hail the carts as they pass, selecting dumplings typically priced at $2 for three to four pieces. Shrimp wrapped in rice noodles, baked buns stuffed with barbecued pork, egg rolls, duck feet, deep-fried taro balls, and sweet-rice sesame balls are a few of the choices. Recently remodeled, Fong Chong has replaced its grocery with a second dining room yet is still often packed at noon. At night, Fong Chong becomes a quiet Cantonese seafood eatery. Decor is sparse—pink Formica tables with shiny black chairs and wood paneling—but the waitstaff works hard to keep teapots filled and plastic chopsticks on every table. **COME HERE FOR TRADITIONAL DIM SUM.** *$; MC, V; no checks; lunch, dinner every day; full bar; no reservations; map:L5*

Foothill Broiler / ★

33 NW 23RD PL, NORTHWEST; 503/223-0287 You don't go to Foothill Broiler for romantic atmosphere or obsequious service—and you won't get it. But the avid lunchtime crowds are testament to Foothill's real attraction—ground beef on a hot grill. What you get in this utilitarian little cafeteria is a straight-up hamburger (plain, or with chili and/or cheese) in quarter-pound and half-pound sizes. A largely all-American menu—frankfurters, BLTs, potato salad—is offset by the occasional Greek item, such as lamb or chicken gyros and lappi cheese sandwiches. Prices are incredibly low (around $3.50 for a burger), and it's hard to resist the array of fresh fruit pies available by the slice. If you've ever been curious about rhubarb, try it here. Tilework, framed prints, and unexpected skylights in the back raise the interior from merely cafeterian to almost stylish. **COME HERE FOR GREAT BURGERS AT BARGAIN PRICES.** *$; MC, V; checks OK; breakfast, lunch, dinner Mon–Sat; no alcohol; no reservations; map:HH7* ⅃

Fratelli / ★★★

1230 NW HOYT ST, PEARL DISTRICT; 503/241-8800 If there's one dining room in the restaurant-saturated Pearl District that embraces the artsy spirit of First Thursday—all month long—it is this Italian gem. The kitchen brings to the table artistry worthy of the district's many galleries. A narrow entrance passageway leads to the rear of a long dining room of rustic minimalist mood, its two-story ceilings and spare wooden tables and chairs illuminated (if not by late-afternoon sun) by the light of single candles. The menu has grown since Fratelli first opened, but it still won't make you think too hard; there are a small number of antipasti, about a half-dozen starters, and eight or nine entrée choices—rounded out with one or two daily specials. Offerings change to reflect the season, but if spring beans with arugula and octopus are available, order them: it's a textured and satisfying dish, with hints of lemon providing a welcome freshness. The pappardelle with lamb, tomato, and horseradish is also memorable, and the house lasagna, with its layers of beef, pork, and béchamel, is a rich favorite. There are also plenty of vegetarian options. Service here is smart, the mostly Italian wine list impressive (there's also a limited bar), and the location unbeatable. **COME HERE FOR CULINARY ARTISTRY.** *$$; AE, DC, MC, V; no checks; dinner Tues–Sun; beer and wine; reservations recommended; map:M2* &

Fujin / ★★☆

3549 SE HAWTHORNE BLVD, HAWTHORNE; 503/231-3753 Here's a little neighborhood treasure that refuses to let you go broke, assuring the wealth and prosperity—the *fujin*—that its name promises. In this simple but comfortable storefront with tile floor, Formica tables, and a small Taoist altar at the rear, friendly Kevin Chan and his family have been serving superb Sichuan, Mandarin, and Hunan cuisine since 1989. Chan's specialty is "pepper-salted" seafood, which you're more likely to find on the specials board than the regular menu. There are so many good things here, it's hard to decide among them, which is why we like Fujin's chicken trio: smaller-size portions of General Tso's, Snow White (steamed with carrots, snow peas, and water chestnuts), and tangy lemon chicken with rice. It's still enough to provide you leftovers for tomorrow's lunch. **COME HERE FOR THE $3.95 LUNCH SPECIALS.** *$; MC, V; no checks; lunch Mon–Sat, dinner every day; beer and wine; no reservations; map:HH5* &

Fusion / ★

4100 SE DIVISION ST, SOUTHEAST; 503/233-6950 The concept of fusion—a creative blend of two culturally distinct cuisines (say, Japanese and French)—may have passed on as a dining trend, but the idea persists as a democratic value at this folksy restaurant. Appetizers, rambling from yucca fries and beet salad to chicken satay and baked chèvre, may not harmonize elegantly with the red-curry mussels or pork chop to follow . . . but who cares? Select a bottle of wine from the eminently affordable list, check your date's reflection in the mirrored tabletop, and take your time. The staff is warm, kooky, and chatty, but also practiced in the graceful art of leaving you alone. The back lounge is an idiosyncratic antiques store of sorts, featuring vintage housewares and furniture that may be sat on as well as sold. **COME HERE FOR A QUIRKY BUT DELIGHTFUL DINING EXPERIENCE.** *$$; MC, V; checks OK; breakfast Sun, lunch, dinner Tues–Sat; beer and wine; no reservations; map:II4* &

Genoa / ★★★★

2832 SE BELMONT ST, BELMONT; 503/238-1464 One of Portland's truly great restaurants for more than three decades, Genoa seduces with rustic simplicity, not haute cuisine. The waiters are older, incredibly knowledgeable veterans who can effortlessly steer your wine selection. The $68 seven-course menu changes every two weeks, but some favorite dishes reappear year after year. The *bagna cauda* antipasto, served with house-made breadsticks, crisp raw carrots, fennel, radicchio, and celery, is one such true-blue dish. Genoa's version of the anchovy-garlic dipping sauce employs cream instead of butter and oil, creating a wonderfully satiny consistency. This might be followed by a bowl

73

of Sicilian-inspired gazpacho, then a fresh egg pasta tossed with chanterelles and black olives. Salmon marinated in fennel, Dijon mustard, and sugar, broiled to coax a caramelized crust, is a popular item occasionally offered as one of three entrée choices—likewise the roasted poussin stuffed with house-made ricotta, marjoram, and pancetta and the Sardinian-style swordfish cooked in a sauce of tomatoes, saffron, mint, and chiles. Naturally, Genoa's pasta course is unerring. Hand-cut pappardelle with rabbit ragout sings with nutmeg. The *ravioli di zucca* enfolds squash, sweet potato, and biscotti crumbs in its thin sheets. After dessert (pear frangipane tart, house-made fig ice cream, chocolate-chestnut cake), the whole extravagant meal comes to a lovely close with wedges of fresh fruit. **COME HERE FOR HONEST, UNFUSSY COOKING.** *$$$$; AE, DC, MC, V; checks OK; dinner every day; full bar; reservations required; www.genoarestaurant.com; map:HH5*

Giant Drive-In / ★

15840 SW BOONES FERRY RD, LAKE OSWEGO; 503/636-0255 Talk about five-napkin burgers! Even though booths at this '50s-style drive-in have cushy orange-padded backs, sloppy sauces on fat burgers keep everyone leaning over the table. Diners may need fancy handwork to prevent tomatoes, avocados, mushrooms, salsa, and whatnot from slipping off the beef patties and right out of the fresh kaiser buns. Consider the Giant Killer, stacked top to bottom with two lean bacon strips, cheddar cheese, an all-beef patty, a slice of real ham, another beef patty, a fried egg, kosher pickles, onion, tomato, and lettuce on a sesame-seed bun. Oh, and special sauce: there's no safe way to eat *that* in public! As Paul Anka croons "Diana," dive into Cajun fries—not as feisty as the name implies, but made with real unpeeled potatoes—and milk shakes made from hard local ice cream. **COME HERE FOR TWO-FISTED BURGERS.** *$; no credit cards; local checks only; lunch, dinner every day; no alcohol; no reservations; map:LL7*

Gino's Restaurant and Bar / ★★☆

8057 SE 13TH AVE, SELLWOOD; 503/233-4613 Anyone who's eaten at Gino's has a favorite dish. It could be the beautifully flavored clams steamed in a white-wine-and-butter sauce revved by chile and fish broth or the perfect Caesar salad served family-style. Perhaps it's Grandma Jean's meaty pasta; over-the-top cioppino; or Gino's classic, caper-studded chicken marsala; or a Prime Painted Hills steak that is specially cut for Gino's. Whichever dish you claim, the effect is the same: it keeps you coming back for more. The casual, airy restaurant exudes neighborly warmth and offers a terrific value, with pastas $13 and under. The kitchen rounds out the list of perennial favorites with seasonal specials such as braised lamb shoulder with bucatini or a winsome stew of butternut squash, Chioggia beets, carrots, and parsnips laid over white polenta. Owner Marc Accuardi is no slouch when it comes to wine: he knows what the good bottles are, he knows you shouldn't drink it too young, and he knows it's a crime to make people pay too much for it. The place can get crowded, but you can eat at the adjoining Leipzig Tavern, which boasts a gorgeous mahogany bar, cozy booths, Guinness on tap, and full dinner service from Gino's. **COME HERE FOR THE UNPRETENTIOUS CHARM.** *$$–$$$; MC, V; checks OK; dinner every day; full bar; reservations recommended; accuardi@earthlink.com; map:KK5* ♿

Giorgio's / ★★★

1131 NW HOYT ST, PEARL DISTRICT; 503/221-1888 Northern Italy meets the Northwest at Giorgio's, which has hovered under the radar since it opened in 2000. It's difficult to say why. The warm bistro ambience is entirely inviting; the service is crisp, the food is sublime, and it's even located in the Pearl District—but for some reason, this isn't a restaurant that gets people talking. It should. Chef Michael Clancy's puréed vegetable soups, spiked with star anise, or the clever mushroom strudel that's dressed up as a spring roll and served with a few wonderfully dry duck slices, are classy starters. Next comes a plate of house-made pasta: choose from among the lacy, rice paper–thin sweet-potato ravioli with sugar snap peas and prosciutto; browned, bullet-sized gnocchi with sprightly spot prawns and fresh artichoke hearts; or foot-long pappardelle noodles tossed with shredded wild boar, fennel, and tomatoes. All are devastatingly delicious. **COME HERE FOR THE ELEGANT SETTING AND DELICATE HOUSE-MADE PASTAS.** *$$–$$$; AE, MC, V; no checks; lunch Tues–Fri, dinner Tues–Sat; full bar; reservations recommended; map:M2* ዿ

Good Dog/Bad Dog / ★

708 SW ALDER ST, DOWNTOWN; 503/222-3410 This eclectic wiener emporium is devoted to homemade sausages and the family pooch, welcome with its owner at a sidewalk table. Regulars don't seem to object that the small place is rarely tidy. Shelves are crammed with stuffed, carved, and ceramic dogs; walls are plastered with customers' pet portraits; dog wrappers are on the floor; and the daily newspaper is scattered about. Accompanied by sausage-spiked chili, maple-bacon baked beans, and potato chips, the main event comes cased in a bun. European specialties (German bratwurst, British bangers, Polish kielbasa, and sweet Italian sausage), plus an Oregon smoky, are available smothered in grilled onions or with other toppings, such as grilled peppers, garlic, cheese, and horseradish sauce. The buns aren't always quite fresh and plates are often sloppy, but the counter service is nothing but friendly. **COME HERE IF YOU LOVE DOGS: CASED AND CANINE.** *$; MC, V; no checks; lunch, dinner every day; beer only; no reservations; map:I3* ዿ

Gotham Building Coffee Shop / ★★

2240 N INTERSTATE AVE, NORTH PORTLAND; 503/493-2646 Occupying the beautifully renovated Gotham Building, this coffee shop is an arm of the edgy culinary outfit known as Ripe—which also encompasses an in-demand catering business—and Family Supper, a semiprivate supper club in the commercial kitchen upstairs. In addition to serving stellar breakfasts and lunches, the Gotham Building Coffee Shop hosts frequent nighttime events that are anything but ordinary. A striking, light-filled space in the middle of a light-industrial sector, the cafe is angular and sparsely decorated, with cool glass artwork and great magazines. Morning brings delicious scones and coffee cakes, hearty granola with fresh fruit, gently scrambled eggs, a gourmet fried-egg sandwich, and a killer waffle with pure maple syrup. For lunch, try a sandwich of roasted, free-range chicken piled on Ken's artisan bread (see Ken's Artisan Bakery & Café review) and dressed with house-made mayonnaise. There are different selections every day; watch for terrific seasonal salads and soups. **COME HERE FOR A DELICIOUS LESSON IN AES-THETICS.** *$; no credit cards; checks OK; breakfast Mon–Sat, lunch Mon–Fri; no reservations; www.ripepdx.com; map:O6* &

Grand Central Baking Company / ★★☆

1444 NE WEIDLER ST, IRVINGTON (AND BRANCHES); 503/288-1614 Everyone knows the secret to making a good sandwich is good bread. Operating on that premise, Grand Central makes some of the best in town: Black Forest ham and Swiss on sour rye, roasted chicken and cranberry chutney on como, hummus and tomato on yeasted corn. The sack lunch—a sandwich with a bag of chips, pickle wedge, and cookie—makes for a tasty and reasonably priced meal (only $1 more than the price of the sandwich). There also are seasonal soups, salads, and grilled sandwiches oozing cheese and roasted vegetables. Tables, countertop seating, wine by the glass, and an expanded menu have successfully changed this spot's image from mere bakery to multitasking cafe. In addition to all the yummy breads and pastries (jammers, flaky croissants, personal-size apple pies), Grand Central sells marvelous cakes—chocolate, lemon, and carrot—by the slice or to take home whole. Branches in the Hawthorne District (2230 SE Hawthorne Blvd; 503/232-0575; map:HH5) and Multnomah Village (3425 SW Multnomah Blvd; 503/977-2024; map:JJ7) sell the same delicious breads, pastries, and sandwiches, with limited seating. **COME HERE FOR CROISSANTS AND JAMMERS.** *$; AE, MC, V; local checks only; breakfast, lunch, dinner every day; no alcohol; no reservations; www.grandcentralbakery.com; map:GG5* &

Green Onion / ★★

636 SW JACKSON ST, DOWNTOWN; 503/274-4294 This affordable Persian restaurant near Portland State University embodies true Iranian cooking, right down to the green onions in the flatbread sandwiches and the barberries (red berries similar to currants) that garnish sumptuous saffron basmati rice. The cuisine is delicious and provocative. Ingredients and preparations are similar to other Middle Eastern countries, but Persian cuisine is distinguished by its reliance on pomegranate, spinach, saffron, and rosewater, as well as meat-and-fruit sauces and a distinctive sour undercurrent in many savory dishes. In *fesenjun,* a slightly sweet sauce of pomegranate, walnuts, and onions blankets extremely tender chicken. It's served with a heap of basmati—and is wonderful. Green-herb-and-beef stew comprises fenugreek, spinach, cilantro, mint, parsley, and soft chunks of meat and carries that characteristic tart flavor. Service can be slow, but the price is right for lovingly prepared food. **COME HERE FOR THE OPPORTUNITY TO TRY GREAT PERSIAN FARE.** *$$; MC, V; no checks; lunch Mon–Fri, dinner Mon–Sat; beer and wine; reservations recommended; greenonion1@juno.com; map:C1* &

Grolla / ★★☆

2930 NE KILLINGSWORTH ST, NORTHEAST; 503/493-9521 Northeast Killingsworth is not a neighborhood used to fine dining in its midst. Chris Lachmann's friendly restaurant is an anomaly of sorts. Its cuisine may be unique in all of Portland, combining Italian and eastern Mediterranean elements with the produce and spirit of the Northwest. Rich, bold colors—burnt orange, sapphire blue, sage green—greet diners as they walk through French doors to a small room marked by antique chandeliers and handcrafted woodwork. The menu offers enticing dishes like king salmon sautéed in lemon juice with artichoke hearts and mushrooms and laid on a bed of pasta; thin-sliced flatiron steak rubbed with olive oil and served with creamy polenta; and duck à la Beirut, with a walnut risotto and fig sauce. Popular weekend brunches feature a smoked-salmon omelet and *ful mudammas*, a fava-bean soup with olives and yogurt. A wine bar offers numerous selections by the glass. **COME HERE FOR THE FRIENDLY NEIGHBORHOOD VIBE.** *$$; MC, V; checks OK; dinner Tues–Sat, brunch Sat–Sun; beer and wine; reservations recommended; map:FF5* &

Hall Street Bar & Grill / ★★

3775 SW HALL BLVD, BEAVERTON; 503/641-6161 For more than two decades, Hall Street has been the only serious, nonfranchise Northwest-American dining choice in very suburban Beaverton. It can be forgiven for catering to the business bunch and to "ladies who lunch." The dated-but-not-shabby look of wood blinds, black leather booths, and a room-length bar give an impression of seriousness backed by a safe, solid grill menu. Indeed, the kitchen takes few chances, preferring to finesse the classics: mesquite-grilled salmon and sirloin steak, rock-salt-roasted prime rib, tempura fish and chips, artichoke crab dip, Dungeness crab–melt sandwiches, vegetable raviolis. Occasionally, you'll find an exception—crispy coconut prawns with citrus marmalade, or Hawaiian ahi with yakisoba and pickled cucumber. Belgian chocolate mousse and a fresh-fruit cobbler highlight dessert offerings. Friendly service keeps pretentiousness on hold. Certainly, the smashing success Hall Street's owners have had in the Pearl District with ¡Oba! (see review) hasn't taken away from the most popular restaurant in Washington County. **COME HERE FOR HAPPY-HOUR DRINKS AND APPETIZERS.** *$$; AE, DC, MC, V; checks OK; lunch, dinner every day; full bar; reservations recommended;* &

Hands On Café / ★☆

8245 NW BARNES RD, WEST SLOPE; 503/297-1480 If only every institution of higher learning had a cafeteria like this one! The campus of the Oregon College of Art and Craft may seem an unlikely place to sit down to dazzling baked goods—from scones to stunning, ever-changing desserts—but the ovens here produce goods every ounce as artful as the kilns next door. With its small open kitchen and informal aura, the cluttered cafe feels a bit like a home-economics classroom, but it opens out to a welcoming patio: a grove of trees beyond the white azaleas creates shade while allowing sun to shine on the half-dozen tables. The eclectic lunch and early-dinner menus change daily, but can include anything from simple vegetable curry to pasta salad with capers to a cabbage roll stuffed with ground veal. Popular Sunday brunches are inspired by regional specialties from New Orleans to Peru. Pumpkin bread and bowls of strawberries sprinkled with candied ginger will keep you busy while you wait for the main course. **COME HERE FOR BAKED GOODS ON THE GARDEN PATIO.** *$; no credit cards; checks OK; lunch Mon–Fri, dinner Mon–Thurs, brunch Sun; no alcohol; reservations recommended; map:HH9* &

The Heathman Restaurant and Bar / ★★★★

1001 SW BROADWAY, DOWNTOWN; 503/241-4100 Philippe Boulot, who came to Portland by way of Paris and New York, has produced a consistently impressive kitchen to go with a dining room that continues to be the center of Portland power breakfasts and lunches. In 2001, he brought home the James Beard Award of Excellence; and he keeps pushing the envelope with his precise cooking. After making his own strong statements about Northwest cuisine—such as salmon in a pesto crust with a shard of crisp salmon skin planted on top—Boulot has returned to his Gallic roots. That means foie gras in a rhubarb sauce, leg of lamb cooked for seven hours, and Alsatian stuffed veal breast. Of course, there are still heartening Northwest dishes, such as roast venison wrapped in smoked bacon or the appealing crab cakes in a red-curry butter sauce. Dinners are accompanied by a marvelous wine list dominated by Northwest and French vintages. King salmon hash prevails at breakfast, and lunch produces its own creations, including rich soups, pungent salads, and savory stews. All possible excuses should be made to dive into dessert creations, such as chocolate pear tart with pear-brandy sauce and *dulce de leche* ice cream. During the holiday season, the Heathman offers a complete high tea in the swanky Tea Court. Make reservations early (September) to ensure a taste of cucumber crostini, scones with mascarpone cheese, and delicate opera cakes. Visit the Heathman's classy lounge for a more affordable nibble of Boulot's handiwork and don't miss the newly added cheese list. **COME HERE FOR HIGH TEA, ARTISAN CHEESES, AND CHEF BOULOT'S FINE FRENCH-NORTHWEST CUISINE.** *$$$; AE, DC, DIS, MC, V; checks OK; breakfast, lunch, dinner every day; full bar; reservations recommended; valet parking; www.heathmanhotel.com; map:G2* &

Henry's Café / ★★

2508 SE CLINTON ST, CLINTON; 503/236-8707 Restaurants are like love affairs: when you least expect it, one comes along and steals your heart. Henry's, a lovely cafe painted in coffee shades with lots of dark wood, fir floors, antique leather chairs, soapstone tables, gilt-framed mirrors, and a long bar that runs the length of this narrow storefront, is serious crush material. The breakfast menu satisfies a variety of appetites, from simple pastries to the upgraded continental called Parisian Brunch (French-press coffee, a bowl of seasonal fruit, croissant, and jam) and heartier plates like the three-egg meat-and-potatoes omelet. There are only a few choices for lunch—spinach salad, soup du jour, and a handful of sandwiches—but coffeehouse specials abound. Whether for breakfast or between meals, you'll find plenty within the glass pastry case: zucchini bread, cookies, tortes, and cakes. Dinner is unbelievably reasonable; for less than $12 you can sup on sautéed prawns, pan-seared salmon, or on a pork chop with mashed potatoes. **COME HERE FOR A SERIOUS BREAKFAST.** *$-$$; MC, V; no checks; breakfast, lunch every day, dinner Wed–Sat; beer and wine; no reservations; map:II5* &

Higgins / ★★★½

1239 SW BROADWAY, DOWNTOWN; 503/222-9070 Pioneering chef Greg Higgins cooks with skill and principle, distilling dazzling dishes from Northwest soil and seas. Dedicated to local producers and the idea of sustainability, Higgins crafts deft, creative dishes: medallions of pork loin and foie gras, crab and shrimp cakes with chipotle crème fraîche, saffron bourride of regional shellfish. Part of Higgins's policy is to always provide a compelling vegetarian entrée; examples include a forest-mushroom tamale with hazelnut mole and tangerine salsa, and a black-and-white truffle risotto. Spectacular presentation endures, especially in desserts, which might be a roasted pear in phyllo or a chocolate-almond-apricot tart. The adjacent bar, a favorite après-theater haunt, offers a cozy, less-formal environment; its very reasonable bistro menu features a peerless ground-sirloin burger, a mound of herbed chèvre with olives, roasted heirloom potatoes with red pepper rouille, and a house-cured pastrami sandwich. The bar's enormous stable of imported beers can, in one cool swig, transport the drinker to Belgium or Germany. Also among Higgins's classy bistro plates are Oregon-grown hazelnuts, seasoned with honey and chilies, then roasted—a preparation that renders spicy-sweet nuts with notable crunch. Served in a clear-glass coffee mug for $4.50, the nuts are simple yet unpredictable . . . just like the restaurant. **COME HERE TO DISCOVER WHAT PACIFIC NORTHWEST CUISINE IS ALL ABOUT.** *$$–$$$; AE, DC, DIS, MC, V; local checks only; lunch Mon–Fri, dinner every day; full bar; reservations recommended; higgins@europa.com; map:G2* &

Hiro Sushi / ★★

6334 SW MEADOWS RD, LAKE OSWEGO; 503/684-7521 A bland mall location hides this unexpected suburban treasure, a home-away-from-the-Rose Garden for many Portland Trail Blazers. Around an L-shaped, black-Formica bar that attracts savvy sushi aficionados, Chef Hiro skillfully handcrafts his signature special roll, spooning creamy scallops gently onto molded, nori-wrapped rice. Impeccably fresh fish and a daily-special board keep several sushi chefs busy, sometimes preparing unusual choices such as giant clams and monkfish liver. While sushi-bar customers are entertained by the chef's theater, table diners may choose from among a variety of traditional bento dinners: seven or eight assorted meats are beautifully arranged with seafood, rice, and soup in compartments of black lacquer boxes. Also served are gyoza, tempura, deep-fried tofu, and sashimi. **COME HERE FOR THE SUSHI BAR.** *$$–$$$; AE, MC, V, no checks; lunch Mon–Fri, dinner Mon–Sat; beer and wine; reservations recommended; map:MM8* &

Hoda's Middle Eastern Cuisine / ★

3401 SE BELMONT ST, BELMONT; 503/236-8325 It's really no surprise that husband and wife Hani and Hoda Khouri so quickly established this hotbed for vibrant Middle Eastern food: Hoda is the daughter of Nicholas, founder of landmark Lebanese joint Nicholas' Restaurant (see review). Items such as heavenly pita bread, which arrives puffed up like a Chinese lantern, and the smoky baba ghanouj evince the care and love that's poured into the food at this sunny little cafe. Pitas cradle the bargain falafel sandwich, whose condiments include pickles and lettuce as well as the usual tahini sauce and tomatoes. The solid menu provides good reason to move on from hummus and tabbouleh and add shawarma (marinated beef) or a sautéed okra dish to your repertoire. **COME HERE FOR HOT, FRESHLY BAKED PITA BREAD.** *$; no credit cards; checks OK; lunch, dinner Mon–Sat; beer and wine; reservations recommended; www.hodas.com; map:HH5* &

79

Holden's / ★★

524 NW 14TH AVE, PEARL DISTRICT; 503/916-0099 Holden's used to be the kind of place where you could walk in dripping with rain, grab a section of the *New York Times,* and happily ensconce yourself at a booth, satisfying sandwich in hand. This Pearl District nosh spot has souped up its menu and its image, venturing a tricky transition from rough-hewn breakfast-and-lunch counter to nighttime bar and bistro. The cuisine, a little bit Asian, a little bit homegrown, a little bit continental, offers an interesting range of well-articulated flavors and textures. One taste of the velvety lamb ragout, for example, and you'll be craving it for weeks to come. One of the most satisfying salads in town is the magnificent Chopped Cobb, teeming with romaine, avocado, grilled chicken, shredded bacon, tomato, and blue cheese. The Bima Burger, a yummy, hearty half-pounder, is made even better accompanied by highly addictive Stealth fries. Seasonal specials, deft cocktails, and late dining hours add up to one fab destination for the nocturnal set. **COME HERE FOR THE CHOPPED COBB AND STEALTH FRIES.** *$–$$; AE, DIS, MC, V; local checks only; dinner Tues–Sat; full bar; reservations recommended; www.holdenspdx.com; map: M1* &

Horn of Africa / ★⚹

3939 NE MARTIN LUTHER KING BLVD, NORTHEAST; 503/331-9844 Walk through the door, veer to the right, get a specialty East African grocery store stocking fenugreek and custard powder. Veer to the left, get Horn of Africa, the friendly storefront cafe whose proprietors, Mohamed and Khadija Yousuf, serve authentic fare from Somalia, on Africa's northeast coast. Seating and lighting are utilitarian, but the Horn serves a meal as warm and well-balanced as if it came from a family kitchen. The finger-food platter of vegetarian *hoe-dra* will keep you in legumes and greens for days—collards, navy beans, basmati rice, and lentil salad lie fanned on a bed of cabbage with all the colorful diversity of a nutrition diagram. Poultryvores should try *luukun habasha,* a chicken dish seasoned with garlic, paprika and, like most things on the menu, "African spices." Scoop it up with a spongy bread known as *biddeena.* A mango lassi will make all this health go down easier. The meal finishes with good-and-good-for-you gobs of fried dough, gratis, on the same tray as the check. **COME HERE FOR DELICIOUS EAST AFRICAN HOME COOKING.** *$; MC, V; checks OK; lunch Tues–Fri, dinner Tues–Sat; no alcohol; no reservations; map:FF6* &

Hunan / ★

515 SW BROADWAY, DOWNTOWN; 503/224-8063 There's finer, fancier Chinese food in town, but downtown veteran Hunan has a traditional poise and panache that's tough to beat. On a rainy day, the dim lighting, plush banquettes, and eerie aquarium tanks make you feel like you're dining in an underwater cave. Cuisine from Hunan province is typically spicier than other Chinese food, and Portland's own Hunan doesn't disappoint. Indulge in the guilty pleasures on the menu—a lip-smackingly sweet General Tso's Chicken, Lake T'ung T'ing shrimp dumplings in hot oil, or fried pot stickers—but don't miss the relatively simple dishes like sautéed green beans and hot-and-sour soup. Piping hot Chinese tea (complimentary, with endless refills) warms the cockles before you head back out in the cold. **COME HERE FOR CLASSIC HUNAN CUISINE.** *$$; MC, V; no checks; lunch, dinner every day; full bar; no reservations; map:I3* ⟨⟩

Il Fornaio / ★★

115 NW 22ND AVE, NORTHWEST; 503/248-9400 Though this location—one of 24 U.S.-based restaurants and a whopping 2,500 in Italy—follows a corporate model, it never behaves like a groupie. Instead it feels distinctive in a warm, welcoming way. Three separate dining areas share a menu of authentic Italian regional cuisine. A bright bustling bar with polished plank floors, surrounded by windows open in summer, is family-friendly and casual. A softly lit, linen-dressed space offers intimate dining; an enclosed brick patio has a fireplace and roll-away roof. An exhibition kitchen parades chefs who stir asparagus risotto, turn dry-aged rib-eye steaks over mesquite, slide pizza margheritas into the wood oven, and rotate sizzling chickens on a rotisserie. Crusty artisan bread, baked in the downstairs bakery, complements yellow-tomato and dry-aged ricotta salad, butternut-squash-and-sage ravioli, gnocchi with smoked salmon, and stuffed baby artichokes. For dessert, *affogato al caffe* is heavenly: espresso over vanilla ice cream draped in softly whipped cream. Italian wines selected from small, regional wineries pair naturally with aromatic sauces. **COME HERE TO EAT PIZZA IN THE BAR ON WARM DAYS.** *$$; AE, DC, MC, V; local checks only; lunch, dinner every day, brunch Sun; full bar; reservations recommended; www.ilfornaio.com; map:HH7* ⟨⟩

Il Piatto / ★★★
Sala / ★★

2348 SE ANKENY ST, BUCKMAN; 503/236-4997 / 3200 SE MILWAUKIE BLVD, BROOKLYN; 503/235-6665 Portland thrives on restaurants like Il Piatto: a cozy, ever-inviting nook tucked quietly into a residential neighborhood, almost qualifying as a secret. Eugen and Lenor Bingham have created a restaurant that draws fans from across the city, with nearly 20 pastas (notably, a punchy puttanesca and a sweet-potato gnocchi), deft risottos, and signature dishes such as pork saltimbocca and wild-mushroom crepes with smoked-pear crème fraîche. It's a particularly good place for midweek lunches, discreet and otherwise. The attraction is heightened by decor resembling an overstuffed Venetian apartment, complete with a comfy sofa on which to wait for your table, and personable service. **COME HERE TO DINE AS YOUR ITALIAN GRANDMOTHER WOULD HAVE WANTED.**

The Binghams' new, bistro-style restaurant, Sala, is more casual than Il Piatto, its menu is shorter and less classically oriented. But it boasts new creativity: try the seafood lasagna layered with rock shrimp, scallops, salmon, spinach, and fennel, with lobster béchamel and a pine-nut crust. Sunday brunch features a beautiful salmon hash. **COME HERE FOR MEDITERRANEAN-STYLE SEAFOOD.** *$$; AE, MC, V; checks OK; lunch Tues–Fri, dinner every day, brunch Sun (Sala); beer and wine; reservations recommended; www.ilpiatto.citysearch.com; map:GG5; map:II5* ⟨⟩

India House / ★★☆

1038 SW MORRISON ST, DOWNTOWN; 503/274-1017 The tandoori chicken here could draw people right off the light-rail trains that run by the door, and the crispy pakoras could make them miss the next train. Some Portland Indian restaurants may be more elaborate and formal, but this storefront has consistently and skillfully maintained its place near the top of the list. The pleasant restaurant serves the full range of Indian food with a consistency that has attracted a solid, happy constituency of downtown diners. Dishes from north and south India, including tandoori-roasted specials, make weekend dinner a crowded, festive affair, and the daily lunch buffet has caught on, too. Bring a group to adequately sample the generous menu. **COME HERE FOR THE TANDOORI CHICKEN.** *$$; AE, DC, DIS, MC, V; no checks; lunch Mon–Sat, dinner every day; beer and wine; reservations recommended; map: I2* &

J+M Café / ★★☆

537 SE ASH ST, BUCKMAN; 503/230-0463 A stalwart breakfast and lunch joint, J+M Café added dinners near the close of 2002, only to discontinue them a few months later. Luckily, J+M never forgot its roots along the way: breakfast scrambles, rustic French toast, and eclectic sandwiches still satisfy. With its industrial-height ceilings, cobalt floor, and mosaic art, this breezy cafe radiates light on the dreariest days. J+M doesn't purport to be fancy, but the food is refined and wholesome. French toast is made from baguette sliced lengthwise (a whopping five pieces) and served with pure maple syrup. Other top ingredients make their way into 10-grain hot cereal, cornmeal waffles, and creative scrambles. A winning sandwich at lunch is the J+M grilled cheese, with onions, tomatoes, fontina, and red-pepper pesto on sturdy como bread. Stumptown coffee and water are self-serve, ensuring that you never have to wait for either . . . even if you have to wait a while for a table on weekend mornings. **COME HERE FOR QUIET WEEKDAY BREAKFASTS.** *$; no credit cards; local checks only; breakfast every day, lunch Mon–Fri; beer and wine; no reservations; map:HH6* &

Jake's Famous Crawfish / ★★

401 SW 12TH AVE, DOWNTOWN; 503-226-1419 Jake's probably makes more tourist itineraries than any other Portland restaurant. Behind its sociable, trendy scene lies a vigorous 112-year history, still apparent in the clubby wood bar, high-backed booths, and shiny mahogany paneling. Servers in white coats and black trousers hustle through crowds carrying 1-pound platters of crawfish, boiled in spices and served in the shell. Though no longer harvested from basement ponds, they meet Jake's promise: if the seafood isn't fresh, it isn't on the menu. What's more, any fish can be ordered simply broiled with lemon butter or prepared "to match its origins": catfish with pecans and jalapeño chutney, for instance. Signature clam chowder, cedar-plank salmon, popcorn shrimp, and whole-leaf Caesar salad take honors. Secondary dishes (mashed potatoes, vegetables) might fail to dazzle; and in a city of great artisan bakers, Jake's still serves mediocre sourdough. Chocolate truffle cake, however, became so popular that it's sold commercially, and three-berry cobbler earns raves. The bar scene is legendary and a dense wine list showcases some of Oregon's finest vintages. A part of three centuries, Jake's *is* Portland—not the top cuisine but a favorite son. **COME HERE FOR THE HISTORY.** *$$; AE, DC, DIS, MC, V; no checks; lunch Mon–Fri, dinner every day; full bar; reservations recommended; www.mccormickandschmicks.com; map:J2* &

Jake's Grill / ★★

611 SW 10TH AVE (GOVERNOR HOTEL), DOWNTOWN; 503/241-2100 Sure, this is part of the McCormick & Schmick's stable, so fresh seafood features prominently on the menu. But this steak house also serves three meals a day as the Governor Hotel dining room. Typical of hotel eateries, the menu offers a little bit of everything—nearly 100 choices. There's a comfort-food section with a decent meat loaf and fettuccine Alfredo. Super-traditional choices include classic club sandwiches, prime rib, and sides of cottage cheese and steamed broccoli. Choose among 10 varieties of juicy steak, fist-thick double lamb chops, and a boneless half-chicken. Oriental chicken salad, rock-shrimp penne, and cedar-plank salmon provide contemporary options. Appetizers (mainly seafood) and desserts (try the gooey bread pudding) are familiar from other M&S outposts, as is the high-ceilinged, circa-1900 saloon decor. Styles shift during the day: lunch is a casual mix of downtown workers and out-of-town browsers, while dinner is more flashy, drawing birthday celebrants and gussied-up couples on dates. **COME HERE FOR TRADITIONAL MAHOGANY-AND-BRASS-RAIL ATMOSPHERE.** *$$–$$$; AE, DC, MC, V; no checks; breakfast, lunch, dinner every day; full bar; reservations recommended; valet parking; www.mccormickandschmicks.com; map:I2* &

Jam on Hawthorne / ★

2239 SE HAWTHORNE BLVD, HAWTHORNE; 503/234-4790 There's a certain kind of sweet Portland morning, when sunlight beams through the windows, filters through the steam rising from all those coffee cups, and sets the butter-colored walls of Jam on Hawthorne aglow. For that moment, all is right in the world. The replacement to longtime artists' and poets' haunt Café Lena, Jam has taken the baton and run with it, bringing fresh air and fresh recipes to its Buckman-Hawthorne neighborhood. Lively scrambles full of sassy ingredients (pieces of smoked salmon, grainy mustard, rough-chopped scallions, torn spinach leaves) join an abundance of sweet morning treats (including some almost-famous lemon ricotta pancakes). **COME HERE FOR—WHAT ELSE?—HOUSE-MADE JAMS, CONCOCTED FRESH EVERY COUPLE OF DAYS.** *$–$$; DIS, MC, V; no checks; breakfast, lunch Tues–Sun; beer and wine; map:HH5* &

Jarra's Ethiopian Restaurant / ★

1435 SE HAWTHORNE BLVD, HAWTHORNE; 503/230-8990 During years as Portland's prime place to go for an explosive, sweat-inducing Abyssinian stew, Jarra's has had different incarnations. Its current one may be its most formal. Rising from the basement of an old Portland home up to the main floor, this is the neighborhood's unequaled heat champ, its Chez Wat. Indeed, Jarra's is the restaurant to teach you what's *wat*: made with chicken, lamb, or beef, the *wat* (stews) are deep red, oily, and packed with peppery after-kicks. There's *doro wat* (with chicken), *zilzel wat* (with sirloin tip), and *miser* and *yedenitch wats* (vegetarian, with split lentils or potatoes).

83

Full dinners come with assorted stewed meats and vegetables, all permeated with vibrant spices and mounded on *injera*—the spongy Ethiopian bread that doubles as plate and fork. **COME HERE FOR HOT AND SPICY STEWS.** *$; MC, V; no checks; dinner Tues–Sat; full bar; reservations recommended; map:HH5* &

Jo Bar and Rotisserie / ★★

715 NW 23RD AVE, NORTHWEST; 503/222-0048 Papa Haydn's (see review) younger sibling has emerged as a big player in the Nob Hill restaurant stakes, with loyal customers returning to feast on succulent chicken, duck, pork loin, and leg of lamb roasted in one of the two huge wood-burning ovens. Ablaze at the rear of the restaurant, the ovens cast a picture-perfect glow, enhancing the complexions of well-heeled patrons. Jo Bar is known for its flamboyant concoctions—chocolate martini, anyone?—and satisfying bistro fare. The rotisserie chicken always does the trick; crispy pizzas, piquant crab cakes, and the upscale Jo Burger are other good bets. And if decadence strikes, why not knock back a couple of oyster shooters? Weekend brunch breaks away from standard fare, serving up chilaquiles, frittatas, and brioche French toast. Check the chalkboard for daily cocktail specials, often made with house-infused liquors like the cinnamon rum in the Maple Leaf—a chilled autumnal number that also includes maple syrup, and orange and lemon juices. **COME HERE FOR THE JUBILANT ATMOSPHERE AND WELL-CONCEIVED COCKTAILS.** *$$; AE, MC, V; no checks; lunch Mon–Sat, dinner every day, brunch Sun; full bar; reservations recommended; jobarhaydn@aol.com; map:GG7* &

John Street Café / ★★

8338 N LOMBARD ST, SAINT JOHNS; 503/247-1066 With its sunny disposition and lack of airs, this cafe has established firm roots in its North Portland neighborhood. Co-owner Marie Noehren tends the kitchen as her partner-husband Jamie stays out front, serving dense banana bread with omelets of cheese, beans, guacamole, and salsa. Painted lavender outside and in, this corner cafe (at N John Ave) displays eclectic local art on its walls—a helpful distraction during weekend waits for tables. The cuisine follows no culinary themes. It's straightforward and nicely done without too much fuss. On weekends, regulars know to order the corned-beef hash for breakfast. Other days, lightly scrambled eggs with chives, Brie, and oven-roasted potatoes, or plate-covering pancakes with currants and filberts or apples, answer morning needs. At lunch, the kitchen stretches a bit, offering blackened snapper on a bun, linguine with shrimp in aromatic tomato-leek broth, and a Reuben that is among the best in town: toasted sour rye, heaps of corned beef, Gruyère, Russian dressing, and a very tangy sauerkraut. Desserts are often limited to cookies and lemon cheesecake. **COME HERE FOR A REUBEN SANDWICH.** *$; MC, V; local checks only; breakfast, lunch Wed–Sun; no alcohol; no reservations; jmarine@spiritone.com; map:EE9* &

Justa Pasta / ★★☆

1336 NW 19TH AVE, NORTHWEST; 503/243-2249 Slowly, steadily, Justa Pasta has made a stellar name for itself. A wholesaler of fresh pasta to many Portland establishments, Justa also has grown into a full-fledged restaurant that offers one of the best values in town. The clean-lined, unassuming eatery is nonstop busy at lunchtime, presenting nonpareil Caesar salads and bowls of bucatini with marinara, served with perfect timing. Patrons can enjoy their Pearl Bakery baguette with olive oil and balsamic vinegar and a two-course lunch and still get out in 45 minutes. Dinner is sleepier, though Justa is making headway in this trade, serving intricate lasagnas and seafood specials. Day and night, several types of pasta and ravioli are available with sauces ranging from woodsy sautéed mushroom and garlic to subtle Alfredo. The menu changes with the seasons, but if you get too attached to that Swiss chard–ricotta ravioli, you can always buy a pound of it to go, along with a container of Justa's nutty pesto. Beer, affordable wine, and outrageous layer cakes complete the supremely satisfying dining experience. **COME HERE FOR RESTRAINED PASTA DISHES AT ROCK-BOTTOM PRICES.** *$; AE, MC, V; checks OK; lunch Mon–Fri, dinner Mon–Sat; beer and wine; reservations for 8 or more; www.justapasta.com; map:GG7* &

Ken's Artisan Bakery & Café / ★★

338 NW 21ST AVE, NORTHWEST; 503/248-2202 What started as a bread-focused bakery and coffee shop has grown to include a critically acclaimed wholesaling business and wine bar. Owner Ken Forkish's meticulously crafted breads are demanded by top restaurants all around town; loyal bread lovers regularly swing by to pick up a chewy baguette, airy ciabatta, or dense walnut campagne loaf. Ken's specializes in rustic loaves made with organic ingredients, baked to perfection in an enormous steam oven. Forkish's love of good bread and dedication to making exemplary varieties can be witnessed at the bakery, where workers ply their craft in the open kitchen. Besides this show, the cafe also is a great place to linger over a cup of coffee and croissant or spongy quenelle. Simple French-inspired sandwiches and soups, and yummy fruit tarts and macaroons, are available at lunchtime. More recently, Ken's has begun serving wine and light fare in the evening. Table service begins at 5pm and the menu offers salads, cheese and bread, and seasonal hot dishes. **COME HERE FOR A DOSE OF EUROPEAN CAFE CULTURE.** *$; MC, V; checks OK; breakfast, lunch Tues–Sun, dinner Tues–Sat; beer and wine; no reservations; www.kensartisan.com; map:HH7* &

Ken's Place / ★★

1852 SE HAWTHORNE BLVD, HAWTHORNE; 503/236-9520 Longtime comfort-food caterer Ken Gordon has refocused his operations in the low-slung storefront that once housed his catering kitchen. His Place has the elbows-on-the-table informality of a diner, with an open kitchen and a Formica counter arrayed with vinyl stools. The menu is aw-shucks affordable, maybe because the no-frills presentation (paper napkins, jelly-jar water glasses) allows for lower prices. Substantial entrées like steak au poivre and pork chops are served with familiar accompaniments souped up for the dining-out crowd: mashed potatoes in a garlicky cake, applesauce spiked with ginger. In homage to American homestyle cooking, salty, sweet, and buttery flavors dominate the side dishes, which include gooey scalloped spuds and sautéed spinach. But there are also light-handed treats, like Ladd's Rad Salade, blending harvested field greens with fennel, pickled onion, asparagus, and kalamata olives. Even if the desserts weren't arrayed in a tiered display near the front entrance, it would be a crime to pass them up, especially Ken's Chocolate Bites, a sampling of brownies, tiny mousse tarts, chocolate chip cookies, and hand-formed truffles dusted with confectioners' sugar. **COME HERE FOR HEALTHY HOMESTYLE COOKING.** *$–$$; MC, V; checks OK; lunch, dinner Tues–Sat; beer and wine; no reservations; map:HH5*

Khun Pic's Bahn Thai / ★★

3429 SE BELMONT ST, BELMONT; 503/235-1610 Culinary DNA must account for the success of two Thai sisters, daughters of a mother who owned one of Portland's first popular Thai restaurants. Shelley Siripatrapa has Lemongrass Thai (see review), while Mary Ogard operates Khun Pic's. The sisters' independence and competitive spirit show up in subtle ways. Here, Ogard restored a Victorian home to create welcoming spaces, adding orchids and gold wall borders reminiscent of Thailand's gilded temples. A streetside brick patio—screened by lush foliage and bamboo—offers seasonal outdoor dining. Husband Jon manages the dining rooms, freeing Mary to run the kitchen solo. Since food is made to order, service can be interminably slow. Despite the pace, diners forgive all when her intensely seasoned food arrives at their table, served on mismatched china. Most offerings are familiar: phad thai (including a great vegetarian version); tom yum goong (hot-and-sour prawn soup); crispy fried tofu with peanut sauce; fragrant yellow, red, and green curries; freshly grated green-papaya salad; and mango sorbet. **COME HERE FOR THAI HOME COOKING.** *$$; No credit cards; checks OK; dinner Tues–Sat; beer and wine; reservations recommended; map:HH5*

Koji Osakaya / ★

7007 SW MACADAM AVE, JOHNS LANDING (AND BRANCHES); 503/293-1066 Sushi bars are everywhere, but this operation is clearly one of the better full-service Japanese restaurants around—especially since it's multiplied by four. From the original Southwest Portland restaurant featuring sumo wrestling broadcasts, to the always jammed nooks downtown (606 SW Broadway; 503/294-1169; map:I3) and near the Lloyd Center (1500 NE Weidler St; 503/280-0992; map:GG5), to the newest outpost in restaurant-rife Nob Hill (539 NW 21st Ave; 503/222/0962; map:HH7), Koji's offers consistently good Japanese cuisine. Customers create combination dinners by choosing among yakitori (teriyaki chicken skewers), prawn and vegetable tempura, deep-fried pork loin with panko breading, and yakiniku (sautéed rib-eye with onions). Served with the daily sushi roll, miso soup, salad, and rice, it's a heaping value meal. Or opt for delicate noodle soups, sweet *unagi* (eel) donburi or curry. As chain restaurants go, Koji has strong links. **COME HERE FOR WALLET-FRIENDLY JAPANESE MEALS.** *$–$$; AE, MC, V; no checks; lunch, dinner every day; full bar; reservations for 7 or more; map:II6* &

Kornblatt's Delicatessen / ★

628 NW 23RD AVE, NORTHWEST; 503/242-0055 Kornblatt's is the closest thing this West Coast city has to a New York–style deli, and it comes without the intimidating attitude and abrupt service. Though not up to high Manhattan standards, the inclusive menu—long for such a small deli—covers many Jewish soul-food choices: chopped liver, smoked fish, knishes, matzo ball soup, bagels, kosher franks, and cheesecake. A breakfast your mother could love—cream cheese–tomato omelet, home-fried potatoes, and bagel—carries you all day, and the fat pastrami on rye, sided by sauerkraut and macaroni salad, feeds two. Mirrored walls, baskets of bagels, and a deli case that displays a seven-layer champagne cake frosted in white coconut, raise the ambience beyond a typical sandwich shop. **COME HERE FOR PASTRAMI ON RYE.** *$–$$; MC, V; checks OK; breakfast, lunch, dinner every day; beer and wine; no reservations; map:GG7* &

La Calaca Comelona / ★★

2304 SE BELMONT ST, BELMONT; 503/239-9675 La Calaca Comelona has always presented a substantial and intriguing menu, and with its move to a larger Belmont storefront, the menu's scope has broadened further. The authentic Mexican fare once consisted mainly of inexpensive, bulging tacos, tostadas, and quesadillas (never burritos!), but it has evolved into a full-service restaurant with sophisticated entrées and a full liquor license. The expanded menu offers *especialidades de casa* that run as high as $20, including *mole en pipián*, a medium-hot green mole comprising pasilla and serrano chiles, bell pepper, tomatillo, lettuce, and spinach. Ladled over hunks of chicken breast and thigh, studded with pepitas (hulled pumpkin seeds), it's a sumptuous, more delicate alternative to chewy black mole. *Puerco con chile negro* couples a grilled pork loin with smoky-black chile sauce and grilled almonds. The nuts, along with handmade tortillas, serve to balance the startlingly sharp flavor of the chile. Given the rustic quality of these dishes, 20 bucks seems a steep asking price, but it's worth it, considering just how much time is required to produce mole and other complex chile sauces. **COME HERE FOR AUTHENTIC MEXICAN DISHES WITH GREAT TEXTURE AND FLAVOR.** *$–$$; AE, DC, DIS, MC, V; no checks; dinner Mon–Sat; full bar; reservations recommended; www.lacalacacomelona.com; map:HH5* &

La Cruda / ★

2500 SE CLINTON ST, CLINTON; 503/233-0745 A gleaming beacon of affordable, healthy chow just down the street from the Clinton Street Theater, La Cruda's full menu until midnight has made it a late-night Mex mecca. On a hot night, you'll find groups of shorts-clad denizens at the outdoor tables, fanning themselves with baseball caps and sipping bottles of Pacifico. Year-round, locals troop in for the orange juice–marinated tofu tacos, carne asada, and bottomless limeade. The house-made tamales come stuffed to bursting with shredded chicken, black beans, and melted cheese. Entrées arrive with more beans, rice, and salad than you can shake a taquito at, while extras like from-scratch guacamole and four fresh salsas (free at the bar) give bulking-up a touch of class. Margaritas are some of the best quenchers in town. Check out the oddly lifelike paintings of tractor trailers barreling up parched desert highways. **COME HERE FOR A LATE-NIGHT CARB FIX.** *$; AE, DIS, MC, V; local checks OK; breakfast, lunch, dinner every day; full bar; reservations for 8 or more; map:II5*

La Prima Trattoria / ★

4775 SW 77TH AVE, RALEIGH HILLS; 503/297-0360 This restaurant features a stylish Italian ambience of tiles, wood tables, and booths and an open kitchen with a wood-fired oven. This easily overlooked neighborhood favorite defies its suburban mall location. The engaging but occasionally noisy space—divided between bar and restaurant—is daytime bright and evening soft. Peasant-crusted pizzas arrive slightly charred for immediate consumption. Linguini draped in classic pomodoro and penne with pork loin, asparagus, portabello mushrooms, and herbs attract enthusiasts, while *pollo saltimbocca* and veal marsala easily please. Weekend breakfasts feature Italian scrambled eggs, polenta muffins with sausage gravy, and bruschetta. Carefully selected wines and moderate pricing complement the accessible menu. **COME HERE FOR WOOD-FIRED PIZZA AND A GLASS OF RED WINE.** *$$; AE, MC, V; checks OK; breakfast Sat–Sun, lunch, dinner every day; beer and wine; reservations recommended; map:II8* &

Lauro Kitchen / ★★

3377 SE DIVISION ST, SOUTHEAST; 503/239-7000 Chef/owner David Machado is known as the man whose magic hands made Pazzo Ristorante and Southpark Seafood Grill and Wine Bar (see reviews) into suppertime sensations. He's left the boardroom for the kitchen for his latest venture, Lauro Kitchen, bringing marvelous Mediterranean oddities to suddenly booming Division Street. A beautifully designed space painted in shades of cocoa and maize provides the perfect background for rustic salads glistening with jewel-like chunks of tomato, light and brothy seafood fillets and stews, and spicy-smoky chocolate desserts. The influences of Spanish, Moroccan, Portuguese, Greek, and Middle Eastern cuisine dart in and out of the dishes with a flair and sophistication that continually delight and surprise Lauro's diners. But all this fancy footwork hasn't kept burgers, pizza, and fries off the menu—these familiar and affordable comforts make Lauro even more inviting. **COME HERE FOR INTRIGUING MEDITERRANEAN FLAVORS.** *$$; AE, DC, DIS, MC, V; no checks; dinner Tues–Sat; full bar; no reservations; www.laurokitchen. com; map:II5* &

Le Bistro Montage / ★★

301 SE MORRISON ST, INNER SOUTHEAST; 503/234-1324 Every night is Mardi Gras at Montage, where miles of aluminum-foil ornaments hang from the ceilings and cooks sling panfried oysters from an open kitchen. Serious diners come early; later on, you'll wait in line with a young alternative crowd for a spot at one of the long and noisy tables. Until 2am (4am Fri–Sat), Montage serves such Cajun best sellers as The Old Mac (glorified macaroni in garlic and heavy cream), blackened catfish, and jambalaya topped with crawfish or alligator meat. Dinners are both ambitious and unique—from spicy frogs' legs to gator pâté to green eggs and Spam—and make up in visceral satisfaction what they lack in finesse. (When Montage says spicy, it's not kidding.) If you're Atkins dieting, order Meat . . . & That's It!, a plate of chicken, pork loin, and andouille sausage. If you're not, finish your meal with a slice of pecan pie. Wines, offered by the glass, are promptly refilled in jelly jar–like vessels. Portland's definitively hip late-night hangout is also open for weekday lunches: you won't get the energy of the wee hours, but you will get the same unexpectedly good, cheap Southern cuisine. **COME HERE FOR THE PARTY.** *$–$$; no credit cards; checks OK; lunch Mon–Fri, dinner every day; full bar; no reservations; map:G9* &

Le Bouchon / ★★

517 NW 14TH AVE, PEARL DISTRICT; 503/248-2193 Elegant? *Non.* Pretentious? *Non.* Fine French dining? *Oui.* Here is a Left Bank bistro that is perfectly compatible with the Northwest lifestyle. The emphasis is on charm, not intimidation. Classically trained chef Claude Musquin holds forth in the kitchen while his ebullient wife, Monique, controls the dining room with a warm *"Bonjour!"* and a raised eyebrow approving your wine selection. The intimate space—with closely staged tables, banquette seating, and a bar—demands tête-a-tête for private conversation, but diner buzz adds authenticity. Claude Musquin excels in French country and traditional bistro fare, and his wonderful sauces are a highlight of dining here: provençal, bourguignon, deux vinaigres. Dishes prepared *à la minuit* include salmon draped in fresh dill sauce with potatoes au gratin. Classic French onion soup, baked in a crock, requires a spoon to break through a perfect cheese crust to reach rich broth and onions. After your escargot, lamb chops, and *grand-mere*'s noodles, you won't forgive yourself if you haven't left room for a dense white-and-dark-chocolate mousse in a martini glass. **COME HERE IF YOU CAN'T AFFORD FRANCE.** *$$; AE, DIS, MC, V; no checks; lunch Fri, dinner Tues–Sat; beer and wine; reservations recommended; map:M1* &

Legin / ★

8001 SE DIVISION ST, SOUTHEAST; 503/777-2828 At first glance, this huge, garish building among the fast-food outlets of SE 82nd Avenue looks like the chop-suey palace of all time. It's only when you get inside the cavernous dining room, and see the huge Chinese menu and the tanks of live seafood, that you discover one of Portland's better Asian eateries. Some items you just won't find elsewhere in this city—bamboo marrow, two kinds of shark's fin soup—and you can accompany them with live geoduck or a whole tilapia. Try anything that's alive when you order it, try to find a place for the pepper-and-salt lobster, and take a shot at something you don't recognize: Cantonese ham, perhaps. Some diners complain, however, that common dishes may be sloppily prepared. And, although dim sum lunch is served every day, you should come on Sunday if only because you can watch so many chicken feet dispensed. **COME HERE FOR THE SHARK'S FIN SOUP.** *$$; MC, V; no checks; lunch, dinner every day; full bar; no reservations; map:II3* &

Le Happy / ★★

1011 NW 16TH AVE, NORTHWEST; 503/226-1258 Wedged between a real-estate office and a scruffy karaoke tavern is this closet-sized crêperie. With its cheerful red door and lace curtains, Le Happy seems out of place in the somewhat rundown neighborhood formerly known as Slabtown. Yet its cozy interior, and a view of the streetcar yard below I-405's underbelly, exert an off-kilter allure perfectly in sync with area businesses. The menu is mainly crepes—savory and sweet—but also includes terrific salads (don't miss the spicy steak salad) and a lone steak. Many crepes—such as Ma Provençe, a stick-to-your-ribs mix of roasted chicken, garlic, tomato, Gruyère, and goat cheese—are hearty enough for a regular entrée. Even meatless crepes are filling. The Oeuf Deluxe, with a poached egg yolk exposed and glistening at the crepe's center, and Faux Vegan, a double-whammy of chèvre and crème fraîche with spinach and cremini mushroom sauce, are especially good. Don't leave without ordering a dessert such as the Belle-Helène, which folds poached pear, chocolate, toasted almonds, and whipped cream into a delicate vanilla crepe. **COME HERE FOR THE OFFBEAT LOCALE AND EXPERT CREPES.** *$–$$; MC, V; no checks; dinner Mon–Sat; beer and wine; no reservations; www.lehappy.com; map:GG7* &

Lemongrass Thai / ★★☆

1705 NE COUCH ST, BUCKMAN; 503/231-5780 Shelly Siripatrapa's Lemongrass is nestled in a sweet, subdued Victorian house in leafy Buckman, where she prepares and serves much of the food herself. The zesty noodle dishes and be-still-my-heart curries (an impressive array of yellow, red, and green, available with chicken, prawns, and other proteins) have a spiciness scale that runs from 1 to 20—but even the most intrepid, Thai-philic westerner will probably be comfortable with a 3. Besides the spice, Lemongrass cuisine is notable for its emphasis on crisp textures and the heady scents of Thai herbs and spices: grassy basil and cilantro, aromatic kaffir leaves and lemongrass, potent red chiles, tart slivers of lime. Because of the skeletal staff, service can be very slow, but patient diners still pour in for the crispy-chewy salad rolls, the creamy tom yum soup, and the palate-scorching Thai Noodle (known in some circles as phad thai). **COME HERE FOR THE SINUS-CLEARING CURRIES.** *$$; no credit cards; checks OK; lunch Tues–Fri, dinner Tues–Sat; beer and wine; no reservations; map:HH5*

Little Wing Café / ★☆

529 NW 13TH AVE, PEARL DISTRICT; 508/228-3101 Adored for its fresh, filling sandwiches and CD-size cookies, lunch landmark Little Wing is making headway as a dinner destination. Owners Barbara and Bob Weisman were among the first restaurateurs to open an eatery in the Pearl District—before the neighborhood even had its name. The cafe's high ceilings, big windows, quick counter service, and stack of newspapers make Little Wing an ideal lunch spot. In warm weather, the outside deck holds enough tables for everyone to have their moment in the sun. Clever sandwiches, crisp salads, and a vast array of formidable desserts make mincemeat out of regular grab-and-go deli fare. You can get a crunchy Caesar or a spicy carrot-ginger soup. At night, the menu is all over the map, running the gamut from classic dishes such as skirt steak and mashed potatoes and a grilled half chicken to Caribbean-inspired shrimp-and-vegetable skewers. No matter what the time of day, Little Wing's cakes and pastries are always irresistible. **COME HERE FOR KILLER SANDWICHES AND COOKIES.** *$–$$; AE, DIS, MC, V; checks OK; lunch Mon–Sat, dinner Tues–Sat; beer and wine; no reservations; map:M1* &

London Grill / ★★

309 SW BROADWAY (BENSON HOTEL), DOWNTOWN; 503/295-4110 At the core of the Benson Hotel, this place has been a Portland institution since before software, or jogging, or even Mark Hatfield: definitely a 20th-century classic. The deep seats and rococo chandeliers speak to a traditional idea of what a power restaurant should be, and much of the menu harkens back to that ideal:

chicken Oscar, veal medallions, and chateaubriand for two. On the other hand, there are signs of today: Dungeness crab cakes in a green coconut curry, pan-seared Muscovy duck on spinach risotto, and medallions of Oregon ostrich (although presented in the crab-meat-and-béarnaise Oscar manner). London Grill has deeply loyal fans, high-quality ingredients—its seafood treatments may be traditional, but it's treating fine seafood—and a harpist. The service is highly professional, although it seems fewer dishes now involve tableside preparation. The longest wine list in town is especially strong on French bottlings; settle into your cushy chair as you consider your decision. **COME HERE FOR CLASSIC CONTINENTAL CUISINE AND PAMPERED SERVICE.** *$$$; AE, DC, DIS, MC, V; checks OK; breakfast, lunch, dinner every day, brunch Sun; full bar; reservations recommended; www.benson hotel.com; map:J4* &

Lucère / ★★

1510 SW HARBOR WAY (RIVERPLACE HOTEL), DOWNTOWN; 503/228-3233 Since Lucère first dropped anchor as resident restaurant of the RiverPlace Hotel, its fortunes have ebbed, flowed, and finally caught a swell. Former complaints about service and flat preparation have been addressed, and there are many delights on the menu crafted by Matthew Young, chef since the restaurant's name was changed from Esplanade. Pacific Northwest produce provides much of the flavor here, from the wild mushrooms in a perfectly al dente risotto, to the heirloom tomatoes in a chilled salad, to that daub of triple-cream on the artisan cheese plate. True to the restaurant's elegant setting and its own high expectations, execution of the bistro-style entrées is expert—the grilled fillets of beef and pork tenderloin are prepared with delicately rendered sauces and careful, artistic plating. An intelligent wine list contains dozens of Northwest entries, many available by the glass. Lucère provides a tantalizing taste of Oregon for travelers—and a celebration of well-loved favorites for locals. **COME HERE FOR ELEGANT RIVERSIDE DINING.** *$$$; AE, DC, DIS, JCB, MC, V; checks OK; breakfast, lunch, dinner every day; full bar; reservations recommended; valet parking; www.riverplacehotel.com; map:D5* &

Lucy's Table / ★★★

704 NW 21ST AVE, NORTHWEST; 503/226-6126 What you really must know about Lucy's Table is that pound for pound, it's less expensive than many of its peers. The richly hued dining room maximizes capacity without cramping diners; attractive bamboo arrangements are used to buffer a pair of tables from the busy corridor near the kitchen, so there's not a bad table in the house. Chef Thomas McLaughlin's brief weekly menu follows the seasons and veers from fragrant braised duck breast to a deep bowl of risotto that teems with some of the meatiest wild mushrooms you've ever met. Roast pork loin is stuffed with a complimentary mix of plump Carnaroli rice, nuts, and dried fruits, served with a similarly bulging sweet, roasted onion, and is surprisingly reasonably priced. For more deals, park it at the bar 5–6:30pm weeknights for discounted plates of goat-cheese ravioli and baby-back ribs. Owner Peter Kost stocks an impressive and reasonably priced cellar of local and imported wines. **COME HERE FOR THE SURPRISINGLY REASONABLE PRICES.** *$$; AE, DC, MC, V; checks OK; dinner Mon–Sat; full bar; reservations recommended; www.lucystable.com; map:GG7* &

Madame Butterfly / ★

425 SW STARK ST, DOWNTOWN; 503/525-0033 Some Japanese restaurants are lauded for uncommon presentation or the extraordinary freshness of the fish. Madame Butterfly wins the prize for sushi style and late-night cool. The sleek and modern dining room is painted in shades of khaki and deep red, with stalks of living bamboo reaching toward the high ceilings. Though it may not be strictly accurate to call the food "French Japanese," as MB does, there's an undeniably fashionable flair to the misozuke beef—steak marinated and grilled, then sliced with spinach and cream cheese, and sauced with a *yuzu* dressing. This dish is one of MB's "box entrées," but as DJs and dancing turn the dining room into cocktail central Thursday through Saturday nights, lighter fare—such as familiar soba and teriyaki dishes—holds sway here. **COME HERE FOR THE LATE-NIGHT HIPSTER SCENE.** *$–$$; AE, MC, V; no checks; lunch, dinner every day; full bar; reservations recommended; map:I4* &

Malanga / ★★☆

4627 NE FREMONT ST, BEAUMONT; 503/528-2822 In this vibrant new restaurant in Northeast Portland, popular chef Eric Laslow has stepped into the arena of Cuban-inspired *cocina*. Strong primary colors brighten a storefront space that has housed a procession of restaurants: sunshine yellow now floods the walls, a Havana pink ribbon around the room draws focus together, and a line of photos from Cuba sets the location. Malanga sizzled immediately, for who can resist this menu language? *Frituras de Malanga* are crispy, round taro fritters spiked with tons of heady garlic. *Yuca frita con mojo* are sticks of cassava fried in a crisp shell with garlic-citrus sauce. *Filetes de pargo al horno* is red snapper baked with potatoes, tomatoes, and lime. Drawing on his own Cuban heritage and proven culinary skills, Laslow pleases with an authentic menu, clear through *café con leche*. A reasonable wine list draws mostly from Spanish-speaking countries, and ethnically lively Cuban cocktails (think mojitos) entertain. The brick patio is one of the city's nicest. **COME HERE FOR CAMARONES AL AJILLO (GARLIC PRAWNS).** *$$; AE, MC, V; checks OK; dinner every day; full bar; no reservations; map:FF4* &

Manzana Rotisserie Grill / ★★☆

1203 NW GLISAN ST, PEARL DISTRICT; 503/248-1690 A huge patch of premier real estate in the middle of the highfalutin Pearl District has been given over to sweetly spiced, cheese-enhanced comfort food. It's the latest concept from Pacific Coast Restaurants, which owns Portland City Grill (see review) and the Newport Bay and Stanford's chains. The menu comprises 25 of the most requested restaurant items in the country, so don't expect anything too daring. The food may be prosaic, but it's prepared well and satisfies cravings. Among the starters, Southwest chicken-tortilla soup is a highlight: crunchy tortilla strips and buttery smooth avocado make a winsome combination with the cheesy soup. A large artichoke, finished on the wood-fired grill and coupled with piquant rémoulade, begs to be shared by a group. Butter and cream make the mashed potatoes an irresistible side to citrus- and honey-glazed pork loin and Manzana's trademark applewood-roasted rotisserie chicken. Order the generous plate of tender pork medallions or deliciously sweet and moist chicken and you won't be disappointed. **COME HERE FOR CROWD-PLEASING AMERICAN STANDARDS.** *$$; AE, DC, DIS, MC, V; no checks; lunch, dinner every day; full bar; no reservations; www.manzanagrill.com; map:M2* &

Marco's Café and Espresso Bar / ★★

7910 SW 35TH AVE, MULTNOMAH VILLAGE; 503/245-0199 Thank goodness for charming, comfortable Marco's. This is the cafe every city craves, although it's quite at home in quaint Multnomah Village. Lodged in a restored 1913 corner grocery, this longtime neighborhood favorite draws a regionwide audience for all-day breakfast, friendly servers, mammoth berry muffins and espresso, and a well-stocked news rack. Snug between sunny yellow walls, beneath umbrellas that dangle upside down from the ceiling, regulars often forgo the menu. They already know they'll order red spuds with spinach, salsa, and cheddar, brioche French toast, or 10-grain cereal. Lunch offers a parade of seven burgers, Indonesian rice salad, or a delightful chicken-salad sandwich on hazelnut bread. The dinner menu roams the world to find dishes like Spanish paprika pasta and lime-basil sturgeon. Thursday night's tradition is mulligatawny, a curried vegetable soup with apples. The wine list offers bottles and glasses from small, independent wineries, most under $20 per bottle. Never skip dessert: there's bread pudding, huckleberry pie, and usually something chocolate. **COME HERE FOR GREAT AMBIENCE AND MULLIGATAWNY SOUP.** *$$; AE, DC, DIS, MC, V; local checks only; breakfast, lunch every day, dinner Mon–Sat; beer and wine; no reservations; www.marcoscafe.com; map:JJ7* &

Marrakesh / ★★☆

1201 NW 21ST AVE, NORTHWEST; 503/248-9442 Step into Marrakesh and take a magic carpet ride to a place where low lights reveal tapestried walls and yards of fabric draped tentlike from the ceiling. The appeal at this exotic restaurant is in the atmosphere and drama of the evening; and although the food falls short of fabulous, you may be so occupied with the scene (including belly dancers Wednesday through Saturday nights) that you won't notice. Get comfortable on a cushion at a knee-high dining table: you're here for five courses. The meal begins with a finger-washing ceremony and ends with the sprinkling of orange water over your hands. In between, you eat without benefit of utensils (unless you order rice-like couscous, in which case you might wangle a fork). The first course is a cumin-and-coriander lentil soup; next comes an eggplant salad. The sweetened *b'stilla royale* (chicken pie) paves the way for your entrée—maybe lamb *m'rouza* (with onions, raisins, and honey sauce) or braised hare in a rich cumin-and-paprika sauce. The easiest way to sample the fare is to go with three friends and sample the Royale Feast. **COME HERE FOR THE EXOTIC ATMOSPHERE.** *$$; AE, DC, DIS, MC, V; no checks; dinner every day; beer and wine; reservations recommended; map:GG7* &

McCormick & Schmick's Seafood Restaurant / ★★
Harborside / ★★
McCormick's Fish House and Bar / ★★

235 SW 1ST AVE, DOWNTOWN; 503/224-7522 / 0309 SW MONTGOMERY ST, RIVERPLACE; 503/220-1865 / 9945 SW BEAVERTON-HILLSDALE HWY, BEAVERTON; 503/643-1322 Curiosity surrounds the fresh sheets printed daily at the McCormick & Schmick's family of seafood restaurants. How can they offer so many fresh, unusual seafood choices, each identified by where they were caught? Call it ambitious purchasing, but the seafood variety has made a success of this sophisticated homegrown chain-gone-national. In fish-house style, the kitchens prepare crawfish from Lake Billy Chinook, razor clams from Polly Creek, Alaska, and Suva Fiji yellowfin tuna simply—with lemon butter or adorned to complement each seafood's origins, yet without ever stretching culinary boundaries. Each club-like restaurant is solidly styled, with high-backed wood booths ideal for business conversation or urban banter. Servers in white coats and black bow ties hustle plates of halibut in lemon-thyme butter and swordfish with risotto primavera. The international wine list and beers on tap encourage a brisk bar scene. M&S Seafood is in the restored 1886 Henry Failing Building; Harborside oversees a luscious Willamette River view; and the suburban Fish House and Bar is an oasis on a busy road. COME HERE FOR ABSOLUTELY FRESH FISH. $$–$$$; AE, DC, MC, V; no checks; lunch Mon–Sat, dinner every day; full bar; reservations recommended; www.mccormickand schmicks.com; map:I6; map:C5; map:JJ9 &

Milo's City Café / ★★☆

1325 NE BROADWAY, IRVINGTON; 503/288-6456 In a city blessed with great cafes, distinguishing yourself can be a challenge. This urbane contender along browsable NE Broadway is so popular for breakfast, fans demanded that a few select morning items be served all day. The lengthy early menu follows the crowd with multiple variations of egg scrambles, hash and eggs, and eggs Benedict (including pepper, bacon, and tomato). At noon, find a fine wilted-spinach salad, hot and cold sandwiches, pastas, and full meals like pesto salmon with potato crust and rice pilaf or apple brandy pork loin. An exposed industrial ceiling, sunny walls, black accents, bright light, and friendly bustle create daylight cheerfulness. Evenings turn softer as Milo's lures the morning crowd back for filet mignon, roast duck, rosemary chicken linguini, and an Oregon-Washington wine list at moderate prices. COME HERE FOR A SANTA FE OMELET. $$; AE, MC, V; local checks only; breakfast, lunch, dinner every day; full bar; no reservations; miloscitycafe@msn.com; map:GG5 &

Mint / ★★☆

816 N RUSSELL ST, ALBINA; 503/284-5518 A beautiful bauble of a restaurant, Mint has brought understated chic to this old industrial neighborhood and has turned into a hopping destination for the cocktail set. It's little wonder, given that owner Lucy Brennan is a master mixologist, turning out intelligent drinks that have the power to become instant classics. One such triumph is the blended avocado daiquiri, a supple surprise that is neither cloying nor heavy. Take a seat in the modern, cool-hued restaurant and your server will bring a bowl of toasted

pepitas to stave off your hunger. The Caribbean-spiced menu features a fair amount of seafood . . . and intense flavors. The calamari salad, rich with avocado and diced tomatoes, is a pleasing mix of textures. The fish of the day regularly sells out but is a good bet when available. A lamb burger offers a departure from the standard beef, turkey, and vegetable varieties—plus, it's topped with a nice mint *chimichurri*. In the adjoining sophisticated 820 Lounge, the cocktails don't have to compete with food for attention. **COME HERE FOR A FASHION SHOW.** *$$; AE, MC, V; no checks; dinner Mon–Sat; full bar; reservations recommended; www.mintrestaurant .com; map:GG6* &

Misohapi / ★

1123 NW 23RD AVE, NORTHWEST (AND BRANCHES); 503/796-2012 The name's silly play on pronunciation actually states the truth about this straightforward (yet eclectic) Thai-Vietnamese shop: diners *are* happy with things here. Prices are unbelievably reasonable for darn good food, served efficiently, in a sleek, lantern-hung ambience. Healthy and flavorful lunches (all $5.50) include Asian soup or shaved-cabbage salad with bowls of noodles or rice—for instance, grilled pork and shrimp over rice vermicelli with lettuce, bean sprouts, mint, cilantro, peanuts, shallots, and carrot-fish sauce. There's also black-bean garlic chicken with rice, pho (noodle soup), and several vegetarian dishes. Dinner values continue on a 99-item menu that includes fresh salad rolls, coconut curry soup, noodle bowls, vegetarian curries, and drunken seafood. Branches in Swan Island (3449 N Anchor St; 503/285-3151; map:FF7) and Irvington (2226 NE Broadway; 503/281-6213; map:GG5) spread the happiness. **COME HERE FOR THE CHARCOAL CHICKEN BOWL.** *$; MC, V; no checks; lunch, dinner Mon–Sat; beer and wine; no reservations; map:GG7* &

Morton's of Chicago: The Steakhouse / ★★★☆

213 SW CLAY ST, DOWNTOWN; 503/248-2100 Portland has several fine steak houses, but none carries the reputation of Morton's—and none has earned it more. Consistently outstanding food, compelling service, and expense-account prices are earmarks of this establishment, whose 64 restaurants can be found in most major U.S. cities and abroad. Chances are you'll order a tender and juicy steak, of which there are several, including a house-specialty 24-ounce porterhouse and a 20-ounce New York sirloin. There are a few nonbeef specialties (lamb, chicken, fish, and that lobster), but this *is* a steak house. Everything is ordered à la carte, which means you'll pay extra for your appetizer of bacon-wrapped sea scallops, for your house salad, for your enormous baked Idaho potato, and for your steamed fresh asparagus. The short list of wines by the glass doesn't maintain the quality of the outstanding steak menu, but there are excellent choices by the bottle. **COME HERE FOR THE OUTSTANDING STEAKS AND TABLESIDE SERVICE.** *$$$$; AE, DC, MC, V; checks OK; dinner every day; full bar; reservations recommended; valet parking; www.mortons.com; map:E4* &

Mother's Bistro & Bar / ★★★

409 SW 2ND AVE, DOWNTOWN; 503/464-1122 This is the way your mother should have cooked but almost certainly didn't, unless you're closely related to proprietor Lisa Schroeder. After cooking in Paris and New York, Schroeder opened the most comfortable of comfort-food restaurants in Portland, offering the likes of matzo-ball soup, pot roast, and chicken with dumplings. The place flies in H&H bagels from New York but cures its own smoked salmon. The substantial three-meals-a-day menu is not only reassuring but impressively skilled, and every month Schroeder focuses on a different ethnic group, providing offbeat specials ranging from Italian to Moroccan Jewish. Portions are sized to put meat on your bones. Playing on a motherly theme, the space is decorated in maternal memorabilia, from old advertisements to particularly heart-tugging prints and personal photos. Inviting, overstuffed furniture and a warm wooden bar outfit the lounge, which is a great, under-the-radar place to swing by for after-dinner drinks and dessert. Unsurprisingly, Mother's turns out mean cookies and wicked devil's food cake. **COME HERE FOR THE ECLECTIC THEME AND FOR FOOD JUST LIKE MOM USED TO MAKE.** *$$; AE, MC, V; no checks; breakfast, lunch Tues–Sun, dinner Tues–Sat; full bar; reservations recommended; map:I5* &

Navarre / ★★★

10 NE 28TH AVE, LAURELHURST; 503/232-3555 Suffering from been-there, done-that syndrome? Try airy new Navarre. The menu—its choices and presentation—wakes you from dining doldrums. Long and skinny, it's a checklist of about 32 choices, loosely grouped into bar snacks, appetizers, salads, starches, and entrées, though you won't see any headings as such. Bucking the trend of elaborately detailed dishes, you'll find no descriptions telling you where the baby lettuces were grown nor from which waters a fish was plucked. This menu simply reads: Mushrooms. Lentils and Beets. Bird. "Trout baked in parchment" is about as explicit as it gets. The diner's job is to craft a meal from as few or as many dishes (all are petite, tapas-size portions) as desired, marking items on the list and handing it to the waiter. For those accustomed to highly informative menus, ordering from Navarre's oblique list will be a leap of faith. But you will be richly rewarded for your daring. Don't miss chef/co-owner John Taboada's gorgeous foie gras, delicate crab crepes, signature braised greens, perky fried-green tomatoes (in season), and frico (crispy-fried cheese). As befits a wine bar, the vintage selection is unique and flawlessly chosen. **COME HERE FOR THE REFRESHING MENU AND SIMPLE, EXPERT COOKING.** *$$; AE, MC, V; checks OK; dinner Mon–Sat; beer and wine; reservations recommended for large groups; www.navarrepdx.com; map:HH5* &

Nicholas' Restaurant / ★★

318 SE GRAND AVE, INNER SOUTHEAST; 503/235-5123 Talk about a family success story: Nicholas' Restaurant started slinging pizza and calzones in 1986, adding more adventurous Lebanese and Middle Eastern food as their customers grew curious. Now, Nicholas and Linda Dibe are retired (mostly) and daughter Hilda runs the show. You'll find local indie rock stars, lunching business-people, and families crammed into this tiny restaurant, all happily munching on excellent kafta kabobs and pitas. Despite two potential drawbacks—no alcohol served, no credit cards accepted—Nicholas' is packed noon and night simply because the food induces cravings for more. It's a dive, but one with character, and basics such as rich baba ghanouj, light and creamy hummus, and crisp falafel are reliably excellent. Mountainous meze platters come in three equally satisfying varieties: meaty, vegetarian, and vegan. Definitely try the Lebanese cheese pizza, which is nothing more than tangy mozzarella and sesame seeds on fresh dough but is absolutely addictive. **COME HERE FOR UNERRING LEBANESE FOOD.** *$; no credit cards; checks OK; lunch, dinner every day; no alcohol; reservations for large groups; www.nicholasrestaurant.com; map:HH6* &

Noho's Hawaiian Café / ★

2525 SE CLINTON ST, CLINTON; 503/233-5301 As anyone who has spent an extended time in Hawaii can tell you, Noho's is "Shaka, brah!" (That's to say, "It's awesome, brother!") A veritable beach hut (surfboard on the wall) nestled on a street corner in bohemian Clinton, Noho's serves the truest *da kine* meals you're likely to find this side of Honolulu. Korean-cut short ribs, marinated in honey, garlic, and sesame-seed sauce, are sublime; Phil's *ono* chicken is infused in a ginger sauce and cooked until the bird is as tender as tuna. You can get ahi along with mahimahi, teriyaki pork, and vegetarian tofu. There's also Japanese-style saimin, a noodle soup beloved by *kamaaina* (longtime Hawaii residents), and a yakisoba noodle plate with four choices of sauce. As in Hawaii, lunch wagons serve "two scoop rice" and macaroni salad with entrées. **COME HERE FOR ISLAND TASTES WITH TWO SCOOP RICE.** *$–$$; AE, MC, V; checks OK; lunch, dinner every day; no alcohol; no reservations; www.nohos.com; map:II5* &

¡Oba! / ★★★

555 NW 12TH AVE, PEARL DISTRICT; 503/228-6161 ¡Oba! has two identities. There's ¡Oba! the restaurant—a subdued, serious dining room serving one nuevo Latino concoction after another—and there's ¡Oba! the bar, a cavernous expanse where trendy clothes and high-pitched revelry rule. Chef Scott Neuman rocked the city with his jazzy renditions when the place opened in 1998, and he continues to please palates with herbed ricotta enchiladas with pasilla-tomato sauce, Cuban pulled flank steak, and crispy coconut prawns with jalapeño marmalade. The chopped-vegetable salad with avocado-buttermilk dressing, and ¡Oba!'s Caesar with roasted corn and Manchego cheese, are definite highlights. If you don't mind loud, alcohol-embellished speech reverberating off the bar's apricot walls, visit the lounge to try some of the most alluring cocktails in town. A bumpin' bar scene assures fashion gazing or eavesdropping, but the star attraction is hand-crafted drinks, and the reasonable tapas menu is a close second. ¡Oba!'s exotic fresh-fruit margarita, shaken and served on the rocks in a tall pint glass, invites customers to veer from the traditional lime variety. Try the prickly pear 'rita, a robust drink whose luscious crimson color and sweet-and-sour taste come from the cactus fruit popular in Mexico. **COME HERE FOR OUTRAGEOUSLY FLAVORFUL FISH ENTRÉES.** *$$; AE, DC, MC, V; no checks; dinner every day; full bar; reservations recommended; www.obarestaurant.com; map:M2* &

Obi / ★★☆

101 NW 2ND AVE, OLD TOWN; 503/226-3826 Obi's atmosphere may not win your heart—decor in the dark, wood-paneled dining room runs toward pinned-up T-shirts and beer pennants—but the sushi in this Old Town lunch haunt is love inspiring. An exhaustive roster of fresh seafood, from *ama ebi* (raw shrimp) to *mirugai* (giant clam), provides ample variety to novices and sushi studs alike. A vegetarian-friendly menu marks nonseafood items with a prominent V, and there are several rarities, including *natto* (fermented bean curd), *kampyo* (pickled gourd), and *gobo* (burdock root). It's hard to get servers to crack a smile, but there are some flirty items to try—like the Marilyn Mon-Roll, with *maguro* (tuna) and *ika* (squid), and the Bonsai Tree, which wraps fresh flaked crab and radish sprouts into a "trunk" of cucumber. **COME HERE FOR SUSHI YOU WON'T FIND ELSEWHERE.** *$$; AE, DIS, MC, V; no checks; lunch Mon–Fri, dinner Mon–Sat; full bar; no reservations; map:K6* &

Old Wives' Tales / ★

1300 E BURNSIDE ST, BUCKMAN; 503/238-0470 Were there a sensitivity award for Portland dining, Old Wives' Tales would be a top nominee. If you are vegetarian or vegan; if you have particular allergies, such as wheat or dairy, or special dietary requirements; if you are the single mother of toddlers; or if you just want breakfast at 6pm, owner Holly Hart is glad to oblige. Every selection on the multiethnic menu and on the buffet has its full ingredients listed, from the delectable Hungarian mushroom soup (a meatless stroganoff) and the carrot-cashew burgers to hot pastrami sandwiches for unconverted carnivores. When Hart opened the restaurant 20 years ago, it doubled as a feminist gathering place, with an indestructible playroom for the younger set. The playroom is still an important part of the ambience, along with a children's menu that meets parental approval, with pancakes, grilled cheese, and burritos. **COME HERE FOR THE MOST CREATIVE BUFFET IN PORTLAND.** *$; AE, DIS, MC, V; checks OK; breakfast, lunch, dinner every day; beer and wine; reservations recommended; map:HH5* &

Original Pancake House / ★★☆

8600 SW BARBUR BLVD, BURLINGAME; 503/246-9007 Show some respect the next time you come here for Swedish or banana or simply perfect pancakes. In 1999, the Original Pancake House was designated by the James Beard Foundation as a regional landmark restaurant, a thick-battered legend. Indeed, patrons have waited patiently in line for pancakes since the place opened in 1955. The Original hums from the time it opens at 7am practically until it closes in midafternoon. The sourdough flapjacks—from wine-spiked cherry to wheat germ to a behemoth apple pancake with a sticky cinnamon glaze—are made from scratch. A good bet is the egg-rich Dutch baby, which arrives looking like a huge, sunken birthday cake, dusted with powdered sugar and served with fresh lemon. Omelets big enough for two (made from a half-dozen eggs) arrive with a short stack. The billing may mention just the pancakes, but this is a place that knows how to handle eggs. The service, from waitresses clad in pink aprons and bobby sox, is efficient; after all, people are waiting for your table. **COME**

HERE FOR THE DUTCH BABIES. *$; no credit cards; checks OK; breakfast, lunch Wed–Sun; no alcohol; no reservations; www.originalpancakehouse.com; map:KK7* &

Paley's Place / ★★★★

1204 NW 21ST AVE, NORTHWEST; 503/243-2403 Though it's been nearly 10 years since Vitaly and Kimberly Paley waltzed into Portland from New York and swept diners off their feet, Paley's continues to dazzle, warm, and thrill Portlanders. Kimberly is known to dance around the intimate, thoughtfully designed dining room the way she once did on national stages, closely watching everything her husband—a Russian-born former concert pianist—sends out from the kitchen. Together, they maintain an atmosphere as artful as the French-influenced Northwest regional cuisine Vitaly prepares. In winter, their seasonal menu might offer crispy veal sweetbreads with a pomegranate demi-glace and a potato-bacon galette, or roasted rabbit with mustard cream and Gruyère mashed potatoes. You might get started with warmed Pacific oysters served with leeks and a curry cream sauce over a cheddar biscuit, or the mussels with mustard aioli that have become a local addiction. Other seasons might bring a bisque of spring asparagus, broccoli, or steelhead set off by smoked seafood sausage. Menus change with the harvests, but the dessert tray is consistently impressive. From one of the city's best crème brûlées to the warm chocolate soufflé cake to house-made sorbets and ice creams, there's something to satisfy every sweet tooth. In summer, porch and sidewalk seating dramatically increase the size of the dining area. **COME HERE FOR A SYMPHONY OF UNFORGETTABLE FLAVORS.** *$$$; AE, MC, V; no checks; dinner every day; full bar; reservations recommended; www.paleysplace .com; map:GG7* &

Pambiche / ★★

2811 NE GLISAN ST, LAURELHURST; 503/233-0511 To have experienced Pambiche without a crowd is to have dined here shortly after it first opened. With only 10 tables and limited counter seating, it's entirely common to wait for a table. Perhaps it's the otherworldly feel of this tiny storefront, tucked behind a huge colonnade and painted inside and out in bold colors, that makes it so popular. Or the friendly staff, whose conversation slides back and forth between English and Spanish. Maybe it's the lip-smacking taro-root fritters, tostones, grilled Cuban sandwiches, or the pollo criollo: chicken stewed in a Creole sauce with fresh herbs and orange. Or possibly the large glasses of South American wines? And though it is most definitely the café con leche that attracts neighbors between mealtimes, it's the dessert case that makes the largest impression anytime, day or night. Classic tortes, cheesecakes, and tarts spilling over with tropical fruits, liqueurs, chocolate, and nuts, are a force unto themselves. **COME HERE FOR A MINIVACATION TO CUBA.** *$–$$; MC, V; no checks; lunch, dinner every day; beer and wine; no reservations; map:HH5* &

Papa Haydn / ★★

701 NW 23RD AVE, NORTHWEST; 503/228-7317 / 5829 SE MILWAUKIE AVE, WESTMORELAND; 503/232-9440 There are better desserts in Portland than those at Papa Haydn, but it's tough to compete with the expansive pastry cases in terms of sheer volume. Cakes, tortes, and tarts are towering architectural marvels as pretty as debutantes bedecked in tulle and chiffon. Cassata (Kahlua-soaked sponge cake with chocolate-ricotta filling), chocolate-buttermilk Saint Moritz cake with coconut-pecan filling, and lemon Bavarian are just a sampling of the confections. As a prelude to the last course, Papa Haydn offers lunchtime salads and sandwiches (try the chicken club with avocado and sun-dried-tomato mayonnaise) and daily dinner choices such as pasta with scallops and gorgonzola cream, succulent grilled chicken breast marinated in apple brandy and mustard, and filet mignon bresaola. The Northwest Portland outpost extends across most of a block, incorporating Jo Bar and Rotisserie (see review). The Westmoreland location is more low-key with a few menu variances, but don't think that's a way to avoid the lines—it carries most of the famed desserts. **COME HERE FOR GREAT PEOPLE WATCHING.** *$$; AE, MC, V; no checks; lunch every day (Northwest), Mon–Sat (Westmoreland), dinner every day, brunch Sun; full bar (Northwest), beer and wine (Westmoreland); reservations for large groups; jobarhaydn@aol.com; map:GG7; map:JJ5* &

Paragon Restaurant & Bar / ★★

1309 NW HOYT ST, PEARL DISTRICT; 503/833-5060 Like nearby ¡Oba! (see review), Paragon is equal parts lively bar and striving dining room. The food doesn't wow but chef Charles Flint turns out boldly flavored dishes that certainly satisfy. Start with fun, sassy appetizers like the gorgonzola "cheesecake" with tomato coulis, or a bay-shrimp martini with avocado, tomato, and sprouts. Potato-crusted snapper in a tomato-saffron broth and chicken stuffed with wild mushrooms (accented by Oregon blackberry jus and toasted polenta) are good bets for dinner. Paragon also does brisk trade at lunchtime, churning out colorful salads, two-fisted burgers, and fried calamari. Any dedicated cocktail maven should put Paragon on her list: bar manager Bob Brunner concocts sublime drinks, combining seemingly incongruous ingredients to great effect. His contemporary take on the hot toddy, the Karkady Toddy, employs hot hibiscus tea instead of water and Captain Morgan rum instead of whiskey. **COME HERE FOR SUPERLATIVE INFUSED-LIQUOR COCKTAILS.** *$$; AE, DC, MC, V; no checks; lunch, dinner every day; full bar; reservations recommended; portlandparagon@earthlink.net; map:M1* &

Park Kitchen / ★★★

422 NW 8TH AVE, PEARL DISTRICT; 503/223-7282 Former Tapeo chef Scott Dolich jumped ship in late 2002 to open his own place, choosing a quiet locale that has been home to a couple of other restaurants over the years. It hasn't been subdued since Park Kitchen opened the following spring: happy diners have kept the small space buzzing morning, noon, and night. A substantial remodel resulted in a rearranged bar area and a casually elegant, pear-green dining room. Because the tables are squeezed close together (out of necessity), real privacy is pretty much out the window—unless you come at an off hour. The market-driven menu, which changes every two weeks to take advantage of fresh local produce, offers small plates for sharing and nibbling, as well as entrées. You might start with a dish of lightly seasoned fava beans or a mellow leek tart, then advance to delicate cod fritters or tender slices of flank steak. Green beans fried in tempura batter, a clever take on french fries, have become a local favorite, as has Park Kitchen's weekend brunch. Homey desserts, and inventive cocktails made with fruit purées and infused liquors, sweeten your meal no matter what the season. **COME HERE FOR PURE FLAVORS AND BOCCE VIEWING IN THE PARK BLOCKS ACROSS THE STREET.** *$$–$$$; MC, V; breakfast, lunch Tues–Fri, dinner Tues–Sat, brunch Sat–Sun; full bar; no reservations; www.parkkitchen.com; map:L3* &

Pastini Pastaria / ★

1426 NE BROADWAY ST, IRVINGTON; 503 288-4300 / 1506 NW 23RD AVE, NORTHWEST; 503/595-1205 You can bet a restaurant that offers *People* magazine as waiting-room reading material doesn't put on airs. That's the case at Pastini, which knows well why the masses have long loved Italian food: it's filling, cheap, and tasty. The Pastini formula—alas, it is a formula—is incredibly savvy. Bowls of steaming pasta mixed with quality tomatoes, fennel sausage, Gorgonzola, and the like deliver instant comfort. They're served up quickly and pleasantly in a honey-colored setting that feels cheery even on dreary days. Pastini offers noodles for every taste, from weighty baked ziti spiked with pancetta, to a mild kid's plate of fusilli with butter and Parmesan, to the pasta *magra* (low-fat) options. Highlights include *spaghetti al gamberetti*, which sees plump prawns and fresh mozzarella swimming in olive oil and garlic, and spaghetti puttanesca, extra salty thanks to the inclusion of ricotta salata. **COME HERE FOR PASTA EVERY WHICH WAY.** *$; AE, MC, V; local checks only; lunch, dinner every day; full bar; no reservations; www.pastini.biz; map:GG5; map:GG7* &

Pazzo Ristorante / ★★

627 SW WASHINGTON ST (HOTEL VINTAGE PLAZA), DOWNTOWN; 503/228-1515 This bustling hotel restaurant, situated inside the elegant Vintage Plaza, consists of a dining room perfumed by a wood-fired oven, a lively bar overlooking SW Broadway, and a wine cellar that seats private parties. Under former chef Nathan Logan, Pazzo served both locals and travelers well with its groaning pasta portions, Piedmont truffles, and impressive wine list. Now that Logan has departed, it's difficult to say how the menu will fare. But there's little doubt the emphasis will remain on crowd-pleasing, northern Italian cuisine. Popular dishes have included spaghetti with wild mushrooms, chunks of pancetta, and garlic; slices of rare Muscovy duck breast atop bitter greens; risotto with fava beans and morel mushrooms; and braised beef short ribs in a Sangiovese-tomato-broccoli jus with cannellini beans and rapini. For a quick and reasonably priced breakfast or lunch, head next door to Pazzoria (621 SW Washington St; 503/228-1695) and grab a strong cup or coffee or gooey panino. **COME HERE FOR THE EVER-BUSTLING ATMOSPHERE.** *$$; AE, DC, DIS, JCB, MC, V; checks OK; breakfast, lunch, dinner every day; full bar; reservations recommended; valet parking; www.pazzoristorante.citysearch.com; map:J4* &

Perry's on Fremont / ★★☆

2401 NE FREMONT AVE, ALAMEDA; 503/287-3655 Holding court in Portland's tony Alameda neighborhood, Bill and Anna Perry's eponymous restaurant is a favorite snazzy stop for a date or family dinner. Mostly American fare (burgers, pasta, halibut fish and chips) mingles well with more sophisticated specials. The Cajun Fisherwoman's Stew, despite the rough-and-tumble name, is actually a subtle, slow-cooked cassoulet of salmon, prawns, catfish, and a school of other sea creatures. Although risotto and pasta entrées are priced comparably with the fresh seafood fillets and steaks, your money is better spent on the meatier choices, which arrive daintily accompanied by fresh sautéed vegetables and starchy whipped garlic potatoes. The large patio is a lovely place to enjoy happy hour and flashy house drinks. (Try the Flirtini—a cosmopolitan souped up with pineapple juice and champagne.) **COME HERE FOR THE CHEAP HAPPY-HOUR SPECIALS.** *$$; AE, DIS, MC, V; no checks; lunch Sat, dinner Tues–Sat; full bar; reservations recommended; map:FF5* &

Pho Thanh Thao / ★

902 N KILLINGSWORTH ST, NORTH PORTLAND; 503/289-3326 An offshoot of a popular Thai cafe in Hawthorne, Pho Thanh Thao specializes in Vietnamese cuisine. This new restaurant boasts uncommonly tasteful decor, its walls painted sage and straw and adorned with cool lanterns. But Pho Thanh Thao's loyal clientele are here for two reasons other than design. First, the price: nothing on the menu exceeds $10, and an enormous, nicely presented cauldron of pho with all the fresh fixings goes for just $5. Second is the impressive variety of dishes: a large family of Vietnamese specialties includes rice plates, vermicelli noodle dishes, and such delicacies as grilled ground beef wrapped in lotus leaves. Plan to skip the spring rolls and opt for a salad of lotus root, pork, and shrimp; they're crisp and very firm, with a coconut-sweet flavor that is also a bit tangy. The parent restaurant, Thanh Thao (4005 SE Hawthorne Blvd; 503/238-6232; map:HH4), has some of Portland's best Thai soups. **COME HERE FOR EXOTIC VIETNAMESE DISHES AT ROCK-BOTTOM PRICES.** *$; MC, V; no checks; lunch, dinner Wed–Mon; beer and wine; no reservations; map:FF6*

Pho Van / ★★★

1012 NW GLISAN ST, PEARL DISTRICT (AND BRANCHES); 503/248-2171 When army officer Khiet Van fled South Vietnam with his young family in 1981, he could never have dreamed that, two decades later, he'd be one of the toasts of a foodie American city. Van's original SE 82nd Avenue cafe has earned a sterling reputation for aromatic pho, presented nearly a dozen ways. His snazzy new bistro serves two skinnier soups: one with round steak and lean brisket, the other a chicken noodle with *rau ram* (Vietnamese coriander). That leaves room for refreshing salads (banana blossom with chicken, grapefruit, and jicama, for example), grilled pork and chicken dishes, and delicate seafood entrées. Hints of honey punctuate more than a handful of Pho Van's offerings, from the highly recommended fishes—a lightly battered tilapia fillet with garlic sauce and a snowy, steamed Chilean sea bass—to the caramelized chicken and pork stews served in clay pots. The sugary flavors are never cloying and pair well with hoppy Asian beers such as Tiger and Tsingtao. Don't overlook the unusual hand rolls such as *chao tom*, a viscous pâté of finely minced shrimp and chicken molded around sugarcane stalks and grilled. The bistro's casual ambience features lithe, beautiful servers in traditional *ao* robes who present the dinner menu on a scroll sheathed in a bamboo husk. In addition to the original pho house (1919 SE 82nd Ave, Southeast; 503/788-5244; map:HH3), Pho Van has a new shop in Beaverton Town Square (11665 SW Beaverton-Hillsdale Hwy, Beaverton; 503/627-0822; map:II9). **COME HERE FOR THE MOST SOPHISTICATED VIETNAMESE FOOD IN TOWN.** *$$; AE, DIS, MC, V; no checks; lunch and dinner Mon–Sat; beer and wine; reservations for 5 or more; map:*M2 &

Piazza Italia / ★★

1129 NW JOHNSON ST, PEARL DISTRICT; 503/478-0619 Casual but special, Piazza Italia has an infectious spirit that is so strong it can sometimes trump the menu. You can hear *la dolce vita* in the clatter of Italian conversation, smell it in the aromas oozing from the kitchen, taste it in the house Chianti, and see it in the grins on customers' faces. The most important authentic ingredient in Italia's winning equation isn't the fresh mortadella, the hand-crafted Roman ceramics, nor the Illy coffee: it's the Italians who run and frequent the place. The concise menu changes frequently, but some dishes are available year-round. *Squarciarella*, a prized family recipe of egg noodles with prosciutto, pepper, garlic, and oil, is Piazza's most popular dish. Pasta specialties include seasonal risottos and raviolis punctuated by wild mushrooms, plump prawns, and fresh cheeses. Bookend any meal with *insalata Caprese* (tomatoes, fresh mozzarella, basil, and olive oil) and a cannoli, and you'll certainly go home happy. **COME HERE TO FEEL LIKE PART OF THE FAMILY.** *$$; DIS, MC, V; no checks; lunch, dinner every day; beer and wine; reservations recommended; www.piazzaportland.com; map:* N2 &

Pizzicato Gourmet Pizza / ★★☆

705 SW ALDER ST, DOWNTOWN (AND BRANCHES); 503/226-1007 By paying close attention to little details—heavy silverware, thoughtful beer and wine selections, casually classy decor—this upscale local pizza chain has cornered the market on gourmet pizza. Quick expansion has put a Pizzicato into most of Portland's prominent neighborhoods and bigger suburbs, as well as across the Columbia River in Vancouver. Service and setup vary from location to location (the Northwest branch offers whole pies only), but the menu is essentially the same. The cornerstone dish is inventive, sometimes wild, pizza combinations: the Thai chicken number boasts a peanut-sauce base, and everything from chipotle chiles to baby corns can turn up on pies. More often than not, the concoctions are tasty, not jarring. A wild-mushroom pizza, loaded with meaty chanterelles, roasted peppers, roasted garlic, onions, and chèvre, is pure Northwest. Ample slices and fresh salads make Pizzicato a great choice for lunch. The addition of a velvety red wine and a brownie make it just right for dinner as well. **COME HERE FOR INVENTIVE PIZZA AND ROBUST SALADS.** *$; AE, DIS, MC, V; no checks; lunch, dinner every day; beer and wine; no reservations; www.pizzicattogourmetpizza.com; map:*I3 &

Plainfield's Mayur / ★★

852 SW 21ST AVE, PORTLAND HEIGHTS; 503/223-2995 Richard and Rehka Plainfield pioneered the Indian cuisine scene in Portland, way back in 1977. Family members still tend the kitchen and oversee service in the restored Victorian home that houses Plainfield's. Two small dining rooms set out linens and silver—although close inspection reveals the wrinkles and tarnish of an empire in decline. Yet the kitchen remains sharp. India's cultural and geographical diversity, stretching from the Himalayas in the north to the tropical south, provides inspiration for familiar papadums and curries and for exotics such as duck in almond sauce with cheese-stuffed apricots, and vegetables braised in cardamom-nut sauce. Regulars rave about *bhel* salad, an Indian street food of fried lentils, spinach, potatoes, and tomatoes in a tamarind dressing that dances on your tongue. A tandoor oven bakes naan, chicken, and fish. Plainfield's has assembled a credible wine list and Richard will happily discuss the merits of a pinot or Gewürztraminer with *saag paneer*. **COME HERE FOR THE FRIED LENTIL BALLS IN GINGER-CORIANDER-YOGURT SAUCE.** *$$; AE, DIS, MC, V; checks OK; dinner every day; full bar; www.plainfields.com; map:HH7* &

Portland City Grill / ★★★

111 SW 5TH AVE (UNICO US BANK TOWER, 30TH FLOOR), DOWNTOWN; 503/450-0030 One of the most hyped openings of 2002 was Portland City Grill, the penthouse restaurant that replaced Atwaters in the Unico US Bank Tower. A $3-million makeover begat a homey lodgelike ambience replete with purely decorative fir ceiling beams, slate walls (think patio surface), crammed seating, and garish paintings of Oregon landmarks. The dinner menu is bona fide corporate America, promising prime steaks; lobster; pork, veal, and lamb chops; and no surprises. The kitchen's decision to spice things up with Asian twists and turns is an attempt at ingenuity that is not fully realized, resulting in miso, shiitake, and ponzu glazes instead of original dishes. The steaks are outstanding, however, and they really are cooked to your preference. If you love rare meat, the crew here listens, delivering a New York strip that is red and fleshy in the middle and pink throughout. The full sushi menu, incongruous though it may be, is a highlight. Maki are exemplary and affordable, with ample combination plates starting at $10.75. Of course, the sweeping views and be-here-now vibe provide more than enough magic to satisfy most diners. **COME HERE FOR THE VIEW.** *$$–$$$; AE, DIS, MC, V; no checks; lunch Mon–Fri, dinner every day; full bar; reservations recommended; www.portlandcitygrill.com; map:J4* &

Portland Steak and Chophouse / ★★

121 SW 3RD AVE (EMBASSY SUITES HOTEL), DOWNTOWN; 503/223-2995 Dusky lighting, the carafe of giveaway golf tees in the lobby, and decor in the vein of a "gentleman's club" tell the diner (if the name didn't) what you're in for at the Chophouse. Meat-heavy entrées dominate, although non–beef eaters can find plenty to gorge on in the way of fresh seafood, salads with nods to nouveau cuisine (the seared ahi tuna is a standout), and all sorts of gutsy pub fare like thick-cut onion rings. Despite the reach of the menu, the Chophouse does best with food that doesn't stray too far from tradition: the London broil loaded with mushroom gravy and mashed potatoes heartily gets the job done. Owing in part to the Chophouse's stature as the anchor restaurant of the massive and historic Embassy Suites hotel, you can expect an anonymous crowd and service that hustles during busy lunch and dinner hours. Be sure to request a table away from the kitchen, where a narrow walkway exposes diners to the onrush of servers. **COME HERE FOR THE STIFF MARTINIS.** *$$$; AE, DC, DIS, MC, V; no checks; breakfast, lunch, dinner every day; full bar; reservations recommended; map:J5* &

The Purple Parlor / ★

3560 N MISSISSIPPI AVE, NORTH PORTLAND; 503/281-3560 Dan and Molly Sadowsky have lovingly restored a turn-of-the-20th-century house to greater than former grandeur. The green, gold, and (of course) purple domicile shelters not only the couple (in an upstairs apartment) but one of the city's finest breakfast cafes. The menu is all-vegetarian with vegan options in the savory dishes, baked goods, and desserts. Not that eating vegetarian has to mean eating light: the tasty Scramble of the Greek Gods blends eggs (or tofu) with generous heaps of spinach, diced tomato, feta, basil, and garlic, while the Mayan Volcano provides a mountain of beans and roasted vegetables over brown rice. Fruit-topped porridge, pancakes, and granola are equally satisfying and more civilized. Feeling stuffed? Pour a cup of Stumptown coffee from the self-service pots and stroll around to gaze at the shadow boxes in each room. They display artifacts—tin toys, medicine bottles, old shoes—found during renovation of the house. **COME HERE FOR THE VEGETARIAN BREAKFASTS.** *$; MC, V; no checks; breakfast, lunch Tues–Sun; no alcohol; no reservations; www.thepurpleparlor.com; map:FF6*

Red Star Tavern & Roast House / ★★⯪

503 SW ALDER ST (5TH AVENUE SUITES), DOWNTOWN; 503/222-0005 A wall-size mural of the chef as workingman—a modern rendition in WPA style—is a centerpiece of this lofty restaurant in the 5th Avenue Suites hotel. And Rob Pando is, indeed, a workingman's chef. His regional American cuisine covers the continent impressively, from seared Nantucket scallops to Kansas City baby-back ribs to Pacific Northwest halibut, using the huge wood-burning grill and rotisserie at the back of the restaurant. Pando exercises the kind of culinary subtlety that produces splendid crab-and-smoked-salmon cakes or ravioli of winter squash and goat cheese. Also on the menu are some longtime favorites, including hearty soups and a skillet of moist corn bread. For dessert, try the pear in house-made mascarpone with candied hazelnuts and Oregon pinot noir sauce. The range is considerable, portions are sizable, the atmosphere is entertaining, service is uniformly excellent and knowledgeable, and you couldn't be closer to the middle of downtown. It's a great place for breakfast, too, and weekend brunches are a hit. **COME HERE FOR FINELY CRAFTED REGIONAL AMERICAN COOKING.** *$$; AE, DC, DIS, JCB, MC, V; checks OK; breakfast, lunch, dinner every day, brunch Sat–Sun; full bar; reservations recommended; valet parking; www.5thaavenuesuites.com; map:I4* &

Restaurant Murata / ★★★

200 SW MARKET ST, DOWNTOWN; 503/227-0080 Because this tiny, exquisite Japanese restaurant maintains tradition, it attracts both savvy locals and visiting Tokyo businessmen who seek authentic food, service, and atmosphere. All the classic elements are here in Zen-like simplicity—shoji screens, tatami rooms, female servers clad in kimonos—yet customers dine at ease amid gracious hospitality. Behind an eight-seat, L-shaped sushi bar, Japanese master chef Murata deftly slices *toro* (tuna belly) and *uni* (sea urchin) and molds them over rice, displaying the confidence of more than 50 years' experience. At lunch, traditional *teishoku* (set meals) include tempura, teriyaki, and tonkatsu, plus hot and cold udon and soba noodle bowls. Another specialty is *nabemono*, a one-pot beef or seafood dish cooked in earthenware on an iron pot at the table. Murata is one of the few places offering *kaiseki-ryori*, a traditional ceremonial meal of set dishes chosen by the chef to embody the elegance and serenity of each ingredient. Priced slightly higher than other Japanese restaurants, Murata offers the superb quality that justifies the difference. Located directly opposite Keller Auditorium, it's a great place to come before a show—provided you start early, as this is a restaurant to savor, not rush. **COME HERE FOR THE KAISEKI-RYORI.** *$$$; AE, DC, JCB, MC, V; no checks; lunch Mon–Fri, dinner Mon–Sat; beer and wine; reservations recommended; murata@teleport.com; map: E3* &

Rheinlander (including Gustav's Bier Stube) / ★★

5035 NE SANDY BLVD, HOLLYWOOD; 503/288-5503 Missed Oktoberfest this year? Can't get to Munich for a while? Get your fill of Bavarian food and culture at this restaurant and bar. With a roaming floor plan and wandering, lederhosen-clad accordionists to match, the Rheinlander is an amusement-park experience backed up by good German cuisine. From fondue to sauerbraten, the menu is Teutonic through and through. Sausages—bratwurst and weisswurst—are excellent partners for lacy potato pancakes with applesauce and sour cream. A great choice for families (be as loud as you want!) and large groups, the restaurant has private and semiprivate rooms to accommodate parties of various sizes. Adjacent Gustav's is less expensive and devoid of musicians, but just as much fun. Order a glass of smooth Warsteiner Dunkel and watch as your waiter delivers it balanced atop his head. Snag a cozy two-person booth by the gorgeous wooden bar to catch the action in the kitchen. This slice of Bavaria offers a full menu of German specialties as well as lighter entrées such as a salad of prawns, cabbage, and lettuces in horseradish dressing. **COME HERE FOR GREAT BEER AND GOOFY GERMAN AMBIENCE.** *$$–$$$; AE, MC, V; no checks; lunch, dinner every day; full bar; reservations for 8 or more; map:GG4* &

Riccardo's Restaurant / ★★

16035 SW BOONES FERRY RD, LAKE OSWEGO; 503/636-4104 Come summer, the backyard here blossoms, with a welcoming courtyard that features flowers and a Tuscan-style fountain. The challenge is to get the diners to leave after dinner—especially considering the place's intriguing selection of grappas. Owner Richard Spaccarelli is a serious oenophile, as his more than 300 bottles of Italian-only wine (and Riccardo's own wine shop across the way) attest. The kitchen makes a great lasagna and is strong on veal dishes, from an impressively meaty veal chop (with a lively brandy demi-glace) to a pungent, tender saltimbocca. The menu also includes juicy lamb chops and a half-dozen mostly meatless pastas, and it can surprise you with something such as a slow-roasted pork shank with garlic, sage, and rosemary. Some diners complain of spotty service and long waits despite reservations; others attribute that to Riccardo's local popularity. **COME HERE TO DINE IN THE COURT-YARD.** *$$; AE, DC, MC, V; checks OK; lunch Mon–Fri, dinner Mon–Sat; full bar; reservations recommended; map:MM8* &

The Ringside / ★★☆
Ringside East / ★★

2165 W BURNSIDE ST, NORTHWEST; 503/223-1513 / 14021 NE GLISAN ST, GLENDOVEER; 503/255-0750 Some surveys rank the Ringside as one of the top 10 independent steak houses in the country, but nobody needed to tell Portlanders that. For six decades, this restaurant has staked out the territory here, and the only real question for most fans is, which cut? The New York, filet mignon, or prime rib? People come here for beef, and that's what they get—in large, juicy slabs. The steaks appear at the table in black cast-iron platters, preceded by the sound of sizzling. Against the designer starches of newer steak houses, the Ringside holds to the standards and doesn't charge extra. Starring on the side are plump, light, slightly salty onion rings (made with Walla Walla sweets) that single-handedly made the place famous. For those with an aversion to beef, there is well-reputed fried chicken, and there's something to be said for the seafood Caesar. The dignified black-jacketed and bow-tied waiters are eminently professional and the wine list is 530 bottles deep, ideal if you're looking for something red to go with beef. And here's a deal: come before 5:45pm or after 9pm and you can get a three-course dinner, including the marvelous flambéed bananas Foster à la Firestine, for just $25. Lunch is served at the eastside location only. **COME HERE FOR THE STEAKS.** *$$; AE, DC, MC, V; checks OK; lunch Mon–Fri (Glendoveer), dinner every day; full bar; reservations recommended; www.ringsidesteakhouse.com; map:HH7; map:HH1* &

Rivers Restaurant / ★★☆

0470 SW HAMILTON CT (AVALON HOTEL & SPA), SW MACADAM; 503/802-5850 It can't be easy to carry Rolland Wesen's pedigree. But Wesen—executive chef at Rivers and the son-in-law of famed French chef Jacques Pepin—is equal to the task. In this fine-dining establishment adjacent to the Avalon Hotel & Spa off SW Macadam Avenue, behind big windows that look upon the broad Willamette River, the affable Wesen prepares a synthesis of modern American comfort food and classic French bistro fare. Panfried Dungeness crab cakes are served with a frisée salad and peppercorn aioli. A fresh arugula salad pairs wonderfully with roasted garlic and a balsamic vinaigrette. A simmering iron skillet loaded with local seafood delicacies—clams, prawns, mussels, halibut, and salmon—is served in a bouillabaisse-inspired "fire pot" of tomato and saffron broth. Roasted chicken with garlic-sautéed spinach and mashed potatoes competes for your attention with cassoulet-style halibut on fava-bean risotto and an oh-so-Gallic plate of duck livers and hearts. Seasonally inspired desserts feature local fruits and berries, and there's always a mouth-watering triple chocolate cake. **COME HERE FOR RIVERSIDE COMFORT FOOD.** *$$$; AE, DC, DIS, MC, V; checks OK; breakfast, lunch, dinner every* *day; full bar; reservations recommended; valet parking; www.avalonhotelandspa .com; map:II6* ᕪ

Rose's Deli & Bakery / ★

838 NW 23RD AVE, NORTHWEST; 503/222-5292 This iconic bakery and deli has returned to the neighborhood of its heyday in the '50s and '60s. The retro-styled deli is comfortable and not overly kitschy but the menu is a throwback. Reviving original recipes, Rose's specializes in mile-high Reubens (six varieties, including a vegetarian with all the traditional condiments), curative soups, and old-fashioned dinner plates. Flavorful chicken noodle and chicken matzo-ball soups are available daily, providing a cold cure when you can't make your own. The Executive sandwich is a big crowd pleaser: inches of Virginia ham and sliced turkey topped with Gruyère, lettuce, tomato, and Thousand Island dressing, stacked in dark rye bread. Meat loaf is served in warm sourdough at lunch and paired with mashed potatoes and gravy at dinner. In the morning, swing by Rose's for bagels with lox or a whopping cinnamon roll. **COME HERE FOR KOSHER FOODS AND MID-20TH-CENTURY NOSTALGIA.** *$; AE, DIS, MC, V; no checks; breakfast, lunch, dinner every day; beer and wine; reservations for large groups; www.rosesdeli.com; map: GG7* ᕪ

Ruth's Chris Steak House / ★★★

309 SW 3RD AVE, DOWNTOWN; 503/221-4518 Portlanders, those acolytes of salmon, are not shy about enjoying Ruth's steaks, even at $30 a pop. Presented on bone-white china in an atmosphere of high-cholesterol reverence, the steaks— notably the steer-size porterhouse for two—are rich and beefy, with an alluring tenderness. For diners who just had a porterhouse lunch, there are sizable (and sizably priced) lobsters, and there's the chance to pick one that's alive—which is more than you can do with the steak. You'll be paying extra for everything else, but it's still worth exploring the various potatoes and the creamed spinach. The space is massive, and so are the portions; you'll still be eating your dinner for tomorrow's lunch. **COME HERE FOR BIG BEEF.** *$$$; AE, DC, MC, V; no checks; dinner every day; full bar; reservations recommended; www.ruthschris.com; map:I5* ᕪ

Saburo's / ★★

1667 SE BYBEE BLVD, WESTMORELAND; 503/236-4237 It might not be law enforcement, but rules are rules. When ex-policewoman Joyce Nakajima established the precepts that would govern the eclectic Japanese spot run by her and husband Saburo, she posted plenty of them on the walls. For years, Portlanders have tolerated Saburo's with a loyalty that sometimes borders on idolatry. It's a patronage that defies gruff service—if you can even get anyone's attention—and a no-reservations policy that keeps fans loitering on the sidewalk, awaiting a seat at the sushi bar or a table in this shoebox-size space. Prices for exceptionally fresh sushi are rock bottom and portions are larger than at more expensive sushi bars. Teriyaki and tempura dinners, curry udon soup, gyoza, and pork katsu-don round out the inclusive menu. Saburo's tough reputation is part of the charm; and by the way, it isn't foolproof. Servers *do* smile and orders eventually find their way to diners. **COME HERE FOR**

NO-FRILLS, VALUE SUSHI. *$–$$; AE, MC, V; no checks; dinner every day; beer and wine; no reservations; map:JJ5* &

Saigon Kitchen / ★★

835 NE BROADWAY, NEAR LLOYD CENTER; 503/281-3669 / 3829 SE DIVISION ST, SOUTHEAST; 503/236-2312 Still the spring rolls for all seasons, the two branches of this restaurant are among the best of Portland's seemingly endless supply of Vietnamese eateries. The menu—more than 120 items long—features some Thai dishes as well as the predominantly South Vietnamese offerings. Standouts are the spicy soups—try the sour catfish concoction with pineapple—and the stews and ragouts, which go well with white or fried rice. Also wonderful is *tó chim*, which has prawns, scallops, pork, chicken, and vegetables nested in a rice-noodle basket. Service is brisk and efficient at both busy locations. Enjoy patio dining at the Southeast branch. **COME HERE FOR FOUR-COURSE COMBINATION DINNERS.** *$–$$; AE, DIS, MC, V; no checks; lunch Mon–Fri, dinner every day (Southeast closed Sun); beer and wine; reservations for large groups; map:GG6; map:II4* &

Salvador Molly's / ★★

1523 SW SUNSET BLVD, HILLSDALE; 503/293-1790 / 3350 SE MORRISON ST, BELMONT; 503/234-0896 The vitality of Salvador Molly's is half the reason to go to this Caribbean-by-way-of-Mexico restaurant in a Hillsdale strip mall. The other reason, naturally, is for a bellyful of Molly's signature pirate cooking: rich, rib-sticking food with all the spice, smoke, and mojo of Latin cuisines with a dash of Northwest flavor thrown in. The festive lighting, brightly colored walls, and cheeky decorations—an Elvis shrine complete with a Velvet Elvis and tabloid clippings—set the stage for fun dining either in the main room, on the glassed-in sun porch, or on the outdoor patio. Nosh on unshelled peanuts to stay your hunger, but don't let them dissuade you from ordering an appetizer. Starters such as *arepas* (corn griddle cakes) and *bollitos* (black-eyed pea fritters) rarely show up on Portland menus. Yucatán chicken and artichoke-and-*cotija* tamales are must-haves, and though it's impossible to eat with your hands, the overstuffed Ensenada fish taco has many redeeming qualities. Foot-long tamarind pork ribs, served with rich sides, are best consumed when you're really hungry. Salvador Molly's new location in the old Belmont Dairy serves the same menu but offers lunch weekends only. **COME HERE TO EAT LIKE A PIRATE.** *$–$$; AE, MC, V; checks OK; lunch, dinner every day (Hillsdale), lunch Sat–Sun (Belmont); full bar; no reservations; www.salvadormollys.com; map:JJ7; map:HH5* &

Sammy's Restaurant and Bar / ★★

333 NW 23RD AVE, NORTHWEST; 503/222-3123 A list of the day's fresh fish—maybe six or eight choices—hangs proudly at either end of the dining room, noting one of the themes that's made this restaurant last in what had been a turnover spot. When Sam Pishue, founder and longtime successful proprietor of the late lamented Opus Too, decided to open another restaurant, he stayed with what he knew. As a result, the best things here are hot off the grill—steaks, chops, and seafood—although the menu is flecked with pastas and Greek specialties. Subtlety may not be a strong point, but the meats are good, the room is comfortable, and the artfully assembled bar is popular and crowded. Sunday brunch is a particular success, especially on warm weekends when brunchers spread out on tables that stretch along so-called "Trendy-Third" Street, and the atmosphere of urban sophistication makes the just-baked cinnamon twists taste even better. **COME HERE FOR GRILLED FISH.** *$$; AE, DC, DIS, MC, V; no checks; lunch Mon–Fri, dinner every day, brunch Sat–Sun; full bar; reservations recommended; map:HH7* &

San Felipe Taqueria / ★

6221 SE MILWAUKIE AVE, WESTMORELAND 503/235-8158 Outstanding restaurants aren't usually situated next to 7-Elevens, but the upbeat San Felipe Taqueria is no ordinary neighborhood joint. The specialty of the house is a fish taco ($2.50) that puts to shame fish tacos you've endured elsewhere: perfectly fried halibut is topped with pico de gallo, cilantro, and a honey mustard–mayo sauce. You may also want to try tacos or burritos filled with pollo verde (chicken with green-chile sauce); spicy, grilled-pork carnitas; or beef tongue. The taqueria's space is cheerful, clean, and always bustling—and definitely worth the drive even if you're coming from clear across town. **COME HERE FOR THE FISH TACOS.** *$; MC, V; checks OK; lunch, dinner Tues–Sat; beer and wine; no reservations; map:JJ5* &

Saucebox / ★★★

214 SW BROADWAY, DOWNTOWN; 503/241-3393 Portland wouldn't be half as hip without this chic pan-Asian restaurant-cum-boîte. Proprietor Bruce Carey never lets things get stale at this hole-in-the-wall hotspot—as evidenced by a constantly updated menu and a recent expansion. Salty edamame and addictive, fried sweet-potato spring rolls make a promising start to a meal or serve as an ideal bar-snack accompaniment for cocktails. Move on to the coveted Korean baby-back ribs, snowy steamed halibut, or perennial favorite Javanese roasted salmon—crisped in soy, garlic, and ginger, topped with frizzled leeks and served with perfumed jasmine rice. A chef's tour of Southeast Asia in early 2003 added new dishes to the menu, including banana-blossom salad and Laotian catfish in a coconut broth. The creative entrées are made with fresh, top-quality ingredients—as are the widely touted drinks. The Mirrorball, combining house-infused watermelon vodka with lemon, lime, and cranberry juices and a splash of champagne, is a prime example of Saucebox's inventive mixology. While you may be distracted by the stylish crowd (often including visiting celebs), the exquisite art and plate presentation warrant second glances. Saucebox takes on a clubbier feel after 10pm, when DJs turn up the juice and only a bar menu is offered. **COME HERE FOR CELEBRITY SIGHTINGS.** *$$; AE, MC, V; local checks only; dinner Tues–Sat; full bar; reservations recommended; www.saucebox.com; map:J4* &

Savory Bistro / ★★

4323 NE FREMONT ST, BEAUMONT; 503/331-6696 Your wife is in the mood for Asian food, you're thinking continental, and your kid—well, he just wants a hamburger. Here's a casual spot that'll make everybody happy. Brian Raab and his Vietnamese wife, Fawn, opened this Viet-Euro-American bistro and wine bar in a little Beaumont-neighborhood house in early 2003, added a broad front deck, and it's been hopping ever since. Lunch has anything from *bún tom thit nuóng*, a Vietnamese noodle soup, to a one-third-pound Radon Ridge burger, to penne pasta with salmon. At dinner, you can go Asian (salad rolls, Asian slaw, ginger-crusted salmon) or European (start with a *charcuterie et fromage* plate, then dive into pork loin in a light-cream pinot grigio reduction sauce). House-made desserts are ever changing, but if the German-style apfelstrudel is available, you won't want to miss it. **COME HERE IN SUMMER TO DINE ON THE STREETSIDE DECK.** *$$; AE, DC, DIS, MC, V; local checks OK; lunch Tues–Fri, dinner Tues–Sun, brunch Sat–Sun; beer and wine; no reservations; www.grubnow.com; map:FF4* &

Sayler's Old Country Kitchen / ★★

10519 SE STARK ST, SOUTHEAST; 503/252-4171 / 4655 SW GRIFFITH DR, BEAVERTON; 503/644-1492 Still independent after almost half a century and into its second generation of management, the Sayler family proudly follows traditional steak-house rules, sending out sizzling red-meat dinners priced by the ounce. Dinners include relish trays, soup or salad, potato, bread, and ice cream. Sure, there are deep-fried fish and chicken dinners, crab Louie, lobster, lunch salads, and (discreetly hidden in a corner of the menu) a vegetarian burger, but contemporary trends haven't usurped the beef protein centerpiece. The Beaverton steak house resembles a brick Presbyterian church; both locations wear meticulously maintained '70s-style decor. Heavy beams, seasoned wood walls, a lounge with swivel chairs, padded booths, and friendly uniformed servers complement the consistent value menu. **COME HERE FOR CARNIVORE CRAVINGS.** *$$; AE, DIS, MC, V; checks OK; lunch Mon–Fri (Beaverton), dinner every day; full bar; reservations recommended; map:HH2; map:JJ1* &

Seasons & Regions / ★★

6660 SW CAPITOL HWY, HILLSDALE; 503/244-6400 This seafood-oriented bistro may be off the beaten path, but it doesn't stray far from the celebrated Northwest-French cooking that put Portland on the culinary map. The low-slung brick building in suburban Hillsdale houses a funky dining room where diners stream in for fresh fish prepared at least a dozen different ways. S&R crab cakes are 100 percent Dungeness, with just enough bread-crumb filler to hold them together. Choose them as part of a mixed grill that also includes a chunk of halibut, a small chinook salmon fillet seared with a honey-ginger-lime sauce, and a mound of mango-pineapple salsa. There's an extensive vegetarian menu as well, plus a limited selection for the meat eaters among us. S&R is proud of its Cheap Food Menu, which includes a $2.95 burger, and its Curlers and Fuzzy Slippers Take-Out Up Window, where diners on the go can slink around back to retrieve whole dinners. **COME HERE FOR THE FRIED-OYSTER CAESAR SALAD.** *$–$$; MC, V; no checks; breakfast Sat–Sun, lunch, dinner every day; full bar; reservations recommended; www.seasonsandregions .com; map:JJ7* &

Second Story Bistro / ★★

208 NW COUCH ST, OLD TOWN; 503/827-5113 Climbing the stairs to this bistro, you might be ascending to Narnia or Middle Earth: Second Story sports a Gothic arched doorway, a steep, narrow stairway, a curved tree branch for a banister, and an off-kilter foyer festooned with ferns. Cuisine is continental with a Pacific Northwest accent. Several country French dishes—quaint square meals you might make at home but seem forgotten by restaurant chefs—pepper the menu. Juicy coq au vin comes with rice pilaf and fresh sugar-snap peas, while gorgonzola-mashed potatoes accompany the whopping pork-loin entrée. Italian influences show up in a couple of pastas and breakfast frittatas. Also on the morning menu are uncommon stratas—fluffy egg-and-bread casseroles made with seasonal ingre-dients—along with fresh-fruit crepes and griddle classics like buttermilk pancakes. **COME HERE FOR LEISURELY BREAKFASTS.** *$–$$; AM, MC, V; local checks only; breakfast, lunch every day, dinner Tues–Sun; full bar; reservations recommended; 2ndstory@quik.com; map:K6* &

Serratto / ★★☆

2112 NW KEARNEY ST, NORTHWEST; 503/221-1195 From the cavernous dining room with its exposed beams, tall casement windows, and warm amber glow, to the informal wine bar and sturdy sidewalk tables, Serratto is lovely inside and out. Fortunately, the cooking lives up to the restaurant's good looks, satisfying demanding palates. Handmade tagliatelle with braised rabbit, for instance, is something you're unlikely to find elsewhere. Ditto albacore carpaccio with fennel salad and poached halibut with truffle oil. The menu and extensive wine list draw from all regions of Italy. There's not an overwhelming amount of pasta on offer, but there are a few well-chosen bowls, such as classic spaghetti alla bolognese. In lieu of pasta, you'll find a strong focus on Pacific Northwest seafood, such as the elegant Dungeness crab crespelle that pairs creamy crab filling with wispy Italian pancakes and wilted leeks. And the daily preparation of steamed clams or mussels is a sure bet. From time to time, Serratto offers informal wine dinners, providing a relaxed way to learn more about a wine-producing region while enjoying terrific chef's specialties designed to complement the featured vintages. **COME HERE FOR THE WIDE-OPEN DESIGN AND SUBLIME CUISINE.** *$$–$$$; AE, DC, DIS, MC, V; no checks; dinner every day; full bar; reservations recommended; serratto@aol .com; map:GG7* &

750 ml / ★★

232 NW 12TH AVE, PEARL DISTRICT; 503/224-1432 Bedecked in ivory and chocolate hues, this rehabbed Pearl District wine bistro/bar/retail shop feels fresh and breezy. Wine and food receive equal billing and a sheaf of menus encourages nonlinear sipping and grazing. Dozens of wines can be ordered by the taste, glass, or bottle, and the dinner menu consists of first plates (starters) and second plates (entrée-type offerings). All plates are bitsy, so you can rack up a sizable bill if you're fairly hungry; but the small portions also allow for broader sam-pling of 750's yummy offerings. Pork tenderloin, a ubiquitous restaurant standby, is anything but ordinary here: pounded thin, rolled around plumped cherries and prunes, and cut into rounds, it's pink in the center and fork-tender. Each grain of rice in the spinach risotto is properly articulated, but the dish is Cool Whip–creamy as a whole. Braised lamb with silky, house-made pappardelle, chopped artichoke, and olives vanishes from your plate much too quickly. And there is no better starter combo than 750's clams steamed in a broth of white wine, garlic, shallots, and parsley—paired with amazing truffle-scented pommes frites. **COME HERE FOR THE WHIMSICAL APPROACH TO WINE.** *$$; AE, DIS, MC, V; checks OK; lunch, dinner Mon–Sat; full bar; reservations recommended; www.750-ml.com; map:L2* &

Sin Ju / ★★★

1022 NW JOHNSON ST, PEARL DISTRICT; 503/223-6535 Seated in breezy tatami rooms and sequestered alcoves, surrounded by orchids, potted bamboo, and trickling fountains, it's easy to forget the food at pretty Sin Ju. But the well-chosen trappings are not mere gloss masking mediocre meals; they amplify the ultrarefined Japanese food. Sin Ju prepares a full range of traditional items, from teriyaki to maki, but the restaurant keeps its list brief and focused, offering a few favorites and introducing diners to unfamiliar rolls. It's fun to order a mix-and-match meal of sushi and cooked dishes, perhaps starting with a plate of excellent grilled squid or broiled eel and some miso soup before moving onto the Rainbow Roll. This colorful wonder elevates the veggie-packed California roll by topping it with glistening salmon, albacore, shrimp, and so forth, and is a prime example of Sin Ju's exquisite presentation. Hot entrées are served in lidded lacquered boxes as if they were ruby-and-diamond necklaces, and sushi arrives atop enormous wooden boats and bridges that provide ample space to indulge a chef's penchant for artistic arrangement. **COME HERE FOR DYNAMITE SASHIMI AND GORGEOUS PRESENTATION.** *$$; AE, DC, DIS, MC, V; no checks; lunch Mon–Fri, dinner every day; full bar; reservations recommended; map:N2* &

Southpark Seafood Grill and Wine Bar / ★★

901 SW SALMON ST, DOWNTOWN; 503/326-1300 Sometimes sexy starters outshine the main course. This is true at Southpark, the downtown Mediterranean- and North African–leaning restaurant known for its spirited wine list and European-style sidewalk seating. Here there are some two dozen "small bites" that include exquisite warm dates stuffed with Marcona almonds cloaked in ribbons of serrano ham. Piping hot shrimp redolent of garlic are baked with creamy feta, tomatoes, and oregano, begging you to mop up any remaining sauce with hunks of bread. One often-featured soup is a seriously seductive purée of almonds and saffron. And steamed mussels with chunks of fennel sausage, blanketed by fragrant anisette and marinara sauce, are some of the most unusual bivalves in town. For entrées, stick to chicken tagine, a Moroccan stew with falling-off-the-bone chicken and a heady cinnamon aroma; Catalan fish stew, which teems with shrimp, clams, and mussels in romesco sauce; and that perennial favorite, butternut squash ravioli with sage and hazelnuts. Whatever you choose to eat, you'll be able to find an appropriate liquid partner in Southpark's witty, thorough wine list. **COME HERE FOR UNFOR-GETTABLE APPETIZERS AND THE FESTIVE WINE BAR.** *$$; AE, DC, DIS, MC, V; no checks; lunch Mon–Sat, dinner every day; full bar; reservations recommended; www.southpark.citysearch.com; map:H2* &

Stickers Asian Café / ★

6808 SE MILWAUKIE AVE, WESTMORELAND; 503/239-8739 For such a tiny place, Stickers has quite a grand menu, one that reaches well beyond its namesake pot stickers. Owners John Sinclair and Joan Frances spent several years in China sampling regional variations of pot stickers, the quintessential Sino street food. Their renderings of the chubby pork and vegetable packets, available steamed and panfried, prove that the couple did their homework. The menu also includes some of the best-loved curries, satays, and noodle dishes from Thailand and India. Prawn satay marinated in coconut milk and sweet chili sauce, and milder chicken satay, are especially memorable. And you won't forget the spooky Ninja martini. Made with Blavod, a vodka that employs the highly tannic herb catechu to color it black, it coordinates nicely with Stickers's blood-red walls. **COME HERE FOR PANFRIED VEGETABLE POT STICKERS WITH SHANGHAI DIPPING SAUCE.** $; MC, V; checks OK; lunch Mon–Sat, dinner every day; full bar; no reservations; map:JJ5 &

Sungari Restaurant / ★★☆
Sungari Pearl / ★★☆

735 SW 1ST AVE, DOWNTOWN; 503/224-0800 / 1105 NW LOVEJOY ST, PEARL DISTRICT; 971/222-7327 Like any estimable restaurant, Sungari uses fresh, quality ingredients, and right there, that sets it apart from lazier Chinese joints whose scallops don't taste as sweet and whose broccoli is past its prime. Sungari passes up red dragon decor in favor of austere, dove-gray walls and understated art. Though not strictly Sichuan, many of its entrées are peppery, a main characteristic of this particular Chinese cuisine. Yet even with the spiciest dishes, heat does not obscure the pure flavors in components of, say, kung pao shrimp. Diners can taste the individual flavors of plump prawns, peanuts, water chestnuts, and celery, each intensified by chiles, garlic, and ginger. What really makes Sungari special are the creations you don't find at the average Chinese restaurant. Sungari Duck Slices is a fantastic medley of tender duck, snow peas, carrots, and mushrooms in a subtly spiced sauce. And small culinary touches such as ginger chicken made with young ginger—a type with pale skin possessed of a milder zing than mature ginger—go a long way. The new Sungari Pearl, in the Streetcar Lofts building, boasts chic environs and a broader menu than the original downtown location, plus a small, elegant bar near the entrance. **COME HERE FOR THE ABSENCE OF CHINESE KITSCH.** $$; AE, DC (Pearl), MC, V; no checks; lunch Mon–Fri (Downtown), every day (Pearl), dinner every day; full bar; reservations recommended; www.sungarirestaurant.com; map:H5; map:O2 &

Swagat / ★★

2074 NW LOVEJOY ST, NORTHWEST; 503/227-4300 / 4325 SW 109TH AVE, BEAVERTON; 503/626-3000 Swagat means "welcome" in the Hindi language, and that spirit rules at both locations—although you'd never know it from the atmosphere. Cozy, dark, and moody, Swagat in Portland feels more British colonial than postindependence India. And the casual Beaverton location, in a small, renovated house and garage, is anything but stylish. But the cuisine is sensual, perfumed, and complexly spiced—and that's all that really matters. Offering traditional curries, pakoras, biryanis, and vegetarian choices, the diverse dishes cover north and south India. Fans of lamb saag applaud the depth of spicing; papery-thin dosa crepes enclose vegetable curry; and the tandoor oven turns out nicely charred tear-shaped naan, plus yogurt-marinated chicken kabobs, halibut fillet, and skewered shrimp. The inclusive menu brings no surprises to those familiar with Indian cuisine and never ventures beyond expected dimensions. The lunch buffet is a good bargain at both locations. **COME HERE FOR RAVA MASALA DOSA.** *$$; AE, DIS, MC, V, no checks; lunch, dinner every day; full bar (Northwest), beer and wine (Beaverton); no reservations; map:GG7; map:II9* &

Sweet Basil Thai / ★★☆

3135 NE BROADWAY ST, IRVINGTON; 503/281-8337 Part of the fun at Sweet Basil comes with looking before touching: beholding the artfully arranged platters that whet your appetite just before you dig in. Hawaiian fried rice arrives warm and sweet inside a carved-out whole pineapple. Scooping out the aromatic mix, you discover chicken and shrimp pieces mingling with egg, pineapple chunks, raisins, cashews, carrots, and green peas. Phad thai arrives on colorful dishes with chopsticks jutting out at jaunty angles and a spray of bean sprouts on the side. It tastes as good as it looks, spiked with mild to wild heat per your request; pieces of chicken breast and egg mix with cracked peanuts in a tangle of wide noodles, which thankfully aren't overly saturated with sweet sauce. With shrimp, this classic dish costs just a bit more. Another bonus, weather-permitting, is the gorgeous deck. **COME HERE FOR THAI FOOD THAT'S WELL ABOVE AVERAGE.** *$–$$; AE, DIS, MC, V; no checks; lunch, dinner every day; full bar; reservations recommended; www.sweetbasilor.com; map:GG5* &

Syun Izakaya / ★★

209 NE LINCOLN ST, HILLSBORO; 503/640-3131 Imitating a neighborhood *nomiya* (drinking place)—an affordable, affable style of pub ubiquitous in Japan—this downtown Hillsboro sushi-and-sake bar draws locals and expatriate Japanese techies. Housed in the old Carnegie library building, it offers a lively informal mood, but the sushi and traditional dishes are first rate—as fresh and carefully prepared as you'd find in any more formal setting. And the 35-bottle sake collection is impressive. Nearly overdecorated with bamboo, sake bottles, and ceramic cats, the Syun experience is pure Tokyo. Chef Shiro, who trained in French cuisine in Japan, presides over an intimate sushi bar that is often full; wooden tables in two rooms accommodate overflow crowds. An extensive menu offers snacks such as edamame, yakitori, soba, and chilled tofu with ginger and bonito. You'll also get meals of donburi, grilled mackerel, tempura, and tonkatsu, plus eclectic desserts such as banana tempura with red-bean paste and black-tea pudding. Even if Hillsboro weren't short of fine restaurants, Syun would attract loyalty. **COME HERE FOR SUSHI AND SAKE.** *$$; AE, DC, DIS, MC, V; local checks only; lunch Mon–Fri, dinner every day; full bar; reservations recommended* &

Tabla / ★★★

200 NE 28TH AVE, LAURELHURST; 503/238-3777 Like 28th Avenue itself, which has blossomed almost overnight with chic little wine bars and cafes, Tabla began as a blank slate—on which its trio of ex-Serratto chefs and co-owners have drawn a serious bistro. A sinuous modern bar dominates the entrance, yielding to a snug scattering of blond wooden tables in back. The menu tends toward tapas-like plates with Italian and Mediterranean notes. Grilled calamari is served crisp and hot over garlic-dressed arugula and desiccated olives; short ribs are accompanied by a savory bread pudding made from panzanella; duck confit is seared crispy with a port-poached orange. The chilled cucumber soup is an instant winner. Although portions are small, few dishes are priced over $10. An intimate meal can be made by ordering and sharing several plates, and a wine flight ($15 for four half glasses of any pour) adds to the adventure. The wine list is extensive and includes lovely *moscatos* and other dessert wines. For the night-owl set, the full menu is available until 1am Thursday through Saturday. **COME HERE FOR THE HOUSE-MADE TAIARIN PASTA WITH TRUFFLE BUTTER.** *$$; AE, DC, DIS, MC, V; no checks; dinner every day; full bar; reservations recommended; map:HH5* &

Taqueria Nueve / ★★★

28 NE 28TH AVE, LAURELHURST; 503/236-6195 Eastside favorite Taqueria Nueve has expanded into an adjacent storefront and has shed its former rustic cantina ambience. Now, a soft leather banquette runs the length of a freshly painted fuchsia wall and wood paneling slants down from the ceiling to quell the restaurant's din. Part of this sleek package is a tiled bar twice the size of the old one and a hefty wooden table big enough to accommodate large parties. The menu has also been refurbished, though quite a few original dishes fortunately made the cut: piquant ceviche, *coctel de pulpo* (spicy lime-cured octopus), and several taco varieties—including the wonderful achiote-seasoned pork, wild boar, and roasted beef tongue. In other offerings, familiar ingredients are presented in invigorated guises. The intricate mole no longer smothers a quarter chicken; it tops a plate of tortillas, shredded chicken, cheese, and crema. Instead of steak with tequila salsa, delicious grilled top sirloin is paired with sweet-and-sour onions and chipotle salsa. In addition to its wonderful, orange-tinged flan, Taqueria Nueve has introduced a three-milk layer cake with chocolate mocha icing and pecans. Sweet and creamy, it's a chocolate dessert that doesn't oppress you with its chocolateness. **COME HERE FOR CREATIVE TACOS AND KILLER MARGARITAS.** *$$; AE, MC, V; no checks; dinner every day; full bar; reservations for 6 or more; map:HH5* &

Tara Thai Northwest / ★

1310 NW 23RD AVE, NORTHWEST; 503/222-7840 There used to be three branches of this family-run Thai restaurant, but now there is only one; owner Lavanny Phommaneth chose to channel her time and energy into the Northwest location. Oh, the lucky residents of Nob Hill! Everything about the converted former home is pleasant: the modest dining room, the understated but knowledgeable servers, and the fresh and flavorful food. The menu concentrates on the foods of northern Thailand and Laos, including such recognizable dishes as fresh salad rolls, *tom kah kai* (ginger–coconut milk soup with chicken), green curry, and phad thai, as well as less familiar Lao specialties: *khao poon nam kai* (a delicious chicken–rice noodle soup flavored with fresh banana leaves, basil, and galangal) and *soop pak* (steamed vegetables in a roasted ginger paste). For dessert, there's a murky gray—but nonetheless tasty—rice pudding with bananas and, in season, mangoes over sweet sticky rice in coconut milk. **COME HERE FOR UNIQUE LAOTIAN DISHES.** *$–$$; AE,*

DIS, MC, V; no checks; lunch, dinner every day; beer and wine; reservations recommended; map:GG7 &

Tartine / ★★

1621 SE BYBEE BLVD, WESTMORELAND; 503/239-5796 Were it not for the warm hospitality, you'd swear this French country-style bistro were on a backstreet in Haute-Savoie. That's no coincidence, as co-owner and chef Gigi Machet, a native of Lyon, spent years as a ski instructor in that Alpine province. In a friendly room previously occupied by Fishtales, Machet hops back and forth from the kitchen to the tables, conversing with each guest (in French, if you're able) and recommending numerous dishes from the unpretentious menu. Her warm scallop salad (*salade de Saint Jacques*), with citrus slices and house-made Dijon vinaigrette dressing, might precede a meal of *lapin aux pruneaux*—rabbit with prunes, served with polenta—or classic duck à l'orange. Forgo dessert for a plate of five imported cheeses. A *tartine* is a hot, open-faced sandwich, and these are what dominate the lunch menu: try the *montagne*, with ham, mushrooms, onions, and Swiss cheese. **COME HERE TO PRACTICE YOUR FRENCH.** *$$; AE, DIS, MC, V; checks OK; lunch, dinner Mon–Sat; full bar; reservations recommended; map:JJ5* &

Taste of Asia / ★

7113 SW MACADAM AVE, JOHNS LANDING; 503/452-5002 / 14795 SW MURRAY SCHOLLS DR, BEAVERTON; 503/452-1058 In a city replete with Asian cuisine, Khmer food is a rarity. Here it's delivered with heart and courage by the Chhim family, who fled their native Cambodia in 1981. Similar to but distinct from neighboring Thailand and Vietnam, the cuisine of Cambodia uses abundant ginger, but otherwise restrained, delicate seasonings highlight ingredients. The Chhims recommend traditional dishes such as the French-influenced rice-flour crepe, a crispy-chewy omelet-style envelope for shrimp, chicken, and bean sprouts with a sweet-and-sour dressing. Tucked into strip malls, these casual, welcoming spaces feature open kitchens. Watch the chef prepare a sweet-and-sour chicken-pineapple soup and traditional rice noodles fragrant with garlic, dried shrimp, pickled papaya, and peanuts. The menu includes popular Thai, Vietnamese, and Chinese dishes, and modest prices encourage experimentation. **COME HERE FOR A RARE TASTE OF CAMBODIAN CUISINE.** *$; AE, MC, V; no checks; lunch Mon–Fri, dinner Mon–Sat; www.houseofasiapdx.com; map:JJ6* &

Thai Orchid / ★★

2231 W BURNSIDE ST, NORTHWEST (AND BRANCHES); 503/226-4542 With nine locations so far, from Salem to Vancouver, Thai Orchid is competing with Typhoon! (see review) to grow into the region's largest Thai chain. Owners Na and Penny Saenguraipron stylishly design each location, avoiding the chain feel, and phad thai at number 9 is as carefully prepared and served as at their first. Orchid flowers grace the entrance of the low-profile W Burnside location; golden yellow and royal purple color curving walls, and as tradition requires, the king's photo is hung. An ambitious, safe menu covers Thai favorites without straying far into unusual regional specialties. Whole fried catfish or pomfret with chili and garlic sauce, a specialty too messy for home prep, is best enjoyed here; beneath crispy skin, the flaky fish and bold sauce pairs perfectly. Look for *khao soi*, an elegant northern Thai soup of egg noodles in thick, golden coconut curry broth with shallots. Chewy wide rice noodles with meat, broccoli, and gravy taste as good in Portland as in Bangkok; grilled, lemongrass-marinated chicken with peanut sauce, green papaya salad, and traditional curries round out reasonably priced choices. **COME HERE FOR DELICIOUS PHAD THAI.** *$$; AE, DIS, MC, V; no checks; lunch, dinner every day; beer and wine; reservations recommended; www.thaiorchidrestaurant.com; map:HH7* &

3 Doors Down / ★★⯪

1429 SE 37TH AVE, HAWTHORNE; 503/236-6886 You play by the rules at this humble Hawthorne restaurant, with its closet-size dining room and no-reservations policy. The gaggle of patrons waiting patiently outside for tables suggests that the food must be worth it, and it is. 3 Doors Down has found its rhythm, and unusual seasonal experiments—like seared scallops tossed with peaches in a mild basil cream sauce—have become house standards that attract a loyal and appreciative following. In fact, it's the menu's lighter, more playful items that carry the day, particularly on a hot evening when the room approaches sauna temperatures. The Tuscan bread salad, served at the height of summer's harvest of heirloom tomatoes and sweet peppers, has a refreshing tang and texture. Entrées—usually a choice between red meat, fresh fish, and roast chicken—stick to what works with a seasoned broth or sauce (a veal demi-glace, in the case of the pork loin) and with accompaniments of greens, potatoes, or polenta. An informed and voluble staff will tell you what you want to know about the encyclopedic wine list, the food, or its preparation. Save room for dessert, perhaps banana cream pie or double-chocolate mousse cake. **COME HERE FOR A CULINARY ADVENTURE.** *$$; AE, MC, V; checks OK; dinner Tues–Sat; beer and wine; no reservations; map:HH5* &

Three Square Grill / ★★

6320 SW CAPITOL HWY, HILLSDALE; 503/244-4467 Textured potato chip–yellow walls set a sunny scene at this storefront in the Hillsdale Shopping Center, which behaves as both a casual American bistro and an upscale cafe. Barbara and David Barber's Southern-focused menu also roams from coast to coast, assuring less theme than abundant creativity. Local contemporary wall art, table linens, affable servers, and seasonal produce have drawn attention beyond the neighborhood. Just about everything is prepared from scratch: Carolina barbecue pork, pickles, fruit preserves, and buns. House-smoked salmon hash and fresh-squeezed orange juice shine at breakfast; Caesar salad, meat loaf, grilled-onion sandwiches, one-third-pound natural beef burgers, and Louisiana-style jambalini pasta score at lunch. Dinner can be light and casual (black-bean chili and spinach salad) or more substantial (soy- and maple-glazed salmon over sticky rice with shrimp-cucumber salad). There are plenty of Southern sides—hushpuppies, collard greens, fried okra—plus old-fashioned rice pudding to keep the regulars satisfied. **COME HERE FOR NEIGHBORHOOD AMBIENCE.** *$$; MC, V; checks OK; lunch Tues–Fri, dinner Tues–Sat, brunch Sat–Sun; beer and wine; reservations recommended; www.threesquare.com; map:JJ7* &

Tin Shed Garden Café / ★★

 1438 NE ALBERTA ST, ALBERTA; 503/288-6966 Imagine a cafe that is adorable without succumbing to preciousness, low-key but not lackadaisical, its food simultaneously simple and inspired. It's here at the Tin Shed. A zero-attitude vibe permeates the place, from the funky, artsy interior to the sprawling outdoor patio replete with herb garden and huge brick hearth. The food is good and simple, ingredients are hopping with freshness, and helpings are generous and well priced. At breakfast, boulder-size buttermilk biscuits accompany all egg or tofu dishes; they arrive warm and buttered, with delicious berry jam on the side. Savory plates include scrambles like Keepin' It Simple (eggs with Black Forest ham, Tillamook cheddar, and tomato) and Veggie Pesto (roasted vegetables, eggs or tofu, pesto, and cream cheese). Lunch offers much to cheer about, too. Tuna salad mixed with diced cantaloupe, pickle, and onion in a pita is anything but leaden, and the Quesadilla That Did, jazzed by pepper-jack cheese and mango–black bean salsa, is outstanding. **COME HERE FOR THE HOUSE-MADE BISCUITS.** *$; MC, V; no checks; breakfast, lunch Wed–Mon, dinner (summer only) Wed–Fri; beer and wine; no reservations; tinshedgardencafe@hotmail.com; map:FF5* &

Todai Restaurant / ★★

340 SW MORRISON ST, DOWNTOWN; 503/294-0007 You have never seen so much sushi, nor so many people in quest of it. This branch of a California chain of Japanese seafood buffets—on the third floor of the Pioneer Place mall—draws crowds (especially weekend evenings) in search of unlimited salmon-skin hand rolls for $22.95, the fixed dinner-buffet price. (On Thursdays the price drops $1; children to age 11, and under 5 feet, 4 feet, and 3 feet, get respective price breaks.) The sushi is decent, and if it's not comparable to the most exquisite sushi bars in town, the range of choice—and did we mention the unlimited quantity?—helps compensate. The hot side of the buffet is a mixed catch. Although it features multiple varieties of shrimp and regular appearances by fresh scallops and lobster, they tend to end up overcooked, and the teriyaki doesn't have its gingery bite. Still, you can always head back for more spicy tuna seaweed rolls—or to the dessert buffet that runs about 15 feet, East to West. **COME HERE FOR THE VERITABLE SEA OF SUSHI.** *$$; AE, MC, V; no checks; lunch, dinner every day; beer and wine; reservations for 6 or more; www.todai.com; map:H4* &

Tokyo Restaurant / ★★

2331 NW 185TH ST, HILLSBORO; 503/690-1891 Restaurants in Japan often specialize in one cuisine—soba, sushi, one-pot stews—but on these shores, they mainly fall into the category of *nihon-ryori*: literally, assorted Japanese cuisines. In Hillsboro's Tanasbourne Shopping Center, this little blond-wood, shoji-screened *nihon-ryori* packs them in, especially at noon. Diners choose from a wide menu of Japanese classics. With no room for a sushi bar, the kitchen still prepares it to order: *unagi* (eel) and *ebi* (shrimp) nigiri sushi, salmon-skin and tempura rolls. Typical lunch plates—salmon teriyaki, ginger pork, chicken katsu served over rice—are generous and moderately priced, as are bento boxes and soba or udon bowls. Tokyo also serves ramen bowls as a full meal: Chinese egg-noodle soup topped with meat or vegetables, very popular in Japan. Easily overlooked by larger, higher-profile restaurant neighbors, this place merits attention. **COME HERE FOR YAKISOBA NOODLES.** *$$; AE, DIS, MC, V; no checks; lunch, dinner Mon–Sat; beer and wine; no reservations; www.tokyorestaurant.net* &

Touché / ★

1425 NW GLISAN ST, PEARL DISTRICT; 503/221-1150 Dining room downstairs, pool hall upstairs—and often the twain shall meet. Long popular with a dating crowd that likes to sup grown-up style before trooping upstairs for a rowdy round of billiards, Touché offers a uniquely schizophrenic dining experience. Its 1913 building retains vestiges of its original architectural grandeur—exposed brick walls, grand staircase, wedding-cake columns and arches—and may be the most formal thing about Touché. The food is a kind of elbows-out Mediterranean designed to suit the professional drinking that goes on here (the full menu is served until 2am). Wood-fired oven pizzas offer beer-busting flavors and contrasts—the Bianca is four white cheeses, blackened broccoli, and pine nuts, while the al Funghi mingles mushrooms with prosciutto, sage, provolone, and fontina. An array of fairly standard spaghetti, ravioli, and linguini dishes lends an elegance to the menu, but Touché knows its crowd—reasonably priced platters of fried calamari (dressed up with capers, red pepper flakes, garlic, and lemon) and hummus (yours for less than 5 bucks) adorn almost every table. **COME HERE FOR LATE-NIGHT EATS AND A LITTLE 8-BALL.** *$$; AE, DIS, MC, V; no checks; dinner until 2am every day; full bar; reservations recommended; map:M1*

Tucci / ★★

220 A AVE, LAKE OSWEGO; 503/697-3383 An elegant addition to downtown Lake Oswego's evolving pedestrian scene, Tucci is a chic trattoria whose copper-backed open kitchen gives it a rustic allure. A wood-burning stove produces sophisticated pizzas, like crispy pancetta with asparagus and caramelized onions; but chef Pascal Chureau is at his best with elaborate entrées. Grilled sea bass is served with a ragout of eggplant and roasted garlic, drizzled with an olive-and-truffle vinaigrette. Filet mignon comes with porcini risotto cake, grilled broccolini, and a pancetta Chianti sauce. Don't miss the antipasti: black mussels steamed in pinot grigio with oregano, and sweet white anchovies with baby arugula and vine-ripened tomatoes. The lunch menu has a nice selection of salads and panini sandwiches; if the sun is shining, enjoy them on a pleasant outdoor patio. (Inside, tables are tightly clustered beneath a balloon-like chandelier.) A stunning menu of desserts and coffee drinks makes this an outstanding after-dinner stop as well. **COME HERE FOR WARM CHOCOLATE POLENTA CAKE ON THE PATIO.** *$$; AE, MC, V; no checks; lunch Mon–Sat, dinner Tues–Sun, brunch Sun (except summer); full bar; reservations recommended; www.tucci.biz; map:MM6* &

Tuscany Grill / ★☆

811 NW 21ST AVE, NORTHWEST; 503/243-2757 With stunning Italian restaurants packed cheek-by-jowl along NW 21st, it could be easy to overlook Tuscany Grill. Don't. Decorated to resemble the interior of a crumbling stone villa, the restaurant serves the robust, rustic classics of Tuscan cuisine—fresh, house-made mozzarella, pancetta-wrapped prawns over cannellini beans and minced red onion, crisp-tart leaves of arugula and radicchio in salads, and masterfully prepared pastas (including an outstanding orecchiette with chicken confit and braised rapini). Everything seems to be drizzled with fruity, fragrant olive oil . . . which makes a bottle of wine a must. The vintage list showcases close to 100 Italian reds; any of the staff will gladly walk you down the dizzying roster to find a bottle to suit your meal and your money belt. On a busy night, diners frustrated by the impossibility of finding a table elsewhere in the neighborhood can take their ease and their Chianti at Tuscany Grill's comfortable bar. **COME HERE FOR THE ORECCHIETTE.** *$$; MC, V; no checks; dinner every day; full bar; reservations recommended; map:GG7* &

Typhoon! / ★★★

2310 NW EVERETT ST, NORTHWEST; 503/243-7557 / 400 SW BROADWAY (HOTEL LUCIA), DOWNTOWN; 503/224-8385 Typhoon! is expanding into a small empire. The original Northwest Portland space—where the atmosphere is a bit more upscale than much of the Thai competition in town—has been joined by a larger and stylish downtown location in the elegant Hotel Lucia, by two new cafes in suburban Portland, and by two more in the Seattle area. Notice by the national food magazines can do that, and besides, Bo Kline is a deeply gifted chef. From openers of *miang kum* (spinach leaves filled with any of a half-dozen ingredients) and mouth-filling soups, the menu moves into a kaleidoscope of flavors. You can't go wrong with curries (especially the green curry), inspired seafood dishes (such as seasonally available rainbow trout wrapped in lettuce with peanuts and vegetables), and multiple pungent Thai noodle dishes. Try the King's Noodles to know why it's good to be king. Scored into a checkerboard grid, a fried fish blossoms into a pinecone, and dishes with names like Fish on Fire and Superwild Shrimp turn out to be named exactly right. Typhoon! also offers 145 different teas—including one that goes for $35 a pot. If you're in the suburbs, consider visiting the Gresham (543 NW 12th St; 503/669-9995) or Beaverton (12600 SW Crescent St; 503/644-8010) restaurants. **COME HERE FOR THE NORTHWEST'S FINEST GOURMET THAI CUISINE.** *$$; AE, DC, MC, V; no checks; breakfast every day (Downtown), lunch Mon–Sat (Northwest), every day (Downtown), dinner every day; full bar; reservations recommended; www.typhoonrestaurants.com; map:GG7; map:J4* &

Umenoki / ★

2330 NW THURMAN ST, NORTHWEST; 503/242-6404 In sleepy North-by-Northwest Portland, Umenoki serves sushi in a quiet, uncrowded enclave. Rice-paper panels shield the booths from the street and from each other, and every dining chair is covered with one or two quilted satin cushions. A large—and largely unsurprising—menu offers upwards of 50 sushi specialties, as well as soba, somen, and udon dishes. (For a little more flavor, sample the curry udon: slices of beef, carrots, and potatoes in a spicy, fragrant broth poured over thick noodles.) The bento box lunches are affordable (all around $8) and although preparation is mostly average to good, there's virtue in the sole pleasure of dining in relative tranquility: many Portlanders have yet to discover Umenoki. **COME HERE FOR THE SERENE SURROUNDINGS.** *$$; MC, V; no checks; lunch Mon–Fri, dinner Mon–Sat; beer and wine; reservations recommended; map:GG7* &

Vat and Tonsure / ★★

911 SW TAYLOR ST, DOWNTOWN; 503/225-9118 Rare is the restaurant that can get away with being staunchly indifferent to the times. You've gotta stay hip and sexy to survive in this business—unless you happen to be a classic. The Vat and Tonsure earned that status a decade ago. A clubby place that catered to suits at lunchtime and culture hounds by night, it was characterized by Rosemarie Quinn's homey cooking, a steady supply of good wine, and ultraeducated, often imperious waiters. Canonization came as the Vat was forced to close to make way for the looming Fox Tower. And now it's back, its original bar, paintings, and severe wooden booths intact in a comely storefront mere blocks from its former location. The menu is much the same and opera again pours from the sound system, jolting diners with particularly intense arias. You won't find another menu like the Vat's anywhere in town: it could have been plucked from a 1950s time capsule. Whole Cornish game hen, sherry roast pork, sautéed prawns, pork or lamb chops—these no-nonsense entrées include a vegetable (broccoli on every visit thus far) and choice of salad, but no starch and little embellishment. But the food's not really the thing. **COME HERE FOR A GLASS OF WINE, A SHOT OF CLASS, AND THE MEMORIES.** *$$; MC, V; checks OK; lunch Mon–Fri, dinner Mon–Sat; beer and wine; reservations for dinner only; map:H2* &

Veritable Quandary / ★★★

1220 SW 1ST AVE, DOWNTOWN; 503/227-7342 Peppered with local ingredients ranging from Fraga Farm goat cheese to Cotton Creek lamb, the VQ's market-driven menu is a swell representation of what the rain-soaked Northwest brings to table. That wasn't always the case at this cozy, 33-year-old mainstay, once a mere tavern. But since chef Anne Barnette entered the kitchen in 1995, she's been chipping away at the pub fare, replacing it with the likes of bacon-wrapped dates stuffed with Marcona almonds and fork-tender duck confit that boasts a contrasting crispy skin. When available, the must-have appetizer is Gruyère-and-Granny Smith beignets, weightless fritters oozing melted cheese and sweet-tart apple pieces. For the main course, if not Barnette's signature osso bucco, try one of the fresh fish specials, such as red snapper and sweet crab paired with piquant kumquat slices. The VQ still boasts a convivial bar, where downtown workers congregate and aromas of smoke and whiskey snake up from wooden booths. The narrow, high-ceilinged dining rooms are quieter; but true intimacy can be found on the meticulously landscaped patio during fair weather. The VQ's approach to wine is as original as the food. It boasts an extensive by-the-glass program of about 50 wines and a smart cellar with plenty of bottles in the $20–$30 range. **COME HERE FOR OSSO BUCO AND GREAT WINE IN A CLASSIC TAVERN SETTING.** *$$–$$$; AE, DC, DIS, MC, V; no checks; lunch Mon–Fri, dinner every day, brunch Sat–Sun; full bar; reservations recommended; www.veritablequandary.com; map:F4* &

Vista Spring Café / ★

2440 SW VISTA AVE, PORTLAND HEIGHTS; 503/222-2811 You could live in Portland for years completely unaware of Vista Spring's existence—unless you lived in the West Hills. This inviting, comfortable perch is a true neighborhood restaurant. Families and couples swing by for casual weekday suppers of pizza, chicken pot pie, and gargantuan salads. Though Vista Spring offers a full menu of burgers, sandwiches, and pasta, its reputation is primarily built on gourmet pizza. It subscribes to the wildly creative school of pizza-making, combining unusual ingredients such as prosciutto, Thai-spiced chicken, walnuts, and Montrachet cheese with the likes of pedestrian olives, onions, and pepperoni. Pizzas come in personal, medium, and large sizes, and the generous personal can feed more than one if you order a salad or soup as well. **COME HERE FOR GREAT PIZZA AND A FRIENDLY NEIGHBORHOOD VIBE.** *$; DIS, MC, V; no checks; lunch, dinner every day; beer and wine; no reservations; map:HH7* ♿

Wild Abandon / ★★

2411 SE BELMONT ST, BELMONT; 503/232-4458 Red velvet booths, murals of voluptuous nudes, and gilt, gilt, gilt—for a restaurant deep in dreadlock-Birkenstock Belmont, Wild Abandon sure knows how to dress up. The menu's sumptuous offerings include pork loin with an apple-balsamic glaze, rich tomato-flecked pastas, and a fragrant seafood stew—dishes as rich and stylish as the interior. Wines from all over the world find their way to the parlorlike dining room. Order a lush, worldly rioja and stay a while: servers here are used to whispering couples who linger for hours over a shared tiramisù in a bittersweet coffee-chocolate sauce. An outdoor patio covered in climbing vines and nasturtiums provides an idyllic, pre-Raphaelite setting for a fair-weather brunch, while new late-night hours turn the restaurant into the Red Velvet Lounge on Fridays and Saturdays. That's when things get really Bacchanalian. **COME HERE FOR OLD-FASHIONED ROMANCE.** *$$; AE, DIS, MC, V; local checks only; breakfast Mon–Sat, lunch, dinner every day, brunch Sun; full bar; reservations recommended; map:HH5* ♿

Wildwood / ★★★½

1221 NW 21ST AVE, NORTHWEST; 503/248-9663 Wildwood's reputation as one of Portland's top tables is completely deserved. Recipient of the James Beard Award for the region's best chef in 1998, native son Cory Schreiber never gets lazy in his quest to create explosively flavorful food. Driven by the seasons, Wildwood's menu changes weekly but is always solidly Northwest, taking full advantage of local bounty. Schreiber and his loyal team let quality ingredients do most of the work, building dishes around beautiful shell beans, Chioggia beets, abalone, crayfish, and leg of lamb. Robust heirloom tomatoes make a wedge of snowy halibut sing, while a zingy gremolata massages lamb's deep flavor. Pork loin would never be served with mashed potatoes and steamed broccoli here; instead, it's stuffed with lobster mushrooms and sausage and paired with white corn grits and peaches bathing in a maple-syrup glaze. Classic cocktails, a pleasing wine list, and intense fruit desserts, such as a gushing blueberry turnover and roasted apricots with honey ice cream, further the delicious dining experience. In the dining room, high-backed booths create cozy spaces for tête-à-têtes under a sloping wood-paneled ceiling recently installed to blanket the often-noisy restaurant, while the bar and Chef's Counter facing the open kitchen offer more casual seats. Watching your dining budget? Check out the bar's Chalkboard

Menu, a smart selection of uncomplicated pizzas, shellfish, salads, and a $10 burger. **COME HERE FOR EXCELLENT, MARKET-DRIVEN COOKING.** *$$–$$$; AE, MC, V; checks OK; lunch Sun, dinner every day; full bar; reservations recommended; www.wildwoodrestaurant.com; map:GG7* &

Winterborne / ★★★

3520 NE 42ND AVE, BEAUMONT; 503/249-8486 This tiny, almost ritualistic seafood restaurant is always highly ranked by Portlanders as well as outsiders, suggesting that people know what they want. The limited menu, which reflects the style of Alsatian chef Gilbert Henri, includes sautéed oysters with a tangy aioli, escargots in a garlicky herb butter, mussels steamed in white wine, ahi à la Niçoise, and the wonderful Bouillabaisse Royale: a flavorful stew rife with lobster, salmon, and various shellfish. To another dish, Henri adds a touch of Southeast Asia: prawns à la Thailandaise are laced with garlic, basil, ginger, and coconut milk. And in crab Juniper, he blends Dungeness crabmeat with a pear sauce that graces delicate whitefish. Bringing new continental inspiration to Northwest seafood, this chef can stretch a halibut from Astoria to Alsace. Winterborne is an intimate restaurant of a mere seven tables, manned by a single waiter: another charming Frenchman. Guests feel the warmth and care that such a size allows. **COME HERE FOR EXQUISITELY PREPARED SEAFOOD IN THE FRENCH STYLE.** *$$; AE, DIS, MC, V; local checks only; dinner Wed–Sat; beer and wine; reservations recommended; map:FF5* &

Wu's Open Kitchen / ★

17773 SW BOONES FERRY RD, LAKE OSWEGO (AND BRANCHES); 503/636-8899 The flames leaping high behind the windows in the back of the restaurant are firing the large woks in the kitchen, and you can watch the cooks deftly preparing dishes while you wait for dinner. Chef Jimmy Wu's extended family helps run this place, serving a variety of spicy and not-so-spicy dishes from all over China. But the cooks reckon on the American palate; the hot dishes won't wilt too many taste buds. Seafood is fresh, vegetables are crisp, sauces are light, and service is speedy and attentive. Kids will feel right at home and parents will appreciate the modest prices. Prepare for a wait on weekends, though. Wu's is well-known by locals—not only in Lake Oswego, but at its Beaverton and two Tigard stores. **COME HERE FOR THE MOO SHU PORK.** *$–$$; MC, V; no checks; lunch, dinner every day; full bar; reservations recommended; map:LL7* &

Ya Hala / ★★

8005 SE STARK ST, MOUNT TABOR; 503/256-4484 Ya Hala traces its roots to Nicholas' Restaurant (see review), the hole-in-the-wall Lebanese joint that's won Portlanders' hearts for more than three decades: co-owner Mirna Attar is the daughter of Nicholas' founders, Nicholas and Linda Dibe. But Ya Hala is hardly a replica; the menu is clearly its own. Extensive and unusual, it tempts with specialties you may not have encountered elsewhere—such as *soujouk* (broiled spicy beef sausages) and vegetarian artichoke hearts, stuffed with potatoes, onions, carrots, and squash, covered in a creamy garlic sauce. Ya Hala is best enjoyed with a large group, allowing diners to sample and share several meze delights served appetizer-style. Stuffed grape leaves, *labneh* (yogurt cheese topped with kalamata olives and dried mint), a cheese platter spanning Bulgaria, Hungary, Cyprus, and Canada, and deep-fried cauliflower with tahini sauce are recommended. The service is incredibly speedy and friendly; Mirna and her husband, Jean, may even swing by your table to see how you like your meal. **COME HERE FOR THE MULTITUDE OF MENU CHOICES.** *$–$$; AE, DC, DIS, MC, V; checks OK; lunch, dinner Mon–Sat; full bar; no reservations; www.yahalarestaurant.com; map:HH3* &

Yam Yam's Southern Style Barbecue / ★

7339 NE MARTIN LUTHER KING BLVD, NORTHEAST; 503/978-9229 Order at the counter and grab lots of napkins: you're in for a messy but tasty ride. This no-frills barbecue joint doesn't offer much in the way of ambience, but it's the outdoor smoker—with its tempting aromas—that will lure you in, not the nondescript digs. One bite of the beef brisket or shredded pork (available as sandwiches or dinner plates) and you realize that slow smoking is worth the time. Super-tender and spicy-sweet, the meats are very satisfying. Barbecued chicken and pork ribs should not be overlooked, either. For sides, stick to the piquant collard greens, red beans and rice, and succotash. If the sterile atmosphere brings you down, get your food to go. **COME HERE FOR RIBS, BRISKET, AND PULLED PORK.** *$; MC, V; no checks; lunch, dinner every day; no alcohol; no reservations; map:FF6* &

Yuki Japanese Restaurant / ★

1337 NE BROADWAY, IRVINGTON; 503/281-6804 This bamboo-clad joint on bustling Broadway provides fine sushi of stunning freshness. The selection of seafood is enormous: green mussels, halibut, creamy scallops, deep-fried oysters, even *toro*—the elusive tuna belly that brings sushi aficionados at a trot. Yuki's sushi menu is a two-sided broadsheet offering all the usual suspects as well as an intriguing array of novelty and house rolls. Outstanding are the Hawaiian roll (fresh-cut maguro tuna, salmon, avocado, and a sliver of mango) and the Jamaican Dream (steamed lobster and tobiko). Much of the exotic seafood can be found in rolls that have been tempura-battered and flash-fried. Sushi purists may gasp, but Yuki's knack for pairing the cool saltwater flavors of fish with crunchy and spicy complements keeps any morsel from feeling heavy. Yuki also serves full dinners, including a lovingly presented salmon teriyaki meal. **COME HERE FOR THE FRESH FISH.** *$$; AE, DIS, MC, V; no checks; lunch, dinner every day; full bar; reservations recommended for large groups; www.pdxyuki.com; map:GG5* &

Zell's: An American Café / ★★

1300 SE MORRISON ST, BUCKMAN; 503/239-0196 Many restaurants pride themselves on their seasonally changing menus, but how many alter their breakfasts? At Zell's, the market-driven menu can produce pumpkin pancakes, a fresh nectarine waffle, or a daring German pancake with rhubarb, all of which are skillfully executed. Simply put, Zell's serves one of the best breakfasts in this time zone. The brilliance of the hot-from-the-griddle specialties (try the ginger pancakes when available) is matched by a medley of inspired egg dishes. The trademark chorizo-and-peppers omelet is joined by a worthy Brie-and-tomato effort. If you prefer scrambles, you won't be disappointed by the gently mixed eggs with smoked salmon, Gruyère, and green onions. Lunchtime brings an entirely different

FISHING IN PORTLAND

Ask a Portlander to recommend a seafood restaurant and you will most often get steered to Jake's Famous Crawfish or McCormick & Schmick's (see reviews in this chapter). Although both offer fine preparations of fish, Portland also offers a whole world of exotic seafood just waiting to transport you—one bite at a time—without ever leaving the confines of the city.

It's summertime. You're in Southeast—the Hawthorne District, and the heat is stifling on the street. You will wait for a long time to get a table at 3 Doors Down (1429 SE 37th Ave; 503/236-6886). When you do get your table, pay close attention to the scallop dishes—the house specialties that have gathered a cultish following among lovers of fine seafood. Enormous rounds of diver-caught sea scallops from the icy waters off Maine arrive at the table, anointed with the most original sauces and garnishes around. Fresh, sweet peaches with basil-tinted cream one night and a confetti of roasted peppers and white corn with salty chunks of pancetta the next. Don't miss the seafood entrees either. The sautéed halibut in a porcini mushroom crust will haunt your dreams.

A little past midnight, Saturday. On the way to the bright dining room of Golden Horse (238 NW 4th Ave; 503/228-1688), you pass a churning saltwater tank; you peer inside at its doomed occupants. A half dozen resigned Dungeness crabs defy you to order them dismembered in black bean sauce, sluglike sea cucumbers await steaming with bok choy, and one or two geoducks gape lewdly, not seeming to care what happens to them. But tonight a solitary eel nods its head above the surface of the water and mouths to you—"Eat me!" A stout man in a bloody apron appears from the kitchen and seizes your eel by the neck. In less time than it takes for you to order another drink, your eel reappears, transformed by ancient Chinese secrets into clouds of ginger-scented steam and nuggets of glistening meat. Prices are ludicrously low here, and portions are ample. All seafood choices are respectable, consistent, and about as far removed from the ordinary as is possible.

—Troy DuFrene

set of delights, including meat loaf, vegetarian sandwiches, and clam cakes, but it's hard to compete with the expert breakfasts. The catch, especially on weekend mornings, is a long wait for a table—but it probably won't be long enough for the nectarines to go out of season. **COME HERE FOR A BRILLIANT BREAKFAST.** *$; AE, DIS, MC, V; checks OK; breakfast, lunch every day; beer and wine; no reservations; map:HH5* &

Further Afield
Vancouver, Washington

Bacchus / ★

3200 SE 164TH AVE, VANCOUVER; 360/882-9672 Perhaps no restaurant in Greater Portland has a more stunning view of the Columbia River than this artsy east Vancouver establishment. The sweeping views from the spacious and elegant dining room look across Government Island toward the Portland airport, and on summer evenings, the sunset glow on Mount Hood is memorable. The menu is upscale fish and chop house, with some notable nods to original seafood concoctions and wild game. The Dungeness-crab-and-corn ravioli is delicious as a starter; wholesome entrées like buffalo osso buco and venison flank steak (with a huckleberry demiglace) will have you thinking of the mountain wilderness just to the east. The lounge gets lively later at night, when a happy-hour solo guitarist gives way to a live rock band and dancing. **COME HERE FOR THE VIEW AND THE BAR SCENE.** *$$$; AE, DIS, MC, V; no checks; lunch Mon–Fri, dinner every day; full bar; reservations recommended; map:DD1* &

Beaches Restaurant & Bar / ★★

1919 SE COLUMBIA RIVER DR, VANCOUVER; 360/699-1592 Think Seaside during spring break: youthful culture, hibiscus-splattered shirts, footprints in the sand, high-decibel acoustics. With undisturbed views high above the Columbia River, the beach is more wishful than actual . . . but who cares? Not the Match.com-ers flocking to happy hour; or parents chaperoning kids who like wood-fired pepperoni pizza and a s'mores-style dessert; or the business crowd lunching affordably. Preparation styles follow beach cooking, mostly by grill or wood; the menu is an expanded, trendier steak-house style minus pretension. The crowds sometimes overwhelm the kitchen and create slowdowns. But there's pretty good Caesar salad, famous Jack Daniels flaming wings, rib-eye steaks, garlic mashers, cilantro-lime chicken pasta, Black Angus burgers, and wood oven–baked fruit crisps. A newer Beaches in Scholls Town Center (14550 SW Murray Scholls Dr, Beaverton; 503/579-3737; map:JJ9) overlooks a man-made lake and features a similar menu. **COME HERE TO ESCAPE SOLITUDE.** *$$; AE, DIS, MC, V; checks OK; lunch, dinner every day; full bar; no reservations; map:CC6* &

Cactus Ya Ya / ★

15704 SE MILL PLAIN BLVD, VANCOUVER; 360/944-9292 This popular Southwestern-style cafe bundles enthusiasm and contagious camaraderie into a colorful package of great service, tons of fun, and surprisingly good food. Margaritas flow like the Rio Grande, their energy well suited to beer-battered halibut tacos with shredded cabbage, pico de gallo, and cilantro sauce. Enchiladas, fajitas, and jalapeño poppers join playful hybrids such as a turkey Reuben, and seasonings may speak up when least expected. That velvety white sauce over the mashed potatoes? Potent garlic cream sauce. The burrito tastes Asian? It's the peanut sauce. Many menu choices can be ordered in large or small sizes, or à la carte. Owners Jim and

Cheryl Rettig wished for a place to hang out with friends, and that's what they have. **COME HERE FOR FUN AND FULL FLAVORS.** *$; AE, MC, V; no checks; lunch, dinner every day; full bar; no reservations; map:CC1* &

Fa Fa Gourmet / ★★

11712 NE 4TH PLAIN BLVD, VANCOUVER; 360/260-1378 If you saw the wonderful 1994 Chinese movie, *Eat Drink Man Woman*, then you pretty much know the Chia family: a Taiwan-trained chef, his wife, five daughters, and relatives. Fa Fa means "prosper," a wish extended by this hospitable family to its customers. In a metro region where outstanding Thai and Vietnamese restaurants outnumber Chinese, it's worth crossing the Columbia to Vancouver's gourmet oasis of Hunan and Sichuan cuisine. Search the extensive menu beyond the familiar choices—cashew chicken, spring rolls—to discover unique house specials. Consider crisply fried prawns with honey-roasted walnuts in deep-red chili sauce, or the yin/yang of beef in a spicy ginger sauce paired with chicken and snow peas in light wine sauce. The partially open kitchen oversees a Northwest-flavored dining room where regional wines and beers highlight the drink menu. **COME HERE FOR THE BEST CHINESE FOOD IN VANCOUVER.** *$–$$; MC, V; no checks; lunch Mon–Sat, dinner every day; full bar; reservations recommended; map:AA3* &

Hudson's Bar & Grill / ★★★☆

7801 NE GREENWOOD DR (HEATHMAN LODGE), VANCOUVER; 360/816-6100 The dramatic log-and-stone Heathman Lodge, Hudson's hotel home, looks like it should be nestled in old-growth firs rather than standing beside a busy state highway opposite Vancouver Mall. Inside, grand, WPA-style hand-hewn wood beams, a massive slate fireplace, a real dugout canoe, and plush, rugged comfort set the scene for indigenous Northwest cuisine from an open, red-tiled kitchen. Without pretension, chef Mark Hosack prepares meals designed for taste and pleasure, not to dazzle. In the morning, there's a custardy bread-pudding French toast and a halibut Benedict. Midday, a crab-cake sandwich with chipotle aioli, grilled halibut with smoked mozzarella and bacon, and beer-battered onion rings are superb. In the evening, oven-roasted venison with sweet-potato hash and Northwest seafood stew in a charred tomato broth illustrate respect for local seasonal ingredients. Breads and pastries, baked in-house, appear as flatbread appetizers, pear and apple tart, and summertime lemonade cake. The location may be out of context with its neighborhood, but once you're cocooned inside, it becomes a beautiful escape. **COME HERE FOR GOURMET LODGE-STYLE DINING.** *$$$; AE, DC, DIS, JCB, MC, V; local checks only; breakfast, lunch, dinner every day; full bar; reservations recommended; www.heathmanlodge.com/hudsons; map:AA3* &

Little Italy's Trattoria / ★

901 WASHINGTON ST, VANCOUVER; 360/737-2363 / 204 NE PARK PLAZA DR (CASCADE PARK), VANCOUVER; 360/883-1325 In the spirit of Nona's kitchen, this friendly trattoria still dares to dress in red-and-white-checked tablecloths while other Italian restaurants have changed to linens and black. Homestyle design and honest cuisine—forget updated sophistication—reign. These family-owned restaurants trace roots to Naples, where pollo cacciatore and clams in white wine with linguini are rooted in recipes passed through generations. Without fuss or pretension, but dosed with Italian pride, the kitchen sticks close to tradition: spinach ravioli in sun-dried tomato pesto on a bed of marinara, ziti with crumbled meatballs and tomato sauce, pizza, and soft garlic bread. The simple approach has bred a local minichain: in addition to the two trattorias, look for Pasta Cucina at Fishers Landing (212 NE 165th St, Vancouver; 360/882-5122; map:CC1) and Little Italy's Cucina in Portland (2601 SE Clinton St, Clinton; 503/239-4306; map:II5). **COME HERE FOR PASTA AND RED SAUCE.** *$$; MC, V; no checks; lunch Mon–Sat (Washington St), lunch every day (Cascade Park), dinner every day; beer and wine; reservations recommended; www.littleitalysinc.com; map:CC6; map:CC2* &

Oregon Wine Country

Dundee Bistro / ★★

100 SW 7TH ST (AT HWY 99), DUNDEE; 503/554-1650 Wine pioneers Nancy and Dick Ponzi, founders of acclaimed Ponzi Vineyards, have never acknowledged limitations. After the vineyard, these industry leaders and advocates not only founded Oregon's first microbrewery (BridgePort, in 1984), they built the Dundee Bistro and Ponzi Wine Bar complex as a wine-and-food destination on the road through the heart of lush vineyards. The caramel-brushed stucco walls house a country-contemporary space brightened with natural light, an exhibition kitchen with a tandoori oven, and bistro bustle. Cuisine focuses on Willamette Valley organic and sustainable agricultural products—and, of course, an in-depth wine list with ample by-the-glass selections. An ambitious menu includes Manila clams in a garlic-shallot wine-and-cream sauce, asparagus-olive tapenade, house-made sausage-fennel pizza, prosciutto-wrapped scallops, a fall foragers' mushroom plate, frizzled onions, and Muscovy duck confit. For dessert, the dark chocolate soufflé cake with house-made vanilla ice cream is dreamy, and it's especially delightful served in the courtyard on a warm day. **COME HERE FOR FISH-AND-CHIPS AND PONZI WINE.** *$$$; AE, MC, V; local checks only; lunch, dinner every day; full bar; reservations recommended;* &

The Joel Palmer House / ★★★½

600 FERRY ST, DAYTON; 503/864-2995 Jack and Heidi Czarnecki came to Oregon in 1996 to find the perfect marriage of wild mushrooms and civilized pinot noir, and they've created a restaurant that no gastronome will want to miss. A mushroom scholar, hunter, author, and award-winning chef, Jack forages in secret locations for hat-shaped morels and black, trumpet-shaped chanterelles, two of the many mushrooms that define his menu at the historic Palmer House. The restaurant occupies a lovingly restored, white-pillared home with lush gardens, built in 1857 by pioneer Joel Palmer. European service—each server does every job—governs two small, elegant dining rooms. Not all dishes are built around wild mushrooms and wine, but Heidi's three-mushroom tart has graced the menu from the start and is a regionwide, glamorous classic: rich, textured, and tall like a wedge of chocolate pie. The Czarneckis call their cooking "freestyle," as it applies global inspiration to locally farmed and fished ingredients, organic when possible. Signature mushroom soup, using puréed suillus mushrooms, is a third-generation family recipe; upgraded beef stroganoff swims with Oregon white truffles; local pork tenderloin stars with applewood bacon, Spanish rice, and tomatillo sauce; wild salmon complements curried couscous with porcini duxelles. Heidi fashions desserts (so far, without mushrooms) such as apricot-walnut bread pudding, rhubarb Napoleon, and strawberry-rosewater sorbet. Naturally, a fantastic wine list offers pairings specially selected for the menu. It's a 45-minute drive from Portland, but worth it—and then some. **COME HERE FOR A FEAST OF WILD MUSHROOMS.** *$$$; AE, DIS, MC, V; checks OK; dinner Tues–Sat; full bar; reservations recommended; www.joelpalmerhouse.com;* &

Nick's Italian Café / ★★★

521 NE 3RD ST, MCMINNVILLE; 503/434-4471 Back in 1977, long before Yamhill County became Oregon's wine mecca, charismatic Nick Peirano was entertaining local winemakers with fine, prix-fixe Italian dinners. Over Nick's grandmother's pesto minestrone soup, always served in a tureen to encourage seconds, these winemakers held informal wine tastings and shared new bottlings. The historic downtown McMinnville storefront still has the feel of a North Beach haunt, reflecting Nick's childhood in San Francisco's Italian community. A wine list deep in Oregon vintages—including a few choice '70s pinot noirs aging in the cellar—complements house-made pasta offerings that, like the menu, change regularly. The five-course menu might include Caesar salad, minestrone soup, crab-and-pine-nut lasagna, rabbit braised in pinot gris and rosemary, and chocolate brandy hazelnut torte. Or pears with prosciutto, ravioli, salt-grilled salmon, Gorgonzola polenta, and gin-and-tonic ice. Each dish is prepared with a wine pairing in mind. Nick himself makes the fresh pasta and minestrone, then takes his charisma to the dining room, where he chats with loyal customers, celebrates a successful harvest with winemakers, and assures that each guest enjoys a gracious visit. **COME HERE FOR GRANDMA'S PESTO MINESTRONE SOUP.** *$$$; AE, MC, V; checks OK; dinner Tues–Sun; beer and wine; reservations recommended;* &

Red Hills Provincial Dining / ★★☆

276 HWY 99W, DUNDEE; 503/538-8224 Nestled snugly in a 1912 Craftsman-style house, Red Hills deserves a healthy share of the attention directed to its higher-profile wine-country neighbors. For years it has quietly and unpretentiously lavished exceptional service, reliable European country cuisine, and a strong, award-winning wine list upon devoted patrons. Dinner is served on the deck and in the cozy living and dining rooms, which are personalized with souvenir plates on the walls and wine bottles displayed on a high encircling shelf. Changing its menu by season, the kitchen leans to solid preparations such as oysters with sesame-seed crust, hand-cut organic beef filet, veal osso buco, sautéed sole with corn-arugula salsa, and wild-mushroom pasta with sherry-rum cream sauce. A perfectly accomplished salad of field greens couples toasted hazelnuts, Parmigiano-Reggiano, and balsamic vinaigrette. Desserts made in-house include white-chocolate crème brûlée, espresso-chocolate torte, ice creams, and sorbets. **COME HERE FOR GREAT FOOD**

WITHOUT PRETENSION. *$$; AE, MC, V; checks OK; dinner every day; full bar; reservations recommended;* &

Tina's / ★★☆

760 HWY 99W, DUNDEE; 503/538-8880 A tiny jewel, this modest single-story home with an emerald-and-garnet palate hides culinary treasures coveted by savvy Oregonians. Tina Landfried and husband David Bergen share ownership and chef responsibilities in two updated and classy but simply designed dining rooms, divided by a fireplace. They offer warm hospitality, excellent service, and exemplary cuisine: clean, classic French techniques with impeccably fresh local ingredients, including herbs raised in the front garden and a few fruits and vegetables grown at home. The limited menu, which adds an occasional dash of Asian inspiration, delights diners with salmon spring rolls accompanied by hazelnut dipping sauce, corn soufflé, carrot soup, rib-eye with portobello mushrooms and hand-cut fries, duck breast with ginger-fig sauce, and buttermilk-almond cake with fresh strawberries and cream. Full-flavored, house-made sourdough baguettes use a 13-year-old wild yeast starter built from local chardonnay grapes. Don't be surprised if you share the dining room with winery owners—many of whose vintages are carried on Tina's beverage list—and workers fresh from the fields. **COME HERE FOR SEASONAL SOUPS, BAGUETTES, AND WINE.** *$$$; DIS, MC, V; checks OK; lunch Tues–Fri, dinner every day; full bar; reservations recommended;* &

LODGINGS

LODGINGS

Hotels by Star Rating

★★★★
The Heathman Hotel

★★★
The Benson Hotel
5th Avenue Suites Hotel
Hilton Portland & Executive Tower
Portland's White House
RiverPlace Hotel
The Westin Portland

★★⯪
Embassy Suites Hotel Portland–
 Downtown
The Governor Hotel
Heathman Lodge
Hotel Lucia
Hotel Vintage Plaza
The Lion and the Rose
The Paramount Hotel
Portland Marriott City Center

★★
Avalon Hotel & Spa
DoubleTree Hotel Portland–
 Columbia River, Jantzen Beach
DoubleTree Hotel Portland–Lloyd
 Center
Embassy Suites Hotel Portland–
 Washington Square
Heron Haus Bed and Breakfast
Inn @ Northrup Station
MacMaster House
Portland Marriott Downtown
Rose Cottage
Sheraton Portland Airport Hotel

★★⯪
Courtyard Portland Downtown/
 Lloyd Center

Edgefield
Greenwood Inn and Suites
Hilton Garden Inn Portland/Lake
 Oswego
Holiday Inn Crowne Plaza
Holiday Inn Portland–Downtown
The Kennedy School
The Mark Spencer Hotel
Portland Guest House
Residence Inn Portland Downtown/
 Lloyd Center
Residence Inn Portland Downtown at
 RiverPlace

★
Century Garden
Clyde Hotel
Days Inn
Four Points by Sheraton Portland
 Downtown
The Georgian House Bed and Break-
 fast
Hostelling International–Portland,
 Hawthorne District
Hostelling International–Portland,
 Northwest
Lakeshore Inn
Mallory Hotel
Mount Scott Hideaway
Park Lane Suites
River's Edge Bed and Breakfast
RiverView GuestHouse Bed &
 Breakfast
Silver Cloud Inn
Sullivans' Gulch B&B

Downtown/Southwest Portland

Avalon Hotel & Spa / ★★

0455 SW HAMILTON CT, SW MACADAM; 503/802-5800 OR 888/556-4402 An oasis of calm a short hop from downtown, the Avalon overlooks the Willamette River from the John's Landing district off Macadam Avenue (Route 43). The contemporary, red-brick boutique hotel, which opened in 2002, includes a popular day spa. Commissioned works by Northwest artists hang in the two-story lobby, where guests relax beside a fireplace in velvet-upholstered sofas. Yet there's an Asian flair to the seven-story hotel's design, which strives to bring the outside in with tall floor-to-ceiling windows and contemporary wood furnishings. Seventy-eight of the Avalon's 99 rooms, including all 18 fireplace suites, have riverview balconies; all feature marble baths with double vanities, CD players, and high-speed Internet access. If you're headed downtown, leave your car parked here and take the complimentary town car service. The beautiful, 13,000-square-foot Avalon Spa & Fitness Club (503/802-5900) offers traditional European (Hungarian spa kur) and Asian (shiatsu) treatments. Adjacent Rivers Restaurant (503/802-5850; see review in the Restaurants chapter) thrives with the culinary touch of Rolland Wesen, who happens to be the son-in-law of famed chef Jacques Pepin. *$$$; AE, DC, DIS, MC, V; checks OK; www.avalonhotelandspa.com; map:II6* &

The Benson Hotel / ★★★

309 SW BROADWAY; 503/228-2000 OR 800/426-0670 Although the 21st century has brought a slew of new luxury hotels to downtown Portland, the Benson, open since 1913, remains the grand dame of them all. Many locals who want to spend a night downtown opt for the Benson (rates start at $169 per night, with packages and special rates often available), and it's still the first choice for politicos and film stars; with 287 rooms, there's space for everyone. The palatial lobby—a fine place to linger over a drink—features a stamped-tin ceiling, mammoth chandeliers, stately columns, and a generous fireplace, surrounded by panels of carved Circassian walnut imported from Russia. Guest rooms may lack the grandeur of the public areas, but they are dignified and sophisticated, with modern furnishings in conservative blacks and beiges. Characterized by service that's impeccably competent if sometimes impersonal, the Benson is literally and figuratively corporate (it's now owned by Coast Hotels & Resorts) but the place is well loved nonetheless. London Grill (see review in the Restaurants chapter), with its white linens, upholstered chairs, tableside steak Diane, and formal service, caters to an old-fashioned dining crowd; the newer El Gaucho (also reviewed in the Restaurants chapter) features fresh seafood and steak and is also quite formal. *$$$–$$$$; AE, CB, DC, DIS, JCB, MC, V; checks OK; www.bensonhotel.com; map:J3* &

Clyde Hotel / ★

1022 SW STARK ST; 503/224-8000 A simple European charm extends from the mahogany-paneled, mosaic-tiled lobby to the overlooking breakfast mezzanine of the newly renovated Clyde. Built as a hotel in 1912, the National Register property retains its original Commercial-style architectural

135

DAY SPAS: I FEEL PRETTY

While Portland's economy waxes and wanes, spa business just continues to wax—both literally and figuratively. Each neighborhood has its oases where patrons step out of corporate life into plush robes and plastic slippers, where oiled fingers are ready to knead away a workweek of stress.

AEQUIS: AN INCLUSIVE RETREAT (130 NW Hoyt St, Pearl District; 503/223-7847). This spa has an anonymous storefront, but walk up a flight of stairs and you'll enter a soft-focus world of dark walls, pale lights, elegant sofas, and a staff of geishas. Owner Megan Klein was hired by self-help guru Tony Robbins to create the Aequis magic at his Namale Resort in Fiji.

BAREFOOT SAGE (1844 SE Hawthorne Ave, Hawthorne; 503/239-7116). Here detoxification starts at the lowest extremity. A menu of 24 foot massages are geared toward flushing energy through the system, detoxifying the blood and pumping up circulation. They're fun, too.

JENNIFER'S SPA AT THE BOB SHOP (555 SW Oak St, Downtown; 503/226-2886). The hands of aesthetician/owner Jennifer Stoloff have been providing expert massage for 25 years. This facialist of choice for local professionals also provides services as diverse as permanent eye makeup, ayurvedic treatments, microdermabrasion, and sophisticated European facials.

PAT WARREN'S FACES UNLIMITED (25 NW 23rd Pl, Northwest; 503/227-7366). Former model and teacher Warren—a grandmother with flawless skin—brings decades of experience as an aesthetician to her broad range of European skin treat-

design, including tripartite windows with embellished brick pilasters and cast-stone cornice detailing. New owners are refurbishing all 96 guest rooms, retaining original woodwork, mosaic tilework, Victorian claw-foot tubs, and steam heating; at this writing, the 30 fourth-floor rooms have been completed. There are TVs but no individual room phones, although phone and Internet service are available in a guest lounge. A handful of rooms without attached baths appeal to budget-oriented travelers. Rates include continental breakfast. *$$; AE, DIS, MC, V; no checks; www.clydehotel.com; map:J2*

Days Inn / ★

1414 SW 6TH AVE; 503/221-1611 OR 800/899-0248 The nearest hotel to Portland State University flies below the radar of many Portland visitors. The five-story motor inn, though nondescript, offers clean, comfortable, well-maintained rooms with all standard amenities at bargain prices. Prints of Ansel Adams's famed national-park photographs decorate the walls. There's a full-service restaurant and lounge, a heated outdoor swimming pool (open seasonally), and onments, from the exclusive renovator facial to body masking and polishing.

SALON NYLA (Embassy Suites Hotel, 327 SW Pine St, Old Town; 503/228-0389). Nyla offers facials to full body treatments using all Aveda products in a peaceful, contemporary space. The facial produces a spellbinding glow, and Giorgio is a master at haircuts and color treatments.

SYLVIE DAY SPA AND SALON (1706 NW Glisan St, Northwest; 503/222-5054). A full range of body treatments, hand massage, facials, and waxing services are available here. The signature clay facial says *hasta la vista* to wrinkles, stress lines, and weary eyes.

TED ISAACS SALON (1620 SE Bybee Blvd, Westmoreland; 503/223-0639). Facialist and makeup artist Karen Acheson has exclusive rights to Epicuran products— magic little jars of colored liquids designed for medical use in treating patients with burned or discolored skin. They just happen to make regular skin shine with new life.

WILD OATS (3535 NE 15th Ave, Alameda; 503/288-3414). Imagine a spa atop a grocery shop. Then imagine your surprise when you enter this posh getaway designed with spacious dressing, waiting, and service rooms. Treatments range from seaweed wraps to Vichy showers to Dr. Hauschka holistic skin-care treatments.

After all that body work, the best spot in Portland for the finishing touch is **THE MAKE-UP STUDIO** (621 SW Alder St, Downtown; 503/233-4286), run by Darbey Bacchus Budd. A nationally recognized makeup artist and broadcast celebrity with his own line of cosmetics, Budd makes up news anchors and provides personalized group and individual lessons at his startling black-walled studio near Pioneer Courthouse Square.

—Gail Dana

site parking. Breakfast is included in the room price. *$; AE, CB, DC, DIS, JCB, MC, V; checks OK; www.thedaysinn.com/portland05313; map:E2* &

Embassy Suites Hotel Portland–Downtown / ★★☆

319 SW PINE ST; 503/279-9000 This newish hotel on the edge of Old Town has a pedigree: it's the former Multnomah Hotel, a lavish hostelry that hosted U.S. presidents and royalty, plus many of the Hollywood stars who passed through town, from 1912 until its closure in 1965. For the next 30 years the place led a sort of Orwellian existence as home to a large number of boxy federal offices until the Embassy Suites chain bought it in 1997 and remodeled it to restore some of its original grandeur. The spacious lobby is easily the finest room, with its gilt-touched columns and grand piano; it opens into the Portland Steak and Chophouse, a fine-dining option (see review in the Restaurants chapter). The 275 guest rooms, all two-room suites, boast lots of nice touches—marble baths, queen-size sofa sleepers, wet bars with microwave ovens and minirefrigerators, and a coffee-table book describing the building's history. In underground Arcadian Gardens, complimentary hot breakfasts and happy hours are offered. An hourglass-shaped pool is great for

children; there's also an exercise room, two saunas, and a pair of spa pools. *$$$;*
AE, DC, DIS, MC, V; no checks; www.embassysuites.com; map:J5 &

5th Avenue Suites Hotel / ★★★

506 SW WASHINGTON ST; 503/222-0001 OR 800/711-2971 When you walk into your room at the 5th Avenue Suites, don't be surprised to see the teddy bear on your pillow. Teddy was a "cinnamon bear" who, according to an old radio series, lived at the Lipman Wolfe department store in downtown Portland. In fact, this *is* the Lipman Wolfe store. Built in 1912, the elegant but aging structure was transformed into a fine 10-story hotel by the Kimpton Group in 1996. Nearly two-thirds of the 221 rooms are spacious suites, but even those that are not have a sense of grandeur. Two sets of French doors usher guests in; yellow-and-white-striped wallpaper makes the rooms look like well-wrapped presents. Each suite has three phones (with data ports), a couple of televisions, plus such traveler-choice details as ironing boards, hair dryers, and plush cotton robes. The workout room is open 24 hours a day. The staff is gracious and the bellhops are extremely attentive; and, like its sister inn, the Hotel Vintage Plaza (see review), the 5th Avenue Suites welcomes the occasional dog or lizard. The Kimpton Group has covered its bases: everything from indoor parking (with an unloading area to protect you from rain) to the stunning but welcoming lobby with its large corner fireplace, where you'll find complimentary coffee and newspapers in the morning and wine tastings come evening. The Red Star Tavern & Roast House is a very good open-spaced bistro (see review in the Restaurants chapter), and you'll find an art gallery and a small Aveda day spa on the ground floor. *$$$; AE, DC, DIS, JCB, MC, V; checks OK; www.5thavenuesuites.com; map:I4* &

Four Points Sheraton–Portland Downtown / ★

50 SW MORRISON ST; 503/221-0711 OR 888/627-8263 Business travelers looking for convenient yet modestly priced downtown lodging may gravitate to this Starwood-operated property, the former Riverside Inn. Located opposite Gov. Tom McCall Waterfront Park near the foot of the Morrison Bridge, the Four Points prides itself on a European inn style of hospitality. Its 140 rooms (16 with balconies overlooking the Willamette River) are cozy but provide all basic amenities, from a desk (with a two-line speaker phone and data port), to on-site parking, to free passes for Bally's next-door fitness club. If you've brought Fido, he's welcome here, too. The spacious Riverside Restaurant opens into an intimate nonsmoking lounge. *$$; AE, DC, DIS, MC, V; checks OK; www.starwood.com/fourpoints/; map:H6* &

The Governor Hotel / ★★★

611 SW 10TH AVE; 503/224-3400 OR 800/554-3456 In these years of the Lewis and Clark bicentennial, the Governor is certain to have added appeal: spanning one wall of its lobby is Melinda Morey's dramatic four-panel mural depicting scenes from that landmark journey of discovery. Opened in 1909 in the heady days following Portland's 1905 Lewis and Clark Exposition, the hotel lives and breathes the Northwest. Arts and Crafts–style furnishings, leather club chairs, yards of mahogany, and a wood-burning fireplace give the lobby a clubby feel that carries into Jake's Grill (see review in the Restaurants chapter), the storied adjoining restaurant. The 100 spacious guest rooms are decorated in earth tones and hung with early photos of Northwest Indian tribes, circa 1900; all have standard furnishings and upscale amenities. Some also have whirlpool tubs, while suites feature gas-burning fireplaces, wet bars, and balconies. Although we find access to the West Wing (the 1923 Princeton Building) a little awkward, the upper-floor rooms on its northeast corner sport the best city views. (Rooms 5013 and 6013 are the only standard rooms with private balconies.) Guests have 24-hour maid service and business-center access, as well as use of the adults-only athletic club. *$$$; AE, DC, DIS, JCB, MC, V; checks OK; www.govhotel.com; map:I2* &

The Heathman Hotel / ★★★★

1001 SW BROADWAY; 503/241-4100 OR 800/551-0011 A revolutionary personal-service concept has helped the intimate, elegant Heathman rise like cream to the top of Portland's downtown lodging brew. In late 2001, the traditional front desk was replaced by "floating consoles"— staffed by young men and women who act not only as desk clerks but as personal concierges, room-service attendants, and even tour guides. "We wanted to achieve a more direct interaction with our guests," explained general manager Jeff Jobe. The Heathman's location in the heart of the Cultural District (a breezeway links it to Arlene Schnitzer Concert Hall and the Portland Center for the Performing Arts) is underscored by its commitment to the arts; 20 signed Andy Warhol lithographs are just part of a collection that includes a fanciful Henk Pander mural and two large 18th-century oils by Claude Galle. The common rooms are handsomely appointed with Burmese teak or eucalyptus paneling, and the elegant Tea Room is a great place to enjoy an afternoon cup or evening jazz performance. Among the 150 guest rooms, the Symphony Suites, with a sofa and king bed, and the Warhol Suite, featuring that artist's original paintings, are our favorites. Depending on your interests, you might be impressed by the video collection, the library (with author-signed volumes from those who have stayed here), or the fitness suite (personal trainer available). And you're just steps (or room service) away from one of the city's finest restaurants, where chef Philippe Boulot designs culinary masterpieces (see review of the Heathman Restaurant and Bar in the Restaurants chapter). *$$$–$$$$; AE, DC, DIS, JCB, MC, V; checks OK; www.heathmanhotel.com; map:G2* &

Hilton Portland & Executive Tower / ★★★

921 SW 6TH AVE; 503/226-1611 OR 800/HILTONS With 782 rooms in two catty-corner buildings at Sixth and Taylor, the Hilton is easily Oregon's largest hotel. Its new 20-story Executive Tower, which opened in June 2002, added 327 nonsmoking "boutique-style" rooms to the mix; eight floors of parking surmount the ground-level lobby before accommodations begin at higher levels. In the original 24-story hotel, a sweeping staircase rises from a grand lobby to meeting areas and the spacious Pavilion Ballroom; original artwork is by prominent Oregon artists. Both buildings have full-service athletic clubs with indoor swimming pools, saunas, steam rooms, and whirlpools. All guest rooms are elegantly decorated and technologically ahead of the pack with high-speed Internet access, Web TV, ergonomic chairs, and other features that modern business people savor; especially notable are the 31 Business Kings on the top floor of the Tower, with leather recliners, 32-inch televisions, and L-shaped computer desks with modems and color printer-copier-fax-scanner units. Upper-floor rooms rise above surrounding high-rises to afford views either of the West Hills or Mount Hood. Alexander's, on the 23rd floor, offers gourmet Northwest fare and a city panorama; the casual streetside Bistro 921 has an open kitchen. In the new Tower, the Porto Terra Tuscan Grill & Bar serves fine Mediterranean cuisine. *$$$; AE, DC, MC, V; checks OK; www.portland.hilton.com; map: H3* &

Hotel Lucia / ★★☆

400 SW BROADWAY; 503/225-1717 OR 877/225-1717 Black-and-white photographs by Pulitzer Prize–winning journalist David Hume Kennerly, a former Oregonian and one-time official White House cameraman, give this innovative hotel a touch of contemporary class. Opened in April 2002 after a $5 million redesign, the Lucia boasts an ambience of sophisticated minimalism that extends from the lobby to the 128 guest rooms. The white-limestone lobby is accented by walls of dark *sapele*, an African rain-forest tree. Chrome and stainless steel is evident in the decor of the spacious rooms, which feature plush bedding, high-speed wireless Internet access, and top-of-the-line amenities. Room service is from the fine Thai restaurant, Typhoon! (see review in the Restaurants chapter), which adjoins the Lucia's lobby. *$$$; AE, DC, DIS, MC, V; checks OK; www.hotellucia.com; map:J4* &

Hotel Vintage Plaza / ★★☆

 **422 SW BROADWAY; 503/228-1212 OR 800/243-0555** Oregon has some of the nation's finest wine country, and the Vintage Plaza celebrates that heritage. From the wine-colored palette and playful glass "grapes" in the decor, to the happy-hour Northwest wine tasting, this intimate (107-room) Kimpton Group boutique hotel is as playful yet satisfying as a glass of good pinot noir. Lodged in a restored 1894 National Register building with an upscale European-inn appeal, the 10-story hotel has a gracious staff and a charming lobby with antique furnishings and a marble fireplace. The wine theme extends to the guest rooms, most of which are named for Oregon wineries and vineyards—although the layered-tapestry look is more reminiscent of Italy. Particularly delightful are the top-floor Starlight rooms, with angled, greenhouse-style windows for romantic bedtime planet viewing. Below are nine two-story townhouse units. If you have a pet, you'll find it so welcome that the desk staff serves "treats"; the hotel also has a small fitness center. Pazzo Ristorante on the main floor serves excellent northern Italian cuisine in a variety of settings (see review in the Restaurants chapter). Pazzoria, next door, sells pastries, crusty Italian breads, and panini sandwiches to take out or eat in. This hotel is a good value, especially on weekends, when rates drop. *$$–$$$; AE, DC, DIS, JCB, MC, V; checks OK; www.vintageplaza.com; map:J4* &

Mallory Hotel / ★

729 SW 15TH AVE; 503/223-6311 OR 800/228-8657 Rufus Mallory was 81 years old when the hotel that bears his name opened for business in 1912. It was a "strictly modern, high-class, eight-story, fireproof structure." That was 45 years after he had, as a young congressman, passionately advocated the impeachment of President Andrew Johnson. No one wants to get rid of Mallory's hotel—certainly not the dedicated regular guests, many of whom have been staying here since they were kids. Though it may feel long in the tooth, the homey Mallory is one of the best bargains in town: $90 for a spotless double, $165 for a suite. If $20 a night downtown valet-parking charges have you shaking your head, know that the Mallory—on a quiet hillside just a 10- to 15-minute stroll from Pioneer Courthouse Square—offers free parking in its garage. Crystal chandeliers, the hotel's trademark, hang above sturdy, leather-upholstered furniture in the broad lobby. Guest rooms aren't fancy, but they have refrigerators and wireless Internet access, and your pet is welcome ($10 fee). A continental breakfast is included, or opt for German pancakes in the charming cafe, where service is almost motherly. Before retiring, enjoy a drink in the quirky Driftwood Lounge. *$$; AE, DC, DIS, JCB, MC, V; checks OK; www.malloryhotel.com; map:J1* &

The Mark Spencer Hotel / ★★☆

409 SW 11TH AVE; 503/224-3293 OR 800/548-3934 Perhaps no Portland hotel is more dedicated to the local arts community than the Mark Spencer. Powell's City of Books and the Pearl District galleries have dubbed it their "official" hotel; arts packages include admission to major shows or Portland Art Museum exhibits; and at any time of year, you'll find touring thespians making a home-away-from-home in the 101 modestly priced rooms and suites of this low-key, European-style inn. Every room is nicely but not ostentatiously decorated, with a fully equipped kitchen and wireless Internet access; suites also have sofa sleepers. The pet-friendly property rises around an entry courtyard; amenities include a guest laundry, library, and rooftop garden, complimentary continental breakfast and afternoon tea, and a copy of the *New York Times*. Three entire floors are dedicated to nonsmokers. *$$; AE, DC, DIS, MC, V; checks OK; www.markspencer.com; map:J2* &

The Paramount Hotel / ★★★

808 SW TAYLOR ST; 503/223-9900 OR 800/663-1144 If the South Park Blocks represent downtown Portland's ties to the earth, one could imagine the new Paramount as reaching for the stars. The 15-story luxury hotel opened in early 2000 one block north of the greensward, at the corner of SW Park Avenue, and it has since built a reputation for sophistication and innovation. A compact yet elegant seating area sits front and center in the marble-floored lobby, from which doors on either side open to the Dragonfish Asian Café (see review in the Restaurants chapter). Elevators rise to 154 guest rooms, each one simply yet impressively decorated with Biedermeier furnishings (including a polished wood desk and armoire) and provided with a granite-finished bathroom, high-speed wireless Internet, and a top-end amenities package. The roomy Executive rooms have corner views and jetted bathtubs. The hotel also has a modern fitness center, a business center, and a staff that will take the time to help you with any directions or arrangements. *$$$–$$$$; AE, CB, DC, DIS, JCB, MC, V; checks OK; www.paramounthotel.net; map:G2* &

Portland Marriott City Center / ★★★

520 SW BROADWAY; 503/226-6300 OR 800/228-9290 What a concept: a new boutique-style hotel specifically designed with the business traveler in mind. All 249

141

rooms have high-speed Internet and other essentials, such as a two-line speaker phone (with voice mail and data ports) on a well-lit work desk with roll-out computer table, a daily newspaper, and satellite TV. Bold room decor, with heavy dark-wood furnishings accented by deep reds and greens, extends to three concierge levels that share broad city views from the 20th-floor lounge. The streetside entrance lobby is small but elegant, its full-wall maple panels curving around a sweeping staircase that rises to a mezzanine lounge and the casual Bannisters on Broadway restaurant. Added bonuses for Marriott visitors are a 24-hour fitness center (with whirlpool) and a guest laundry. *$$$; AE, CB, DC, DIS, JCB, MC, V; checks OK; www.marriotthotels.com/pdxct; map:I3* ♿

Portland Marriott Downtown / ★★

1401 SW NAITO PKWY; 503/226-7600 OR 800/228-9290 There's lots of glitter, bustle, and convention hustle at this large hotel that would be a standard business lodging except for one important quality: a terrific location beside the Willamette River yet just two blocks from Keller Auditorium. There are 503 cozy rooms in this the 14-story, V-shaped Marriott; we especially like the riverview kings, though all rooms offer the same subdued decor, deluxe amenities, and high-speed Internet access. The 24-hour health club—with access free to hotel guests—ranks among the best in town with its indoor swimming pool, state-of-the-art cardio and universal equipment, free weights, and men's and women's saunas off the full locker rooms. Allie's American Grill serves breakfast and lunch buffets, as well as full dinners; Champions Sports Bar offers light meals; and there's another lounge and espresso shop in the lobby, along with a business center and a gift-and-sundry shop. *$$$; AE, CB, DC, DIS, JCB, MC, V; checks OK; www.marriott.com/pdxor; map:E4* ♿

Residence Inn Portland Downtown at RiverPlace / ★★☆

2115 SW RIVER PKWY; 503/552-9500 OR 800/331-3131 Popular among business people who want to escape the hectic city-center scene but still be close enough for a quick shuttle, this new (2003) hotel beside the Willamette River has 258 units, every one a suite. Although there's no restaurant—the nearest are a few blocks away on the RiverPlace esplanade—each room has a full kitchen; and if you provide a list, the hotel will do your grocery shopping. Skip the eggs, though: a hot buffet-style breakfast is served in the lobby daily, along with the morning paper. Each room has a king-size bed and such business-sensitive amenities as high-speed Internet access and dual-line phones with data ports. There's also an indoor pool, jetted spa, and exercise facility. *$$$; AE, CB, DC, DIS, JCB, MC, V; checks OK; www.marriott.com/pdxri; map:B6* ♿

RiverPlace Hotel / ★★★

1510 SW HARBOR WY; 503/228-3233 OR 800/227-1333 If you're looking for a room with a view, look no further than RiverPlace. Facing directly upon the busy Willamette River (and the boat show that comes with it), this casually elegant hotel is lovely to look in at and glorious to look out from. The best rooms among 74 kings, doubles, and suites face the water or look north across park lawns to the downtown cityscape. Decor has a Cape Cod appeal, with beiges and powder blues picking up the river's nuances. Live plants and botanical prints bring the outside in. Plush furnishings include teak and oak paneling, wingback chairs, overstuffed sofas, hand-woven rugs, and CD players. Ten adjacent private condominiums—with dining and living rooms and wood-burning fireplaces—are popular with visiting entertainers and athletes. Concierge service is among the best in the city; room service is available 24 hours from the stunning Lucère restaurant (see review in the Restaurants chapter); and a complimentary continental breakfast can be brought to your room along with the day's newspaper. Massage and spa treatments are available by appointment. There's no charge to use the adjacent RiverPlace Athletic Club (including an indoor pool and running track), but on nice days there's plenty of opportunity for outdoor exercise: wide, paved paths lead through the fountains and monuments of adjacent Governor Tom McCall Waterfront Park. *$$$–$$$$; AE, DC, DIS, JCB, MC, V; checks OK; www.riverplacehotel.com; map:D5* &

The Westin Portland / ★★★

750 SW ALDER ST; 503/294-9000 OR 800/937-8461 If your bed is the single most important furnishing in your hotel room—and Westin says it is—then this hotel has got it right. With its 1999 opening, Westin introduced its trademark Heavenly Bed, a 10-layer nest of goose down, duvet, comforter, and pillows that will have you convinced you're resting on cloud nine. (If Rover has joined you, the hotel will provide a Heavenly Dog Bed.) All but 28 of the hotel's 205 rooms are classified as "deluxe" (most of the rest are suites); they also feature high-tech work areas with ergonomic leather desk chairs, and very spacious bathrooms with walk-in showers and separate tubs, marble-top vanities, and makeup mirrors. If they're available, request one of the 32 corner rooms. The Westin's handsome design blends modern European elements with natural stone and wood; a ground-floor "living room" with a large fireplace, and a separate and intimate library, are charming places to take morning coffee. The Daily Grill serves three meals daily; a fitness center features an array of weight and cardio machines. *$$$$; AE, CB, DC, DIS, JCB, MC, V; checks OK; www.westin.com/portland; map:I3* &

Northwest Portland/King's Hill

Heron Haus Bed and Breakfast / ★★

2545 NW WESTOVER RD; 503/274-1846 Hostess Julie Keppeler loves "stuff that moves." Her spacious 1904 English Tudor home, at the foot of the West Hills just four blocks from NW "Trendy-Third" Street, is a tasteful museum of mobiles and motion toys. From the original oak-parquet floors of the elegant parlor to the mahogany paneling of the library, from the living room to the conservatory that overlooks a fountain patio, you'll also find books, fine art, and ethnic basketry. A collection of family photos reminds you that you're a guest in the Keppeler home—which is entirely nonsmoking. Each of the six guest rooms (with Hawaiian names) has a king- or queen-size bed, private bath, fireplace, air-conditioning, cable TV, and computer jack: a midweek corporate rate attracts single business people.

The Kulia Room features an elevated spa tub with a city view and deluxe bathing accoutrements. Breakfast is an artistic affair—a full continental breakfast designed with advice from Sinclair Philip of Vancouver Island's famed Sooke Harbour House. *$$$; MC, V; checks OK; www.heronhaus.com; map:GG7*

Hostelling International–Portland, Northwest / ★

1818 NW GLISAN ST; 503/241-2783 Frequent hostellers know that a drawback to this budget-lodging system is the need to share a dormitory room with a dozen or more fellow travelers. That's not the case here. Lodged in a restored circa-1900 home two blocks from McMenamins' Mission Theater, this hostel's dorms (separated by gender) have no more than four beds, and private rooms may be reserved by couples or families. Bathrooms are shared, as are coin-op laundry and a community kitchen and dining area. A courtesy phone and Internet access are available in the lounge, which features a coffee bar. Unavailable to anyone residing in the greater Portland area, rooms are $15–$18 a night for Hostelling International members, $18–$21 for nonmembers; private rooms range $30–$52. More private rooms may be available in a nearby hostel-operated guesthouse. *$; DIS, JCB, MC, V; no checks; www.2oregonhostels.com; map:HH7*

Inn @ Northrup Station / ★★

2025 NW NORTHRUP ST; 503/224-0543 OR 800/224-1180 The sole hotel in the heart of trendy Northwest Portland, the Inn @ Northrup Station is also, beyond a doubt, the city's most eclectic in decor. Industrial chic with nods to Art Deco and '70s retro, this all-suite boutique hotel startles the newcomer with colors the hotel defines as "energetic": lime green, lemon yellow, plum purple. Parking is free, and there's a streetcar stop (the "station") outside the front door. Opposite the small registration desk is a sleek lobby—fused-glass art hanging from its ceiling—where continental breakfast is served daily beside a fireplace. Long hallways lead to the suites, all with marble bathrooms, executive desks (with two-line phones and data ports), and private balconies or patios. The fully furnished kitchens (with granite countertops and maple cabinets) may inspire you to stay in and cook, but several of Portland's finest restaurants are just around the corner on 21st Street. If you're clueless as to how to spend your time, the desk will provide you a toll-free number for a tarot reading. *$$–$$$; AE, DC, DIS, MC, V; checks OK; www.northrupstation.com; map:HH7* &

MacMaster House / ★★

1041 SW VISTA AVE; 503/223-7362 OR 800/774-9523 Contrasts set the tone at this centrally located bed-and-breakfast inn. A massive portico flanked by Doric columns makes for an imposing exterior, but the interior of the 1895 mansion feels more like Dr. Doolittle's library. Though the decor is florid and eclectic, the rooms, like the innkeepers, are quiet and gracious. There are a half-dozen rooms, ranging from small and bookish to large and fanciful. All have antiques . . . and CD players. Four rooms boast fireplaces and two have private baths. Our favorite, the Artist's Studio on the third floor, has the feel of a Parisan garret apartment, complete with a claw-foot tub in the bath. The dining table is a great place to socialize over an oven-fresh country-style breakfast; or, if you'd rather keep to yourself and have breakfast in your room, so be it. Located in the King's Hill Historic District, the manor is two blocks from the east entrance to Washington Park and a straight shot down to NW 23rd Avenue. *$$; AE, DIS, MC, V; checks OK; www.macmaster.com; map:HH7* &

Park Lane Suites / ★

809 SW KING AVE; 503/226-6288 OR 800/532-9543 A renovated former apartment building on the lower slope of King's Hill, this no-frills hotel has a lot going for it. Each of its 44 suites—studio, one-bedroom, and two-bedroom units—has custom-designed cherry furniture, a warm pastel color scheme, and a business-size desk with two-line phone and data port. The kitchen has a large refrigerator, stove top, microwave oven, dishwasher, and coffeemaker, as well as a full complement of kitchenware. The roomy lobby always has books to read and games to play; the friendly staff is always ready with a smile. There's a guest laundry, and parking is free. Ask about extended-stay rates. *$$; AE, CB, DC, DIS, MC, V; checks OK; www.parklanesuites.com; map:HH7* &

Silver Cloud Inn / ★

2425 NW VAUGHN ST; 503/242-2400 Just off Hwy 30 near the Fremont Bridge, location alone would recommend this motor hotel. It's clean and well priced, and has plenty of parking. Spacious guest rooms, with bright pastel decor, feature mini-refrigerators and big marbletop working desks with high-speed Internet access—plus such amenities as clock radios, ironing boards, and hairdryers. Jacuzzi and kitchen units are available. A continental breakfast, featuring pastries from local bakeries, is served with designer coffee; there's also a fitness room and a guest laundry. *$$; AE, DC, DIS, MC, V; checks OK; www.cheaprooms.com/silvercloudinn/; map:GG7* &

North Portland/Jantzen Beach

DoubleTree Hotel Portland–Columbia River / ★★
DoubleTree Hotel Portland–Jantzen Beach / ★★

1401 N HAYDEN ISLAND DR; 503/283-2111 OR 800/643-7611 / 909 N HAYDEN ISLAND DR; 503/283-4466 OR 800/643-7340 These similarly sized, twin motor hotels, poised right on the Columbia River beneath the I-5 bridge 7 miles north of downtown, have 672 rooms between them and a corner on tour-group and convention business. But there are ample reasons for others to consider a stay here. One is the range of sports activities: not only does each hotel have its own outdoor pool, riverside Jacuzzi deck, and fitness center; between them, they have tennis courts, a putting green, and a jogging path, and the 27-hole Heron Lakes Golf Course is a two-minute shuttle away. Another is free parking and complimentary airport transportation (flight crews often stay here); when the MAX light-rail line begins service to the Expo Center (scheduled September 2004), downtown will be a short shuttle-and-train run away. Third are the fine restaurants and lounges: at the Jantzen Beach, the Hayden Island Steak House is highly rated, while Maxi's Lounge has live dance music on weekends; at the Columbia River,

Brickstone's Riverside Grill serves Native American–influenced Northwest cuisine, and the adjacent sports bar has a lively billiards scene. Both inns also have casual coffee shops. Comfortable guest rooms all have balconies or patios (many overlooking the river) along with standard amenities; wireless Internet is due in 2004. *$$; AE, DC, DIS, MC, V; checks OK; www.doubletreehotel.com; map:CC6* &

RiverView GuestHouse Bed & Breakfast / ★

3909 N OVERLOOK TERRACE; 503/287-3937 Sitting on a hilltop above the Willamette River and the Swan Island industrial zone, this quiet B&B in the Overlook Park neighborhood is at once off the beaten track but convenient to downtown. Of the three guest rooms, we like room 3, with a queen bed and river view; it shares a bath with full-bedded room 1. Room 2 has a queen and a private bath. Each room has a telephone and cable TV; smoking is permitted on a lovely outdoor deck, but not in the house. Children are welcome; guests may choose between a continental or home-cooked breakfast. *$; AE, DIS, MC, V; no checks; www.riverviewguesthousebb.com; map:FF7*

Northeast Portland

Courtyard Portland Downtown/Lloyd Center / ★★☆

435 NE WASCO ST; 503/234-3200 OR 800/321-2211 Designed specifically for business travelers, this five-year-old, six-story Marriott hotel is a short walk from both the Oregon Convention Center and the Lloyd Center. Each of its 202 comfortable rooms (nearly three-quarters of them standard kings or king spas) are outfitted with working desks, featuring free high-speed Internet access and voice mail. A 24-hour business center also provides printing and copying services. Other services include a fitness center, indoor pool, whirlpool, and guest laundry. Free shuttles are offered to the airport and train station; for those who drive, underground garage parking is $9 per night. Charley's Restaurant and Bar has a daily breakfast buffet and a lunch/ dinner menu that features American and Mediterranean cuisine. *$$; AE, CB, DC, DIS, JCB, MC, V; checks OK; www.courtyard.com/pdxcl; map:GG6* &

DoubleTree Hotel Portland–Lloyd Center / ★★

1000 NE MULTNOMAH ST; 503/281-6111 OR 800/222-TREE Opposite the Lloyd Center and close to the Rose Quarter, this 476-room property is one of Oregon's largest convention hotels. Premium king rooms in the North Tower are decidedly more spacious than standard queens in the South Tower, which have showers but no bathtubs. All rooms are nicely decorated and have balcony views of downtown Portland or Mount Hood. Amenities include a large parking garage, an outdoor pool, a fitness room with plenty of cardio equipment, and two restaurants: the Multnomah Grille coffee shop and Eduardo's, a Mexican eatery. The focus, however, is on business travelers: open in April 2004 is the Executive Meeting Center, whose 10 conference rooms, corporate training complex, and expanded business center complement an expansive exhibit hall and ballrooms. *$$$; AE, DC, DIS, MC, V; checks OK; www.portlandlloydcenter.doubletree.com; map:GG6* &

The Georgian House Bed and Breakfast / ★

1823 NE SISKIYOU ST, IRVINGTON; 503/281-2250 OR 888-282-2250 On a summer day, most guests can be found outside in the garden amid the fragrant lavender and roses, perhaps helping themselves to berries that grow along the back fence. With its lovely grounds and quiet neighborhood, this handsome 1922 brick B&B in historic Irvington—for architecture buffs, one of three true Georgian Colonials in Portland—combines the respite of a rural getaway with a convenient location: downtown is about 10 minutes away by car. Antique furniture and collectibles blend with a contemporary country motif. There are four rooms; the three upstairs are all air-conditioned. We like the East Lake for its private veranda and the Lovejoy Suite for its claw-foot bathtub. Ms. Willie Canning, the likable host, has guests sign up for breakfast times. *$–$$; MC, V; checks OK; www.thegeorgianhouse.com; map:GG5*

Holiday Inn Portland–Downtown / ★★

1441 NE 2ND AVE; 503/233-2401 OR 877/777-2704 Holiday Inn, which bought this Rose Quarter property from the Radisson Group in 2003, gave it a thorough makeover in 2004. All 239 rooms—75 kings, 104 double queens, and 60 single corner queens—were refurbished; each one boasts a microwave oven, refrigerator, coffeemaker, armoire with television, and working desk with a high-speed Internet link. The lobby was redecorated in earth tones to encompass the pre-existing lounge and to open onto the Three Forks restaurant. The outdoor pool was enclosed for year-round recreation, along with a Jacuzzi; and work on a new ballroom began. The striking, tri-arc-shaped hotel retained its gracious staff and surprisingly large fitness center, with multiple cardio machines. *$$; AE, CB, DC, DIS, E, JCB, MC, V; checks OK; www.ichotelsgroup.com; map:GG6 &*

The Kennedy School / ★★

5736 NE 33RD AVE; 503/249-3983 If you're not familiar with the McMenamin brothers' brewpub/movie theater/B&B enterprises, you may find this place perplexing, but if you're in the loop, you're bound to like the Kennedy School. Located in a former public-school building in the Concordia neighborhood, built in 1915 in Italian Renaissance style, this enterprise is part community center, part meeting facility, part fun house. The Kennedy School features 35 bed-and-breakfast guest rooms—two to a classroom—each featuring a private bath, the McMenamins' signature commissioned artwork (think Grateful Dead posters), Indonesian antiques, and (in some) chalkboards still in place. There are the requisite bars—Detention (cigars and jazz), Honors (smoke-free and classical)—plus a brewery and the Courtyard Restaurant in the old cafeteria. There are also some not-so-common public areas: an excellent movie theater (with a bar of its own), a gymnasium, a wine bar/dessert room with an open-air patio (the Cypress Room), and a hot-water soaking pool in a garden courtyard. *$$; AE, DIS, MC, V; checks OK; www.mcmenamins.com; map:FF5 &*

The Lion and the Rose / ★★★

1810 NE 15TH AVE, IRVINGTON; 503/287-9245 OR 800/955-1647 Occupying the 1906 Freiwald House, a Queen Anne mansion with Craftsman flair in the historic Irvington district, the Lion and the Rose maintains its status as one of Portland's finest B&Bs. Steve Unger and Dustin Carsey, the genial hosts, let few details go unchecked: from candles in the baths, to beverages in the refrigerator, to extra blankets upon request. Our favorites of the six rooms are Joseph's (rich colors contrast with ample natural light), the Starina (strong, dark colors with a map theme), and the Lavonna (done in lavender and white, with a spacious reading nook in the turret); throughout, the inn is indisputably decorated with rich drapery, fine rugs, and antiques. Breakfast, served in the formal dining room, is lavish, and tea is offered to guests 4–6pm. Those set on relaxing will appreciate the two elegant living rooms, known as the Front Parlor and Middle Parlor, and the porch swing (roofed to guard against rain); business travelers find plenty of phone lines (with data ports) and other amenities. *$$$; AE, DC, DIS, MC, V; checks OK; www.lionrose.com; map:GG5*

Portland Guest House / ★★

1720 NE 15TH AVE, IRVINGTON; 503/282-1402 Since 1987, owner Susan Gisvold has maintained this simple urban retreat just off busy NE Broadway in the historic Irvington neighborhood. White carpets and antique linens lend the classy air of an intimate hotel, and comfortable mattresses ease the separation from home. Gisvold doesn't live here, but she's usually around to advise you on Portland doings and to make sure the flowers in the window boxes are watered. In the morning, she'll drop in to serve a home-cooked breakfast of low-fat cottage-cheese pancakes, scones, fresh strawberries, and coffee or tea. Each of the seven rooms (five have private baths) has its own phone and clock, making this a good place for business travelers, too; but the house's only (very small) TV is in the living room. Three of the rooms have multiple beds for travelers rooming together but sleeping separately. *$–$$; MC, V; checks OK; www.teleport.com/~pgh/; map:GG5*

Portland's White House / ★★★

1914 NE 22ND AVE, IRVINGTON; 503/287-7131 Owners Lanning Blanks and Steve Holden hired a historian to help with the restoration of this stately old home, built in 1911 of solid Honduran mahogany and oak by local timber baron Robert F. Lytle. Now the exquisitely furnished interior replicates the original Lytle home. On the outside, Portland's White House looks a bit like its Washington, D.C., namesake, complete with fountains, a circular driveway, and a carriage house that contains three guest rooms with baths. Inside are five more guest rooms, all with private baths. The Canopy Suite features a large canopied bed and bright bath; the Baron's Suite is adorned in blues and golds and boasts a Victorian claw-foot tub. A full gourmet breakfast is served in the main dining room every morning; the signature dish is salmon eggs Benedict with an orange hollandaise. Evenings, wander down to the formal parlor for a turn at the grand piano or a game of chess. Blanks, a flamboyant South Carolina native, loves to show off his collection of Miessen porcelain from Germany—one that makes museums salivate. Active in the Irvington community, the White House is a catering specialist, and it hosts numerous weddings and social gatherings in its garden. *$$–$$$; AE, DIS, MC, V; checks OK; www.portlandswhitehouse.com; map:GG5*

Residence Inn Portland Downtown/Lloyd Center / ★★☆

1710 NE MULTNOMAH ST; 503/288-1400 OR 800/331-3131 Planning to bring the family and stay a few days, maybe more? This residential community might fit the bill. With 168 rooms in apartment-like 12-plexes, the property is ideal for visitors who may plan to spend extra time at the hotel. Every room (studios, one-bedrooms, and two-bedroom split levels) is a suite with a full kitchen, executive desk and phone, and living area—in most, facing a wood-burning fireplace. A renovation in late 2003 introduced a new color palette of forest greens and beiges. Guests enjoy a heated outdoor pool and Jacuzzi; a nominal daily fee provides membership at the Lloyd Center Athletic Club. A daily breakfast buffet with eggs and waffles, and weekday afternoon hors d'oeuvres, are served in the lobby area. The hotel has a guest laundry and is only two blocks from the MAX light-rail line. *$$; AE, DC, DIS, JCB, MC, V; no checks; www.marriott.com/pdxlc; map:GG5* &

Sullivans' Gulch B&B / ★

1744 NE CLACKAMAS ST; 503/331-1104 A 1907 Victorian home on a quiet, tree-lined street almost next door to the Lloyd Center, this charming residence features a cozy garden where breakfast is served amid the flowers on sunny days. The Red and Green suites each have private baths, sitting rooms, ceiling fans, refrigerators, and private phones with modem links; guests in the Northwest Room have similar amenities but must cross a hall to their bathroom. All three rooms are decorated with traditional western and American Indian art. Well-behaved pets who get along with the resident dog are welcome. *$$; AE, MC, V; checks OK; www.sullivansgulch.com; map:GG5* &

Airport

Sheraton Portland Airport Hotel / ★★

8235 NE AIRPORT WY; 503/281-2500 OR 800/808-9497 Some Portlanders opt to spend the night here before an early flight: it's conveniently close to the terminal (Delta and United arrival and departure times are broadcast via video screen at the hotel's main entrance), and guests can park a car for up to eight days with no charge. For the traveling business person, this Sheraton's 213 rooms provide ergonomic work stations and free high-speed Internet access; the hotel has a small but complete business center (with a computer, printer, fax machine, and secretarial service) and multiple meeting rooms. There's an indoor swimming pool, Jacuzzi, sauna, and 24-hour fitness center, and room service from the excellent Premiere Restaurant is also available around the clock. Mount Hood stands tall to the east, but you'd never know it from the airport-facing rooms. *$$; AE, DC, JCB, MC, V; corporate checks OK; www.sheratonportland.com; map:EE3*

Southeast Portland

Century Garden / ★

1960 SE LARCH AVE, LADD'S ADDITION; 503/235-6846 The diminutive Century Garden offers a private three-room, upstairs suite in a 1909 house in the engaging Ladd's Addition, near the Hawthorne District (see the Exploring chapter). Vintage and antique furniture tastefully decorate walls and fill corners. In the Garden Room, lace curtains hang from birch-branch rods, and a queen-size bed looks feather soft beneath a cream-colored down comforter and blue-and-white sheets. The Century Room's queen bed is covered in quilts and pillows, located beneath windows that spill light everywhere. Guests share a bath. The den has a TV, phone, microwave, refrigerator, and a collection of coffees and teas; everything is immaculately clean. Innkeeper Carol Olpin prepares breakfast when you'd like it; gingerbread muffins are a constant, but you can choose the rest from a menu of standard items. In nice weather, meals are served on the back balcony overlooking a manicured garden. *$$; MC, V; checks OK; www.centurygarden.com; map:HH5* &

Hostelling International–Portland, Hawthorne District / ★

3031 SE HAWTHORNE BLVD, HAWTHORNE; 503/236-3380 OR 866/447-3031 This Hawthorne District hostel location, in a charming early-20th-century house, couldn't be better for budget travelers; within blocks are great used bookstores, good eats, and plentiful coffee and microbrew hangouts. This place will seem familiar to those who know hostels: clean linens are available; check in by 10pm and enjoy 24-hour access with a security access code. Shared showers, bunk beds, blankets, a kitchen, and two small living areas are the amenities—plus all-you-can-eat pancakes come morning. The hostel encourages groups and has a couple of private rooms, good for families. Hostelling International membership is not required but lessens the price; you can buy an HI membership ($25 for the year) when you arrive. Rooms are $16–$18/night (private $38–$42) with membership, $19–$21 (private $44–$48) without. *$; MC, V; no checks; www.portlandhostel.org; map:GG4*

Mount Scott Hideaway / ★

9350 SE 92ND AVE; 503/777-6170 Sharon Jacobs's charming bed-and-breakfast, just east of I-205 at Johnson Creek Boulevard, sleeps seven—so children are welcome! Climb to the fully furnished duplex via a long private driveway; a west-facing deck offers panoramic views of city lights. Guest rooms, decorated in turn-of-the-20th-century style, have TVs, phones with data ports, refrigerators, and coffeemakers. A hot multicourse breakfast is served in the morning. Smoking is not permitted indoors. *$; MC, V; checks OK; www.mtscotthideaway.com; map:KK2*

Lake Oswego

Hilton Garden Inn Portland/Lake Oswego / ★★☆

14850 KRUSE OAKS BLVD, SOUTHWOOD, LAKE OSWEGO; 503/684-8900
Ideally located for businesspeople whose affairs may be focused in Southwest Portland, this handsomely landscaped, bright-yellow hotel faces I-5 directly. Each of the 181 rooms (including 7 king spa units) has a working desk with two-line phone, voice mail, data port, and high-speed Internet access. Each room also has a microwave, refrigerator, coffeemaker, ironing board, and hair dryer. A breakfast-only cafe is adjacent to the lobby, along with a lounge and a 24-hour convenience store. Also open around the clock is a business center. Guests have use of an indoor pool, whirlpool, fitness center, and laundry. *$$; AE, DC, MC, V; checks OK; www .portlandlakeoswego.gardeninn.com; map:MM8* &

Holiday Inn Crowne Plaza / ★★☆

14811 KRUSE OAKS BLVD, SOUTHWOOD, LAKE OSWEGO; 503/624-8400 An atmospheric business hotel, the Crowne Plaza—sitting right off I-5—has a six-story waterfall cascading into a fountain in its central atrium. The 161 rooms, including 12 suites, are fairly standard (although they have high-speed Internet and CD player/clock radios), unless you request one of the posh sixth-floor rooms on the concierge level. All guests receive free van service within 5 miles (downtown Portland is 7). The High Rock Steakhouse and Lounge provides meals and cocktails. The hotel has an indoor/outdoor pool, sauna and whirlpool, a fitness center, and bicycles (there are trails behind the hotel); and if that's not enough, you can get a free pass to a nearby athletic club. There's also a laundry, newsstand, and business center. *$$; AE, DC, DIS, MC, V; checks OK; www.ichotelsgroup.com; map:MM8* &

Lakeshore Inn / ★

210 N STATE ST, DOWNTOWN, LAKE OSWEGO; 503-636-9679 OR 800/215-6431
From the street or parking lot, this four-story motor hotel might look like any other located on a main thoroughfare; but this one happens to be right next door to the new and impressive Millennium Plaza Park on the lakefront, a short walk from downtown Lake Oswego. All 33 rooms have windows on the lake, and the view is uncannily rural and picturesque. Although the one- and two-bedroom suites offer more room, the studios allow a view of the water without getting out of bed. Every room is nonsmoking and has a kitchenette and TV. Guests have year-round use of the pool (heated only in summer), perched over the lake; lakeside rooms have private sun decks. *$$; AE, DC, DIS, MC, V; checks OK; www.thelakeshoreinn.com; map: MM6* &

West Linn

Rose Cottage / ★★

2248 5TH AVE, DOWNTOWN, WEST LINN; 503/650-6053 Sally Palmer's modern home, built in traditional English style and surrounded by lovely gardens, has two guest rooms a short stroll from Willamette Park, at the confluence of the Tualatin and Willamette Rivers. Spacious and high-ceilinged, each has a king-size bed with reading lamps, a table and chairs, an armoire with a TV/VCR, a refrigerator and coffeemaker, a portable phone with a data port, and a tiled bathroom. The garden theme carries indoors, with fresh flowers in each room. Take morning coffee beside the fireplace in a sitting room stocked with books, then enjoy a three-course breakfast with dishes like apple-filled poppy-seed scones and zucchini corn cakes. No smoking. *$$; AE, DIS, MC, V; checks OK; www .rosecottagebb.com; map:PP5*

Tigard

Embassy Suites Hotel Portland–Washington Square / ★★

9000 SW WASHINGTON SQUARE RD, TIGARD; 503/644-4000 OR 800/362-2779 Ideally situated for visitors shopping at the adjacent Washington Square complex or doing business in the south side's Silicon Forest, this immense suburban hotel has more character than one might initially expect. Its 354 rooms, all of them two-room suites, surround a central atrium with waterfalls that tumble into a lush central garden, accented by flowing streams and koi ponds. Rooms have sleeper sofas for additional guests, kitchenette facilities, and high-speed Internet access. The hotel is also a swank conference center with an elaborate ballroom. A full complimentary breakfast is served each morning, and happy-hour drinks are on the house at the nightly manager's reception in the atrium. Guests enjoy an indoor pool, Jacuzzi, sauna, free video games, and the casual Crossroads Restaurant and Bar. *$$; AE, DC, DIS, MC, V; checks OK; www.embassysuites.com; map:KK9* &

Beaverton

Greenwood Inn and Suites / ★☆

10700 SW ALLEN BLVD, DOWNTOWN, BEAVERTON; 503/643-7444 Billed as a city hotel with resort-style comfort, this Best Western complex delivers—for the most part. Located just off Hwy 217, the Greenwood oddly has 217 standard guest rooms—as well as 35 two-room Jacuzzi or kitchen suites. Each room is pleasantly decorated, with standard amenities. Working guests find an office nook with a spacious desk and phone (with data ports for Internet access), and the hotel offers full business services. The courtyard and trapezoidal pool are quite pretty; there's also a second heated outdoor pool and hot tub, plus a fitness center and guest laundry. Free shuttle service is offered within a 5-mile radius. Inside the Pavilion Trattoria, the menu features Italian cuisine, the lights are soft, and the service treads the delicate line between chummy and concerned. *$$; AE, CB, DC, DIS, MC, V; checks OK; www.greenwoodinn.com; map:JJ9* &

Sauvie Island

River's Edge Bed and Breakfast / ★

22502 NW GILLIHAN RD, SAUVIE ISLAND; 503/621-9856 Wes and Beverley Westlund's rural B&B is poised on the bank of the Columbia River on Sauvie Island, a hamlet devoted to farming and wildlife. Less than a half hour's drive from downtown Portland, it offers year-round viewing of waterfowl and river traffic from its spacious deck, as well as fishing, boating, strolling, and even swimming in summer. The private guest house has two bedrooms, the Pink Room and the Blue Room, both simply but comfortably decorated; they share a bath, a kitchenette stocked with cookware, and a living room with a wood stove, TV, VCR, and two-line phone. One door opens to a parking area, a second to the riverside beach and picnic area (with its own brick fireplace). Smoking is not permitted. *$$; AE, MC, V; checks OK; www .riversedge-bb.com; map:AA9*

Troutdale

Edgefield / ★★☆

2126 SW HALSEY ST, TROUTDALE; 503/669-8610 OR 800/669-8610 The McMenamin brothers of microbrew fame did a terrific job of turning the former Multnomah County Poor Farm into a quirky but winning place to visit. There's the brewpub, of course, but there's also the movie theater, the winery, the distillery, the respectable Black Rabbit Restaurant and Bar (see review in the Restaurants chapter), the Power Station pub, the amphitheater (which draws some big-name bands in the summer), the 18-hole par-3 golf course, the meeting and party sites, and 114 guest rooms spread throughout three buildings. All rooms are furnished with antiques and cozy linens and are embellished with custom artistry; most share a bath, although the 13 suites have private baths. Because Edgefield is billed as a European-style bed-and-breakfast, the first meal of the day is included in the room rate, and glasses and pitchers are readily available for fetching beer. There is also a men's and women's hostel, a great alternative for the budget traveler, as well as family rooms that sleep up to six. Hallways are lined with unique murals and wall paintings by an unconventional variety of artists. The proximity to (and location away from) the airport makes Edgefield less ordinary than the usual airport-area lodging alternatives. *$-$$; AE, DIS, MC, V; checks OK; www.mcmenamins.com* &

Vancouver, Washington

Heathman Lodge / ★★☆

7801 NE GREENWOOD DR, VANCOUVER MALL, VANCOUVER; 360/254-3100 OR 888/475-3100 Vancouver's first luxury hotel—run by the pros who until recently owned Portland's venerable Heathman Hotel—gives a distinct first impression: it's simply stunning but somewhat out of place. The hotel looms like a national-park lodge as you approach it from busy Route 205, but it's set squarely in a Clark County suburb, near a shopping mall and high-tech office space. Huge timbers support the porte cochere; nearby, a carved cedar totem pole and a bronze sculpture of a Chinook chief enrich your first impressions, which only grow more positive as you step inside. There's a striking lobby with a basalt fireplace, bright pool and fitness rooms, the top-drawer Hudson's Bar & Grill, a range of suites and guest rooms attractively furnished in Northwest style (complete with bedspreads created by Pendleton), and plenty of amenities for the business traveler. Perhaps best of all is that promise of excellent, understated service for which the Heathman Lodge's parent company has made itself known. The lodge is unlikely to become a destination in itself because of the surrounding neighborhood, but for those travelers making Vancouver their destination, the Heathman Lodge should be at the top of their accommodations list. *$$$; AE, DC, DIS, MC, V; checks OK; www.heathmanlodge.com* &

EXPLORING

EXPLORING

Top 20 Attractions

1) WASHINGTON PARK

BETWEEN SW CANYON RD (HWY 26) AND W BURNSIDE RD, THREE BLOCKS WEST (UPHILL) OF VISTA AVE VIA SW PARK PL; 503/823-2223 Portland is a city of parks: there are some 280 green spaces in the city. At 4,683 acres, **FOREST PARK** (see Parks and Beaches in this chapter) is by far the most sprawling and primitive, while the 24-square-inch **MILL ENDS PARK** (SW Naito Pkwy and Taylor St) is decidedly the city's smallest. And lovely Washington Park may well be the most civilized.

The 129½-acre plot, originally purchased by Portland's founders in 1871, is the home of several different gardens, including the well-kept trails of the **HOYT ARBORETUM** (see no. 11 in this section) and its inspiring **OREGON VIETNAM VETERANS' LIVING MEMORIAL** (4000 SW Fairview Blvd, next to the Forest Discovery Center; 503/823-3654).

Whether to obtain a blossom-framed snapshot of Mount Hood or to scrutinize a new hybrid, the **INTERNATIONAL ROSE TEST GARDEN** (400 SW Kingston Ave; 503/823-3636) is an obligatory stop for any visitor to the City of Roses. The garden (established in 1917) is the oldest continually operating testing program in the country. With more than 8,000 plants (more than 400 varieties) and a knockout setting overlooking downtown Portland, it's an unmatched display of the genus *Rosa*. The garden's 4½ acres are a riot of blooms from June through October, from dainty half-inch-wide miniatures to great, blowsy 8-inch beauties. And you'll find fragrant old-garden varieties on the east side of the Washington Park tennis courts. While you're here, check out the **ROSE GARDEN STORE** (850 SW Rose Garden Wy; 503/227-7033), which sells rose-themed merchandise, including rose-patterned tea sets and floral wreaths; proceeds from the store benefit these gardens and Portland parks youth programs.

The park also is home to the elegant **JAPANESE GARDEN** (see no. 7 in this section) and the **OREGON ZOO** (see no. 8 in this section), famed for its successful breeding of Asian elephants. The westside light-rail line, MAX (503/238-RIDE), stops at the zoo; take time to notice the geological timeline exhibit on the walls of this 260-foot-deep train stop—the **DEEPEST UNDERGROUND TRANSIT STATION** in North America (elevators take you up and down in 20 seconds). At the entrance to the above-ground plaza sits a sculpture made from columnar basalt and etched granite, telling the story of creating the light-rail tunnel. Those who arrive at the zoo by car take a chance with overflow parking, especially on the weekend.

In the vicinity of the zoo are the educational **FOREST DISCOVERY CENTER** and **CHILDREN'S MUSEUM 2ND GENERATION** (see Museums in this chapter). One-way roads wind through Washington Park, and in warm-weather months a narrow-gauge train runs through the zoo to the rose garden (see Train and Trolley Tours in

PORTLAND'S TOP 20 ATTRACTIONS

1) Washington Park
2) Central Downtown/Pioneer Courthouse Square/South Park Blocks
3) Gov. Tom McCall Waterfront Park/
   RiverPlace
4) Portland Art Museum
5) Oregon Museum of Science and
   Industry
6) Portland Classical Chinese Garden
7) Japanese Garden
8) Oregon Zoo
9) Pearl District
10) Northwest Portland

11) Hoyt Arboretum
12) Oregon History Center
13) River Cruises on the Columbia
    and Willamette Rivers
14) Oregon City Historic Sites
15) Powell's City of Books
16) Breweries and Brewpubs
17) Hawthorne District
18) Pittock Mansion
19) Fort Vancouver National
    Historic Site
20) Saturday Market

this chapter). Other facilities include four lit tennis courts, covered picnic areas, an archery range, a playground, public restrooms, and an outdoor amphitheater that features free musical and stage performances in summer (call 503/823-2223 for schedule). *www.parks.ci.portland.or.us/parks/washington.htm; map:HH7* &

2) CENTRAL DOWNTOWN/PIONEER COURTHOUSE SQUARE/ SOUTH PARK BLOCKS

BORDERED BY I-405 ON THE WEST AND SOUTH, W BURNSIDE ON THE NORTH, AND THE WILLAMETTE RIVER ON THE EAST Portland's history lives in well-maintained historic structures and dramatic modern and postmodern edifices. These buildings reflect the economics of their time, the sponsors who backed them, and the architects' visions. An afternoon tour of some of the more interesting architectural designs in the city core requires little more than a sturdy umbrella, a durable pair of boots, a raincoat, a camera, and a strong sense of wonder.

During the mid-to-late 1800s Portland's business center ran alongside the west bank of the Willamette River. Here, streets were lined with cast-iron-fronted architecture. Portland's Front Avenue then looked very much like San Francisco's Montgomery Street—a study in masonry and cast-iron facade. After the San Francisco earthquake in 1906, Portland was left with the largest collection of cast-iron structures on the West Coast. These structures declined as the city center moved west. The area was largely demolished in the 1940s.

Today, Pioneer Courthouse Square (715 SW Morrison St; map:H4) is Portland's living room. Designed by Will Martin, the Square features an amphitheater-like design well suited to people watching. Here is *The Weather Machine*, a sculpture that delights with its quirkiness; there is the J. Seward Johnson statue, *Allow Me*, of a man with an umbrella, extending his hand. Elsewhere, there are bits of cast-iron fence from the grand hotel that one graced this spot, as well as a Starbucks to duck into out of the rain. Most of the Square's 45,000 bricks bear the names of individual contributors who helped pay for the project, completed in 1984. The Square hosts a number of festivals, and during the Christmas season a huge fir is lit with great fanfare.

Before leaving Pioneer Courthouse Square, stop at the **VISITOR INFORMATION AND SERVICES CENTER** (701 SW 6th Ave; 503/275-8355; map:H3), on the lower west side, to pick up a city map and other information. If you take a wrong turn as you walk these pedestrian-friendly half-size blocks, keep an eye out for the green-jacketed **PORTLAND GUIDES**, employees of the Association for Portland Progress. They roam the downtown core in pairs just to answer questions about the city.

PIONEER COURTHOUSE (555 SW Yamhill St; map:H3) itself faces the Square from the east. Built from 1869 to 1875 as the second-oldest federal building west of the Mississippi River, the three-story sandstone-walled structure persists today; it has a gracefully refurbished post office on its main floor. From the cupola of this historic building you get great views of the city. Next to the eight windows are historic photos of the area you're looking at, so you can see how Portland has changed. (To get to the cupola, take the elevator to the third floor, turn left, go through the door, and walk two flights up.)

Numerous early-20th-century buildings surround the Square. The 1912 **JACKSON TOWER** (800 SW Broadway; map:H3) provides a beautiful example of Portland's early "White City" look, reflected in banks, department stores, and government offices. The Tower, built by Sam Jackson, founder of the *Oregon Journal*, stood an astonishing (at the time) 186 feet, from the ground floor to the flagpole base. The building that housed Jackson's competitor, the *Oregonian*, then rose only 138 feet. Jackson Tower once housed presses in its basement and the business of writing on its main floors; it shot newspapers out to boys on roller skates who made distribution swift.

Architecture often corresponds to the music of its time and, that being the case, the 1902 **CHARLES F. BERG BUILDING** (615 SW Broadway; map:I3) is pure Jazz Age razzle-dazzle. Its Art Deco architecture is considered the finest in Portland. The joint just stuns the inner eye: the black facade is frosted with pounds of gilt; inset designs range from chevrons to peacocks, sunbursts to rain clouds. Built by an eccentric businessman, the building—which once housed his elaborate fine women's clothing store—now provides space for a number of retailers.

The **MULTNOMAH COUNTY CENTRAL LIBRARY** (801 SW 10th Ave; map:I2) dates from a similar era: 1912–13. Beautifully restored in the mid-1990s at a cost of $24 million, this Georgian architectural gem is worth a visit even if you're not feeling bookish.

It isn't hard to find Portland's tallest building, the **UNICO US BANK TOWER** (555 SW Oak St; map:J4): just stand anywhere downtown and look up. This astonishing study in light, mass, and space takes on a different color and shape depending on the time of day and viewpoint. It appears multidimensional from one side, but seen from a different angle, it seems flat as a credit card. A sculptural skyscraper, the 1983 building affectionately known as Big Pink was designed by Skidmore, Owings, and Merrill, with Pietro Belluschi as consulting architect.

Belluschi's first big commission after World War II was the Equitable Building (1948), now known as the **COMMONWEALTH BUILDING** (421 SW 6th Ave; map: I4). It's an outstanding example of how existing patterns can be combined with new materials and structural systems to produce an elegantly proportioned building. It features a detailed aluminum and glass-curtain wall that was the first of its type in the United States.

The **PORTLAND BUILDING** (1120 SW 5th Ave; map:G3) was one of architect Michael Graves's first major designs. Portlanders love it or hate it; mostly, they love to hate it. Flamboyantly blue, wrapped with a brown ribbon design, and fit with tiny windows, it reflects a reverence for both classicism and cubism. Built in 1982, this is *the* best example of Portland's flirtation with postmodernism. Close-up the building loses much of its grandeur, due more to economically driven compromises on materials than a failure of artistic vision. Perhaps the most important legacy of this building is *Portlandia*, Raymond Kaskey's famous hammered-copper statue above the entrance that has become one of the city's icons.

Closer to the river, the bold, brick, 1984 **KOIN CENTER** (222 SW Columbia St; map:E4), like a blue-tipped pen, has left its indelible mark on Portland's skyline; inside are six cinemas and offices for its namesake, KOIN-TV. Across from that is the **KELLER AUDITORIUM** (SW 3rd Ave and Clay St; map:E4), where many local and traveling performers take the stage. Also check out the 1963 **STANDARD INSURANCE BUILDING** (1100 SW 6th Ave; map:G3), at once very subtle and exquisitely designed. Often described as an architect's building, it is a modernist glass box built to the highest standard.

A peaceful component of Portland's downtown is the elm-lined oasis known as the **SOUTH PARK BLOCKS**. If Pioneer Courthouse Square is the heart of the city, the Park Blocks are its green backbone; sandwiched between SW Park and Ninth Avenues, the blocks are reserved almost entirely for public use. In 1852 a 25-block stretch running parallel to Broadway was set aside for a park. However, in 1871, 8 blocks ended up in private hands, and they continue to be developed.

THE SOUTH PARK BLOCKS (demarcated on street signs as the Cultural District) begin in a pedestrians-only zone on the Portland State University campus and continue north for 12 blocks, hedged neatly along the way with student apartments, upscale condominiums, and public institutions such as the **PORTLAND ART MUSEUM** (1219 SW Park Ave; map:G2) and the **OREGON HISTORY CENTER** (1200 SW Park Ave; map:G2); see nos. 4 and 12 in this section. In summer months the **PORTLAND FARMERS MARKET** sells fresh produce in the South Park Blocks on Wednesdays and Saturdays (see "The Portland Growing Season" in the Shopping chapter).

Sculpture abounds in the South Park Blocks. Tipped-over granite monoliths adorn the three-church block between SW Columbia and Jefferson Streets, Theodore Roosevelt and his horse guard the next block north, and a somber statue of Abe Lincoln stands outside the art museum's North Wing. At the Portland Center for the Performing Arts (1111 SW Park Ave; map:G2) be sure to view the Henk Pander mural, *Portland Town*, through the glass on the west side of the building. Just across SW Main Street (a block closed during concerts) is the larger **ARLENE SCHNITZER CONCERT HALL** (SW Broadway and Main St; map:I2), aka "The

Schnitz"; this plush and ornate theater, built in 1928 to host vaudeville shows, is home to the Oregon Symphony and the Portland Arts and Lectures Series (see the Arts Scene chapter).

The Park Blocks seem to end on SW Salmon Street, but they pick up again at SW Washington Street and **O'BRYANT SQUARE** (named for Portland's first mayor, Hugh Donaldson O'Bryant), with a jet engine–like fountain encircled by brick steps—a good spot to catch noontime rays in summer. *Map:B1–J6*

3) GOV. TOM MCCALL WATERFRONT PARK/RIVERPLACE

WEST SIDE OF THE WILLAMETTE RIVER FROM THE MARQUAM BRIDGE NORTH TO THE STEEL BRIDGE; 503/823-2223 It's a rare city that has both the planning sense and the political will to reclaim territory taken over by the automobile, but that is precisely what Portland did at the eastern edge of its downtown. In the early 1970s, Portlanders decided they didn't like the way the city had grown: an expressway called Harbor Drive impeded access to the otherwise-scenic Willamette River. So the Portland Development Commission did what the locals asked. It took the road away and replaced it with a showcase riverfront park.

GOV. TOM MCCALL WATERFRONT PARK—named for the state leader (1967–75) credited with giving Oregon its reputation as a "green" state—has become indispensable. Its 73 acres of sweeping lawns are the hardest-working turf in the city; from Cinco de Mayo through Labor Day, it's rare to find a weekend when something (Rose Festival, Brewers Festival, Blues Festival) isn't going on here. The riverside promenade is shared by anglers, walkers, runners, rollerbladers, and cyclists; and in the summer, many adults join children cooling off with a dash through the **SALMON STREET SPRINGS** fountain at the foot of SW Salmon Street.

A 1½-mile north-to-south stroll through the park begins at *Friendship Circle.* This sculpture emits the sounds of a Japanese flute and drum and honors the strong sister-city relationship between Portland and Sapporo, Japan. It's located by the west end of the Steel Bridge. The walkway next passes 100 Japanese cherry trees in the **JAPANESE AMERICAN HISTORICAL PLAZA**, which honors the Japanese Americans interned during World War II. Memorable quotes by captive Oregonians are set in boulders along the pathway.

WATERFRONT STORY GARDEN, just north of the Burnside Bridge, is a whimsical sculptural tribute by artist Larry Kirkland to storytellers of all ages, complete with etchings in granite and cobblestone of animals, queries ("What do you remember?"), and "safe havens." The Burnside's buttresses offer their own safe haven to the bustling **SATURDAY MARKET** (see no. 20 in this section).

A ship's mast at the **BATTLESHIP OREGON MEMORIAL**—built to honor the 1893 "Bulldog of the U.S. Navy"—is your clue to start looking for the **OREGON MARITIME CENTER AND MUSEUM** (see Museums in this chapter). Its main exhibit is the steam-powered stern-wheeler *Portland*, moored in the Willamette opposite the foot of SW Pine Street. Continuing past the Morrison Bridge, you'll need a keen eye to find **MILL ENDS PARK**, located in the SW Naito Parkway median at Taylor Street. In season, it's planted with colorful flowers. A plaque at the site tells how a hole for a lamppost became the smallest park in the nation, and probably the world. Despite its size, weddings are occasionally held at the spot.

In the heart of McCall Waterfront Park, near the Salmon Street Springs fountain, sits McCall's Waterfront Cafe (1020 SW Naito Pkwy; 503/248-9710). This is a fine place to congregate on a sunny day. River cruises on the *Portland Spirit* (see no. 13 in this section) depart daily from a nearby dock. An amphitheater south of the Hawthorne Bridge, a few blocks farther, is center stage for many of the park's festivals.

When Harbor Drive was demolished, Portland was left with 15 acres of undeveloped riverfront land between the Hawthorne and Marquam Bridges, at the south end of McCall Waterfront Park. That acreage is now **RIVERPLACE**, a multimillion-dollar development that includes two hotels, several restaurants, 480 condominium units, extensive office and specialty retail space, and a broad promenade tying all this together with a marina, beach, and fishing pier. The esplanade ends at the new world headquarters for PG&E Gas Transmission Northwest—thus establishing an attractive and efficient "mixed-use" neighborhood. *www.parks.ci.portland.or.us/ Parks/TomMcCallWaterfront.htm; map:C5–M7* &

4) PORTLAND ART MUSEUM

1219 SW PARK AVE, DOWNTOWN; 503/226-2811 This is the oldest art museum in the Pacific Northwest. Its southern wing has been a landmark building on the South Park Blocks since 1932, when celebrated Portland architect Pietro Belluschi bucked tradition to build a modernist brick structure trimmed in Italian travertine.

The museum, known to its friends as PAM, got its start in 1892, when Portland business leader and art connoisseur Henry Corbett paid $10,000 for a collection of Greek and Roman antiquities. The extraordinary sculptures are still part of the museum holdings. So, too, are 750 Japanese prints purchased in 1932; Claude Monet's impressionistic *Water Lilies*, purchased in 1959; and a collection of other work spanning 35 centuries: prehistoric Chinese artifacts, tribal art from Cameroon, and modern European and American sculpture. In all, PAM retains 32,000 pieces of art; its 240,000 square feet make it one of the 25 largest museums in the country.

And it continues to grow. In 2000, the museum built a new Center for Native American Art and Northwest Art, underscoring PAM's importance to the regional art community. It also added an impressive outdoor sculpture garden, two special-exhibition galleries, a new community education center, a state-of-the-art auditorium, a museum shop, and a cafe (serving lunch every day but Monday). Currently under construction in the newly acquired North Wing (formerly the Masonic Temple, built in 1924 in grand classical style) is a Center for Modern and Contemporary Art, plus an elaborate ballroom, museum offices, and resource library. An underground gallery between museum buildings, a new home for the Northwest Film Center, and a rental sales gallery are to be completed by spring 2005.

PAM attracts some of the world's top touring exhibitions. Past presentations have included priceless objects from the Imperial Tombs of China and Russia's Stroganoff Palace. Renowned collections of Pre-Raphaelite and ancient Egyptian art are scheduled for exhibition in 2005 and 2006.

From October through April, Museum After Hours tempts businesspeople to stay downtown on Wednesdays for two hours of live music, beginning at 5:30pm (tickets are $7, or $4 for museum members). Museum admission is $10 for adults,

$9 for students and seniors (over 55), $6 for children 5–18, and children under 5 are free. *Tues–Wed 10am–5pm, Thurs–Fri 10am–8pm, Sat 10am–5pm, Sun noon–5pm; www.portlandartmuseum.org; map:G2* &

5) OREGON MUSEUM OF SCIENCE AND INDUSTRY

1945 SE WATER AVE, SOUTHEAST; 503/797-4000 With its knockout view of downtown from the east bank of the Willamette, OMSI is a delightful diversion no matter the weather—and it's not just for kids. The facility features six immense exhibit halls, a planetarium that doubles as a theater in the round, an Omnimax theater, a great science store (see the Shopping chapter), and a riverfront cafe. There's even a naval submarine, the USS *Blueback*, permanently docked for tours by those 4 years and older (admission is $5 extra).

You can't miss this angular brick showpiece, capped with a copper dome, topped by a Ferrari-red smokestack and a glass pyramid atrium. The 18½-acre industrial location (formerly owned by Portland General Electric, which donated the land) is ideal for a museum where science and industry are the emphasis: the Marquam Bridge soars just above, and a PGE substation still operates at one corner of the property.

Inside, you can poke around an old turbine, stand on a platform and feel an earthquake, touch a tornado in the Natural Science Hall, observe nutrient cycling in the Greenway, or cruise the Internet in the High Tech Hall. The numerous hands-on exhibits are popular with people of all ages, but for the very young—and their grateful parents—there's Discovery Space, a tots' room with tennis balls to feed into a pneumatic tube, a Lego table, and live reptiles. The Murdock Planetarium features a new state-of-the-art Digistar projection system, which displays 10 times as many stars as the former system and can simulate three-dimensional space travel (admission is $5 extra). Traveling exhibits—robotics, for example, or early humans—are both educational and entertaining.

Museum admission is $8.50 for adults, $6.50 for seniors (63 and older) and for children 3–13; Omnimax admission is an additional $8.50 for adults, $6.50 for seniors and children. But ask about the $20 package admission if you'd like to see a little of everything. And from after Labor Day until mid-June, every Thursday after 2pm, OMSI offers two-for-the-price-of-one admission to all attractions. Evening laser-light extravaganzas in the planetarium cost $7.50. Memberships are available. *Every day 9:30am–7pm (mid-June–Labor Day), Tues–Sun 9:30am–5:30pm (after Labor Day–mid-June), closed Thanksgiving and Dec 24–25; www.omsi.edu; map: HH6* &

6) PORTLAND CLASSICAL CHINESE GARDEN

NW 3RD AVE AND EVERETT ST, CHINATOWN; 503/221-8131 The largest urban classical Chinese garden in the country, Lan Su Yuan—the Garden of the Awakening Orchid—grew out of a partnership between Portland and its Chinese sister city. Suzhou, 50 miles west of Shanghai, is known for its compact, intricate urban gardens; the city sent designers and artisans to build an authentic Ming Dynasty garden in Portland. Over the course of 10 months, beginning in November 1999, the Chinese planned and built the garden, funded by private, foundation, and government monies.

Although tall buildings ring the garden, inside its walls is an oasis of beauty and calm that covers an entire city block. Serpentine walkways lead through open colonnades, over a bridge across Zither Lake, and into serene courtyards and pavilions such as Painted Boat in Misty Rain and Celestial House of Permeating Fragrance. Meticulous rock groupings, and Chinese and Northwest native trees and shrubs, create a landscape that stays fixed—though the visitor's view, framed through windows, doors, and lattice screens, continually shifts. A rockery with waterfalls embodies the Chinese philosophy that a garden must embrace mountains and water.

From the Tower of Cosmic Reflections, an elegant two-story teahouse, you can have a bird's-eye view of the garden. Virtually everything you see—from the 500 tons of cloud-shaped limestone to the elaborately carved ginkgo-wood panels—came from China. Zither Lake links the garden's elements, with the midlake Moon Locking Pavilion reached by a zigzag bridge. Were you fortunate to stand here on a clear night under a full moon, you would see the moon's reflection framed by the shadow of the pavilion's sweeping roof line.

Essential to a Chinese garden is poetry. Baked into the roof tiles of the garden's nine buildings are symbols of life's five blessings: health, wealth, long life, love of virtue, and happy ending. Poetic phrases illuminate literary allusions in inscriptions on rocks, screen panels, gateways, and pillars. Were you able to read Chinese, you might discover this one on the outside of the Reflections in Clear Ripples Pavilion:

Slanted the path; crooked the stream; soft is the water's song
Shadow of bamboo; layers of rockery; dark is the pine's hue

Public tours are offered daily at noon and 1pm. A gift shop sells a variety of books and souvenirs. Admission is $7 for adults, $6 for seniors, $5.50 for students; kids under 6 are free. *Every day 9am–6pm (Apr–Oct), 10am–5pm (Nov–Mar); www.portlandchinesegarden.org; map:K5*

7) JAPANESE GARDEN

611 SW KINGSTON AVE, WASHINGTON PARK; 503/223-1321 In 1988, the Japanese ambassador to the United States pronounced this the most beautiful and authentic Japanese garden outside of Japan, and it continues to enthrall visitors. An extraordinarily peaceful spot, it actually comprises five gardens: the traditional raked-sand Flat Garden; the serene and flowing Strolling Pond Garden with its colorful koi fish; the Tea Garden, with a *chashitsu* (ceremonial teahouse); the stark Dry Landscape Garden, nearly devoid of foliage; and the Natural Garden, lush with moss and maples.

In contrast with the exuberant rose blossoms down the hill, this is an oasis of lush greenery, winding paths, and tranquil ponds. Flowering cherries and azaleas accent the grounds come spring; in summer, the Japanese irises bloom; in autumn, the laceleaf maples glow orange and red. Eaves and posts of the Japanese pavilion frame the Flat Garden to the west and Mount Hood to the east.

A garden shop stocks books on such topics as the art of Japanese flower arrangement and traditional tea ceremonies, as well as one on Portland's garden itself. Guided public tours are offered Tuesday through Sunday at 10:45am and daily at 2:30pm, mid-April through October. Admission is $6 for adults, $5 for seniors, and $4 for students and children over 5. *Mon noon–7pm, Tues–Sun 10am–7pm (Apr–Sept), Mon noon–4pm, Tues–Sun 10am–4pm (Oct–Mar); map:HH7*

8) OREGON ZOO

4001 SW CANYON RD, WASHINGTON PARK; 503/226-1561 What began
more than a century ago as a seaman-turned-veterinarian's menagerie on SW Third Avenue and Morrison Street has since grown into an outstanding 64-acre zoo, winning awards for exhibits showcasing the fauna of the Cascades as well as a colony of endangered Peruvian Humboldt penguins, well protected (and thriving) here.

Born in 1962, Packy—the first Asian elephant born in the Western Hemisphere—blazed the trail for the pachyderm breeding program. Now, some two dozen newborns later, the elephant program continues apace, with excellent viewing opportunities no matter the weather. The unique Lilah Callen Holden Elephant Museum not only documents Packy's story, but highlights elephants' historic role as workers and cultural icons while decrying illegal poaching by ivory hunters.

The zoo has a complex primate exhibit, featuring an arena architecturally designed in keeping with the natural behavior of chimpanzees and other apes. The African savanna exhibit features black rhinoceros, giraffes, impalas, zebras, and birds; the African rain-forest exhibit features hourly rainstorms and more than two dozen animal species, including the naked mole rat.

The newest exhibit is Great Northwest: a Crest to Coast Adventure, where visitors can journey through lush mountain forests and wild coastlines. Located on the north end of the zoo, it's being completed in phases: the first was Cascade Crest, where mountain goats roam a simulated rocky cliff face, and the second was Steller Cove, home to Steller's sea lions, sea otters, and a kelp forest. Eagle Canyon and the Trillium Creek Family Farm, along with a breeding center for the highly endangered California condor, were scheduled to open in mid-2004. When completed, the exhibit will include black bears, wolverines, bald eagles, and other Northwest animals in a 90-year-old forest.

The cafeteria-style Cascade Grill restaurant serves better-than-average zoo food; its carpet and metalwork chandeliers are commissioned art pieces that reflect the Pacific Northwest. During warm-weather months, a small steam train chugs through the zoo and down to the rose garden ($3 for adults; $2.25 for seniors and children 3–11); in spring and for special events the train makes a shorter run around the zoo's perimeter. On the second Tuesday of each month, zoo admission is free after 1pm; regular admission is $8 for adults, $6.50 for seniors, and $5 for kids 3–11.

On summer evenings crowds throng to the grassy outdoor amphitheater for live music concerts by nationally acclaimed artists. In fall, the zoo hosts a World Animal Festival, and on the weekend before Halloween, kids trick-or-treat at the Howloween party. In December, the Zoo Lights Festival is an incandescent holiday tradition. *Every day except Christmas, gate hours are 9am–6pm (Apr 1–Sept 30), 9am–4pm (Oct 1–Mar 31), visitors can stay in the zoo for 1 hour after the gate closes; www.oregonzoo.com; map:HH7* &

9) PEARL DISTRICT

W BURNSIDE ST NORTH TO NW NORTHRUP ST, BETWEEN NW 8TH AND 15TH AVES Since the mid-1980s, warehouses and wholesalers' storefronts in the aged industrial Northwest Triangle district have taken on new lives. Empty spaces have been turned into clean-lined art galleries, antique showrooms, furniture stores, bookstores, and lofts for upscale urban dwellers. Construction and renovation continue along the cobblestone streets (built at the turn of the 20th century from stones used as ballast by sailing vessels); the recent multiblock redevelopment of the Brewery Blocks, formerly Henry Weinhard's Burnside brewery, is the latest (but certainly not the last) office/retail/housing metamorphosis to take place. When the dust finally clears, the area will be substantially transformed and considerably more populated.

The Pearl is the place to gallery-browse, especially on the **FIRST THURSDAY** of each month, when galleries throw open their doors to show off their collections (see Galleries in the Arts Scene chapter) and beautiful people stroll the sidewalks. If you're lucky enough to catch First Thursday on a warm evening, the show on the sidewalk may be the best: artists of all stripes come to hawk their wares, creating a vibrant street scene. Besides the fine-art galleries, the Pearl District is saturated with "functional art" galleries and hot furniture stores. Wine bars and fine-dining restaurants have sprung up throughout the district, offering respite to gallery-goers on *every* night of the month.

Start a stroll through the Pearl at **POWELL'S CITY OF BOOKS** (1005 W Burnside St; 503/228-4651; map:K2), the country's largest independent bookstore (see no. 15 in this section). A visit to this literary institution is a tour in itself, with 68,000 square feet—a city block's worth—of new and used books. The surrounding, newly redeveloped five-block neighborhood is known as the **BREWERY BLOCKS**; after the Blitz-Weinhard Brewery, established in 1864, closed in 1999, it underwent urban renewal to the tune of 1.7 million square feet of retail, office, and residential space. Among the refurbished buildings in this complex are the 1908 Tuscan-brick **BLITZ-WEINHARD BREWERY BUILDING** (1133 W Burnside St; map:K2); the 1929 **A. B. SMITH AUTOMOTIVE BUILDING** (1207 W Burnside St; map:K2), with cast-stone eagles and Art Deco ambience; and the fortresslike **PORTLAND ARMORY BUILDING** (NW 10th Ave between Couch and Davis Sts; map:K2), built in 1891, site of the first professional hockey game in the United States in 1912.

Next door to the Armory is the **ART INSTITUTE OF PORTLAND** (1122 NW Davis St; 503/228-6528; map:K2), which offers degree programs in digital media production and graphic design. Catty-corner is the five-story 1910 Ice House, now the **WIEDEN + KENNEDY BUILDING** (224 NW 13th Ave; map:K1). Renovated to the tune of $36 million in 1999, the understated structure—home to a major advertising agency and **BLUEHOUR** restaurant (see review in the Restaurants chapter)—is focused on a central skylit atrium.

At NW 11th Avenue and Flanders Street is **THE GREGORY** (map:L2), a 12-story Art Deco–style monument completed in 2001. A prototype for other modern mixed-use developments in the Pearl, this full-city-block giant boasts such architectural features as curved corners and futuristic detailing. Similarly spectacular is the new—2004—**REI BUILDING** (1405 NW Johnson St; map:N1), its climbing wall

165

clearly visible behind a two-story glass facade (see review in the Shopping chapter). Nearby NW Glisan and Hoyt Streets, especially between 10th and 14th Avenues, are the hubs of Pearl District nightlife; here are such fine restaurants as **FRATELLI, GIORGIO'S, MANZANA ROTISSERIE GRILL, iOBA!,** and **PARAGON RESTAURANT & BAR** (see reviews for all in the Restaurants chapter).

Construction is fast and furious around **JOHNSON SQUARE,** a charming neighborhood park between NW Johnson and Kearney Streets and between 10th and 11th Avenues. But the Pearl District extends yet farther northwest to the **BRIDGEPORT BREWING CO. BUILDING** (1313 NW Marshall St; map:O1), built in 1888 and one of the oldest industrial buildings still in use in Portland. Virginia creeper vines cover much of the rough-hewn structure, once a marine cordage company. (See review in the Nightlife chapter.)

On the west, I-405 separates the Pearl District from Northwest Portland. On the east, the **NORTH PARK BLOCKS** create a division between the district and Chinatown. Stretching from Burnside to Glisan Streets, these five blocks are home to the Art in the Pearl celebration each Labor Day weekend. The 1901 **U.S. CUSTOM HOUSE** (220 NW 8th Ave; map:L4) faces the park between Davis and Everett Streets; a majestic French Renaissance structure, it boasts a granite colonnade and beautiful open courtyard. It is currently home to the Army Corps of Engineers. *www.thepearl.citysearch.com; map:K1, 2, 3–O1*

10) NORTHWEST PORTLAND

NORTH OF W BURNSIDE ST, CENTERED ON NW 21ST AND 23RD AVES For thousands of Portlanders, "Northwest" means home, but for nonresidents it mostly means shopping and dining along two of the most bustling avenues in the city. Lively, urbane NW 23rd Avenue purposefully combines elements of funk with high fashion, making for a smart street scene. Two blocks away, though somewhat more downscale, NW 21st Avenue is home to several of Portland's finest restaurants.

In block after block along NW 23rd Avenue, from Burnside to Thurman Streets, there is a wealth of cosmopolitan attractions. Down the avenue, many Victorian homes have been remodeled into small retail enclaves, and attractive new developments have also been built, nosing out less sightly structures. "Trendy-Third," as the street is affectionately known, draws an eclectic crowd: neighborhood first-graders on scooters weave among open-mouthed tourists, determined shoppers busily compare goods in the many housewares and clothing stores, and the cafe crowd lingers at tables along the sidewalk. (This crowd may surprise you: look for the lineup of Harleys parked every evening outside the local Starbucks). It's easy to pass a day here. Parking can be tough; your best bet for spaces may be on the east–west cross streets. Many visitors prefer to take Tri-Met or the new Portland Streetcar from downtown. (See Getting Around in the Lay of the City chapter.)

A good way to see Nob Hill, as the heart of this district is sometimes known, is to walk up NW 23rd Avenue and back down NW 21st Avenue. Start at the **UPTOWN SHOPPING CENTER** (W Burnside St and NW 24th Ave; map:HH7), then wander north up 23rd, past shops like **MOONSTRUCK CHOCOLATIER** and the **LENA MEDOYEFF STUDIO** and such restaurants as **TYPHOON!** and **PAPA HAYDN.** Turn the corner at Pettygrove Street, just past the Good Samaritan Hospital, and cut over

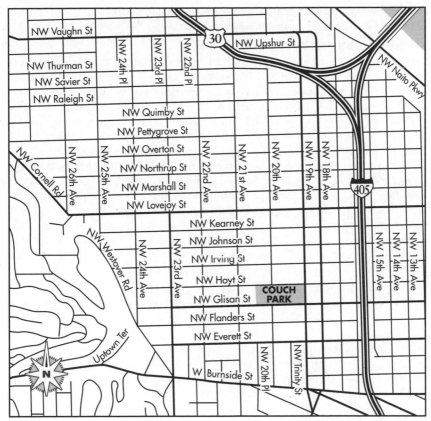

NORTHWEST PORTLAND

to 21st, where the slew of fine-dining establishments includes Cory Schreiber's cutting-edge **WILDWOOD** and Vitaly Paley's intimate **PALEY'S PLACE**. (See reviews in the Restaurants and Shopping chapters.) Two spots worthy of special note are **CITY MARKET** NW (735 NW 21st Ave; 503/221-3007; map:GG7), where individual purveyors of the finest pasta, seafood, fruits, vegetables, and meats are gathered under one roof; and **CINEMA 21** (616 NW 21st Ave; 503/223-4515; map:GG7), an old-fashioned movie house, where rocking chairs provide seating for art-house and foreign-film patrons.

Northwest's other cinema is the **MISSION THEATER** (1624 NW Glisan St; 503/223-4031; map:M1), where the McMenamins' brewing-and-hospitality group has its head offices. Built in 1912 and operated as a Swedish evangelical mission for four decades, it was later occupied by the Longshoremen's Union. Three blocks west, **TEMPLE BETH ISRAEL** (1931 NW Flanders St; map:HH7) is unique in Oregon—a distinctive, turreted Byzantine synagogue with a domed tower and sculpted bronze doors, completed in 1927. Twelve blocks north, motorists on the Hwy 30 ramp pass close by the 1891 **SAINT PATRICK'S ROMAN CATHOLIC CHURCH** (1635 NW 19th Ave; map:GG7) and its Renaissance Revival dome.

11) HOYT ARBORETUM

4000 SW FAIRVIEW BLVD, WASHINGTON PARK; 503/228-8733 Sweeping views, 12 miles of trails, and more than 1,000 species of plants—all neatly labeled—make up Portland's 185-acre tree garden. It's an international collection of woody plants, including the nation's largest assortment of conifer species. Blossoms dust the Magnolia Trail in spring; pink and white flowers shower the Dogwood Trail in midsummer. Maps are available at the visitors center, where one-hour guided walks (2pm Sat–Sun, Apr–Oct) begin. Some trails are paved for wheelchair access.

In Hoyt Arboretum's southwest corner is the **OREGON VIETNAM VETERANS' LIVING MEMORIAL**, an inspiring outdoor cathedral (built in 1987) that honors the 759 Oregonians who died, and the 32 still missing in action, in Vietnam. From the Garden of Solace at its heart, a slowly rising trail spirals clockwise over a bridge and past six monuments, whose poignant text integrates news from the warfront with stories of day-to-day life back home between 1959 and 1976. *Grounds open every day 6am–10pm, visitors center open Mon–Fri 9am–4pm, Sat 9am–3:30pm, except Thanksgiving, Christmas, Jan 1; www.hoytarboretum.org; map:HH7*

12) OREGON HISTORY CENTER

1200 SW PARK AVE, DOWNTOWN; 503/222-1741, 503/306-5198 An eight-story-high trompe l'oeil mural, overlooking the spacious new plaza and glass facade of this museum and research library, is a landmark on the South Park Blocks. Headquarters of the Oregon Historical Society (OHS) since 1966, the building reopened in the fall of 2003—after being closed a full year for renovation and expansion—with new permanent exhibits and bigger plans for the future.

The "Oregon, My Oregon" exhibit, whose scheduled opening was July 2004, occupies an entire floor with more than 50 separate displays (several of them hands-on) interpreting state history—from ancient Native Americans to modern corporate culture—through artifacts, documents, photographs, and video. Other permanent exhibits depict Oregon's early maritime history and showcase miniature horse-drawn vehicles. Temporary exhibits in 2004 through 2006 will focus on the Lewis and Clark Expedition; this museum will be the West Coast's only venue for the National Bicentennial Exhibition, scheduled to open in November 2005.

The redesigned OHS Research Library, open to the public three days a week, contains 30,000 books, 25,000 maps, and more than 2.5 million photographs in its archives. There's also a fine store (SW Broadway and Madison Street) with books and gift items. Museum admission is $6 for adults, $5 for students and seniors, $3 for youth, and children 5 and under are free. *Museum open Tues–Sat 10am–5pm, Sun noon–5pm, library open Thurs–Sat 1–5pm, both closed major holidays; www.ohs.org; map:F2* &

13) RIVER CRUISES ON THE COLUMBIA AND WILLAMETTE RIVERS

VARIOUS LOCATIONS Before the arrival of railroads and paved roads, people could hail a steamboat just about anywhere between Portland and Eugene, Astoria, and

The Dalles. Stern-wheelers still navigate the waters of the Columbia and Willamette Rivers and offer some relief from today's crowded highways. But more importantly, they give patrons an opportunity to see the region from a riverine viewpoint.

The *Portland Spirit* (503/224-3900) and her sister vessels, the *Willamette Star* and *Crystal Dolphin*, offer fine dining, dancing, and sightseeing cruises up and down the Willamette River. The *Portland Spirit* leaves from its berth near the Salmon Street Springs in Gov. Tom McCall Waterfront Park; catch the *Willamette Star* and *Crystal Dolphin* at the RiverPlace Marina. You may want to reserve this activity for special occasions. The cost of dinner cruises has climbed to $56, a midday lunch tour costs $29, and the Sunday champagne brunch cruise is $38 (all prices are lower for seniors and children). Two less expensive options are available without dining: sightseeing tours cost $16, and occasional dance cruises are $15. *www.portlandspirit.com* &

WILLAMETTE JETBOAT EXCURSIONS (503/231-1531) offer perhaps the most exciting way to experience the Willamette River on a public boat, if you don't mind the possibility of getting splashed. The open-air jet boats ride close to the water and take sightseers upriver, past riverfront homes—the spectacular and the modest—all the way to Willamette Falls in Oregon City and downriver to Portland's cargo docks and shipyards. Two-hour, 37-mile tours depart from the Oregon Museum of Science and Industry (OMSI) every day from May 1 to early October. Adults are $27, children (4–11) are $17, and kids 3 and under are free. One-hour tours are also available. *www.jetboatpdx.com*

The *Sternwheeler Rose* (503/286-7673), a 92-foot stern-wheeler replica, also sails from the OMSI dock on the east side of the Willamette. The downriver trip has an industrial look, passing shipyards, grain terminals, seven of Portland's 12 bridges, and one of the world's largest dry docks. Upriver toward Milwaukie is more scenic, passing John's Landing, Oaks Park, Sellwood, and gracious old homes on the bluffs overlooking the Willamette. Public meal cruises on the 130-passenger, double-deck boat run $28 for brunch, $38 for dinner. *www.sternwheelerrose.com.*

From its base at Marine Park in Cascade Locks, about 45 minutes east of Portland, the *Sternwheeler Columbia Gorge* (541/374-8427), a triple-deck paddle-wheeler, voyages through the dramatic Columbia River Gorge. Sound a bit touristy? There are plenty of Portlanders who've taken the scenic trip several times and still love it. In December, the 147-foot vessel docks at Gov. Tom McCall Waterfront Park in Portland and takes guests up and down the Willamette River on dinner-dance, brunch, and special holiday cruises. Fares range from $15 to $65. *www.sternwheeler.com.*

14) OREGON CITY HISTORIC SITES

OREGON CITY, 13 MILES SOUTHEAST OF PORTLAND VIA HWY 99E (AT I-205, EXIT 10) The official end of the Oregon Trail, Oregon City (then "Willamette Falls") became the first incorporated city west of the Rocky Mountains in 1844. The story of the arduous cross-country route, and the hardy pioneers who undertook the journey, is related today in giant covered wagon–shaped buildings at the END OF THE OREGON TRAIL INTERPRETIVE CENTER (1726 Washington St; 503/657-9336). Visitors see a mixed-media dramatization of mid-19th-century life; an exhibit hall with displays on Northwest life between the fur-trading era and the coming of the railroads; and the **WILLAMETTE TRADES & CRAFT WORKSHOP** with hands-on activities. Admission is $7.50, $6.50 for seniors, $5 for children 5–12, and children under 5 are free. *Mon–Sat 9:30am–5:30pm, Sun 10:30am–5:30pm, shows hourly (Memorial Day–Labor Day), Mon–Sat 9:30am–5pm, Sun 10am–5pm, shows hourly (Mar–May and Sept–Oct), Wed–Sat 11am–4pm, Sun noon–4pm, shows twice daily (Nov–Feb), closed Thanksgiving, Christmas, Jan 1; www.endoftheoregontrail.org; map:OO3* ⚹

Oregon City also can lay claim to the first public library west of the Rockies (1842) and the Northwest's first navigation locks (1873)—still operational today. Much of the city's history is portrayed in murals on its downtown buildings. The Oregon City Municipal Elevator (at the foot of the bluff on 7th St), one of only four municipal elevators in the world, takes you from the town's river level up to the top of the bluff.

A few blocks away is the **MCLOUGHLIN HOUSE NATIONAL HISTORIC SITE** (713 Center St; 503/656-5146). Dr. John McLoughlin, the "Father of Oregon," built this house in 1846 when he was forced to retire as chief factor of the British Hudson's Bay Company at Fort Vancouver (see no. 19 in this section). Here you can learn how the Quebec-born McLoughlin helped claim the Oregon Territory for the United States and see some of the home's original furnishings, including the dining-room table and chairs, Staffordshire china, and a hand-carved bed from Scotland. Admission is $4 for adults, $3 for seniors, $2 for children 6–17. *Wed–Sat 10am–4pm, Sun 1pm–4pm, closed Jan and holidays; www.mcloughlinhouse.org; map:PP4*

About 10 blocks south, the **MUSEUM OF THE OREGON TERRITORY** (211 Tumwater Dr; 503/655-5574), operated by the Clackamas County Historical Society, displays ancient petroglyphs, a 12-foot-high statue of Lady Justice, and the original plat map of San Francisco (filed here in 1850 because Oregon City had the only federal courthouse in the territory). From the museum's third floor you get a panoramic view of Willamette Falls, where Native Americans gathered for centuries to catch and trade salmon; and whose power later settlers used for saw, grain, and paper mills. Adult admission is $4; less for seniors and children. *Mon–Fri 10am–4pm, Sat–Sun noon–4pm; www.orcity.com/museum; map:PP4*

15) POWELL'S CITY OF BOOKS

1005 W BURNSIDE ST, DOWNTOWN; 503/228-4651 National bookseller chains can open as many superstores in town as they please, but Powell's will always be top dog in Portland. Even those who prefer smaller, more intimate bookstores find themselves lured to Powell's out of sheer gluttony. With more than 1 million volumes filling a city block at the main Burnside store, it is the largest independent bookstore in the country (see sidebar, "A Literary Legend"). Tourists should plan at least an afternoon here, if just to say they've seen it.

The store provides floor maps to help buyers find their way through its myriad sections, from Automotive to Zen. Tucked into the maze are a rare-book room and a children's book area. Several times each week, touring authors of national repute read from their work in the Pearl Room, part of the store's latest expansion. The Pearl Room also houses the Basil Hallward Gallery, which displays art and

A LITERARY LEGEND

Powell's City of Books (main store at 1005 W Burnside St, Downtown; 503/228-4651; www.powells.com; map:J2) is one of the world's great bookstores, and one of the most successful dot-coms in the world of books. But that wasn't always the case.

The store's roots go back to Chicago, circa 1970. Portlander Michael Powell was a graduate student at the University of Chicago when he took out a $3,000 loan to assume a lease on a small bookstore. With friends and professors (among them Nobel Prize–winning novelist Saul Bellow) as regular patrons, he repaid the loan in two months.

Michael invited his father, Walter, a retired painting contractor, to spend the summer in Chicago working at the store. So gratifying did Walter find the experience, he returned to Portland and opened his own used bookstore. Walter wasn't selective like Michael: he bought every marketable volume that found its way through his door and soon had no room in his little shop for the merchandise. By the end of 1971, he had taken over a derelict car dealership at 10th and Burnside in Northwest Portland. And Powell's City of Books was born.

When Michael returned to Portland to join his father in 1979, he found a book business that was unorthodox at best. Not only were hardcover and paperback books together on the same shelf; used books were stacked together with new ones. What's more, Powell's was open 365 days a year, well into the late-night hours.

"I had no sympathy," Michael said, in recalling his initial reaction. "Used and new on the same shelf? It seemed crazy."

But—surprise!—the dual approach worked. "If you put all the new books in one store and all the used books in another, each wouldn't get half the total business," Michael said. "They drive each other."

Powell's has undergone many expansions and mutations over its three-plus decades of business. The store entered the computer age when it went online in 1994 and within two years had its entire inventory listed on the Web. Powells.com today ships books all over the world.

—*John Gottberg*

photography from local and international artists. The new northwest entrance to the store is anchored by the Pillar of Books, a nine-foot column of Tenino sandstone in which eight of the world's great books have been carved. Powell's even has a parking garage (enter on NW 11th Ave).

Powell's has spawned a half-dozen offspring, each with its own specialty. **POWELL'S TRAVEL STORE** (SW 6th Ave and Yamhill St, Downtown; 503/228-1108; map:H4), in the southeast corner of Pioneer Courthouse Square, carries guidebooks to everywhere. On your way out of town at the airport, check out **POWELL'S BOOKS AT PDX** (503/249-1950; map:EE3), which stocks mostly new volumes. A few blocks from the main store, **POWELL'S TECHNICAL BOOKSTORE** (33 NW Park Ave, Downtown; 503/228-3906; map:K3) has the city's best selection of computer, electronics, and engineering books. **POWELL'S BOOKS IN BEAVERTON** (8725 SW Cascade Ave, Beaverton; 503/643-3131; map:KK9) has an excellent children's selection, but much more. **POWELL'S ON HAWTHORNE** (3723 SE Hawthorne Blvd, Southeast; 503/238-1668; map:HH5) carries a healthy selection of new and used general titles, while two stores down, **POWELL'S BOOKS FOR COOKS AND GARDENERS** (3747 SE Hawthorne Blvd, Southeast; 503/235-3802; map:HH5) specializes in (what else?) cookbooks and gardening guides. *Powell's main store is open every day 9am–11pm; www.powells.com; map:J2* &

16) BREWERIES AND BREWPUBS

VARIOUS LOCATIONS More than a century has passed since Henry Weinhard proposed pumping beer through the Skidmore Fountain. But even before that, Portlanders loved beer. Today, although Weinhard's beer is brewed elsewhere (and the former brewery has been developed into housing and retail space), the city has almost as many places to drink beer as to drink coffee.

More than 40 craft breweries and brewpubs call Portland home, more per capita than any other American city (check out www.oregonbeer.com for a listing). The Northwest in general—and Portland in particular—is the national center for craft breweries: small, independent companies that turn out specialty beers, generally in small batches and according to traditional methods. Aficionados argue that Northwest brews are distinctly different from even the best imports. They claim that the western barley, hops from the Willamette and Yakima Valleys, and Cascade water give local concoctions their particular character.

One place to get a free tour of the brewing process is the **WIDMER BREWING COMPANY**, which produces the city's favorite hefeweizen in its facility on an industrial byway in North Portland. Tours (with beer sampling) are available Fridays at 3pm and Saturdays at 1pm and 2pm; simply show up at the attached beer hall, the attractive **WIDMER GÄSTHAUS** (955 N Russell St, Albina; 503/281-3333; www.widmer.com; map:GG6), which also is a fine place to sample Widmer suds with a plate of sausage and kraut or a pretzel.

Head to the waterfront along the RiverPlace esplanade for **FULL SAIL BREWING COMPANY'S** Portland brewery (0307 SW Montgomery St, RiverPlace; 503/222-5343; www.fullsailbrewing.com; map:C5). Tours are by appointment only, but you can see the works from the adjoining **HARBORSIDE PILSNER ROOM** pub (503/220-1865) and sample 12 beers, including Full Sail's best-selling Amber Ale, Golden Ale, and Nut Brown Ale.

One brewery that's garnered attention on the international level is **HAIR OF THE DOG** (4509 SE 23rd Ave, Brooklyn; 503/232-6585; www.hairofthedog.com; map: HH5), which produces sublime "bottle-conditioned" (it improves with age) strong beer. British beer writer Michael Jackson has picked the brewery as one of the best in the country, and their Adam beer is one of his personal favorites. It's a small operation, but the beer makers at Hair of the Dog are happy to give tours (call ahead).

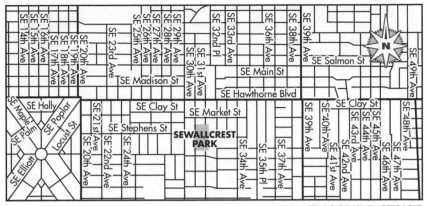

HAWTHORNE DISTRICT

You can read about the history of Portland brewing, and learn about more than a dozen pubs offering custom-brewed suds, in this book's Nightlife chapter. One way to sample brews from multiple places is to head down to Gov. Tom McCall Waterfront Park the last full weekend in July for the **OREGON BREWERS FESTIVAL** (503/778-5917; www.oregonbrewfest.com) to sample beers from about 70 different craft breweries.

17) HAWTHORNE DISTRICT

SE HAWTHORNE BLVD FROM ABOUT SE 20TH TO 49TH AVES The lengthy strip that is Hawthorne Boulevard might well be considered Portland's own little Haight-Ashbury. And while those who dream about the Summer of Love feel right at home here among the purveyors of tie-dye and incense, an increasing number of upscale retail shops and eateries are locating here as well. As commercial activity creeps east and west along the boulevard, this district—just southeast of downtown—may come to resemble a funkadelic, four-lane version of NW 23rd Avenue.

The hub of Hawthorne is McMenamins' brightly colored **BAGDAD THEATER AND PUB** (3710 SE Hawthorne Blvd; 503/230-0895; map:HH5). Built in 1927 with financing from Universal Studios, the Mediterranean-style building with the neon Middle Eastern marquee still packs in patrons for pizza, brewski, and celluloid. In 1975, actor Jack Nicholson saw the premiere of his Oscar-winning performance in *One Flew Over the Cuckoo's Nest* from a seat at the Bagdad.

For blocks in either direction from the Bagdad are quaint stores, coffee shops, and wonderfully idiosyncratic dining establishments like the **BREAD AND INK CAFÉ** (3610 SE Hawthorne Blvd; 503/239-4756; map:HH5), which serves up a Yiddish brunch with great blintzes, and **3 DOORS DOWN** (1429 SE 37th Ave; 503/236-6886; map:HH5), which offers Mediterranean-inspired dinners in a warm, bistro-style setting (see reviews in the Restaurants chapter). There are a half-dozen unique bookstores between SE 31st and 37th Avenues, and a variety of quirky specialty shops providing everything from crystals to clocks to cat-scratch furnishings (see Shopping).

At its west end, between SE 12th and 20th Avenues, the Hawthorne District brushes the northern edge of **LADD'S ADDITION**, one of Portland's most intriguing neighborhoods. Extending south to Division Street, it was developed between 1903 and 1925 on the earlier plan of pioneer entrepreneur William S. Ladd, who had been impressed by the radial street pattern of Washington, D.C. The main streets in this residential district, SE Ladd and Elliott Avenues, form a large X that meets in a central park, Ladd's Circle; secondary streets come together at four diamond-shaped rose gardens. *Map:HH5*

18) PITTOCK MANSION

3229 NW PITTOCK DR, PITTOCK ACRE; 503/823-3624 Henry Pittock (1835–1919) had the advantage of watching over Portland from two perspectives: from behind the founder's desk at the daily *Oregonian* and, in his later years, from this home 1,000 feet above the city. Built between 1909 and 1914 by San Francisco architect Edward T. Foulkes, the stately, 16,000-square-foot mansion stands on 46 acres that look across North Portland to Mount Hood. A fortresslike chateau of French Renaissance style, it boasts sandstone-faced walls and a red-tiled roof broken up by turrets and dormer windows. It stayed in the Pittock family until 1964, when the property—in poor repair and threatened by the wrecker's ball—was sold to the City of Portland for $225,000. Restoration has since been ongoing; the historic gatehouse was scheduled to be reopened in summer 2004 after extensive work.

The house has two main wings that meet in a central drawing room. A graceful marble staircase sweeps from the basement to the second story; another, less conspicuous stairway leads to the servants' quarters on the top floor. The 22 rooms, furnished with antiques, include an oval parlor and a Turkish smoking room. Everywhere, it seems, is beautiful wood paneling and crystal chandeliers. Regular tours are conducted in the afternoon, and the manicured grounds around the mansion and Pittock Acres (with numerous hiking trails) are open to the public until dark. Admission to the mansion is $5.50 for adults, $5 for seniors, $3 for kids 6–18, and free for children 5 and younger. *Every day 11am–4pm (June–Aug), noon–4pm (Feb–May and Sept–Dec), closed Jan, late Nov, and Christmas; www.pittockmansion .com; map:HH8* &

19) FORT VANCOUVER NATIONAL HISTORIC SITE

612 E RESERVE ST, VANCOUVER, WA; 360/696-7655 Anyone with even a mild curiosity about life in the Oregon Territory in the 19th century should head to Fort Vancouver across the Columbia in Washington. The headquarters (1825–60) and main supply depot for the Hudson's Bay Company regional fur-trading operation, it was the political, commercial, and cultural center of life in the Pacific Northwest. A U.S. military reservation beginning in 1849, it has been reconstructed as a historic site within the 366-acre Vancouver National Historic Reserve.

Stop at the **VISITORS CENTER** (1501 E Evergreen Blvd, via Mill Plain Blvd off I-5; map:CC6) to gather maps and visit the museum, which presents a 12-minute video of the fort's history. The old fort and officers' quarters are in different areas: a map will help.

Plan to spend a couple of hours in reconstructed **FORT VANCOUVER**. There are living-history demonstrations in the kitchen and bakehouse, blacksmith, and carpenter shops. (Admission is $3 per person, $5 per family, with children under 17 free.) Newly arrived Oregon Trail immigrants purchased supplies from the trade and retail stores to launch their new settlements; the fort operated sawmills and grist-mills, livestock and dairy farms, and had a hand in salmon fishing and shipbuilding. Up to 1,000 people of diverse ethnic backgrounds lived in the adjacent Company Village, stretching south to the bank of the Columbia River: it was the largest community between San Francisco and Russian-controlled Sitka, Alaska.

Just outside the palisade, the 1840s **GARDENS OF FORT VANCOUVER** continue to flourish. Some consider these gardens the seedbeds of Northwest horticulture and agriculture. It's the first known organized local planting of vegetables, herbs, and flowers in a formal plot, reflecting the garden's English origins as well as some exotic additions—purple Peruvian potatoes, for instance, and West Indian gherkins.

The **VANCOUVER BARRACKS** and the grand officers' quarters along **OFFICERS' ROW** have all been restored. Note the impressive quarters of the Hudson's Bay Company's first chief agent, Dr. John McLoughlin, later the founder of Oregon City. Several Civil War generals—including Ulysses S. Grant, later U.S. president—launched their military careers here. The showpiece building is the antique-filled **MARSHALL HOUSE**, named for commanding officer George C. Marshall, who headed training for the Civilian Conservation Corps in the 1930s. The rest are townhouses and offices.

Troops from Vancouver Barracks provided protection and support for Oregon Trail immigrants. After the Hudson's Bay Company pulled up stakes in 1860, the Barracks sent men to fight in the Indian Wars, to quell labor strikes, to keep order during Alaska's Klondike gold rush, and to serve in the Philippines during the Spanish-American War. Portions of the Barracks today are home to two divisions of the U.S. Army Reserve. In 1905, **PEARSON FIELD** (1115 E 5th St, Vancouver; 360/694-7026; www.pearsonairmuseum.org; map:CC5) was established nearby; it became an important U.S. Army Air Corps base in the 1920s and 1930s. *Every day 9am–5pm (Mar–early Sept), 9am–4pm (early Sept–Feb), closed Thanksgiving, Dec 24–25, Dec 31, and Jan 1; www.nps.gov/fova; map:CC5–6* &

20) SATURDAY MARKET

108 W BURNSIDE ST, UNDER THE BURNSIDE BRIDGE BETWEEN SW 1ST AND FRONT AVES; 503/222-6072 In 1974 a group of Portland artists assembled the beginnings of what may today be the largest continuously operating outdoor craft market in the country. This is no occasional street fair: every weekend for 10 months, and during the week before Christmas (known as the "Festival of the Last Minute"), more than 350 craft and food vendors cluster under the Burnside Bridge and beyond to peddle handmade items ranging from stained glass to huckleberry jam, wool sweaters to silver earrings. On any given weekend (and especially around holidays or during summer), musicians, jugglers, magicians, face painters, and clowns entertain the crowd. A main stage, with scheduled entertainment, is at the hub of the food court, where the bites are usually beyond what you'd expect from a cart.

Tri-Met buses and the MAX light-rail serve the market in Fareless Square; disembark at Skidmore Fountain, under the Burnside Bridge. Street parking is free on

Sundays, but with a $25 purchase at the market you can also get two hours of free parking at the **SMARTPARK** garage on NW Davis Street and Naito Parkway.

While in the area, wander through the year-round stalls in the nearby **NEW MARKET VILLAGE** and the **SKIDMORE FOUNTAIN BUILDINGS** (see Old Town/ Skidmore/Chinatown in the Neighborhoods section of this chapter). *Sat 10am– 5pm, Sun 11am–4:30pm (Mar–Dec 24), every day the week before Christmas; www.portlandsaturdaymarket.com; map:J6* &

Neighborhoods

ALAMEDA/BEAUMONT

NE FREMONT ST BETWEEN 41ST AND 51ST AVES In the heart of the Alameda neighborhood, a beautiful residential district developed between 1910 and 1940, is the portion of NE Fremont Street known as Beaumont Village. The quaint shops and refurbished homes have created a place where Northeast Portlanders like to shop, eat, and browse. The **BEAUMONT MARKET** (4130 NE Fremont St; map:FF4) has the sensibility of an old-time general store; next door, the unique **DUTCH VILLAGE** building (NE 41st Ave and Fremont St; map:FF4) houses several shops. The new **FIFE** restaurant (4440 NE Fremont St; 222-3433; map:FF4) occupies a handsome and distinctive, brownish cube of a building in the heart of the Village (see review in the Restaurants chapter).

Klickitat Street parallels Fremont just one block to the south. If you're a fan of author Beverly Cleary and her children's novels, you'll want to visit the neighborhood where Ramona ("the Pest") Quimby lived. Then check out the statues of Ramona, Ribsy, and Henry Huggins in **GRANT PARK**, about six blocks off Fremont Street via 33rd Avenue. *www.bwna.org; map:FF4–5*

ALBERTA

NE ALBERTA ST BETWEEN 13TH AND 31ST AVES The best time to visit multicultural and arty NE Alberta Street is on the last Thursday evening of the month: galleries and shops in a 20-block stretch come alive in a happy bustle of art, food, and bodies known as **ART ON ALBERTA** (www.artonalberta.com) or Last Thursday— not to be confused with First Thursday in the Pearl District and downtown. The scene is quieter the rest of the time, but is no less intriguing.

NE Alberta is rapidly becoming not only a commercial success story but an ever-strengthening ribbon of community that ties together several residential neighborhoods (King, Vernon, Concordia, and Sabin). Yes, such restaurants as **BERNIE'S SOUTHERN BISTRO**, and **GROLLA** (see reviews in the Restaurants chapter) fill the bellies of the locals; but those establishments' art-hung walls also fill more aesthetic cravings. Numerous studios and art galleries line the street, including the **GUARDINO GALLERY** (2939 NE Alberta St; 503/281-9048), **ONDA STUDIO AND GALLERY** (2215 NE Alberta St; 503/493-1909), and **GLASS ROOTS** (2921 NE Alberta St; 503/460-3137). You'll see a Malcolm X mural on one corner, a Mexican grocer on another, and an art exhibit of Central Asian textiles on a third. It all adds up to a lively, groovy, youthful scene—a diamond in the rough that is being polished all the time. *www.alberta.urbanlivingmaps.com; map:FF5*

CENTRAL DOWNTOWN

See no. 2 in Top 20 Attractions.

HAWTHORNE DISTRICT

See no. 17 in Top 20 Attractions.

IRVINGTON

APPROXIMATELY FRAMED BY NE 7TH AND 26TH AVES, BROADWAY AND FREMONT STS One of Portland's oldest eastside neighborhoods, Irvington was initially the 1851 land claim of Scottish Captain William Irving. Purchased by the Prospect Park Company in the late 1880s and developed as an exclusive residential enclave, it was built up between 1905 and 1930 with a variety of Arts and Crafts bungalows, Victorian houses, and (toward Broadway) apartment buildings. Today an easy mile-and-a-quarter stroll down Irvington's wide sidewalks reveals beautiful large homes (several of them now bed-and-breakfast inns) and attractive gardens, as well as a hip shopping district.

From Broadway, walk a block north on NE 15th to the **GUSTAV FREIWALD HOUSE** (1810 NE 15th Ave), now a B&B called **THE LION AND THE ROSE** (see review in the Lodgings chapter). The turreted Queen Anne Victorian was built in 1906 for an early microbrewer. The stone Gothic **WESTMINSTER PRESBYTERIAN CHURCH** (1624 NE Hancock St), another block north and east, was built in 1912 through 1914 and trimmed with black basalt.

Turn east on Thompson to see the 1909 **MARCUS DELAHANT HOUSE** (1617 NE Thompson St), a beautiful prairie-style home with oversize porch, eaves, and support pillars. The architect, John Bennes, had been an office boy for Frank Lloyd Wright, and his mentor's hand is evident. Pass the **IRVINGTON CLUB** (2131 NE Thompson St), a tennis and swimming club established in 1898; its two-story Craftsman-style home was built in 1912 by member Ellis Lawrence, founder of the School of Architecture at the University of Oregon in Eugene. The large 1910 **WILLIAM KENNARD HOUSE** (2230 NE Thompson St) is also in the Craftsman style; architect Raymond Hockenberry, best known for Oregon's Crater Lake Lodge, used concrete blocks to imitate natural stone. Just around the corner stands Portland's **FIRST ARTS AND CRAFTS HOME** (2210 NE 23rd Ave), also designed by Ellis Lawrence.

Turn south again to **PORTLAND'S WHITE HOUSE** (1914 NE 22nd Ave), the 1911 estate of timber baron Robert F. Lytle. Now a luxurious bed-and-breakfast inn (see review in the Lodgings chapter), the oak-and-Honduran-mahogany house does resemble the president's mansion with its pillared portico and circular drive. A block west is Pietro Belluschi's **CENTRAL LUTHERAN CHURCH** (2104 NE Hancock St), built in 1948 through 1951. An architectural rebel best known for the Portland Art Museum, Belluschi designed a Scandinavian-style church with a Japanese gateway. The interior displays a Northwest simplicity in its use of wood and stained glass.

On the neighborhood's south end, small stores, boutiques, restaurants, and coffee shops line NE Broadway and Weidler Street, a block farther south. Shops like **MATISSE** (1411 NE Broadway) and **TRADE ROOTS** (1831 NE Broadway) have

NE Fremont St

IRVING PARK

NE Klickitat St

NE 15th Ave · NE 16th Ave · NE 17th Ave · NE 18th Ave · NE 19th Ave · NE 20th Ave

NE Siskiyou St

NE 28th Ave · NE 29th Ave · NE 30th Ave · NE 31st Ave · NE 32nd Ave

99E

NE 10th Ave · NE 11th Ave · NE 12th Ave · NE 13th Ave · NE 14th Ave

NE Stanton St

NE Knott St

Russell St

Brazee Ct

NE Brazee St

NE Sacramento St

IRVINGTON SCHOOL PARK

NE Thompson St

NE 21st Ave · NE 22nd Ave · NE 23rd Ave · NE 24th Ave · NE 25th Ave · NE 26th Ave · NE 27th Ave

Martin Luther King Jr Blvd

NE 7th Ave · NE 8th Ave · NE 9th Ave

NE Tillamook St

NE Hancock St

NE Schuyler St

NE Broadway St

NE 28th Ave · NE 30th Ave

Grand Ave · NE 6th Ave

NE Weidler St

NE Halsey St

84

IRVINGTON

strong followings, as do such cafes as **COLOSSO** (1932 NE Broadway) and **CHEZ JOSÉ** (2220 NE Broadway). If you're eating in, you can pick up everything you need at **IRVINGTON MARKET** (1409 NE Weidler St), home to **NEWMAN'S FISH COMPANY** (503/284-4537) and **KRUGER'S PRODUCE** (503/288-4236). See the Shopping and Restaurants chapters for more information on these establishments.

One Sunday in mid-May, the Irvington Community Association sponsors an open-house tour ($20) of the neighborhood's historic homes. Year-round, the Web site provides a wealth of detailed information. *www.irvingtonhometour.com; map: GG5*

LAKE OSWEGO

8 MILES SOUTH OF PORTLAND ON THE WEST BANK OF THE WILLAMETTE RIVER; 503/636-3634 Before white settlement, Native Americans fished for abundant salmon in narrow, 3½-mile-long Lake Oswego, which they called Waluga for the wild swans that gathered. White settlers first came in 1846, and a thriving iron industry (1865–94) gave the newly established town early prosperity. As the iron industry declined, the 405-acre lake became a popular recreation area and the city grew around the lake, becoming an upscale community now rife with trendy shops and restaurants.

Lake Oswego is an 8-mile drive south from downtown Portland via SW Macadam Avenue (Hwy 43); the road first becomes Riverside Drive and then State

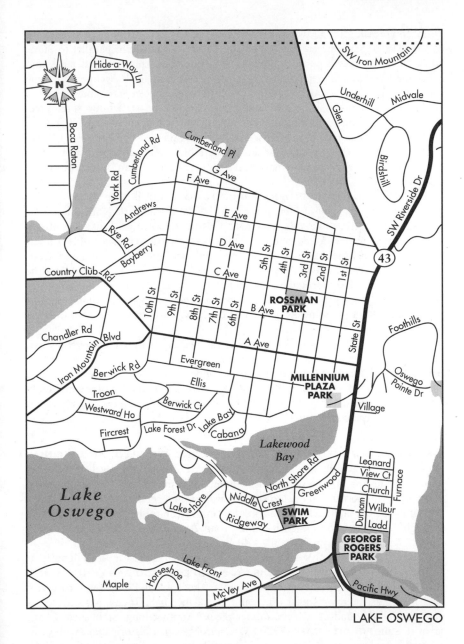

LAKE OSWEGO

Street, when you cross into Clackamas County. Or take the **WILLAMETTE SHORE TROLLEY** (503/222-2226) from RiverPlace along the Willamette River into Lake Oswego (see Train and Trolley Tours in this chapter).

In downtown Lake Oswego, lettered avenues (A, B, C, D) run perpendicular to the west of State Street. Numbered streets run north–south, parallel to State. More than two dozen public sculptures—in bronze, marble, stainless steel, and other media—have been placed along both sides of broad A Avenue and some cross streets. The new **LAKE VIEW VILLAGE** (A Ave between State and 1st Sts), a six-building complex that began opening in fall 2003, boasts 84,000 square feet of restaurants, shops, and offices beside **MILLENNIUM PLAZA PARK** (200 1st St), an inviting lakeside public square itself only four years old. The park has a lovely fountain and reflecting pond, benches, picnic tables, and public rest rooms; site of a summer Saturday farmers market, it also hosts concerts and numerous other events.

Elsewhere downtown, **GOURMET PRODUCTIONS** (39 B Ave; 503/697-7355) will prepare a tasty take-out lunch for you to take to the park (with a bottle of Oregon wine). Stores like **THE ELEGANT BASKET** (450 5th St; 503/636-4041), selling wines, gourmet foods, and other gifts; **RED DOOR COTTAGE** (425 2nd St; 503/635-3520), with a variety of handmade doll furniture and clothes; and **KILN-MANJARO** (41 B Ave; 503/636-9940), a colorful pottery workshop, address the town's creativity. The thoroughly English **LADY DI BRITISH STORE** (420 2nd Ave; 503/635-7298) serves tea with finger sandwiches and crumpets; fine-dining options include **CLARKE'S** (455 2nd Ave) and **TUCCI** (220 A Ave) (see reviews in the Restaurants chapter).

Some of Lake Oswego's earliest homes can still be seen in the **OLD TOWN** district, just south of downtown, east of State Street, and north of George Rogers Park. In particular, look for the 42-foot iron-smelter chimney stack (on the riverfront at the foot of Furnace Street); dating from 1866, it is the last reminder of a community settlers had hoped to turn into the "Pittsburgh of the West." *www.ci.oswego.or.us, www.lake-oswego.com; map:MM6*

MULTNOMAH VILLAGE
SW CAPITOL HWY FROM 30TH AVE TO MULTNOMAH BLVD, AND VICINITY
Hidden among the hills and vales of Southwest Portland is a jewel of a district known to most as Multnomah Village. (Some longtime residents insist on calling it simply "Multnomah," its name when it was an independent town.) No doubt, part of its quaint, laid-back charm comes from the Capitol Highway, which winds through the district like an English country road. Antique shops, art galleries, bookstores, and specialty shops make the Village a window shopper's delight.

Curiously, Multnomah's acknowledged heart isn't on the Capitol Highway at all, but a block's jog south. **MARCO'S CAFÉ AND ESPRESSO BAR** (7910 SW 35th Ave) occupies a 1913 building constructed as the Thomas Bungalow Grocery; it later served as the town's post office and as a dance hall. Today, Marco's serves breakfast all day and an eclectic dinner menu. Another long-established Village favorite is the **FAT CITY CAFE** (7820 SW Capitol Hwy), a historic diner with walls covered in traffic signs, that has played a key role in civic politics. See reviews in the Restaurants chapter.

A few blocks east, in the old Multnomah School, is a multipurpose neighborhood treasure: the **MULTNOMAH ART CENTER** (7688 SW Capitol Hwy; 503/823-ARTS).

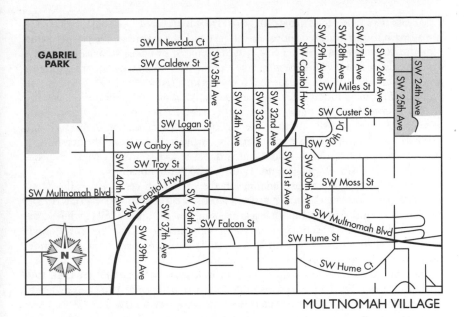

MULTNOMAH VILLAGE

Any time of year, you'll find a variety of cultural events and community classes offered here. Across the street, a vintage Masonic meeting hall now is home to the **LUCKY LABRADOR** brewpub (7675 SW Capitol Hwy). *Map:JJ7*

NORTHWEST PORTLAND
See no. 10 in Top 20 Attractions.

OLD TOWN/SKIDMORE/CHINATOWN
NORTH OF W BURNSIDE ST TO NW HOYT ST AND 8TH AVE, SOUTH OF W BURNSIDE TO SW OAK ST AND 4TH AVE Once the heart of the city's commercial core, the Skidmore and Old Town districts (Skidmore to the south of Burnside, Old Town to the north) have undergone major revitalization since the mid-1970s. Today they abound with good restaurants, nightclubs, and art galleries. Chinatown, with its magnificent gate on Fourth Avenue and W Burnside, is a relatively small area highlighted by the new classical Chinese garden. Overall, these districts contain one of the largest collections of restored brick and Italianate cast-iron buildings in the country, making the neighborhoods popular with film producers for period movie sets.

Start an exploration at the **SKIDMORE FOUNTAIN** (SW 1st Ave and Ankeny St; map:J6), the city's oldest and most gracious fountain, in cobblestone Ankeny Square. Built in 1888 from the estate of city councilman Stephen Skidmore, the cast-iron fountain features two handmaidens dispensing water through lions-head spouts into drinking troughs earmarked "for horses, men and dogs." These days, it's mainly appreciated by dogs.

Across the square, the **SKIDMORE FOUNTAIN BUILDING** has been remodeled as a mall with tourist-oriented shops. At the east end of the square, the **JEFF MORRIS MEMORIAL FIRE MUSEUM** (35 SW Ash St; map:J6) provides what is basically a window view of vintage fire engines; take a peek. West of Ankeny Square is a courtyard with tables for eateries inside the **NEW MARKET THEATER** (120 SW Ankeny St; map:J6). This magnificent brick and terra-cotta building, of Victorian Renaissance style, was considered the finest theater north of San Francisco after it opened (with *Rip Van Winkle*) in 1875. In fact, the 1,200-seat theater was on the second and third floors; a fresh-produce market with 28 marble stalls occupied the first floor. It was restored in 1984 to a jewel-like standard. Nearby, the Saturday Market bustles beneath the Burnside Bridge (see no. 19 in Top 20 Attractions).

One of Portland's grandest buildings in the early 20th century was the Multnomah Hotel, now the **EMBASSY SUITES HOTEL PORTLAND–DOWNTOWN** (319 SW Pine St; map:J5). A mammoth brick structure that occupies a full city block, the 1912 hotel has hosted celebrities from Charles Lindbergh to Elvis Presley to John F. Kennedy. Its enormous lobby, with 24 decorated marble columns, impresses visitors even today. (See review in the Lodgings chapter.)

Notable restaurants in these precincts include **DAN AND LOUIS' OYSTER BAR** (208 SW Ankeny St; map:J6), an institution in these parts since 1907 (see review in the Restaurants chapter), and **KELLS IRISH RESTAURANT & PUB** (112 SW 2nd Ave; map:J6), ensconced in the last cast-iron building (with Art Nouveau touches) constructed in Portland: the 1889 Glisan Building. Nearby is the spacious **ELIZABETH LEACH GALLERY** (207 SW Pine St; map:J6), considered one of Portland's premier art spaces (see review in the Arts Scene chapter).

Down the middle of SW First Avenue runs the MAX light-rail line. Follow it north, under the Burnside Bridge, to the carefully restored historic district of **OLD TOWN**. As in the Skidmore district, you'll see all manner of Italianate cast-iron architectural treasures, including the 1888 **SKIDMORE BLOCK** (32 NW 1st Ave; map:J6), which now houses an antiques market. Many of the buildings here now provide office or warehouse space. On the exterior of the modern (1983) **ONE PACIFIC SQUARE** building (between NW 1st and 2nd Aves, Davis and Everett Sts; map:L6), find a plaque that indicates the high-water mark of the Willamette River flood of June 7, 1894: 3 feet above the present sidewalk level.

From the 1920s until the onset of World War II, when Americans of Japanese ancestry were moved to internment camps, the area between SW Ankeny and NW Glisan Streets, and between First and Sixth Avenues, was known as Japantown. The bustling community had more than 100 businesses concentrated especially between NW Second and Fourth Avenues. Today the **OREGON NIKKEI LEGACY CENTER** (121 NW 2nd Ave; 503/224-1458; www.oregonnikkei.org; map:K6) preserves the heritage and offers walking maps of Japantown. (See Museums in this chapter.)

Portland's diminutive **CHINATOWN** blends into Old Town at about NW Third Avenue, but the serpent-adorned **CHINATOWN GATE** stands on NW Fourth Avenue at Burnside Street. Yu Tang Wang's 40-foot portal, dedicated in 1986, supports five roofs and 64 dragons. Although Portland's original Chinatown in the late 1800s was focused five blocks south of here, around Alder Street, the Chinese population slowly moved north. This area was designated a National Historic District in 1989;

it's small enough that fiery red-and-yellow lampposts are needed to remind you of your whereabouts.

The highlight of Chinatown is the new **PORTLAND CLASSICAL CHINESE GARDEN** (NW 3rd Ave and Everett St; 503/221-8131; map:K5). The largest of its kind in the United States, this Garden of the Awakening Orchid opened in 2000, the result of a partnership between Portland and its Chinese sister city, Suzhou. (See no. 6 in Top 20 Attractions.)

While several restaurants here will fill a craving for good Chinese food, the oldest, **FONG CHONG** (301 NW 4th Ave; map:L5), has been serving Portlanders since the 1930s. It harbors the city's finest dim sum parlor, a Sunday morning tradition. (See review in the Restaurants chapter.)

The Old Town/Chinatown neighborhood extends north to **UNION STATION** (800 NW 6th Ave; map:N4), eight blocks north of Burnside. A city landmark with its 150-foot, red-brick, Tuscan-style clock tower at the foot of the Broadway Bridge, the handsome Renaissance structure was built between 1890 and 1896. Pietro Belluschi remodeled the interior in the 1930s, and the building underwent a full restoration in the late 1990s. It remains a transportation hub today.

One caveat: Although lawyers, architects, and artists dominate the work force in and around Old Town, the perpetually unemployed consider the area prime turf too. Officially designated a "drug-free zone," Old Town has yet to be freed of drug dealers. While visitors should spend time in this area, they may not want to linger long after dark. *www.portlandalliance.com/otct/; map:J6–N4*

SELLWOOD/WESTMORELAND

SE 13TH AVE FROM MALDEN TO UMATILLA STS, SE MILWAUKIE AVE FROM KNIGHT TO MALDEN STS At the east end of the Sellwood Bridge, these two adjacent neighborhoods are one of Portland's best areas to go shopping for antiques and collectibles.

Sellwood, for six years a separate town on the east bank of the Willamette, was annexed to Portland in 1893, and it's proud of its past: shop owners have placed signs on their buildings identifying the structures' original uses and construction dates. One of the oldest buildings is the 1851 **OAKS PIONEER CHURCH** (455 SE Spokane St; www.oakspioneerchurch.org; map:KK6), a popular wedding site, but it is not a Sellwood original: built upriver in Milwaukie as Saint John's Episcopal Church by pioneer shipbuilder Lot Whitcomb, it was barged here in 1961.

The better part of a day can be spent browsing in this old neighborhood, a repository of American country furniture (both antique and new), lace, quilts, toys, hardware, china, jewelry, and trinkets. Particularly noteworthy are the **1874 HOUSE** (8070 SE 13th Ave; 503/233-1874; map:KK5), crammed with brass and copper hardware, light fixtures, and architectural fragments; and **R. SPENCER ANTIQUES** (8130 SE 13th Ave; 503/238-1737; map:KK5), with furniture and collectibles. At the **HANDWERK SHOP** (8317 SE 13th Ave; 503/236-7870; map:KK5), you can buy high-quality new and old Mission-style furniture. (See the Shopping chapter.) **OLD SELLWOOD SQUARE** (8235 SE 13th Ave; map:KK5) has several shops that surround a charming courtyard; among them is the Antique Row Cafe, serving light lunches Tuesday through Saturday. **GINO'S RESTAURANT AND BAR**

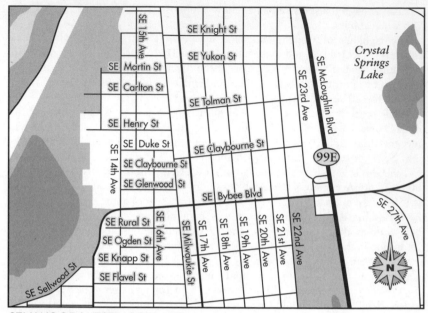

SELLWOOD/WESTMORELAND

(8051 SE 13th Ave; 503/233-4613; map:KK5), once the Original Leipzig Tavern, is a longtime Italian favorite in this neighborhood; **ASSAGGIO** (7742 SE 13th Ave; 503/232-6151; map:KK5) is a better bet for a romantic dinner. (See reviews in the Restaurants chapter.)

Several blocks north and east, **WESTMORELAND** has become a destination in itself, especially for foodies. This is where one of Portland's favorite chefs, Caprial Pence, and her husband, John, have their restaurant, store, and cooking school. At **CAPRIAL'S BISTRO** (7015 SE Milwaukie Ave; 503/236-6457; map:JJ5), Pence serves eclectic Northwest fare with her own special touches. Around the corner, **CAPRIAL & JOHN'S KITCHEN** (1608 SE Bybee Blvd; 503/233-4382; map:JJ5) takes the PBS series, *Cooking with Caprial & John*, to a whole new level with hands-on cooking classes. For reviews of Caprial's and other fine Westmoreland restaurants, see the Restaurants chapter.

Westmoreland doesn't have as many antique stores as its sister neighborhood of Sellwood, but it *does* have **STARS, AN ANTIQUE MALL** (7027 SE Milwaukie Ave; 503/239-0346; map:JJ5), which is actually *three* malls in one, incorporating **STARS AND SPLENDID** (7030 SE Milwaukie Ave) and **MORE STARS** (6717 SE Milwaukie Ave). Nearby independent bookstore **WALLACE BOOKS** (7241 SE Milwaukie Ave; 503/235-7350; map:JJ5) offers a houseful of new and used books and will help you track down that out-of-print volume.

The western fringe of this dual neighborhood is marked by the Willamette River and its newly extended **SPRINGWATER CORRIDOR** walking and biking trail, stretching south 3 miles from the Oregon Museum of Science and Industry. The corridor slices past **OAKS PARK** (foot of SE Spokane St; 503/233-5777; www. oakspark.com; map:KK6), one of the oldest operating amusement parks in the country, famous for its huge roller rink and 1921 carousel; and transits the **OAKS BOTTOM WILDLIFE REFUGE** (SE Oaks Dr off Milwaukie Ave; 503/823-2223; www.portlandparks.org; map:JJ5), a 160-acre woodland haven for bird watchers. (See the Recreation chapter for details.) *Map:JJ6–KK5*

Museums

American Advertising Museum

211 NW 5TH AVE, CHINATOWN; 503/226-0000 Who could forget Burma Shave signs, Will Vinton's California Raisins, and Texaco's sign of the flying horse? All-American artifacts are preserved at AAM, the first museum of its kind in the world. Time-line displays chart the development of advertising from the 15th century to the present. Memorable moments from radio days replay continuously: not just commercials, but broadcasts that marked the course of history, such as FDR's final oath of office and CBS's Bob Trout announcing the end of World War II. Video recordings of the all-time best TV commercials can keep you glued in place all day. Periodic rotating exhibits bring Portland some of the best print and broadcast advertising around. Admission is $5 for adults, seniors (60 and over), and students, and children are $4; free for children under 4. *Thurs–Sat 11am–5pm; www.admuseum .org; map:L5* &

Children's Museum 2nd Generation

4105 SW CANYON RD, WASHINGTON PARK; 503/223-6500 Now located in the old OMSI building in Washington Park, directly opposite the Oregon Zoo, Children's Museum 2nd Generation (CM2) is the museum that's not really a museum: it's a play and learning center for children from babies up to preteens. The "please touch" exhibits include a fantasy forest, where babies crawl along a fantasy stream and play with flowers and trees; a child-size grocery store and cafe, complete with shopping baskets, a checkout line, and a cash register where kids can ring up groceries; a water room that features everyday objects like kitchen tools and car windshield wipers used in unexpected and wacky ways; and a giant ball tower, where kids experiment with balls that don't always behave as they'd expect. Older children love the drop-in clay studio, where they can make a sculpture to be fired and glazed; artists are on hand to help. Various craft and music activities, puppet shows, costume parades, and other events are scheduled daily. Admission is $5.50 for ages 1–54 and $4.50 for seniors (55 and older); museum members and infants are admitted free. *Mon–Sat 9am–5pm, Sun 11am–5pm; www.portlandcm2.org; map:HH7*

End of the Oregon Trail Interpretive Center

1726 WASHINGTON ST, OREGON CITY; 503/657-9336 See no. 14 in Top 20 Attractions.

Forest Discovery Center

4033 SW CANYON RD, WASHINGTON PARK; 503/228-1367 The talking tree that greets visitors to this branch of the World Forestry Center will delight young and old alike: the 70-foot-high fir literally tells about its natural functions. Permanent exhibits focus on old-growth stands in the Pacific Northwest and tropical rain forests (in cooperation with the Smithsonian Institution); there also are cross-section displays of 200-million-year-old petrified logs. While the kids are exploring the Forest Discovery Lab, adults can enjoy traveling shows on art, history, and culture that cover such things as papermaking, wood carving, and James Audubon's original engravings. Admission is $5 for adults, $4 for seniors over 62, and $3.50 for children 5–18; kids under 5 are free. *Every day 10am–5pm, closed Thanksgiving and Christmas; www.worldforestry.org; map:HH7* &

Oregon History Center

1200 SW PARK AVE, DOWNTOWN; 503/222-1741 See no. 12 in Top 20 Attractions.

Oregon Maritime Center and Museum

GOV. TOM MCCALL WATERFRONT PARK AT SW PINE ST; 503/224-7724 When Portland was founded in the early 1840s on the banks of the Willamette River, the town thrived because of its deep harbor: any ship that could come into the mouth of the Columbia could go all the way to Portland, and shipping was by far the cheapest way to move cargo. The Maritime Museum celebrates this history aboard the *Portland*, the last steam-powered stern-wheel tugboat built in the country (in 1947), now moored at Gov. Tom McCall Waterfront Park. Here you can see the crew's quarters and the engine room, then climb up to the Pilot House, 32 feet above the water, for a great view. Many of the exhibits once in a nearby museum building have been moved onto the ship; they include model sailing ships, photographs from Portland's shipbuilding heritage, and navigational instruments. Admission is $4 for adults, $3 for seniors, $2 for students 8–17, and $10 for families. Children under 8 are free. *Wed–Sun 11am–4pm (May–Aug), Fri–Sun 11am–4pm (Sept–Apr); www.oregonmaritimemuseum.org; map:I7*

Oregon Museum of Science and Industry

1945 SE WATER AVE, SOUTHEAST; 503/797-4000 See no. 5 in Top 20 Attractions.

Oregon Nikkei Legacy Center

121 NW 2ND AVE, OLD TOWN; 503/224-1458 This small museum in the heart of what was once Portland's Japantown serves as a focal point for understanding Oregon's Japanese citizens and preserving their history—from the arrival of the first immigrants in the 1880s, to the thriving communities of the 1930s, to their displacement in World War II internment camps and their postwar resettlement. With rotating exhibits, a resource library of books and videotapes, educational programs and speakers, and performances of such groups as the Portland Taiko drummers, the center provides public education. Admission is free. *Mon–Fri 10am–3pm; www.oregonnikkei.org; map:K6* &

Portland Art Museum

 **1219 SW PARK AVE, DOWNTOWN; 503/226-2811** See no. 4 in Top 20 Attractions.

Gardens

Portland has been called the gardening capital of the United States. That may or may not be true, but there's no disputing the fact that it's a fantastic place to get your hands dirty. The Willamette Valley's mild climate makes for a long growing season that supports a variety of plant life about which most American gardeners only fantasize, and the diversity, expertise, and wild enthusiasm of the local green thumbs make it fertile ground in more ways than one.

Accomplished Portland gardeners are not a recent phenomenon. In 1889 the nation's first rose society was established here, soon followed by the first primrose and rhododendron societies. By the 1920s, Portland boasted more garden clubs than any other city in the nation; they now total more than 20.

This predilection for plant life means that visitors will encounter gardens in unexpected places. A small bamboo garden, for example, is tucked between exhibits at the Oregon Zoo (see no. 8 in Top 20 Attractions). There are more than 101 named varieties of camellias on the **UNIVERSITY OF PORTLAND** campus (5000 N Willamette Blvd, North Portland; 503/943-7911; map:EE8). A third-floor courtyard in **GOOD SAMARITAN HOSPITAL** (1015 NW 22nd Ave, Northwest; 503/413-7711; map:FF6) includes a rose garden; the **KAISER PERMANENTE CLINIC** in Rockwood (19500 SE Stark St, Gresham; 503/669-3900; map:HH1) maintains a sinister garden of common poisonous plants, designed to alert parents to backyard dangers.

The **COMMUNITY GARDENS PROGRAM** (503/823-1612) took root in Portland in the 1970s; it has spread to 21 neighborhood locations. Both year-round and summer 20-by-20-foot plots are available; some gardens have waiting lists. For those who would rather look than dig, the **FRIENDS OF PORTLAND COMMUNITY GARDENS** has established a demonstration site at Fulton Garden (SW 3rd Ave and Barbur Blvd; map:A2) featuring raised beds, irrigation and composting methods, heirloom seeds, and new plant varieties. A backyard wildlife habitat cozies up to the **CLINTON GARDEN** (SE 18th Ave and Clinton St; map:II5), and a demonstration orchard spreads its limbs next to the **GABRIEL GARDEN** (SW 41st Ave and Canby St; map:JJ8).

The following gardens are among the city's horticultural highlights. All are free and open daily, unless otherwise noted.

Berry Botanic Garden

11505 SW SUMMERVILLE AVE, RIVERWOOD; 503/636-4112 Berry's quarter-acre rock garden is more than an extraordinary accumulation of alpine plants; it's also part of this garden's nationally recognized effort to preserve endangered plant species of the Pacific Northwest in their native habitats. Three other plant groups (primulas, rhododendrons, and Northwest natives) are featured on the 6¼-acre estate of Mrs. Rae Selling Berry. Groups may schedule tours with volunteer guides by calling at least two weeks in advance. Admission is $5 for adult nonmembers; members and children under 12 are free. Call ahead to tell them you're coming and to get directions; it's just past Lewis and Clark College. The garden is partially wheelchair accessible. *Every day during daylight hours, visitors center open Mon–Fri 9am–4:30pm; www.berrybot.org; map:LL6* &

Crystal Springs Rhododendron Garden

SE 28TH AVE, 1 BLOCK NORTH OF SE WOODSTOCK BLVD, WOODSTOCK; 503/771-8386 Kodachrome was invented for places like this. This nationally acclaimed garden near Reed College is a peaceful green retreat for bird watchers and neighborhood strollers for most of the year. In April, May, and June, however, Crystal Springs becomes an irresistible magnet for color-happy camera and video buffs, as some 2,500 rhododendrons, azaleas, and companion plants blaze on the 7-acre grounds. Japanese maples, sourwood trees, and fothergillas paint the garden in fall, and the spring-fed lake, home to a sizable colony of waterfowl, is a year-round attraction. The annual plant sale and show is held on Mother's Day, when loads of Portlanders traditionally promenade through at peak bloom, and Crystal Springs is the spot for a spring wedding. Although the garden is free to view on Tuesdays and Wednesdays and every day after 6pm, a $3 admission fee is charged Thursday through Monday, March through Labor Day; children under 12 are free. *Every day dawn to dusk; www.parks.ci.portland.or.us/Parks/CrysSpringRhod Gar.htm; map:JJ5*

The Elk Rock Garden of the Garden of the Bishop's Close

11800 SW MILITARY LN, DUNTHORPE; 503/636-5613 This 13-acre estate at the edge of the exclusive Dunthorpe neighborhood serves as the headquarters of the Episcopal Diocese of Oregon, which explains the name: "close" is a British term for an enclosed place or garden around a church or other sacred place for quiet and meditation, where monks used to march in peace. This garden's genesis, however, dates back 75 years to the collaboration between its owner, Scottish grain merchant Peter Kerr, and New York landscape architect John Olmsted, son of Central Park designer Frederick Law Olmsted. Together they created an exquisite terraced garden facing Mount Hood and overlooking pristine Elk Rock in the Willamette River. Both native and rare plants are featured, including a multitude of madrones and 70 varieties of magnolia. Other highlights are lily ponds, a landscaped watercourse fed by a natural spring, a large rock garden, a formal boxwood-hedged terrace, and some of the finest specimens of wisteria you're likely ever to see. Tread respectfully. *Every day 8am–6pm (summer), 8am–5pm (winter); www.diocese-oregon.org/ theclose/; map:LL5*

The Grotto

NE 85TH AVE AND SANDY BLVD, NORTHEAST; 503/254-7371 Out-of-towners sometimes introduce longtime Portlanders to the National Sanctuary of Our Sorrowful Mother, commonly known as the Grotto. Tended by Friars of the Order of the Servants of Mary (the Servites), the Grotto is both a religious shrine and a lovely woodland garden. Mass is held daily year-round in the chapel; from May to September, Sunday Mass faces the Grotto itself, a fern-lined niche in the 110-foot-tall cliff, which houses a marble replica of Michelangelo's Pieta. Throughout the 62-acre grounds, rhododendrons, camellias, azaleas, and ferns shelter religious statuary, providing both the prayerful and the plant lover with ample material for contemplation, while giant sequoias tower above. Upper-level gardens and a panoramic view of the Cascades and the Columbia River (seen from floor-to-ceiling windows in the Meditation Chapel as well as from the gardens) are reached via a 10-story elevator ride ($2). In December, the Grotto radiates with its spectacular Festival of Lights. *Every day 9am–7:30pm (summer), 9am–5:30pm (spring and fall), 9am–4pm (winter); closed Thanksgiving and Christmas; www.thegrotto.org; map:FF3*

Home Orchard Society Arboretum

19600 S MOLALLA AVE, OREGON CITY; 503/657-6958 Adjacent to the John Inskeep Environmental Learning Center (at Clackamas Community College) is a dazzling assortment of fruit-bearing plants. The Home Orchard Society cultivates dwarf fruit trees, with terrific samplings of apple and pear varieties. If you've been wanting to add a blueberry bush to your yard—or a kiwi vine, persimmon, papaw, or plum-apricot cross—this is the place to decide on the variety. *Tues and Sat approximately 8:30am–12:30pm (Mar–Oct); map:QQ3*

Hoyt Arboretum

4000 SW FAIRVIEW BLVD, WASHINGTON PARK; 503/228-8733 See no. 11 in Top 20 Attractions.

International Rose Test Garden

400 SW KINGSTON AVE, WASHINGTON PARK; 503/823-3636 See no. 1 in Top 20 Attractions.

Japanese Garden

611 SW KINGSTON AVE, WASHINGTON PARK; 503/223-1321 See no. 7 in Top 20 Attractions.

John Inskeep Environmental Learning Center

19600 S MOLALLA AVE, OREGON CITY; 503/657-6958 What was once an 8-acre plot of ravaged land—the wastewater lagoons and parking lots of a berry-processing plant—is now home to shady paths, ponds, and wildlife habitat in an urban setting. The learning center at Clackamas Community College demonstrates environmentally sound solutions to landscape problems, incorporating recycled plastic "logs" in footbridges and utilizing solar- and compost-heated greenhouses in the nursery. Kids flock to the ponds, home to three kinds of turtles (red-eared sliders, western pond, and painted) as well as ducks; parents appreciate the more delicate butterfly garden. The observatory's 24-inch refractor telescope is open during cloudless Friday and Saturday evenings. A $2 donation is suggested. *Every day dawn to dusk; depts.clackamas.edu/elc/; map:QQ3*

Leach Botanical Garden

6704 SE 122ND AVE, SOUTHEAST; 503/761-9503 The emphasis on native Northwest plants in this garden is fitting: one of the garden's creators discovered 2 genera and 11 species in Northwest wildernesses. Well-known amateur botanist Lilla Leach and her husband, John, began their 5-acre garden along Johnson Creek in the early 1930s; today, its 15 acres are home to 2,000 species and cultivars of both native and nonnative plants, as well as a variety of different habitats, including a sunny rock garden; a cool, shady riparian area; and a xeric plant display. The Leaches' 1930s manor can be rented for weddings, receptions, and meetings. *Tues–Sat 9am–4pm, Sun 1pm–4pm, with tours at 2pm Wed and 10am Sat; www.parks.ci.portland .or.us/Parks/LeachBotanicalGar.htm; map:JJ2*

Portland Chinese Classical Garden

 NW 3RD AVE AND EVERETT ST, CHINATOWN; 503/221-8131 See no. 6 in Top 20 Attractions.

Parks and Beaches

PORTLAND PARKS AND RECREATION (1120 SW 5th Ave, room 1302, Downtown; 503/823-5132; www.parks.ci.portland.or.us; map:F3) offers a wide variety of natu-ralist-led excursions in many of the regions parks, green spaces, and waterways, including hikes, walks, bicycle rides, bird-watching trips, and kayaking and canoe trips. Pick up their brochure, *Outdoor Recreation*, at libraries and stores around town or visit the Parks and Recreation offices.

Blue Lake Park

BLUE LAKE RD AT N MARINE DR AND 223RD AVE, TROUTDALE; 503/797-1850 OR 503/665-4995 Although there is a 5-acre natural wetlands area here, most of Blue Lake Park's 185 acres is unabashedly developed, with plenty of parking, swimming, boat rentals, volleyball courts, paved paths, playfields, and other facilities. Each Wednesday in summer, from 2pm to 2:45pm, kids can drop by for activities such as Asian drumming and folktales, talks on Northwest birds of prey, a globe-trotting comedy cowboy show, or Tears of Joy puppet theater. Park admission is $3 for cars and free for walkers and cyclists (no pets). *Every day 8am–sunset; map:FF1* &

Council Crest Park

TOP OF MARQUAM HILL, A 10-MINUTE DRIVE SOUTHWEST OF DOWNTOWN; FOLLOW SW VISTA AVE FROM W BURNSIDE ST, THEN CONTINUE ON SW TALBOT RD Set atop one of the tallest peaks in the Tualatin Mountains, Council Crest Park is valued for its nearly panoramic views of the Coast Range and the Cascades. Park at the top. Frustratingly, it's closed at night due to vandalism. The Marquam Hill Trail crosses through the Douglas firs and maple forest on the north-west side of the hill. *Every day 10am–8pm; map:II7*

Elk Rock Island

SE 19TH AVE AND BLUEBIRD ST, MILWAUKIE Each spring, high waters on the Wil-lamette impede access to this pristine island, but at other times you can step from Milwaukie's Spring Park across the gravel-scrubbed bedrock to the island. Great blue herons feed in the little bay between the island and Spring Park. Migrating Canadian geese graze on the shelf of grass on the island's west side. A sublime natural rock formation cascades out of the oak forest on the northwest end, while the deepest waters of the Willamette (home to many sturgeon) slice by. Local lore attributes the name to Native Americans driving elk over the bluff and floating them to the island for processing. Watch for poison oak if you've a notion to wander into the woods. *Map:LL5*

Forest Park

NORTH OF W BURNSIDE ST TO NW NEWBERRY RD, WEST OF NW ST. HELENS RD (HWY 30) TO SW SKYLINE RD; 503/223-5449 In 1948, after more than 40 years of citizen effort, 4,200 acres of forestland were formally designated Forest Park. The land had survived logging, wildfire burns, subdivision into private lots, and an aborted scenic-road project. Now expanded to more than 5,000 acres, Forest Park is the largest city park in the nation. The forest wilderness includes 50 miles of trails and 30 miles of gated roadways for mountain biking along northwest Portland's Tualatin Mountains, and is an easy 10-minute drive from downtown. Leif Erikson Drive, an 11-mile gravel road that stretches from NW Thurman Street to Germantown Road, is all that remains of an ambitious real-estate agent's 1914 plans for a subdivision. Now closed to cars, the popular hiking, running, and mountain-biking lane is bumpy in spots but affords good views north; it parallels the Wildwood Trail. An indispensable reference to the park is Marcy Cottrell Houle's *One City's Wilderness: Portland's Forest Park*, which includes maps, park history, and flora and fauna checklists. *www.parks.ci.portland.or.us/Parks/ForestPark.htm; map:DD9–GG8*

Gov. Tom McCall Waterfront Park

WEST SIDE OF THE WILLAMETTE RIVER FROM THE MARQUAM BRIDGE NORTH TO THE STEEL BRIDGE; 503/823-2223 See no. 3 in Top 20 Attractions.

Hoyt Arboretum

4000 SW FAIRVIEW BLVD, WASHINGTON PARK; 503/228-8733 See no. 11 in Top 20 Attractions.

Kelley Point Park

N KELLY POINT PARK RD AND N MARINE DR, SAINT JOHNS This is an isolated park across the channel from Sauvie Island at the convergence of the Willamette and Columbia Rivers. Biking, hiking, and wildlife viewing are best in the spring and fall. In the summer, Kelley Point is inundated with picnickers and sunbathers. Despite abundant wildlife, the slow-moving waters are polluted, and water experts advise against swimming and fishing. As in all urban-area parks, leave your valuables at home and lock your car. *Map:BB9*

Mary S. Young State Park

HWY 43, JUST SOUTH OF MARYLHURST COLLEGE, WEST LINN Along the Willamette River, this suburban refuge is stalwartly defending itself from surrounding development. A favorite of urban birders, the 160-acre park has baseball diamonds, soccer fields, picnic spots, 2 miles of dense forest trails, a half-mile bike path, and restrooms. The state maintains it in as close to its original natural condition as possible. *Map:OO4*

Oxbow Regional Park

8 MILES EAST OF GRESHAM VIA SE DIVISION ST AND OXBOW PKWY; 503/663-4708 OR 503/797-1850 In the oxbow bends of the Sandy River Gorge, old-growth forests and wildlife thrive (in part because no dogs are allowed, not even on a leash). The park formally covers more than 1,000 acres, but the ecosystem appears to extend upstream to the Sandy River Preserve (owned by the Nature Conservancy) and downstream to the YMCA camp. The Sandy River is part of the National Wild and Scenic River system; evidence exists that Native Americans lived here 9,000 years ago. The second weekend in October every year, the park hosts its annual Salmon Festival, focusing on the spawning salmon. About 15 miles of hiking trails follow the river and climb the ridges, and some are open to horses. The park includes 45 camping sites, probably the closest public campground to Portland proper. Year-round interpretive hikes, programs, films, and lectures are available; call for reservations.

Powell Butte

SE POWELL BLVD AND 162ND AVE (UNMARKED STREET), SOUTHEAST Plenty of horses, mountain bikes, and hikers share this park's trails, which on sunny days can be downright crowded. From the meadows at the 630-foot summit, you can see north to Mount St. Helens and south to Mount Jefferson. A 2-mile loop circles the volcanic mound on the way to the top. Watch out for poison oak. *Map:II1*

Rooster Rock State Park

TAKE I-84 EAST TO EXIT 25 IN THE COLUMBIA GORGE; 503/969-8254 On a warm weekend, all 1,800 parking spaces for this mile-long sandy beach are full. The familiar Crown Point viewpoint rises on the other side of I-84. There's a logged-off swimming hole in the Columbia River, a boat launch, and docks for boats and anglers. On the far east end, a separate beach has been designated "clothing optional." When the east wind is blowing, windsurfers crowd the beaches. Park admission is $3 per car. *www.prd.state.or.us/parks.html*

Sauvie Island Wildlife Management Area

AT THE CONFLUENCE OF THE WILLAMETTE AND COLUMBIA RIVERS (10 MILES NORTHWEST OF PORTLAND VIA HWY 30), ON THE NORTH END OF SAUVIE ISLAND; 503/621-3488 The hinterlands of Sauvie Island offer great birding opportunities, but in the past two decades, both human and car traffic in this area have tripled. To finance toilets, parking, a viewing platform, and maintenance, the Oregon Fish and Wildlife Commission charges $3.50 daily and $11 annually for car-park permits for this 12,000-acre state wildlife preserve. Walton Beach, one of the few sandy beaches on the Columbia (and open for swimming), is located at the end of the paved portion of NW Reeder Road. Warrior Rock Lighthouse is a 3-mile hike from the north unit parking facility. Non-wildlife-related activity is discouraged; open fires are prohibited, and there are no picnic facilities. *Open year-round are the road to Warrior Rock Lighthouse, bird-watching areas at Coon Point and NW Reeder Rd, the Columbia River beaches, and the eastside viewing platform; the rest of the park is closed Oct 1–Apr 15; map:AA9*

Smith and Bybee Lakes Wildlife Area

NORTH PORTLAND PENINSULA BETWEEN DELTA AND KELLEY POINT PARKS In industrial North Portland, this designated natural area—encompassing nearly 2,100 acres of lakes and wetlands—is yet another haven where urbanites can hike, watch wildlife, and listen to birds call. The bird blinds (camouflaged viewing spots) offer a good place to spy on wildlife, especially blue herons in the slough. *Map:CC8*

Springwater Corridor

16¾ MILES, FROM SELLWOOD EAST TO BORING See description under Bicycling in the Recreation chapter.

Tryon Creek State Park

11321 SW TERWILLIGER BLVD, 1 MILE OFF HWY 43 IN LAKE OSWEGO; 503/636-9886 OR 503/636-4398 Like Forest Park, the Tryon Creek canyon was threatened with a housing project. Thanks to the Friends of Tryon Creek State Park, a citizens' group organized to raise money to buy the land, it's now a park consisting of 645 protected acres between Lewis and Clark College and Lake Oswego. There are 14 miles of intersecting trails, including the paved half-mile Trillium Trail (the first all-abilities trail in an Oregon state park) and a 3-mile bike trail along the park's border with Terwilliger Boulevard. The Nature Center features a bookstore, exhibits, and a meeting room. The Trillium Festival is hosted in early spring, when these delicate flowers blossom. *Park is open every day dawn till dusk, Nature Center open Mon–Fri 9am–5pm, Sat–Sun 9am–4pm; map:LL6* &

Organized Tours

MOTOR TOURS

ART: The Cultural Bus (aka Tri-Met bus 63)

503/238-7433 ART hits all the city's cultural hot spots: the Portland Art Museum, Oregon History Center, Oregon Museum of Science and Industry, and the Oregon Zoo, to name a few. Wildly designed by beloved Portland artist Henk Pander and his sons, Arnold and Jacob, ART is itself a masterpiece. Prices are the same as for all Tri-Met buses. Board at most attractions or in the Downtown Transit Mall. (See Getting Around in the Lay of the City chapter.)

Eco Tours of Oregon

3127 SE 23RD AVE; 503/245-1428 You don't have to be politically correct to book a tour with these folks, but if you pride yourself on being politically progressive, you'll definitely want to check out their tours. As its name implies, this tour company specializes in environmentally and culturally conscious tours, including a full-day Old Growth Forests and Mountain Walks tour; a Native American Cultural tour to the Warm Springs Indian Reservation, where participants are guests of a tribal member; rafting in white or calm water; or whale watching from Newport. Not all tours are active; they'll also take you to the northern Oregon Coast, the Columbia Gorge, and Mount St. Helens volcano; there's even an evening Microbrewery Tour and a full-day Winery Tour. Or custom-design your own tour. Prices range from $39 (microbreweries) up to $100 (whale watching). *www.ecotours-of-oregon.com*

Evergreen–Gray Line of Portland

503/285-9845 This touring agency offers several bus-tour choices, including a northern Oregon Coast tour, three Portland city tours, a 4½-hour tour to Multnomah Falls and the Columbia River Gorge, and a 9-hour tour that includes the gorge, Timberline Lodge, and Mount Hood. Pickup can be arranged from any major hotel. Prices range from $30 to $52, with children under 12 half price. Call for times and days. Reservations are required. *www.grayline.com*

Portland Parks and Recreation Historical Tours

503/823-5132 These educational day trips sponsored by the Outdoor Recreation Department of Portland Parks and Recreation cover a gold mine of historic places: the Oregon Trail, Lewis and Clark's route to Astoria, the Columbia Gorge, Portland cemeteries, and four- and five-day trips to eastern Oregon to see Native American petroglyphs, rock carvings, and the Lost Blue Bucket Gold Mine. Portland historian and writer Dick Pintarich leads the popular van tours. Most span the entire day (8am–7pm), give or take a few good stories; tours operate April through October only and reservations are required. For more information, pick up the Parks and Recreation brochure, *Outdoor Recreation*, at libraries and stores around town or at the agency's offices (1120 SW 5th Ave, Rm 1302).

VanGo Tours

503/292-2085 Like other minivan tour companies, VanGo will take you just about anywhere you want to go around Portland and northern Oregon: half-day city trips, half-day Columbia Gorge tours, full-day Mount Hood Loop trips, full-day Oregon Coast tours, and more. Call for details.

WALKING TOURS

Peter's Walking Tours

503/665-2558 Former elementary school teacher Peter Chausse offers walking tours of the downtown area, any day of the week. A knowledgeable and enthusiastic guide, Chausse focuses on the city's art, architecture, parks, fountains, and history and emphasizes his points with hands-on activities such as sidewalk rubbings and using magnets to see whether a building is made of cast iron. A 2½-hour, 1½-mile tour costs $10 for adults, $5 for teens, and nothing for children 12 and under. Call to reserve a time. *www.walkportland.com*

Portland Parks and Recreation Art and Architecture Walking Tours

503/823-5132 Portland Parks and Recreation sponsors a variety of tours around Portland that focus on architectural history, public art, and what's new in the various downtown neighborhoods. For more information, pick up the Parks and Recreation brochure, *Outdoor Recreation*, at libraries and stores around town or drop by agency offices (1120 SW 5th Ave, Rm 1302).

Portland Public Art Walking Tour

503/823-5111 Request the map at the Regional Arts and Culture Council (620 SW Main St, Ste 420, Downtown), the Oregon Convention Center (NE Martin Luther King Jr Blvd and Holladay St, Rose Quarter), the main lobby of the Portland Building (1120 SW 5th Ave, Downtown), or the Visitor Information and Services Center (Pioneer Courthouse Square). See Art in Public Places in the Arts Scene chapter for more information on public art and architecture.

Urban Tour Group

503/227-5780 For more than 25 years, schoolchildren and adults alike have learned Portland history from UTG volunteers. Teachers, round up the kids—school groups are free. Private tours cost $5 per person ($25 minimum); reservations are a must. Tourists can choose one of three stock tours or have one custom made.

Waterfront Bridge Walks

503/823-5132 OR 503/222-5535 There are few cities that offer such diverse bridge-work as Portland, and fewer yet that feature tours by such a lively and devoted guide as Sharon Wood-Wortman, whose *Portland Bridge Book* was first published in 1989 and is now in a new edition. Besides tours offered through the Portland Parks and Recreation, Wood-Wortman also offers private tours.

BOAT TOURS

See no. 13 in Top 20 Attractions.

TRAIN AND TROLLEY TOURS

Molalla Miniature Train–Pacific Northwest Live Steamers

31803 S SHADY DELL DR, MOLALLA (SOUTHEAST OF PORTLAND); 503/829-6866 All-volunteer hobbyists drive these miniature trains along a 0.7-mile route. Passengers can bring their own lunches and relax in the shaded picnic area, admiring the fine, detailed antique trains. *Sun and major Mon holidays noon–5pm (May–Oct); www.pnls.org*

Mount Hood Scenic Railroad

110 RAILROAD AVE, HOOD RIVER (60 MILES EAST OF PORTLAND VIA I-84); 541/386-3556 OR 800/872-4661 The restored Pullman cars of the Mount Hood Railroad chug from Hood River to Parkdale, linking the Columbia Gorge to the foothills of Mount Hood. Tickets are $23 for adults, $21 for seniors 60 and over, and $15 for children 2–12. The Saturday dinner train is $70, and the Sunday brunch train is $57. The spring run gives rail riders spectacular views of blossoming orchards. There's also a Native American Celebration, featuring dancers from the Warm Springs Reservation, and a Western Train Robbery and Country Barbecue. (Don't worry: the sheriff comes to the rescue.) In December, the Christmas Tree Train gives riders a chance to join Santa and Christmas carolers and buy a tree, which is loaded onto the train. Call for a full list of events. *Mar–Dec; www.mthoodrr.com*

Oregon Zoo Railway

OREGON ZOO, 4001 SW CANYON RD, WASHINGTON PARK; 503/226-1561
The zoo railway boasts the only surviving railroad post office in the country, so mailing a postcard while you're on board is a must. A round-trip ticket to ride the train from the zoo to the rose garden costs $3, $2.25 for seniors and children 3–11 (in addition to zoo admission). You'll get a dose of history and some nice scenery along the 35-minute loop, which runs in warm-weather months; in spring the route is shorter. *www.oregonzoo.com; map:HH7*

Samtrak

503/653-2380 A bright, red-and-white, open-air train allows you to take in the riverine scenery of the Oaks Bottom wetlands between the Oregon Museum of Science and Industry and the legendary Oaks Amusement Park near the Sellwood Bridge. The round trip takes about an hour, and you can get off to enjoy the sights and return on a later trip. Board the train at OMSI (1945 SW Water Ave, Southeast), at the Oaks Park Station (SE Oaks Parks Dr at the foot of SE Spokane St), or at the Sellwood Station (8825 SE 11th Ave). Round-trip fare is $5 for ages 13 and up, less for youngsters. *Sun 11am–5pm (mid-June–Labor Day), Sat–Sun 11am–5pm (after Labor Day–mid-Sept); wheelchairs can board at the OMSI station*

Vintage Trolley

503/323-7363 Four oak-paneled and brass-belled trolleys—replicas of the city's old Council Crest trolley—follow the MAX route (catch the trolley at any light-rail station) from Lloyd Center to the downtown turnaround at SW 11th Avenue and back. Top speed is 35 miles an hour, and the round trip takes about 40 minutes. The trolley is free. Vintage Trolley is owned by Portland General Electric and is operated by Tri-Met. *Sun noon–6pm*

Willamette Shore Trolley

503/697-7436 The Willamette Shore Trolley has been running along the river between downtown Portland and Lake Oswego since 1990, keeping the track warm for eventual mass transportation development. Two trolleys, one built in 1902 in Blackpool, England, another a 1932 model from Portland, run for 7 miles from RiverPlace to the State Street terminal in Lake Oswego. Round-trip tickets are $9 for adults, $8 for seniors (55 and over), and $6 for children 3–12. Charter runs are available for large groups. Reservations are required for the December Christmas boat-watching tour and the Fourth of July trip to watch fireworks. Call for current schedule. *www.oregonelectricrailway.org*

SHOPPING

SHOPPING

Neighborhoods, Districts, and Malls

Portland has grown up. Long gone are the "forgettable small city" days when travelers seeking cosmopolitan delights would pass over this community in favor of Seattle or San Francisco. Portland has quickly acquired an urban sophistication that, when married to the town's famed livability and manageable size, make for a uniquely vibrant and approachable city. A bustling downtown is surrounded by a cluster of neighborhoods, each with its own distinct character and the shops and services to go with it. Locals are loyal to independently owned businesses and intensely proud of the city's devotion to sound urban planning and community building. As a result, characterless strip malls and big-box megaretailers have been banished to the outskirts—much to the benefit of the city's homegrown atmosphere.

DOWNTOWN PORTLAND

Continued investment by community and business has made Portland's downtown a model for revitalizing urban areas across the nation. Buses, light-rail, and a new streetcar system crisscross the city center, making it incredibly easy to maneuver to the big retailers that we expect from a big city, as well as to the small boutiques that give Portland its unique character. A handful of large department stores (Nordstrom, Saks Fifth Avenue, Meier & Frank) and the Pioneer Place mall—a glass-roofed two-building complex full of chain retailers, on SW Fifth Avenue between Morrison and Taylor Streets—dominate the downtown grid. But the Brewery Blocks—a massive mixed-use redevelopment project just northwest of the city core—has begun to attract slick national retailers even before completion. The Brewery Blocks link downtown Portland with the Pearl District, a former industrial area turned gallery scene that has rapidly shape-shifted into a chic shopping district.

Meier & Frank

621 SW 5TH AVE, DOWNTOWN (AND BRANCHES); 503/223-0512 The family-friendly Meier & Frank department store has been a marketplace mainstay since 1857. That year, two enterprising families opened a block-long, full-service department store in mid-downtown at SW Fifth Avenue and Morrison Street. Now the chain is owned by the St. Louis–based May Company. The original flagship store, though it has lost some luster over the years, still offers the signature services you expect from a big downtown department store: a beauty salon, a bridal registry, picture framing, jewelry repair, a travel agency, and a photo studio. M&F's biggest treat is the 10th-floor Georgian Room restaurant, where white tablecloths and a tinkling piano greet elderly shoppers and lunching office workers with reminders of more graceful times. Also in Lloyd Center (1100 Lloyd Center; 503/281-4797; map:GG5), Clackamas Town Center (12100 SE 82nd Ave; 503/653-8811; map:LL3), Washington Square (9300 SW Washington Square Rd, Tigard; 503/620-3311; map:KK9), and Vancouver Mall (8208 NE Vancouver Mall

Dr, Vancouver; 360/256-4411; map:AA3). *Every day; www.maycompany.com; map:I4*

Nordstrom

710 SW BROADWAY, DOWNTOWN (AND BRANCHES); 503/224-6666 Nordstrom was once Portland's most sophisticated shopping experience; the apparel retail giant has long been a downtown fixture. But the city's growing sophistication, and the arrival of other upscale chains, has left Nordstrom somewhere in the middle. The store no longer offers the exemplary "At Your Service" concierge desk downtown; it's there only at Christmastime and during big sales. But Nordy's notorious sales—the Half-Yearly men's and women's sale and the Anniversary Sale in July—still draw hordes who paw the sweaters and shoes looking for, and finding, fairly good deals. Nordstrom's well-appointed staff is still more knowledgeable (and fashionable) than average store help. The downtown location was Oregon's first but the Washington Square branch (see Suburban Malls below) is more elegant, with a wider range of merchandise. Nordstrom Rack (401 SW Morrison St, Downtown; 503/299-1815; map:H4; and 8930 SE Sunnyside Rd, Clackamas; 503/654-5415; map:LL3) carries clearance merchandise at up to 70 percent off full Nordstrom prices. *Every day; www.nordstrom.com; map:I3*

Saks Fifth Avenue

850 SW 5TH AVE, DOWNTOWN; 503/226-3200 The Northwest got its first look at this distinguished New York–based department store when the 47th branch opened in 1990. Saks has since expanded its reach with a three-story shop in the expanded Pioneer Place mall. Although its range of merchandise has waned since those halcyon days of the early '90s (once-plentiful fur coats are hardly in evidence), Saks still offers top-quality clothing and an unmistakable "luxury retail" experience. The ground floor is a plush walk-through of designer handbags, shoes, and accessories, while the cosmetics counter offers solicitous service and a host of big-ticket beauty brands unavailable elsewhere in town. The 5th Avenue Club offers customers personal shopping services, including wardrobe consultation and gift selection, at no extra charge. *Every day; www.saksfifthavenue.com; map:H3*

NEIGHBORHOODS

You'll get the most shopping per square foot on NW 23rd Avenue (from W Burnside St north to NW Thurman St; map:GG7), where stores—stocking chic apparel, gifts, housewares, and funky odds and ends—join a number of coffee shops and cafes. The **PEARL DISTRICT** (north of W Burnside St and west of the North Park Blocks; map:K3–P1), recently dominated by art galleries and home to a thriving First Thursday scene, is quickly being overtaken by upscale restaurants and furniture retailers. The **BREWERY BLOCKS**, a cluster of converted buildings left over from the Blitz-Weinhard days, borders the Pearl and hosts the city's newest big shops, including Diesel footwear and REI. Down toward the river is the restored **SKIDMORE/OLD TOWN** (between Naito Pkwy and 4th Ave from SW Oak to NW Glisan Sts; map:H5–L5), which has a growing number of shops and galleries that have been edged out—or priced out—of the Pearl. On weekends, Skidmore perks up with the Saturday Market, a food and craft fair.

THE PORTLAND GROWING SEASON

Recent hosannas in national publications like *Gourmet* magazine have broadcast to the nation what many Oregonians already knew: Portland's farmers markets are at the top of their class.

Strategically located in the beating heart of the agriculturally prolific Willamette Valley, Portland welcomes the return of growers' produce to the city every spring; most markets run through mid-October. Shoppers can find not only unbelievably fresh corn, carrots, and spinach at the city's open-air markets, but also exotic and niche produce like Asian greens and long beans, heirloom tomatoes, edible nasturtium blossoms, and lobster mushrooms in vivid orange bloom.

Though prices are often higher than at grocery stores, the caliber of produce—much of it organically grown—makes up for the extra nickels and dimes. And there's an added benefit in supporting small family and community farms rather than the agribusinesses that supply large grocery chains; such support brings vitality to rural areas and new generations to farming, guaranteeing this quality will persist. Many farmers drive long distances to set up their booths in the heart of the city.

The city's most heavily attended market is the **PORTLAND FARMERS MARKET** (503/705-2460; www.portlandfarmersmarket.org), which runs from April through October in the South Park Blocks. It sets up Saturdays, 8am–1pm, near Portland State University (SW Park Ave and Montgomery St; map:E1), and Wednesdays, 10am–2pm, by the Arlene Schnitzer Concert Hall (SW Park Ave and Salmon St; map:H2). Though nowhere near the biggest market, the Portland Farmers Market is one of the oldest, established in 1992 by the Albers Mill grain elevators on the Willamette River; its central location and twice-a-week-schedule make it a prominent part of city life. Besides superstar vegetables, fruit, and nuts, this market boasts baked and dairy goods, organically raised meat and seafood, salsas and sauces, herbs, cut flowers, and live plants. On any

Southwest of town is the charming **MULTNOMAH VILLAGE** (just off SW Multnomah Blvd on SW Capitol Hwy; map:JJ7), with a quaint, small-town personality revolving around several eateries, an excellent bookstore, a few arty shops, and about a dozen antique stores. Across the Sellwood Bridge in the city's southeast corner are **SELLWOOD** (SE Tacoma St and 13th Ave; map:KK5), which is saturated with stores selling antiques, and **WESTMORELAND**, whose shops, cafes, and antique malls crowd around SE 17th Avenue and Bybee Boulevard (map:JJ5).

The **HAWTHORNE** area (SE Hawthorne Blvd between SE 20th and 49th Aves; map:HH5) and **BELMONT STREET** (SE Belmont St between SE 30th and 39th Aves; map:HH5) are two neighborhood arteries with a funky, artsy vibe. Browsers can spend hours pawing through secondhand record shops and vintage clothiers, enjoy an excellent Italian foods specialty shop, a comprehensive cookbook store, bath market day there are cooking demonstrations, soil-management lectures, live music performances, and other events.

Another popular market is the **BEAVERTON FARMERS MARKET** (SW Hall Blvd between 3rd and 5th Aves; 503/643-5345; map:II9), the state's largest agriculture-only market. (There are no crafts sellers here.) On a Saturday (8am–1:30pm, May–Oct) in peak season, as many as 10,000 people descend upon 100 vendors for things as prosaic as snap peas or as special as wedding flowers. (July to September, there's also a Wednesday market.) Fetzer's German deli, which closed its beloved Beaverton store a few years back, has a sausage booth that welcomes long queues hungry for grilled bratwurst and kraut.

Other thriving farmers markets, mostly on Saturdays, are in the Pearl District (Ecotrust Building parking lot, NW 10th Ave and Johnson St; map:N2); Gresham (NE Roberts Ave between 4th and 5th Aves; 503/695-2698); Hillsboro (Courthouse Square, NE 2nd Ave and Main St; 503/844-6685); Hollywood (NE Hancock St between 44th and 45th Aves; 503/233-3313; map:GG4); Lents (SE 91st Ave and Foster Rd; 503/227-5368; map:JJ3); and Buckman (SE 20th Ave between Hawthorne and Belmont Sts; map:HH5). There's even an all-organic market every Wednesday (2–7pm) outside the People's Food Co-op (3029 SE 21st Ave, Brooklyn; 503/232-9051; map:II5). The U.S. Department of Agriculture publishes a current Web directory (www.usda.gov/farmersmarkets/states/oregon.htm) of markets; check for times before you venture out, as some change location and others have irregular (i.e., non-Saturday) schedules.

One caveat: In peak season, it's not surprising to see golden-sweet Suncrest peaches or hand-picked marionberries sell out long before 10am. Farmers market shoppers have passionate natures and aren't afraid to rise with the rooster (or, for that matter, the growers) to be there for the first flat of fresh fruit. Set that alarm clock for the best selection.

—*Elizabeth Dye*

and body-care shops, and several boutiques. Farther south, the **DIVISION/CLINTON** area (SE Division and Clinton Sts near SE 25th Ave; map:II5) has enjoyed a recent boom, adding a number of new cafes and boutiques to the scattering of book and record shops and natural foods grocery stores. To the north, **NE BROADWAY** (east from NE 7th Ave; map:GG5), bordering Irvington and the Lloyd Center, has taken on a freshly minted elegance, with clothing, kitchenware, and book shops; a trendy hair salon; a good wine store; and several above-average restaurants.

SUBURBAN MALLS

Long a Portland anchor, the **LLOYD CENTER** (east across the Broadway Bridge, bordered by NE Broadway and Multnomah St, and NE 9th and 16th Aves; open every day; map:GG5) remains Oregon's largest mall. A multimillion-dollar renovation in the early '90s put a glass roof over the entire structure (including the ice rink); these days there are three levels with nearly 200 shops. Nordstrom bookends the massive shopping center; Meier & Frank and Sears are also there. Lloyd Center's proximity to downtown (connected by MAX light-rail), as well as to the Oregon Convention Center and the Rose Quarter, helped give this formerly faltering mall a fresh start.

The west side is crawling with malls. Between Beaverton and Tigard is the largest, **WASHINGTON SQUARE AND SQUARE TOO** (just off Hwy 217; open every day; map:KK9). A food court, lots of specialty shops, and the quintessential Nordstrom (ritzily refurbished) are the big draws. **BEAVERTON TOWN SQUARE** (off SW Canyon Rd and SW Beaverton-Hillsdale Hwy, off Hwy 217; open every day; map: II9), marked by its clock tower, and the **BEAVERTON MALL** (take SW Walker Rd exit off Hwy 217; open every day) are smaller westside shopping stops.

Back across the river lie **MALL 205** (take the SE Stark St exit off I-205; open every day; map:HH2), with a much-needed remodel in progress, and the booming **CLACKAMAS TOWN CENTER** (take the Sunnyside Rd exit from I-205; open every day; map:LL3), the place where Tonya Harding learned to skate. Up north is **JANTZEN BEACH CENTER** (just off I-5 at Jantzen Beach; open every day; map: CC6), which stands out from the crowd with a 72-horse merry-go-round in the center of the mall ($1 a spin).

Circling the city are a number of popular factory outlets. The Columbia River hamlet of Troutdale beckons eastbound traffic to the **COLUMBIA GORGE PREMIUM OUTLETS** (450 NW 257th Wy; 503/669-8060; www.premiumoutlets.com), which features discounted merchandise from big brands like Levi's, Gap, American Tourister, and Adidas. The **WOODBURN COMPANY STORES** (1001 Arney Rd, Woodburn; 888/664-SHOP; www.woodburncompanystores.com) houses one of Oregon's best selections of higher-end retailers, featuring well-known labels such as Banana Republic, Ralph Lauren, Tommy Hilfiger, and Timberland.

Merchandise from A to Z

ANTIQUES AND COLLECTIBLES

Antique Alley

2000 NE 42ND AVE, HOLLYWOOD; 503/287-9848 Antique Alley, in the basement of the 42nd Street Station, is a fun place to find funky collectibles and cool stuff. There's not much in the way of authentic antiques, but it's a good place to rummage for neat stuff from the 1930s, '40s, and '50s, including ashtrays and cigarette boxes, Hawaiian shirts, art prints, and World War II memorabilia. *Every day; map:GG4*

Bernadette Breu Antiques & Ornament

1134 NW EVERETT ST, PEARL DISTRICT; 503/226-6565 Be prepared for a surprise when you enter this highly personal shop. Vintage bureaus, desks, and tables overflow with decorative items. Owner Breu applies her eye for whimsy, and her talent for dramatic tableau, to this big gallery space with the look and feel of Old World Europe. All goods—including vintage jewelry and an impressive collection of

Bakelite jewelry—were collected from local estate sales. *Every day; www.bernadetteb .com; map:L2*

Circa, A.D.

1204 NW GLISAN ST, PEARL DISTRICT; 503/221-1269 Recreate a corner of the 19th century in your home or garden with help from owner Elizabeth Orme. She regularly visits Europe to bring back brightly painted home items and garden furniture from Denmark, Sweden, France, and Holland. *Tues–Sat; map:M2*

Geraldine's

2772 NW THURMAN ST, NORTHWEST; 503/295-5911 Once you discover this little antique shop tucked between a pottery gallery and a tapas restaurant, you'll want to visit often. Geraldine's features a constantly changing display of antique and restored furniture: English pine dressers, iron bed frames, outdoor garden gates and architectural elements, antique braids and trim, and decorative items and assorted other oddities. Owner Geraldine Buchholz makes frequent shopping trips to Europe and the East Coast. Get on the mailing list for trunk shows of imported Italian linens. *Mon–Sat; map:GG7*

Hollywood Antique Showcase

1969 NE 42ND AVE, HOLLYWOOD; 503/288-1051 More than 70 dealers and 10,000 square feet of floor space make this a star-quality antique mall. On the main level are collectibles, from Depression-era glass to jewelry, while handsome vintage furniture and home accessories are found in the basement. *Every day; map:GG4*

Jerry Lamb Interiors and Antiques

2304 NW SAVIER ST, NORTHWEST; 503/227-6077 Interior designer Lamb showcases an outstanding collection of Asian antiques and English and American antique furniture, silver, and porcelain. Take note too of the fine embroidery and woodblock prints from China and Japan and the wide selection of porcelain—Imari, blue-and-white Canton, celadon, and Rose Medallion—from the Far East. *Tues–Fri; map: GG7*

Marcella Peterson

619 SW 10TH AVE, DOWNTOWN; 503/223-5538 Peterson's small but excellent shop, just down the block from the Governor Hotel, is a treasure trove of fine European and Asian antique decorative arts. Come here for tea sets, vases, paintings, jewelry, porcelain, and silverware. *Tues–Sat; map:I2*

Partners in Time

1313 W BURNSIDE ST, PEARL DISTRICT; 503/228-6299 A friendly, knowledgeable staff can provide history on most items, including restored European furniture from England, Austria, Holland, and Germany. In addition to the antique imports, you'll find good-quality period reproductions, Oriental rugs, and such decorative objects as painted wooden boxes and toile trays. *Every day; www.partnersintimeantiques.com; map:K1*

Stars, an Antiques Mall

7027 SE MILWAUKIE AVE, SELLWOOD; 503/235-5990 Stars has expanded into three vintage-goods and antique malls within two blocks of one another in the village-like neighborhood of Sellwood. From country kitsch to Belleck china and Tiffany silver, these outlets encompass an enormous 27,500 square feet. You can spend an entire afternoon searching through the offerings of nearly 300 dealers. *Every day; www.starsantique.com; map:KK5*

Vestiges

4743 NE FREMONT ST, BEAUMONT; 503/331-3920 Bring a friend and embark on an impromptu treasure hunt at Vestiges. You can each take a floor, taking plenty of time to explore the ever-changing array of furniture, books, kitschy artwork, and collectible kitchen goodies. The shop is separated into miniature "rooms" of collectibles, each one set up by a different vendor—just like a never-ending estate sale without the dust bunnies. *Every day; map:FF4*

APPAREL

Aubergine

1100 NW GLISAN ST, PEARL DISTRICT; 503/228-7313 This airy, elegant boutique features clean-lined women's clothing in innovative textures and fabrics. Owners Margaret Block and Tanya Doubleday regularly travel to New York in search of unique designs, including Dosa silk garments based on traditional Indian and Korean layering, austere styles in unusual fabric hybrids by Su-zen, and Lilith pieces designed for layering woven fabrics over stretch garments. *Mon–Sat; map:M2*

Barbara Johnson Clothing Outlet

18005 SW LOWER BOONES FERRY RD, TIGARD; 503/620-1777 If you're a sample size (from 6 to 12), you're in luck, because Barbara Johnson is the place where sales reps unload their merchandise. Women's dresses, suits, blouses, and lingerie are priced 20 percent above wholesale, and well-known brands (Sigrid Olsen, Carol Anderson, Marisa Christina) hit the racks here one to two seasons ahead of the stores. *Mon–Sat; www.barbarajohnsons.com; map:NN8*

Changes—Designs to Wear

927 SW YAMHILL ST, DOWNTOWN; 503/223-3737 An extension of the Real Mother Goose (see Jewelry and Accessories), this shop carries clothing designed by regional and national artists. There are often new and wonderful surprises: blocked silk shirts, tooled-leather purses, burned-velvet scarves, hand-woven suits cut to flatter real women's bodies. Earthy and unusual jewelry complements all of the above. *Mon–Sat; map:I2*

Elizabeth Street

635 NW 23RD AVE, NORTHWEST; 503/243-2456 This trendy Northwest boutique consistently brings an L.A.-style chic and urban sensibility to its range of dresses and separates. Flirty frocks, designer denim, and eye-catching pieces from the likes of Trina Turk and Woo round out the handpicked inventory. Check the glass case at the front of the store for sleek eyewear, jewelry, and gloves. An interior passage to the adjacent Zelda's Shoe Bar (see Shoes) makes for head-to-toe dressing. *Every day; map:GG7*

Gazelle

4100 NE FREMONT ST, BEAUMONT; 503/288-3422 An oasis of comfortable, natural fiber clothing, Gazelle stocks "real" clothes: flowy linen dresses, roomy cotton cardigans, cozy wool jackets. Other distractions include soft cotton shirts for men, hemp bags, and the delightful imported toys and housewares that line the perimeter of the store. *Every day; map:FF4*

Girlfriends

904 NW 23RD AVE, NORTHWEST; 503/294-0488 This shop carries a solid collection of cotton T-shirts, chic dresses, sweaters, comfy pants, pajamas, and stockings (not to mention soaps, scents, and candles). Think of it as slumber-party wear—and then some. The savvy owners provide treats like lemonade in the summer and see to it that even shoppers' companions can enjoy lounging in the shop. *Every day; www.girlfriendsboutique.com; map:GG7*

Jane's Vanity

521 SW BROADWAY, DOWNTOWN; 503/241-3860 An elegant lingerie outlet owned by Jane Adams, Vanity features the best in European bras, panties, garter belts, nightwear, and accessories. Acquired every January in Paris, elegant bits of silk and lace are displayed on racks, in glass cases, and across the walls. *Every day; janesvanity.com; map:I3*

La Paloma

6316 SW CAPITOL HWY, HILLSDALE SHOPPING CENTER; 503/246-3417 Kim Osgood and Mike Roach oversee one of the city's best finds for relaxed, contemporary women's natural-fiber clothing. The emphasis is on easy-care pieces that pack well, a must for well-dressed travelers. Brands such as Flax, Cut Loose, and Mishi mean breezy linens and separates and sweaters in cotton or rayon. There's also Indonesian batik and ikat clothing and silver jewelry from Southeast Asia. *Every day; www.palomaclothing.com; map:JJ7*

Lena Medoyeff Studio

724 NW 23RD AVE, NORTHWEST; 503/227-0011 Portland designer Lynn Medoff learned her craft from a woman in a small town in Guatemala during a stint in the Peace Corps—not exactly your average fashion schooling. Her luxurious creations are equally extraordinary. She employs exquisite imported fabrics (lots of silk and hand-stitched, ornate textiles) in straightforward dresses, skirts, blouses, jackets, and pants. Spoil yourself rotten in the rich beauty of Medoff's studio/retail space amid her infectious enthusiasm. *Every day; www.lenadress.com; map:GG7*

Lit

214 SW 8TH AVE, DOWNTOWN; 503/827-3300 Since opening in late 2001, owner Kenny Wujek has built a reputation for his stylish boutique that draws hipsters citywide—and, occasionally, the attention of national fashion magazines. The compact shop is home to designer denim by Paper Denim + Cloth and Blue Cult, as well as hard-to-find indie brands like Modern Amusement and Gsus. For regulars in the know, Lit is Portland's ground zero for modern urban casual clothing. *Every day; www.litpdx.com; map:J4*

Mario's

921 SW MORRISON ST, DOWNTOWN; 503/227-3477 For more than six decades, men demanding the best in designer fashion have shopped Mario's. Armani, Vestimenta, Hugo Boss, Canali, and Zegna suits keep elegant company here with fine sweaters, top-notch cotton shirts, and tasteful Friday casual wear. *Every day; www.marios.com; map:I2*

Matisse

1411 NE BROADWAY, NEAR LLOYD CENTER; 503/287-5414 Anyone who revels in femininity will adore this enchanting store, the bedroom/walk-in closet of girly-girl dreams. Stunning dresses (from formal to casual), adorable separates (not to mention vibrant tees and tanks), and silk and rayon dresses fill the racks. Romantic necklaces and other accessories displayed in antique cases accent the gorgeous garments. *Every day; map:GG5*

The Mercantile

735 SW PARK AVE, DOWNTOWN; 503/223-6649 Owners Victoria Taylor and Dottie Johnson love fashion, and their store seems at once a gallery of their favorite up-to-the-minute styles and an elegant, comfortable shopping destination. Clothing here suits mature women looking for tailored, upscale style as well as young professionals seeking sophisticated, contemporary fashion. The sprawling space houses evening and sportswear by designers like Nicole Miller and Eileen Fisher, with a smattering of sleepwear, eclectic accessories, and household objects. *Every day; www.mercantile.citysearch.com; map:I3*

Michael Allen's

915 SW 9TH AVE, DOWNTOWN; 503/221-9963 Polished, professional men's clothing is the mainstay here, with a bonus: many of the classically tailored men's shirts and pants are available in the kind of sumptuous wools and silks too often reserved for women's apparel. In addition to the retail showroom, Allen runs a thriving custom clothing business for both men and women—consider consulting with him about a special garment straight from your imagination. *Mon–Sat; map:H2*

Mimi and Lena

823 NW 23RD AVE, NORTHWEST; 503/224-7736 Named for the grandmothers of the two shop owners, Mimi and Lena specializes in contemporary dresses that range from simply casual to bridesmaid dressy (think Nicole Miller). Mimi and Lena also offers local designs like rustic printed dresses by Kara-Line and a large collection of feminine footwear with names like Giraudon and Kenneth Cole, along with fabulous bags and jewelry that'll spice up whatever you've got on. *Every day; www.mimiandlena.com; map:GG7*

Monkey Wear

811 NW 23RD AVE, NORTHWEST; 503/222-5160 Want to strut your stuff? Monkey Wear is jam-packed with contemporary, sometimes provocative garb and accessories for the teen and twenty-something set. Shoppers peruse both floors for flirty dresses, slinky evening wear, wild lingerie, tiaras, inexpensive jewelry, and bright wigs. *Every day; map:GG7*

M. Sellin Ltd.

3556 SE HAWTHORNE BLVD, HAWTHORNE; 503/239-4605 Formerly El Mundo for Women, M. Sellin carries natural-fiber clothing cut to wear easy and still look sophisticated—classic Northwest style. Eileen Fisher, Flax, and Tommy Bahama are the names on the labels; sizes go up to 3X. And the shoes are quite possibly Hawthorne's best-kept secret; Kenneth Cole and American Eagle top the list of familiars. Browse the bath care, well-priced jewelry, stockings, scarves, and hats while you're there. A branch outlet is on the Oregon Coast at Cannon Beach. *Every day; www.msellinltd.com; map:HH5*

New American Casuals

326 SE MORRISON ST, INNER SOUTHEAST; 503/294-0445 Independent boutique pioneer Jason Brown closed his popular PokerFace store to open NAC, a street-smart venture that's part retail shop, part art gallery, part DJ'd chillout room. Shoppers can expect the same range of hip esoterica—from Marc Jacobs jeans to edgy tops and sweaters by Mint, Ulla Johnson, and Grey Ant—as well as an expanded men's section. Sales are frequent and generous, with markdowns as much as 75 percent on otherwise pricey items. *Tues–Sun; map:G9*

Norm Thompson

1805 NW THURMAN ST, NORTHWEST; 503/221-0764 Displaying a dependable conservatism that almost flirts with dowdy, this venerable local retailer keeps a low profile and an incredibly loyal clientele. Though the inventory of flannel nightgowns, plaid shirts, and pleated slacks may not inspire MasterCard mania, the place fairly bustles during the holiday season with shoppers drawn to Norm Thompson's fine service, folksy gifts, and packaged foods. There's another branch at Portland International Airport (503/249-0170). *Every day; www.normtom.com; map:GG7*

Odessa

718 NW 11TH AVE, PEARL DISTRICT; 503/223-1998 It's easy to forget that you're in Portland while shopping at Odessa; the fashion lies ahead of the game, relative to most local offerings, and the space feels like a SoHo gallery. Shop here for coveted fashions spied in the latest magazines—not the high-end couture lines, but the more affordable, hip styles from young designers. Browse the racks for sumptuous evening wear, or the sweater you won't find anywhere else for six months (if ever). The latest footwear and imported Indian bedding add to the appeal. *Every day; map:M2*

Phillip Stewart

1202 SW 19TH AVE, GOOSE HOLLOW; 503/226-3589 Sold by founder Stewart to a former employee, Jim Maer, the store still stocks the same fine wool jackets and gabardine trousers it has carried for a quarter century. Expect to find more custom lines and updated sportswear, displayed like treasured objects throughout the main floor of this historic house turned shop. Hidden away near downtown, this is a beautifully tailored secret, with more than 300 choices of fabric for custom shirts and other garments. *Mon–Sat; pstewart@xann.com; map:HH7*

The Portland Pendleton Shop

900 SW 5TH AVE, DOWNTOWN; 503/242-0037 A passing knowledge of Pendleton's wool products—and at least one well-worn, button-down shirt—is vital to being an Oregonian. The Portland shop, in the Standard Insurance Building, offers the most complete collection of Pendleton clothing anywhere in Oregon, including petite sizes, skirt-and-shirt matchables, and summer silk and rayon combinations. Of course, it wouldn't be Pendleton without the wool chemises and blankets, endearingly familiar to virtually every northwesterner. *Mon–Sat; www.pendleton-usa.com; map:H3*

Retread Threads

931 SW OAK ST, DOWNTOWN; 503/916-0000 Once an all-resale store with an emphasis on funky, whimsical clothes from the '60s and '70s, Retread Threads has gradually evolved into an all-purpose fashion outlet for the teen and early-20s set. Heavily dominated by Paul Frank merchandise, you'll find everything from pajamas to undies to cute cords and jackets bearing his popular illustrated characters. The store's second floor loft and a couple of the racks on the main floor are still devoted to affordably priced vintage and mostly casual tops, pants, and skirts. *Every day; www.retreadthreads.com; map:J3*

Savvy Plus

3204 SE HAWTHORNE BLVD, HAWTHORNE; 503/231-7116 Plans to close were thwarted by a clamor from longtime customers, and this plus-size boutique is as vital and popular as ever. Women's resale clothing, sizes 12 and up, is offered in a comfy atmosphere by a supportive sales staff. Recognizing that women who wear larger sizes don't have to sacrifice style, the store has loads of pretty jewel-toned tops, stretchy skirts, feminine knits and dresses. As plus-size women tend to fluctuate a size or two, the buy-and-sell policy makes it possible to maintain a fashionable wardrobe that always fits. *Tues–Sun; map:HH5*

Seaplane

3356 SE BELMONT ST, BELMONT; 503/234-2409 Owner-designers Kathryn Towers and Holly Stalder met just a few doors down from their Belmont shop, while working at the Pied Cow cafe. Their friendship became a business partnership and yielded Seaplane, where clothes—designed by more than 60 locals—are mostly one-of-a-kind pieces of wearable art. Styles are offbeat, and the average skirt won't cost you any more than one from the Gap. CDs from Northwest musicians, handmade jewels, and a monthly rotating art show round out the collection. *Every day; www.e-seaplane.com; map:HH5*

Sheba House of Elegance

2808 NE MARTIN LUTHER KING JR BLVD, NORTHEAST; 503/287-8925 Since moving her shop to the refurbished Standard Dairy Building, Assefash Melles has solidified her reputation as Portland's best source for dramatic ethnic pieces from

Africa and Asia. There's some alternative office and career wear here, plenty of caftans, and unique evening looks, as well as great jewelry by local designers. *Every day; map:GG6*

The Showroom

 604 SW 9TH AVE, DOWNTOWN; 503/223-9252 Since 1994, Brent Collier has specialized in bringing designer stock from labels like Versace, Issey Miyake, and Dolce & Gabbana to style-starved Portlanders. Though most pieces are from past seasons and not necessarily the pick of the litter, shoppers in the know should still make a stop for occasional couture-quality scores. The men's inventory is particularly good. Add slashed prices and solicitous service, and a visit to the Showroom can be a delicious digging experience. *Every day; map:I3*

Spartacus Leathers

300 SW 12TH AVE, DOWNTOWN; 503/224-2604 A longtime downtown denizen, Spartacus has downplayed its seedy sex-shop origins in favor of a streetwise, slightly left-of-center collection of novelty lingerie and accessories. The selection is huge and, to the store's credit, not all geared toward the fetish crowd. There are racks of sexy, elegant nighties and robes, nice bras and panties, and a wide range of men's underwear in addition to the wilder garb. *Every day; www.spartacusleathers.com; map:J2*

Tumbleweed

1804 NE ALBERTA ST, ALBERTA; 503/335-3100 Local designer Kara Larson opened this delightful store in the flourishing and eclectic Alberta Street neighborhood to showcase her rustic, prairie-inspired Kara-Line clothing line. The timeless, sizeless dresses and separates are romantic and feminine, yet comfortable and cowboy boot–worthy. Wild Carrots gingham jumpers for the toddler set, beautiful beaded jewelry, novel wallets and journals, and dresses and separates by Kara's fave designers are also charmingly displayed here. *Mon–Sat; www.kara-line.com; map:FF5*

Uncle Zach's Earth Friendly

4314 SE HAWTHORNE BLVD, HAWTHORNE; 503/295-6677 The only shop of its kind in Portland, Uncle Zach's is an all-organic clothing and housewares store, stocking the finest and most stylish in organic cotton and hemp textile products. Find fashion-forward Blue Canoe fitted yoga wear, Ecolution hemp pants and tops, and absolutely adorable baby clothes. The selection of organic sheets and towels is positively luxurious. *Tues–Sat; map:HH4*

BODY CARE

Escential Lotions & Oils

710 NW 23RD AVE, NORTHWEST; 503/248-9748 This Earth-friendly boutique invites customers to select mood-enhancing fragrances to infuse unscented lotions, massage oils, and body shampoos. Emily Mann runs the business begun by her mother, Margaret, in 1979. This is the perfect place to put together a gift basket for someone who loves luxurious baths and essential oil-scented skin treats. Classic shaving supplies, cosmetics, and incense round out the selection. A second branch is in the Hawthorne District (3638 SE Hawthorne Blvd; 503/236-7976; map:HH5). *Every day; www.escentialonline.com; map:GG7*

Faces Unlimited

25-7 NW 23RD PL, NORTHWEST; 503/227-7366 Former model Pat Warren began this business in the 1970s, offering a full line of body-care treatments—from polishing scrubs and moisturizing wraps to bikini and brow waxing, manicures, pedicures, and (of course) facials. Now a Portland skin-care institution, Faces keeps an ample supply of European body-care products in stock, including Payot, Murad, and T. LeClerc among others. *Mon–Sat; www.facesunlimited.com; map:HH7*

The Perfume House

3328 SE HAWTHORNE BLVD, HAWTHORNE; 503/234-5375 Don't be put off by the imitation greenery in the planters: Chris Tsefelas's Perfume House has been praised as the ultimate source of rare authentic scents from abroad, from hard-to-come-by Russian perfumes to Corina (from the Patrician House), introduced at the 1962 Seattle World's Fair. *Mon–Sat (Tues–Sat Sept–May, every day in Dec); www.theperfumehouse.com; map:HH5*

Sylvie Day Spa & Salon

1706 NW GLISAN ST, NORTHWEST; 503/222-5054 A cool tropical ambience marks the transition from the urban jungle to this urban oasis for body and spirit. Sylvie devotes itself to naturopathic pampering with botanicals and algae products. Facials, body treatments, and massage are *de rigueur*; hair care services also are available. *Mon–Sat; www.sylviedayspa.com; map:HH7*

Trade Secret

700 SW 5TH AVE (PIONEER PLACE), DOWNTOWN (AND BRANCHES); 503/228-4488 It's OK to play with your hair at Trade Secret. In fact, it's encouraged. Stock up on products from KMS, Sebastian, Back to Basics, and other well-known brands. Promotions and sales encourage you to shop often and spend the bucks you save on your next haircut. Other area locations are at Clackamas Town Center, Jantzen Beach, Lake Oswego, Lloyd Center, Tanasbourne, and Washington Square. *Every day; www.tradesecret.com; map:H4*

Ziva Salon-Store

610 NW 23RD AVE, NORTHWEST; 503/221-6990 Don't be surprised by the professional quality hair and cosmetics lines in this vast body-care emporium. Ziva stocks an astounding selection of products for locks and skin, as well as pro tweezers, styling tools, and heavy-duty metal cases to tote your goods. Lines like Bumble & Bumble, Rene Furterer, Phytologie, L'Occitaine, and Dermalogica are just the tip of the iceberg. Salon and spa services are available in back. *Every day; www.ziva net.com; map:GG7*

BOOKS AND PERIODICALS

Annie Bloom's Books

7834 SW CAPITOL HWY, MULTNOMAH VILLAGE; 503/246-0053 Readers from all over the city are drawn to this independent bookstore. Staff recommendations pepper the extensive selection of fiction, parenting, and children's literature, the last of which surrounds a colorful play area at the back of the store. The Judaica section is quite strong, and special orders are no problem. The shop presents readings from local fiction and poetry writers. Cushy armchairs, a house cat named Oscar Wilde, and complimentary tea make you feel at home. *Every day; www.annieblooms.com; map:JJ7*

Broadway Books

1714 NE BROADWAY, IRVINGTON; 503/284-1726 Together, Gloria Borg Olds and Roberta Dyer have been in the book biz in Portland for some 35 years, and they provide personal, educated service. There's a sizable selection of biographies and memoirs, the shop's specialty; but also fiction, Judaica, and contemporary fiction. Any book not already in stock can be special ordered. *Every day; map:GG5*

A Children's Place

4807 NE FREMONT ST, BEAUMONT; 503/284-8294 This adorable store goes beyond being the neighborhood book nook. Toys, puzzles, and kid-friendly music complement an extensive selection of books for you and your pint-size bookworm. The selection varies from bedtime classics (*Goodnight Moon* and *Madeline*) to kid's reference books and survival guides for parents. And it's an excellent resource for educators, who receive a 20 percent discount. *Every day; www .achildrensplacebooks.com; map:FF4*

Future Dreams

2205 E BURNSIDE ST, LAURELHURST; 503/231-8311 Future Dreams is one part sci-fi bookstore and one part comic art store. New and used magazines, books, and comics range from classic favorites to esoteric, hard-to-find titles. There's also a good selection of back issues and a reservation service for new volumes. *Every day; fdb@hevanet.com; map:HH5*

The Great NW Book Store

3314 SW 1ST AVE, LAIR HILL; 503/223-8098 From its new location in an 1895 church—in the Lair Hill neighborhood off Barbur Boulevard south of downtown—GNW specializes in used books with an emphasis on Americana and western literature. First-edition modern and older literature and sports are particularly strong. The shop offers an appraisal service and a rare-book room; book buying is by appointment. *Every day; www.greatnorthwestbooks.com; map: II6*

Hawthorne Boulevard Books

3129 SE HAWTHORNE BLVD, HAWTHORNE; 503/236-3211 Roger and Ilse Roberts invite the public into their Hawthorne home to browse their used and antiquarian books. They're particularly fond of classic literature and American history. A fireplace makes it difficult to leave in the chilly months. During the commemmoration of the Lewis and Clark expedition—through 2005—they are featuring a collection of topical literature as well as a first-edition printing of the expedition's journal. *Tues–Sat; hbb@teleport.com; www.abebooks.com; map:HH5*

In Other Words

3734 SE HAWTHORNE BLVD, HAWTHORNE; 503/232-6003 Here you'll find herstory written by womyn. This nonprofit store provides a repository of feminist, women-centered, lesbian, and holistic literature not available at mainstream retail venues, as well as "women-positive" videos to rent. The children's section is an excellent source for nonsexist literature. In Other Words has expanded with a gallery for local women artists. *Every day; othrwrds@teleport.com; www .inotherwords.org; map:HH5*

Laughing Horse Books

3652 SE DIVISION ST, SOUTHEAST; 503/236-2893 Activists, heretics, and visionaries run this politically progressive and environmentally sensitive nonprofit bookstore and coffeehouse collective. The schedule of events features discussion groups, speakers, and community potlucks that focus on social change. There are strong sections on U.S. and world politics and economic globalization. *Mon–Sat; map:HH5*

Longfellow's Books

1401 SE DIVISION ST, SOUTHEAST; 503/239-5222 Tucked between a school and a residential neighborhood, this gem of a used bookstore will delight the dedicated book browser. Jon Hagen has run Longfellow's for more than two decades and is quick to help new customers find their area of interest. He has a special focus on Oregon- and Portland-specific books, collectible periodicals, and books he remembers from childhood. *Mon–Sat; longfellowspdx@hotmail.com; www.abebooks.com; map:II5*

Looking Glass Bookstore

318 SW TAYLOR ST, DOWNTOWN; 503/227-4760 Now three decades old, this much-loved shop, with its skylit and polished trilevel interior, is probably one of the nicest-looking bookstores around. Its titles include many that other stores might skip over: offbeat comic books, contemporary graphic arts, and science fiction, plus notable psychology, health, and modern literature sections. *Mon–Sat; lookglas@teleport. com; map:H4*

Murder by the Book

3210 SE HAWTHORNE BLVD, HAWTHORNE; 503/232-9995 Mystery lovers and all fans of thriller and spy fiction adore this shop. An expanded selection of imported British books has introduced readers to many interesting but lesser-known European writers, as well as volumes out of print in this country. Friendly, knowledgeable staff are excited to unite you with new authors. New and used books to buy, sell, and even die for. *Every day; www.mbtb.com; map:HH5*

New Renaissance Bookshop

 1338 NW 23RD AVE, NORTHWEST; 503/224-4929 Two adjacent Victorians house some 15,000 titles and a varied selection of accoutrements to help you take your next spiritual step—whether it be recovery, growth, business prosperity, or self-transformation. Lectures, tarot readings, and discussions are also part of this harmonic convergence, as are chimes, rainbow crystals, videos, and a wide selection of DVDs. A play area has holograms, science toys, fairy costumes, and books on children's spirituality. *Every day; map:GG7*

Oregon History Center Museum Store

1200 SW PARK AVE, DOWNTOWN; 503/306-5230 See no. 10 in Top 20 Attractions in the Exploring chapter.

Periodicals and Book Paradise

 3315 SE HAWTHORNE BLVD, HAWTHORNE; 503/234-6003 Two huge stores are combined under one roof, meaning more to look at and less room to do it in. With nearly a million issues in stock, Periodicals Paradise has one of the largest magazine collections in the West. Issues published within the past year sell for 75 percent off the cover price. Book City, part and parcel of this "Paradise," offers everything from mysteries to religion, health to children's books. *Every day; mookeymags@aol.com; map:HH5*

Powell's City of Books

1005 W BURNSIDE ST, DOWNTOWN (AND BRANCHES); 503/228-4651 See no. 15 in Top 20 Attractions in the Exploring chapter.

Rich's Cigar Store

820 SW ALDER ST, DOWNTOWN; 503/228-1700 / 706 NW 23RD AVE, NORTHWEST; 503/227-6907 This is perhaps the best place in town to find a broad selection of current magazines and newspapers, including national and foreign publications. Tobacco, pipes, and stylish lighters fill the glass cases. Helpful staff can assist you in choosing a gift for the smoker in your life. *Every day; www.richscigarstore.com; map:I3; map:GG7*

Title Wave Bookstore

216 NE KNOTT ST, ALBINA; 503/988-5021 Ever wonder where old library books end up? More than 20,000 volumes from the Multnomah County Library sell for bargain prices here at the old Albina Library, a 1912 Spanish Renaissance Revival–style Carnegie Library building. Volunteers organize the books by—what else?—the Dewey decimal system. There are also magazines, CDs, books on tape, and videos. Prices start at $1 for hardbacks. *Mon–Sat; map:GG6*

Twenty-Third Avenue Books

1015 NW 23RD AVE, NORTHWEST; 503/224-5097 This Nob Hill store is just what a bookstore should be: low-key and well organized with a strong sense of its authors and customers. Contemporary fiction predominates in the original store area, while the adjoining room allows plenty of space for lovely cooking, gardening, and design books. Author readings occur frequently; call for details. *Every day; books23@teleport.com; www.23rdavebooks.com; map:GG7*

CARDS AND STATIONERY

In the Bag

708 NW 23RD AVE, NORTHWEST; 503/223-3262 Like a well-packed suitcase, this shop makes the most of its precious real estate. Sensory overload might hit as you stroll in and see rack after rack of colorful cards, many of them all the way from London. Fancy gift bags, ribbon, and wrapping paper turn any gift into a fabulous feast for the eyes. Wrapping service is complimentary when you buy the materials. *Every day; map:GG7*

Oblation Papers and Press

516 NW 12TH AVE, PEARL DISTRICT; 503/223-1093 There's no other place in town like this when it comes to buying paper—or is that *fresh* paper? A peek from the retail space into the working studio reveals a day in the life of the papermaker and letterpress printer. Beautiful handmade floral paper, cards, fountain pens, and French wax seals make up the bulk of the merchandise, but there's also custom-designed invitations and announcements to behold. *Every day; www.oblationpapers.com; map:M2*

Present Perfect

700 SW 5TH AVE (PIONEER PLACE), DOWNTOWN; 503/228-9727 This downtown destination for gift wrapping offers cheery papers sold by the sheet, gift bags galore, bows, and ribbons. Gifts and collectibles from Mary Englebert to Winnie the Pooh are ready to wrap. Stationery here also hits a higher plane. There's a mammoth selection of cards—some exquisite handmade works of art—for every mood and occasion. *Every day; map:H4*

Presents of Mind

3633 SE HAWTHORNE BLVD, HAWTHORNE; 503/230-7740 Here, shopping for a birthday is as much an occasion as the celebration itself. Find a gem among the well-rounded and frequently rotated selection of cards. Picture frames, candles, photo albums, blank books, jewelry, and scarves make special gifts. Just for fun, toss in a glow-in-the-dark insect, plastic fish, candy necklace, or rubber stamp. *Every day; presentsofmind@qwest.net; map:HH5*

Wham!

617 NW 23RD AVE, NORTHWEST; 503/222-4992 Fun is the name of the game here, with lots of pop-culture cards and toys. You may find yourself longing to play with the sea monkeys, stink bombs, potato guns, and classic Gumby—the original yogi. Take a few minutes to browse the racks and racks of postcards, T-shirts, and refrigerator magnets with classic TV and cartoon themes. *Every day; map:GG7*

CHILDREN'S CLOTHING AND ACCESSORIES

Bambini's Children's Boutique

16353 SW BRYANT RD, LAKE OSWEGO; 503/635-7661 Little-girl glamour abounds at this dress-up paradise, from the sassy striped pants, iridescent puffy coats, and gossamer party gowns to the hundreds of hair bows and shelves of glittery kid-cosmetics. Bambini's has added a preteen boutique called Che Bella, making the sweet and smart clothes (often kid versions of trendy adult items like Petit Bateau and Three Dots T-shirts) available in a greater size range. *Mon–Sat; map:NN8*

The Bee and Thistle

2328 NW WESTOVER RD, NORTHWEST; 503/222-3397 Even if you don't know anyone with an immediate need for a miniature kimono or a T-shirt with sequins that spell "baby," the urge to buy is undeniable at the Bee. You'll also find cleverly displayed treasures like beaded jewelry, candles, and shiny business-card cases: good things come in small packages here. *Every day; map:HH7*

Generations

4029 SE HAWTHORNE BLVD, HAWTHORNE; 503/233-8130 Founded in 1981, a new generation now patronizes this reliable favorite for natural-fiber children's and maternity clothing. The store focuses on all-cotton basics for outerwear, sleepwear, and play clothes, with sweet, nature-inspired prints on T-shirts and dresses. A well-stocked resale rack in the store makes gently worn all-cotton kid's clothing available in sizes from newborn to 6X. *Mon–Sat; generations.citysearch.com; map:HH4*

Haggis McBaggis

6802 SE MILWAUKIE AVE, WESTMORELAND; 503/234-0849 This store's delightful interior is a wild playhouse, complete with enough toys, slides, and brightly colored murals to divert any shop-weary little one. Parents will be pleased with the selection of kids' all-weather gear, dominated by functional but stylish shoes (including Robeez, infant slippers reported to be un-pull-off-able). Service is helpful and personalized. And if there were an award for Best Changing Room in the Universe, this shop would win—hands down, bottoms up. *Tues–Sun; mcbaggis@aol.com; map:JJ5*

Hanna Andersson

327 NW 10TH AVE, PEARL DISTRICT; 503/321-5275 / 7 MONROE PKWY, LAKE OSWEGO; 503/697-1953 Best known around the country for its catalog of Swedish-style cotton clothing for kids (and moms and dads, too), Hanna Andersson is one of Portland's brighter retail success stories. With colors this vivid and fabric this sturdy, could it be anything but? The quality of Hanna's goods is usually very high, and the styles are irresistible. And for the family who likes to dress alike, there are pj's, T-shirts, and sweatshirts in every size. Buy reduced-priced irregulars and last season's stock at the spacious outlet store in Oswego Town Square. *Every day; www.hannaandersson.com; map:L2; map:LL7*

Lads and Lassies Frocks and Britches

BEAVERTON TOWN SQUARE, BEAVERTON; 503/626-6578 The name says it all—this is the place for a first-class get-up for a formal tea party or a first Communion. Unique and classy pieces abound for infants, toddlers, boys up to size 7, and girls up to size 14. The toy and book departments are centered on proven classics and stylish newcomers; the same goes for the doll collection. *Every day; map:II9*

Mako

732 NW 23RD AVE, NORTHWEST; 503/274-9081 Colorful sweaters, vests, and hats hand-knit by Mako and her sister are one of the biggest draws to this shop under the stairs, but there's also practical rain gear, bright bathrobes, flashy underwear, a fanciful sock collection, and shelves of toys, puzzles, and bath accessories for kids. Everywhere you look, it's lots of cotton—a great selection of rainbow-hued leggings and T-shirts—at everyday prices. *Every day; map:GG7*

Second to None

6308 SW CAPITOL HWY, HILLSDALE SHOPPING CENTER; 503/244-0071 Tucked into a strip mall, this children's shop features a good selection of used clothing (often name brands like Guess, Gap, and Hanna Andersson) and colorful new cottonwear and polar-fleece jackets. Unfinished and hand-painted wooden toy chests and child-size chairs, American Girl clothes and accessories (some custom made), dress-up costumes, and used goods such as car seats and toys in good condition set this store apart from other consignment shops. *Mon–Sat; map:JJ7*

Spoiled Rotten

1622 SE BYBEE BLVD, WESTMORELAND; 503/234-7250 Specializing in playful, bright designs with that French je ne sais quoi, this neighborhood boutique offers a whimsical range of versatile clothes for small fry: cotton dresses by Petit Bateau and Le Top, Nowa Li moccasins, T-shirts, pants, and sweaters by Catimini and Baby LuLu. Gifts like eeBoo growth charts and Juwel blankets, plush toys, and a selection of classic children's books are also on hand. *Every day; map:JJ5*

Zipadees

806 NW 23RD AVE, NORTHWEST; 503/493-3390 If Portland has an anti–Gap Kids, this is it. Owner Pam Small gravitates toward funky, eclectic designs, including her own handmade line, which she offers in the shop under the name Wasabi. From Asian-print pj's to faux fur and leopard-print accessories, kids who shop here will find those fashionable must-haves they didn't know they needed. Most inventory is in girls sizes newborn to 12, and boys, newborn to 7; there's also a small selection of adult clothing. *Every day; map:GG7*

FLORISTS AND NURSERIES

The Bovees Nursery

1737 SW CORONADO ST, LAKE OSWEGO; 503/244-9341 This specialty nursery features hundreds of types of rhododendrons—each neatly labeled— in the display garden. The star rhodies and deciduous azaleas bloom nearly six months of the year, but trees, hardy perennials, and Northwest natives are no less visible. Catalog on request. *Wed–Sun (closed Jan and Aug 1–Sept 15); www.bovees.com; map:LL7*

Cornell Farm

8212 SW BARNES RD, WEST SLOPE; 503/292-9895 A 1926 Dutch Colonial house, with a towering monkey-puzzle tree and lovely flower gardens, is the centerpiece of this 5-acre nursery. Owners Ed Blatter and Deby Barnhart grow more than 700 varieties of perennials and 150 types of annuals on the former goat and strawberry farm. Growing beds, open to the public, are across the road from the nearby Oregon College of Arts and Craft. *Every day; map:HH9*

Flowers Tommy Luke

1225 NW EVERETT ST, PEARL DISTRICT; 503/228-3140 This high-volume florist's shop is a Portland tradition, with designs that range from standard to airy English-garden arrangements. A large loftlike gallery is an ideal showroom for an eclectic selection of giftware, pottery, and vases. *Mon–Sat; map:L1*

Geranium Lake Flowers

555 SW OAK ST, DOWNTOWN; 503/228-1920 Painter and floral artist Kim Foren has built an oasis of blooms in the middle of the US Bancorp Tower. The brightly colored space specializes in whimsical artistry and caters to those looking for a hip edge in floral display. You won't find any baby's breath here. *Mon–Sat; www.geraniumlake.com; map:J4*

Gifford-Doving Florists

704 SW JEFFERSON ST, DOWNTOWN; 503/222-9193 / 200 SW MARKET ST, DOWN-TOWN; 503/222-5029 Family-owned since 1938, Gifford-Doving stocks one of the better selections of cut flowers in town. In the late afternoon, it's one of Portland's busiest florists. Several kinds of greens are on hand at both shops, making this a favorite of do-it-yourself arrangers. Friendly staff are always ready to help select the blooms that best suit the sentiment. *Mon–Sat; www.giffordflorist.com; map: F2; map:E4*

The Orchid Exchange

404 NW 12TH AVE, PEARL DISTRICT; 503/295-6899 Satisfy your craving for exotic blossoms at this exquisite floral shop. Reasonably priced, potted orchids start at $25; rare exotics can range up to $500. Owners Lisa and Adam Heim keep you coming back for more: any plant can be exchanged for a discount on your next purchase. At any one time, there are around 150 orchids in bloom in the store—some of them fragrant, some not. The shop also features sculptural wall pieces by Adam Heim. *Mon–Sat; map:L2*

Portland Nursery

5050 SE STARK ST, SOUTHEAST; 503/231-5050 / 9000 SE DIVISION ST, SOUTHEAST; 503/788-9000 A venerated landmark spread over 5 acres, Portland Nursery supplies city gardeners with the greatest variety of annuals, perennials, bushes, shrubs, and trees. A weekend visit is a cultural outing. An easy-to-follow layout takes you directly to the type of greenery you want, whether it be ground cover or climbing vine. The store's reputation owes much to its knowledgeable and helpful staff, ready to track down the answers to any questions they can't promptly resolve. This is also a good source for basic yard and deck furnishings, trellises, garden globes, and more. A second branch on Division Street specializes in ponds and houseplants. *Every day; www.portlandnursery.com; map:HH4; map: II3*

Sammy's Flowers

2120 NW GLISAN ST, NORTHWEST; 503/222-9759 A choice of more than 50 varieties of cut flowers, plus a larger selection of tropicals, makes Sammy's a Northwest institution. A mixed bouquet can cost as little as $15. The shop keeps later hours than most—7am to 10pm—and it offers delivery. *Every day; map:HH7*

Tualatin River Nursery

65 S DOLLAR ST, WEST LINN; 503/650-8511 John and Lori Blair's nursery is known for its relaxed atmosphere. There's a lovely pathway and a coffee shop that serves light meals; some years, there's been a children's garden. It has a wide variety of annuals and perennials and a selection of shrubs and trees. *Every day; map:PP5*

FURNITURE

Design Within Reach

1200 NW EVERETT ST, PEARL DISTRICT; 503/220-0200 Perhaps the work of the classic furniture designers of the 20th century is indeed within reach—but it comes at a price. Names like Eames, Aalto, Breuer, Le Corbusier, and Jacobsen share center stage with such current designers as Phillipe Starck, Ron Arad, Enrico Franzolini, and Michael Goldin. This San Francisco–based gallery devotes itself to delivering products of quality workmanship, so don't expect knock-off prices. *Every day; www.dwr.com; map:L2*

Goodnight Room

1517 NE BROADWAY, IRVINGTON; 503/281-5516 This is the place to shop for a child's "home." This colorful store houses almost everything to outfit, or at least to decorate, a child's nursery or bedroom: furniture, linens, hand-painted mirrors, lamps, and pint-size rocking chairs. If you don't have a grand to spend on a Maine Cottage dresser or bunk bed, at least stop by for one of the less expensive items: Groovy Girl dolls, bath toys, and towels, whimsical bibs, hand puppets, books, and games. *Every day; map:GG5*

The Handwerk Shop

8317 SE 13TH AVE, SELLWOOD; 503/236-7870 Customers become fast friends at this neighborly store south of Sellwood's antique row. Mission oak furniture, textiles, and pottery from the Arts and Crafts period vie for space with distinguished artwork and antiques in-the-making. Co-owner and master craftsman Brent Willis makes Morris chairs, settees, accent tables, and picture frames in the spirit of design legend Gustav Stickley. *Thurs–Sun and by appointment; map:KK5*

H.I.P.

1829 NW 25TH AVE, NORTHWEST; 503/225-5017 This is not your grandmother's furniture store. H.I.P. sets an urbane stage for modern living with streamlined furniture buffed to a fare-thee-well. Sofas, chairs, dining sets, and entertaining systems come in modern combinations of steel, wood and glass, leather, and contemporary upholstery fabrics. *Every day; www.ubhip.com; map:GG7*

J. D. Madison Rug & Home Co.

1307 NW GLISAN ST, PEARL DISTRICT; 503/827-6037 One of Portland's top sources for classic contemporary furnishings of high quality, J. D. Madison has a look of maximum minimalism. Custom upholstery, sofas and chairs, tables, and cabinetry of elegant simplicity are displayed in a living room–sized showroom of sophisticated aesthetic. Handcrafted rugs and carpeting provide a virtual couture line of floor coverings. *Every day; www.jdmadison.com; map:M1*

The Joinery

4804 SE WOODSTOCK BLVD, WOODSTOCK; 503/788-8547 For many years a fine place for custom-made Mission and Shaker-style furniture, the Joinery has expanded its style vocabulary to include wooden French country– and Pacific-Asian–style designs. The shop also carries a selection of well-hewn wooden accessories—table lamps, mirrors, boxes, spinning tops—from all over the world. *Mon–Sat; www.thejoinery.com; map:JJ4*

Kinion Furniture Company

1979 COLVIN CT, MCMINNVILLE; 503/2233-6165 Though its Southeast Portland store has closed, Kinion continues to produce beautiful, mostly cherry-wood furniture at its McMinnville workshop. These are contemporary renditions of Shaker furniture—tables, chairs, desks, and beds—with a little Mission and Arts and Crafts thrown in for good measure. Traditional joinery techniques guarantee furniture built to last. *Mon–Sat; www.kinionfurniture.com*

P. H. Reed Furniture

1100 NW GLISAN ST, PEARL DISTRICT; 503/274-7080 Upscale upholstered furniture and sophisticated Italian lighting dazzle the eye at this gallery-like furniture boutique. Owner Pieter Reed represents local artists and designers, so expect close-up looks at one-of-a-kind, cast-glass side tables, hand-loomed carpets, and incredible lamps. Directly across the street, P. H. Reed Bedroom (1101 NW Glisan St; 503/227-1742) makes sweet dreams come true with a truly adorable and seductive selection of bed and bedding accessories. *Tues–Sun; map:M2*

Rejuvenation House Parts

1100 SE GRAND AVE, INNER SOUTHEAST; 503/238-1900 This store has built a national reputation (and a booming catalog business) around superior reproductions of Craftsman-style lighting fixtures and Mission-style furniture. You'll also find salvaged doors, windows, tubs, and kitchen sinks. If you're having trouble getting started, a variety of workshops assist do-it-yourself weekend warriors as well as accomplished pros. Powell's Books supplies interior-design and building books for this home refinishers' hangout. In the store's southwest corner is the Daily Café, a delicious place to break for coffee or lunch (see review in the Restaurants chapter). *Every day; www.rejuvenation.com; map:F9*

Simon Toney and Fischer

105 SE TAYLOR ST, INNER SOUTHEAST; 503/721-0392 Cabinet makers David Simon and Bill Toney, and designer Susan Fischer, create wood furniture of astonishing beauty. Each piece is a custom-designed, one-of-a-kind work of artisanship for the client. The central east-side showroom features a broad sample of their work. This is comfortable, unfussy furniture that exhibits influences of Mission and Arts and Crafts eras. Rarely used woods of walnut, pear, yew, and chinquapin predominate the collection, and each board is handpicked. Luminous finishes and color kick up the luxe quotient. *Tues–Sat; map: F9*

Urbino

638 NW 23RD AVE, NORTHWEST; 503/220-0053 Its two Trendy-Third shops consolidated into one overstuffed furnishings gallery, Urbino specializes in the country-style furniture of Italy and southern France. The sunny, aromatic shop has also assembled a collection of other home accessories and giftware, including Italian and French kitchenware; lamps and pillows; and candles, soaps, and jewelry. *Every day; map:GG7*

GIFTS

Callin's Novelties and Magic

909 SW WASHINGTON ST, DOWNTOWN; 503/223-4821 This little shop of ha-ha's employs a staff of professional magicians who can show you how to pull off pranks (or at least your finger) in style: for every "trick" you buy, you get a lesson in how to perform it. Not so much a gift shop, Callin's is a theatrical prop and costume store for adolescent schemes and dreams—and for anyone who spent his or her childhood buried in the back pages of a comic book. Among the boomer-era gag gifts are sea monkeys, magic rocks, and X-ray specs to make your friends blush. *Mon–Sat; www.callinsmagic.com; map:I3*

Dazzle

704 NW 23RD AVE, NORTHWEST; 503/224-1294 From the spotted pony mascot outside to an interior that looks like it was decorated by Salvador Dali, Dazzle's chaotic collection of kitschy collectibles lives up to its name. And it's an ideal place to find the perfect gift for someone who needs a little whimsy in their life. *Every day; map:GG7*

Friends Library Store

801 SW 10TH AVE, DOWNTOWN; 503/988-5911 Multnomah County's Central Library not only makes room for its own Starbucks outlet; it has its own gift shop. Operated by the Friends of the Multnomah County Library, this niche-filled nook is full of everything for the book lover—colorful bookends, tiny book lights, and writing implements (costly and not)—plus children's gifts and jewelry. But you aren't going to find any books: you have to check those out. *Mon–Sat during library hours; www.friends-library.org/store; map:I2*

Greg's

3707 SE HAWTHORNE BLVD, HAWTHORNE; 503/235-1257 A treasure of the Hawthorne District, Greg Klaus's shop offers an abundance of goodness. There are good things to smell (candles scented with ginger or cinnamon), to induce laughter (hilarious quotable cards), or to make a bath a delicious treat (Tub Tea, Pre de Provence soaps). Rub shoulders in the smallish space with other similar-minded shoppers on a Saturday afternoon, or stop in during the week for a more serene walk-through. *Every day; map:HH5*

Made in Oregon

921 SW MORRISON ST (THE GALLERIA), DOWNTOWN (AND BRANCHES); 503/241-3630 If it's made, caught, or grown in this state, it's sold at Made in Oregon. Visitor essentials include smoked salmon, berry jams, chocolate, and hazelnuts that can be packed for traveling along with souvenir wooden slugs, myrtlewood, and warm-and-cozy Pendleton blankets. There are 10 stores around the state, including 5 others in Greater Portland: at the airport, in Old Town, Lloyd Center, Clackamas Town Center, and Washington Square. For a catalog, call 800/828-9673. *Every day; www.madeinoregon.com; map:I2*

The Nature Store at Portland Audubon Society

5151 NW CORNELL RD, NORTHWEST; 503/292-9453 Going bird-watching in Belize? Before you take flight, be sure to swoop down to this resource center and gift shop on the edge of Forest Park within the Audubon sanctuary. Inside, there's a treasure trove for naturalists: worldwide field guides, natural-history books, binoculars, bird feeders, and more. About one-third of the inventory is children's books; there are also stuffed animals, model insects, and jigsaw puzzles. *Every day; www.audubonportland.com; map:GG8*

Topanien

7832 SW CAPITOL HWY, MULTNOMAH VILLAGE; 503/244-9683 This world-friendly shop brings global treasures to the comfy Village confines. Alongside a colorful stock of beeswax sheets for candle making, educational gifts from all over the world include wall hangings, noise-making toys, and necklaces. And for the home, there's a collection of tablecloths and mats, vases, and frames. *Every day; map:JJ7*

Twist

30 NW 23RD PL, NORTHWEST; 503/224-0334 / 700 SW 5TH AVE (PIONEER PLACE), DOWNTOWN; 503/222-3137 On a blustery day, the bright, cheery entryway provides a warm Northwest welcome. Twist playfully

221

displays some of the world's top jewelry designers alongside unique American Arts and Crafts artifacts. The gallery focuses on exclusive designers, delicate glassware, hand-painted ceramics, crafts, and a smattering of furniture. While the Pioneer Place shop is geared for the traveler, it maintains the same level of quality merchandise and mystique. *Every day; www.twistonline.com; map:HH7; map:H4*

HARDWARE

A-Ball Plumbing Supply

1703 W BURNSIDE ST, NORTHWEST; 503/228-0026 A-Ball's surprise-filled windows have amused passing motorists while attracting customers for over 30 years. A locally founded, nationally recognized emporium of posh porcelain goods, this on-the-ball spot sells high-end kitchen fixtures and bathroom fittings. If the fine claw-foot tubs are out of your price range, consider a towel bar or a toothbrush holder. *Mon–Sat; www.a-ball.com; map:HH7*

1874 House

8070 SE 13TH AVE, SELLWOOD; 503/233-1874 Local architectural remnants that homeowners ripped out and discarded decades ago have found a new home at the 1874 House. An organized jumble of high-quality light shades and fixtures, antique as well as reproduction hardware, windows, shutters, and mantels all wait to be reinstalled in the bungalow of your dreams. A tad bit younger than most of its contents, this place has been around for more than three decades. *Tues–Sat; map:KK5*

Environmental Building Supplies

819 SE TAYLOR ST, BUCKMAN; 503/222-3881 EBS has three criteria for its products: they must be natural, low in toxicity, and renewable or recyclable. With that mission, this eastside store (formerly in the Pearl District) offers a wide range of hard-to-find floor coverings and finishes, cabinets and countertops, paint and plumbing supplies, all safe for the home and easy on the environment. You'll find sustainable hardwoods, wool carpets from New Zealand, and linoleum from Holland. A second store is in the central Oregon city of Bend. *Mon–Sat; www.ecohaus.com; map:N1*

Hippo Hardware and Trading Co.

1040 P BURNSIDE ST, BUCKMAN; 503/231-1444 / 7829 SW CAPITOL HWY, MULTNOMAH VILLAGE; 503/293-8017 Hip, hippo, hooray! This place can hook you up with a kitchen sink and just about every other house part you can think of. Built on a foundation of buy, sell, and trade, Hippo is always on the prowl for architectural elements—doors, windows, molding, and trim—as well as hardware from the 1800s through the 1940s. Pre-1970s lighting fixtures and specialized plumbing fixtures are also sought after. Hippo's wonderfully quirky staff keeps you smiling as you sort through design treasures and organized bins of clutter. If you can't find something, ask; if they don't have it, they just might be able to splice, dice, or file something to fit. *Mon–Sat; www.hipponet .com; map:HH6; map:JJ7*

Winks Hardware

200 SE STARK ST, INNER SOUTHEAST; 503/227-5536 We're not too sure that owner Anne Kilkenny's grandfather intended to stock 50,000 items when he opened this hardware store in 1909. But everything, from 1,000 sizes of springs to hundreds of styles of hinges, gives Winks a full house for your house. With its impressive array of hard-to-find, unusual, and useful things, Winks caters to the trade (hence the weekday-only hours), but experienced clerks happily share advice with do-it-yourselfers. Relocated in 2001 from the Pearl District, this is about as old-fashioned as it gets today. *Mon–Fri; map:I9*

Woodcrafters

212 NE 6TH AVE, BUCKMAN; 503/231-0226 This is where Portland's builders and woodworkers spend their fun money: a friendly warehouse filled with tools, woodstains, and high-quality lumber, mill ends, and hardwood carving blocks. An enormous book section (with back issues of *Fine Homebuilding*) serves as an unofficial library for do-it-yourselfers and craftspeople and makes this the logical destination after an episode of *This Old House*. Free demonstrations of wood turning and other specialized skills are offered most Saturdays. *Every day (closed Sun June–Sept); map:HH6*

HOME DECOR

The Arrangement

4210 NE FREMONT ST, BEAUMONT; 503/287-4440 This friendly shop in the Alameda/Beaumont neighborhood beckons with an ever-changing flow of decorative items. Around holiday time, the winter-wonderland quality of the shop is as inviting as a cup of warm hot cocoa on a blustery day, and the helpful staff will assist you in designing just the right wreath or table arrangement. Like a mini department store with tons more personality, The Arrangement boasts casual clothing and jewelry, housewarming decor, and stationery. *Every day; map:FF4*

The Compleat Bed & Breakfast

615 NW 23RD AVE, NORTHWEST; 503/221-0193 This is a store where you can indulge in some civilized pampering: you'll find enough luxurious linens and billowy comforters, duvets, and pillow shams to supply sweet dreams for a lifetime. If it's not on the shelf, pick out fabric—Waverly or other top-drawer lines—and the shop will have it made to order. There's a large selection of Crabtree & Evelyn toiletries as well. *Every day; map:GG7*

Dieci Soli

304 NW 11TH AVE, PEARL DISTRICT; 503/222-4221 Featuring artful treasures for the table, smack-dab in the middle of the Pearl's gallery and furniture store district, Dieci Soli carries an enormous selection of gorgeous hand-painted Italian pottery from espresso cups to jardiniere. Table linens from Italy and France are available in all sizes. Traditional oilcloth for casual table coverings is available by the yard as well. *Every day; www.dieci-soli.com; map:L2*

French Quarter

1444 NE BROADWAY, NEAR LLOYD CENTER; 503/282-8200 / 536 NW 14TH AVE, PEARL DISTRICT; 503/223-3879 "Crème de la crème" describes this boutique, which caters to Francophiles who don't want to use up their frequent-flier miles in search of a gift but still want to wrap themselves in Parisian panache. Every square inch of the French Quarter is filled with something to lust after: plush bath mats, unbelievably soft flannel sheets (100 percent cotton, unbleached and undyed), aromatic candles, fancy French soaps and bath salts, colorful towels, downy bathrobes, and dreamy pajamas. A second shop nestles between cafés and artists' lofts—so French—in the Pearl District. *Every day; www.eurolinens.com; map:GG5; map:M1*

Hunt & Gather

1302 NW HOYT ST, PEARL DISTRICT; 503/227-3400 Treasures from around the globe make for an interesting mix of home accessories at this Pearl District favorite. Beyond global goodies for the table, Hunt & Gather features custom-made, decadent down sofas and chairs sure to be the focus of any elegant home. Check out the nifty candle selection too. *Every day; www.huntgather.com; map:M1*

Natural Spaces

6401 SW MACADAM AVE, JOHN'S LANDING; 503/892-2373 What goes around, comes around, in this . . . well . . . natural space, tucked neatly into the John's Landing neighborhood. All furniture, glassware, and home-refurbishment accessories are made from recycled and sustainable materials. And this stuff's made to last a lifetime—just when you were convinced that they don't make 'em like they used to. *Every day; www.naturalspaces.com; map:JJ6*

Pendleton Woolen Mills Store

8550 SE MCLOUGHLIN BLVD, MILWAUKIE; 503/535-5786 This is the drop-off spot for products from the research and development department of the Pendleton Woolen Mills, an Oregon pioneer. Prototypes for new products—from theme blankets to wool-upholstered furniture—are offered here at discount prices. *Mon–Sat; www.pendleton-usa.com; map:KK5*

Pratt & Larson Tile Co.

1201 SE 3RD AVE, INNER SOUTHEAST; 503/231-9464 With what seems to be tile by the mile, lining every surface, this is one of the country's largest custom tile manufacturers. The shop is like a large working studio with examples of kitchen and bathroom treatments that use both imported tiles and one-of-a-kind work by potter Michael Pratt and fabric artist Reta Larson. For bargains, check out their seconds room, where mistakes are practically given away. *Mon–Sat; www.prattandlarson.com; map:E9*

Relish

433 NW 10TH AVE, PEARL DISTRICT; 503/227-3779 The ultramodern aesthetic of Relish is right at home with the Pearl District's loft lifestyle. Here you'll find an eclectic collection of beautifully made tableware, including wood vessels from Costa Rica; ceramic dishware from Italy, London, and Japan; and kitchen utensils from Denmark and Germany. Relish also features arty jewelry of silver, enamel, and feathers; plus steel and acrylic jewelry from Ann Brumby of Portland. *Tues–Sun; www.relishstyle.com; map:L2*

The Whole 9 Yards

1033 NW GLISAN ST, PEARL DISTRICT; 503/223-2880 The *Oregonian* calls this gem "one of the nation's top interior fabric stores," One step inside reveals why: seamsters come here in droves not only for the luxurious silks, velvets, and jacquards, but also for ideas and inspiration. Need a second opinion? The gracious staff double as design consultants. A custom furniture line and classes on making curtains and pillows are added bonuses. *Every day; www.w9yards.com; map:M2*

IMPORTS

Arthur W. Erikson Fine Arts

1030 SW TAYLOR ST, DOWNTOWN; 503/227-4710 This astonishingly eclectic mélange of traditional tribal artifacts will appeal to the novice and experienced collector alike. The focus is on Native American and Eskimo arts and crafts. Bronze figurines from the Horn of Africa and Kashmiri shawls are among the out-of-the-ordinary offerings. *Wed and by appointment; map:H1*

Cargo

734 NW 14TH ST, PEARL DISTRICT; 503/209-8349 Welcome to another world. Where else but in this 10,000-square-foot warehouse will you find all the world's treasures under one roof? Big-ticket home-furnishing items include Chang dynasty beds and a Ming puppet theater (with puppets) for just under $10,000, or entire walls from a faraway island in Indonesia. Folding iron chairs, seed baskets from Borneo, Indonesian hutches, Mexican pottery and glassware, and funky doodads from everywhere fill this eclectic store to its rafters. This is a shopping oasis for those who want to create a homespun Shangri-la. *Every day; www.cargoinc.com; map:N1*

Scandia Imports

10020 SW BEAVERTON-HILLSDALE HWY, BEAVERTON; 503/643-2424 Finnish glassware, gleaming brown stoneware by Arabia, and heavy pewter candelabra from Denmark dazzle at surprisingly low prices. Homesick Scandinavians can buy birthday cards in their native languages, good Swedish mint pastilles, linens, and enough candles for a hundred Santa Lucia nights. *Mon–Sat; www.scandiaimports.com; map:II9*

Signature Imports

638 SW ALDER ST, DOWNTOWN; 503/222-5340 / 920 NW 23RD AVE, NORTHWEST; 503/274-0217 Signature Imports runs a brisk business in Latin American imports, including colorful sweaters and jewelry. It carries rough-hewn furniture and gorgeous handblown glass from Mexico, handcrafted figures from Oaxaca, and (stretching the map) masks from Ghana. Signature supports its own knitting co-op in Bolivia, so craftspeople benefit directly from their labors. *Every day; map: I3; map:GG7*

Trade Roots

1831 NE BROADWAY, IRVINGTON; 503/281-5335 Folk art at this friendly shop includes brightly painted coconut-shell masks from Mexico, Peruvian amulets, and handwoven place mats from Nepal. Gauzy skirts, embroidered vests, batik dresses, and other colorful apparel (including pieces from Putumayo), plus lots of silver jewelry, are available at good prices. *Every day; www.traderoots.com; map:GG5*

JEWELRY AND ACCESSORIES

Carl Greve

731 SW MORRISON ST, DOWNTOWN; 503/223-7121 Exclusive representation of the world's top jewelry designers is the specialty of the house at the fourth-generation, family-owned Carl Greve. On the second floor is a gift boutique: a fantasyland of shimmering china, stemware, and home accessories. Like the jewels and gems, much of it is exclusive to this chic boutique. Many of Greve's trunk shows and events are the talk of the social season. *Mon–Sat; www.carlgreve.com; map:I3*

Dan Marx

511 SW BROADWAY, DOWNTOWN; 503/228-5090 For more than a century, Portlanders and visitors have been buying from Oregon's oldest jewelry store. Clean-lined jewelry, gorgeous colored stones and diamonds, and the staff's quiet politeness set the tone. Eighteen-karat gold and platinum are showcased throughout this immaculate little family-owned shop full of small and delicate treasures. *Tues–Sat; map:I3*

Gary Swank Jewelers

840 SW BROADWAY, DOWNTOWN; 503/223-8940 Custom designer Gary Swank does on-the-spot creations, from bold earrings to necklaces that could have come from an Egyptian tomb. And he'll set anything from a diamond to a scarab. A great selection of newly minted wristwatches, and Swank's coveted collection of antique timepieces (restored to perfect ticking order), are an extra lure for ladies and gentlemen. *Tues–Sat; www.garyswank.com; map:H3*

Gilt

720 NW 23RD AVE, NORTHWEST; 503/226-0629 An eclectic collection of contemporary local designs and vintage Americana jewelry mingles with work from such faraway places as India and China. Jewels arrive weekly from trusted sources, adding to the ever-changing selection of precious, semiprecious, and costume pieces. Standouts include contemporary rings with unusual stones and settings. *Tues–Sat; map:GG7*

Goldmark

1000 SW TAYLOR ST, DOWNTOWN; 503/224-3743 Cal Brockman, Goldmark's owner, loves working with customers to create one-of-a-kind jewelry designs. Endlessly fascinated with the variety of colored gemstones, he has been designing, updating, and restyling jewelry for more than 25 years. *Tues–Sat and by appointment; map:H2*

Margulis Jewelers

800 SW BROADWAY, DOWNTOWN; 503/227-1153 Many of David Margulis's fetching designs—in 18- and 22-karat gold as well as platinum—are inspired by classical themes. You'll find Heracles-knot bracelets, Celtic-style rings adorned with granulation, and elegant pearl earrings that resemble those in a Rubens painting. Established in 1932, this family-owned business was the first to sell estate jewelry in Portland. *Mon–Sat; www.margulis.com; map:H3*

The Real Mother Goose

901 SW YAMHILL ST, DOWNTOWN (AND BRANCHES); 503/223-9510 Since 1971, this fairy-tale shop—an American Crafts Gallery of the Year award winner—has showcased the finest of Northwest designers. A jeweler and goldsmith create wedding rings and other custom pieces, while holiday shoppers and travelers find choice gifts that reflect the region's spirit. The downtown furniture gallery carries contemporary pieces in creative blends of fine (and sometimes exotic) woods, and you can buy distinctive Northwest gifts at the airport branch (7000 NE Airport Wy, Northeast; 503/284-9929; map:EE3) on your way out of town. Also in Washington Square (9300 SW Washington Square Rd, Tigard; 503/620-2243; map: KK9). *Mon–Sat; map:I2*

Something Silver

700 SW 5TH AVE (PIONEER PLACE), DOWNTOWN; 503/248-0221 While most mall-bound jewelry stores leave something to be desired, this one offers a surprisingly whimsical collection of sparkling silver earrings, bracelets, pendants, and the like. Celebrate baby's arrival with a silver spoon or baby cup—or commemorate that all-important silver anniversary (25 years!) with something special. *Every day; www.somethingsilver.com; map:H4*

Zell Bros.

800 SW MORRISON ST, DOWNTOWN; 503/227-8471 More than three floors of jewelry, watches, sterling silver, china, and crystal mark the Zell brothers' legacy. Since 1912, when Julius and Harry Zell opened a small jewelry store near Union Station, the Zell family has offered the finest in jewelry and other precious things. *Mon–Sat; map:I3*

KITCHENWARE

In Good Taste

231 NW 11TH AVE, PEARL DISTRICT; 503/248-2015 This is a place for people who are passionate about food and wine. What began as a cooking school has grown into retail space for professional-quality kitchen utensils, from copper and stainless cookware to Laguiole knives. A wine shop carries an extensive selection from Oregon, Washington, and California, plus imports; the foodie in your life will love the Scharffen Berger chocolate. Cooking classes are taught by well-known local chefs and visiting professionals, and most are small enough (14 max) to allow for hands-on participation. *Every day; www.ingoodtastestore.com; map:K2*

Kitchen Kaboodle

8788 SW HALL BLVD, BEAVERTON (AND BRANCHES); 503/643-5491 Top-of-the-line cookware, tons of gadgets, and beautiful, reasonably priced tableware make this a favorite haunt of food enthusiasts. Novelty accessories, like salt and pepper shakers in the shapes of tomatoes, are complemented by purely practical tools, appliances, and furniture: cherry dressers, ash side tables, and custom-made couches. Kitchen Kaboodle's January sale brings cooks out of the kitchen and into the store. The locally owned company has expanded its original Beaverton location and now has five other shops in Greater Portland. *Every day; www.kitchenkaboodle.com*

MUSIC (CDS, RECORDS, AND TAPES)

Crossroads

3130-B SE HAWTHORNE BLVD, HAWTHORNE; 503/232-1767 This cooperative of 35 vendors in a storefront is modeled much like an antique mall. That makes sense, considering that they specialize in collectibles and hard-to-find records—they even offer a computerized record-search service. If you need *Meet the Beatles* on the black label, green label, red label, or Apple label to complete your collection, pay this place a visit. It will definitely be worth the trip. *Every day; www.xro.com; map:HH5*

Django's

1111 SW STARK ST, DOWNTOWN; 503/227-4381 As befits Portland's first used record store, this shop offers a nostalgic, old-school browsing experience: racks and racks of used CDs and vinyl and windows papered with posters of long-past live shows. But Django's is a lot more than a trip down memory lane; it's a Portland landmark with a good selection across many genres—particularly jazz and classic rock. Dedicated rummagers can also find used videos and DVDs. *Every day; www.django.com; map:J2*

Everyday Music

1313 W BURNSIDE ST, PEARL DISTRICT (AND BRANCHES); 503/274-0961 Combined with a little browsing at nearby Powell's Books, a leisurely visit to Everyday Music makes for a fine afternoon . . . or evening (they're open 'til midnight). The huge space is stocked with new and pre-loved CDs, cassettes, and LPs from the worlds of rock, jazz, and dance music. The next-door annex has a great classical selection. Try before you buy at one of the listening stations. Other branches are in Northeast Portland (1931 NE Sandy Blvd, Buckman; 503/239-7610; map:HH5) and in Beaverton (3290 SW Cedar Hills Blvd, Beaverton; 503/350-0907; map:II9). *Every day (including Christmas); www.everydaymusic.com; map:K1*

Jackpot Records

3736 SE HAWTHORNE BLVD, HAWTHORNE; 503/239-7561 Owner Isaac Slusarenko provides what mega music vendors can't—a cross-genre wealth of knowledge and a hands-on approach to selling music. Come here if you're looking for obscure reggae, rare vinyl, esoteric local artists, or an incredible array of independent rock

MERCHANDISE FROM A TO Z

and punk music. Just don't come looking for Britney Spears or the Backstreet Boys. *Every day; www.jackpotrecords.com; map:HH5*

Locals Online.com

916 W BURNSIDE ST, DOWNTOWN; 503/227-5000 "True talent but not a very big spotlight" is how the owners of Locals Online describe the store's focus. The shop stocks new releases by up-and-coming regional bands and maintains a regular best-sellers list to educate customers about popular picks. Prepurchase listening is welcome (and recommended). *Tues–Sat; www.localsonline .com; map:K3*

Music Millennium

3158 E BURNSIDE ST, LAURELHURST; 503/231-8926 / 801 NW 23RD AVE, NORTHWEST; 503/248-0163 Since 1969, the independently owned Music Millennium has stayed competitive with larger record chains. Its stock is truly impressive: an amazing variety of rock CDs plus separate areas for oldies, rap, jazz, blues, reggae, country, and New Age. The east-side store has a separate classical music annex. Check out their intimate in-store miniconcerts with big-name artists like the Cowboy Junkies. The Northwest shop also hosts special appearances. *Every day; www.musicmillennium.com; map:HH5; map:GG7*

Ozone Records

701 E BURNSIDE ST, BUCKMAN; 503/227-1975 / 2 NW 10TH AVE, PEARL DISTRICT; 503/227-1981 Formerly a fixture at 11th and Burnside, Ozone's owners split the business in 2002 into two stores. O3:Ozone Records, on the east side, carries forward the store's reputation as a solid alternative record store—decently augmented by local releases. Ozone UK, near the old location, focuses on hard-to-find import releases; its selection of goth, industrial, and experimental music is the best in town. *Every day; www.ozonerecords.com; map:HH6; map:K3.*

Platinum Records

104 SW 2ND AVE, OLD TOWN; 503/222-9166 This DJ-centric shop is the place to go for dance music and hard-to-find musical genres. The stock is mostly LPs—not surprising, as DJs don't mix with cassettes or CDs. There's also a good selection of DJ equipment, including mixers, PA systems, and a few glittering disco balls. *Every day; www.platinum-records.com; map:J6*

2nd Avenue Records

400 SW 2ND AVE, DOWNTOWN; 503/222-3783 Definitely not a grab-and-go music shop, 2nd Avenue is a shrine to the record-hunting experience. Stacks of collectible and imported vinyl share scant store space with CDs; these are unfortunately kept behind glass, which requires requesting them from the sales staff. All genres—including hip-hop, punk, ska, and rock—are represented, but selection is on a try-your-luck basis. *Every day; map:I5*

OUTDOOR GEAR

Alder Creek Kayak and Canoe

250 NE TOMAHAWK ISLAND DR, JANTZEN BEACH; 503/285-0464 If it floats and you paddle it, Alder Creek probably sells it—whether it's a canoe, sea kayak, or river kayak. Demos in the nearby Columbia River are free (note to self: this is a great way to find out how much you're willing to lug around on the dock). The store carries an extensive line of gear, books, and videos and emphasizes group and private instruction and guided tours. *Every day; www.aldercreek.com; map:CC6*

Andy & Bax Sporting Goods

324 SE GRAND AVE, INNER SOUTHEAST; 503/234-7538 This is ground zero for the sports lover/camper or for the person who just likes to wear campy sport clothes. Huge helpings of personality are split three ways between rafting and whitewater equipment, piles of Army/Navy surplus, and family camping and cold-weather gear. From commercial inflatables to information on guides and beginner classes, Andy & Bax is one of Portland's better rafting and whitewater resources. Prices are reasonable, and there are some awesome bargains (like European army surplus blankets for cheapie cheap). *Mon–Sat; www.andyandbax.com; map:GG5*

Bicycle Repair Collective

4438 SE BELMONT ST, BELMONT; 503/233-0564 The Bicycle Repair Collective has only a handful of peers nationwide. It sells parts and accessories, repairs bikes, and gives personal assistance in a rental work space. For $75 a year or $10 an hour, cyclists can tune their bikes and adjust their chains. *Mon–Sat; map:HH4*

The Bike Gallery

5329 NE SANDY BLVD, HOLLYWOOD (AND BRANCHES); 503/281-9800 The Bike Gallery is to cycles what Saks is to clothing. With humble origins as a small, family-run shop, it's now one of the country's finest bike dealers. All sales are guaranteed, whether you buy a bicycle (road, mountain, crossover, tandem, child's, or adult), Burly, or jogging stroller. Branches are in Downtown (1001 SW Salmon St; 503/222-3821; map:H2), in Lake Oswego (200 B Ave; 503/636-1600; map:MM6), and in Beaverton (3645 SW Hall Blvd; 503/641-2580). *Every day; www.bikegallery.com; map:GG4*

Bob's Bicycle Center

10950 SE DIVISION ST, SOUTHEAST; 503/254-2663 Bob's started as a small BMX store and is now one of the largest cycling shops in the Northwest. The stock has grown to 2,000-plus bikes (everything from BMX to touring), and the store even sponsors a bicycle team. Attentive staff cater to all customer needs, from free bicycle fits to full-service bike repairs. *Every day; www.bobsbicyclecenter.com; map:II2*

Columbia Sportswear

911 SW BROADWAY, DOWNTOWN (AND BRANCHES); 503/226-6800 While Gert Boyle, mother figure and CEO of Columbia Sportswear, has become a national icon through savvy advertising and an insistence that everyone dress warmly, her business has exploded internationally. Located in the 1888 United Carriage Company Building, this is Columbia's flagship store: 17,000 square feet of outdoor apparel and footwear reflecting the latest in high-tech fabrics and technologies. Got a sport? Boyle has the shoes, the socks, and the practical advice. Outlet stores in Sellwood (1323 SE Tacoma St; 503/238-0118; map:KK5) and Lake Oswego (3 Monroe Pkwy at Boones Ferry Rd; 503/636-6593; map: LL7) carry irregulars, closeouts, and overstocks of active outdoor apparel and footwear fresh from the factory, at 30 to 50 percent below retail prices. *Every day; www.columbia.com; map:H3*

Country sport

126 SW 1ST AVE, OLD TOWN; 503/221-4545 For the fly-fishing aficionado, Country sport is a simple yet gorgeous store with antique reels, bamboo fly rods, wicker creels, and canoe chairs displayed on hardwood floors. Clothing includes technical rainwear, canvas shirts, and fleece, as well as tropical wear. There's a huge selection of flies, feathers, and thread and practical gear such as float tubes and pontoon boats. Fly-fishing classes, guided tours, travel planning, and catalog sales are available. This is a weekend-minded retreat for the downtown workforce. *Every day; www.csport.com; map:J6*

Ebb & Flow Paddlesports

0604 SW NEBRASKA ST, SW MACADAM; 503/245-1756 Donna Holman, co-founder of OOPS (Oregon Ocean Paddling Society), has rented sea kayaks and canoes for nearly 20 years. Behind her intimate shop, off Macadam Avenue, is a warehouse full of reliable boats. You can put a kayak on a portage cart, wheel it across the street to Willamette Park's boat ramp, and try out different kinds of paddles to ensure a perfect fit. Whitewater instruction is offered at all levels of experience. *Tues–Sun; map:JJ6*

Exit Real World

206 NW 23RD AVE, NORTHWEST; 503/226-3948 Bored? Grab a board. Established in Salem in 1993, this is the ultimate shop for the new generation of snowboarders and skateboarders. Boards, bindings, boots, and cold-weather attire are all here or at Exit's mountain shop on Mount Hood (Government Camp). Skateboarders find everything from wheels and bearings to decks and fashions. And Exit's demonstration teams offer expert instruction. *Every day; www.exitrealworld.com; map:HH7*

Fat Tire Farm

2714 NW THURMAN ST, NORTHWEST; 503/222-3276 This shop has the advantage of immediate access to the nation's largest municipal playground: Forest Park. Novice mountain bikers can rent a bike and helmet here, load up on equipment, grab a water bottle and a fistful of Power Bars, and tour the park with a map and expert advice. Bikes and accessories, clothes, and literature are sold by a friendly, informed staff. *Every day; www.fattirefarm.com; map:GG7*

Kaufmann's Streamborn Inc.

8861 SW COMMERCIAL ST, TIGARD; 503/639-6400 Kaufmann's has been Portland's consummate fly shop since 1970. The knowledgeable staff can outfit you for fishing on the Clackamas River, or they can equip you for specialty fishing trips, local or overseas. Along with one of the finer selections of flies in the country, Kaufmann's offers fishing classes and fly-tying materials. Its free catalog has made the store world famous. *Mon–Sat; www.kman.com; map:MM9*

The Mountain Shop

628 NE BROADWAY, NEAR LLOYD CENTER; 503/288-6768 Established in 1937, this store may well be the area's best one-stop shopping center for downhill and back-country ski gear, both Nordic and tidemark. It's certainly the most unabashed, with three floors of skis, boards, and accessories to help you refine your technique—and a full line of footwear and apparel to help you perfect your style. The shop also outfits backpackers and four-season climbers who would rather go up and down the mountain without skis. Summer and winter rental packages are available. *Every day; www.mountainshop.net; map:GG6*

Oregon Mountain Community

60 NW DAVIS ST, OLD TOWN; 503/227-1038 OMC is a four-season outfitter. As winter approaches, patrons of this popular Old Town store come for backcountry ski equipment; in spring and summer, they look for packs, tents, sleeping bags, and rock-climbing equipment. All manner of outdoor equipment, as well as men's and women's clothing, are sold year-round by an active and experienced sales staff. And a travel desk helps in planning that long-awaited backpacking trip to New Zealand. *Every day; www.e-omc.com; map:K6*

Pace Setter Athletic

4306 SE WOODSTOCK BLVD, WOODSTOCK; 503/777-3214 Wear your old running shoes to this store and the staff will check them out, then recommend—based upon tread-wear patterns—an appropriate new pair from among the 10 dozen models it stocks. The casual, friendly salespeople include some of the area's better competitive runners (several of them on Pace Setter's own race team), so the merchandise reflects a slightly more technical bias than a typical running store. Students get discounts. *Every day; www.pacesetterathletic.com; map:JJ4*

Portland Niketown

930 SW 6TH AVE, DOWNTOWN (AND BRANCHES); 503/221-6453 This state-of-the-art, showcase store displays all the latest from the entire Nike line. Fans come not only to buy but to gawk at this sports enthusiasts' love fest. The young and fit clerks—athletes one and all—know what they're talking about. And, though you'll rarely find stuff on sale, there's plenty to purchase no matter what your budget. For less show and better prices, shop at the Nike Factory Store (2650 NE Martin Luther King Jr Blvd, Northeast; 503/281-5901; map:FF5). The Nike store on the mini retail row at Portland's International Airport (503/284-3558) packs as much as it can into a small space. *Every day; niketown.nike.com; map:G3*

The Portland Running Company

11355 SW SCHOLLS FERRY RD, BEAVERTON; 503/524-7570 Since the mid-1960s, when University of Oregon track coach Bill Bowerman and athlete Phil Knight germinated the seed that became the Nike corporation, the Willamette Valley has been a focus of the runner's world. Sales staff fit shoes based upon a careful analysis of running or walking style and injury history; many customers are referred by their doctors. But this is more than a shoe and apparel store: it's a complete running service providing route maps, event information, and training and nutritional tips. *Every day; www.portlandrunningcompany.com; map:KK9*

Recreational Equipment Inc. (REI)

1405 NW JOHNSON ST, PEARL DISTRICT (AND BRANCHES); 503/221-1938 A spectacular Pearl District store, with a freestanding climbing pinnacle behind a two-story glass facade, solidified REI's longtime Portland presence upon opening in early 2004. All inventory and more than 100 knowledgeable employees were relocated from the former Jantzen Beach store, established in 1976 as the third of this Seattle-based consumer cooperative's now 66 stores in 24 states. The new 35,000-square-foot store stocks REI's full line of clothing and gear for hiking, camping, climbing, skiing, cycling, and water sports—and offers test areas for hiking boots, camp stoves, and water filters. A onetime $15 fee earns roughly 10 percent cash back on nonsale purchases. REI also has a store in Tualatin (7410 SW Bridgeport Rd; 503/624-8600; map:NN9); another in Hillsboro is planned for the end of 2004. *Every day; www.rei.com; map:N1*

River City Bicycles

706 SE MARTIN LUTHER KING JR BLVD, INNER SOUTHEAST; 503/233-5973 Open since 1994, this bike shop is among the finest wheel winders in town. With an 11,000-square-foot showroom, including a slow-speed indoor test track, it's certainly the largest. The friendly experts who run River City stock the store with all kinds of riding gear: tricycles, tandems, mountain and road bikes, helmets, shoes, a huge clothing section . . . you name it. This is a great place to outfit the family. *Every day; www.rivercitybicycles.com; map:H9*

Running Outfitters

2337 SW 6TH AVE, LAIR HILL; 503/248-9820 At the foot of the popular Terwilliger Boulevard running route, two blocks from Duniway Park's track, is the city's oldest running-only store: smaller than your garage, but well stocked. Owner Jim Davis is, of course, an avid runner, and his store has a cultlike local following. *Mon–Sat; map:II6*

SHOES

Al's Shoes & Boots for Men

5811 SE 82ND AVE, SOUTHEAST; 503/771-2130 Third-generation owners continue the tradition—started in 1947—of supplying Portland's men and boys with handsome soles in time-tested styles. Work, cowboy, and hiking boots are plentiful, but Al's also offers a range of popular sneakers and other street shoes. This is where firefighters shop for indestructible Wesco Smoke Jumper boots; but a hipster seeking the perfect black slip-on will be treated with equal respect by the friendly and knowledgeable staff. *Mon–Sat; alsshoes.citysearch.com; map:JJ3*

Bad Doll

808 NW 23RD AVE, NORTHWEST; 503/525-2202 What's bad? This is a *good* place to find screamin' deals on right-now styles. The enthusiastic staff will take you on a tour that begins with Pumas and Converse in a pleasing palette of colors (some are imported) and ends up with Diesels, Fornarinas, and Simples. *Every day; www.baddoll.com; map:GG7*

Birkenstock Haus

730 SW 11TH AVE, DOWNTOWN; 503/227-4202 Since opening Portland's first Birkenstock store in 1976, Marcia Hanna has seen the übercomfortable walking shoe grow in popularity and style. The store keeps pace by stocking classic Birks, as well as the company's new, sleeker styles. Other options include snappy Dansko clogs and a wide range of comfortable socks. In-house repairs are affordable and prompt. *Every day; birkenstock.citysearch.com; map:I2*

Halo

1425 NE BROADWAY, NEAR LLOYD CENTER; 503/331-0366 This intimate shoetique stocks incredibly rich leather styles, many of them from Europe. They range from updated Mary Janes to ultrafeminine heeled sandals and other classy styles for women of impeccable taste . . . and with a couple hundred dollars to spend. Men's shoes and unique leather bags are worth a look too. *Every day; map:GG5*

Imelda's Designer Shoes

1431 SE 37TH AVE, HAWTHORNE; 503/233-7476 Consistently named by local shoe fanatics as Portland's favorite shoe store, Imelda's strikes a balance between high fashion and affordable prices. The store's buyers have a knack for finding unique styles by such European manufacturers as Giraudon and Fornarina. Also available are trendy Puma sneakers, handbags and hats, and a good array of men's shoes. *Every day; map:HH5*

Johnny Sole

815 SW ALDER ST, DOWNTOWN; 503/225-1241 Owner John Plummer's got sole. He keeps a close watch on the fashion trend meter and stocks his once-tiny shoe boutique—now a two-story, shoe-hound heaven—accordingly. You'll find Italian and Spanish imports, steel-toed work boots, sexy women's flats and heels, beloved Fluevogs, and classy Kenneth Cole styles. (The funkiest stuff is upstairs.) With so much space, there's no excuse not to take your favorite pairs for a test stroll. *Every day; map:I3*

Nob Hill Shoes

921 NW 23RD AVE, NORTHWEST; 503/224-8682 Shopping here is akin to making a lasting friend: the store offers lifetime cleaning, conditioning, waterproofing, and minor repair on all shoes. And the foot-friendly styles—including Dansko clogs and Naot sandals—will have you smiling as you walk out the door. A downtown location (611 SW 6th Ave; 503/223-0046) is a repair shop only, where cobblers will revive your tattered footwear with expert skill. *Every day; www.nobhillshoes.com; map:GG7*

Oddball Shoe Company

1639 NW MARSHALL ST, NORTHWEST; 503/827-7800 Brothers Zac and Seth Longaker weren't just serving their own size-16 feet when they opened this store, specializing in men's large-size shoes (12 and up). The popularity of their concept has led to inventory expansion—an impressive selection of sneakers and athletic shoes (brands like Adidas and New Balance), fashion-forward street shoes, and European-made dress shoes. *Every day; www.oddballshoe.com; map:GG7*

Zelda's Shoe Bar

633 NW 23RD AVE, NORTHWEST; 503/226-0363 To a well-heeled clientele thirsty for style, this bar serves only cutting-edge shoes, straight up. Zelda's exhibits its carefully selected styles on sleek, copper-topped counters with the austere elegance of a shoe museum. Trendy, high-fashion European brands are straight from the pages of *InStyle* magazine. But high fashion doesn't come cheap; bargain hunters can check the sale section in the back of the store for markdowns. *Every day; map:GG7*

TOYS

Child's Play

907 NW 23RD AVE, NORTHWEST; 503/224-5586 This store is packed to the gills with uncommon American and European toys for every stage of a child's development, from rattle shaking to puzzle building. The selection of dolls and doll accessories is particularly strong, and there's an excellent art-and-science section. Go often (and well before Christmas) to see Child's Play at its finest. *Every day; www.toysinportland.com; map:GG7*

Finnegan's Toys and Gifts

922 SW YAMHILL ST, DOWNTOWN; 503/221-0306 The biggest and best toy store in town, Finnegan's can keep you and your child enthralled for the better part of an afternoon. There's plenty of room for test drives of the windup cars, building blocks, and whatnot. Look for Playmobil gear, Brio trains, dollhouses, craft supplies, board games, dress-up clothes (including a number of amusing animal snouts), and a great selection of puppets and stuffed animals. *Every day; www.finneganstoys.com; map:I2*

Kids at Heart

3445 SE HAWTHORNE BLVD, HAWTHORNE; 503/231-2954 It's playtime all the time at Kids at Heart, and the smiley, enthusiastic staff will help you make the most of it. Highlights include Brio and Playmobil toys, dollhouses and furnishings, dress-up

235

wings and fairy garlands, glow-in-the-dark soccer balls, puzzles, and stuffed animals. A quick stop on the way to a birthday party yields the perfect less-than-$10 gift: craft kits, finger puppets, harmonicas, maracas, and cards too. *Every day; map: HH5*

Oregon Museum of Science and Industry Science Store

1945 SE WATER AVE, SOUTHEAST; 503/797-4626 In addition to a great selection of thought-provoking, fun, science-oriented toys, games, puzzles, and project kits, the OMSI store boasts an awesome selection of science books. Virtually every major category is here, from astronomy to zoology, with books for readers of every age and level of know-how. *Tues–Sun; www.omsi.org; map:HH6*

Paint the Sky Kites

828 NW 23RD AVE, NORTHWEST; 503/222-5096 Enter this colorful store through the curtain of windsocks hanging on the front porch. You'll find yourself amid a friendly collection of kites and other stuff to fly in the great blue yonder: boomerangs, flying disks for Ultimate and disk golf, banners, and flags. There are kite-making supplies for do-it-yourself types, as well as wind chimes, yo-yos, and bubble-blowing toys. *Every day; www.paintthesky.com; map:GG7*

Tammie's Hobbies

12024 SW CANYON RD, BEAVERTON; 503/644-4535 A budding engineer's dream store, Tammie's is packed floor-to-ceiling with plane and boat kits, radio-controlled cars, rockets, and model trains. It's one of the only Portland stores to carry German LGB electric train sets (and spare parts). The exhaustive inventory of model-building accessories and paint supplies will thoroughly outfit the home hobbyist. *Every day; www.tammieshobbies.com; map:II9*

Thinker Toys

7784 SW CAPITOL HWY, MULTNOMAH VILLAGE; 503/245-3936 Tye and Joan Steinbach, two science teachers who founded Thinker Toys in 1994, have christened their expanded 3,500-square-foot shop "Portland's most hands-on toy store"—and with good reason. An in-house fairy cottage and pirate ship, activity tables, and train sets provide ample diversion for kids, while plush armchairs await fatigued parents. Merchandise focuses on tactility, learning, and fun: Brio, Playmobil, dress-up clothing, and puzzles. *Every day; www.thinkertoysoregon.com; map:JJ7*

VINTAGE AND CONSIGNMENT

Avalon Antiques

203 SW 9TH AVE, DOWNTOWN; 503/224-7156 Avalon is one-stop shopping, especially for men. It's easy to walk out of this well-stocked vintage emporium with a dashing suit, dress shirt, shoes, fedora, watch, and tie. From Victorian to '50s-era wear, the selection for both men's and women's clothing is outstanding. Those who adore '20s styles will be especially pleased. Antique lockets, scarves, and other accents are quite impressive, and the staff is knowledgeable and friendly. *Every day; map:J3*

Buffalo Exchange

1420 SE 37TH AVE, HAWTHORNE; 503/234-1302 / 1036 W BURNSIDE ST, DOWNTOWN; 503/222-3418 Buy, sell, or trade in your wardrobe: this Arizona-based resale chain carries mostly used, current styles of clothes and shoes. There are jeans for both sexes, trendy new bags, belts, and jewelry on the cheap. The vintage racks offer an occasional treasure, but customers are more likely to walk out with a J. Crew sweater or a Gap shirt than anything truly retro. The downtown location is opposite Powell's Books. *Every day; www.buffaloexchange .com; map:HH5; map:K2*

Decades Vintage Company

328 SW STARK ST, DOWNTOWN; 503/223-1177 Specializing in men's and women's vintage fashions from the '30s to the '70s, Decades offers impeccable quality: items are spotless and often still have their original tags. The men's selection is especially dashing—charcoal tweed jackets and hand-painted ties from the '40s. Vintage eyeglass frames, '50s cocktail frocks, costume jewelry, and deco bar collectibles also await shoppers who value workmanship and condition. *Every day; www .decadesvintage.com; map:I5*

Glamour Gallery

9 SE 28TH AVE, LAURELHURST; 503/231-0888 This tiny boutique is filled to the rafters with vintage accessories, knickknacks, and beauty products. Dig through the dresser drawers to find ancient flasks of perfume and crumbling lipsticks, or check out the selection of novelty jewelry and retro eyewear. For those fickle about their frames, the collection of sunglasses—including wild mod styles from the '60s—is enough to summon anyone's inner Austin Powers. *Wed–Sun; map:HH5*

Hattie's Vintage

729 E BURNSIDE ST, BUCKMAN; 503/238-1938 Since moving into a new outlet on E Burnside's "vintage strip," 14-year vintage veteran Hattie Shindler has expanded her offering of crisp vintage dresses, satin jackets, and go-go boots. Finds include dead-stock Jantzen beach sarongs, gloves and jewelry, and those in-demand men's western shirts. Prices are affordable, and you can often find extraordinary pieces— like Italian-made wedge heels from the '50s—tucked amid the usual retro flotsam. *Every day; map:HH6*

Lady Luck Vintage

1 SE 28TH AVE, LAURELHURST; 503/233-4041 Stepping into Lady Luck is like sneaking into the boudoir of a '40s film star. Wild nighties, metallic cha-cha heels, and frothy dresses are plentiful in this large, browse-worthy boutique. There's a pink, marabou-trimmed salon in the back, with dressing rooms where countless racks of glamour gowns are ready to dance the night away. Most garments are in great condition, and the store offers plenty of guayabera shirts and action slacks to woo the men too. *Every day; www.ladyluckvintage.com; map: HH5*

Ray's Ragtime

1021 SW MORRISON ST, DOWNTOWN; 503/226-2616 If you're a fan of Gus Van Sant films, you may have seen some of Ray's finest duds onscreen in *Drugstore Cowboy* or *My Own Private Idaho* (both filmed in Portland). Hundreds of gowns and glittery party dresses hang chronologically inside the store, with the valuable pieces out of reach. If you see something you fancy, Ray will gladly fetch it for a closer look. Next door, Ray's Cheap Date (1027 SW Morrison St) focuses on wild disco-era getups from the '60s and '70s and features boas, crinoline skirts, and wigs in not-so-natural hues. *Every day (closed Sun Nov–Dec); www.raysragtime.com; map:I2*

Red Light Clothing Exchange

3590 SE HAWTHORNE BLVD, HAWTHORNE; 503/963-8888 Tacee Webb's used-clothing boutique is a great place to build a one-of-a-kind costume; to shop for wild party togs; or to score that perfect, ancient Mötley Crüe T-shirt. The "clothes bought and sold" policy means inventory changes daily and is always surprising. Prices are affordable, and the men's selection rivals the women's in volume and variety. *Every day; www.vintageclothes.com; map:HH5*

Torso Boutique

36 SW 3RD AVE, OLD TOWN; 503/294-1493 John Hadeed has an unmistakable edge over many vintage dealers. He trains his eye on truly incredible pieces and fills his store with delights—pleated and pintucked Victorian cottons, dazzling bugle-beaded flapper gowns, frothy frocks from the '30s, satin dressing gowns from the '40s. Prices here reflect the extraordinary quality of the inventory, but penniless browsing is still a treat. *Wed–Sun and by appointment; map:J5*

Xtabay

2515 SE CLINTON ST, CLINTON; 503/230-2899 Fabulous and full of fun, Xtabay was born when Liz Gross left Lady Luck to open her own boutique. Peruse the racks for slinky evening gowns, filmy negligees, and an inspiring range of funky, one-of-a-kind finds in this small neighborhood shop. Don't miss the cheap rack out front, or the cases near the register, which hold enough ritzy-looking costume jewelry to sink a cruise ship. *Every day; map:II5*

Food from A to Z

BAKERIES

Beaverton Bakery

12375 SW BROADWAY, BEAVERTON; 503/646-7136 / 16857 SW 65TH AVE (SOUTHLAKE CENTER), LAKE OSWEGO; 503/646-7136 Elaborately decked wedding and birthday cakes are what this bakery is best known for, but the crusty breads and frosted seasonal shortbread cookies (pumpkins in October, baby chicks in April) are equally pleasing. It's part of the experience to take a number from the old-fashioned dispenser and wait in line . . . but impatient shoppers can visit the less-crowded Lake Oswego location. *Every day; map:II9; map:NN8*

The German Bakery

10528 NE SANDY BLVD, PARKROSE; 503/252-1881 Atmosphere isn't everything—especially when you're a completely authentic bakery that tumbles out Bavarian Landbrot, Jägerbrot, and other German varieties from your ovens every day. The marzipan and sugar-dusted sweets, loafs of rye, and spongy rolls are comforting even if you don't have a single drop of German blood. If you do, the array of curious pickles available up front may have extra appeal. *Tues–Sat; map:FF1*

Grand Central Baking Company

 2230 SE HAWTHORNE BLVD, HAWTHORNE (AND BRANCHES); 503/232-0575 See review in Restaurants chapter.

Great Harvest Bread Company

810 SW 2ND AVE, DOWNTOWN; 503/224-8583 / 8926 SE SUNNYSIDE RD CLACK-AMAS; 503/659-5392 Healthy, fundamental, fresh—this is bread of the "staff of life" variety. This bakery chain, based in Montana, grinds its own wheat—a practice compared to grinding one's own coffee for freshness and flavor. Here you can snag a just-baked sandwich loaf that will take you through the week, although the fruit bread varieties and baked sweets are equally tempting. *Mon–Sat; map:G5; map: LL3*

JaCiva's Chocolates and Pastries

4733 SE HAWTHORNE BLVD, HAWTHORNE; 503/234-8115 Taking its name from its owners, Jack and Iva Sue Elmer, this delectable pastry and chocolate shop has specialized in producing European-style sweets—"a necessary indulgence"—since 1986. Under the burgundy and white awning, you'll find bakery, chocolate factory, retail, and wholesale operations (JaCiva chocolates are distributed all over the country). Everything's delicious, but the cakes are legendary. There's even a room where brides and grooms can sample wedding cakes (pictures and "dummy cakes" help you decide). *Mon–Sat; www.jacivas.com; map:HH4*

Ken's Artisan Bakery

 338 NW 21ST AVE, NORTHWEST; 503/248-2202 See review in Restaurants chapter.

Pearl Bakery

102 NW 9TH AVE, PEARL DISTRICT; 503/827-0910 Testament to Pearl Bakery's floury artistry comes in the lunchtime hordes—and in the appearance of the blue paper–wrapped loaves in fine markets all over town. The irresistible pastries and breads are leavened by traditional methods, hand-formed, and baked before your very eyes in massive ovens. For lunch there's a delicious selection of sandwiches: eggplant on ciabatta, pears and gorgonzola on walnut levain, even an elegant PB&J. *Mon–Sat; www.pearlbakery.com; map:K3*

Pix Patisserie

3402 SE DIVISION ST, SOUTHEAST; 503/232-4407 French-trained pastry-maker Cheryl Wakerhauser used to wow dessert lovers with her incredible concoctions at the Portland Farmers Market. Though she still maintains a presence there, her charming bakery/cafe is ground zero for sweet inventions with names like "Le Petit Prince" and "Cocoa Chanel." Beautiful presentation and unexpected flavors—pears and rosemary, orange crème brûlée and gold dust—make each dessert a treasure. Stay and enjoy yours with a dessert wine or a steaming cup of café au lait, or take a box of goodies home. You'll also find savory snacks like breakfast crepes and grilled-cheese sandwiches on brioche. *Wed–Sun; www.pixpatisserie.com; map:II5*

CANDY AND CHOCOLATE

Moonstruck Chocolatier

608 SW ALDER ST, DOWNTOWN (AND BRANCHES); 503/241-0955 This small retail shop showcases probably the prettiest chocolates in town . . . and the tastiest. Some Moonstruck truffles (many of them hand-dipped) are spiked with tipsy fillings like Chambord, Clear Creek apple brandy, and Bailey's Irish Cream; but the wild huckleberry and extra-bittersweet truffles are equally intoxicating. There are also shops in Northwest (526 NW 23rd Ave; 503/542-3400; map:HH7) and at Portland International Airport (503/247-3448; map:EE3). *Mon–Sat; www.moonstruckchocolates.com; map:I3.*

Sweets, Etc.

7828 SW CAPITOL HWY, MULTNOMAH VILLAGE; 503/293-0088 Multnomah just wouldn't be the same without a candy store on its main street. Expect to find a good mix of old and new: hard candies, saltwater taffy, malt balls, chocolate turtles, penguin gummies, truffles. If you want to sit for a spell with an ice-cream cone or Italian soda, you'll find a couple of seats. Of special interest are sugar-free and kosher candy. *Every day; map:JJ7*

Teuscher Chocolates of Switzerland

531 SW BROADWAY, DOWNTOWN; 503/827-0587 First concocted by Dolf Teuscher in a small Alps village in the 1940s, these Swiss-made chocolates contain the most costly all-natural cocoa, marzipan, fruits, and nuts available. Air-shipped from the Zurich factory to this tiny, ribbon-festooned boutique, the truffles and pralines arrive fresh and beautifully packaged. Toothsome wedding favors are a specialty of this shop. *Every day; www.teuscher.com; map:I3.*

Verdun Fine Chocolates

421 NW 10TH AVE, PEARL DISTRICT; 503/525-9400 Specializing in candies, chocolates, and confections imported from Lebanon, this little shop displays its wares like fine jewels—in beds of excelsior and in glass-topped cases. The chocolate base is *gianduja* (cocoa, cocoa butter, and emulsified hazelnut), which makes for a rich flavor that's sweet but not cloying. Foil-wrapped *drajee* (chocolate or candy-coated almonds) make popular gifts and wedding favors, and the shop also sells silver platters—to more elegantly display the chocolate, naturally. *Every day; www .verdunfinechocolates.com; map:L3*

COFFEE AND TEA

Peet's Coffee & Tea

1141 NE BROADWAY, NEAR LLOYD CENTER; 503/493-0192 / 508 SW BROADWAY, DOWNTOWN; 503/973-5540 To the delight of many of Northern California transplants, Berkeley-born Peet's Coffee & Tea has brought its signature dark-roasted style north. The opening day of its NE Broadway store lived up to its anticipatory buzz, with droves of curious coffee hounds snatching up pounds of beans. With such a positive response, Peet's wasted no time in opening a second location, this time downtown. Whichever side of the river you find yourself on, you'll find consistent coffee, knowledgeable employees, and a respectable selection of coffee and tea accessories. *Every day; www.peets.com; map:GG5, map:I3*

Stumptown Coffee Roasters

128 SW 3RD AVE, OLD TOWN (AND BRANCHES); 503/295-6144 Since opening its airy, modern-casual Old Town cafe, the legend of Stumptown's signature, super-strong brew has spread to the city's four corners—if not the world. The Southeast location (4525 SE Division St; 503/230-7702; map:II4) has a garage door that opens on nice, breezy days; Belmont (3356 SE Belmont St; 503/232-8889; map:HH5) is packed with neighborhood hipsters reading the latest issue of *Giant Robot*. Beans are also sold by the pound in familiar and exotic roasts, including several organic varieties. (See also review in the Nightlife chapter.) *Every day; www.stumptowncoffee.com; map:J5*

The Tao of Tea

3430 SE BELMONT ST, BELMONT (AND BRANCHES); 503/736-0198 In the yin/yang cycle of life, sipping tea out of a ceramic vessel to the sound of trickling water is the natural counterweight to sucking coffee out of a paper cup to the sound of an idling motor. The Tao of Tea, a serene stone-lined enclave bedecked with colorful cushions, offers sweet respite from the clamor of modern life. Here, an encyclopedic range of teas (green, black, white, scented, oolong, or herbal) is served in cups unique to each tea's character. In the adjacent Leaf Room you can purchase leaves from the Tao's impressive range and from a wide selection of teaware, from Yixing pots to yerba maté gourds. Newer teahouses are in Northwest Portland (2212 NW Hoyt St; 503/223-3563; map:GG7) and at the Classical Chinese Garden (239 NW Everett St, Chinatown; 503/224-8455; map:L5), the latter with occasional formal tea ceremonies. (Also see review in the Nightlife chapter.) *Every day; tea@taooftea .com; www.taooftea.com; map:HH5* &

The TeaZone

510 NW 11TH AVE, PEARL DISTRICT; 503/221-2130 More than four dozen loose-leaf teas—from Dragonwell green to South American yerba maté—are offered at this soothing European-style tea salon. Enthusiastic owners Jhanne Jasmine and Grant Cull are happy to tell you even more about each variety than you can read on the detailed menu. A range of desserts and snacks is also offered. While you sip, let your eye drift over the elaborate selection of teapots and tea accessories from around the world. *Every day; www.teazone.com; map:M2.*

ODDS AT THE END OF THE TRAIL

Portland is packed full of interesting shops, but some of them are, well, just plain odd. For a souvenir off the beaten track, or to simply explore Portland's more eclectic or goofier side, you'll want to check out the following.

WACKY WILLY'S SURPLUS STORE (2374 NW Vaughn St, Northwest; 503/525-9211; www.wackywillys.com): This no-man's retail land is unlike any store in Portland. Every time you try to label it (surplus store, museum, novelty shop), another strange and oddly wonderful item will catch your eye and make you wonder (or laugh aloud) about what exactly you should do with it. The business card boasts that Willy buys and sells "any type of merchandise," which explains a shifting inventory that might include 27,000 pieces of itty-bitty Plexiglas, 100 old-fashioned dial telephones, Desert Storm postcards, computer components, and tiny purple-and-pink army guys (40 for a buck). It's popular with artists, teachers, hobbyists, and clutter bugs. A second store is in Hillsboro (2900 SW Cornelius Pass Rd; 503/642-5111). *Every day; map:GG7*

THE BUTTON EMPORIUM (914 SW 11th Ave, Downtown; 503/228-6372; www.buttonemporium.com): One of the area's most unusual shops, the Button Emporium is a fabric lover's must-stop. Literally hundreds of thousands of buttons, from the everyday to the exotic, are up for grabs, along with a wide assortment of antique ribbons and trims. Sign up for one of the various hand-crafting specialty classes. *Tues–Sat; map:H1*

DESPERADO (428 NW 11th Ave, Pearl District; 503/294-2952; www

World Cup Coffee & Tea

1740 NW GLISAN ST, NORTHWEST; 503/228-4152 / 721 NW 9TH AVE, PEARL DISTRICT; 503/546-7377 Beginning as a small Northwest Portland shop in 1993, World Cup has grown to be a nationally recognized roaster with two capacious, homey cafes. Beans from all over the world end up in the hopper here; there's an emphasis on shade-grown, organic, and fair-trade varieties. The popular house blend is a warm, full-bodied mix of Indonesian, Central American, and South American coffees. On the tea side, World Cup offers about 12 loose-leaf varieties, as well as wonderful pastries, desserts, and grilled sandwiches. *Every day; www.worldcupcoffee.com; map:GG6; map:N3*

ETHNIC AND SPECIALTY FOODS

Becerra's Spanish and Imported Groceries

3022 NE GLISAN ST, LAURELHURST (AND BRANCHES); 503/234-7785 You're greeted by a friendly "*Hola!*" and the strains of Latin pop music as soon as you step into this neighborhood shop. Disappear into aisles stocking all manner of Mexican, Salvadoran, Spanish, and South American foods and cooking supplies—cellophane cones of *chicharones*, packets of dried tamarind and chiles, tortilla presses, cast-aluminum cookware from Colombia, votive candles, frozen banana leaves, and

.godesperado.com): Although the Pearl District may seem like an unlikely place for a western-themed boutique, "boutique" is the operative word. Desperado carries cowboy boots, dress-up western apparel, jewelry, wool blankets, and nostalgic stuff for kids to fill up your saddle bag, including cowboy pj's, and deerskin moccasins. *Every day; map:L2*

BAZAAR OF THE BIZARRE (7202 NE Glisan St, Northeast; 503/235-3552): This treasure trove of truly tantalizing tidbits (some with a high gross-out factor) now has a new, larger store. Its location—between Providence Medical Center and the old Brainard Cemetery—may or may not explain the amazing array of anatomically correct (but fake . . . we think!) hearts, brains, and eyeballs. There's a fair share of hard-to-find toys and an impressive collection of things that glow in the dark. *Mon–Sat; map:HH3*

For the pet lover, two special shops cater to dogs' and cats' every need. **URBAN FAUNA** (338 NW 6th Ave, Chinatown; 503/223-4602; map:L4) offers doggy day care, grooming, and obedience classes. The shop specializes in quality pet food and supplies (open every day, but no day care on Sundays). **BEAUTY FOR THE BEAST** (3832 NE Sandy Blvd, Hollywood; 503/288-5280; map:GG4) calls itself a "pet launderette" and is the perfect place to pamper your pooch. Choose between do-it-yourself pet washing or the full-service grooming salon. When you're done doing doggy's do, you can shop at the bowwow-tique for treats, sweets, and other gifts (open every day).

acajutla cheese. You can also buy tapes and CDs of that music you're hearing. Other branches are on E Burnside and N Lombard Streets. *Every day; map:HH5*

Elephants Delicatessen

13 NW 23RD PL, NORTHWEST; 503/224-3955 / 812 SW PARK AVE, DOWNTOWN; 503/546-3166 A picnic-perfect supplier of sandwiches, soups from scratch, and other gourmet fare, this Uptown Shopping Center deli is often mobbed at lunchtime. If your order totals $40 or more, you can phone it in, Elephax it (503/238-8143), or order online. Order by 10am and you'll get it delivered by noon: Elephants never forgets. The kitchen bakes 20 kinds of bread, desserts, and a variety of sumptuous take-home dinner entrees. Flying Elephants, the downtown shop in the Fox Tower, draws shoppers and office workers grabbing a bite on the run. *Every day; www.elephantsdeli.com; map:HH7; map:H2*

Hiroshi's Anzen

736 NE MARTIN LUTHER KING JR BLVD, NORTHEAST; 503/233-5111 For all things Japanese—fish and nori for sushi, pickled ginger, live geoduck, fresh yellowfin tuna, and octopus—Anzen is the place. The stock goes well beyond just food: you'll find lacquered dishes, rice cookers, and Japanese books and magazines. The inventory of more than 10,000 items includes prepared deli foods such as sushi and bentos, packaged and canned goods (including shelves of various soy sauces), and a large selection of sake and Asian beers. *Every day; map:N9*

Kruger's Specialty Produce

735 NW 21ST AVE (CITY MARKET NW), NORTHWEST; 503/221-3004 / 1409 NE WEIDLER ST (IRVINGTON MARKET), IRVINGTON; 503/288-4236 You'll find the most beautiful produce in town here. A few exotics—edible flowers, baby bok choy, purple potatoes—are mixed among more familiar capsicums and tubers. Kruger's also sells bulk and packaged natural foods and gourmet items, from breakfast cereals to dried pasta in the shape of artichokes or bicycles. Shopping here is an indulgence, since the impeccable quality is matched by high prices. *Every day; map: GG7; map:GG5*

Martinotti's Café & Delicatessen

404 SW 10TH AVE, DOWNTOWN; 503/224-9028 Once upon a time, Martinotti's was Portland's only Italian foods shop, with one of the first espresso machines in town. Even though the city is now saturated with venues offering Italian flavor, there's still a place for what the Martinotti family has to offer: a solidly Italian grocery of good tastes, good smells, and good products—including towers of boxed panettone at Christmas. The wine selection is rich in Italian varietals as well as French wines and port. For everyday shopping, there are dried pastas and sundry other imports like Italian tomatoes, olive oil, chocolate, and cookies. *Mon–Sat; map:J2*

Pastaworks

3735 SE HAWTHORNE BLVD, HAWTHORNE; 503/232-1010 / 735 NW 21ST AVE (CITY MARKET NW), NORTHWEST; 503/221-3002 Pastaworks is all things Italian: fresh pastas, pesto and mushroom sauces, dozens of olive oils, herbed and aged vinegars, whole-bean coffees, delectable desserts, exotic cheeses, aged prosciutto . . . and the best Italian wine section in town. Don't hesitate to ask for staff help when choosing that Brunello or Montalcino. The inventory of kitchenware has been expanded to include Reidel glassware, Spanish pottery, wooden salad bowls and cutting boards, and top-notch cooking utensils—sometimes turning a quick stop for a wedge of Romano into an hour of lip-smacking loitering. *Every day; www .pastaworks.com; map:HH5; map:GG7*

Sheridan Fruit Co.

408 SE MARTIN LUTHER KING JR BLVD, INNER SOUTHEAST; 503/235-9353 The lower eastside industrial area has become something of a neighborhood, and Sheridan Fruit Co. is its grocery store. Founded in 1916, this is one of the last remnants of the city's old Produce Row. You'll still find remnants of its former glory as a bulk supplier of nature's bounty—oversize sacks of roasted nuts, dried fruit and honey, boxed pasta, and bins of lentils. But the store has also become a full-service supermarket with a meat counter, a kitchen and bakery, a respectable wine section, even a florist. Stop for rare ethnic items like Israeli couscous and curry sauces; and if you ever need a 5-pound bag of sun-dried tomatoes or an industrial-size can of artichoke hearts, check here first. *Every day; map:I9*

Uwajimaya

10500 SW BEAVERTON-HILLSDALE HWY, BEAVERTON; 503/643-4512 This is no pint-size Asian specialty shop, but an American-style supermarket packed with imported canned foods, exotic fruits and vegetables, and sashimi-grade ahi and other fresh seafood—some of it still swimming. Kaffir lime leaves, daikon, and lemongrass are as prolific as apples in the stunning produce department. Grocery offerings are dominated by Japanese foods, but Southeast Asian and Chinese goods are mixed in. A housewares section is as pleasurable as functional. (You can choose from around two-dozen rice cookers.) A branch of the Japanese Kinokuniya bookstore chain is on the premises, as is a soba (noodle) cafe. *Every day; www.uwajimaya.com; map:II9*

Zupan's Market

2340 W BURNSIDE ST, PORTLAND HEIGHTS (AND BRANCHES); 503/497-1088 Though not always reliable for some sundries or more esoteric items, Zupan's strives for full service with its deli, bakery, meat counter, and wine section. The produce section is hard to beat; fresh water chestnuts, starfruit, uglifruit, and boutique salad greens are laid out in freshly misted, parsley-garnished heaps. Best of all, the market is open 24 hours every day but Christmas. Prices can be a little steep, but watch for seasonal produce sales. Look for branches in Belmont, Corbett, Raleigh Hills, and West Linn. *Every day; www.zupans.com; map:HH7*

HEALTH FOOD STORES

Food Front

2375 NW THURMAN ST, NORTHWEST; 503/222-5658 Stocking the largest and freshest selection of organic produce in town, Food Front also carries what may be the city's best crop of vegan and vegetarian groceries. You'll also find no-cruelty body-care products, vitamins and homeopathic remedies, bulk foods, coffee, and fresh juices. A fantastic deli (the sandwiches are dynamite and come wrapped with a delectable honey candy on top) makes a midday stop a pleasure. Discounts and rebates offered to co-op members (a lifetime membership costs $150, a year is $25); and if you work here eight hours a month, you'll get 15 percent off. *Every day; map:GG7*

New Seasons

1214 SE TACOMA ST, SELLWOOD; 503/230-4949 / 7300 SW BEAVERTON-HILLSDALE HWY, RALEIGH HILLS; 503/292-6838 This store was established by former Nature's Fresh Northwest employees when Wild Oats took over the former market. There's an abundance of fresh local produce and meats here, as well as a good deli section and bakery. New Seasons also offers lots of prepackaged, middle-brow stuff, so you don't have to slink off guiltily to Safeway for Oreos. *Every day; map:KK5; map:II8*

People's Food Co-op

 3029 SE 21ST AVE, BROOKLYN; 503/232-9051 Once a pokey neighborhood natural-foods grocery with cramped aisles and a spotty selection, the little co-op that could has blossomed into a full-service market. An elaborate and ecologically conscious remodel in 2002 has expanded more than just the space: inventory now includes necessities like toilet paper and laundry soap, more produce and bulk items, even an ATM. A membership ($30 per year) buys an automatic 4 percent discount at the register. *Every day; www.peoples.coop; map:II5*

Wild Oats

3535 NE 15TH AVE, NORTHEAST; 503/288-3414 Since absorbing the locally owned Nature's Fresh Northwest chain, Wild Oats has taken Portland by storm with its slick, superstore approach to natural foods. This store, off Fremont Street, maintains a deli, gifts and housewares department, meat and cheese counters, bakery, magazine stand, and skin-care "bar" with fresh mixed concoctions available by the ounce. Cooking classes, a wellness center (with movement classes and a naturopath), and a day spa round out the package. The store promises plenty of organic produce, free-range meat and poultry, and high prices. *Every day; www.wildoats .com; map:FF5*

MEATS AND SEAFOOD

Edelweiss Sausage Company and Deli

3119 SE 12TH AVE, BROOKLYN; 503/238-4411 Even if you can resist the aromas of house-made sausage, smoked ham hocks, and exotic wursts drifting from the cases in back, you'll be hard pressed to leave this tiny wonderland without sinking your teeth into something. The deli serves incredible sandwiches made from the dazzling array of German-style meats (almost everything is prepared on-site) and house-made potato salad. Groceries from spaetzle and grainy mustards to imported beers (available by the bottle) join diverting odds and ends—German magazines, lovely European candies—for an immersive Fatherland experience. *Mon–Sat; map:II5*

Gartner's Country Meat Market

7450 NE KILLINGSWORTH ST, NORTHEAST; 503/252-7801 This is the no-flourishes, serious-about-meat store. Busy but ever-pleasant counter people staff a large, open preparation and display-case area. Roasts, steaks, chops, and house-smoked hams and bacons fill the L-shaped meat case. Aromatic smells spice the air, and meat saws whir in the background. *Tues–Sat; map:FF3*

Newman's Fish Co.

1409 NE WEIDLER ST (IRVINGTON MARKET), IRVINGTON; 503/284-4537 / 735 NW 21ST AVE (CITY MARKET NW), NORTHWEST; 503/221-3002 Hands down, fins up, Newman's is the best place in town to buy fresh fish; it has been a business since 1890. The staff is knowledgeable, energetic, and pleasant; helping customers learn to buy and prepare fish is a priority of the owners (who also have a thriving wholesale business). The variety is noteworthy, and freshness is a given. Pacific oysters, Manila clams, green-lipped mussels, and colossal scampi are joined by a fine array of smoked fish, as exotic as Norwegian-style lox or familiar as Columbia River sturgeon and Dungeness crab. Peer into the tanks for your pick of live Maine lobsters. *Every day; map:GG5; map:GG7*

Otto's Sausage Kitchen and Meat Market

4138 SE WOODSTOCK BLVD, WOODSTOCK; 503/771-6714 The deli gets crowded with loyal neighborhood customers at lunchtime, but this good-natured and unpretentious store is famed for its smoked meats and house-made sausages, ground and stuffed in the back room. There's a German flavor here, but you'll find meats in dozens of European styles—pepperoni and pastrami, Black Forest ham, Portuguese linguisa, and good ol' British bangers. A small but decent wine selection emphasizes vintages from the Northwest, Germany, and France. Check out the generous jars of German mustard and cornichons. *Mon–Sat; www.ottossausagekitchen.com; map: JJ4*

Phil's Uptown Meat Market

17 NW 23RD PL, NORTHWEST; 503/224-9541 If there was such a thing as a "meat boutique," this would be it. Located in the Uptown Shopping Center off Westover Road, this black-and-white-tiled shop with white porcelain display cases, butcher blocks, and fan-type scales, marries old-time butcher-shop atmosphere with up-to-the-minute freshness. Cuts of lamb, pork, beef, and poultry are of the highest quality, and there's a small seafood selection. Passersby have trouble resisting the skewers of chicken grilled out front. *Tues–Sat; map:HH7*

Viande Meats and Sausage Co.

735 NW 21ST AVE (CITY MARKET NW), NORTHWEST; 503/221-3012 Viande is renowned for fresh cuts and prepared meat items. All the deli meats and sausages (including a classic Italian pork with fennel) are house-made by a staff of former restaurant chefs. An emphasis on local produce and high-quality exotics (like Kobe beef) means merchandise is always top-notch. Charcuterie is an art here, and the chefs who prepare the duck confit, stuffed quail with figs and polenta, and sage-and-apple breakfast sausage take pride in their work. *Every day; map:GG7*

White's Country Meats

1206 SE ORIENT DR, GRESHAM; 503/666-0967 Gresham residents recommend this straight-forward meat store with its own smokehouse and processing facilities. Expect fresh, honestly trimmed, good-quality meats at reasonable prices. A variety of roasts, steaks, and ground meats are available; the poultry and pork look better than at many other meat counters. *Tues–Sat*

WINE, BEER, AND SPIRITS

Clear Creek Distillery

1430 NW 23RD AVE, NORTHWEST; 503/248-9470 With a gorgeous copper still, fruit from his family's Hood River orchards, and other local ingredients, Stephen McCarthy creates impeccably crafted versions of a variety of classic European liquors. He is best known for his pear brandy, a colorless ambrosia that's available with and without a pear in the bottle, but his range extends from a Calvados-style apple brandy to grappa to Oregon's first single-malt whiskey. He also makes framboise (raspberry *eau de vie*), kirschwasser (cherry brandy), and slivovitz (plum brandy). Clear Creek is open daily during the week, but it's best to let them know you're coming. *Mon–Fri; www.clearcreekdistillery.com; map:GG7*

E&R Wine Shop

6141 SW MACADAM AVE, JOHN'S LANDING; 503/246-6101 Ed ("E") Paladino and Richard ("R") Elden play starring roles in the growing vitality and sophistication of Portland's wine scene. Besides offering many hard-to-find (and—gulp—hard-to-afford) elite selections, they feature a large inventory of lovely, moderately priced vintages. The shop's frequent (and often free) events and tastings are a great opportunity to learn more about, say, Italian whites or prosecco. Also offered are books, accessories, and foodstuffs. *Tues–Sat (every day in Dec); www.erwines.citysearch .com; map:JJ6*

Great Wine Buys

1515 NE BROADWAY, IRVINGTON; 503/287-2897 Founded in 1985, this neighborhood shop was bought by employee John Kennedy in 1999, forever banishing the image of the wine-shop owner as grizzled sage. Young Kennedy—a would-be PhD in French literature—has thrown his heart into making this store a folksy, friendly place, with cozy armchairs and marble-topped tables surrounded by open cases of affordable vintages. The huge Northwest selection is augmented by bottles from the Rhone Valley, and special attention is paid to German and Alsatian Rieslings. Kennedy recently took a group of customers on an insider's wine trip to France; patrons now ask about the next excursion. *Every day; www.greatwinebuys.citysearch.com; map:GG5*

Liner & Elsen Wine Merchants

202 NW 21ST AVE, NORTHWEST; 503/241-9463 The display of empty wine bottles from the '60s and '70s should clue you in to Liner & Elsen's lineage as one of Portland's most venerable wine suppliers. Dimly lit and hushed as a library, this shop is comprehensive, with hundreds of labels from France lining the walls and glamorous vintage ports kept under lock and key. Despite the intimidating vibe, the staff is helpful and approachable, and will point you to a website or another wine shop if they don't stock what you're looking for. *Mon–Sat; www.linerandelsen.com; map:HH7*

Mount Tabor Fine Wines

4316 SE HAWTHORNE BLVD, HAWTHORNE; 503/235-4444 This low-key, tastefully appointed shop caters to penurious and plush oenophiles with equal grace. There's something for everyone here, from Oregon pinot noirs to Italian rosés, and wines are displayed democratically (a $90 Château-Figeac St. Emilion looks right at home next to that $14 Spanish table wine). A monthly broadsheet advertises a selection of reasonably priced wines, and the front of the store is stacked with open cases of colorfully described cheap hits. The crowds at Friday tastings nibble baguettes and sample wines of the world for a nominal fee. *Tues–Sat; www.mttaborfinewines .com; map:HH4*

Oregon Wines on Broadway

 515 SW BROADWAY, DOWNTOWN; 503/228-4655 The name says it all, although there are a few bottles of Washington red here among the ranks of outstanding regional wines. Located in Morgan's Alley, an elegant downtown shopping arcade, the narrow street-facing shop has a woody, classic ambience that suits the garnet-colored nectar available for tasting by the glass. There are 30—count 'em, 30—pinots. *Tues–Sat; map:I3*

750 ml

232 NW 12TH AVE, PEARL DISTRICT; 503/224-1432 Those daunted by the prospect of selecting an impressive bottle for that dinner party with the in-laws can breathe a sigh of relief. By grouping wines according to their character, rather than by varietal or winery (bottles are described as "bodacious" or "self-indulgent"), owner Rena Vatch makes wine shopping a hilarious "Wine for Dummies" jaunt. The inventory hovers at around 80 vintages. The shop has been expanded to include an intimate bistro. (See reviews in the Restaurants and Nightlife chapters). *Mon–Sat; www.750-ml.com; map:L2*

Wizer's Lake Oswego Foods

330 1ST ST, LAKE OSWEGO; 503/636-1414 What looks like an average suburban supermarket houses one of the biggest retail cellars in Greater Portland. Though not necessarily a first stop on a search for a glitzy wine hot off the pages of *Wine Spectator*, this wine department has a wide array of domestic and imported wines with the added advantage of frequent sale items. Ask to explore the cellar, with bottles from places as far-flung as Hungary and South Africa . . . and years as distant as the 1930s. *Every day; www.wizers.com; map:MM6*

Woodstock Wine and Deli

4030 SE WOODSTOCK BLVD, WOODSTOCK; 503/777-2208 The Fujino family's shop and restaurant—which they've operated near Reed College for 18 years—may not be the fanciest, but it has plenty to brag about. Here is one of the largest and most affordable selections of wines in town, including Kosher wines and sake, and an encyclopedic inventory of Oregon and Northwest specialties like pinot noir and merlot. Dozens of tables sit amid the cases and bottles (ranging in price from $7 to $150); diners can enjoy a glass of wine with hearty soups and sandwiches, or purchase a bottle and enjoy it on-site. *Mon–Sat; map:JJ4*

THE ARTS SCENE

THE ARTS SCENE

Portland may be known for shutting its lights off early, but those lights shine on stages around the city every night of the week. Unforgettable art exhibits from around the country and the world are displayed at the ever-expanding Portland Art Museum and a throng of acclaimed local galleries. Moreover, frozen art—the stunning buildings of architects Pietro Belluschi, John Yeon, Michael Graves, David Pugh, and Willard Martin, among others—are on view 24 hours a day, seven days a week.

The city has attracted artists in every discipline. Well-known established artists, like Gus Van Sant in film, James DePreist in classical music, Katherine Dunn in literature, and Keith Scales in classic Greek theater, offer unpredictable but always-vibrant performances. They inspire younger, lesser-known artists—young people with talent, vision, and grit—who move to Portland because of the very lack of an establishment that would lock them out.

"I think Portland is just coming into its own," says architect Stuart Emmons. "We have home-grown talent and new talent moving into the city, and over the next 10 years, the future just looks very bright." Emmons is co-founder of the Design Collaborative, an organization that supports Portland designers engaged in everything from architecture to fashion. "Lots of young designers come here because they have the opportunity to create their own niche," Emmons says.

The real payoff is for local audiences. One week, they can fete adopted son Van Sant with a parade to a premiere screening of his latest film. The next, they can watch Twyla Tharp's latest dance concert onstage. In between, inexhaustible art patrons can fill up on as much experimental theater and music, paintings, and sculpture as their senses can hold.

Fine Arts

PORTLAND ART MUSEUM

The pride of the city's art community is the venerable Portland Art Museum (1219 SW Park Ave, Downtown; 503/226-2811; map:G2), the Northwest's first art museum when it was founded in 1892. Its collection of 32,000 pieces spans 35 centuries; a new Center for Native American Art and Northwest Art underscores its importance in the regional scene. See description in the Exploring chapter's Top 20 Attractions.

GALLERIES

Portland has become a destination for artists and designers looking for an opportunity to produce and show their best work—in an environment open to, and supportive of, pieces that range from exquisite to outrageous. An older echelon of established artists put Portland on the map; they included George Johanson, a painter, printmaker, and portraitist, as well as Jay Backstrand, Louis Bunce, Sally Haley, Lee Kelly, Jack McLarty, Henk Pander, Michele Russo, and Harry Widman. Their energy, and that of early gallery owners (particularly William Jamison), have expanded the creative scene and produced a flourishing business for the gallery culture.

The streets of the Pearl District and adjacent central downtown come alive on **FIRST THURSDAY** (www.firstthursday.org), the first Thursday night of every month, when galleries feature their best and newest work. Roaming visitors jam the streets and crowd the galleries, becoming visions themselves for people watchers. In warm weather, artists without patrons turn the streets into a bazaar of their original work. Even on the rainiest days, the turnout of sturdy, dedicated gallery-goers is impressive.

Galleries can be found in every corner of the city and suburbs, but many cluster in three areas: Downtown, the Pearl District, and Alberta Street. Alberta, a newly gentrifying stretch of Northeast Portland, opens the last Thursday of every month instead of the first; it has developed its own following of mostly young and chic patrons.

Alysia Duckler Gallery

1236 NW HOYT ST, PEARL DISTRICT; 503/223-7595 This intimate and stylish gallery features small shows of consistently fine quality. Located as it is among furniture boutiques and restaurants, Alysia Ducker makes a fine stop on a leisurely stroll. Additional services include framing, shipping, and installation. *Tues–Sat; www.alysiaducklergallery.com; map:M2*

The Art Gym

MARYLHURST UNIVERSITY, 17600 HWY 43, LAKE OSWEGO; 503/699-6243 Once a gymnasium, this 3,000-square-foot space on the third floor of the Marylhurst University administration building (10 miles south of Portland) is a well-respected showcase and testing ground for work by the Northwest's rising stars and established artists. Lucinda Parker, Tad Savinar, and Mel Katz have all shown here. As this is an educational institute, lectures and panel discussions accompany show openings. *Tues–Sun; www.marylhurst.edu/artgym/; map:NN5*

Augen Gallery

817 SW 2ND AVE, DOWNTOWN; 503/224-8182 As one of the largest and most comprehensive galleries in Portland, Augen caters to the tastes and budgets of a diverse clientele with a variety of art—from prints by Robert Motherwell and Jim Dine to paintings by regional artists. Monthly exhibits occupy the central space on the main floor. *Mon–Sat; www.augengallery.com; map:G5*

Blackfish Gallery

420 NW 9TH AVE, PEARL DISTRICT; 503/224-2634 Housed at the sign of the wooden fish, Blackfish is the country's oldest artists' cooperative, primarily displaying the latest work of its members in monthly shows. Over the years, 117 artists have hit the Blackfish roster, their work chosen for an openness to innovation. Media, as varied as the members' styles, run from figurative sculpture and weaving to abstract painting. *Tues–Sat; www.blackfish.com; map:L3*

Blue Sky Gallery and Nine Gallery

1231 NW HOYT ST, PEARL DISTRICT; 503/225-0210 Blue Sky, which opened in 1975, displays outstanding contemporary and historical photography. The contemporary selections often show considerable wit, in distinct contrast to the seriousness of more traditional photography shows. The Nine Gallery, in an adjoining room, is a cooperative run by 10 local artists who take turns dreaming up installations. *Tues–Sat; www.blueskygallery.org; map:M2*

Bullseye Connection Gallery

300 NW 13TH AVE, PEARL DISTRICT; 503/227-0222 Thanks to the presence of Bullseye, Portland is now known for exceptional glass work. This gallery, which markets glass to Murano, Italy, and other locales, shows contemporary kiln-formed glass and related works. Artists in residence show their work in a stunning loft space. *Tues–Sat; www.bullseyeconnection.com; map:L1*

Butters Gallery Ltd.

520 NW DAVIS ST, CHINATOWN; 503/248-9378 This classy gallery features monthly exhibits by such nationally known artists as sculptor Ming Fay and painters David Geiser and Frank Hyder, as well as Portland painter Ted Katz. Highlights might include glass exhibits by West Coast artists. *Tues–Sat; www.buttersgallery.com; map:L4*

Contemporary Crafts Museum and Gallery

3934 SW CORBETT AVE, LAIR HILL; 503/223-2654 The oldest nonprofit gallery in the nation (established in 1937), Contemporary Crafts perches on a hillside with a spectacular city view. The permanent collection features nearly 700 works of textile, furniture, ceramics, glass, and metal that go far beyond functional. Indeed, the line between art and craft may sometimes be hard to distinguish. An acclaimed artist-in-residence program is now more than three decades old. *Tues–Sun; www.contemporarycrafts.org; map:II6*

Elizabeth Leach Gallery

207 SW PINE ST, OLD TOWN; 503/224-0521 This airy space in the historic Hazeltine Building is well-suited to large-scale sculpture. But exhibits here are equally strong in two-dimensional works, including Northwest contemporary painting and photography. You'll find work by such artists as Christopher Rauschenberg, Robert Lyons, Stephen Hayes, Judy Cooke, and Dinh Q. Le, who interweaves 40-by-60-inch photos of everything from war scenes to Hollywood celebrities. *Tues–Sat; www.elizabethleach.com; map:J6*

Froelick Adelhart Gallery

817 SW 2ND AVE, DOWNTOWN; 503/222-1142 An attractive, long space, the Froelick Adelhart Gallery exhibits and represents contemporary Northwest artists in sculpture and on canvas, as well as national and international painters and printmakers. *Tues–Sat; www.froelickgallery.com; map:G5*

SOARING WITH WHITE BIRD

When White Bird flew into Portland in 1997, the local dance scene was grounded by budget cuts and a dearth of vision. Enter East Coast entrepreneurs and White Bird founders Walter Jaffe, a PhD in German literature, and Paul King, a pastry chef—partners who saw in Portland a stage for international dance presentations.

White Bird (503/245-1600; www.whitebird.org) has since feted its new home with visits by 45 dance companies. It has commissioned 15 original dance works and entertained more than 120,000 individuals. Under White Bird's wing, headliners Mikhail Baryshnikov, Steve Petronio, Bill T. Jones, and Merce Cunningham have flown to Portland, performing remarkably between works by local companies like BodyVox and individuals like Gregg Bielemeier and Michael Curry.

The company is named for its mascot, Barney, a 15-year-old white cockatoo whose passion for flight and fancy mirrors White Bird's mission to seek out and deliver dancers who make the soul soar. The company is committed to outreach and regularly collaborates with local arts and dance schools, public schools, and private colleges. Jaffe and King seek to enrich and uncover layers of meaning in the design and performance of fine and outrageous dance.

—Gail Dana

Interstate Firehouse Cultural Center

5340 N INTERSTATE AVE, PATTON SQUARE; 503/823-4322 A performance space, gallery, and workshop make up the body of this multifaceted arts showcase, housed in a refurbished 1910 firehouse. The emphasis is on the work of the city's artists from all heritages, and often the IFCC scores with shows not likely to be seen at other venues. The Kwanzaa celebration in December is a major event. *Tues–Sat; www.ifcc-arts.org; map:GG6*

Laura Russo Gallery

805 NW 21ST AVE, NORTHWEST; 503/226-2754 Laura Russo maintains a strong commitment to contemporary Northwest artists and represents many of the most respected ones. Russo does not shy away from the controversial and experimental; her artists work in painting, sculpture, works on paper, and fine-art prints, with a scope ranging from landscape to abstract expressionism. The handsome gallery is one of a handful with space enough for large-scale works. *Tues–Sat; www.laurarusso.com; map:GG7*

Lawrence Gallery

903 NW DAVIS ST, PEARL DISTRICT; 503/228-1776 Northwest landscape painters Romona Youngquist, Charles Palmer, and Hans Schiebold are among the 150-plus premier artists represented by this outstanding gallery, established in 1977 in Oregon's Wine Country and now the state's largest. Inside, you'll find works on canvas, photography, mixed media creations, bronze sculptures, porcelain, and pottery; outside, a newly created sculpture garden (facing Ninth Avenue) displays fountains, wood art, and metal landscaping accents. The Lawrence is renowned for encouraging young artists like Amanda Dunbar, a 20-year-old university student whose work goes for $75,000 and up. Additional galleries are in Sheridan and McMinnville. *Every day; www.lawrencegallery.net; map:L3*

Littman Gallery and White Gallery

SMITH MEMORIAL CENTER, PORTLAND STATE UNIVERSITY; 503/725-5656 The Littman has an excellent regional reputation for its engaging photographic exhibits. The White features paintings and sculptures, and often hosts such touring exhibits as the Harlem Renaissance display, showcasing 20 artists including Jacob Lawrence. *Mon–Fri; map:E1*

Mark Woolley Gallery

120 NW 9TH AVE, PEARL DISTRICT; 503/234-5475 This spirited upstairs gallery puts on great shows and knows how to throw a preview party (on the Wednesday before First Thursday art walk). The work found here is almost always kinetic and dynamic, representing quite a range of styles, but often the work is mixed-media and three-dimensional. *Tues–Sat; www.markwoolley.com; map:K3*

Oregon College of Art and Craft

8245 SW BARNES RD, WEST SLOPE; 503/297-5544 There's eye-pleasing detail and design in every corner of this college and its grounds. Enter the Hoffman Gallery through a gate of elaborate, swirling wrought iron to see work in wood, metal, glass, fiber, and ceramics; student art is sometimes featured. Buy hand-crafted gifts in an adjacent gallery, and stop for a bite at the Hands On Café (see review in the Restaurants chapter). *Every day; www.ocac.edu; map:HH9*

Pacific Northwest College of Art

1241 NW JOHNSON ST, PEARL DISTRICT; 503/226-4391 This huge space is broken into two galleries—the Manuel Izquierdo gallery and the Philip Feldman Gallery. There's always something interesting going on, whether it be a retrospective of Oregon printmaker Gordon Gilkey, a new-media exhibit, or an open-studio show of student work. *Every day; www.pnca.edu; map:N2*

PDX Gallery

604 NW 12TH AVE, PEARL DISTRICT; 503/222-0063 Critically acclaimed nationally, this tiny pearl of the Pearl represents highly original Native American painter James Lavadour and more than two dozen up-and-coming Portland artists. Intellectually driven pieces by Ellen George, Malia Jensen, Joe Macca, Storm Tharp, Marie Watt, and others are exhibited because they invite contemplation. *Tues–Sat; www.pdxcontemporaryart.com; map:M2*

Photographic Image Gallery

240 SW 1ST AVE, OLD TOWN; 503/224-3543 This is the place to go for fine prints by such well-known artists as Phil Borges and William Neill. Rotating monthly exhibits feature the work of more than 50 nationally recognized photographers, including Portland's Christopher Burkett and Frank DiMarco. There's a small but excellent selection of posters and cards as well. *Mon–Sat; www.photographic image.com; map:I6*

Pulliam Deffenbaugh Gallery

522 NW 12TH AVE, PEARL DISTRICT; 503/228-6665 The diversity and quality of the contemporary art selections featured in this Pearl District gallery are often stimulating and rewarding. The gallery, which once focused on figurative pieces, has switched its viewpoint toward abstract and expressionistic works. Noted artists include Laurie Reid, Jeffrey Mitchell, and Hildur Bjarnadottir. *Tues–Sat; www .pulliamdeffenbaugh.com; map:M2*

Quintana Gallery

120 NW 9TH AVE, PEARL DISTRICT; 503/222-1729 The only Portland gallery dedicated to Inuit and Northwest Coast Native American arts, this establishment features contemporary and antique works—sculptures, carved masks, and totems from such tribes as the Haida, Inupiaq, Kwaguilth, and Tlingit. Some Southwest Indian and Mexican pieces are displayed as well. *Tues–Sat; www.quintana galleries.com; map:K3*

S K Josefsberg Gallery

403 NW 11TH AVE, PEARL DISTRICT; 503/241-9112 This consistently fine gallery is dedicated to classic, vintage, and contemporary photography. It may present a show of surf photography one month and rarely seen Soviet or Japanese photography the next. Look also for custom hardwood frames, made by master craftspeople and shipped internationally. *Tues–Sat; www.skjstudio.com; map:L2*

The Talisman Gallery

1476 NE ALBERTA ST, ALBERTA; 503/284-8800 This cooperative gallery in the heart of Alberta Street displays the diverse work of 22 member painters and sculptors. "We let people work from their heart and their spirit," says artist Serena Barton. "What we get is work with a contemporary edge." *Thu–Sun; www.talisman gallery.com; map:FF5*

Yoshida's Fine Art Gallery

206 NW 10TH AVE, PEARL DISTRICT; 503/227-3911 Formerly in suburban Troutdale, Yoshida's represents 50 artists whose work ranges from original oils and acrylics, watercolors, and photographs, to bronze sculpture and Raku pottery. The gallery sometimes hosts jazz performers in its small wine bar and bistro. *Tue–Sun; www.yoshidagallery.com; map:L3*

Art in Public Places

Public art is everywhere in Portland, thanks to the patronage of its citizens—and a program that requires all new, large-scale commercial, and public building construction to include public art in the budget. Every City of Portland office building, lobby, and park boasts a signature mural, sculpture, painting, relief, or fountain. With artwork spread out across the city, you needn't try to cram a tour into an afternoon. Choose a few arty blocks, stop for a soda along the way, and enjoy.

Start at Portland's **VISITOR INFORMATION AND SERVICES CENTER** (701 SW 6th Ave at Morrison St; 503/275-8355 or 877/678-5263; www.pova.com; map: H3), located on the lower west side of Pioneer Courthouse Square. Pick up a free map indicating the location of public art works. Then begin looking around **PIONEER COURTHOUSE SQUARE**, where Portlanders gather any and every hour of the day. The amphitheater-style design of the square is well suited to people watching. Just before noon the *Weather Machine*, a shiny sphere atop a 25-foot pole, plays a musical fanfare and sends forth one of three creatures, depending on the day's weather. When it's clear, you'll see the sun figure Helia; on stormy days, a dragon; and on gray, drizzly days, a great blue heron. Equally popular is the bronze sculpture by J. Seward Johnson, *Allow Me*, a life-size replica of a businessman with an umbrella. On either side of the historic **PIONEER COURTHOUSE** building, on SW Sixth Avenue at Yamhill and Morrison Streets, look for Georgia Gerber's delightful bronze bears, beavers, ducks, and deer wandering down the sidewalk and playing in small pools of water (map:H3).

On SW Yamhill Street between Third and Fourth Avenues (map:H4), the **SIDEWALK** speaks, thanks to author/artists Katherine Dunn and Bill Will. Engraved in the right-of-way are thought-provoking phrases and quotes, ranging from a Pablo Picasso quip to "Step on a crack, break your mother's back." Across the parking lot to the north is Gary Hirsch's *Upstream Downtown*, 18 colorful aluminum fish that decorate the south side of the parking structure at SW Third Avenue and Alder Street. Backtrack a bit to catch John Young's *Soaring Stones* on SW Fifth Avenue between Yamhill and Taylor Streets.

One of the city's most familiar landmarks is the bronze *Elk* by Roland Perry, set in the fountain on SW Main Street between Third and Fourth Avenues (map: G4)—a middle point between Lownsdale and Chapman Squares. It once served as a watering trough for both horses and humans and remains the primary watering hole for the Portland Police's mounted patrol. The **JUSTICE CENTER** (between SW 2nd and 3rd Aves and SW Madison and Main Sts; map:F4) houses a fine 19th-century Kwaguilth carving of an eagle and an array of contemporary pieces. At the entrance are Walter Dusenbery's untitled travertine sculptures representing the various paths to justice. Near them is a wall of stained-glass windows by Ed Carpenter.

The famous **PORTLAND BUILDING** (1120 SW 5th Ave; map:G3) is a provocative landmark. The first major work by architect Michael Graves, it has been described with adjectives ranging from "brilliant" to "hideous." Kneeling above its entrance on SW Fifth Avenue is Raymond Kaskey's monumental *Portlandia*. In 1985, locals cheered as the nation's second-largest hammered-copper sculpture (only the Statue of Liberty is larger) was barged down the Willamette River, trucked through downtown, and hoisted to a ledge three stories up. Most Portlanders have forgotten that *Portlandia* is fashioned after Lady Commerce, the figure on the city seal.

Directly across the street from *Portlandia* is Don Wilson's abstract limestone sculpture, *Interlocking Forms*. Nearby is **CITY HALL** (1220 SW 5th Ave; map:F3), whose east courtyard contains the oldest of Portland's artworks: petroglyphs carved into basalt rock near Wallula, Washington, some 15,000 years ago. Inside City Hall are numerous interesting pieces of art, including Jim Blashfield and Carol Sherman's *Evolution of a City*, a photographic tour through time.

The **TRANSIT MALL** on SW Fifth and Sixth Avenues (map:E2–G3) is lined with sculptures, including Kathleen McCullough's *Cat in Repose* (a children's favorite) and Norman Taylor's *Kvinneakt*, the notorious nude that Portlanders know as former mayor Bud Clark's accomplice in an "Expose Yourself to Art" poster. At the southern end of the transit mall, Portland State University has created a city-block-sized plaza at the heart of its **COLLEGE OF URBAN AND PUBLIC AFFAIRS** (between SW 5th and 6th Aves and SW Montgomery and Mill Sts; map:E2), with a variety of attractive stone sculptures and stair-stepping fountains.

North of PSU, facing the South Park Blocks, are two of the city's cultural institutions. The inviting, newly renovated **SCULPTURE GARDEN** on the north side of the Portland Art Museum (1219 SW Park Ave; map:G2) features rotating exhibits of historic and contemporary sculpture from the museum's collection. Across the Park Blocks, cast a lingering eye at a modern application of trompe l'oeil effects on the south and west walls of the **OREGON HISTORY CENTER** (1200 SW Park Ave; map: G2). The Richard Haas murals depict figures from Oregon history: Lewis and Clark, Sacagawea, fur traders, and pioneers who journeyed westward on the Oregon Trail. For another rendering of the Lewis and Clark expedition, visit the lobby of **THE GOVERNOR HOTEL** (611 SW 10th Ave; map:I2), where Melinda Morey's sepia-toned murals cover the south wall.

Some of Portland's best privately financed artwork is set inside the **PACIFIC FIRST FEDERAL CENTER** (SW Broadway between Taylor and Yamhill Sts; map: H3): Larry Kirkland's suspended woven panels cascade into the lobby, catching the changing light throughout the day. More of Kirkland's work, including an intricately carved staircase and an enormous golden light fixture on the second floor, can be found in the **MULTNOMAH COUNTY LIBRARY** (801 SW 10th Ave; map:I2).

Fountains abound in central Portland; here are some to consider. The smallest are the ornamental bronze drinking fountains found all around the downtown core, called **BENSON BUBBLERS** after lumberman and civic leader Simon Benson; he gave them to the city in 1917 hoping people would drink water instead of whiskey. The city's most popular fountain may be the ever-changing **SALMON STREET SPRINGS**, in Gov. Tom McCall Waterfront Park, where SW Salmon Street meets Naito Parkway (map:F5). To the southwest, in front of Keller Auditorium (SW 3rd Ave between Market and Clay Sts; map:E3), is the **IRA KELLER FOUNTAIN**, also known as the Forecourt Fountain. It's a cool resting place in the middle of downtown, a full city block of waterfalls and pools built specifically with summer splashing in mind. Less well known but equally playful is the **LOVEJOY FOUNTAIN** (between SW 3rd and 4th Aves on Hall St; map:C2), built to resemble a cascading mountain stream. In Old Town stands Portland's first piece of public art, the 1888 cast-iron **SKIDMORE FOUNTAIN** (SW 1st Ave and Ankeny St; map:J6); two handmaidens hold an overflowing bowl above their heads.

William Wegman's **PORTLAND DOG BOWL** is a functioning bronze water fountain for pets in the North Park Blocks, north of Burnside Street between NW Eighth and Park Avenues (map:L3). This whimsical take on a dog's water bowl, an homage to Portland's Benson Bubblers, sits atop a floor reminiscent of kitchen linoleum.

PICA AND THE CUTTING EDGE

During its roaming, formative years in the mid-1990s, the Portland Institute of Contemporary Art (PICA) gained a reputation for bringing truly edgy artists and performers to town, ones who local audiences might never have expected to see this side of New York City. Now, under the tireless leadership of executive director and curator Kristy Edmunds, the cutting-edge arts group has found itself a permanent address (219 NW 12th Ave, Pearl District; 503/242-1419; map:L2) and a base of operation. PICA's spacious new galleries, housed in the same building as local ad giants Wieden + Kennedy, are located at the very pulse of Portland's creative center, the Pearl District. Thus situated, PICA continues doing what it does best: commissioning artists to develop work and designing exceptional performance seasons for its audiences.

A typical season might include anything from New York theatrical group Elevator Repair Service to a screening of early 20th-century avant-garde films with live accompaniment by Tom Verlaine. PICA's first exhibition in its new space was a gutsy show entitled *Fictional Cities* by two young contemporary French artists, each fascinated in his own way with themes of cities and migration. This show was followed by a salon-style art show open to all local artists who cared to participate.

Every autumn, PICA hosts an annual fund-raising event called the Dada Ball. The ball is a social high point, a celebration of the weird and wonderful not to be missed for its creative and conceptual costuming.

Performances take place all over town. For upcoming events and current shows, check the *Oregonian* and *Willamette Week* or visit www.pica.org.

—Michaela Lowthian

The revitalized Pearl District has added color and vibrancy to Jamison Square (NW 11th Ave and Johnson St; map:N2) with Kenny Scharf's **TIKITOTEMONKI** totems, selected in 2002 by *Art in America* magazine as one of the top 10 examples of new public art in the United States.

For a different perspective on Portland's public art, take a MAX ride across the river. The **OREGON CONVENTION CENTER** (NE Martin Luther King Jr Blvd and Holladay St; map:N9) is home to one of the state's most impressive public art collections. From the Sound Garden, created with bronze bells and chimes donated by Portland's Pacific Rim sister cities, to local artist Lucinda Parker's painting, *River Song*, the works at the Convention Center define the spirit of the state's people. The vision is universal, as seen in Kristin Jones and Andrew Ginzel's *Principia*—a pendulum hanging in the north tower above a 30-foot halo of suspended rays and a circular blue terrazzo floor inlaid with brass and stones. The vision is also provincial, as in a series of 30 etched and color-filled plaques noting key events and figures in Oregon history, by Terrence O'Donnell, Dennis Cunningham, and John

Laursen. And it's witty, as in Elizabeth Mappelli's enameled-glass panels of Oregon waterfalls, installed above men's-room urinals. Particularly telling and provocative is Seattle artist Buster Simpson's outdoor installation facing NE Martin Luther King Jr Boulevard. The work-in-progress is a nurse log pulled from Bull Run Reservoir; seedlings sprout from the irrigated, decaying wood, generating a bit of forest in the middle of the city.

While in Northeast Portland, don't miss the works scattered around the **LLOYD CENTER** mall, including Larry Kirkland's fountain, *Capitalism*. Outside the **ROSE GARDEN** stadium, children love *Essential Forces*, whose 500 computerized jets of water may or may not qualify as art: the fountain was a gift to the city from high-tech tycoon Paul Allen, owner of the Trail Blazers. Farther east, at **GRANT PARK** (NE 33rd Ave between Knott St and Broadway; map:GG5), children's books come alive in the **BEVERLY CLEARY SCULPTURE GARDEN FOR CHILDREN**, as cast-bronze statues of Ramona Quimby, Henry Huggins, and Henry's dog Ribsy cavort through a fountain, inviting real kids to join them.

Literature

Rainy days and Mondays may get some folks down, but those people must not have a good book to curl up with for a long, lazy read. Portland has enough rain and bookshops to satisfy any rainy-day (or sunny-day!) reader.

POWELL'S CITY OF BOOKS stands front and center on the literary canvas. With its multiple floors and gigantic collection—open 14 hours a day, 365 days a year—Powell's (1005 W Burnside St; 503/228-4651; www.powells.com; map:J2) is the nation's largest individual bookstore and is indeed one of the city's Top 20 Attractions (see the Exploring chapter). The store underwrites dozens of literary projects and events; local readers crowd appearances or readings by noted authors.

The large national bookstore chains like Barnes & Noble and Borders have arrived in Portland full force. As well, smaller stores equipped with espresso bars, deep reading chairs, and great lighting dot the city. There are dozens of independent new-book shops and probably just as many, if not more, dealers in used and rare books. (See Books and Periodicals in the Shopping chapter.) And the **FRIENDS OF THE MULTNOMAH COUNTY LIBRARY** (503/248-5439) each fall conducts an enormous used-book sale that raises as much as $150,000 for the library.

Many shops host touring authors to discuss their books and the writing life, and open-house readings are regularly scheduled at coffeehouses on both sides of the river. Check calendar listings in local newspapers. Book clubs, meanwhile, are prolific; members meet in libraries and small shops.

Among the best-known **PORTLAND-AREA WRITERS** are Jean Auel (*Clan of the Cave Bear*), Katherine Dunn (*Geek Love*), Matt Groening (*The Simpsons*), Ursula K. LeGuin (*The Left Hand of Darkness*), Phillip Margolin (*Wild Justice*), Chuck Palahniuk (*Fight Club*), Robert Sheckley (*Immortality, Inc.*), and Tom Spanbauer (*The Man Who Fell in Love With the Moon*). Some of them produce their work in the urban environment; others have studios in secluded venues not far from the city.

Portland is one of the few cities in the country to have its own nonprofit literary organization. **LITERARY ARTS** (503/227-2583; www.literary-arts.org) enriches readers and writers through fellowships, book awards, and the hugely popular **PORTLAND ARTS AND LECTURE SERIES**. Created in 1984, the series, which runs September to May, surprises even the nation's best-known authors with the enthusiasm of its audience. Readers from Salman Rushdie to Gore Vidal, Sandra Cisneros to David Guterson, take the stage to read from their work, discuss the writing process, and answer audience questions.

After 30 years, the **MOUNTAIN WRITERS SERIES** (www.mountainwriters.org) has become one of the largest poetry-reading series in the United States, offering readings, workshops, and lectures by distinguished writers. MWS works with more than 90 literary sponsors around the Northwest to bring great writers to local communities. The series maintains the **MOUNTAIN WRITERS CENTER** (3624 SE Milwaukie Ave, Brooklyn; 503/236-4854), where you can hear readings, read a literary journal, take a class or workshop, and chat up an accomplished writer or poet.

You need not be a full-time student to take advantage of Lewis and Clark College's **NORTHWEST WRITING INSTITUTE** (0615 SW Palatine Hill Rd, Riverdale; 503/768-7745; www.lclark.edu/dept/nwi/; map:JJ6), headed by poet-writer and local literary stalwart Kim Stafford, with its ever evolving list of courses and workshops.

Performing Arts

THEATER
Portland theater offerings range from long-running local hits to imported Broadway blockbusters, from Greek tragedy to experimental theater to the premier of an original play. There's also children's fare that can tease and delight adults. Check local newspapers for current schedules.

Artists Repertory Theatre
1516 SW ALDER ST, DOWNTOWN; 503/241-1278 One of Portland's best small theaters, ART features acclaimed local actors and directors overseen by artistic director Allen Nause. Company focus is on cutting-edge American plays juxtaposed with relevant classics. A sparkling black-box theater, built in 1998, has given ART a dream space to work in: Portland's small theaters often appear in makeshift settings, but here, the stage and seating—which can be reconfigured as needed—are gems. *www.artistsrep.org; map:J1*

Broadway in Portland
211 SE CARUTHERS ST, SOUTHEAST; 503/241-1802 This is the big shot in the theater scene, importing extravagant touring blockbusters like *Stomp, 42nd Street,* and *Oklahoma!* for presentation on the local stage—most often, the Keller Auditorium (222 SW Clay St, Downtown; map:E3). Tickets are sold through the Portland Opera. *www.portlandopera.org/broadway.php; map:HH6*

CoHo Productions and Stark Raving Theatre

2257 NW RALEIGH ST, NORTHWEST; 503/220-2646 OR 503/232-7072 These two companies share a 100-seat Northwest Portland theater. CoHo offers previously produced works in collaboration with local artists (Eugene O'Neill's *Moon for the Misbegotten* was a hit in 2003); Stark Raving is committed to regional premieres of provocative new works. The theater's annual New Rave festival is a summertime celebration of original work by local playwrights. *www.cohoproductions.org, www.starkravingtheatre.org; map:GG7*

Cygnet Theatre

VARIOUS LOCATIONS; 503/493-4077 Founded in 1992 by Louanne Moldevan, this small, critically acclaimed theater company performed for years in the back of a used bookstore. When the shop closed, they moved to a warehouse before becoming a roving theater. Moldevan's original work, *Vitriol and Violets: Tales from the Algonquin Round Table*, will appear in the fall of 2004 at the Lakewood Theater for the Arts (368 S State St, Lake Oswego; map:MM6). A previous performance in 2003 played to sellout crowds. *www.cygnettheatre.org*

Imago Theatre

17 SE 18TH AVE, BUCKMAN; 503/231-9581 With its blend of mask, mime, and vaudeville, this whimsical, movement-based company astonishes young and old alike. From a skit with comical penguins in a game of musical chairs, to a play based on the male ego and cloning, Imago captures the human spirit and melds it with the spirit of the times. *www.imagotheatre.com; map:HH5*

Northwest Children's Theater

1819 NW EVERETT ST, NORTHWEST; 503/222-4480 From *Jack and the Beanstalk* to *Arabian Nights*, this theater presents a variety of plays each year. Its 450-seat theater, and theater school for Portland's youngest thespians, is lodged in the Northwest Neighborhood Cultural Center. *www.nwcts.org; map:HH7*

Oregon Children's Theatre

600 SW 10TH AVE, DOWNTOWN; 503/228-9571 Children's fave stories—from *The Chronicles of Narnia* to *The Velveteen Rabbit*—come to life in an annual handful of engaging works. They are presented at the Portland Center for the Performing Arts' Keller Auditorium (222 SW Clay St, Downtown; map:E3) and Newmark Theatre (1111 SW Broadway, Downtown; map:G2). *www.octc.org; map:I2*

Portland Center Stage

PORTLAND CENTER FOR THE PERFORMING ARTS, 1111 SW BROADWAY, DOWNTOWN; 503/274-6588 Portland's leading professional theater company is on a par with the country's best regional theaters. Founded in 1988, Center Stage mounts seven annual productions (September through May) in the Newmark and Winningstad Theatres. Director Chris Coleman, who took over the company in 2000, has a distaste for complacency; he has upgraded every element of the Portland Center Stage, bringing in seasoned actors and plays that illumine the stage. Coleman twists even the most conventional plays with energy and wit: expect to be surprised. *www.pcs.org; map:G2*

263

Tears of Joy Puppet Theatre

321 NE WYGANT ST, NORTHEAST; 503/248-0557 From *Rumpelstiltskin* to ancient Greek epics, Tears of Joy always awes the family. A three-decade tradition, the award-winning company thrills with over-the-top, puppet-enhanced retellings of classic tales and original works. Each year, Tears of Joy mounts 100 performances of six productions at the Winningstad Theatre (1111 SW Broadway, Downtown; map:G2) and in Vancouver, Washington's Royal Durst Theatre (3101 Main St; map:CC6). Its outreach programs extend throughout the West. This company is a local treasure; everything it does is a class act. *www.tojt.com; map:FF6*

Teatro Milagro

425 SE 6TH AVE, BUCKMAN; 503/236-7253 "Miracle Theater" tours internationally, crafting current global issues into cutting-edge drama infused with Latino culture, the Spanish language, and original music. But since its inception in 1985, it has evolved into more than a performing-arts group: El Centro Milagro is now a regional cultural center for Portland's large Hispanic community, and its Bellas Artes division stages a variety of music festivals and other events. *www.milagro .org; map:HH6*

Theatre Vertigo

2512 SE GLADSTONE ST, BROOKLYN; 503/306-0870 Located in the Electric Company, this small company produces edgy, often hilarious, ensemble works, occasionally in collaboration with other local companies. Watch as they produce an updated work by Aeschylus or a remake of Oscar Wilde. *www.theatrevertigo.org; map:II5*

Classical Music and Opera

During the symphony season, Portland audiences have many opportunities to listen to classical music, both by the powerful Oregon Symphony Orchestra and by smaller orchestras, ensembles, and choral groups. The highlight of the year, however, comes midsummer with Chamber Music Northwest—a five-week celebration that is among the finest festivals of its type in the nation (see listing, below). If you're in town during July, investigate ticket availability. The rest of the year, look to local newspapers for a schedule of the best performances in Portland.

Chamber Music Northwest

CATLIN GABEL SCHOOL, 8825 SW BARNES RD, WEST SLOPE / REED COLLEGE, 3203 SE WOODSTOCK BLVD, WOODSTOCK; 503/294-6400 A talented group of musicians, recruited from New York's Chamber Music Society of Lincoln Center and other Big Apple ensembles, puts the annual summer festival (in 2004, June 21–July 24) in an elite class. Longtime artistic director David Shifrin is committed to a wide-ranging repertoire from duos and trios to large ensembles, from baroque and classical masterpieces to world and West Coast premieres. More than two dozen concerts, held at Reed College or the Catlin Gabel School, range from solo recitals to evenings for small orchestras, from Bach to Bartok, and from chamber music staples (Brahms, Schubert, Beethoven) to surprises. Between October and April, the company presents a concert series (often featuring touring chamber groups) at venues around the city; watch local media, or call for information. Keep an eye out for Portland's own Floristan Trio, an internationally acclaimed violin-cello-piano group. *www.cmnw.org; map:HH9; map: JJ5*

Oregon Repertory Singers

1925 NE PACIFIC ST, NORTHEAST; 503/230-0652 Thirty years of innovative concerts have given Gilbert Seeley's 65-voice adult ensemble a reputation for creative programming. In four shows from October to May, Seeley specializes in new commissions and neglected classics; he is also a gifted orchestral conductor. Collaborations with other ensembles on works by Hayden, Bach, Mozart, and Handel are high-quality repertoire staples. Most performances are in area churches; call for locations. A youth choir mounts three productions a year. *www.oregonrepsingers .org; map:GG5*

Oregon Symphony Orchestra

ARLENE SCHNITZER CONCERT HALL, 1037 SW BROADWAY, DOWNTOWN; 503/228-1353 One of the largest arts organizations in the Northwest and a Portland institution since 1896, the OSO is one of the major orchestras in the United States. Legendary conductor James DePreist (who remains as laureate music director) has transferred his baton to Carlos Kalmar, who plans a return to a core orchestral repertoire. An all-star roster of guest artists, including Wynton Marsalis and Art Garfunkel in spring 2004, will join him. (Past visitors have included Aaron Copland, Maurice Ravel, Igor Stravinsky, and Yo-Yo Ma.) The Portland Symphonic Choir chimes in a couple of times a year. Pops and youth series fill out the 39-week calendar. *www.oregonsymphony.org; map:G2*

Portland Baroque Orchestra

1020 SW TAYLOR ST, DOWNTOWN; 503/222-6000 The Baroque has gained enormous stature since 1995 under the baton of English superstar violinist Monica Huggett. The Portland early-instrument specialists tackle music written between 1600 and 1825 in performances designed to recreate the sound of period ensembles. Visiting soloists on trumpet, cello, violin, harpsichord, and recorder, plus a crack 24-voice chorus, conspire in brisk versions of Bach, Handel, Vivaldi, Mozart, Haydn, and Beethoven. From October to April, Friday- and Saturday-night concerts are at the First Baptist Church (909 SW 11th Ave, Downtown; map:F2); most Sunday matinees are in Reed College's Kaul Auditorium (3203 SE Woodstock Blvd, Woodstock; map:JJ5). *www.pbo.org; map:H2*

Portland Opera

KELLER AUDITORIUM, 222 SW CLAY ST, DOWNTOWN; 503/241-1802 Over the years, Portland's homegrown opera company has lived up to its self-description: "anything but stuffy." Always sparkling, theirs are sounds that shock the senses. New director Christopher Mattaliano may continue former director Robert Bailey's commitment to classic repertoire staples, juxtaposed with a season-ending Broadway offering and occasional premieres. Then again, the passionate Mattaliano has a history as a stage director, so he's likely to add a heavy dose of the theatrical. Operatically speaking, this is the only game in town, and tickets go quickly. *www.portland opera.org; map:E3*

Third Angle New Music Ensemble

VARIOUS LOCATIONS; 503/203-2836 This ensemble—eight permanent members and a revolving roster of guest artists—specializes in 20th-century chamber music by American composers, refreshingly not just those of European descent. You might hear a commissioned piece by Guyanian master drummer Obo Addy (who makes Portland his home), a concert devoted entirely to tango, or the work of New Romantic composers. Four to six polished, provocative programs are presented each year at locales that vary from Reed College to Winningstad Theatre and the Arlene Schnitzer Concert Hall. *www.thirdangle.org*

Dance

Portland's dance explosion can be readily traced to a single event: the creation, in 1997, of White Bird. This nonprofit organization (see sidebar) has brought a wealth of national and international concert performers to the city, from Mikhail Baryshnikov and Alvin Ailey to Paul Taylor, Twyla Tharp, and Urban Bush Women. Reviewers have described their works as "diamond-edged dancing" and "a world where madness waltzes with grace." Performances, scheduled October through May, cost $12 to $25, with a half-price student rush special. Performances run monthly.

Numerous dance companies make their home in Portland, chief among them the much celebrated Oregon Ballet Theatre. For both local and national appearances, keep on eye on newspaper listings.

BodyVox

1300 NW NORTHRUP ST, PEARL DISTRICT; 503/224-8499 Launched almost coincidentally with White Bird (see sidebar), this high-energy contemporary dance theater operates out of a studio loft above the BridgePort Brew Pub. Choreographers/founders Jamey Hampton and Ashley Roland bring a bold athleticism and inherent theatrical spirit to their troupe. Dynamic and emotional, the touring company has won rave international reviews. *www.bodyvox.com; map:O1*

Do Jump! Extremely Physical Theater

1515 SE 37TH AVE, HAWTHORNE; 503/231-1232 These tremendously energetic dancers fuse acrobatics with athletics using props from hand trucks to ladders, breaking down the boundary between audience and performers. Over two decades, director Robin Lane has created 16 full-length works. Do Jump! is the resident company of the Echo Theatre, where **THE DANCE CARTEL** (503/972-7709) also performs its showcase work. *www.dojump.org; map:HH5*

The Northwest Afrikan American Ballet

77 NE KNOTT ST, ALBINA; 503/287-8852 The first traditional African dance company in the Northwest, this 16-member troupe has been inspired for 20 years by

PINK MARTINI: A TOP-SHELF INDULGENCE

Pink Martini is Portland's hottest musical exponent of international chic. A concert never fails to deliver a vibrant and stylish good time to its audience. The 10-piece band, which tours both nationally and abroad, plays several sold-out concerts in Portland each year and continues to enjoy the success of its 1997 album, *Sympathique*. The second CD is in the works.

Much of the credit for the group's success and appeal goes to its inimitably talented artistic director and pianist, Thomas Lauderdale. Vocalist China Forbes lends her strong and lovely voice to the music, often singing in French or Spanish. The result is a frothy mix of percussion, brass, and strings. One moment the band might play a big band bossa nova number, and the next a catchy reworked version of Barry Manilow's "Copacabana." Pink Martini is one of the few bands to blend classical chamber music, Cuban jazz, and an occasional French dance-hall song—appealing to young and old alike.

Pink Martini performed alongside Elton John and Ringo Starr at the 1998 Cannes Film Festival and welcomed 2004 with a New Year's Eve performance at the new Walt Disney Concert Hall in Los Angeles. Don't be surprised to hear strains of *Sympathique* playing in the background of such television shows as *The Sopranos* and *The West Wing*.

From the rumba to the waltz, from Taiwan to Spain, from the Hollywood Bowl to Broadway, Pink Martini jet-sets across the musical globe, always (thankfully!) arriving back in Portland. What they bring back is never kitschy and always first class. Check www.pinkmartini.com for upcoming concerts.

—*Michaela Lowthian*

drummer/dancer/director Bruce Smith. Performing indigenous dances of Senegal, Gambia, Mali, and Guinea to the insistent beat of a virtuoso drum contingent, and clad in the gorgeous fabrics of those West African nations, the athletic troupe recreates village festivals that celebrate marriage, coming of age, harvest time, and the passing of seasons. An annual Rose Festival fixture, the company appears in schools and other locations up and down the West Coast. *Map:GG6*

Oregon Ballet Theatre

818 SE 6TH AVE, BUCKMAN; 503/222-5538 This energetic company of talented dancers wowed critics in New York with its strong blend of classical and modern ballet when it toured in 2000. A wellspring of youth and daring, the troupe satisfies both the cravings of Portland's traditional ballet fans and the appetites of the MTV generation. New director Christopher Stowell, who succeeds the enthusiastic James Canfield, plans to celebrate the evolution of ballet through a series of works inspired both by the great masters and by the hottest of young talents. OBT's obligatory holiday *Nutcracker* is pure guilty joy, with a dance narrative set in tsarist St. Petersburg and dancers in superb costumes and sets. Performances are in Keller

267

Auditorium (222 SW Clay St, Downtown; map:E3) and the Newmark Theatre (1111 SW Broadway, Downtown; map:G2). *www.obt.org; map:HH6*

Oslund + Co./Dance

918 SW YAMHILL ST, 4TH FLOOR, DOWNTOWN; 503/221-5857 Artistic director and choreographer Mary Oslund stages a concert when the spirit moves her: several times a year. Noted for erratic, gestural movement, she combines modern dance and live, newly composed music with excellent scenery and lighting, giving her shows a spirit both postmodern and avant-garde. The efforts of musicians, poets, visual artists, and filmmakers put Oslund in the best tradition of collaborative art. Usually at home in the cozy Conduit Contemporary Dance Studio, above the MAX tracks downtown, Oslund also performs at the larger Imago Theatre (17 SE 18th Ave, Buckman; map:HH5). *wwww.conduit-pdx.org; map:I2*

Performance Works NorthWest

4625 SE 67TH ST, SOUTHEAST; 503/777-1907 Founded in 1999 by dancer/choreographer Linda Austin and technical director Jeff Forbes, this company—ensconced in a former Orthodox church off Foster Road—both produces its own imaginative works and performs that of other artists. Austin herself emcees the off-the-wall Cabaret Boris & Natasha, an occasional tongue-in-cheek mix of dance, music, theater, and performance art, and Holy Goats!, an almost-monthly Sunday afternoon improv session. *www.performanceworksnw.org; map:II3*

Film

Portland is the hub of a booming movie industry. More and more film companies—small independent filmmakers as well as big Hollywood conglomerates—are discovering the variety of venues the region can provide. Films like *The Ring* (2002), *The Hunted* (2001), *Pay It Forward* (2000), and *Men of Honor* (1999) were filmed, in part, in the Portland area. Since 1999, in fact, more than three dozen feature films have been shot in Oregon.

Cutting-edge filmmaker Gus Van Sant moved to Portland from New York in the late 1980s. In his own new backyard, he directed Matt Dillon and Kelly Lynch in *Drugstore Cowboy* (1989) and Keanu Reeves and River Phoenix in *My Own Private Idaho* (1991). By the time Van Sant scored box-office gold with *Good Will Hunting* (1997), other international-caliber artists had followed him to Portland. Among them is director Todd Haynes, acclaimed for *Far From Heaven* (2002) and *Velvet Goldmine* (1998). In 2003, Van Sant won the top prize at the Cannes Film Festival for *Elephant*, a film he shot in North Portland casting real high-school students.

This city loves the movies. Movie theaters keep expanding to meet the demand not only for first-run flicks but for art films and other efforts that studio-bound theaters fail to book. For complete movie listings check out the entertainment section of the *Oregonian* (www.oregonianlive.com), the *Portland Tribune* (www.portland tribune.com), or *Willamette Week* (www.willametteweek.com).

Broadway Metroplex

1000 SW BROADWAY, DOWNTOWN; 503/225-5555, EXT 4607 This is a multiplex, true—but it's in central downtown, and its coffee bar serves first-rate mochas and quality chocolates. Enjoy the old Portland theater marquees hanging in the lower lobby and the continuous classic film footage that entertains you as you wait in line for tickets. By the way, don't hang up when you call this theater (or any other Regal Cinema house) and reach the *Oregonian*'s automated information service: punch in the extension and eventually you'll get what you called for. *www.regalcinemas .com; map:H3*

Cinemagic

2021 SE HAWTHORNE BLVD, SOUTHEAST; 503/231-7919 This independently owned rep house serves up the classics as well as near-first-run faves. You might see *My Fair Lady* one week and a recent feature the next—or even an East Indian film. Seats are soft and comfy and theater ambience is calm and pretty. Popcorn is drenched in real butter. *Map:HH5*

Cinema 21

616 NW 21ST AVE, NORTHWEST; 503/223-4515 Portland's best movie house is one of a dying breed: the single-screen neighborhood theater. Spacious and clean, it still has a roomy balcony and rocking-chair seats, and it features a crying room for troubled tots. Films range from way-left documentaries to art-house intrigues to premieres. Watch for the annual festival of animation. *www.cinema21.com; map: GG7*

Fox Tower 10

SW PARK AVE AND TAYLOR ST, DOWNTOWN; 503/225-5555, EXT 4604 Tall escalators deliver patrons from the street into this huge, 10-auditorium theater in the central shopping district. Cozy individual theaters feature tiered seating, retractable armrests for snuggling (or arm wrestling) with your popcorn partner, and digital everything. Look for both major Hollywood releases and alternative fare. *www.regalcinemas.com; map:H2*

Hollywood Theater

4122 NE SANDY BLVD, HOLLYWOOD; 503/281-4215 Opened as a vaudeville theater in 1926, the grand and garish Hollywood now serves classic, family, and second-run fare to frequent sellout audiences. This is also a site for concerts, live performances, and other public events. Concessions include fat-free, sugar-free, and vegan options. *www.hollywoodtheater.org; map:GG4*

KOIN Center Cinemas

SW 3RD AVE AND CLAY ST, DOWNTOWN; 503/225-5555, EXT 4608 Hollywood releases, foreign films, and art-house movies appear on the KOIN's six screens. Parking lots dot the area, but street parking is tight. Children's crying rooms are available in two of the theaters. *www.regalcinemas.com; map:E4*

Laurelhurst Theater and Pub

2735 E BURNSIDE ST, LAURELHURST; 503/232-5511 It doesn't get much better than this: $3 admission, a slice of Pizzicato pizza (see review in the Restaurants chapter), and a draft microbrew or a glass of wine. Get comfy in the wide seats at this friendly neighborhood cinema, a 1923 Art Deco classic. Set your snacks on the tables between seats in each of the four theaters, and take in a classic or recent first-run film. No one under 21 is admitted after 4pm. *www.laurelhursttheater.com; map:HH5*

Lloyd Center and Lloyd Cinemas

1510 NE MULTNOMAH BLVD, LLOYD CENTER; 503/225-5555, EXT 4601 AND 4600 With 10 screens in the mall and 10 across the street, this is the biggest movie site in the city. Both theaters are owned by the Regal Cinemas chain, so films are traditional, first-run Hollywood fare. The Lloyd Cinemas building features a long, neon-lit interior corridor and an espresso bar. *www.regalcinemas.com; map:GG5*

McMenamins Theater Pubs

VARIOUS LOCATIONS; 503/225-5555, EXT 8830 What may well be Portland's favorite movie-theater chain is actually a group of brewpubs that show movies: you gotta love the concept of a pint of suds with a frisky flick! Admission is $3; children are allowed during matinees. There are six options in Greater Portland: the Mission (1624 NW Glisan St, Northwest; map:HH7); the Bagdad (3710 SW Hawthorne Blvd, Hawthorne; map:HH5); the St. Johns (8203 N Ivanhoe St, Saint Johns; map:EE9); the Kennedy School (5736 NE 33rd Ave, Northeast; map:FF5); the Edgefield (2126 SW Hawley, Troutdale); and the Grand Lodge (3505 Pacific Ave, Forest Grove). *www.mcmenamins.com*

Northwest Film Center

1219 SW PARK AVE, DOWNTOWN; 503/221-1156 A steady menu of art films, independent features, and documentaries appear here, as do guest filmmakers presenting their recent work. This nonprofit organization, a branch of the Portland Art Museum, also presents several annual festivals. The Portland International Film Festival screens international indie films over two weeks in February; the Northwest Film & Video Festival highlights work by regional artists in November; and the Young People's Film & Video Festival honors school-age filmmakers in July. *www.nwfilm.org; map:G2*

Roseway Theater

7229 NE SANDY BLVD, ROSEWAY; 503/287-8119 This classic, family-owned neighborhood theater—a throwback to days of yore—has high ceilings, wide aisles, comfortable seats with spacious leg room, an elegant lobby, and great attitude. Theater here is a gift to the community. Quality second-run films are presented with pleasure and flair. *Map:FF3*

NIGHTLIFE

Nightlife by Feature

ALL AGES
All coffee houses
BridgePort Brewpub
Huber's
Laurelwood Public House & Brewery
The Lucky Labrador
Meow Meow
Nocturnal
Port Halling Brewing Company
Quest
Roseland Theater

BAR GAMES/BILLIARDS
Berbati's Pan
Bitter End
The Egyptian Club
Goodfoot Lounge
Horse Brass Pub
Laurelthirst Public House
The Matador
Meow Meow
Ponderosa Lounge at Jubitz Truck
  Stop
Pub at the End of the Universe
Quest
Rialto Poolroom Bar and Cafe
Ringler's
Sam's Hollywood Billiards
Shanghai Tunnel
Uptown Billiards Club

BLUES/FOLK
Aladdin Theater
Billy Ray's Neighborhood Dive
Bitter End
Laurelthirst Public House
Produce Row Cafe
Roseland Theater
Spare Room
St. Johns Pub and Theater
The Tugboat Brewery

CABARET
Berbati's Pan
Dante's

Wilf's Restaurant and Piano Bar

CIGARS
The Brazen Bean
Greater Trumps
Uptown Billiards

COMEDY
Dante's
Harvey's Comedy Club

COUNTRY
Ponderosa Lounge at Jubitz Truck
  Stop

DANCE FLOORS
Berbati's Pan
Cañita
Cobalt Lounge
Crush
The Crystal Ballroom
The Egyptian Club
Fernando's Hideaway
Fez Ballroom
Goodfoot Lounge
The Grand Cafe/Andrea's Cha Cha
  Club
Greek Cusina
Heaven Cafe
Holocene
Laurelthirst Public House
Level
The Lotus Cardroom
Madame Butterfly
Nocturnal
The Ohm
Ponderosa Lounge at Jubitz Truck
  Stop
Quest
The Red Sea
Ringler's
Roseland Theater
Spare Room
1201 Club
The Viscount Ballroom

DIVE BARS
Billy Ray's Neighborhood Dive
Chopsticks Express II
The Matador
Space Room at the Brite Spot
Tony's Tavern
Virginia Café

GAY/LESBIAN
Cobalt Lounge
Crush
Darcelle XV
The Egyptian Club
Panorama
Three Sisters

HAPPY HOUR/ LATE-NIGHT GRUB
Basta's Trattoria
Brasserie Montmartre
Cassidy's
Dante's
Dragonfish Asian Café
Harborside
Heaven Cafe
The Rock Bottom Brewpub
Veritable Quandary
Voodoo Doughnut

HIP-HOP
Ash Street
B Complex
The Crystal Ballroom
East Chinatown Lounge
Fez Ballroom
Holocene
Level
Madame Butterfly
Meow Meow
Quest
The Red Sea
Ringler's
Roseland Theater

JAZZ
The Benson Hotel Lobby Court
Billy Reed's
Blue Monk

Brasserie Montmarte
Goodfoot Lounge
The Know
Jimmy Mak's
Produce Row Cafe
Saucebox
Sapphire Hotel
The Tugboat Brewery

KARAOKE
The Alibi
Bush Garden
Chopsticks Express II
The Egyptian Club
The Grand Cafe/Andrea's Cha Cha
   Club
Panorama

LATIN/SALSA
Cañita
820 Lounge at Mint
Fernando's Hideaway
The Grand Cafe/Andrea's Cha Cha
   Club
The Viscount Ballroom

MARTINIS
Alexander's
The Benson Hotel Lobby Court
The Brazen Bean
Crush
The Heathman Hotel
Jake's Grill
M Bar
Saucebox
Wilf's Restaurant and Piano Bar

PIANO BAR
Alexander's
The Heathman Hotel
Wallbangers
Wilf's Restaurant and Piano Bar

POETRY (LIVE)
Coffee Time

PUBS/ALEHOUSES
Alameda Brewhouse

273

Beulahland
Biddy McGraw's
Bitter End
BridgePort Brewpub
Captain Ankeny's Well
Goose Hollow Inn
Horse Brass Pub
Laurelthirst Public House
Laurelwood Public House & Brewery
The Lucky Labrador
McMenamins
Portland Brewing Company
Produce Row Cafe
Pub at the End of the Universe
The Rock Bottom Brewpub
Rogue Ales Public House
The Tugboat Brewery
Widmer Brewing and Gasthaus

PUNK
Aladdin Theater
Meow Meow

REGGAE/WORLD BEAT
Aladdin Theater
The Crystal Ballroom
The Red Sea

RETRO
The Alibi
Bar of the Gods
Beuhlahland
The Crystal Ballroom
The Gypsy `
Hung Far Low
The Lotus Cardroom
Quest

Space Room at the Brite Spot
Wilf's Restaurant and Piano Bar

ROCK
Aladdin Theater
B Complex
Berbati's Pan
Bitter End
Cobalt Lounge
The Crystal Ballroom
Laurelthirst Public House
Meow Meow
Roseland Theater
Spare Room
White Eagle Rock 'n' Roll Hotel

SMOKE-FREE
Aladdin Theater
Harvey's Comedy Club
Uptown Billiard Club

TECHNO/ELECTRONIC
B Complex
The Crystal Ballroom
Holocene
Level
Madame Butterfly
Nocturnal
Panorama
Saucebox
Tube
1201 Club

VIEW
Alexander's
Harborside
Windows Skyroom & Terrace

Nightlife by Neighborhood

ALBERTA
The Know
Star E. Rose Cafe

ALBINA
820 Lounge at Mint
White Eagle Rock 'n' Roll Hotel
Widmer Brewing and Gasthaus

BEAUMONT
Alameda Brewhouse

BELMONT
Blue Monk
The Pied Cow
Stumptown Coffee Roasters
The Tao of Tea

BROOKLYN
Aladdin Theater
C-Bar
Pub at the End of the Universe

BUCKMAN
Crush
Nocturnal
Rimsky-Korsakoffee House

CHINATOWN
East Chinatown Lounge
Harvey's Comedy Club
Hung Far Low
Level
Roseland Theater
The Tao of Tea

CLINTON
Dots Café

DOWNTOWN
Alexander's
The Benson Hotel Lobby Court
Brasserie Montmartre
Bush Garden
Cassidy's
The Crystal Ballroom
Dragonfish Asian Café
Fernando's Hideaway
Fez Ballroom
Greek Cusina
The Heathman Hotel
Heaven Cafe
Huber's
Jake's Grill
The Lotus Cardroom
Madame Butterfly
Market Street Pub
Panorama
Quest
The Red Sea
Rialto Poolroom Bar and Cafe
Ringler's
Ringler's Annex
The Rock Bottom Brewpub
Saucebox
Stumptown Coffee Roasters

Three Sisters
Torrefazione Italia
The Tugboat Brewery
1201 Club
Veritable Quandary
Virginia Cafe
Wallbangers
World Cup at Powell's City of Books

GOOSE HOLLOW
Goose Hollow Inn

GRESHAM
Port Halling Brewing Company

HAWTHORNE
Bagdad Theater and Pub
Bar of the Gods
Diedrich Coffee People
The Empire Room
Greater Trumps
Sapphire Hotel
Space Room at the Brite Spot

HOLLYWOOD
Laurelwood Public House & Brewery
Sam's Hollywood Billiards

INNER SOUTHEAST
B Complex
Back to Back Cafe
The Grand Cafe/Andrea's Cha Cha
    Club
Holocene
Meow Meow
Produce Row Cafe
The Viscount Ballroom

LADD'S ADDITION
Palio Dessert & Espresso House

LAURELHURST
Beulahland
Chopsticks Express II
Goodfoot Lounge
Laurelthirst Public House
Navarre
Noble Rot
Wine Down

275

MULTNOMAH VILLAGE
The Lucky Labrador

NEAR LLOYD CENTER
Grand Motor Moka
Windows Skyroom & Terrace

NORTH PORTLAND
The Alibi
Fresh Pot
Ponderosa Lounge at Jubitz Truck
    Stop

NORTHEAST
Biddy McGraw's
Billy Ray's Neighborhood Dive
Billy Reed's
Kennedy School
Spare Room
Torrefazione Italia

NORTHWEST
Basta's Trattoria
Bitter End
Blue Moon Tavern
The Brazen Bean
Coffee Time
Diedrich Coffee People
The Gypsy
M Bar
The Matador
Mission Theater and Pub
Portland Brewing Company
The Ram's Head
Staccato Gelato
The Tao of Tea
Tony's Tavern
Torrefazione Italia
Uptown Billiards Club

OLD TOWN
Ash Street
Berbati's Pan
Cañita

Captain Ankeny's Well
Cobalt Lounge
Dante's
Darcelle XV
The Ohm
Shanghai Tunnel
Stumptown Coffee Roasters
Tube
Voodoo Doughnut

PEARL DISTRICT
BridgePort Brewpub
Jimmy Mak's
Rogue Ales Public House
750 ml
Torrefazione Italia
Vigne

RIVER DISTRICT
Wilf's Restaurant and Piano Bar

RIVERPLACE
Harborside

SAINT JOHNS
St. Johns Pub and Theater

SOUTHEAST
Barley Mill Pub
The Egyptian Club
Horse Brass Pub
The Lucky Labrador
Pix Patisserie

SOUTHWEST
Fulton Pub and Brewery

TROUTDALE
Edgefield

NIGHTLIFE

Because the Portland nightlife palette has so much to offer, you might want to sketch out a plan before going out. Like the city's neighborhoods, Portland's clubs are often separated into areas; the majority of venues and bars are located downtown, but clusters of genre-oriented clubs sprout up here and there. For instance, Stark Street, between SE 9th and 14th Avenues, is sometimes known as the Pink Strip, where the majority of Portland's gay bars are located. Over on SE Hawthorne, a host of clubs and bars cater to a more rootsy, hippie-oriented crowd. Because the city is so spread out, if you want to hit more than one event per night, a little preplanning will help in the long run.

Music, Clubs, and Lounges

Aladdin Theater

116 SE 11TH AVE, BROOKLYN; 503/234-9698 The Aladdin began as a venue for vaudeville acts (including Jack Benny), evolved into a family movie theater, and landed a 20-year stint as a notorious porn house (*Deep Throat* played here). Today it enjoys a reputation as one of Portland's classier venues, featuring a choice selection of musical acts as diverse as its beginnings. Popular bluegrass, acoustic, rock, R&B, even indie and art-punk bands have filled this hall; its ornate architecture and old wooden seats dictate the no-smoking policy. *MC, V; checks OK; open during events only; beer and wine; www.aladdin-theater.com; map:II5* &

Alexander's

921 SW 6TH AVE (HILTON HOTEL), DOWNTOWN; 503/226-1611 Alexander's meaty gourmet menu (duck strudel, lamb chops with Cajun dipping sauce), dapper piano bar, and sweeping view of the West Portland hills with their luxury homes is straight out of a movie. Romance, intrigue, and drama are all here, atop the glam Hilton Hotel—the only things missing are J. Lo and George Clooney. Alexander's staff is friendly and unexpectedly cool; go for an upscale experience without any semblance of attitude. *AE, DC, DIS, MC, V; no checks; Wed–Sat; full bar; map:H3* &

Ash Street

225 SW ASH ST, OLD TOWN; 503/226-0430 Renovation has turned this modest bar into a decent small venue with a hodgepodge of musical acts. It's still one of the only places in Portland to see live hip-hop at least once a week. There's not much in the way of atmosphere—a few tables and high-backed booths make it comfortable—but it's a regular hangout for the many bike messengers who, in a way, represent the real heart of Portland. *AE, DC, DIS, MC, V; no checks; every day; full bar; www.ashstreetsaloon.com; map:J6* &

B Complex

320 SE 2ND AVE, INNER SOUTHEAST; 503/235-4424 B Complex occupies a large bi-level in Portland's hip warehouse district, and the concrete walls and modern

THE PORTLAND SOUND: DEFINING A SUBCULTURE

Portland is a city of young transplants, and it's in constant flux. It sometimes feels as if no one was actually born here, that everyone migrated en masse via bicycle. Thanks to a particularly high recent volume of youth migration, numerous nationally prominent bands now call Portland their home: among them **ART ALEXAKIS** and **EVERCLEAR**, pride-of-the-city female band **SLEATER-KINNEY**, ex-Pavement iconoclast **STEPHEN MALKMUS**, pop group **THE SHINS**, and cabaret piano quartet **GET HUSTLE**. Record labels (including Aesthetics and Temporary Residence) have relocated here, too, attracted to Portland's fiercely independent mentality of inevitable achievement. At the same time, longtime Portland residents—pop duo **QUASI**, hip-hop preachers **THE LIFESAVAS**, disco minimalists **GLASS CANDY**, druggy Britpopists **DANDY WARHOLS**, live electronic artists **NUDGE**, and electro encyclopedia **DJ BROKEN-WINDOW**—have gained widespread notoriety through national label support.

For many years Portland was known as the indie-rock town where Elliott Smith penned his Grammy Award–nominated song, "Miss Misery" (from the *Good Will Hunting* soundtrack). In recent years, however, the city's music scene has grown so broad and diverse that Smith's exodus to (and sudden death in) Los Angeles has become almost symbolic. While a pervasive independent aesthetic shapes the musical landscape, there's no single defining sound—making the music scene one of the city's most flourishing attractions.

While stellar jazz drummer **MEL BROWN** (a regular at Jimmy Mak's; see review under Music, Clubs, and Lounges in the Nightlife chapter) has played with artists from the Beatles to the Temptations, the future for another type of beat is just as promising.

furniture give it a gritty, urban feel. Formerly a site for raves, its warehouse parties are now legit and mostly feature national electronic, hip-hop, and rock acts. The bar serves natural juices and teas, and smoking is relegated to an upstairs balcony overlooking downtown. *Cash only; open during events only; no alcohol; www.bherenow.net; map:I9*

The Benson Hotel Lobby Court

309 SW BROADWAY, DOWNTOWN; 503/228-2000 It's always fun to have a drink in one of your town's nicest hotels. You can pretend you're from some foreign port, just in for the weekend. Have a drink in the opulent Benson lobby court while pretending to be a visiting dignitary from some exotic land. The classy lobby is dark, lined with imported Russian walnut, and furnished with comfortable black leather chairs—great for sinking into and catching live jazz Wednesday through Saturday. *AE, DC, DIS, MC, V; no checks; every day; full bar; www.benson-hotel.com; map:J4*

The **LIFESAVAS**, a trio of Portland natives, have earned substantial national attention for their soulful record, *Spirit in Stone* (Quannum Projects) and on world tours with the likes of feel-good hip-hop stalwarts Blackalicious. The group's CD release party, which drew more than 1,000 people to the Roseland Theater, is already seen as a galvanizing moment for Portland hip-hop. Add rap entrepreneur **COOL NUTZ**, live groups like **QUIVAH** and **REPARATIONS**, stalwart regular DJs like **WICKED** and **MELLO-CEE**, and collective **CLAN OF THE CAVE MACKS** to the picture, and it's clear the city is establishing itself as a strong hip-hop center.

With flourishing electronic, noise, and more experimental music scenes, Portland has come a long way from its days as a grunge outpost where Courtney Love hung her hat. Since you can't throw a rock without hitting an independent record store in Portland, you'll have no trouble discovering more about local music and its history from the staff at an Ozone or Jackpot shop (see reviews under Music in the Shopping chapter). For a hip-hop and electronic music perspective, seek out 360 Vinyl (214 NW Couch St, Old Town; 503/224-3688; map:K6) or Platinum Records (see review under Music in the Shopping chapter).

An influx of musical acts has meant an influx of venues. There are always at least three or four interesting events every night of the week, an incredible number for a city the size of Portland. Check the listings in the *Oregonian's A&E*, the *Tribune's Cue* (both out Fridays), *Willamette Week* (out Wednesdays), or for the edgier listener, the *Portland Mercury* (out Thursdays).

—*Julianne Shepherd*

Berbati's Pan

231 SW ANKENY ST, OLD TOWN; 503/248-4579 This popular club was an afterthought to the adjoining Greek restaurant, but it has grown considerably in physical size and prominence. Featuring a long bar, large dance floor, and separate cafe and game rooms, the club showcases acts that range from burlesque cabarets to eclectic DJ nights, local bands, and smaller national touring acts like Interpol and the Gossip. Because the schedule is always full of interesting offerings, Berbati's is a favored destination for live-music lovers. *AE, DIS, MC, V; checks OK; every day; full bar; map:J6* &

Billy Ray's Neighborhood Dive

2216 NE MARTIN LUTHER KING JR BLVD, NORTHEAST; 503/287-7254 Housed in a rickety A-frame that looks like a barn fallen from the sky, Billy Ray's is most definitely a dive. But it's friendly, charming, and very much a local staple for eclectic DJs, acoustic musicians, and those who just want to drink a cheap beer and meet some eccentric people. Its next-door papa, Billy Reed's, is preferred by less rough-and-tumble types and hosts great live jazz, blues, and soul on a regular basis. *Cash only; every day; beer and wine; map:GG6*

Bitter End

1981 W BURNSIDE ST, NORTHWEST; 503/517-0179 This British-style pub serves up hefty beer concoctions—an Irish Car Bomb hoists like a feather compared with a Black and Tan (India Pale Ale and Guinness)—to a backdrop of live bluegrass, folk, and rock music. Should the weighty brew leave you groggy, relax on an antique-backed velvet couch or perk up with a game of Foosball. *DIS, MC, V; no checks; every day; full bar; www.bitterendpub.com; map:HH7* &

Blue Monk

3341 SE BELMONT ST, BELMONT; 503/595-0575 With great jazz in the basement and rich meals upstairs, Blue Monk is the kind of place you go for dinner and don't leave for the rest of the night. The unassuming, casual yet classy restaurant features a hearty, pasta-heavy menu with a great, refined selection of microbrews and imported ales. In the downstairs club, indulge in live local and national jazz five nights a week, and peruse a "jazz museum" with a photo history of Portland jazz, past and present. *MC, V; no checks; Tues–Sun; full bar; www.thebluemonk .com; map:HH5* &

Brasserie Montmartre

626 SW PARK AVE, DOWNTOWN; 503/224-5552 At this dressed-up down-town nook, you might catch a Trail Blazer hanging out late at night in his extra-long finest, or see a few head-over-high-heels couples doing their best crayon scribblings on the paper tablecloths. (Prize-winning drawings decorate the walls.) The columnous, high-ceilinged decor is splendid, and the jazz is free and top flight. The charming Brasserie is packed with the professional crowd after work and into the evening; a full bistro menu is served till 3am on weekends and till 1am Sunday through Thursday. (See also review in the Restaurants chapter.) *AE, DIS, MC, V; checks OK; every day; full bar; map:I3* &

Cañita

503 W BURNSIDE ST, OLD TOWN; 503/274-4050 You can't miss Cañita; it's the giant purple-and-orange building breaking up Burnside's dirty gray motif. Week-ends, live Cuban music goes down smoothly with the Cuban restaurant's delicious fresh rum mojitos. It's the only place downtown to gnaw on sugarcane while dancing merengue, a sunny and delightful respite from dreary, rainy days. (See also review in the Restaurants chapter.) *MC, V; no checks; every day; full bar; map:K5* &

Cobalt Lounge

32 NW 3RD AVE, OLD TOWN; 503/225-1003 The former home of one of Portland's dirtiest dives has been cleaned up considerably and now showcases a variety of entertainment, usually of the dance-floor variety. Especially popular is the weekly Queer Night, which features dancing, DJs, and often a wacky pirate theme. *MC, V; no checks; Wed–Sun; full bar; map:K5* &

The Crystal Ballroom

1332 W BURNSIDE ST, DOWNTOWN; 503/225-0047 The chandelier-bedecked icing on the McMenamin brothers' entertainment cake, this refurbished dance parlor/rock club/whatever is a sensory experience to sink your feet into. The floating dance floor can make you feel slightly seasick during a raucous rock show but light on your feet during a ballroom dance soiree. Note the attention to detail: artistic motifs abound on the walls, re-creating the room's past incarnations as a soul shack and hippie hangout. The offerings are eclectic: indie rock shows, jam bands, electronic, hip-hop—even plain-old, non-genre-specific rock. On the second floor, Lola's Room has DJs, dancing, and smaller acts on off nights. *AE, DIS, MC, V; no checks; open during events only; full bar; www .danceonair.com; map:K1* &

Dante's

1 SW 3RD AVE, OLD TOWN; 503/226-6630 This steamy, sexy hangout is dark and red enough to make you assume everyone here is drop-dead gorgeous. An open oil-drum fire blazes near the windows; a naughty stage flirts through its rich, red-velvet curtains; between them, a glowing red bar smolders with anticipation of your imminent intoxication. It's the perfect ambience for a melange of cabaret-style performances, live bands, and such special events as theme parties, go-go girls, and comedy acts. A walk-up pizza window offers late-night slices. *MC, V; no checks; every day; full bar; map:K5* &

Darcelle XV

208 NW 3RD AVE, OLD TOWN; 503/222-5338 Portland's only long-running drag house has been purveying glitz since 1967, thanks to the sharp and teasing, blonde-wigged, false-eyelashed Darcelle herself. The Queen Mother of Portland, Ms. Darcelle is also involved in city politics and holds special shows on voting days, along with a cornucopia of ongoing banquets, drag coronations, and New Year's extravaganzas worthy of champagne and feather boas. Dinner reservations are recommended. *AE, MC, DIS, V; no checks; Wed–Sat; full bar; www .darcellexv.com; map:L5*

The Egyptian Club

3701 SE DIVISION ST, SOUTHEAST; 503/236-8689 This Sapphic social club comes complete with DJ dancing Thursday through Sunday, a wet T-shirt contest every Memorial Day, and free pool on Tuesday nights. What's more, there's an ever-changing roster of special events (open mic, karaoke, dancers), singer-songwriters, and Portland's cutest lesbians. *AE, DIS, MC, V; no checks; every day; full bar; map: II5*

Fernando's Hideaway

824 SW 1ST AVE, DOWNTOWN; 503/248-4709 Spain visits Portland at Fernando's, from the colorfully tiled entryway to the very traditional tapas menu and drink selection (including Licor 43, Spain's national liqueur, and the largest selection of Spanish wines on the West Coast). In the loftlike upstairs, a dance club offers free salsa lessons on Thursday, Friday, and Saturday starting at 9pm. Thursdays are more packed; some weekends, Portland's professional salsa dancers will show up in sequins to set the dance floor afire. (See also review in the Restaurants chapter.) *AE, DIS, MC, V; checks OK; every day; full bar; www.fernandosportland.com; map:G5* &

Fez Ballroom

316 SW 11TH AVE, DOWNTOWN; 503/226-4171 A dark ballroom with a distinctly Middle Eastern ambience up three flights of stairs, the Fez is a classy yet laid-back venue with a good variety of music. From live hip-hop to *desi* (South Asian) parties hosted by *bhangra* DJs playing Punjabi dance music, the club's faraway feel is furthered by rolls of chiffon wafting from the ceiling and comfortable velour couches. It's a great place to escape. *AE, DIS, MC, V; no checks; open during events only; full bar; map:J2* &

Goodfoot Lounge

2845 SE STARK ST, LAURELHURST; 503/239-9292 This unpretentious, bi-level Southeast hangout comes equipped with an upstairs haven of pool tables, but downstairs is where it's really at. The basement bar showcases a range of jazz and funk (with tendencies toward the hippie); on Friday nights, shake a tail feather to Soul Stew, a popular weekly soul night that attracts neighborhood denizens and Portland break-dancers alike. *AE, DIS, MC, V; no checks; every day; beer and wine; map:HH5* &

The Grand Cafe/Andrea's Cha Cha Club

832 SE GRAND AVE, INNER SOUTHEAST; 503/230-1166 The Grand Cafe is a strange place indeed. The sprawling interior is red, red, red, and lined with mirrors. Occasionally the menu stretches into the stratosphere to include such delicacies as ostrich meat or "bull's balls" (Rocky Mountain oysters), which you can nibble while checking out the karaoke action. Downstairs in a smallish, wood-paneled basement party room—Andrea's Cha Cha Club—which is home to some of the most happening Latin dance events around. Get lessons or jump right in with the big kids and pump your pelvis to recorded salsa. *AE, DIS, MC, V; no checks; every day; full bar; map:G9* &

Greek Cusina

404 SW WASHINGTON ST, DOWNTOWN; 503/224-2288 By day, this is a quiet Greek deli marked by a giant purple octopus emerging from its second floor. Every Friday and Saturday night, however, the upstairs bar gets as wild as that unlikely marine creature. Arrive before 9:30pm to watch the transformation: at first the musical trio seems to be dozing off, but before long, the host peps things up by giving Greek dancing lessons. By midnight the floor is packed with as many as 100 people—including comely belly dancers—caught up in frenzied dancing, ouzo drinking, and plate smashing ($2 a plate). *AE, DIS, MC, V; no checks; every day; full bar; www.greekcusina.com; map:I4* &

Harvey's Comedy Club

436 NW 6TH AVE, CHINATOWN; 503/241-0338 The only continuous comedy-only club in town, Harvey's has all the intimacy of an auditorium, but the comedy can be first-rate, often including big national names. There's no drink minimum, but the joke's on you, pawns of nicotine: Harv's is a nonsmoking establishment. *DC, DIS, MC, V; no checks; open during events only; full bar; map:M4* &

Holocene

1001 SE MORRISON ST, INNER SOUTHEAST; 503/239-7639 Holocene is a hip mecca for DJs, dancers, and diners, pairing some of the world's most creative electronic music with a unique, reasonably priced selection of drinks, an intriguing menu, and a gaping concrete dance floor. Electro, house, techno, hip-hop, new wave—you name it, they spin it, even during Sunday brunch (12–5pm). Local and national DJs and live bands bump the system in the stark white, warehouse atmosphere, with a blank screen for overhead projections and visuals. A designated smoking room features rotating art installations. *DIS, MC, V; no checks; Tues–Sun; full bar; www.holocene.org; map:G9* &

Jimmy Mak's

300 NW 10TH AVE, PEARL DISTRICT; 503/295-6542 Jimmy Mak's is nationally renowned as a classy, great place to hear jazz, and with good reason. Legendary jazz drummer Mel Brown (who has worked with Marvin Gaye, Stevie Wonder, and the Temptations) plays with his band in this informal environment every Tuesday and Wednesday; top regional performers like bassist David Friesen and guitarist Dan Balmer hold down the weekends. *AE, DIS, MC, V; no checks; Mon–Sat; full bar; www.jimmymaks.com; map:L3* &

The Know

2022 NE ALBERTA ST, ALBERTA; 503/284-6397 Portland has a longstanding tradition of underground art spaces, basement parties, do-it-yourself venues, and makeshift bike-in theaters. These spots rotate depending upon who's organizing them, but The Know is a continuous venue that truly captures the eclectic feel of Portland's grassroots arts and music scenes. Events range from live jazz to experimental and noise musics; local mini–film festivals in the adjacent microtheater are common, as are online zine-publishing classes and quirky art exhibitions. *Cash only; every day; no alcohol; info@theknow.info; theknow.info; map:FF5*

Level

13 NW 6TH AVE, CHINATOWN; 503/228-8888 Here's another classic example of a vacant theater transformed into something else: this time, a large dance club. Marked by its majestic ceilings and original balcony seats, the vibe here is geared toward mainstream, high-visibility house, trance, hip-hop, and techno DJs. If you get tired of light shows and four-on-the-floor beats, walk through a tunnel to Electrofish, the adjacent sushi bar. *MC, V; no checks; Thu–Sat; full bar; map:K4* &

The Lotus Cardroom

932 SW 3RD AVE, DOWNTOWN; 503/227-6185 When the Lotus opened in 1924, it's unlikely that its patrons could have imagined hordes of sweaty downtowners bumping and grinding to Donna Summer. But that's the setting: dance-floor denizens shaking it to the backdrop of an elaborate antique bar. The dance floor is in the back, though, so those looking to escape the mainstream '70s disco and '80s new wave scene can grab a drink in the central restaurant or out-of-the-way bar. *AE, DIS, MC, V; no checks; every day; full bar; map:G4* &

Meow Meow

520 SE PINE ST, INNER SOUTHEAST; 503/230-2111 Though its atmosphere may feel like a basement or a tomb, most of the bands that play here like it that way; Meow Meow is the best midsize all-ages club in town, hosting a healthy melange of teen-centric pop punk mixed with underground hip-hop, hardcore, and the occasional rock opera. Get jittery on black-cherry soda and licorice in the Glitter Box, the adjacent candy bar/retro video arcade. *Cash only; open during events only; no alcohol; www.themeowmeow.com; map:HH6*

Nocturnal

1800 E BURNSIDE ST, BUCKMAN; 503/239-5900 For such a giant venue, the friendly staff and creative theme nights make Nocturnal seem more like a living room. Upstairs, an airy, colorful room stages all-ages shows, break dancing and tango lessons, and theme-oriented craft nights. Downstairs, over-21s can drink beer and wine, munch on fun snacks (fried potatoes are a house fave), and hit the Scrabble decks, while DJs spin new wave, rockabilly, techno, and more. A newer venue with a clean atmosphere, its patrons are of the more down-to-earth, artier ilk. *MC, V; local checks OK; every day; beer and wine; contact@nocturnalpdx .com; www.nocturnalpdx.com; map:HH5*

The Ohm

31 NW 1ST AVE, OLD TOWN; 503/223-9919 This slick, Miami-style club features an outstanding sound system, surprisingly elegant and tasty food, and after-hours dancing. Entertainments vary from turntable and DJ nights to live bands of all genres. The well-designed interior is complemented by an artfully lit outdoor patio in back. *AE, MC, V; no checks; every day; full bar; www.clubohm.com; map:K6* &

Panorama

341 SW 10TH AVE, DOWNTOWN; 503/221-7262 Sophisticated grown-ups, young rebels, and suburban slummers check each other out in the murky light, multiple bars, and fantasy decor of Panorama, a once-gay club now almost completely straight on weekends. Next door (under the same cover charge) is the Brig, where Panoramians take in a DJ mix of disco and new wave from the '70s and '80s, techno, trance, and high-energy house tunes. Also here is Boxxes, a dark boy-bar with big-screen porn and bingo, karaoke, dating games, and the occasional special-occasion party (such as Pride Week, Madonna's Birthday, episodes of *Will and Grace*). Adjoining the gigantic clubplex—earning its boast as "Portland's Largest Nightclub Complex"—is the Red Cap Garage, a partially open-air bar that is an ideal spot to catch the cruising action on the gay-friendly Pink Strip. *AE, DIS, MC, V; no checks; Tues–Sun (Boxxes, Red Cap), Fri–Sat (Brig, Panorama); full bar; www.boxxes.com; map:J2* &

Ponderosa Lounge at Jubitz Truck Stop

10310 N VANCOUVER WY, NORTH PORTLAND; 503/283-1111 There's more testosterone pumping through this truck stop, near East Delta Park, than there would be on a battlefield. But the dance floor at the Ponderosa Lounge—lined with lit-up tailgates—offers burly drivers, cowboys, and spectators an outlet for their hormones and relief from highway stress. Live country-western bands play seven nights a week. If that's not entertainment enough, you'll find pool tables and video games off to the side. Handily, there's a motel and weigh station next door. *AE, DIS, MC, V; no checks; every day; full bar; map:DD6*

Quest

126 SW 2ND AVE, DOWNTOWN; 503/497-9113 Quest is the most popular club in town for those aged 16 to 21. The kids who stand patiently in weekend lines to disco down '90s-style range from suburban cherubic to urban slick. Some of Portland's most wizardly DJs spin industrial, house, hip-hop, and retro Thursday through Sunday. This place is smokier than most, but if you can't drink, you gotta indulge somehow; for those who don't dance, there's pool. *Cash only; open during events only; no alcohol; map:J6*

The Red Sea

318 SW 3RD AVE, DOWNTOWN; 503/241-5450 One of the more internationally and racially diverse crowds in town throbs in sweaty, cathartic unison on the expanded dance floor in this oddly shaped, right-angle hideaway behind an Ethiopian restaurant. Reggae, dance hall, and hip-hop DJs and live bands play regular gigs to a lively, dance-passionate crowd. The drinks are stiff, and the vibes and tunes continue even after the bartender stops pouring. *AE, MC, V; no checks; Wed–Sun; full bar; map:J5* &

Roseland Theater

10 NW 6TH AVE, CHINATOWN; 503/224-2038 Once a two-story Apostolic Faith church, the Roseland is now a comfortable midsize concert hall for mostly out-of-town acts. It's smoky, boozy, and noisy with metal, rock, hip-hop, and folk music (some shows are all ages). Whether you dance or not, be prepared to sweat, especially in the balcony, which commands an excellent view of the stage. The Roseland also has a full restaurant and bar, with separate stage, downstairs. *Cash only; open during events only; full bar; www.doubletee.com; map:K4* &

Spare Room

4830 NE 42ND AVE, NORTHEAST; 503/287-5800 This twinkle-lit, mirror-walled bar is packed with regulars (septuagenarians and hipsters alike) tearing it up to swing, rock, and blues on the dance floor. Tuesday through Friday nights, Teri and Larry—a charming, husband-and-wife cover band—make cute-cheesy "married couple" jokes and take pop/rock requests. *AE, MC, V; no checks; every day; full bar; map:FF4* &

Three Sisters

1125 SW STARK ST, DOWNTOWN; 503/228-0486 If you're feeling adventurous, get an eyeful at the heart and soul of Portland's queer district. This all-male revue goes full monty, and its strippers have exceptional gymnastic skills besides, often swinging from monkey bars and literally hanging from the rafters. It's a clean, festive environment, usually populated equally with gay boys and women having bachelorette parties. However, the cover goes up from $3 to $6 for those with the double-X chromosome. *MC, DIS, V; no checks; Wed–Sat; beer and wine; map:J2*

1201 Club

1201 SW 12TH AVE, DOWNTOWN; 503/225-1201 Portland has its share of dance clubs, but the 1201's small, airy room has a unique, mellow charm. Perhaps it's the dark, modern interior—hip, but not oppressively so—or the dance floor, which keeps you at an intimate eye-level with the DJ. A good selection of up-and-coming, regional techno, down-tempo, and other dance music spins regularly on 1201's decks. *MC, V; no checks; Tues–Sat; full bar; map:H1* &

The Viscount Ballroom

722 E BURNSIDE ST, INNER SOUTHEAST; 503/233-7855 The Art Deco ballroom of this renovated Masonic Temple is lovely, ringed by a balcony and adjoining salons that are perfect for viewing the action from afar or enjoying a quiet tête-à-tête with a new partner. Live bands and DJs run the gamut from big band to salsa; on weekends, dinner shows and dancing feel almost glamorous. Lessons are free with cover ($6–$25 for dinner shows) about an hour before the music starts. *MC, V; no checks; Mon, Tues, Fri, Sat; full bar; www.viscountballroom.com; map:HH6* &

Wallbangers

915 SW 2ND AVE, DOWNTOWN; 503/274-4386 Dueling pianos are center stage at this rollicking, audience-request establishment. If you've never heard two madcap musicians at matching, fire-engine-red keyboards trading licks of Jerry Lee Lewis's "Great Balls of Fire," here's where you can see what you've been missing. The pianists lead partygoers in rounds of college fight songs, Irish jigs, and Billy Joel's "Piano Man" as they munch on Wally's Wieners and other snacks. *AE, MC, V; no checks; Tue–Sat (lunch Mon–Fri); full bar; www.wallbangers.net; map:G5* &

Wilf's Restaurant and Piano Bar

800 NW 6TH AVE (UNION STATION), RIVER DISTRICT; 503/223-0070 The gold-flecked red-velvet wallpaper fell victim to Wilf's 1995 remodel, but this piano bar in the train station has retained its old-fashioned nightclub feel. The Rat Pack would be proud. The bar makes an excellent cosmopolitan, served in its own beaker and nested in a bowl of ice. There's cabaret every Tuesday night; solo pianists play Sinatra-like standards Thursday to Saturday. *AE, DC, MC, V; no checks; Mon–Sat; full bar; wilfs.citysearch.com; map:N4* &

Bars, Pubs, and Taverns

The Alibi

4024 N INTERSTATE AVE, NORTH PORTLAND; 503/287-5335 Lured here by the hypnotic, Route 66–like pageantry of neon that throws a glow over Interstate Avenue, you don't need an alibi to go to the Alibi. It's simply one of Portland's best blasts from the past, an authentic tiki lounge where the service is sharp and the waitstaff all wear palm trees on their shirts. Friendly karaoke hosts lead a wholesome lung-powered jamboree starting at 9pm, Wednesday through Saturday nights. (A complimentary midnight buffet makes Saturday really busy, so if you're itching to bust a move, try the Thursday-night fest.) *AE, DIS, MC, V; no checks; every day; full bar; map:FF6*

Bar of the Gods

4801 SE HAWTHORNE BLVD, HAWTHORNE; 503/232-2037 From its name, you might expect an exalted temple of insobriety, but instead you'll find a small, dark, very personable, well-populated hole-in-the-wall. Nods to its sobriquet are given in various depictions of the Bacchae, in the grapevine-wrapped beams and in the regular mixing of an eclectic crowd that spans Portland's social strata. *MC, V; no checks; every day; full bar; map:HH4* &

Basta's Trattoria

410 NW 21ST AVE, NORTHWEST; 503/274-1572 Basta's vast selection of wine and drinks are perfectly poured by its handsome and knowledgeable bartenders and, despite the swanky Roman-style decor, it's all done in a decidedly comfy environment. Jovial owner Marco Frattarolli enjoys the fruits of his own establishment at night, chatting up customers as barkeep. The best time to go, however, is during the much-too-short happy hour (5–6pm weekdays), when upscale Italian appetizers and cocktails are slashed to the near-crazy price of $3 each. (See also review in the Restaurants chapter.) *AE, MC, V; no checks; every day; full bar; map:HH7* &

Beulahland

118 NE 28TH AVE, LAURELHURST; 503/235-2794 A museum-quality assortment of quirky old restaurant and bar fixtures have been hauled out of retirement and placed into service at Beulahland, creating an atmosphere rich in Mayberryesque character. Oddball signage, vintage advertising paraphernalia, and quirky local art completes the *mise-en-scène* that draws the neighborhood's vintagewear denizens. In keeping with the Southern-fried atmosphere, it tends to get steamy rather quickly in here. But respite from the heat can be taken on the charming back patio. *MC, V; no checks; every day; beer and wine; map:HH5* &

Biddy McGraw's

6000 NE GLISAN ST, NORTHEAST; 503/233-1178 If a sweaty, smoky, jigging joint fits the bill, Biddy's is your place. You'll swoon to hear half the patrons using a brogue straight from the land o' the green. And along with the good times, these folks have brought their politics from the Old Country: the whitewashed walls are decked with posters urging sentiments such as all-party peace talks. You can get Guinness as well as a full spectrum of drafts, hard cider, an Irish Sunday brunch—and whiskeys, of course. Celtic, Irish, and rock musicians ignite the crowd into a toe-to-the-sky frenzy. *MC, V; no checks; every day; full bar; www.biddys.com; map:HH4* &

Bush Garden

900 SW MORRISON ST, DOWNTOWN; 503/226-7181 You might not expect to find such a scene in the middle of a serene Japanese restaurant (complete with low tables), but this is one of the most jamming karaoke spots around. Bold college students, good-time Asian businessmen, and lovely Nordstrom clerks take turns fulfilling their secret rock-star dreams on stage. Occasionally, they'll switch off karaoke in lieu of a live band or DJs; check local listings to see what will accompany your sake sipping. (See also review in the Restaurants chapter.) *AE, DC, DIS, MC, V; no checks; every day; full bar; map:I2* &

Captain Ankeny's Well

50 SW 3RD AVE, OLD TOWN; 503/223-1375 Named after a sailor who left his stamp on Old Town, this pizza-and-potables pit stop has become a home for a different kind of traveler. On any given day you can catch a gaggle of bike messengers hanging around the outdoor tables or staring out of the glass-walled bar. Captain Ankeny's has a full bar but is best known for its wide variety of beers (20 on tap, 20 in bottles) and the fact that you can order up a pitcher as you watch downtown Portland passing by. *AE, MC, V; no checks; every day; full bar; www.ankenys.com; map:J5* &

Cassidy's

1331 SW WASHINGTON ST, DOWNTOWN; 503/223-0054 The dim, circa-1900 environs are conducive to heavy thoughts and heavier conversation. In this night-owl place, you can knock 'em back until 2:30am in the company of personable staff and off-duty barkeeps from surrounding establishments. Keep an eye on the windows, as the entertaining antics of Cassidy's colorful neighbors often transpire within full view of the bar. For a late-night meal—maybe a veggie quesadilla or a plate of calamari with roasted peppers—it doesn't get much better than this. *AE, DC, DIS, MC, V; no checks; every day; full bar; www.cassidysrestaurant.com; map:J1* &

Chopsticks Express II

2651 E BURNSIDE ST, LAURELHURST; 503/234-6171 This divey lounge in the back of a fast-food Chinese restaurant is a popular hub for Portland karaoke fanatics. Sometimes frequented by members of semifamous local rock bands, from Quasi to Sleater-Kinney to Unwound, it's better to go early to ensure maximum performance time—the place can pack quickly, especially on weekends. Karaoke starts at 9pm Monday through Saturday. *V; no checks; every day; full bar; map:HH5*

Dots Café

2521 SE CLINTON ST, CLINTON; 503/235-0203 The popularity of this Clinton nightspot may be inversely related to its waitstaff's seeming disdain for patrons. Regardless, the drinks and vegan-friendly menu are creative and affordable. The ambience is appropriately kitsch, dark, and adorned with doe-eyed Margaret Keane paintings. And it's a sure thing you'll be gazing at a healthy cross section of Portland hipsters by night's end. (See also review in the Restaurants chapter.) *No credit cards; checks OK; evervy day; full bar; map:II5* &

Dragonfish Asian Café

909 SW PARK AVE (PARAMOUNT HOTEL), DOWNTOWN; 503/243-5991 If there's one thing Dragonfish has a lot of, it's spunk—not what you'd expect for the hotel lounge of the fancy Paramount. Its shiny red ambience is achieved through comfy couches, perky waitstaff, and a flashing wall of decorative pachinko machines (the Japanese equivalent to pinball). However, though it's a fun atmosphere, you might want to get serious about the happy-hour sushi specials from 4 to 6pm and 10pm to close; $1.45 is an absurdly cheap price for spicy tuna rolls. (See also review in the Restaurants chapter.) *AE, DIS, MC, V; no checks; every day; full bar; www.dragonfishcafe.com; map:H2* &

East Chinatown Lounge

322 NW EVERETT ST, CHINATOWN; 503/226-1569 East is smaller than it looks; it's dark and red and, if you're not careful, you might run into one of its mirrored walls. The bar's sleek, expensive modern interior attracts a bevy of upper-crust hipsters and aspiring graphic designers; its selection of DJs spinning great new wave and hip-hop attracts everyone else—but forget about dancing unless you do it on the sidewalk outside. Special drinks include the daunting Wasabi Bloody Mary. *AE, MC, V; no checks; Tues–Sun; full bar; map:L5* &

820 Lounge at Mint

820 N RUSSELL ST, ALBINA; 503/284-5518 The lounge adjoining Mint—a trendy, new, upscale restaurant with a neighborhood feel—is perfect for those hoping to escape the hustle of NW 23rd. The dark, murky interior lends a sense of mystery, but the drinks are überfresh, so you feel more like you're on a night train to Paris than hanging out in a cave. (See review of Mint in the Restaurants chapter.) *AE, MC, V; no checks; Wed–Sat; full bar; map:GG6* &

Goose Hollow Inn

1927 SW JEFFERSON ST, GOOSE HOLLOW; 503/228-7010 For decades, the Goose was a hotbed of political debate and discussion. Not surprisingly, it remains a social institution, given its continued ownership by former Portland Mayor J. E. "Bud" Clark, the JFK of city politics. Join the hundreds who came before you and surreptitiously carve your initials into a dark wooden booth. Or sink your teeth into one of the thick Reuben sandwiches that have made this place as much a classic as the proudly displayed "Expose Yourself to Art" poster, featuring Clark flashing one of Portland's street sculptures. *MC, V; checks OK; every day; beer and wine; map:HH7* &

The Gypsy

625 NW 21ST AVE, NORTHWEST; 503/796-1859 The retro Gypsy ought to hand out vintage bathing trunks with every order, because you can practically swim in their gigantic, yummy drinks. The excellent collection of pinball art, Sputnik-style space-age fixtures, and extra-comfy booths are more slick than kitsch for that retro-NASA vibe, but without all of the mildew. *AE, DIS, MC, V; no checks; every day; full bar; map:HH7* &

Harborside

0309 SW MONTGOMERY ST, RIVERPLACE; 503/220-1865 The lounge at McCormick & Schmick's RiverPlace restaurant is perhaps the best water-front drinking-with-a-view spot in Portland. The crowd tends toward yuppie elders in business casual, but the beer selection is large—Full Sail is brewed right next door—and you can get a decent mixed drink as well. Park yourself near one of the floor-to-ceiling windows and look out onto the esplanade and the Willamette beyond. From 4 to 6pm and 9:30pm to closing, there are killer happy-hour specials: under $3 a plate with a $3 minimum drink. (See also McCormick & Schmick's review in the Restaurants chapter.) *AE, DC, MC, V; no checks; every day; full bar; map:C5* &

The Heathman Hotel

1001 SW BROADWAY, DOWNTOWN; 503/241-4100 The bars in the Heathman are among Portland's swankiest. There's the cool ambience of the Marble Bar, where symphony crowds rendezvous around the grand piano after a performance and executives convene for lunch; the high-ceilinged Lobby Lounge and Tea Court is as formal as a Tudor drawing room, with a fire blazing in the hearth. For a delicious light meal, a gourmet bar menu is served in both of the ground-floor bars. (See also review in the Restaurants chapter.) *AE, DC, DIS, MC, V; no checks; every day; full bar; www.heathmanhotel.com; map:G2* &

Horse Brass Pub

4534 SE BELMONT ST, SOUTHEAST; 503/232-2202 Truly a slice of merry olde England, the Horse Brass is a magnet for British expats and Portland Anglophiles alike. It's also a favorite of beer fanatics, with more than 50 microbrews, imports, and cask-conditioned ales. The convivial bar staff will guide you to the perfect pint while flatly refusing any cocktail order more complex than gin and tonic. Enjoy your brew over a hot game of darts on one of the four highly competitive boards. The Brass also serves an extensive selection of Scotch and other whiskeys. English pub fare, served well into the evening, is filling. *AE, DIS, MC, V; no checks; every day; full bar; www.horsebrass.com; map:HH4* &

Huber's

411 SW 3RD AVE, DOWNTOWN; 503/228-5686 Said to be Portland's oldest extant bar (it opened in 1879), Huber's is a fabulous rendezvous spot for famous, flaming Spanish coffees and turkey sandwiches—two great tastes that actually go well together. Its Gothic architecture and Old World panache add to the flair of the tableside service. Although the menu has more bird recipes than a post-Thanksgiving weekend, it's the passing sidewalk show that lures regulars and tourists alike. *AE, DC, DIS, MC, V; no checks; Mon–Sat; full bar; map:I5* &

Hung Far Low

112 NW 4TH AVE, CHINATOWN; 503/223-8686 This small, dark bar in the back corner of a brightly lit restaurant (which, by virtue of its name, has made the pages of *National Lampoon*) is the place to meet friends for a preshow drink. The cocktails are among the strongest and cheapest in the whole city; the AM radio pumping through the speakers, the '70s mystical decor, and the eccentric bartenders make it a near-Lynchian experience. *MC, V; no checks; every day; full bar; map:K5*

Jake's Grill

611 SW 10TH AVE (GOVERNOR HOTEL), DOWNTOWN; 503/241-2100 Career dress dominates at the Grill, located in the exquisitely refurbished Governor Hotel. But all walks of Portland life gravitate here after work to see the original 1909 mosaic tiled floor, slow-turning fans, gold-framed mirrors, and big-game heads staring down at the plates of onion rings on the bar. The Grill's parent establishment, **JAKE'S FAMOUS CRAWFISH** (401 SW 12th Ave, Downtown; 503/226-1419; map: J2), is much the same, but with a little less elbow room. (See also review in the Restaurants chapter.) *AE, DIS, MC, V; no checks; every day; full bar; map:I2*

Laurelthirst Public House

2958 NE GLISAN ST, LAURELHURST; 503/232-1504 If it were located near a college campus, the Hacky Sack types would simply call this chill place "home." Tavern by night, cafe by day, the Laurelthirst always has someone hanging out—either munching on a late breakfast, playing pool with a pitcher of brew, or taking in live local music. A beautiful antique bar and comfy leather booths add to the zero-pretension atmosphere. On the billiards side, you can cram around a small table and catch up on gossip. In the main section, live bands—blues, rock, acoustic—keep the karma flowing and get people dancing. *AE, MC, V; no checks; every day; full bar; map:HH5* &

Madame Butterfly

425 SW STARK ST, DOWNTOWN; 503/525-0033 You may be intrigued by Madame Butterfly's cuisine—Japanese "with a French flair"—but perplexed by its lack of a bigger dance floor. This swank sushi bar boasts refreshing cucumber margaritas and an excellent selection of DJs spinning electronic and hip-hop music amid a soft-lit, almost dainty, glassy decor. An igloo-like reflective light sculpture gives the place more of a club feel. (See also review in the Restaurants chapter.) *AE, MC, V; no checks; every day; full bar; map:I4* &

The Matador

1967 W BURNSIDE ST, NORTHWEST; 503/222-5822 Every town worth its salt has at least one perfect dive bar, and Portland is no exception. The Matador has all the essentials: an old jukebox loaded with esoteric classics, cheap drinks that'll put hair on your chest, a couple of well-used pool tables, lots of booths, and plenty of seedy patrons to keep the adrenaline flowing. If it's *too* flowing, as the popular hangout is wont to be, try walking up the block to the second-most-perfect dive bar in Portland,

Tony's Tavern (1955 W Burnside St; 503/228-4574). *MC, V; no checks; every day; full bar; map:HH7* &

M Bar

417 NW 21ST AVE, NORTHWEST; 503/228-6614 If you're in the mood for good conversation and a reasonably priced glass of beer or wine, squeeze yourself into what is certainly the tiniest bar in town. The bar itself seats only five people (uncomfortably), but with all walls practically within reach and the few tables easily within earshot, everyone weighs in on the topic at hand. There is sidewalk seating for the claustrophobic. *Cash only; every day; beer and wine; map:HH7*

Produce Row Cafe

204 SE OAK ST, INNER SOUTHEAST; 503/232-8355 Hunker down at a rough-hewn table on the Produce Row patio and contemplate a selection of 200 bottled beers, 29 drafts, and fresh cider. Much loved since it opened in the early '70s, the Row is a friendly spot to mix with a melange of Portlanders as freight trains whistle past. Monday-night jazz and Tuesday-night bluegrass jam sessions draw supportive friends and music lovers, while Wednesday's open mic attracts hopeful musicians. In summer, the back deck is filled with imbibers enjoying an open sky framed by the neighborhood's industrial walls. *No credit cards; checks OK; every day; beer and wine; map:I9* &

Pub at the End of the Universe

4107 SE 28TH AVE, BROOKLYN; 503/238-9355 It's not far-fetched to believe that liberal Reed College is, indeed, the End of the Universe. Many Reed students frequent this hard-to-find pub, yukking it up with local residents, shooting pool, avoiding being bull's-eyed by the continuous dart games going down, and drinkin' 'em down in this lounge-away-from-home atmosphere. *MC, V; no checks; every day; beer and wine; map:II5* &

Rialto Poolroom Bar and Cafe

529 SW 4TH AVE, DOWNTOWN; 503/228-7605 A hustler's paradise, this pool hall also boasts video poker, a great jukebox (essential to any shark's game), and a basement wonderland of off-track betting. Sixteen pool tables usually ensure a weekday table, but big booths abound if you've gotta wait your turn. Not only are the drinks generous and reasonably priced, but the cheese fries are to die for. *AE, DC, MC, V; no checks; every day; full bar; map:I5* &

Sam's Hollywood Billiards

1845 NE 41ST AVE, HOLLYWOOD; 503/282-8266 A mural on an outside wall—of men immersed in a billiards game—tips off visitors that pool sharks may lurk within. But it's not just Minnesota Fats types who find joy here. All sorts gather at Sam's on weekends to test their hand-eye coordination on 10 regulation-size (plus a couple snooker) tables. Sunday and Wednesday tournaments heat up the action. *MC, V; no checks; every day; full bar; map:GG4*

Saucebox

214 SW BROADWAY, DOWNTOWN; 503/241-3393 The artfully appointed interior is awash with well-coiffed up-and-comers—and occasional visiting celebrities like Vince Vaughn and Benicio del Toro—enjoying expensive but perfect cocktails alongside tasty appetizers. When the kitchen closes, the DJ turns up the hot wax, including house, electro, down-tempo, and nu-jazz. Exceptionally attractive staff accept the moony stares of a devoted public as their due, without the slightest bit of pretension or conceit. (See also review in the Restaurants chapter.) *AE, DC, MC, V; local checks only; Tues–Sat; full bar; map:J4* &

Shanghai Tunnel

211 SW ANKENY ST, OLD TOWN; 503/220-4001 Portland sits atop a maze of tunnels just below its blacktop, leftovers from the days when "Puddletown" was a port of call for sailors and smugglers. Most of the passageways were bricked up long ago—a defense, perhaps, against the ghosts rumored to reside there. But at this subterranean hipster oasis, you can enjoy a Pabst Blue Ribbon or Spanish coffee, a game of pool, or a yummy bowl of noodles while you're waiting for your "spirited" captain to reassign you. *MC, V; no checks; every day; full bar; map:J6* &

Space Room at the Brite Spot

4800 SE HAWTHORNE BLVD, HAWTHORNE; 503/235-8303 Divey, tacky, and oh-so-'80s—so much so that even *Wonder Years* cherub Fred Savage has been sighted here—the Space Room's Saturn lamps and glowing murals of Portland (downtown on the south wall, Mount Tabor on the north) beckon Southeast hipsters and old-school regulars alike. Watch out for the inexpensive yet dramatically strong cocktails: a lone mai tai could blast you to Neptune. *MC, V; no checks; every day; full bar; map:HH4* &

Tube

13-D NW 3RD AVE, OLD TOWN; 503/241-8823 Überhip and extra-sterile, Tube's white-and-clear atmosphere could be a space station, a surgical theater, or the inside of a television. The ultramodern bar was built so that experimental films could be projected on its windows, though it's so tiny you'll wonder how they could even fit a projector inside. Wear your best German Spock outfit and kick it with the bar staff. *No credit cards; checks OK; every day; full bar; map:K5*

Uptown Billiards Club

120 NW 23RD AVE, NORTHWEST; 503/226-6909 Uptown Billiards is a find for pool aficionados who detest cigarette smoke clouding their vision: it's a smoke-free cueing zone in Northwest's tony zone. With 10 immaculate replicas of French-style billiards tables, exposed brick walls, and a liberal supply of pool stools, this posh hall is a great place to shoot some serious stick, though be prepared for serious drink prices as well. On occasion the club hosts a cigar night, but afterward they air the place out, erasing any malodorous memories. *AE, MC, V; no checks; Tues–Sun; full bar; map:HH7*

A SHORT HISTORY OF PORTLAND BREWING

Oregon's Liquor Control Commission watches the flow of alcohol like a hawk, which may be one explanation for the proliferation of independent breweries in Portland: nothing does more for a vice than making it harder to get.

Henry Saxer, a German immigrant, opened Portland's first brewery in 1852. After 10 years, he sold his operation to another German, Henry Weinhard, who in 1863 opened the City Brewery in the Pearl District, a next-door neighbor to what is now Powell's City of Books. The brewery gave the city a distinct, wafting-hops smell for 136 years, until its 1999 closure. Weinhard loved his beer. In 1888, for the unveiling of the Skidmore Fountain, he offered to pump his special brew through the fountain from the brewery using fire hoses—a spectacular plan that was nixed by the fire chief. Thirty-one years later, all alcohol everywhere was nixed by the U.S. government in a 13-year lapse of judgment known as Prohibition. Weinhard managed to get through the drought by manufacturing soft drinks and, eventually, by merging with the Portland Brewing Company owned by Arnold I. Blitz.

Blitz-Weinhard had no competition until 1981. The Cartwright Brewing Company established in that year didn't last, but the subsequent decade brought an onslaught of new breweries. The vineyard-owning Ponzi Brothers opened BridgePort Brewing in 1984. A year later, Kurt and Rob Widmer established the German-style Widmer

Veritable Quandary

1220 SW 1ST AVE, DOWNTOWN; 503/227-7342 The narrow, galleylike shape of this exposed brick and dark-wood bar encourages body contact. By day, you rub up against corporate types and politicos who come for the efficient business lunches. After dark, a dressy crowd moves in and transforms the VQ into a sultry late-night spot with outdoor seating that invites you to kiss your date under the moonlight. (See also review in the Restaurants chapter.) *AE, DC, DIS, MC, V; no checks; every day; full bar; www.veritablequandary.com; map:F4* &

Virginia Cafe

725 SW PARK AVE, DOWNTOWN; 503/227-0033 This homey mainstay has twice survived fire and flood—but never famine, as the bar food is hearty and moderately priced. Historical photos of Portland adorn the walls, and all sorts of urbanites stop in for a drink before catching a film at the nearby Guild Theatre. A visit to the ladies' room, with its napkin art and vintage magazine ads, is a cultural experience. *MC, V; no checks; every day; full bar; map:I3*

Windows Skyroom & Terrace

1021 NE GRAND AVE (RED LION), NEAR LLOYD CENTER; 503/235-2100 With all of Portland's glamorous hotel bars, it seems unlikely that one of the best is in a Red Lion. Yet, nesting at the very top of the chain hotel near the Convention Center, sits

Brothers Brewing Company; their wildly popular hefeweizen (wheat beer) was considered a first step in creating mass customer interest in craft beers.

It was also in 1985 that the Oregon legislature passed a law enabling brewers to sell beer directly to the public. Mike and Brian McMenamin immediately opened a small brewery and tavern in the Hillsdale neighborhood. In the years since then, the McMenamin brothers have established a brewing-based empire of more than 50 pubs, theaters, music venues, and inns.

In 1987, the Full Sail Brewing Company—one of the first to market its product in bottles—was established an hour's drive east of Portland in Hood River. (Today, Full Sail is the country's only brewery owned by its employees.) By 1990, Portland was honored as "America's Microbrew Capital," with more microbreweries and brewpubs than any other city in the country.

Today, microbrewing has become an economic cornerstone in Portland, thanks in part to the vast Oregon Brewers Guild, a nonprofit that lobbies for policy and protection of Portland's brewing industry while promoting what matters most in a craft quality beer: flavor. And each July, the Oregon Brewers Festival welcomes more than 80,000 beer enthusiasts to a three-day celebration of the art of brewing in Gov. Tom McCall Waterfront Park.

—*Julianne Shepherd*

Windows Skyroom. Its vantage point, from just across the river, affords the best view of downtown in the whole city. Drinks are stiff at hotel prices, but the excellent vista—from an outdoor patio terrace—is worth the extra expense. *DIS, MC, V; no checks; Mon–Sat; full bar; map:GG6* &

Brewpubs

Alameda Brewhouse

4765 NE FREMONT ST, BEAUMONT; 503/460-9025 This modern brewpub boasts huge fiberglass partitions, lofty ceilings, and a long, sinuous bar to complement its tasty selection of handcrafted ales—made distinct with ingredients like sage, juniper, and Willamette Valley fruit. Above-average pub fare includes classics like fish-and-chips and burgers with big leafy salads but ventures into less standard territory with tahini-soy tiger prawns, salmon gyros, and whiskey barbecue baby-back ribs, augmenting the Alameda's one-of-a-kind feel. Located in a charming (even "cute") neighborhood, this is not your typical brewpub. *AE, MC, V; no checks; every day; full bar; map:FF4* &

BridgePort Brew Pub

1313 NW MARSHALL ST, PEARL DISTRICT; 503/241-3612 The Ponzi family's vision of producing beer as good and as complex as their Oregon wines was realized in 1984 with the opening of this self-contained brewery and pizza pub. After several expansions and a change in ownership, this former cordage factory (with gargantuan wooden rafters) remains a favorite nightspot for 20-ounce pints of thick, creamy Black Strap Stout or floral India Pale Ale. Great pizza and Caesar salads add to the appeal. The upper Pearl locale, near cobblestone streets and busy loading docks, is the essence of Northwest Portland—though an influx of *Fountainhead*-like condos and the Portland Streetcar are transforming the landscape. *MC, V; checks OK; every day; beer and wine; www.bridgeportbrew.com; map:O1* &

Laurelwood Public House & Brewery

1728 NE 40TH AVE, HOLLYWOOD; 503/282-0622 A bright neighborhood pub with Applebee's-like decor, this is a place where brewskis and kidskis mix harmoniously—where adults can enjoy a finely crafted brew while children run wild in the adjoining play area. Though not the most romantic of atmospheres, it is friendly to moms and pops looking to relax in adult ambience without having to leave the kids behind. And the food meets the challenge: artichoke chicken, grilled sirloin, Thai peanut salad, and a portobello mushroom and roasted-garlic linguine complement a long list of burgers and other sandwiches. *MC, V; local checks OK; every day; beer and wine; map:GG4* &

The Lucky Labrador

915 SE HAWTHORNE BLVD, SOUTHEAST; 503/236-3555 / 7675 SW CAPITOL HWY, MULTNOMAH VILLAGE; 503/244-2537 Opened by a band of BridgePort defectors, this eastside hangout follows a path similar to its crosstown model with an easygoing atmosphere and flavorful, British-inspired brews. Instead of filling up on pizza, pub sandwiches, and curried bento dishes, leave room for beer consumption. A vast covered patio, with nearly three dozen picnic tables, welcomes your favorite canine. Several brews are named after dogs—Black Lab Stout, Dog Day India Pale Ale, Top Dog Extra Special Ale—and if you're the owner of a lab, you can bring a photo for framing and wall-hanging. The Multnomah Village location occupies a vintage Masonic meeting house . . . and *does* have pizza. *DIS, MC, V; checks OK; every day; beer and wine; pub@luckylab.com; www.luckylab.com; map:HH6; map: JJ7* &

McMenamins

MULTIPLE LOCATIONS; 503/669-8610 Like the old Roman Empire, the McMenamins' pub chain (spawned in 1983 when Mike and Brian McMenamin opened the Barley Mill Pub) continues to expand into all corners of the Northwest, from Roseburg north to Seattle. Its Vatican City, if you will, is the **CRYSTAL BALLROOM** (see Music, Clubs, and Lounges in this chapter), a renovated entertainment venue glowing with so much history that the founders commissioned an entire book to be written about it. Beneath the ballroom sits **RINGLER'S** (1332 W Burnside St, Downtown; 503/225-0543; full bar; map:K1), a youthful hot spot to shoot pool, practice pickup lines, and dance to DJ hip-hop on unlikely Mondays.

From this epicenter, all roads lead out to other McMenamins. While each pub has its own quirky traits, all maintain a few sacred characteristics—namely, great beer and wine (produced at the McMenamins' local brewery and winery, of course), crispy fries and burgers, and an unintrusive, hippie-meets-yuppie ambience. At the **MISSION THEATER AND PUB** (1624 NW Glisan St, Northwest; 503/223-4031; beer and wine; map:M1), where McMenamins has its head offices, you can sink into a comfy couch and sip on a trademark intoxicant while enjoying a second-run film—or a Blazers game of movie-epic proportions. Similarly, the **BAGDAD THEATER AND PUB** (3710 SE Hawthorne Blvd, Hawthorne; 503/230-0895; beer and wine; map:HH5) offers cheap dollar films in a cavernous (and haunted!) big-screen environment reminiscent of cinema's halcyon days. Neighborhood residents gather at outdoor tables at the adjacent pub to gawk at passing tourists. The McMenamins' signature mosaic design and recurrent court-jester theme mark both the Mission and Bagdad theaters. **ST. JOHNS PUB AND THEATER** (8203 N Ivanhoe St, Saint Johns; 503/283-8520; full bar; map:EE9) has a nice pub feel and a beautiful historic dome in which to catch second-run films and occasional rock or bluegrass shows. Around the corner from the Bagdad lies **GREATER TRUMPS** (1520 SE 37th Ave, Hawthorne; 503/235-4530; beer and wine; map:HH5), a smoky yet alluring cigar-and-port room.

Less cinematic and more pragmatic is the **FULTON PUB AND BREWERY** (0618 SW Nebraska St, Southwest; 503/246-9530; beer and wine; map:II6), a compact eatery south of downtown with a functional and friendly flower-trimmed beer garden out back. The **BLUE MOON TAVERN** (432 NW 21st Ave, Northwest; 503/223-3184; beer and wine; map:HH7) and the **BARLEY MILL PUB** (1629 SE Hawthorne Blvd, Southeast; 503/231-1492; beer and wine; map:HH5) are casual lunch and dinner neighborhood joints with sidewalk seating. The **MARKET STREET PUB** (1525 SW Park St, Ste 100A, Downtown; 503/497-0160; full bar; map:F1) caters to urbanites and Portland State students alike. Equally upscale—if upscale could be applied to a pub chain—is **THE RAM'S HEAD** (2282 NW Hoyt St, Northwest; 503/221-0098; full bar; map:GG7), fronting bustling NW 23rd Avenue. Perhaps the hippest of the pubs is **RINGLER'S ANNEX** (1223 SW Stark St, Downtown; 503/525-0520; full bar; map:J2), an old radio station wedged into a pie-cut corner and redesigned into a three-level den of revelry. The dank basement bar is moody and intriguing, lit predominantly by dripping candles, while the top seating area offers a nice view.

McMenamins operate three other historic properties in Greater Portland. The **WHITE EAGLE ROCK 'N' ROLL HOTEL** (836 N Russell St, Albina; 503/282-6810; map:GG6), a circa-1905 former brothel and opium den in the North Portland industrial district, has live bands seven nights a week and European-style sleeping rooms on the second floor. The **KENNEDY SCHOOL** (5736 NE 33rd Ave, Northeast; 503/249-3983; full bar; map:FF5) is a really pleasing pub, performance space, movie theater, and bed-and-breakfast-style inn (see review in the Lodgings chapter) housed in a charming old elementary school that the brothers rescued from bulldozers. **EDGEFIELD** (2126 SW Halsey St, Troutdale; 503/669-8610; full bar) is a rambling former poor farm located at the gateway to the Columbia Gorge. It combines multiple pubs and restaurants with a working vineyard and winery, distillery, live stage, movie theater, and inn (see review in the Lodgings chapter). *AE, DIS, MC, V; checks OK; every day; www.mcmenamins.com*

Port Halling Brewing Company

333 N MAIN ST, GRESHAM; 503/674-4906 Nautical decor dominates at this suburban establishment. Imaginative handcrafted beers—the Knaughty Weissen Wheat Beer boasts "banana, clove, and bubblegum characteristics"—are served in an atmosphere of casual elegance with a beautiful fireplace and a children's play area. Menu offerings range from Chilean blue mussels and Jamaican jerk-chicken salad to steak and seafood entrees, pizzas, and sandwiches. Live bands perform Thursday through Saturday nights. *AE, MC, V; no checks; every day; full bar; www.porthallingbrewing.com* &

Portland Brewing Company

2730 NW 31ST AVE, NORTHWEST; 503/228-5269 Founded in 1986, Portland Brewing has survived financial turmoil and a glutted, cutthroat microbrew market. After selling its Pearl District pub (the Flanders Street Brewery and Pub), it tightened its belt and refocused on what it does best: making affable specialty beers and running a convivial in-house restaurant. The flagship MacTarnahan's Ale is its Scottish beacon of light, while seasonal brews, such as a German-style Oktoberfest, are equally robust and drinkable. The Brewhouse Taproom and Grill is highlighted by two large copper kettles and a menu that features honey-beer steamer clams and baby back ribs prepared with Haystack Black Porter. *AE, MC, V; checks OK; every day; beer and wine; info@macsbeer.com; www.macsbeer.com; map:GG8*

The Rock Bottom Brewpub

206 SW MORRISON ST, DOWNTOWN; 503/796-2739 They boldly came north from Boulder, Colorado, in 1995 with a gutsy idea: to bring a chain of Rocky Mountain brewpubs to the very city known for starting the microbrew trend. Corporate interlopers always are met with suspicion around these parts. But such wariness has done little to deter the masses from making this one of the city's favorite yuppie bars, where young professionals gather to talk shop over an Oregonic Amber or Maltnomah Porter and down gargantuan plates of $1.95 happy-hour food. Superb lunches and dinners—from sandwiches and pastas to Brown Ale chicken and Texas fire steak—are served amid hip industrial decor. *AE, MC, V; no checks; every day; full bar; www.rockbottom.com; map:H5* &

Rogue Ales Public House

1339 NW FLANDERS ST, PEARL DISTRICT; 503/222-5910 Originating in Ashland, Oregon, in 1988, the cheeky Rogue Nation populates the Pearl at a homey pub: a "micro meeting hall," as it calls itself. With pub food, a Lego table, a full bar, and ever-popular Golden Tee ale, the Rogue pub is every bit an easy hangout. Its location makes it a busy super-destination on First Thursday, when it fills with parched, famished art crawlers. *DIS, MC, V; no checks; every day; full bar; www.rogue.com; map:L1* &

The Tugboat Brewery

711 SW ANKENY ST, DOWNTOWN; 503/226-2508 Producing only a few barrels of various malted elixirs each week, this most microscopic of microbreweries serves up its delicious homebrew in a library-like space lined with books and staffed by the owner's gregarious relatives. The pints attract a wide swath of Portlanders, from visiting CEOs staying at the nearby Benson to graying hippies en route to Saturday Market. Tuesday through Saturday there's free music (jazz, roots, and folk duos or solos): small acts for a small bar. *Cash only; Mon–Sat; beer and wine; tugboatale@webtv.net; www.d2m.com/Tugwebsite; map:J4* &

Widmer Brewing and Gasthaus

955 N RUSSELL ST, ALBINA; 503/281-3333 Lovers of flavorful, light beer unite: the Widmer Brothers produce Oregon's top-selling microbrew, a delicious hefeweizen that goes great with a lemon wedge. You can sample the ever-evolving seasonal beers at the Gasthaus adjacent to the brewery, where a German-centric menu—sauerkrauts, wursts, fondue, pretzels—awaits the masses. The atmosphere is quite simple, but reminds you that you're drinking a local beer in industrial North Portland. *AE, DIS, MC, V; no checks; every day; beer and wine; www.widmer.com; map:GG6* &

Wine Bars

C-Bar

2880 SE GLADSTONE ST, BROOKLYN; 503/230-8808 Wine bars may tend toward the dark and imposing or the überbright populist, but the C-Bar strikes a near-perfect balance between fashion and function. Painted in mauve with a large marble bar, patio, and wine-related art, it feels neighborhoody and hip, but not too family oriented. It's a charming place to indulge in a dessert wine—the list is short and sharp—and grab a bite of panini. *MC, V; no checks; every day; beer and wine; map: II5* &

Crush

1412 SE MORRISON ST, BUCKMAN; 503/235-8150 Crush turns the idea of being a wine bar into a serious concept, marked by carefree glitz and laid-back classiness. Lined by velvety silver curtains, it's an excellent backdrop for occasional drag shows, which are well-attended, bona fide extravaganzas. On Straight Night, heteros file in for specials on wine and martinis. Rotating evenings, you can take in live music or even modern dance in this friendly, glammy little bar. *MC, V; no checks; Wed–Sun; full bar; map:HH5* &

Navarre

10 NE 28TH AVE, LAURELHURST; 503/232-3555 In a vaguely Old World environment adorned with rustic green chairs and a bevy of pans cascading from the ceiling—just like at grandma's—you can sip from a small but erudite wine list. The menu offers whole, hearty foods like white beans and ham, and toast with eggplant and red peppers. Intimate and subtly homey, Navarre could be a neighborhood stop in Venice or Barcelona. (See also review in the Restaurants chapter.) *AE, MC, V; checks OK; Mon–Sat; beer and wine; map:HH5* &

Noble Rot

2724 SE ANKENY ST, LAURELHURST; 503/233-1999 In this classy bar, enjoy an inexpensive glass of the house wine. Or get a taste of everything with moderately priced flights that complement a rotating menu of light dishes. Hide yourself in the quiet back room to enjoy a romantic tête-à-tête. Attend a wine-appreciation class (Thursdays) or an occasional cooking course (call for info) to learn what you're sipping. *MC, V; no checks; Mon–Sat; beer and wine; map:HH5* ♿

Sapphire Hotel

5008 SE HAWTHORNE ST, HAWTHORNE; 503/232-6633 The Sapphire Hotel is dressed in a decadently beautiful Chinese, Art Deco motif. Bird art adorns the walnut tables and colorful swaths of silk drift from the ceiling, transporting you to 1920s Shanghai. The wine list is largely from California and Spain. Special events—like jazz nights, tarot readings, and singles matchmaking—make this little bar a wonderful destination for those seeking both nightlife and intimacy. Smokers can puff at outdoor benches under the moonlit glow of Mount Hood. *MC, V; no checks; Tues–Sun; beer and wine; map:HH4* ♿

750 ml

232 NW 12TH AVE, PEARL DISTRICT; 503/224-1432 Its interior belies its vibrant, New York aspirations: refined, ultramodern furniture sits under minimally adorned walls, a fun combination of futurism and naturalism. The vast list of wine and sparkly strikes a good balance between Italian, Australian, and Pacific Northwest wines; samples of most hover around $3. The bistro food is light, fresh, exotic, and cheaper than you'd imagine (around $11 a plate). (See also reviews in the Restaurants and Shopping chapters.) *AE, DIS, MC, V; no checks; Mon–Sat; wine only; www.750-ml.com; map:L2* ♿

Vigne

417 NW 10TH AVE, PEARL DISTRICT; 503/295-9536 This Pearl District wine bar is ultrasophisticated and—located next door to the swank Gregory Lofts—it's got a healthy clientele of nouveau riche and hip entrepreneurs. Extremely modern, minimalist design manifests itself in black-leather seating, glass tables, and paper lanterns; the temperature-regulated wine cellar is floor level and encased in glass, defining the atmosphere as a giant aquarium might. *AE, MC, V; no checks; Tues–Sun; wine only; map:L2* ♿

Wine Down

126 NE 28TH ST, LAURELHURST; 503/236-9463 Wine Down's initial environment is intimate—a few oak tables and chairs, a counter, a dessert case—but an adjacent lounge sprawls into several more tables and offers occasional live acoustic music. It's an informal, breezy space with more family than date ambience, if that can be said about a wine bar. Small tapas-style plates complement fine Oregon and other wines. *MC, V; no checks; every day; beer and wine; map:HH5* ♿

Coffee, Tea, and Dessert

Back to Back Cafe

616 E BURNSIDE ST, INNER SOUTHEAST; 503/233-1929 As Portland cafes go, there are a thousand Back to Backs: comfortable, vegetarian-friendly, and fair trade–centric, with charming baristas. What distinguishes this cafe is that it's a worker-owned collective run by the Industrial Workers of the World, whose headquarters are located next door. Thus it's the best place to discuss the leftist politics that flourish in Portland—the politics that led ex-President George Bush (Sr.) to anoint the city "Little Beirut." *No credit cards; checks OK; every day; beer and wine; map: HH6* &

The Brazen Bean

2075 NW GLISAN ST, NORTHWEST; 503/294-0636 The setting is pure nouveau Gothic: lots of candles, velvet, and tables tucked into various nooks and crannies surrounded by deep, saturated colors. Movie-set types of all ages puff cigars (there's a humidor on-site; ask your server), linger over a wide range of beverages (champagne, beer, and creative martinis, as well as coffee and tea), and nibble on the kinds of foods that go perfectly with drinks. For dessert there's chocolate silk pie, apple pie, and messy but delectable chocolate fondue for two. *AE, MC, V; no checks; Mon–Sat; full bar; map:HH7*

Coffee Time

710 NW 21ST AVE, NORTHWEST; 503/497-1090 Just in case you simply can't wait till morning for your daily caffeine fix, Coffee Time is open 24/7. If you think there's absolutely no reason to be drinking coffee in the wee hours of the morning, think again. Any time of day or night, you'll find buzzing yuppies, mellow hippies, and newly existentialist teenagers all bonding over love of java. Perhaps you can write a poem about the mixed crowd and join one of Coffee Time's semiregular open-mic nights. *No credit cards; checks OK; every day; no alcohol; map:HH7* &

Diedrich Coffee People

533 NW 23RD AVE, NORTHWEST (AND BRANCHES); 503/221-0235 Jim and Patty Roberts' Coffee People has come a long way since its humble beginnings on NW 23rd. Now owned by the Diedrich corporation, the Greater Portland enterprise totals some 24 outlets, including a kiosk at PDX called Aeromoka and nine drive-through Motor Mokas: the Grand Motor Moka (525 NE Grand Ave, near Lloyd Center; 503/232-8002; map:HH5) stays open till 11pm for curing late-night caffeine headaches. Coffee People's lengthy menu includes almost every kind of coffee concoction you could imagine, plus coffee-oriented milk shakes and pastries from various bakeries. The shops on NW 23rd and in the Hawthorne District (3500 SE Hawthorne Blvd; 503/235-1383; map:HH5) provide modish backdrops for late-night rendezvous. *AE, MC, V; checks OK; every day; no alcohol; www .coffeepeople.com; map:HH7*

The Empire Room

4260 SE HAWTHORNE BLVD, HAWTHORNE; 503/231-9225 The Empire Room is a stylish place to stall, linger, or stop by for an early evening . . . or a rich snack or dessert. Soft lights, small tables, a very chic waitstaff clad in black, and jazzy music provide the ambience of a French salon. Appropriately, coffee comes in a French press. *MC, V; local checks only; Tues–Sat; beer and wine; map:HH4* &

Fresh Pot

4001 N MISSISSIPPI AVE, NORTH PORTLAND; 503/284-8928 It began with the coffee shop inside Powell's bookstore on Hawthorne, but when the Fresh Pot's owners branched out into the promising Mississippi neighborhood, they almost single-handedly jump-started its now-bustling renaissance of business. Some call it gentrification, but most agree: a cup of Stumptown coffee, or a vegan cookie from local Black Sheep Baking, is better in this neighborhood-friendly stop than any chain coffee shop. *Cash only; every day; no alcohol; map:GG7* &

Heaven Cafe

421 SW 10TH AVE, DOWNTOWN; 503/243-6152 One of Portland's few Internet cafes is equipped with a live DJ on deck and decorated with monthly graffiti-influenced or silk-screened art shows. It's open till 2am weekdays and 5am weekends, with an adjacent dance floor, making it a convenient stop for urban teens and anyone else craving coffee, pastries, Japanese sodas, or *Vice* magazine at 4 in the morning. *Cash only; every day; no alcohol; map:J2* &

Palio Dessert & Espresso House

1996 SE LADD AVE, LADD'S ADDITION; 503/232-9412 This may be the closest you get to great coffee and desserts without feeling like you've left home. Situated in the quaint Ladd's Addition neighborhood between Division and Hawthorne Streets in Southeast Portland, Palio is friendly and cozy: candles and dim lights warmly illuminate this den; and lest you get bored, there are toys, games, and books galore. The desserts change often, but they're always decadently sweet, and you're sure to find a luscious chocolate cake of some sort. *AE, MC, V; checks OK; every day; no alcohol; map:HH5*

The Pied Cow

3244 SE BELMONT ST, BELMONT; 503/230-4866 A bay window, beads, lace curtains, and low couches leave this colorful hangout aglow in Victoriana. But the candlelit backyard-soirée ambience of its patio assures its place as a hip spot in Belmont. It may not be as popular as Stumptown (see review below), but it's an easier place to lose several hours playing cards or contemplating one's existence. This is the ultimate coffeehouse: the food is cheap, the cappuccinos are delicious, and there's always a goopy-sweet chocolate dessert enriching the coffee drinks. *MC, V; no checks; Tues–Sun; beer and wine; map:HH5* &

Pix Patisserie

3402 SE DIVISION ST, SOUTHEAST; 503/232-4407 See Bakeries in the Shopping chapter.

Rimsky-Korsakoffee House

707 SE 12TH AVE, BUCKMAN; 503/232-2640 Laughter and music from the resident piano greet the ear at the threshold of this grand old Victorian mansion befitting its Russian composer namesake. The place is nearly always filled with young lovers sharing ice-cream sundaes (Rasputin's Delight is a favorite) or a decadent mocha fudge cake. The Cafe Borgias are exceptional: coffee, chocolate, and orange harmoniously mingle in one cup. You might drive right by this place—there's no sign marking its presence—but once inside, with a string trio or classical guitarist providing entertainment and a proper cup of coffee to sip, you may not want to leave. *No credit cards; checks OK; every day; no alcohol; map:HH5*

Staccato Gelato

232 NW 23RD AVE, NORTHWEST; 503/231-7100 This charming ice-cream and coffee joint is generally brighter and less formal than its Italian counterparts, but its creamy product is just as authentic. Staccato's fresh gelato—in flavors ranging from melon to banana to straight-up vanilla—is served in cones or festive plastic cups with tiny spoons. Don't forget to order a delicious Segafredo Zanetti coffee, so rich and smooth you can almost bite it. *No credit cards; checks OK; Tues–Sun; no alcohol; map:HH7*

Star E. Rose Cafe

2403 NE ALBERTA ST, ALBERTA; 503/249-8128 Delicious house-made desserts and a friendly, diner-like atmosphere render the Star E. Rose the early-morning location of choice for Alberta Street bike punks. It can be a little on the hippie side, so the service is sometimes slow, but a slice of fresh peach pie à la mode is utterly worth it. And it wouldn't be a Northeast establishment if it didn't have a Scrabble board for fierce caffeine-fueled wordsmithery. *MC, V; no checks; every day; no alcohol; map:FF5* &

Stumptown Coffee Roasters

128 SW 3RD AVE, OLD TOWN (AND BRANCHES); 503/295-6144 Three locations and a roastery have turned this local company into one of Portland's definitive establishments. Stumptown roasts the richest, deepest cup in town: it's so good that many local restaurants hang signs boasting, "Proudly Serving Stumptown Coffee." And owner Duane Sorenson hires some of the most attractive and talented baristas this side of *Friends'* Central Perk. The downtown location serves beer and wine and has a stage where bands and DJs perform on weekends. The Southeast (4525 SE Division St; 503/230-7702; map:II4) and Belmont (3356 SE Belmont St; 503/232-8889; map:HH5) locations are also open late in the evening. (See also review in the Shopping chapter.) *MC, V; no checks; every day; beer and wine; www.stumptowncoffee.com; map:J5* &

The Tao of Tea

3430 SE BELMONT ST, BELMONT (AND BRANCHES); 503/736-0198 Enter the Tao of Tea and you'll soon forget where you are. Trickling water, meditative music, exotic teapots, and feng shui–specific decor instantly draw you into another world. The tea selection seems endless (more than 120 types), with the finest varieties of oolong, green, white, red, and black teas, as well as fruit and herbal infusions. The eclectic vegetarian menu is designed to complement the teas; the green tea, bean curd, and mango ice-cream assortment will complement your palate. And with new teahouses in Northwest Portland (2212 NW Hoyt St; 503/223-3563; map:GG7) and at the Classical Chinese Garden (239 NW Everett St, Chinatown; 503/224-8455; map:L5), you're never far from indulgence. (See also review in the Shopping chapter.) *DIS, MC, V; checks OK; every day; no alcohol; tea@taooftea.com; www.taooftea.com; map:HH5* &

Torrefazione Italia

838 NW 23RD AVE, NORTHWEST (AND BRANCHES); 503/228-1255 This is Portland's own Little Italy. The terra-cotta tile floors and hand-painted earthenware, the frequently overheard dialect and rich smell of dark-roasted coffee—all these add up to a Mediterranean vogue. This is a popular hangout for neighborhood locals, Eurobabes, and Italian wannabes. Classic crunchy, sweet biscotti go perfectly with a foamy cappuccino. The Northeast shop (1403 NE Weidler St; 503/288-1608; map: GG5) offers the same delicious coffee and a large patio for outside sipping; the Pearl branch (1140 NW Everett St; 503/224-9896; map:L2) caters to day trippers, closing at 7 each night; and a downtown location (1001 SW 5th Ave; 503/226-2313; map: G3), open weekdays only, is geared to a business crowd. *MC, V; checks OK; every day; no alcohol; www.titalia.com; map:GG7* &

Voodoo Doughnut

22 SW 3RD AVE, OLD TOWN; 503/241-4704 In the tradition of Portland's late lamented Church of Elvis, you can tie the nuptial knot in this tiny downtown doughnut stop. Effectively a walk-up counter adjacent to Berbati's Pan (see review under Music, Clubs, and Lounges), the 24-hour shop takes Krispy Kreme to task with a wide assortment of flavors most doughnut lovers would never dream of. Some—like Tang, Pepto Bismol, and Froot Loops—are surprisingly delicious. *Cash only; every day; no alcohol; map:J5*

World Cup at Powell's City of Books

1005 W BURNSIDE ST, DOWNTOWN; 503/228-4651 After you orient yourself in the byzantine empire that is Powell's City of Books, meander through the Blue and Yellow Rooms into World Cup, where you can peruse books and magazines over a latte, tea, or pastry. It's usually crowded; with windows overlooking Burnside, it's also a great place to people-watch. But visitors respect an informal, library-like quiet out of respect for readers. *AE, MC, V; no checks; every day; no alcohol; map:K2* &

DAY TRIPS

DAY TRIPS

Situated at the foot of the Willamette River Valley, an easy two-hour drive from both the Pacific Coast and the Cascade Mountains, Portland is a great hub for planning one- to three-day trips. The famed Columbia River Gorge National Scenic Area is just east of the city. Mount Hood, the Oregon wine country, the spectacular coast, and other attractions are nearby.

Sauvie Island

Pastoral Sauvie Island, with its farms, orchards, produce stands, waterways, and wildlife—just 20 minutes from downtown Portland via westbound US Hwy 30—is a quick escape for bicyclists, bird watchers, anglers, and boaters.

The island, formed by the confluence of the Willamette and Columbia Rivers, enticed the Multnomah Indians to make it their summer and fall home with its edible wapatoo root. You too can graze at in-season U-pick farms, or buy fresh produce from one of the local markets, such as the SAUVIE ISLAND FARMS MARKET (503/621-3988) or the PUMPKIN PATCH (503/621-3874). Be warned, though: on rainy days the broad, golden fields of the island turn into mud farms, so take your rubber boots if you're going to pick.

There's only one access route to Sauvie Island, a bridge at the south end of the island, well-marked off Hwy 30. To bicycle around the island, park your car at the east end of the bridge (you can't miss the lot), and from there take the 12-MILE BIKING LOOP. At the halfway point, if you're feeling energetic, a 5-mile loop that branches down to the Columbia offers several bird-watching turnouts.

The northern half of the island is a GAME REFUGE—one that is open to duck hunters from October through January, which means this is no time for either you or the birds to hang around. At other times, the marshes and open fields make a fine playground for enjoying the bountiful wildlife. Look for red foxes, black-tailed deer, great blue herons, geese, ducks, bald eagles, and migrating sandhill cranes. Reeder Road extends to the northern shore's sanctioned COLLINS BEACH CLOTHING OPTIONAL AREA and other short sandy beaches that freighters and small pleasure craft pass by. The western branch of the road follows the dike of the MULTNOMAH CHANNEL, passing the historic Bybee-Howell House, humble houseboats, rickety marinas, and the old site of the Hudson's Bay Company's Fort William (abandoned in 1836; nothing remains) before the road eventually dead-ends. You'll want to purchase a parking permit (daily or yearly) if you plan to venture to the refuge or beaches; permits are available at the grocery on your left immediately as you cross over the bridge onto the island.

The BYBEE-HOWELL HOUSE, in Bybee-Howell Territorial Park, was built in 1858 by James F. Bybee on a donation land claim and was sold to neighbor Benjamin Howell in 1860. The Classical Revival–style, two-story house has nine rooms and six fireplaces. Its hands-on agricultural museum displays equipment used in cultivating and harvesting crops, a complete harness shop, dairy equipment, and hand tools for working wood, leather, and metal. House and museum are open noon to 5pm weekends only, from the first Saturday in June through Labor Day. Suggested admission is a $2 donation. The park makes a lovely place for a summer picnic and can be rented for special events. In the adjacent Pioneer Orchard, there are more than 115 varieties of apple trees (many unknown to modern orchardists) brought here by early settlers. A nice fall tradition at the Bybee-Howell House is the **WINTERING-IN FESTIVAL**, complete with gallons of fresh apple cider; call the Oregon History Center (503/222-1741) for information.

Columbia River Gorge (Oregon)

The federally designated Columbia River Gorge National Scenic Area preserves what is among the most impressive riverscapes in North America. You'll want to explore it by taking I-84 east from Portland. On your return to the city, you can choose one of two routes: either back down the Washington side of the gorge, or a loop around Mount Hood.

In 1792 Boston trader Robert Gray and his crew became the first white people to sail on a strip of then-wild water that flowed into the Pacific Ocean. Gray named it the Columbia, after his ship, and proclaimed it a "noble river." After a week or so, the crew sailed out to sea without much of a second thought; Gray barely acknowledged his find when he returned to Massachusetts. Historians note that Gray sailed on rather hastily because he didn't find any sea-otter pelts to buy from the native people on the banks of the river. Would he have lingered a bit if he'd sailed the *Columbia Rediviva* as far east as the majestic Columbia River Gorge? This landscape, with its magnificent waterfalls, dramatic cliffs, and rock formations cut by the river, is enough to make nature lovers want to explore every crevice.

In decades past, when its highway was narrow and winding, driving in the gorge was not for the queasy. These days, most of the traffic goes down I-84, leaving the beautiful old Historic Columbia River Highway (Hwy 30) for unhurried wanderers. This engineering marvel originally went from Portland to Mosier (just past Hood River), continuing to The Dalles; today the old highway can still be followed for 22 miles from Troutdale to Ainsworth State Park (exit 35). In addition, portions near Bonneville Dam and Hood River have been restored for hikers and cyclists; call the Oregon Department of Transportation (503/731-8200) for details and maps, and see the Hood River section in this chapter.

Start your exploring in charming **TROUTDALE**—home of the McMenamins' unique **EDGEFIELD** complex at a former poor farm (see review in the Lodgings chapter). Merchants have renovated a four-block stretch of the Historic Columbia River Highway (between exits 16 and 17 off I-84) as **HISTORIC OLDTOWN TROUT-DALE**, with various antique shops, art galleries, and specialty shops. Peek into the **TROUTDALE GENERAL STORE** (289 E Historic Columbia River Hwy; 503/492-7912) for a look at an early-1900s soda fountain and confectionary. For a full meal, continue across the Sandy River Bridge to **TAD'S CHICKEN 'N' DUMPLIN'S** (1325 E Historic Columbia River Hwy; 503/666-5337), a riverside dinner destination since the 1930s.

You enter the national scenic area just past Tad's, and popular viewpoints and attractions become numerous. **CROWN POINT**, 733 feet above the river, features a stone visitors center—the 1917 Vista House—with gorgeous views and, sometimes, tremendous winds. Phallic **ROOSTER ROCK** is at the heart of a state park flanked by sandy swimming beaches. Nearby, look for **LARCH MOUNTAIN ROAD**, which leads 14 miles uphill to one of the best sunset-watching spots in western Oregon (unless you're atop Mount Hood). A short road's-end trail leads to Sherrard Point, a rocky promontory at the mountain's summit with spectacular 360-degree views that take in Mount Hood, Mount Adams, Mount St. Helens, Mount Jefferson, the Columbia River Gorge, and all of Portland.

Driving east from Troutdale, the route passes numerous waterfalls; if you stop at only one, make it **MULTNOMAH FALLS** (I-84, exit 31), whose two-step drop of 620 feet makes it the second-highest waterfall in the country. The wood-and-stone Multnomah Falls Lodge, at the foot of the falls, was designed in 1925 by architect Albert E. Doyle (of Portland's Benson Hotel fame); now a National Historic Landmark, the lodge houses a naturalists and visitors center. The large restaurant (503/695-2376) serves good breakfasts (brunch on Sun), lunch, and dinner but does not have overnight facilities. A couple of more miles upriver, **ONEONTA GORGE** is a narrow, dramatic cleft through which a slippery half-mile trail winds through a streambed to secluded Oneonta Falls; the trail is quite rugged and suitable only for the adventurous.

You'll rejoin I-84 at exit 35. Five miles on, stop to visit the **BONNEVILLE DAM** (541/374-8820), first federal dam on the Columbia. Here you can get tours of the dam itself, the fish ladders (seen through underwater viewing windows), and the shipping locks. You can also tour the adjacent **BONNEVILLE FISH HATCHERY** (541/374-8393) year-round, but the best time is September to November, when the chinook salmon are spawning. Be sure also to visit the outdoor pond, where 10-foot sturgeon reside.

The **BRIDGE OF THE GODS**, in the old river town of Cascade Locks, is now steel, but at the site is a fine little museum that recounts the Indian myth about the original, legendary arching-rock bridge that collapsed into the Columbia River long ago. The locks that the town is named for are themselves a sight worth seeing: the stonework is beautiful and the scale awesome, accentuated by the small figures of the people who fish off the walls. The **STERNWHEELER COLUMBIA GORGE** (503/223-3928) departs three times daily, May to September, from Marine Park at the locks (narrated tour $12.95); it stops at Bonneville Dam and also at Stevenson Landing if there are passengers waiting.

HOOD RIVER

Fruit orchards are everywhere near the bustling town of **HOOD RIVER**, an hour's drive east of Portland via I-84. Sunny weather combines with substantial moisture (about 31 inches of rain annually) to create a climate perfect for cultivating pears, apples, and plums. It's pastoral indeed, but there's drama, too: 30 miles to the south, 11,235-foot Mount Hood looms, and from the town itself, the stunning views are of Washington's 12,326-foot Mount Adams.

And then there's **WINDSURFING**, which in the past 20 years has transformed this once-sleepy town into a kaleidoscope of color. In summer you can't miss the brilliant sails dotting the river and the influx of wind chasers who lend the town a distinctly touristy feel. They've come since the 1980s because of the roaring winds that blow opposite the Columbia River current, making Hood River one of the world's top three windsurfing destinations (the other two are in Hawaii and Australia). While Hood River reaps all the sailboard mythology, in fact the waters on the Oregon side of the Columbia are reportedly tame compared with those off the Washington banks, where boardheads claim the wind "really pulls." Hence, the hottest sailors circumvent rocky shores and industrial areas to surf off points on the river's north bank such as Swell City and Doug's Beach. To find them, follow the streams of vans and wagons piled high with boards and masts, tune in to radio station KMCQ-104 for the local wind report, or call 541/386-3300 for a recorded message.

Two fine spectator spots are located right in Hood River. The **HOOD RIVER WATERFRONT CENTER EVENT SITE** (from I-84 follow signs to the visitors center) is a grassy park with a small sandy beach and unrestricted access to the Columbia. Sailing is somewhat easier at the **COLUMBIA GORGE SAILPARK** at Port Marina Park, which features a marina, rental shop, and cafe with enclosed porch. (After all, who wants to dine in the wind?) For lessons or for information on wind conditions, sailboard rentals, or launching spots, investigate the multitude of sailboard equipment shops, including **HOOD RIVER WINDSURFING** (in Doug's Sports, 101 Oak St; 541/386-5787) and **BIG WINDS** (207 Front St; 541/386-6086). **KERRITS** (316 Oak St; 541/386-4187) makes colorful and practical activewear for women (the suit remains on your body when you fall off your board); Kerrits recently added a line of kids' clothing that includes knock-your-socks-off polar fleece and equestrian gear. Down the street, **WINDWEAR** (504 Oak St; 541/386-6209) sells probably the most stylish onshore clothing in town, at boutique prices.

As longtime Hood River residents attest, while acknowledging the economic boost the windsurfers have provided, there was life in this town of 4,500 before they arrived. You can learn its story at the **HOOD RIVER COUNTY HISTORICAL MUSEUM** (300 E Port Marina Dr; 541/386-6772), open every day April through October. The **MUSEUM OF CAROUSEL ART** (304 Oak St; 541/387-4622; admission $5) is a labor of love that restores and displays carousels from around the world.

The local **VISITORS INFORMATION CENTER**, tucked inside the Hood River Expo Building (405 Portway Ave; 800/366-3530), is a friendly place to get informed. If it's closed (as it sometimes is on winter weekends), you can find reading material at the **WAUCOMA BOOKSTORE** (212 Oak St; 541/386-5353), a notable independent bookseller. **PUBLIC RESTROOMS** are located at 2nd and State Streets, on the ground floor of the city hall. **LIBRARY PARK**, above the intersection of Fifth and Oak Streets, sports a great view of both town and river.

Hood River's grandest structure is the **COLUMBIA GORGE HOTEL** (4000 Westcliff Dr; 541/386-5566 or 800/345-1921). Built just west of town by lumber baron Simon Benson in 1922 to crown the first opening of the old gorge highway, it also boasts Hood River's fanciest restaurant. In the heart of the city, the restored 1913 **HOOD RIVER HOTEL** (102 Oak St; 541/386-1900 or 800/386-1859) is a simple but intimate country hotel with 41 rooms, including 9 kitchen suites; its in-house

MOUNT ST. HELENS NATIONAL VOLCANIC MONUMENT

Flat-topped Mount St. Helens, about an hour's drive north of Portland and east of I-5, enthralls visitors. On a clear day it is well worth the trip to see the 8,365-foot remains of the volcano, as well as the vegetation that's sprouted since St. Helens's incredible eruption of May 18, 1980 (it's 1,300 feet shorter than it was before the blast). There are two areas to explore, and each is reached by a different highway. One area covers the south and east sides of the volcano, where climbers ascend and where there are caves to brave; the other is the west side, where a string of visitors centers educate about the blast and the area's regrowth. All visitors must display a monument pass at developed recreation sites; these passes are $10 per person for three days ($5 for seniors, free for children under 15) and can be purchased at visitors centers and information stations throughout the area. Or call 360/449-7800 to reach national monument headquarters.

WEST SIDE

Most visitors take the Spirit Lake Memorial Highway (State Hwy 504) east from Castle Rock, about 40 minutes north of Portland via I-5. Just off the freeway, before you begin the ascent to the ridge, you can see the 25-minute Academy Award–nominated *The Eruption of Mount Saint Helens* projected on the three-story-high, 55-foot-wide screen of **THE CINEDOME** (360/274-8000). About 5 miles east of I-5, on your way up to the volcano, sits the oldest of the visitors centers in the Mount St. Helens area, the wood-and-glass center at **SILVER LAKE** (360/274-2100). Built shortly after the eruption, this center commemorates the blast with excellent exhibits, a walk-through volcano, hundreds of historical and modern photos, geological and anthropological surveys, and a film documenting the area's destruction and rebirth.

The second visitors center, complete with cafe, gift shop, and bookstore, sits atop windswept **COLDWATER RIDGE** (360/274-2131), some 38 miles east. It's a multi-million-dollar facility with a million-dollar view—of the crater just to the southeast, the debris-filled valley of the Toutle River's north fork, and of new lakes formed by massive mudslides. The speed and heat of the blast, estimated at 600 miles per hour and as high as 350 degrees Celsius, scalped at least 150,000 acres surrounding the mountain. The Coldwater Ridge center focuses on the astounding biological recovery of the landscape. From the visitors center, you can descend the short distance to Coldwater Lake, where there's a picnic area and boat launch, or take a guided interpretive walk.

The **JOHNSTON RIDGE OBSERVATORY** (360/274-2140; call for hours, closed in winter) is located at the end of Spirit Lake Memorial Highway, about 8 miles beyond Coldwater Ridge. This futuristic-looking structure, within 5 miles of the crater, offers the best views of the steaming lava dome inside the crater—unless, of course, you climb the volcano.

Two visitors centers can be visited without the monument pass: Cowlitz County's **HOFFSTADT BLUFF** center (milepost 27 on Spirit Lake Memorial Hwy; 360/274-7750), which explores the lives and deaths of those most directly affected by the blast; and Weyerhaeuser's **FOREST LEARNING CENTER** (milepost 33½; 360/414-3439), which focuses on the land's recovery in the wake of the eruption.

SOUTH AND EAST SIDES

State Hwy 503 east from Woodland or north from Battle Ground, less than 20 minutes' drive north of Portland, will take you past Yale Lake to these precincts of the national monument. En route, check out the map at visitors centers in Woodland or Amboy; the St. Helens area has a confusing range of attractions, and it may help to orient yourself at the beginning of your trip.

There are two possibilities for spelunking at the **APE CAVES** on Forest Service Road 8303, an hour from Woodland: the moderately difficult lower cave, ¾-mile long, and the more challenging 1½-mile upper cave. This lava tube, the longest in the continental United States, was formed 1,900 years ago in a St. Helens blast. Rent lanterns and gather more information at the **APES HEADQUARTERS**, open daily mid-May through September. For a dramatic view of a vast pumice plain, travel east and north another 1 hour and 45 minutes, to the **WINDY RIDGE VIEWPOINT**, situated within 4 miles of the volcano's crater.

For information on climbing St. Helens, call the **CLIMBING INFORMATION LINE** (360/247-3961). You'll need to buy a $15 climbing permit; a few are available on a daily basis, but it's best to reserve in advance. Most climbers take one of two trails (Butte Camp or Monitor Ridge) up the south face. It's more of a rugged hike than real alpine climbing, but an ice ax is still recommended. The all-day climb (8 miles round-trip) is ideal for novice alpinists; the only big dangers are some loose-rock cliffs and the unstable edge around the crater. In winter you can ski down.

—John Gottberg

restaurant, Pascuale's, offers an outstanding Mediterranean menu. An inexpensive alternative is the modest **VAGABOND LODGE** (4070 Westcliff Dr; 541/386-2992 or 877/386-2992), located next door to the Columbia River Gorge Hotel; ask for a cliffside room.

Hood River is the home of the country's first employee-owned brewery. You can enjoy light meals with the handcrafted ales at the **FULL SAIL TASTING ROOM AND PUB** (506 Columbia St; 541/386-2247). The outdoor deck (with live music on weekends) is an apt place for tired board sailors to unwind while keeping the river in sight. Another popular spot for brews—as well as steaks, fish, pastas, and house-made desserts— is **BRIAN'S POURHOUSE** (606 Oak St; 541/387-4344). Choices for more substantial dining include three Italian restaurants: **ABRUZZO** (1810 Cascade

Ave; 541/386-7779), **NORTH OAK BRASSERIE** (113 3rd St; 541/387-2310), and **SANTACROCES'** (4780 Hwy 35; 541/354-2511), the latter locally famous for its pizza and house-made bread and sausage. **THE 6TH STREET BISTRO AND LOFT** (509 Cascade Ave; 541/386-5737) has a creative menu of international cuisine. **BETTE'S PLACE** (416 Oak St; 541/386-1880) is a local diner that's been serving almost the same breakfast-and-lunch menu for two dozen years. Charming **STONEHEDGE GARDENS** (3405 Cascade Ave; 541/386-3940) has some of the best food in town, a Northwest bistro menu with continental flair.

The region's bountiful orchards and beautiful landscape are celebrated during the wonderful small-town **BLOSSOM FESTIVAL**, held annually in mid-April. The **MOUNT HOOD RAILROAD** (800/872-4661) makes two- or four-hour round-trips— and dinner-train excursions—from the quaint Hood River Depot into the heart of orchard country; call for the schedule. You can buy the fruit of the orchards at **THE FRUIT TREE** (4140 Westcliff Dr; 541/386-6688), near the Columbia Gorge Hotel; at **RIVER BEND COUNTRY STORE** (2363 Tucker Rd; 541/386-8766); or at one of the many fruit stands that dot the valley. **RASMUSSEN FARMS** (3020 Thomsen Rd, 1 mile off Hwy 35; 541/386-4622), in addition to selling seasonal fruit, also has a pumpkin patch and U-pick flower fields. For wine tasting, visit **HOOD RIVER VINEYARDS** (4693 Westwood Dr; 541/386-3772), known for its pear and raspberry dessert wines.

If you're returning to Portland via the Mount Hood Loop route, this is where you turn south on State Hwy 35. If you're continuing east toward The Dalles, another 20 minutes' drive, be sure to exit I-84 at Mosier (5 miles east of Hood River) and climb to the **ROWENA CREST VIEWPOINT** on old Hwy 30. The grandstand Columbia River view is complemented by a wildflower show in the **TOM MCCALL PRESERVE**, maintained by the Nature Conservancy.

The area's newest hiking and biking option is the 6½-mile restored section of the Historic Columbia River Highway connecting Hood River to Mosier. The highway was decommissioned in 1953, and the **TWIN TUNNELS** were plugged with gravel to keep the curious out. A lengthy and expensive effort reopened (and reinforced) the Twin Tunnel trail in 2000. To reach this spectacular trail, follow the signs to the parking lots from I-84's Hwy 35 exit in Hood River or from exit 69 in Mosier. You'll need $3 in correct change for the parking-fee machine.

THE DALLES

A couple of miles west of The Dalles on Crates Point is the excellent **COLUMBIA GORGE DISCOVERY CENTER/WASCO COUNTY HISTORICAL MUSEUM** (5000 Discovery Dr; 541/296-8600), official interpretive center for the national scenic area. Split into two wings, the center recounts the natural and human history of the Columbia Gorge and of Wasco County—which extended all the way to the Rocky Mountains when it was created in 1854. Multimedia exhibits focus on the life and use, past and present, of this stretch of the Columbia, from Native American culture to the river's current recreational popularity. Special emphasis is placed on the Lewis and Clark Expedition of 1803–1806. The location is stunning and the architecture noteworthy; even the cafe is above average.

Twenty minutes east of Hood River is **THE DALLES**, a small city of about 12,000 people that does a nice job of sharing its unique heritage with visitors. In the 1840s, the Oregon Trail ended here; goods from wagons were loaded onto barges for the final float to Portland or were taken around Mount Hood on the notorious Barlow Road. Later, Fort Dalles was here; today the **FORT DALLES MUSEUM** (500 W 15th St; 541/296-4547; admission $3) displays exceptional pioneer-era relics in its 1856 surgeon's house and 1880s homestead. Stop by **THE DALLES AREA CHAMBER OF COMMERCE** (404 W 2nd St; 541/296-2231) for a *Historic Walking Tours* brochure: more than 100 historic sites are referenced, including numerous handsome buildings in Colonial, Gothic Revival, Italianate, and American Renaissance styles.

As befits a town of historical flavor, The Dalles has several charming bed-and-breakfast inns, including the Dutch Colonial **WINDRIDER INN** (200 W 4th St; 541/296-2607), whose amenities include sailboard storage. Dining options include the delightful 1876 **BALDWIN SALOON** (1st and Court Sts; 541/296-5666), once a steamboat navigational office, warehouse, coffin storage site, and saddle shop. **BAILEY'S PLACE** (515 Liberty St; 541/296-6708) occupies the upstairs of an 1865 hillside Victorian; known for its prime rib, the restaurant also serves up fresh seafood, including razor clams in summer.

At **THE DALLES DAM** (I-84, exit 87, 2 miles east of The Dalles; 541/296-9778), a visitors center has informative displays on Lewis and Clark and on the fishing industry. A free tour train makes stops at the dam, powerhouse, locks, fish ladders, and a picnic area.

Columbia River Gorge (Washington)

To return to Portland from The Dalles, you could cross the Columbia River to the Washington side via US Hwy 197 and turn west on State Hwy 14. We recommend continuing east another 19 miles and crossing on US Hwy 97—at which point you may ask, "Where in the Sam Hill am I?"

You're in Sam Hill country, and the early-20th-century Seattle millionaire left two monuments here to his eccentricity. One of them is the eclectic **MARYHILL MUSEUM OF ART** (Hwy 14, Maryhill; 509/773-3733; open mid-Mar–mid-November), a massive neoclassical edifice perched rather obtrusively upon the river's barren benchlands. In 1907, Hill bought 6,000 acres here with the intention of founding a Quaker agricultural community. When that failed to materialize, friends encouraged Hill to turn his mansion into an art museum. Art collector Alma Spreckels became Maryhill's principal benefactor, and Queen Marie of Romania (whom Hill met during their shared philanthropic work in Europe after World War I) offered Hill much of her royal and personal memorabilia and graced the dedication of the Maryhill Museum in 1926.

Today the museum boasts one of the world's largest collections of Rodin art (78 bronze and plaster sculptures and 28 watercolors), three floors of classic French and American paintings and glasswork, unique exhibitions such as chess sets and 19th-century royal Romanian furnishings, and splendid Native American art. Along with its permanent collection, the museum hosts many traveling collections, often featuring Northwest artists. A cafe serves espresso, pastries, and sandwiches; peacocks roam the lovely landscaped grounds. Take time to explore the intriguing sculptural overlook on the east side of the museum grounds.

Four miles east of the museum on Hwy 14, Hill built a full-scale replica of the inner third of **STONEHENGE**, to honor the World War I veterans of this county. About three degrees off center, Hill's Stonehenge (not stones but poured concrete) functions as an observatory. It embodies Hill's personal vision: a pacifist, he considered his monument a statement on the human sacrifices made to the god of war.

If you let it, Hwy 14 will carry you all the way to Vancouver, Washington—96 miles, which on this two-lane road will take well over two hours. We recommend you follow it at least 60 miles, at which point you can cross back over to I-84 at Cascade Locks's Bridge of the Gods (75-cent toll). En route, you'll pass through one of Washington's lesser-known wine-growing districts. The half-dozen or so wineries here all are open for tastings; we recommend **MARYHILL WINERY** (9774 Hwy 14, Maryhill; 877/627-9445) and **SYNCLINE CELLARS** (307 W Humboldt St, Bingen; 509/365-4361). Near Syncline, you can get some of the best picnic food around at **MOTHER'S MARKET PLACE** (415 W Steuben St, Bingen; 509/493-1700), whose cheerful owners are on a vegetarian food mission. They'll happily give you samples of their homemade vegan cheeses, sandwiches, and fresh-fruit shakes.

People come to **CARSON HOT SPRINGS** (509/427-8292), 20 miles west of Bingen, to take the waters: mineral baths and massages. The women's side is much more crowded than the men's, so if your entourage is mixed, the men will finish sooner. To avoid this problem, reserve a massage in advance. There are also rooms at the lodge and cabins (nothing fancy) for reasonable rates.

For a higher standard of accommodation, travel 15 minutes west to the **DOLCE SKAMANIA LODGE** (1131 Skamania Lodge Wy, Stevenson; 509/427-7700 or 800/221-7117). The lodge was constructed in the early 1990s with the help of a $5 million grant to spur economic development on the Washington side of the river. Built in the style of the old Cascade lodges, with big timbers and river rock, it wasn't intended to be a four-star resort. But the common rooms are grand, the conference center works well, and the setting in the woods overlooking the river is pleasant indeed. The hotel has 254 rooms and numerous amenities: bar, restaurant, lap pool, saunas, outdoor hot tub, 18-hole public golf course, and an original art collection. The Forest Service's small room in the massive lobby offers maps and info on area recreation, wildflower and geology books, and so on. A day pass ($10 for adults, $5 for kids) buys you entrance to the pool, hot tub and workout center without being a hotel guest; anyone can hike the trails. Sunday brunch in the restaurant draws visitors from near and far for a spread that includes fresh crab, smoked salmon, omelets made to order while you watch, and miles of pastries and desserts.

The **COLUMBIA GORGE INTERPRETIVE CENTER** (509/427-8211), located just below the lodge on Hwy 14, displays the history of the gorge via a nine-projector slide show that recreates the gorge's cataclysmic formation. The show also features Native American fishing platforms and a 37-foot-high replica of a 19th-century fishing wheel. Admission is $6 for adults and $4 for kids.

BEACON ROCK STATE PARK, just east of Skamania, surrounds one of the world's largest monoliths, an 848-foot-high volcanic plug with a viewing platform at its summit. (A steep, railed, ¾-mile trail climbs the rock.) It was here that Lewis and Clark first detected the tidal influence of the Pacific Ocean.

Mount Hood Loop Highway

To return to Portland from Hood River via Mount Hood, turn south on State Hwy 35 at Hood River, passing the spectacular Panorama Point viewpoint as you leave town. After 43 miles, turn west (right) on US Hwy 26; Portland is 55 miles away.

When British navigator Captain George Vancouver first spied Mount Hood from the mouth of the Columbia River in 1792, he thought it must have been the highest mountain in the world. It *is* Oregon's tallest, but at just over 11,235 feet, Mount Hood is not even the highest in the volcanic Cascade Range (Washington's Mount Rainier, at 14,411, holds that honor). Nonetheless, Hood's proximity to Portland, its beautiful asymmetry, and its relative ease of ascent make it one of the busiest peaks in the country. According to geologists, Mount Hood still conceals hot magma and is bound to spew at some point. For now, though, all's peaceful in the towns scattered on its flanks.

About 20 miles south of Hood River, Hwy 35 enters Mount Hood National Forest. Soon thereafter, a road climbs to the family-oriented **COOPER SPUR MOUN-TAIN RESORT** (Cooper Spur Rd; 541/352-6692), with gentle slopes for child skiers and a rough-hewn inn with a fine steak house and cabins—with fireplaces and hot tubs. Climb this switchbacking Forest Service road another dozen or so miles to the 1889 **CLOUD CAP INN**, a log landmark at timberline on the north flank of Mount Hood. No longer a hotel, it's anchored to the mountain by cables, and the view alone is worth the detour. If the inn happens to be occupied by a search and rescue team (common in the summertime), ask if they have time to give you a tour. The lodge is also an access point for the Timberline Trail. Call the ranger station in Hood River (541/352-6002).

The largest of Mount Hood's five ski areas is **MOUNT HOOD MEADOWS**, off Hwy 35 about 5 miles north of the Hwy 26 junction. Just after the turn onto Hwy 26, you'll encounter the others: **GOVERNMENT CAMP** and **SKIBOWL/MULTORPOR** are right off the highway, and a detour will take you to **TIMBERLINE**. Information on any of these ski areas, or any other Mount Hood activities, can be obtained from the **MOUNT HOOD INFORMATION CENTER** (503/622-3360).

Tiny Government Camp is the hub—such as it is—of Mount Hood activities. From here, a 6-mile road twists its way to stunning **TIMBERLINE LODGE** (elevation 6,000 feet; 800/547-1406; www.timberlinelodge.com), with its impressive frontal views of Mount Hood's glaciers. The massive timber-and-stone lodge was constructed by government workers in the 1930s, who completed the monument in just 15 months. Throughout the building are structural and decorative pieces made by hand from native materials: the 100-foot-high chimney and enormous central fireplace were fashioned out of volcanic rocks from the mountain, the hand-wrought andirons were made from old railroad tracks, and the hardwood chairs and tables were hand-hewn from Oregon timber. The lodge's rooms with fireplaces get booked early, so call well in advance. The **CASCADE DINING ROOM** (503/

622-0700) serves an array of notable Northwest fare and is popular; reservations are suggested. (Other more modest dining options are also available.) For lodgers dying to shop, **THE GALLERY** on the ground floor has locally made handicrafts and more images of Mount Hood than you can imagine. The Forest Service offers historical tours of the lodge at midday on weekends, and a self-starting movie shows the lodge's history daily.

One of the best hiking trails in the area, the 40-mile **TIMBERLINE TRAIL,** leads 4.5 miles west from Timberline Lodge to flower-studded **PARADISE PARK.** The Timberline Trail is a circuit of the entire peak that traverses snowfields as well as ancient forests. The lower parts can blaze with rhododendrons (peaking in June) and wildflowers (peaking in July); all are easily reachable from trails that branch out from the lodge.

Mid-May to mid-July is the prime time for climbing **MOUNT HOOD,** a peak that looks deceptively easy, although its last 1,500 feet involve very steep snow climbing. **TIMBERLINE MOUNTAIN GUIDES** (541/312-9242) in the Wy'east Day Lodge equips and conducts groups of climbers to the summit. The climb starts early in the morning; allow four to six hours to go up and two or three to come down.

For those looking for an easier route up the mountain, the **MAGIC MILE SKY RIDE** chairlift hoists the brave and curious to the 7,000-foot level year-round, weather permitting. All they ask is that you buy a ticket, wear sturdy shoes, and (no matter how warm you feel in the parking lot) bring a jacket. At the top of the lift you can buy a barbecue lunch, look through the powerful telescope, or find your favorite vantage point for a magnificent view. Call 503/222-2211 for weather conditions, and see Timberline's website (above) for ever-changing year-round activities. (You may see skiers and snowboarders here even in the middle of summer: Timberline is the only year-round ski area in North America.)

The nearby **SILCOX HUT** (503/219-3192) has been gutted and restored to its original stone-and-timber glory. Six cubicles off the large central room provide sleeping quarters for 22. Organize a dozen or more of your best friends: in winter you can ride up on a Sno-Cat, have dinner, stay overnight, wake up to breakfast, and then ski down to the lodge—all for $100 per person, or $90 if you bring your own sleeping bag.

Back in Government Camp, an extreme-sport summer theme park at Skibowl has been luring nearly as much business as winter's snow. **ACTION PARK** (503/222-2695; open Memorial Day–Labor Day, plus Sept weekends) has taken advantage of privately owned land that surrounds its base lodges to establish city-type attractions often frowned upon by the Forest Service. In this case, Mount Hood National Forest is a willing partner, giving its blessing to such attractions as scenic horseback rides, a mountain-biking park, a dual alpine slide, and hay rides on the federally owned ski slopes. Down in the parking lots, Action Park has enough activities to keep a junior-high class buzzing for the summer.

If you dare, begin with a tumble off the 100-foot free-fall bungee tower. If that's not enough, go for an 80-foot fling on the reverse rapid-riser bungee jump. Indy karts, kiddy jeeps, trampolines, miniature and Frisbee golf, Velcro fly trap, body Nerfing, batting cages, and a 40- by 60-foot play zone offer fun for all ages. The mountain bike park has 40 miles of trail and is served by two chairlifts. Scenic heli-copter rides take off from the parking lot for a bird's-eye view of Mount Hood.

The 50-mile, 90-minute drive to Portland—downhill all the way—passes through a series of small resort villages with names like Rhododendron, Zigzag, and Bright-wood. A fine restaurant en route is **THE RENDEZVOUS GRILL** (67149 E Hwy 26, Welches; 503/622-6837), with creative continental cuisine at moderate prices.

Nineteen miles from Portland, the town of **SANDY**—named for the nearby river—makes a nice stop with its century-old buildings, its weekend country market, and its fruit stands. Here you'll find **ORAL HULL PARK** (503/668-6194), designed for the blind but a pleasure for the sighted as well, with splashing water and plants to smell and feel. You'll need permission to walk through the garden unless you're a guest at the conference lodge here. If you're headed up to the snow from Portland, several ski shops can provide equipment and information—including busy **OTTO'S CROSS COUNTRY SKI SHOP** (38716 Pioneer Blvd; 503/668-5947), next to the historic Good Shepherd Episcopal Church.

Oregon Wine Country

Oregon's rolling hills—with their good sunlight exposure, soil composition, and drainage—are choice locations for vineyards. Winemakers are at work in this state as far south as Ashland and as far east as Milton-Freewater, but the majority are clustered west and southwest of Portland in the northern Willamette Valley. State Hwy 99W, through the heart of Yamhill County, is an avenue to the greatest con-centration of wineries in the state, which has developed a worldwide reputation for its fine **PINOT NOIR** and **PINOT GRIS** grapes.

The wineries themselves are delightful to visit for those with even a passing interest in wine. In all seasons, there is much to take in, from misty hills reminiscent of a Japanese woodcut to flaming fall colors to the harvesting of the small, intensely flavored grapes. Almost all wineries have tasting rooms staffed by either winery owners or workers with intimate knowledge of the wines and production methods. Facility tours are often available; and, of course, there are wines to sample, which may include vintages not available elsewhere or small lots from grapes in scarce supply. Do take along bread, cheese, and other wine-friendly foods to enjoy. Calling in advance is always recommended; some wineries close for the month of January.

Start your wine tour by making an advance dinner reservation at one of the fine restaurants in this region (see Farther Afield in the Restaurants chapter). Then enjoy the drive along Hwy 99W, Oregon's official wine road. Local produce stands dot the roadside in summer, and the wineries, antique shops, and galleries will give you many options to follow your whims as you pass through these lush green hills. In particular, between Dundee and McMinnville, drop into the former **LAFAYETTE SCHOOLHOUSE** (Hwy 99W, Lafayette; 503/864-2720), now a 100-dealer antique mall.

With nearly 200 wineries in Oregon, it can be hard for the traveler to know where to stop. These are a few of our favorites, all of them located on or near Hwy 99W in Yamhill County, all with tasting rooms open year-round.

REX HILL VINEYARDS (30835 N Hwy 99W, Newberg; 503/538-0666) was chosen 2002 Oregon Winery of the Year by *Wine & Spirits* magazine. Occupying a restored 1920s fruit-and-nut-drying plant, founder Paul Hart's winery has produced numerous vineyard-designated pinot noirs that received critical attention. Rex Hill's location is splendid, with perennials in bloom even when the grapevines are not, making this one of the state's best visitor facilities.

DUCK POND CELLARS (23145 Hwy 99W, Dundee; 503/538-3199) gets wide commercial exposure for the various wines it produces here from Washington vineyards (mainly Columbia Valley merlots and chardonnays) as well as Oregon pinots. A gourmet food and gift market is on site.

ARGYLE WINERY (691 Hwy 99W, Dundee; 503/538-8520) is producing some of the best sparkling wines in the region as well as fine chardonnays and pinot noirs. *Wine Spectator*'s "Oregon's Best All-Around Winery" in 1999, Argyle has a tasting room ensconced in a restored Victorian farmhouse.

ERATH VINEYARDS (9409 NE Worden Hill Rd, Dundee; 503/538-3318) is one of the pioneer Oregon wineries, noted for wonderful pinots and late-harvest rieslings. Dick Erath's wines are a good value, and his winery is in a beautiful setting uphill from Crabtree Park—good for picnics.

SOKOL BLOSSER WINERY (5000 Sokol Blosser Ln, Dundee; 503/864-2282), high on a hill overlooking the Yamhill Valley, offers visitors a self-guided vineyard tour showcasing grape varieties and seasonal change. The winery is renowned for its pinot noirs and its unique underground barrel-aging cellar, winner of environmental design awards.

CHATEAU BENOIT WINERY (6580 NE Mineral Springs Rd, Carlton; 503/864-2991) is best known for pinots, chardonnays, and German-style white wines. With a marvelous hilltop view, it's popular with picnickers.

LAUREL RIDGE WINERY (13301 NE Kuehne Rd, Carlton; 503/852-7050) has a new location in the Willakenzie district where you can taste excellent sparkling wine and award-winning sauvignon blanc and pinot noir.

Many other wineries are open to the public only on Thanksgiving and Memorial Day weekends, or by appointment. Most offer case discounts over the holiday weekends. For a complete guide to the state's wineries, contact the **OREGON WINE ADVISORY BOARD** (1200 NW Naito Pkwy, Ste 400, Portland; 503/228-8336; www.oregonwine.org).

Conclude your wine touring with a visit to **THE LAWRENCE GALLERY** (19700 SW Hwy 18, Sheridan; 503/843-3633), about 10 minutes' drive beyond McMinnville. There's an outdoor garden where you can picnic among the sculptures, and an indoor display of paintings, jewelry, prints, and pottery by some 200 artists. (Ask to see the tonalist Wine Country landscapes of local painter Romona Youngquist.) Within the gallery is the **OREGON WINE TASTING ROOM** (503/843-3787), where you can sample wines from more than 50 different wineries—including a long and impressive roster of Oregon pinot noirs. Put your new wine knowledge to good use as you order lunch at **FRESH PALATE** (503/843-4400), above the gallery. Eating on the deck feels like dining in the treetops; Northwest cuisine, crab cakes, and sandwiches are all made from scratch.

MCMINNVILLE

With about 27,000 residents, **MCMINNVILLE** is decidedly the population center of Oregon's wine country. One of Oregon's earliest communities (founded in 1843), it is the home of **LINFIELD COLLEGE**, a long-established liberal arts institution. At the Chamber of Commerce (417 NW Adams St; 503/472-6196), pick up a walking-tour map of the **DOWNTOWN HISTORIC DISTRICT**; it points out many late-19th- and early-20th-century buildings up and down Third Street.

Then drop by the new **EVERGREEN AVIATION MUSEUM** (3685 NE Cumulus Ave at the McMinnville airport; 503/472-9361). Howard Hughes's famous "flying boat," the **SPRUCE GOOSE**, is the star attraction here. The largest aircraft in the world, it was built to carry 750 men into World War II battle. The plane has a 335-foot wingspan and took so long to build that the war ended before the plane was completed. The institute also has a '40s-style cafe, a movie theater, and 40 other planes on display.

Another McMinnville attraction is the McMenamin brothers' **HOTEL OREGON** (310 NE Evans St; 503/472-8427), which will celebrate its 100th birthday in 2005. The refurbished four-story hotel has 42 rooms and a popular pub for dining and drinking—making it a great place to stay, whether you're going on the cheap or splurging.

WASHINGTON COUNTY WINERIES

Even nearer to Portland than the Yamhill County wineries are the dozen or so of Washington County's Tualatin Valley. It's easy to pack a picnic lunch and take a short afternoon drive west of the metropolis. Each of the following recommended wineries has a three-decade reputation, and each welcomes visitors daily year-round.

PONZI VINEYARDS (14665 SW Winery Lane, Beaverton; 503/628-1227), designed by Dick and Nancy Ponzi, is now in the hands of their three children. Bottlings of pinot noir, pinot gris, and chardonnay are first-rate. The Ponzis also own and operate the charming Dundee Bistro (see review in the Restaurants chapter).

OAK KNOLL WINERY (29700 SW Burkhalter Rd, Hillsboro; 503/648-8198) produces notable fruit and berry wines (including a raspberry framboise), plus award-winning pinot noir and pinot gris. Founded in 1970 by the Vuylsteke family, its picnic grounds are very popular.

SHAFER VINEYARD CELLARS (6200 NW Gates Creek Rd, Forest Grove; 503/357-6604; open weekends only in Jan), at its tasting room overlooking the Gates Creek Valley, shares an unusually wide range of wines: sparkling wines, pinot noir, pinot gris, chardonnay, riesling, and German-style whites (gewürztraminer and Muller-Thurgau). Be sure to visit Miki Shafer's quaint Christmas shop.

Champoeg-Aurora

A pair of old pioneer communities on opposite sides of the Willamette River, about 20 miles south of Portland via I-5, Champoeg and Aurora can make an interesting half-day trip for the history-minded traveler.

Even before fur traders and settlers arrived in the early 1800s, **CHAMPOEG** (pronounced "sham POO ey") was home to Calapooya Indians. Today it is remembered by the **CHAMPOEG STATE HERITAGE AREA** (8239 Champoeg Rd NE, St. Paul; 503/678-1251), a 568-acre park on the banks of the Willamette. The excellent visitors center describes how, in 1843, local settlers voted to form the first provisional government of the Oregon Country. In **MOTHER'S PIONEER CABIN** (open Mon and Fri–Sat; admission $2 adults, $1 children), an original log cabin maintained by the Daughters of the American Revolution, kids can knead bread dough, card wool, and make fires using flint and steel—just as pioneer children did. The heritage area charges a $3 vehicle fee, allowing picnickers, bicyclists, Frisbee throwers, and volleyball players to enjoy it on summer weekends.

Just west of the park entrance is the **NEWELL HOUSE** (503/678-5537; call for hours, closed Nov–Feb; admission $2 adults, $1 children), a replica of the 1852 original, which serves as a museum of Native American and pioneer artifacts. On the grounds are the Butteville Jail (1850) and a pioneer schoolhouse.

The town of **AURORA**, midway between Portland and Salem on the east bank of the Willamette, is a well-preserved turn-of-the-20th-century village that's been put on the National Register of Historic Places. It's also a well-known antique center. About two dozen clapboard and Victorian houses line a mile-long stretch of State Hwy 99E, and more than half of them have been made into antique shops (most closed Mon). An outstanding restaurant, the popular **CHEZ MOUSTACHE** (21527 Hwy 99E; 503/678-1866) has for many years served French continental cuisine.

In 1856, Prussian immigrant Dr. William Keil led a group of Pennsylvania Germans here to establish a communal settlement of Harmonites; Aurora is named for Keil's daughter. Property, labor, and profits were shared, and the society prospered under his autocratic rule. Farming sustained the economy, but outsiders knew the colony for the excellence of its handicrafts: furniture, clothing, tools, embroidered goods, baskets, and clarinet reeds. After a smallpox epidemic in 1862 and the coming of the railroad in 1870, the colony gradually weakened.

The **OLD AURORA COLONY MUSEUM** (2nd Ave and Liberty St; 503/678-5754) recounts the history of the town with five buildings: the ox barn, the Karus home, the Steinbach log cabin, the communal washhouse, and the farm-equipment shed. Among its annual events, Colony Days in August and a quilt show in October are standouts (call for opening days, which vary annually; admission $3.50 adults, $1.50 children).

Northern Oregon Coast

It won't take you much more than 90 minutes, if that, to drive to the Oregon Coast from Portland. Once you've arrived, however, chances are you'll want to stay for longer than a day. Technically, it's no problem driving our 300-mile loop—Portland to Astoria, south down US Hwy 101 to Lincoln City, then back to Portland—in a single day. Practically speaking, you may want to take three days.

Therefore, we've broken the northern Oregon Coast into three sections: Astoria to Seaside (between US Hwys 30 and 26), Cannon Beach to Tillamook (US Hwy 26 and State Hwy 6), and Tillamook to Lincoln City (State Hwys 6 and 18). Any one of these loops provides you quick access to and from Portland, in case you must cut your journey short.

ASTORIA TO SEASIDE

Situated on the tip of a peninsula where the Columbia River reaches the Pacific Ocean, **ASTORIA** has a unique, edge-of-the-world flavor. Its Victorian architecture, natural beauty, and rich Native American and immigrant history offer much to the visitor.

Take Hwy 30 west from I-405; it's 107 miles from Portland to Astoria. Your first stop might be the **ASTORIA COLUMN**, atop Coxcomb Hill, Astoria's highest point. The 164-step climb to the top is well worth it, affording a seemingly endless panoramic view of the harbor, the Columbia estuary, and the distant headlands of the Pacific. Spiral murals of the region's history wrap around the outside of the column. To get there, drive up to the top of 16th Street and follow the signs.

The history of U.S. exploration and settlement here begins with Captain Robert Gray, who sailed up the river in 1792, naming it after his ship, the *Columbia Rediviva*—which saw only 10 miles of the river before turning back to sea. In 1805–1806, Lewis and Clark spent a miserably rainy winter at Fort Clatsop, now restored as the **FORT CLATSOP NATIONAL MEMORIAL** (6 miles southwest of Astoria; 503/861-2471). Besides audiovisuals and exhibits in the visitors center, there are living-history demonstrations (musket firing, candle making) during the summer.

Five years later, in 1810, New York fur trader John Jacob Astor, one of America's wealthiest individuals, sent to the Northwest the fur-trading company that founded **FORT ASTORIA** (1811–1825). The fort had all but disappeared by the mid-19th century but now has been partially reconstructed (at 15th and Exchange Sts).

The city of Astoria really dates from the late 1840s, when it began to thrive as a customhouse town and shipping center. The well-maintained Victorians lining the harbor hillside at Franklin and Grand Avenues provide glimpses of that era. Astoria today is a museum without walls, an unstirred mix of the old and new that finds common ground along the busy waterfront—once the site of canneries and river steamers, now an active port for oceangoing vessels and Russian fish-processing ships. Salmon and bottom-fishing trips leave from here.

SIXTH STREET RIVER PARK, with its always-open, covered observation tower, provides the best vantage point for viewing river commerce, observing river pilots as they board tankers and freighters, and watching seals and sea lions search for a free lunch. Just down the waterfront is the **COLUMBIA RIVER MARITIME MUSEUM** (foot of 17th St; 503/325-2323; admission $8 adults, discounts for seniors and children), the finest museum of its type in the Northwest. The 1951 Coast Guard lightship *Columbia* is moored outside, and inside are restored small craft and thematic galleries depicting the region's maritime heritage: fishing and whaling, fur trading, navigation, and shipwrecks.

Three other museums devoted to Astoria's history are operated by the Clatsop County Historical Society (503/325-2203). The **CLATSOP COUNTY HERITAGE MUSEUM** (16th and Exchange Sts; 503/338-4849) is in the 1904 city hall building. The **FLAVEL HOUSE** (8th and Duane Sts) is the city's best example of ornate Queen

Anne architecture, built by the Columbia River's first steamship pilot, Captain George Flavel. The **UPPERTOWN FIREFIGHTERS MUSEUM** (2986 Marine Dr) houses an extensive collection of fire-fighting equipment dating back to 1879.

An unpretentious town of about 10,000 residents, Astoria all but shuts down on Sundays. Downtown, art galleries are tucked in next to the fishermen's bars and mom-and-pop cafes, and there are a few notable restaurants as well. If there's a gathering place for the town's intelligentsia, it's **GODFATHER'S BOOKS AND ESPRESSO** (1108 Commercial St; 503/325-8143).

Bed-and-breakfasts have proliferated, particularly in the lovely Victorian homes on the steep hillsides overlooking the river. The **BENJAMIN YOUNG INN** (3652 Duane St; 503/325-6172 or 800/201-1286) has five lavishly decorated guest rooms and stellar views of the Columbia River. The Finnish innkeepers at the **ROSE RIVER INN** (1510 Franklin Ave; 503/325-7175 or 888/876-0028) lend a European flair to their lodging; ask about the sauna paneled in Alaska yellow cedar. The reasonably priced and rambling **ROSEBRIAR INN** (636 14th St; 503/325-7427) has 11 rooms, each with a private bath.

For upscale creative dining, visit the **SILVER SALMON GRILLE** (1105 Commercial St; 503/338-6640) or **T. PAUL'S URBAN CAFE** (1119 Commercial St; 503/338-5133). The Cajun chef at **HOME SPIRIT BAKERY AND CAFE** (in an old Victorian at 1585 Exchange St; 503/325-6846) makes his pastas and ice cream from scratch, and a local forager delivers wild mushrooms and watercress daily. The **RIO CAFE** (125 9th St; 503/325-2409) offers inspired south-of-the-border cuisine. But the place to go in this fishermen's town for Sunday brunch and the catch of the day is the **CANNERY CAFE** (at the foot of 6th St; 503/325-8642), which sits on pilings right over the water. Buy fresh seafood at **FERGUS-MCBARENDSE** (at the foot of 11th St; 503/325-0688) or at **JOSEPHSON'S SMOKEHOUSE** (106 Marine Dr; 503/325-2190), whose superb hot-smoked and cold-smoked seafood includes salmon, tuna, and sturgeon.

Astoria is a natural starting point for excursions to the Oregon and Washington coasts. Get panoramic views of both from the **SOUTH JETTY LOOKOUT TOWER**, Oregon's northwesternmost point. **FORT STEVENS STATE PARK AND HISTORICAL SITE** (Pacific Dr, Hammond), 20 minutes west of Astoria off Hwy 101, preserves a military reservation built at the mouth of the Columbia during the Civil War as part of Oregon's coastal defense. Fired upon in June 1942 by a Japanese submarine, it was the only fort in the continental United States to see action during World War II. Today Fort Stevens is a 3,500-acre park offering 604 campsites, 7 miles of bike paths, uncrowded beaches, and Mongolian yurts (rigid-walled, domed tents) for rent. (Yurts in Oregon state parks have light, heat, and sleeping space for eight people. For reservations and information, call Reservations Northwest; 800/452-5687.) Walk the beach to see the rusted hulk of the British schooner *Peter Iredale*, wrecked in 1906.

Fifteen miles south of Astoria, **SEASIDE** is a horse of a very different color. Just past the charming, almost-bohemian seaside village of **GEARHART**, which lures visitors to its **PACIFIC WAY BAKERY & CAFE** (601 Pacific Wy; 503/738-0245), Seaside is a mini Atlantic City, minus the casinos.

Established at the turn of the 20th century as a summer resort for Portlanders, the town today spreads north and south along Hwy 101, flanking both sides of the tidal Necanicum River. Broadway, its main drag, is lined with souvenir shops, seafood houses, and youth-oriented amusement centers. From the vehicle turnaround at its seaward end, a broad paved pedestrian walk—known as **NORTH PROM** and **SOUTH PROM**—extends a 1½ miles along the shore, sometimes shielded from the waves by bunchgrass.

Seaside's premier attraction is its historic **SEASIDE AQUARIUM** (200 N Prom; 503/738-6211), Oregon's original (1937) marine-life center, though its importance has long since been eclipsed by Newport's Oregon Coast Aquarium. The **SEASIDE HISTORICAL SOCIETY MUSEUM** (570 Necanicum Dr; 503/738-7065) encompasses the 1912 Butterfield Beach Cottage. On the south side of town, you can view a circa-1900 recreation of a **SALT CAIRN** established at the site by the Lewis and Clark expedition (the southernmost point they visited); a touching **UNKNOWN SAILOR'S GRAVE** ("Found on the Beach April 25 1865 Known Only to God"); and a popular cold-water surfing destination at **THE COVE** (watch the dry-suited athletes from benches in Seltzer Park).

The Seaside Chamber of Commerce (800/444-6740) recommends 48 places to stay in town, including the unique **SEASIDE OCEANFRONT INN** (581 S Prom; 503/738-6403 or 888/772-7766). For dining, consider Mediterranean-flavored **KALYPSO** (619 Broadway; 503/738-6309) and the ever-popular **NORMA'S OCEAN DINER** (20 N Columbia St; 503/738-4331).

Four miles south of Seaside, Hwy 101 meets Hwy 26, the most direct route back to Portland from the coast. Cannon Beach is about 3 miles south of the intersection.

CANNON BEACH TO TILLAMOOK

CANNON BEACH relishes its reputation as the Carmel of the Northwest. This artsy community with a hip ambience has strict building codes that prohibit neon and ensure that only aesthetically pleasing structures of weathered cedar and other woods are built. In summer, the town explodes with visitors who come to browse local galleries and crafts shops or to rub shoulders with the coastal intelligentsia on crowded Hemlock Street. Its main draw is the spectacular beach: wide, inviting, and among the prettiest anywhere. Dominating the long, sandy stretch is **HAYSTACK ROCK**, one of the world's largest coastal monoliths at 235 feet high. It's impressive enough just to gaze at, but check it out at low tide to observe the rich marine life in the tidal pools.

ECOLA STATE PARK (on the town's north side) has fine overlooks, picnic tables, and good hiking trails. If you climb to Tillamook Head, you can see the Tillamook Rock Light Station, a lighthouse built offshore under difficult conditions more than 100 years ago and abandoned in 1957. Today it is a columbarium (a facility for storing cremated remains) called "Eternity at Sea." No camping is allowed along the densely wooded trail, except for summer campsites atop the Head.

Shopping is a favorite pastime in Cannon Beach, and there are enough shops and galleries along Hemlock Street, the main drag, to keep you busy until the tide goes out. Especially good ones are **THE JEFFREY HULL GALLERY** (172 N Hemlock

St in Sandpiper Square; 503/436-2600), with notable watercolors; **HAYSTACK GAL-LERY** (183 N Hemlock St in Cannon Beach Mall; 503/436-2547), with prints and photographs; **WHITEBIRD GALLERY** (251 N Hemlock St; 503/436-2681), featuring a variety of arts and crafts; and **RHODES STRINGFELLOW** (219 N Hemlock St; 503/436-8520), with fine paintings and sculptures extending from the gallery into its courtyard.

The **COASTER THEATRE PLAYHOUSE** (108 N Hemlock St; 503/436-1242) has a year-round schedule of mainly comedies and musicals. Its summer repertory theater includes the likes of Ken Ludwig's *Moon Over Buffalo*, George Stiles's and Anthony Drewes's *Honk!*, and Ira Levin's *Death Trap*. Portland State University's **HAYSTACK PROGRAM IN THE ARTS** (in Portland; 503/725-8500) conducts workshops for adult students at the Cannon Beach grade school.

There are several good restaurants in town. The **OCEANFRONT WAYFARER** (Oceanfront and Gower Sts; 503/436-1108) and **JP'S AT CANNON BEACH** (1116 S Hemlock St in the Cannon Beach Hotel; 503/436-0908) are renowned for their seafood. For something more artsy, in keeping with the community's ambience, consider **THE BISTRO** (263 N Hemlock St; 503/436-2661), intimate and rustic, with Mediterranean-style chops, seafood, and pastas; or **THE LAZY SUSAN** (126 N Hemlock St; 503/436-2816), a casual restaurant beside the Coaster Theatre. And don't fail to have at least one breakfast at **CAFE MANGO** (1235 S Hemlock St; 503/436-2393).

For accommodation, a centrally located choice is the clean and comfortable **ARGONAUTA INN** (188 W 2nd St; 503/436-2601 or 800/822-2468), in a series of early-20th-century Victorian beachside cottages, now operated by the Waves Motel. The nicely refurbished **CANNON BEACH HOTEL** (116 S Hemlock St; 503/436-1392) is on the main road through town and three blocks from the beach.

The south side of Cannon Beach is better suited for luxury lodgers. Side by side on a beautiful stretch of sand are two elegant properties. The well-known **STEPH-ANIE INN** (2740 S Pacific St; 503/436-2221 or 800/633-3466) has 46 rooms with ocean or mountain views and a renowned prix-fixe dining room with two seatings nightly (non-Inn guests can also dine here). Its beautiful new, pet-friendly next-door neighbor, **THE OCEAN LODGE** (2864 S Pacific St; 503/436-2241 or 888/777-4047), has 45 rooms with fireplaces and eight beach bungalows.

TOLOVANA PARK, nestled on Cannon Beach's south side, is more laid-back and less crowded than the in-town beach. Leave your vehicle at the Tolovana Park Wayside (with parking and restrooms) and stroll the uncluttered beach. At low tide you can walk all the way to Arch Cape, 5 miles south, but take care: the incoming tide might block your return. **HUG POINT STATE PARK**, south of Arch Cape, comprises a rocky beach nestled between two headlands. Just south of here is **OSWALD WEST STATE PARK**, with one of the finest campgrounds on any coast in the world. You walk a half mile from the parking lot (where wheelbarrows are available to carry your gear) to tent sites among old-growth trees; the ocean, with a massive cove and tide pools, is just beyond. No reservations (open for camping Mar–Oct only), but the walk deters some of the crowds who might otherwise come.

Low-key **MANZANITA** is gaining popularity as a second home for in-the-know Portlanders. The attractions are obvious: the adjacent Nehalem Bay area is a windsurfing mecca, and **NEHALEM BAY STATE PARK**, just south of town, offers hiking and bike trails, miles of little-used beaches, and lodging in yurts. Overlooking it all is nearby **NEAHKAHNIE MOUNTAIN**, its steep, switchbacked trail leading to a 1,600-foot summit with the best viewpoints on Oregon's North Coast. Hundreds of miles of Coast Range logging roads offer unlimited mountain-biking thrills. The nearby, quaint river town of **NEHALEM**, just inland from Manzanita, is becoming a destination for kayakers who find rental craft available here.

Besides a great beach, Manzanita has great food. The sweet **BLUE SKY CAFÉ** (154 Laneda Ave; 503/368-5712) has a menu that is far-flung and ambitious, and lacks any pretension. The best pizza on the North Coast can be had at **MARZANO'S** (60 Laneda Ave; 503/368-3663). For a pampered, adults-only retreat, try **THE INN AT MANZANITA** (67 Laneda Ave; 503/368-6754).

A few miles south of Manzanita, at the head of Tillamook Bay, is the old fishing town of **GARIBALDI**, whose charms are all about fresh seafood. Head out to the fishermen's terminal to buy shrimp, crab, salmon, tuna, lingcod, and bottom fish from **BAY OCEAN SEAFOOD** (608 Commercial Dr; 503/322-3316), or take a table and order some finny delights at the nearby **TILLAMOOK BAY BOATHOUSE** (500 S Biak St; 503/322-3600). Nearby **BAY CITY** is Oyster Central: watch the gritty mollusks harvested and shucked at the **PACIFIC OYSTER COMPANY** (5150 Oyster Dr; 503/377-2323); see them artistically rendered at the **ARTSPACE** gallery and bistro (Hwy 101 and 5th St; 503/377-2782); or stop for a bowl of chowder at **DOWNIE'S CAFE** (9320 5th St; 503/377-2220).

If you're planning to return to Portland, turn east on Hwy 6 in downtown **TILLAMOOK**. The big city is a 78-mile drive.

TILLAMOOK TO LINCOLN CITY

In Tillamook County alone, there are 198 dairy farms and 41,600 cows. So say the displays at the **TILLAMOOK COUNTY CREAMERY ASSOCIATION** (4175 Hwy 101 N; 503/815-1300)—better known as the Tillamook cheese factory. With an international reputation, this cheesery at the north end of town draws hordes of tourists for the self-guided tour (including big windows overlooking the factory floor) and for scoops of rich ice cream in waffle cones. For less kitsch—but no ice cream—you might drive another mile south on Hwy 101 to the **BLUE HERON FRENCH CHEESE COMPANY** (2001 Blue Heron Dr; 503/842-8281), where you can sample a variety of cheeses and other Oregon-made specialty foods, including wine.

The **TILLAMOOK COUNTY PIONEER MUSEUM** (2106 2nd St; 503/842-4553) occupies three floors of Tillamook's 1905 county courthouse. Shipwreck buffs will be particularly interested in the artifacts (including huge chunks of beeswax with Spanish markings) from an unnamed 18th-century Spanish galleon that wrecked near the base of Neahkahnie Mountain. The new **MUNSON FALLS NATURAL SITE** (Munson Creek Rd off Hwy 101), 7 miles south of Tillamook, features a 319-foot waterfall—Oregon's second tallest.

Tillamook lodgings are strictly of the franchise variety, but the town does have a couple of noteworthy restaurants. The **CEDAR BAY RESTAURANT** (2015 1st St; 503/842-8288) offers a wide selection of traditional steaks, seafoods, and pasta dishes. The charming **COYOTE MOON CAFE** (116 Main Ave; 503/842-2666) prepares creative global cuisine, accompanied by a nice wine list.

Unless you're in a tremendous hurry to get to Lincoln City, plan to detour close to the water, following the 22-mile **THREE CAPES SCENIC DRIVE**. This is arguably Oregon's most beautiful stretch of coastline. The narrow, winding road skirts Tillamook Bay, climbs over **CAPE MEARES** (a state park with a working lighthouse), traverses the shores of Netarts Bay, and runs over **CAPE LOOKOUT**, westernmost headland on the north Oregon Coast. The trail from the parking lot at Cape Lookout's summit meanders through primeval forests of stately cedar and Sitka spruce. Camping facilities in the state park include yurts.

The lower side of the drive provides spectacular ocean vistas. Down at sea level, the desertlike dune landscape presents a stark contrast to Cape Lookout's densely forested slopes. The road to **PACIFIC CITY** and the route's third cape, **CAPE KIWANDA**, runs through lush, green dairy country. Pacific City is known for its hang gliders, which swoop off the slopes of the cape and land on the sandy expanses below. Another Haystack Rock sits a half-mile offshore. Even if you've never visited before, this area may look familiar: the late Ray Atkeson, a nationally acclaimed Oregon photographer, made Cape Kiwanda the most photographed spot on the Oregon Coast.

ROBERT STRAUB STATE PARK sits at the south end of town and occupies most of the Nestucca Beach sand spit. The Nestucca River flows idly to the sea right outside the **RIVERHOUSE RESTAURANT** (34450 Brooten Rd; 503/965-6722), a calming, apple-pie sort of place. Gargantuan cinnamon rolls and loaves of crusty bread can be had nearby at the **GRATEFUL BREAD BAKERY** (34805 Brooten Rd; 503/965-7337). At the secluded **EAGLE'S VIEW BED AND BREAKFAST** (37975 Brooten Rd; 503/965-7600), all five guest rooms have private baths. As you might guess, the panoramas are grand.

The Nestucca dairy land inland from here is some of the most fertile in the state. You can pick up Hwy 101 again in **CLOVERDALE**, a town that became famous for a 1986–1987 battle with state officials over two roadside signs (featuring Clover the Cow) that violated a state signage law. Outside Cloverdale, in the middle of nowhere, is the historic 1906 **HUDSON HOUSE BED & BREAKFAST** (37700 Hwy 101 S; 503/392-3533).

OTIS is barely more than a junction, but the busy **OTIS CAFE** (you can't miss it; 541/994-2813) and its down-home breakfasts, shakes, and homemade pies—good enough to have been touted in the *New York Times*—have put this tiny town on the map. Here's where Hwy 18 from Portland (a two-hour drive) joins Hwy 101, just north of Lincoln City.

If local business owners have their way, **LINCOLN CITY** may someday have a more "beach-like" (and thus more tourist-friendly) name. Most locals seem happy with the name as is, though, and it hasn't stopped hordes of Willamette Valley residents from converging on Lincoln City year-round. Whale watchers appreciate the nearby viewpoints, shoppers hunt for bargains at the huge outlet mall on the east side of Hwy 101, and others simply pass through before dispersing to quieter points north and south. This is a good place to pop in your favorite CD: if you're continuing south another 25 miles to Newport, the congestion may slow you down a bit.

Outstanding lodgings are few and far between in Lincoln City, although the scene is slightly improved over years past. The upscale, oceanfront **O'DYSIUS HOTEL** (120 NW Inlet Ct; 541/994-4121 or 800/869-8069) contains 30 sizable units outfitted with such amenities as fireplaces and whirlpool baths. The **INN AT SPANISH HEAD** (4009 SW Hwy 101; 541/996-2161 or 800/452-8127) is a 10-story, 120-room hotel with a large outdoor swimming pool and full kitchens in most rooms.

Consistently the finest place to dine is the **BAY HOUSE** (5911 SW Hwy 101; 541/996-3222), where the food, like the view, is worth savoring. The **BLACKFISH CAFÉ** (2733 NW Hwy 101; 541/996-1007) has a bustling open kitchen that turns out exemplary clam chowder, and much more. At the **LIGHTHOUSE BREW PUB** (4157 N Hwy 101; 541/994-7238), expect the same pub grub as at any McMenamins establishment—and beer made on the premises. Two good shopping stops are **BARNACLE BILL'S SEAFOOD MARKET** (2174 NE Hwy 101; 541/994-3022), famous for fresh seafood and smoked fish—salmon, sturgeon, albacore tuna, and black cod; and **CATCH THE WIND KITE SHOP** (266 SE Hwy 101; 541/994-9500), headquarters for a coastal chain of excellent kite stores.

ITINERARIES

ITINERARIES

Portland is a compact, walkable city, and even on a short stopover visitors can get a sense of what makes it such a livable, well-loved place. The following itineraries include suggestions for meals and for evening entertainment and for ways to enjoy a day in the City of Roses with kids. Information about most of the places shown in boldface can be found in other chapters of the book (Restaurants, Shopping, Exploring, and Nightlife).

Three-Day Tour

DAY ONE

Spend this first day exploring the sights and shops of downtown Portland, arguably one of the busiest and healthiest downtown cores in the country. The best way to get around is on foot, but driving from area to area is not difficult either, although parking can be hit or miss. Tri-Met buses in the downtown core's Fareless Square are free, as is the MAX train; just board at any stop and ride within the parameters of the Willamette River on the east side, I-405 on the west and south, and NW Irving Street on the north. For further information, call Tri-Met (503/238-7433).

MORNING: Start with breakfast downtown on Broadway, a one-way street that runs north to south past such quintessential Portland sights as **PIONEER COURTHOUSE SQUARE** (between SW Morrison and Yamhill Streets), **NORDSTROM** (710 SW Broadway; 503/224-6666), and **THE HEATHMAN HOTEL** (corner of SW Broadway and Salmon St; 503/241-4100). In fact, king salmon hash at **THE HEATHMAN RESTAURANT AND BAR** (reserve through the hotel) is a tasteful and tasty way to begin the day, although if coffee and a pastry are all you need, **PAZZORIA**, about five blocks north off SW Broadway (next to Pazzo, 625 SW Washington St; 503/228-1695) is a fine, fast choice. After breakfast, stretch your legs in **GOV. TOM MCCALL WATERFRONT PARK**, one of Portland's showpiece greenspaces, sandwiched between the Willamette River and a busy north–south thoroughfare, the Naito Parkway. Start just south of the **RIVERPLACE HOTEL** (1510 SW Harbor Wy; 503/228-3233) and walk north on the promenade, browsing the row of retail shops. A picturesque marina is set alongside the river here; procure a frozen yogurt or a cup of coffee, find a bench, and enjoy the passing boat show.

Continue your walk north along the sidewalk; you'll pass close to the **SALMON STREET SPRINGS**, with its waterworks show that's a playground for squealing children throughout the summer months. Continue on beneath the Burnside Bridge and, if it's a weekend day between early March and the end of December, you'll want to pause here at the **SATURDAY MARKET**, for great people watching, better-than-average booth food, and loads of handmade Oregon craft items—from beaded earrings to fireplace pokers—to take home to Kansas or Kyoto.

AFTERNOON: Lunch at the Saturday Market is satisfying and fun, but if it's a weekday and there's no sign of a food booth in sight, make your way to the longtime favorite **BIJOU CAFÉ** (132 SW 3rd Ave; 503/222-3187) for a memorable burger or salad. After lunch, take in the new **PORTLAND CLASSICAL CHINESE GARDEN** (admission $7, discounts for seniors and kids) between NW Second and Third Avenues and between NW Everett and Flanders Streets (enter at NW 3rd Ave and Everett St). The garden is a meditative place, and you might be compelled to spend all afternoon here, sipping tea in what may be the most authentic classical Chinese teahouse in the country, run by the able tea masters of the **TAO OF TEA**. If not, make tracks to the elm-lined **SOUTH PARK BLOCKS**.

Portland State University anchors this string of well-tended blocks at the south end; at the north end sits **SOUTHPARK** (901 SW Salmon St; 503/326-1300), where you can try a glass of Oregon wine or eat a blood-sugar-boosting midafternoon dessert. Art lovers should steer toward the **PORTLAND ART MUSEUM** (1219 SW Park Ave; 503/226-2811), and history buffs can go across the street to the **OREGON HISTORY CENTER** (1200 SW Park Ave; 503/222-1741). Shoppers will be happy to know they can skip the museums altogether, but hit the **MUSEUM SHOPS**, both of which are excellent (the art museum shop is off the courtyard; the history center's is right on SW Broadway). Almost any time is shopping time at **PIONEER PLACE** (on the blocks between SW 3rd and 5th Aves and SW Yamhill and Morrison Sts), but many downtown stores close at 6pm, so you'll want to plan to finish by then.

EVENING: Make a dinner reservation at **HIGGINS** (1239 SW Broadway; 503/222-9070), where local ingredients receive reverential treatment under the careful eye of local food master Greg Higgins; it's located just off the South Park Blocks in the same block as the Oregon History Center. Or if a view is what you crave, head to the **PORTLAND CITY GRILL** (111 SW 5th St; 503/450-0030) on the 30th floor of the US Bancorp Tower (lovingly known as the Big Pink for its pinkish glass exterior). Arrange to see a music or theater performance in the **PORTLAND CENTER FOR THE PERFORMING ARTS' WINNINGSTAD THEATRE** (1111 SW Broadway; 503/796-9293) or across Main Street at the **ARLENE SCHNITZER CONCERT HALL** (same phone). If neither of those options appeals, take a walk along Broadway; even in the waning hours of the evening, pedestrians (residents, late workers, tourists, and gadflies) are still enjoying the city's very vital downtown.

DAY TWO

On the second day, discover the area **IN AND AROUND NORTHWEST PORTLAND**, especially NW 23rd and 21st Avenues, and the arty **PEARL DISTRICT**. Once more, we prefer walking to other modes of transportation, and although the I-405 freeway divides the two areas, there are several easy foot passages that cross from the neighborhood on the west side of the freeway to the Pearl on the east. But other options abound: driving gives you the most flexibility, but Tri-Met bus 15 (to NW 23rd Ave) goes from downtown to NW Thurman Street in a quick 20 minutes, and you don't have to park the bus. The new **PORTLAND STREETCAR** also makes this a quick trip from the downtown core.

MORNING: Begin this day with a four-square breakfast at **BESAW'S** (2301 NW Savier St; 503/228-2619). Thus fueled, head south along NW 23rd Avenue. **WINDOW SHOPPING** is pure pleasure, especially in the area south of Good Samaritan Hospital. Many of the street's original Victorian-era houses have been developed into boutiques and shops, and there are plenty of cool cafes and coffee stops interspersed (one caveat: some shops don't open until 11am). One store that's pure Portland is longtime tenant **MUSIC MILLENNIUM** (801 NW 23rd Ave; 503/248-0163), where you can get Pink Martini's new CD. Another is **URBINO** (638 NW 23rd Ave; 503/220-0053), with its beautiful albeit pricey inventory of goods for your home. Zigzag along NW 23rd (there are shops for 10 blocks straight, and then some) as long as you can stand it, but before you leave the neighborhood be sure to poke into **TWIST** (30 NW 23rd Pl; 503/224-0334), where the selection of dishes, jewelry, furniture, and tabletop items made mostly by American craftspeople would be notable in any city (to reach the shop, turn west off of NW 23rd Ave onto W Burnside St, and double-back onto the half-block-long NW 23rd Pl).

If you follow NW 23rd Avenue across W Burnside Street, it becomes SW Vista Avenue. One of Portland's more exclusive neighborhoods, Portland Heights, is just off this route. SW Vista is also the easiest way to get to the **WASHINGTON PARK'S INTERNATIONAL ROSE TEST GARDEN** or to the **JAPANESE GARDEN** from Northwest Portland. Walk a couple of blocks up—up as in climb—SW Vista Avenue to Park Place and turn right. Here you can catch bus 63 to take you up into Washington Park (or if you haven't climbed enough already, continue your hike). Disembark at the tennis courts to visit either the rose garden (just down the hill to your left) or the Japanese Garden (uphill on your right). Or stay on the bus until it reaches the big parking lot near the **OREGON ZOO** and the **WORLD FORESTRY CENTER**. From here you can also check out **HOYT ARBORETUM**, where dozens of species of trees are labeled. One of Portland's longest, most woodsy hiking trails is the **WILDWOOD TRAIL**; it starts near the **VIETNAM VETERANS' LIVING MEMORIAL**, near the forestry center, and will take you through Washington Park and beyond.

AFTERNOON: Lunch at the Oregon Zoo's **CASCADE GRILL** is possible—and not bad, really, for zoo food—even if you don't actually enter the zoo. Or head back down to Northwest Portland for outstanding Thai food at **TYPHOON!** (2310 NW Everett St; 503/243-7557). Another can't-miss choice is **PAPA HAYDN**, at NW 23rd Avenue and Irving Street (701 NW 23rd Ave; 503/228-7317), where you can get a salad and a voluptuous dessert and have a good view of the people parade along the street. (Both of these restaurants have outdoor seating, a nice choice come summer.) There are also many excellent restaurants along NW 21st Avenue—two blocks east of 23rd Avenue—that serve lunch and dinner, including **SERRATTO** (2112 NW Kearney St; 503/221-1195), a lovely place to linger over a leisurely Italian lunch, and **BASTA'S TRATTORIA** (410 NW 21st Ave; 503/274-1572), for heavenly pasta and other Italian fare.

After lunch, walk east on NW Everett Street or Lovejoy Street to the Pearl District. A onetime warehouse and light industrial area, the Pearl is caught up in a renaissance. This neighborhood continues to be gentrified, with new structures going up among once-decrepit buildings that now house work/live lofts, advertising and high-tech offices, and arty retail space (especially art galleries and furniture stores). Be sure to hit NW Everett, Glisan, or Hoyt Streets, but don't overlook the cross streets either. A few places to be sure to check out are **PICA** (Portland Institute for Contemporary Art; 219 NW 12th Ave; 503/242-1419), in the elegant Wieden + Kennedy (of advertising fame) Building; **IN GOOD TASTE** (231 NW 11th Ave; 503/248-2015), where foodies run amok; and if there's a child in your life, **HANNA**

ANDERSSON (327 NW 10th Ave; 503/321-5275), for Swedish cotton clothing via Oregon.

EVENING: These days the Pearl District has almost as many restaurants as art galleries. For dinner, try **BLUEHOUR** (250 NW 13th Ave; 503/226-3394), for elaborate surroundings and Mediterranean-style food, or **FRATELLI** (1230 NW Hoyt St; 503/241-8800), a romantic and artsy niche serving innovative Italian cuisine. There are plenty of options for lingering over a cocktail, too: **¡OBA!** (555 NW 12th Ave; 503/228-6161) is a popular dinner and night spot, as is **PARAGON** (1309 NW Hoyt St; 503/833-5060). If a fussy dinner isn't what you're needing, consider pizza and a pint at one of the city's longtime microbreweries, **BRIDGEPORT BREW PUB** (1313 NW Marshall St; 503/241-3612).

If you walk on NW 10th Avenue toward W Burnside and downtown, you'll come to **POWELL'S CITY OF BOOKS** (1005 W Burnside St; 503/228-4651); there's also an entrance at the corner of NW 11th Avenue and Couch Street. Depending on how you feel about books and shopping, you could spend a whole day here or be overwhelmed immediately; but start with an evening visit, when the store is hopping and there may be an author reading in the Pearl Room. Don't think twice about walking around with a map (even natives do it, since major remodeling seems to enlarge the store on a regular basis), available at the front door.

Still not ready to call it a day? Stop by the **CRYSTAL BALLROOM** (1332 W Burnside St; 503/778-5625) to see what's playing; it could be anything from bluegrass to bossa nova. The dance floor here is on springs, making an evening of dancing an energizing treat.

DAY THREE
To get the full flavor of Portland, you'll want to spend some time across—and on—the Willamette River. This day starts with a visit to three eastside neighborhoods and ends with a cruise on the river. You may want a car on this day, since the neighborhoods are not adjacent to one another.

MORNING: One of the best breakfasts in town is at **ZELL'S: AN AMERICAN CAFÉ** (1300 SE Morrison St; 503/239-0196). But perhaps more convenient, as you'll start the day in the residential neighborhood of **IRVINGTON**, is for you to grab a hearty cinnamon roll and a fresh orange juice at the **GRAND CENTRAL BAKING CO.** (1444 NE Weidler St; 503/288-1614), on the edge of Irvington. (Zell's is about 20 blocks south.) One of Portland's oldest neighborhoods, Irvington is chock-full of mansions and rambling old houses, most in good repair with appealing gardens. In **GRANT PARK** (NE 33rd Ave between Broadway and Knott St, adjacent to Grant High School), you'll find statues of Beverly Cleary's characters from her *Ramona* series. These beloved statues are not visible from the street; you'll have to walk into the park to find them. (Klickitat Street, where Ramona lives, is about four blocks to the north.) Many shops line NE Broadway between 14th and 28th Avenues, but the traffic along this four-lane conduit to I-5 and downtown is heavy, making for a noisy walking route. A few shops to duck into: **MATISSE** (1411 NE Broadway; 503/287-5414)—rumpled maybe, but frumpy never—for beautiful women's clothing; and **FRENCH QUARTER** (1444 NE Broadway; 503/284-1379), where the linens and everything else are imported from the Continent. There's a

333

lot of coffee in this neighborhood (**TORREFAZIONE, PEET'S, STARBUCKS**); you should have no problem staying on your feet.

AFTERNOON: Lunch is in the **HAWTHORNE DISTRICT**, about 30 blocks south of Irvington. One of the joys of this street is its ambience, a cheerful hippieness that ages gracefully—and it's a real neighborhood, where Gen Xers hanging at one of the strip's many music stores mingle on the street with octogenarians on their way to the Fred Meyer pharmacy. **BREAD AND INK CAFÉ** (3610 SE Hawthorne Blvd; 503/239-4756) is a longtime neighborhood bistro, where the burgers and house-made ketchup are legendary (not to mention the cassata for dessert). After lunch, take in the used-book and music stores and funky furniture vendors. It may come as no surprise that there's a **BEN AND JERRY'S** (SE 36th Ave and Hawthorne Blvd; 503/234-2223) in this neighborhood, with some of the richest and most politically progressive ice cream in town.

At some point in the afternoon, you'll want to head south again, to the **WEST-MORELAND** neighborhood, where there's more shopping and **CAPRIAL'S BISTRO** (7015 SE Milwaukie Ave; 503/236-6457). This renowned, informal lunch and dinner spot is owned by cooking-show host and chef extraordinaire Caprial Pence and her husband, John. If you'd like to stay for dinner—and we recommend you do—but haven't reserved far in advance, you might still find a spot at the counter. Not hungry yet? The heart of Westmoreland is at the intersection of SE Bybee Boulevard and Milwaukie Avenue. If you take SE Bybee west and follow it as it curves around and becomes SE 13th Avenue, you've reached **SELLWOOD**, with its multitude of antique stores.

EVENING: If you haven't already had dinner with Caprial, consider a dinner cruise on the Willamette River. The *Portland Spirit* (503/224-3900) docks at Gov. Tom McCall Waterfront Park, near the Salmon Street Springs fountain. A river cruise is a great way to get a sense of this city on the water and of the many bridges that connect Portland's west and east sides. (You'll pass right under several of them, depending on your route.) Most dinner cruises are two- to three-hour events starting at 7pm, but if you still have a little life in you after this busy day, check out the nightlife in the same place you started this three-day tour, **THE HEATHMAN RESTAURANT AND BAR.**

A Day with Children

Kids and grown-ups alike should appreciate the following itinerary, which is best accomplished with a car.

MORNING: Load up everyone for breakfast at the **ORIGINAL PANCAKE HOUSE**, (8600 SW Barbur Blvd, Burlingame; 503/246-9007), 10 minutes south of downtown (take the Barbur Blvd exit from I-5; the restaurant is immediately on your left). This Portland landmark is popular with tourists, businesspeople, students, grandparents and grandchildren, neighbors—well, you get the picture. Allow plenty of time to be seated, although service from that point is snappy. Afterward, take I-5 south to I-205 and head east, to historic Oregon City. Watch for the giant covered wagon off to the right (exit 10); this is the **END OF THE OREGON TRAIL INTERPRETIVE CENTER**

(1726 Washington St, Oregon City; 503/657-9336). Call ahead to plan your arrival in time for a staging of the multimedia presentation; otherwise, there's not a lot to see besides the well-stocked gift store and some worthwhile hands-on displays.

AFTERNOON: The kids sat still for breakfast, so the airy and spacious **OREGON MUSEUM OF SCIENCE AND INDUSTRY** (1945 SE Water Ave, Southeast; 503/797-4000) might be a good place to head for lunch and the early-afternoon hours. There are plenty of permanent and rotating exhibits here and a special room for the under-3 crowd, plus a perfectly adequate restaurant at which to fortify the troops. If the sun is shining and no one wants to go inside, head to the **OREGON ZOO** (4001 SW Canyon Rd, Washington Park; 503/226-1561). The zoo's new Pacific Northwest areas allow visitors to observe fauna that's native to this part of the country, and there are plenty of exotic creatures from farther afield. Finish the afternoon with a visit to the world's first **NIKETOWN** (930 SW 6th Ave, Downtown; 503/221-6543), a museum-cum-shopping experience, where everything is made by Portland's own mega shoe company (OK, Nike headquarters are actually in Beaverton).

EVENING: At dinnertime, head to NW 23rd Avenue, where there are a couple of pizza options. A quirky but fun place for excellent New York–style pies is **ESCAPE FROM NEW YORK PIZZA** (622 NW 23rd Ave, Northwest; 503/227-5423), although be warned: its list of toppings is basic and its seating options are limited. A more practical choice might be **PIZZICATO** (505 NW 23rd Ave, Northwest; 503/242-0023), where the toppings tend toward the pesto/sun-dried tomato/kalamata olive school (but, of course, they have plain cheese also) and where there's lots of seating. Kids and grown-ups alike will enjoy walking along the street, with the little white lights twinkling in the trees overhead. But if dad and mom really want a beer while the kids run around, head for the excellent **LAURELWOOD PUBLIC HOUSE** (1728 NE 40th Ave, Hollywood; 503/282-0622), which not only has a children's menu but also an extensive play area. For a city view, and a final cap on a busy day, follow NW 23rd Avenue across W Burnside Street to where it becomes SW Vista Avenue, and follow the signs for Scenic Drive. This route takes you up to **COUNCIL CREST PARK**, at 1,073 feet the highest place in Portland and a great spot for viewing the city lights spread out below.

RECREATION

RECREATION

Outdoor Activities

Proud and protective of their parks and greenspaces, Portlanders are never more than a few minutes away from a quick getaway for bird-watching, kayaking, or cycling. A little farther afield, they have the magnificent scenery of the Pacific Coast and the snowy slopes of Mount Hood. As the city continues to grow and freeways clog with newcomers and old-timers alike, harried drivers at least know that where the traffic jams end, the fun begins.

Outdoor Recreation, published four times a year by Portland Parks and Recreation (1120 SW 5th Ave, Rm 1302, Downtown; 503/823-5132; www.parks .ci.portland.or.us; map:F3), is a comprehensive guide to seasonal recreation programs. There's something in it for everyone: from cross-country ski trips and whale watching in winter to hiking, paddling, biking, fly-fishing, tot walks, and historic bridge tours in summer. Pick it up free at libraries and outdoor stores. Metro's department of parks, trails, and greenspaces publishes *GreenScene*, another quarterly guide to the great outdoors, this one focused on wildlife habitats (call Metro to request a copy; 503/797-1850, ext. 3; www.metro-region.org/parks). Other suburban park districts have similar programs.

BICYCLING

In recent years, *Bicycling* magazine has rated the City of Roses the most bike-friendly city in the country. Why? The diverse topography—flat and breezy stretches on the east side, steep and breathless hills on the west—has something for every cyclist, and many streets have bike lanes. In Portland, a lot of people bike to work, and urban messengers work on bikes, as do some of the downtown police patrols. Want to know the quickest and safest bike route to your destination? Grab a copy of the map "Bike There" ($6), published by Metro and available at area cycle shops and at Powell's Travel Store (in the southeast corner of Pioneer Courthouse Square, SW 6th Ave and Yamhill St; 503/228-1108; map:H4). You can take your bike on any Tri-Met bus or MAX train without a special pass, just paying the standard fare; buses and trains are outfitted with racks to make the going easy.

Cyclists looking for organized 30- to 100-mile rides at a touring pace should call the **PORTLAND WHEELMEN TOURING CLUB** (503/257-7982 hotline). As many as 120 people show up for group and nongroup rides—several each weekend and at least one nearly every day of the year—and you don't have to be a member to pedal along. The **BEAVERTON BICYCLE CLUB** (503/649-4632), which sponsors road, track, and criterium events, has a strong group of junior riders but no age limit. The **OREGON BICYCLE RACING ASSOCIATION** (503/661-0686 hotline; www .obra.org) acts as a clearinghouse for race information for two dozen competitive clubs in Oregon. Call the OBRA hotline for event information. From May to mid-September, races are held at **PORTLAND INTERNATIONAL RACEWAY** (West Delta Park; 503/823-7223; map:DD7) on Tuesday nights—women and masters on alternate Mondays—and at the **ALPENROSE DAIRY VELODROME** on Thursday nights (6149 SW Shattuck Rd, Raleigh Hills; 503/244-1133; map:II8). The velodrome is one of the shortest in the country (hence heroically steep) and is situated next to a working dairy farm. Admission is free for spectators. Classes are offered on Wednesdays, and fixed-gear bikes are available to rent.

The annual **CYCLE OREGON** (800/292-5367; www.cycleoregon.com) is organized in Portland but is staged each year in different parts of the state. The weeklong early-September event usually fills its quota of 2,000 riders.

In the interest of protecting environmentally sensitive areas, **MOUNTAIN BIKING** is restricted to a handful of marked trails in the metropolitan region, but the available choices are well managed and rewarding. Trail maps are available from Portland Parks and Recreation (1120 SW 5th Ave, Rm 1302, Downtown; 503/823-5132; www.parks.ci.portland.or.us; map:F3) for Forest Park, Powell Butte, and the Springwater Corridor. Fat-tire cyclists looking for like minds join the **PORTLAND UNITED MOUNTAIN PEDALERS** (www.pumpclub.org), whose motto is "Mountain biking is not a crime," for organized year-round weekend rides (see also the Leif Erikson Drive listing below). Check with a bike store for the latest club contact information, or check PUMP's website. The **BIKE GALLERY** (1001 SW Salmon St, Downtown; 503/222-3821; map:G2; and 5329 NE Sandy Blvd; 503/281-9800; map:FF4; plus two suburban locations) is the biggest bike-shop network. The **WOMEN'S ASSOCIATION OF MOUNTAIN BIKERS** (503/829-8487) stages Tuesday night rides in Forest Park during the summer and weekend rides throughout the year. Men are welcome on some of the rides.

Although one avid **CYCLOCROSS** racer has described that sport as "ballet on wheels," a less biased observer might see it as a mud festival for people who just can't get off their bikes . . . even for a few months each year. (Cyclocross first gained popularity in Europe as a means of breaking up the winter doldrums between racing seasons.) There are a half-dozen races in the annual **FAT TIRE FARM CROSS CRUSADE**, which runs early October through December. A typical cyclocross course takes riders through mud bogs, over barriers, down sharp slopes, and up steep, short hills. Racers spend about 30 percent of the race running with their bikes slung by their sides or over their shoulders. Interest in the sport has grown remarkably over the past five years; more than 200 racers, and an equal number of spectators, show up, rain or shine. For race information, contact Fat Tire Farm Mountain Bike Company (2714 NW Thurman St, Northwest; 503/222-3276; map:GG7).

The following are a few favorite mountain- and road-bike routes in the area. For more rides and details, ask the resident experts at a local bike shop, or pick up a copy of any of a half-dozen cycling guidebooks published in recent years.

Banks/Vernonia State Park

25 MILES WEST OF PORTLAND ON HWY 26 TO THE MANNING TRAILHEAD; 503/324-0606 An old railroad has been converted to a 21-mile-long trail in the eastern foothills of the Coast Range in Washington and Columbia Counties. The northern part of the trail near Vernonia is paved, but the rest of the trail has some missing links where cyclists are diverted to gravel roads, so it's best to ride the trail with a fat-tire mountain bike.

Hagg Lake

7 MILES SOUTHWEST OF FOREST GROVE; 503/359-5732 From early spring to October, cyclists swarm the well-marked bike lane around man-made Henry Hagg Lake in Scoggins Valley Park. The loop follows gentle hills and fields for some 10 miles, passing numerous picnic and swimming spots. Ambitious cyclists can start in Forest Grove and take the Old Tualatin Valley Highway to Scoggins Valley Road.

Leif Erikson Drive

END OF NW THURMAN ST TO NW GERMANTOWN RD, FOREST PARK Have a fat-tire affinity? Forest Park's Leif Erikson Drive is your kind of place. This 11-mile gravel road twists along the park's north side. For the first 6 miles, the road threads in and out of gullies, offering occasional spectacular views of the Willamette River and North Portland; the last 5 miles are the most isolated and peaceful. Leif Erikson is rough going (but possible) on touring bikes. Although the fragile Wildwood Trail is off-limits, four other areas are open for mountain biking. Take the cutoff to NW Skyline Boulevard via Fire Lane 3 (just past the 3-mile marker), NW Saltzman Road (6 miles), Springville Road (9 miles), or NW Germantown Road (11 miles). Then loop back on the precariously busy Hwy 30, or continue to Bonneville Road and Fire Lanes 12 and 15. If you yearn to tread the terrain but don't own gear, Fat Tire Farm Mountain Bike Company (2714 NW Thurman St; 503/222-3276; map: GG7), located about a mile from the Leif Erikson gate into Forest Park, will rent you everything you need. PUMP organizes year-round, after-work rides; meet at the gate to Leif Erikson Drive at 6pm Wednesday evenings. *Map:DD9–GG7*

Marine Drive

KELLEY POINT PARK AT THE CONFLUENCE OF THE WILLAMETTE AND COLUMBIA RIVERS TO THE EAST END OF N MARINE DR Just across the Willamette from Sauvie Island, Kelley Point Park anchors a favorite ride that follows the Columbia east along the airplane-swept flats of N Marine Drive. Most riders take the river road, but you can also cross the Columbia River on I-205 (there's a bike lane) into Washington and back to the bike path alongside roaring I-5 via Evergreen Highway and Columbia Way. The bike lane across the Columbia is part of the I-205 bike path, which extends 15 miles south to the Clackamas River in Gladstone. *Map: AA9–BB6*

Sauvie Island

SAUVIE ISLAND, 10 MILES NORTHWEST OF PORTLAND VIA HWY 30 On this ride, the ends justify the means. Endure 10 miles of pedaling alongside 18-wheelers through the mostly industrial section of Hwy 30 from Northwest Portland to Sauvie Island (or shuttle your bike on Tri-Met bus 17 or on your car), and you'll be rewarded. The island is a bicycle-friendly zone . . . as long as you ride single-file. The standard 12-mile loop has many scenic offshoots. Forgo the head-down hammer for a chin-up view of farm animals, U-cut flower and vegetable farms, great blue herons, and more. Be sure to visit Bybee-Howell Territorial Park, a 100-acre park rich in cultural and natural history. Metro has added a new restroom building and interpretive displays that explain how some of Oregon's earliest pioneers lived. During summer weekends, tours are available of the historic Bybee-Howell House, an authentically restored and furnished farmhouse of the 1850s. *Map:CC9.*

Skyline Boulevard

SKYLINE BLVD BETWEEN NW CORNELL AND ROCKY POINT RDS This 17-mile loop requires pedaling an elevation gain of 1,400 feet, but Skyline Boulevard is truly the most scenic ridgetop road in town, offering broad views of the Willamette Valley. Begin in Portland or in Beaverton (the climb is about the same either way). From Portland, turn off NW Cornell onto 53rd Drive or Thompson Road for a peaceful (albeit steep and winding) climb to Skyline. Pack a few dollars and plan to stop for microbrews and a view at the Skyline Tavern (8031 NW Skyline Blvd; 503/286-4788; map:FF9) or for burgers, fries, and malts at the Skyline Restaurant (1313 NW Skyline Blvd; 503/292-6727; map:GG8). *Map:DD9–GG7*

Springwater Corridor

PORTLAND PARKS AND RECREATION; 503/823-2223 Since 1990, when the City of Portland acquired the land, nearly 17 miles of abandoned rail line between Milwaukie and Boring have been open to mountain bikers, hikers, and horseback riders. The wild and weathered rail bed was replaced by a tamer, smooth surface called "sandseal." While mountain bikes are still the best two-wheel bet in the corridor, narrow road-bike tires can also negotiate the trail. The hardened surface runs from Westmoreland east to Gresham. Signals, crosswalks, and warning signs add a modicum of safety. Trailheads and toilets are located at SE Johnson Creek Boulevard, SE Hogan Road, and at the Main City Park in Gresham. In-line skaters focus on the portion of trail that is paved through Gresham. *Map:JJ1–JJ5*

BIRD-WATCHING/WILDLIFE VIEWING

Water makes Portland a wildlife haven. The infamous rainfall results in lush vegetation, and the confluence of the Columbia and Willamette Rivers lures myriad waterfowl. Streams, lakes, and wetlands form an emerald necklace around the metropolitan area, and there's a regional effort to protect these wildlife habitats and promote responsible use of natural areas. Three times a year, Metro's department of parks, trails, and greenspaces publishes *GreenScene*, a guide to hikes, benefit concerts, history tours, biking, river trips, and other organized activities that increase awareness of local wildlife habitats (call Metro to request a copy; 503/797-1850 ext. 3; www.metro-region.org/parks).

From great blue herons to beavers, minks to muskrats, an impressive array of wildlife calls Portland home. Every glove compartment should include a copy of the *Oregon Wildlife Viewing Guide* ($10; available at bookstores and from Defenders of Wildlife in Lake Oswego, 503/697-3222). Many **VIEWING SITES** are marked with state highway signs depicting binoculars. For nature unleashed, venture to Powell Butte, Sauvie Island Wildlife Management Area, or Kelley Point Park (see the Exploring chapter). Here are a few other notable natural areas.

Beggars-Tick Wildlife Refuge

SE 111TH AVE AND FOSTER RD, SOUTHEAST Named after a native sunflower, the Beggars-Tick Wildlife Refuge serves as a wintering habitat for a diversity of waterfowl: wood duck, green-winged teal, and hooded merganser, to name a few. The marsh dries up during summer, but it still provides a permanent residence for muskrats, raccoons, and other species. *Map:II5*

Heron Lakes Golf Course

3500 N VICTORY BLVD, NORTH PORTLAND; 503/289-1818 Built around wetlands, the course is home to great blue herons as well as other waterfowl. Ask for permission and directions at the pro shop and, once on the course, be sure to keep your eyes open for birdies of the round, white, dimpled sort. *Map:CC7*

Oaks Bottom Wildlife Refuge

TRAILHEADS: SE 7TH AVE AND SELLWOOD BLVD, SELLWOOD PARK; SE MILWAUKIE BLVD AND MITCHELL ST, WESTMORELAND These 160 acres of woods and wetlands form the first officially designated wildlife refuge in Portland. The walk, just short of 3 miles, begins in Sellwood Park. More than 140 species of birds have been spotted here, among them the great blue heron, which feeds on carp in the refuge. Others include pileated woodpeckers and warblers (spring) and green-backed herons (spring and summer). *Map:JJ5*

Portland Audubon Society Sanctuary

5151 NW CORNELL RD, FOREST PARK; 503/292-6855 Every birder in the state ends up here eventually—in part for the winged species that flock to the woods surrounding the facility, but also for the selection of excellent naturalists' books in the store (503/292-9453). This 160-acre sanctuary is surrounded by the vast wildness of Forest Park and connects to the Wildwood and MacLeay Park trails. The trails wrap around a pond and follow the creek. The Audubon House features a nature-oriented store, an interpretive area, and a viewing window overlooking the feeding platforms for local songbirds. Year-round, the Audubon Society sponsors free field trips to teach people about nature. During winter, spring, and summer vacations, the sanctuary offers educational nature classes for kids. To listen to the weekly updated Rare Bird Alert message, call and ask for extension 2. *Map:FF7*

Ross Island

WILLAMETTE RIVER, JUST SOUTH OF ROSS ISLAND BRIDGE The Willamette island south of downtown actually includes the complex of Ross, Hardtack, East, and Toe Islands. All but one are owned by Ross Island Sand and Gravel. The company's dredging permit expires in 2005, and gravel mining is being phased out. On the northwest side of privately owned Toe Island is a 50-nest great blue heron rookery in a black-cottonwood grove. The rookery can be viewed only by boat, or with binoculars from the mainland. The best shoreside views (try for winter, when the trees are leafless) are from the Willamette Greenway, just north of Willamette Park. Look for belted kingfishers nesting on the island's steep banks, as well as beavers and red foxes. Bald eagles have also nested on the island in the past. The nearest boat ramp is in Willamette Park, but don't land on the island. To join an organized kayak tour, contact the Portland River Co. (0315 SW Montgomery St, RiverPlace; 503/229-0551; map:E5). *Map:HH5*

Wallace Park

NW 26TH AVE BETWEEN PETTYGROVE AND RALEIGH STS, NORTHWEST If you loved Alfred Hitchcock's classic *The Birds*, you won't want to miss Wallace Park in late September and early October. For about a two-week period during their migratory route south, Vaux's swifts roost in the several-story-tall chimney of Chapman School on the west side of the park. Each evening thousands of birds circle the chimney and then drop down inside, one by one, for the night; at sunrise they fly out just as dramatically. Spectator conversation usually revolves around the swifts that flew in first: can they actually sleep at the bottom of the pile, and what happens if one bird becomes claustrophobic? *Map:GG7*

CAMPING

Portland residents who want to get away for a quiet weekend camping trip need not drive far. Visitors from outside the city also have the opportunity to explore the city sights, its restaurants, and other attractions while staying inexpensively in a nearby campground. Metro, the Portland area's regional government, has upgraded the closest publicly owned campground to the city at Oxbow Regional Park. Other campgrounds less than an hour's drive from downtown are managed by the Oregon and Washington state park systems and by Clackamas County. Campsite fees range from $12 to $20, depending on the season and the amenities.

OXBOW REGIONAL PARK (6 miles east of Gresham via SE Division St; 503/797-1850) has long been a favored spot for fishing on the Sandy River, hiking through old-growth forests, studying nature (especially the fall chinook salmon run), and for simply getting away from the surrounding hubbub. Recent improvements to the campground make the park much more attractive to campers. Installation of a new water-pumping and treatment system allowed Metro to construct two new restroom buildings, complete with hot running water, showers, and flush toilets. The campground was expanded to include 45 campsites. It's open year-round but does not take reservations. Pets are not allowed in the 1,200-acre park.

The Oregon Parks and Recreation Department manages three state parks close to Portland that have campsites. **MILO MCIVER STATE PARK** (4 miles west of Estacada) has 44 electric sites and 9 primitive tent sites. The main attraction is the park's Clackamas River frontage and its trail system for hikers and equestrians. **CHAMPOEG STATE PARK** (30 miles south of Portland and 7 miles east of Newberg) has 12 full-service sites, 67 electrical sites, 6 cabins, and 6 yurts. The park preserves a historic settlement on the banks of the Willamette River. **AINSWORTH STATE PARK** (37 miles east of Portland in the Columbia River Gorge) has 45 full-service sites and 4 walk-in tent sites. Only Champoeg is open all year. Reservations are available at McIver and Champoeg (800/452-5687). For state park information, call 800/551-6949 or visit www.oregonstateparks.org.

The Washington Parks and Recreation Department has three parks with campgrounds within an easy drive of Portland. **PARADISE POINT STATE PARK** (on the east fork of the Lewis River 16 miles north of Vancouver) has 78 standard sites. **BEACON ROCK STATE PARK** (35 miles east of Vancouver in the Columbia River Gorge) has 29 sites. **BATTLE GROUND LAKE STATE PARK** (19 miles northeast of Vancouver), has 31 standard sites, 2 electrical sites, and another 15 walk-in tent sites. Battle Ground Lake is open for camping all year, but the other parks are seasonal. Reservations are taken May through September for Battle Ground Lake and Paradise Point (888/226-7688). For Washington state park information, call 360/902-8844 or visit www.parks.wa.gov.

Clackamas County offers camping at **BARTON PARK** (9 miles west of Estacada on the Clackamas River), **METZLER PARK** (5 miles south of Estacada on Clear Creek), and **FEYRER PARK** (3 miles southeast of Molalla on the Molalla River). Barton is largest, with 96 sites. Camping season runs May through September. For reservations and information call 503/353-4415 or visit www.co.clackamas .or.us/dtd/parks.

CANOEING/KAYAKING

Many rivers converge in the Portland area, joining the Columbia in its final push to the Pacific. Boaters paddle kayaks and canoes at a leisurely pace along the shores of the **WILLAMETTE, COLUMBIA**, and **TUALATIN RIVERS**, watching for great blue herons, which nest along the banks. Whitewater kayakers surf the rapids of the **SANDY, CLACKAMAS, EAST FORK LEWIS**, and **WASHOUGAL RIVERS**. Pick up a copy of *Oregon's Quiet Waters: A Guide to Lakes for Canoeists and Other Paddlers*, by Cheryl McLean and Clint Brown; it includes more than a dozen lakes within two hours of Portland. Another must-read for Portland paddlers is the second edition of *Canoe and Kayak Routes of Northwest Oregon*, by Philip N. Jones. The **OREGON OCEAN PADDLING SOCIETY** (www.teleport.com/~orops/; or inquire at a paddling store), with 300 active members, also fills a niche.

South of downtown, canoe and kayak rentals are available from either of two shops on opposite sides of the Willamette. On the west side, across SW Macadam Avenue from Willamette Park, **EBB & FLOW PADDLESPORTS** (0604 SW Nebraska St, SW Macadam; 503/245-1756; map:JJ6) rents canoes, kayaks, and accessories for $20 to $45 a day. The store offers sea-kayaking classes and family and private lessons. On the east side, there's the floating **SPORTCRAFT MARINA** (1701 Clackamette Dr, Oregon City; 503/656-6484; map:OO4), which rents flat-water kayaks, canoes, and motorboats. The marina's history dates to the 1920s, when it was just a floating moorage. At the north edge of town, **ALDER CREEK KAYAK AND CANOE** (250 NE Tomahawk Island Dr, Jantzen Beach; 503/285-0464; map:CC6) rents and sells a variety of inflatable kayaks, touring canoes, and whitewater and flatwater kayaks and offers trips, tours, and classes. Many general sporting-goods stores also have boating supplies.

CLIMBING

On July 19, 1894, aided by the complex carbohydrates of an old-fashioned bean bake, 193 persons climbed Mount Hood and initiated themselves as members of the **MAZAMAS** (909 NW 19th Ave, Northwest; 503/227-2345; www.mazamas.org; map:FF6). Now 3,000 members strong, the Mazamas is Oregon's biggest climbing group and the standard local means of acquiring mountain- and rock-climbing skills. This safety-conscious organization is a superb resource, offering seasonal group climbs, weekly lectures at its clubhouse, midweek rock climbs, day hikes, and other adventurous activities both in and outside of the Northwest.

Throughout the year, avid rock climbers—as well as those just starting out—hone their skills at local indoor climbing facilities: the **PORTLAND ROCK GYM** (2034 SE 6th Ave, Brooklyn; 503/232-8310; map:GG5) and **STONEWORKS CLIMBING GYM** (6775 SW 111th Ave, Beaverton; 503/644-3517). The Portland Rock Gym accommodates a 40-foot lead wall; it has 8,000 square feet of climbing, 25 top ropes, and 12 lead routes. Stoneworks features 13 roped sections of wall and a large bouldering area. **CLUBSPORT OREGON** (18120 SW Lower Boones Ferry Rd, Tualatin; 503/968-4500; map:NN9), a sports megastore that includes basketball and volleyball courts and a soccer/hockey field, also boasts the highest indoor rock-climbing wall (45 feet) in the Portland area.

OREGON MOUNTAIN COMMUNITY (60 NW Davis St, Old Town; 503/227-1038; map:K6) rents and sells ice and alpine climbing gear as well as rock shoes. Check out the piles of adventure literature lining the entrance for info on classes and trips, and see the For Sale bulletin board for gear. **RECREATIONAL EQUIPMENT INC.** (1405 NW Johnson St, Pearl District; 503/221-1938; map:N1)—better known as REI—rents shoes, sells climbing equipment, and occasionally holds classes. Portland Parks and Recreation (1120 SW 5th Ave, Rm 1302; 503/823-5132; www .parks.ci.portland.or.us; map:F3) hosts spring/summer events that include rock-climbing classes in Portland and at Smith Rock State Park, and mountaineering ascents of Mount Hood and Mount St. Helens. Free mountaineering slide shows and lectures are a regular feature of the Mazamas, REI, and **THE MOUNTAIN SHOP** (628 NE Broadway, near Lloyd Center; 503/288-6768; map:FF6).

The following are a few of the major climbs (alpine and rock) within three hours of Portland. For a more complete list, talk to the experts at one of the local rock gyms or outdoor stores. The definitive sources for climbing around Portland—*Portland Rock Climbs: A Climber's Guide to Northwest Oregon*, by Tim Olson, and *Oregon High: A Climbing Guide*, by Jeff Thomas—are out of print; consider yourself lucky if you find a used copy. A guide to the volcanoes is *Climbing the Cascade Volcanoes*, by Jeff Smoot.

Broughton's Bluff

LEWIS AND CLARK STATE PARK OFF E HISTORIC COLUMBIA RIVER HWY, TROUT- DALE, ABOVE THE EAST BANK OF THE SANDY RIVER While it pales in comparison to the beauty and quality of Smith Rock in Central Oregon, Broughton's Bluff is just 30 minutes from Portland and offers about 200 midrange to difficult climbs. A new trail was cut in 1990, and the rock is relatively clean. The southwestern exposure protects climbers from the chill winter winds of the Columbia River Gorge.

Horsethief Butte

2 MILES EAST OF THE DALLES BRIDGE, ON HWY 14 IN WASHINGTON Here's a good practice spot 90 miles east of Portland, a basaltic rock mesa offering corridors of short climbs and top-rope challenges.

Mount Hood

50 MILES EAST OF PORTLAND; INFORMATION CENTER ON HWY 26 IN WELCHES; 503/622-4822 At just over 11,235 feet, Mount Hood is Oregon's highest mountain. Its beautiful asymmetry and relative ease of ascent make it one of the busiest peaks in the country for climbers. Still, unpredictable weather and very steep snow climbing (the last 1,500 feet) require either a skilled guide or solid mountaineering skills. During the spring climbing season, smart climbers start early, finishing before the heat of the day turns the snow to mush. By July, rock fall becomes a serious issue and the climbing season is pretty much over. **TIMBERLINE MOUNTAIN GUIDES** (541/312-9242) are based, during climbing season, at the Wy'east Day Lodge at Timberline. The primary guide service on Mount Hood and other Oregon volcanoes, this group teaches mountaineering, mountain-climbing, and ice-climbing courses; rock climbing is taught at Smith Rock State Park and in the Columbia Gorge. *www.fs.fed.us/mthood*

Mount St. Helens National Volcanic Monument

55 MILES NORTHEAST OF PORTLAND VIA I-5; 360/247-3900 (HEADQUARTERS) OR 360/247-3961 (CLIMBING HOTLINE) The flat-topped Mount St. Helens, about an hour's drive north of Portland and east of I-5, enthralls visitors. The 8,365-foot volcano's fame was established in its incredible eruption of May 18, 1980. Most climbers take one of two trails up the south face: Butte Camp or Monitor Ridge. These are more like rugged hikes than real alpine climbs, but an ice ax is still recommended. The all-day climb (8 miles round-trip) is ideal for novice alpinists; the only big dangers are some loose-rock cliffs and the unstable edge around the crater. A $15 climbing permit is required; a few are available on a daily basis, but it's best to reserve in advance. In winter, backcountry adventurers can ski down. For more on Mount St. Helens, see the Day Trips and Itineraries chapter. *www.fs.fed.us/gpnf/mshnvm*

Smith Rock State Park

9 MILES NORTHEAST OF REDMOND OFF HWY 97, 3 HOURS SOUTHEAST OF PORTLAND; 541/548-7501 Its extremely challenging routes (the welded tuff volcanic rock is sometimes soft enough to tear off in your hand), stunning scenery, and arid climate have helped make Smith Rock a mecca for world-class climbers. The park is open year-round, but rock climbers are busiest March to May and September to November, between the brutal heat of summer and the winter snows. There are more than 1,000 routes in the park (as well as great hiking trails and scenic vistas), something for all abilities. The nationwide climbing consensus is that "Just Do It" is still one of the hardest in the country, although several other less famous, but just as difficult, routes have been put up in the park in recent years. Bivouac camping only (hike-in sites; showers available; no reservations) along the Crooked River.

FISHING

To maintain a minimum number of spawning chinook salmon, the Oregon Department of Fish and Wildlife has issued quotas on Portland-area waters. Once, from February through June, fanatical anglers would line their boats from bank to bank across the Willamette, wait for the river's monsters to bite, and be rewarded with 10- to 30-pound salmon. In recent years, quotas of 3,000 or 6,000 fish caught after April 1 have brought the season to a close by mid-May. Indeed, the fishing week has been limited to two days in some instances. Even so, there is a lot of fun to be had: Industrious fishermen will head for other nearby waters with an open season, or spend the off days roaming through the gear at **G I JOE'S** (1140 N Hayden Meadows Dr, Jantzen Beach; 503/283-0318; map:DD6; and branches).

Fishing in Portland is a year-round sport. The Clackamas and Sandy Rivers lure a steady stream of anglers to their banks, with deep pools that hold spring chinook salmon and summer and winter steelhead. The Willamette River is a good place to catch warm-water species such as bass, bluegill, and crappies; Blue Lake Park in the East Portland suburb of Fairview, and Smith and Bybee Lakes in North Portland, are also good bets. For more info on the best bets for local fishing, pick up a copy of *Fishing in Oregon*, by Madelynne Sheehan and Dan Casali, at a local outdoor store. Hogliners and other anglers can find salmon and steelhead tag information at the **OREGON DEPARTMENT OF FISH AND WILDLIFE** (503/872-5268, a 24-hour automated number that provides answers to oft-asked questions; www.dfw.state. or.us/); also, pick up the annual regulations at fishing-tackle stores. **OUT-OF-STATE ANGLERS** can call 800/ASK-FISH for information. The state sponsors a **FREE WEEKEND OF FISHING** on an early Saturday in June. The **OREGON STATE MARINE BOARD** (435 Commercial St NE, Salem OR 97310; 503/378-8587) publishes a guide to the lower Columbia and Willamette Rivers, as well as a statewide facilities guide that includes information on boat ramps, parking, and types of fishing available.

Guide services are numerous and easy to find under "Fishing Trips" in the Yellow Pages. For home-river specialists, try **JACK'S SNACKS AND TACKLE** (1208 E Historic Columbia River Hwy, Troutdale; 503/665-2257), on the Sandy River, or **NORTHWEST FLYFISHING OUTFITTERS** (10910 NE Halsey St, Downtown; 503/252-1529; map:GG2) and **COUNTRYSPORT LIMITED** (126 SW 1st Ave, Downtown; 503/221-0543; map:I7), near the Willamette River.

Two local sport-fishing groups have been especially active in watchdogging area fish populations. The **ASSOCIATION OF NORTHWEST STEELHEADERS** (PO Box 22065, Milwaukie OR 97269; 503/653-4176) promotes fishery enhancement and protection programs, river access, and improved sport-fishing. Since 1958, the **OREGON BASS AND PANFISH CLUB** (503/282-2852) has promoted preservation of, improvement of, and education about warm-water fishing in Oregon. Thanks to the club's efforts, access to warm-water fishing may be stabilizing after an increased amount of privately owned shoreline had been causing access points to diminish.

GOLFING

Portland has more golfers than greens, but additional courses are being built all the time. Currently, about 55 golf courses are less than an hour's drive from the city center, although half of them are private, including the older generation of spectacular courses: the **COLUMBIA EDGEWATER COUNTRY CLUB** (2138 NE Marine Dr, North Portland; 503/285-8354; map:DD5), **PORTLAND GOLF CLUB** (5900 SW Scholls Ferry Rd, Raleigh Hills; 503/292-2778; map:II8), **RIVERSIDE GOLF & COUNTRY CLUB** (8105 NE 33rd Dr, Northeast; 503/288-6468; map:DD5), and **WAVERLEY COUNTRY CLUB** (1100 SE Waverly Dr, Sellwood; 503/654-9509; map:KK5).

The following are among the best of the public courses in the Portland area.

Cedars Golf Club

15001 NE 181ST ST, BRUSH PRAIRIE WA; 360/687-4233 OR 503/285-7548 Just north of Vancouver, the Cedars offers a long, rolling challenge with a lot of water hazards. Clubhouse facilities are especially nice.

Eastmoreland Golf Course and Driving Range

2425 SE BYBEE BLVD, EASTMORELAND; 503/775-2900 Bordered by the Crystal Springs Rhododendron Garden and blessed with venerable trees and lovely landscaping, the second-oldest golf course in the state is a technically challenging championship course. In 1991 Eastmoreland was named one of the top 25 public golf courses in the nation by *Golf Digest. Map:II5*

Heron Lakes Golf Course

3500 N VICTORY BLVD, NORTH PORTLAND; 503/289-1818 OR 503/823-4653 FOR TEE TIMES Designed by renowned golf course architect Robert Trent Jones Jr., Heron Lakes is a championship-quality public golf facility with two 18-hole courses. Great Blue has been described as one of the hardest courses in the Northwest thanks to water and sand on every hole. The Green Back is a bit less challenging and retains the old, economical rates. Located just 15 minutes from downtown, Heron Lakes is one of the busiest courses in the city. *Map:CC7*

Pumpkin Ridge: Ghost Creek Course

12930 NW OLD PUMPKIN RIDGE RD, NORTH PLAINS; 503/647-9977 Pumpkin Ridge's recent claims to fame have been hosting the 2000 U.S. Junior Amateur, the 1997 and 2003 U.S. Women's Open, and the 1996 U.S. Men's Amateur Championship, which Tiger Woods won so easily that he had to turn professional in order to find a challenge. The *Business Journal* ranked it as the toughest course in the Portland area in 2000. And in 1996, *Golf* magazine rated it the fifth-best golf course in America. Designed by Robert E. Cupp, Pumpkin Ridge (20 miles west of Portland off Hwy 26) features natural areas and views of both the Cascades and the Coast Range. A second course at Pumpkin Ridge (Witch Hollow) is private.

The Reserve Vineyards and Golf Club

4805 SW 229TH AVE, ALOHA; 503/649-8191 Opened in 1997 near Beaverton, the Reserve is a 36-hole, semiprivate golf facility with two courses, one designed by John Fought and the other by Robert E. Cupp. Fought's is a championship, traditional, 7,300-yard course with 114 bunkers; Cupp's is a slightly less difficult, open-design course with a lot of water and trees. *www.reservegolf.com*

HIKING

Oregon offers superlative hiking. The cascading waterfalls of the Columbia River Gorge, the alpine lakes of the Cascades, majestic Mount Hood, and the rugged Oregon Coast . . . all are within easy access of Portland. To really get away, however, you barely need to leave the city limits. A 30-mile hike on the Wildwood Trail begins in Northwest Portland in Forest Park; it's part of the 40 Mile Loop hiking/biking/ running system around the city. (The network's distance has actually now surpassed 140 miles).

Looking for company? Metro's department of parks, trails, and greenspaces publishes *GreenScene*, a seasonal guide to organized outdoor activities, including hikes (call Metro to request a copy; 503/797-1850, ext. 3; www.metro-region .org/parks).

For tramping farther afield, good maps of hikes in the gorge and around Mount Hood can be found at the Forest Service information office (800 NE Oregon St, Ste 177, near Lloyd Center; 503/872-2750; map:GG6) and at local outdoor stores. Parking lots at some trailheads are subject to car prowls, so don't leave anything valuable behind.

The following are a few of the better close-in hikes.

Columbia River Gorge

ALONG I-84 IN OREGON AND HWY 14 IN WASHINGTON, FROM 17 MILES EAST OF PORTLAND (AT TROUTDALE) TO 100 MILES EAST (AT THE DESCHUTES RIVER); COLUMBIA RIVER GORGE NATIONAL SCENIC AREA, HOOD RIVER; 541/386-2333 The Columbia's magnificent gorge, unique enough to be the nation's only national scenic area, has dozens of hiking trails. Its closeness to Portland and relatively mild weather make it a year-round destination. The east end, beyond Hood River, is especially beautiful when wildflowers bloom during spring; trails in the midgorge ascend high enough to escape summer's heat; those at the west end are awesome during fall as the leaves change color. Favorite trails are Angels Rest at Bridal Veil, Larch Mountain at Multnomah Falls, McCord Creek at Warrendale, and Eagle Creek near Bonneville. Each spring, the Friends of the Columbia Gorge (503-241-3762; www.gorgefriends.org) leads hikes to lesser-known trails to follow the wildflower bloom. For more on the Columbia Gorge, see the Day Trips chapter. *www.fs.fed.us/r6/columbia*

Lower MacLeay Park

NW 29TH AVE AND UPSHUR ST, NORTHWEST Balch Creek is one of the few creeks that still flows unfettered down the heavily developed West Hills. Lower MacLeay Trail connects NW Upshur Street to Forest Park's long Wildwood Trail, but hikers can make a 2-mile loop up Balch Canyon by taking a right at the first trail intersection (at the stone hut), then right again at the second intersection (near an open meadow), ending up on NW Raleigh Street. A short northeasterly walk through the Willamette Heights neighborhood takes you to the Thurman Bridge above the park; take the stairs on the east side of the bridge back down to the starting point. At the park, the creek disappears unceremoniously into a drainpipe. *Map:FF7*

Marquam Nature Park

TRAILHEADS: COUNCIL CREST PARK; SW SAM JACKSON PARK RD (JUST WEST OF THE CARNIVAL RESTAURANT); SW TERWILLIGER BLVD (NEAR THE OHSU SCHOOL OF DENTISTRY) A series of trails makes this one of the best hilly hiking areas in the city. From the parking lot and shelter off SW Sam Jackson Park Road, the trail to the right climbs 900 feet to Council Crest. To walk to the Oregon Zoo, continue over the top to the intersection of SW Talbot and Patton Roads. A short downhill trail leads to a Hwy 26 overpass. The trail to the left of the shelter follows an old roadbed up and around Oregon Health Sciences University, crosses

Marquam Hill Road, and comes out on Terwilliger Boulevard. At Terwilliger and SW Nebraska, the trail departs from the bike path and goes under Barbur Boulevard and I-5, coming out in John's Landing, four blocks from Willamette Park. A third trail, a 1½-mile nature loop, also begins at the shelter; follow the signs. The trails are all remarkably quiet and peaceful, but be forewarned: it's common to round a corner on a trail and stumble upon folks making a temporary home in the woods. *Map:GG7*

Oaks Bottom Wildlife Refuge

TRAILHEADS: SE 7TH AVE AND SELLWOOD BLVD, SELLWOOD PARK; SE MIL-WAUKIE BLVD AND MITCHELL ST, WESTMORELAND The trail can be damp at times—you're in a wetland, after all—but what an inner-city escape! See Bird-Watching/Wildlife Viewing in this chapter. *Map:HH5*

Springwater Corridor

PORTLAND PARKS AND RECREATION; 503/823-2223 One of the region's best rails-to-trails hikes. See Bicycling in this chapter. *Map:JJ1–JJ5*

Wildwood Trail, Forest Park

TRAILHEADS: W BURNSIDE ST GRAVEL PARKING AREA; WASHINGTON PARK; NW CORNELL RD; NW THURMAN ST; 503/823-2223 One of the country's longer natural woodland trails winding through a city park, the Wildwood Trail is Portland's cherished refuge for hikers and runners. The shady route through groves of fir and aspen officially begins at the World Forestry Center (near the Oregon Zoo) and travels north, linking such attractions as the Hoyt Arboretum, Pittock Mansion, and the Portland Audubon Society Sanctuary, before it plunges into the less-trodden territories of Forest Park. It ends some 30 miles later, at NW Newberry Street. Many spurs cross the trail, joining it to various neighborhoods and parks. The first 10 miles are well used; the last are good for solitude. Large, glass-encased maps of the entire trail are situated at convenient locations along the way. The Hoyt Arboretum Tree House has brochures and maps.

The best place to pick up the southern end of the Wildwood Trail is at its origin, at the World Forestry Center near the Vietnam Veterans' Living Memorial and the light-rail stop at the Oregon Zoo. The trail travels north and crosses W Burnside Street, then climbs up to the Pittock Mansion or farther north to NW Cornell Road (and the Audubon sanctuary). Another option is to explore the branching trails of the Hoyt Arboretum in Washington Park. These are the most-used parts of the trails, and are very hilly. Another trail begins across the Hwy 26 overpass and continues south, connecting the Wildwood Trail to panoramic Council Crest. A walk on this uncrowded mile-long trail is best when timed with the setting sun.

The central 10 miles of the trail (from NW Cornell to NW Germantown Rds) is a departure from the comforting rest stops of zoo, arboretum, mansion, and gardens. This part—a favorite for runners and walkers training for marathons—is composed of long, solitary stretches of rolling hills with just a few brutally steep sections. Bring plenty of water, as there are no drinking fountains. Get to the central section via NW Cornell Road, 53rd Avenue, or the Leif Erikson gate at the end of NW Thurman Street (hike Leif Erikson Dr up to the Wild Cherry Trail, which climbs to Wildwood).

To reach the northern 10 miles, hike north from NW Germantown Road and access it from the BPA Road along Skyline Boulevard. While the weather in recent winters has damaged many sections of Wildwood (especially its access trails), thanks to an amazing trail crew, repairs are fast and thorough. The ultimate guide to the park's trails is *One City's Wilderness: Portland's Forest Park*, by Marcy Cottrell Houle.

HORSEBACK RIDING

Although Oregon is about as west as you can get, it's not the romantic Wild West of the Rocky Mountains. Still, look hard enough and you can find a horse to ride, a sunset to ride into, and bliss along the trail.

Hill Top Riding Stables

SW 204TH AVE AND FARMINGTON RD, BEAVERTON; 503/649-5497 The last public riding stable in the Portland metro area, Hill Top has 50 wooded acres, plus an indoor arena. Cost is $25 an hour; make your reservation on the day you want to ride. Once clients become known by the staff, they can rent horses and ride on their own.

Flying M Ranch

10 MILES WEST OF YAMHILL ON HWY 99W (WATCH FOR SIGNS); 503/662-3222 Known for its Old West down-home flavor, the Flying M is a great place to take the kids (over age 8) riding. The fee is $20 per hour per person, including a guide. Pony rides for the younger set are available. For more adventuresome travel, a handful of two-day overnight rides up Trask Mountain are scheduled each summer, including all meals, lodging, and the singing cowboy's campfire songs at the top of the mountain. Flying M also takes private groups on overnight trail rides and has special steak-dinner, breakfast, day-long, and starlight rides.

ICE SKATING

Even in the deep of winter, you'd be hard pressed to find naturally occurring ice in the Portland area. Skaters settle for indoor rinks, of which there are several.

Lloyd Center Ice Chalet

LLOYD CENTER MALL, NORTHEAST; 503/288-6073 For more than 30 years, only the Portland sky covered the ice rink at Lloyd Center, but in 1990, the rink and the mall went under cover. The facility includes a pro skate shop, where group and private lessons are available. Public skate admission (including skate rentals) is $7.50. *Map:FF5*

Mountain View Ice Arena

14313 SE MILL PLAIN BLVD, VANCOUVER; 360/896-8700 The star among the metro area's neighborhood ice rinks, Vancouver, Washington's twin ice sheets opened in 1998 and quickly became the in place to skate. Portland's junior hockey team, the Winter Hawks, uses it for practice. Frequent public skate sessions cost $6.50, plus $2.50 for skate rental. *Map:CC1*

Sherwood Ice Arena

20407 SW BORCHERS DR, SHERWOOD; 503-625-5757 This rink, southwest of Portland, opened in 2000 with one ice sheet, a pro shop, and a restaurant. Daily public skate sessions are $6, plus $2.50 skate rental.

Valley Ice Arena

9250 SW BEAVERTON-HILLSDALE HWY (VALLEY PLAZA SHOPPING CENTER), BEAVERTON; 503/297-2521 The largest recreational skating rink on the Portland side of the Columbia River has been a fixture at the Valley Plaza Shopping Center for more than 30 years. Lessons are available, and skate rentals are free with a $7 admission (children under 4 skate free). There's public skating most weekday mornings, afternoons, and weekends. *Map:HH9*

RIVER RAFTING

The local rafting season generally runs from April to October. Outfitters rent the necessary equipment to run the closest whitewater rivers—Clackamas, Sandy, White Salmon, and Klickitat—as well as the Deschutes, the busiest of all. Since river conditions can change rapidly, inexperienced rafters should stick to guided trips. To join trips with experienced boaters, try www.oregonwhitewater.org. For those who want to develop their own boating skills, a good place to start gathering equipment and information is **ANDY & BAX SPORTING GOODS** (324 SE Grand Ave, Inner Southeast; 503/234-7538; map:GG5), Portland's premier rafting store.

Clackamas River

The upper Clackamas River is one of the most challenging runs so close to a major American city. The 13 miles from Three Links to North Fork Reservoir, just above Estacada, have Class IV water. Bob's Hole is a favorite play spot for kayakers. For a guided trip, arrange an excursion with **BLUE SKY WHITEWATER RAFTING** (800/898-6398). The 21½ miles of the lower Clackamas, from McIver State Park (near Estacada) to Clackamette Park (at the confluence with the Willamette in Oregon City), provides a good introduction for beginners; it's so placid that inner tubers float it during summer, although cold water during spring runoff makes it potentially dangerous because of the risk of hypothermia. Shorten the trip by using Clackamas County boat facilities at the communities of Barton or Carver.

Deschutes River

Two hours southeast of Portland, the Deschutes is an extremely popular day trip, especially for the 12-mile "splash and giggle" section on either side of Maupin. The river's lower 100 miles can be run as a pair of three-day trips—53 miles from Warm Springs to Sherars Falls and another 44 miles to the Columbia River. With more than 100,000 boater days each summer, the Deschutes has plenty of outfitters. Maupin's big four rental companies are **ALL STAR RAFTING AND KAYAKING** (800/909-7238), **DESCHUTES RIVER ADVENTURES** (800/723-8464), **DESCHUTES U-BOAT** (541/395-2503), and **DESCHUTES WHITE WATER SERVICE** (888/324-8837).

Sandy River

One of the most reputable rental outfitters is **RIVER TRAILS CANOE AND RAFT RENTALS** (336 E Historic Columbia River Hwy, Troutdale; 503/667-1964). For

$55 per raft, up to four people can float the relatively calm section of the Sandy from Oxbow Park 7½ miles to Lewis and Clark State Park, or the more challenging 8 miles from Dodge Park to Oxbow Park. In May and June, more confident rafters can run the longer section that starts 11½ miles from Dodge Park at Marmot Dam; designated an Oregon Scenic Waterway, it features Class III rapids.

White Salmon River

ZOLLER'S OUTDOOR ODYSSEYS (1248 Hwy 141, White Salmon; 509/493-2641 or 800/366-2004) offers guided day trips on the White Salmon River, which enters the Columbia River across from Hood River off Hwy 14, less than a two-hour drive east of Portland. From April to October, the company makes up to five three-hour runs per day down the White Salmon, a federal Wild and Scenic River. Fed by springs, the river has Class II, III, and IV rapids. Prices start at $60 per person; call for reservations. The Klickitat, the next river to the east, is primarily run by rafters with their own gear or with a fishing guide during the steelhead season.

ROLLER AND IN-LINE SKATING/SKATEBOARDING

Remember when skates buckled over your shoes and off you went down the road? These days, roller skating has been joined by roller hockey, in-line skating, and "aggressive skating"—the name given to the actions of those amazing kids who skateboard down railings, catching some serious air and (miraculously) landing back on their boards. In Portland, most action of this sort takes place beneath the east side of the Burnside Bridge, which is pretty much maintained and monitored by those who skate there. Two park districts have also created places to ride. The **TUALATIN HILLS SKATEBOARD PARK** (off NW Blueridge Dr at NW 158th Ave and Walker Rd, Beaverton) is part of the Tualatin Hills Park and Recreation District (503/645-6433). The **CITY OF TUALATIN SKATEBOARD PARK** (SW Tualatin Rd and Boones Ferry Rd; 503/691-3061; map:NN9) is part of the Tualatin Community Park.

For up-to-date information on the best half-pipes, skate parks, and roller hockey leagues, try **CAL SKATE** (210 NW 6th Ave, Chinatown; 503/248-0495; map:K6). In-line skaters who long for open skies have a few options from which to choose in Portland: Gov. Tom McCall Waterfront Park (see Top 20 Attractions in the Exploring chapter), Springwater Corridor (the paved sections along the Willamette River and in Gresham; see the Bicycling section in this chapter), and the bike pathway along I-205.

Oaks Amusement Park

FOOT OF SE SPOKANE ST, NORTH OF SELLWOOD BRIDGE ON THE EAST RIVERBANK, SELLWOOD; 503/236-5722 The Northwest's largest roller-skating rink stays open year-round: its floor is designed so that it can be cut away from the wall to float atop rainwater. A DJ rocks the rollers Friday through Sunday nights, and a giant Wurlitzer pipe organ entertains the rest of the time (the rink is closed most Mondays). A full session costs $5. The rink is available for private parties; call ahead. *Map:II5*

Skate World

1220 NE KELLY AVE, GRESHAM; 503/667-6543 / 4395 SE WITCH HAZEL RD, HILL-SBORO; 503/640-1333 Skate World describes itself as a "clean, family-oriented, modern skate center," and the rinks welcome all sorts of patrons and parties. Public sessions cost $4 to $4.75, plus $1 rental.

ROWING

The Willamette is to Portland what the Charles is to Boston. When the weather is good, it's best to get on the water at sunrise; later in the day, barges and motorboats turn smooth water to chop. Most rowing takes place between the Sellwood and Fremont Bridges, and boathouses on this stretch of water are at a premium. **OREGON ROWING UNLIMITED** (503/233-9426) offers youth programs, coaching, and rack space at Oaks Park. For lessons, check with **LAKE OSWEGO COMMUNITY ROWING** (503/699-7458); for sculling lessons, try **RIVERPLACE MARINA** (503/221-1212, ext. 309).

RUNNING/WALKING

Regardless of the weather, Portlanders like to run . . . a lot. This is, after all, the home of Nike. And those who don't run, walk. The **OREGON ROADRUNNERS CLUB** (4840 SW Western Ave, Ste 200, Beaverton; 503/646-7867) is the premier running/walking club in the Northwest with 1,300 active members ($30 per year for individuals, $40 per family). The club coordinates spring and summer running programs for youths, sponsors running clinics, and publishes a magazine and newsletter. The ORRC also puts on a dozen local races, including the Thanksgiving Turkey Trot at the Oregon Zoo. The annual **PORTLAND MARATHON** (www .portlandmarathon.org and www.teamoregon.com) is held each year in late September or early October. Training clinics (free and fee-based) are held year-round, although the pace picks up in the spring and summer.

Council Crest Park

TOP OF MARQUAM HILL, SOUTHWEST OF DOWNTOWN SW Hewett, Humphrey, and Fairmount Boulevards form a figure eight to the west of this park, creating one of the more popular recreation paths in the city. People walk, run, cycle, even rollerski here. The most heavily used portion is 3½ miles along SW Fairmount Boulevard, which circles Council Crest Park and is a moderately hilly course that on a clear day overlooks virtually everything from the Willamette Valley to Mount St. Helens. Take SW Hewett Boulevard to avoid the busier Humphrey Boulevard during rush hour, making, in fact, a figure nine. *Map:II7*

Duniway Park and Terwilliger Boulevard

NORTH END OF SW TERWILLIGER BLVD TO BARBUR BLVD AND I-5 Runners have worn grooves into the lanes of the Duniway track, which now holds water like a drainage ditch. Up one terrace, however, is the quarter-mile sawdust track. The track has certain conveniences—the adjacent YMCA, an exercise and stretching area, public toilets—but parking is not one of them. At 5pm you won't find a space, legal or illegal, for your car in the tiny lot. Terwilliger continues all the way to Lake

Oswego, although few trot that far, due to the hills and hard asphalt surface. *Map: GG6–II6*

Glendoveer Golf Course

14015 NE GLISAN ST, GLENDOVEER; 503/253-7507 The sawdust trail around the circumference of the 36-hole golf course measures 2 miles 95 feet, according to one coach who measured it for his team's workouts. The north and south sides border sometimes busy streets, but the east-end trail curves through a miniature wildlife refuge in woods overrun with well-fed (and fearless) rabbits. *Open daylight hours; Map:FF1*

Gov. Tom McCall Waterfront Park and Willamette Park

WEST BANK OF THE WILLAMETTE RIVER, STRETCHING 3¼ MILES SOUTH FROM THE BROADWAY BRIDGE Noontime runners flock to the promenade in what's considered by many to be the city's front yard. It runs only 1¾ miles north from RiverPlace; to the south, however (after a brief interruption), the path reappears along the river to Willamette Park, making a round-trip of 6½ miles. *Map:A6–K6*

Greenway Park

SW HALL BLVD AND GREENWAY ST, BEAVERTON A suburban common, Greenway is surrounded by modern commercial and residential developments. The 2½-mile trail follows Fanno Creek to SW Scholls Ferry Road, where the asphalt ribbon doubles back. *Map:HH9*

Laurelhurst Park

SE 39TH AVE BETWEEN ANKENY AND OAK STS, LAURELHURST Once a gully and swamp, Laurelhurst is now a lovely 25-acre parkland where paved and gravel trails crisscross under elegant shade trees, and a pond set amid manicured lawns holds ducks. The mile path rings the park . . . but pay attention to the kids on bikes and roller skates. *Map:FF4*

Leif Erikson Drive/Forest Park

NW THURMAN ST TO GERMANTOWN RD Runners share this road with hikers, dog walkers, and cyclists, but no motorized vehicles. See Bicycling or Hiking (Wildwood Trail) in this chapter. *Map:DD9–FF7*

Mount Tabor Park

SE 60TH AVE AND SALMON ST, MOUNT TABOR The only volcano within city limits in the contiguous 48 states has one of the better eastside views of Portland's West Hills and Mount Hood. Tabor was named in honor of a faraway peak in Biblical Palestine. Asphalt roads loop up the hill; the upper roads are for bikers and walkers only. Dirt trails stretch for 1 to 5 miles. The park has become a focal point for the city's dog-leash laws, leading to increased enforcement but also to more off-leash areas and hours throughout city parks. *Map:GG3*

Powell Butte

SE POWELL BLVD AND 162ND AVE (UNMARKED STREET), SOUTHEAST A hilly 2-mile run on an open butte. See Parks and Beaches in the Exploring chapter. *Map: II1*

YOGA: HOLD THAT POSE

Just a decade ago, yoga studios were unique to Portland and suspect to its conservative populace. Today expensive health clubs, free-standing yoga studios, discount gyms, church clubs, and middle schools offer a variety of yoga classes. These are a few of the studios:

GUDMESTAD YOGA STUDIO (3903 SW Kelly Ave, Ste 210, Corbett; 503/223-8157) offers a variety of yoga styles but focuses tightly on proper alignment. Yoga teachers around the city consider owner Julie Gudmestad's anatomy classes essential to their knowledge.

HOLIDAY'S HEALTH AND FITNESS CENTER (510 SW 3rd, Ste 210, Downtown; 503/224-8611) looks at yoga as serious education. Owner Holiday Johnson has taught yoga for 28 years and founded the Stand On Your Own Two Feet program, targeted at teaching teenage girls self-confidence through body control. Look for a variety of styles and great lunch-hour sessions.

JULIE LAWRENCE YOGA CENTER (1020 SW Taylor, Ste 780, Downtown; 503/227-5524), established in the mid-1970s, focuses exclusively on the Iyengar practice. The studio offers more than 30 classes a week and hosts nationally recognized teachers.

SANCTUARY & CENTER FOR YOGA DHARMA AND HEALING ARTS (4515 SW Corbett Ave, Johns Landing; 503/552-9642) is recognized as one of the finest schools in Portland. Instructor Sarahjoy Marsh is revered in the local yoga community; her classes cover a variety of styles and levels.

YOGA COLLEGE OF INDIA (4831 NE Fremont St, Beaumont; 503/284-0555) is faithful to the Bikram method: a regimen of 26 postures, practiced in a room heated to 104 degrees. Owner Michael Harris hosts the annual citywide yoga championship here, involving students from all yoga disciplines in a friendly competition.

YOGAPADA (532 SE Ankeny St, Buckman; 503/963-8131) turns a serious, focused eye on the business of yoga. Most classes are part of a six-week committed package that helps the student develop a strong self-practice, a study both physically demanding and intensely spiritual.

—Gail Dana

Tryon Creek State Park

11321 SW TERWILLIGER BLVD, 1 MILE OFF HWY 43 IN LAKE OSWEGO; 503/636-9886 Lots of room to stretch out here, with 14 miles of trails. See Parks and Beaches in the Exploring chapter. *Map:KK6*

Tualatin Hills Nature Park

15655 SW MILLIKAN BLVD, BEAVERTON; 503/644-5595 Fortunately, the Tualatin Hills Park and Recreation District has left Saint Mary's Woods virtually untouched since it purchased the 200 acres from the Catholic archdiocese of Portland in the mid-1980s. Deer trails work their way through the woods, but the path (clearly marked) makes a 1-mile loop on the west bank of Beaverton Creek. If it's wet out, the dirt trail is likely to be quite muddy. The new Nature Park Interpretive Center is the focal point of the 1½-mile paved and 3-mile dirt trail system. Westside light-rail stops at the park's north entrance.

SAILING

Scores of speedboats chop up the water on the Willamette River, making a simple summer Sunday sail a fight for survival, especially against the wakeboarders and Jet Skis in the stretch of river just upstream from downtown. And while sailing on the Columbia is certainly pleasant, windsurfing gets more attention on that river these days, mainly upstream from Portland in the Columbia River Gorge. Nevertheless, sailing is a business for the following organizations, which specialize in rentals and instructions.

Island Sailing Club

515 NE TOMAHAWK ISLAND DR, NEAR JANTZEN BEACH; 503/285-7765 This members-only Columbia River club, located east of Jantzen Beach, offers instruction for American Sailing Association certification and rentals (20- to 30-foot crafts). Members are also welcome at the club's two Washington locations. Charters are available. *Year-round; map:CC6*

Portland Sailing Center

3315 NE MARINE DR, NORTH PORTLAND; 503/281-6529 Primarily an American Sailing Association–certified school, the center allows students at all skill levels to practice the particulars of tacking and jibbing on a range of boats. The center also rents to certified parties, when its boats are available, and offers brokered charters far beyond the banks of the Columbia—to Baja or the San Juans, for example. *Every day, 10am–dusk; map:CC4*

Willamette Sailing Club and School

6336 SW BEAVER AVE, JOHNS LANDING; 503/246-5345 The club is a family affair, costing $250 to join and $180 per year. The club-owned school offers adult and youth classes. Most popular are the weekend and Thursday evening classes from May into September and the weeklong, $125 youth session during the summer. *Every day; map:JJ6*

SKIING: CROSS-COUNTRY/SNOWSHOEING

The popularity of cross-country or Nordic skiing has outpaced the availability of new groomed trails, Sno-Parks (designated parking areas), and trail information. Many maps list the popular or marked trail systems, but Klindt Vielbig's guide, *Cross-Country Ski Routes of Oregon's Cascades*, offers a more comprehensive listing. Snowshoeing, which often uses the same locations as cross-country skiing, is booming at Mount Hood, as it is everywhere else with snow. Snowshoers are asked

ON THE RIGHT TRAIL IN URBAN PORTLAND

Like a cyclist on a downhill sprint in the Tour de France, Portland's eastside bike path keeps rolling along—just not quite as quickly as a spin down the Alps. The massive project has taken great strides in recent years, but the missing links are still so very frustrating.

Some history is in order.

Portland jumped on the rails-to-trails bandwagon in the early 1990s by converting an old rail line into a 16-mile bike/pedestrian path called the Springwater Corridor. The paved/hardened-surface trail runs from the inner-eastside neighborhood of Eastmoreland, near Reed College, all the way to the community of Boring in the Clackamas County countryside. The trail is more fun than its end point's name would indicate.

The plan is to link the Springwater Corridor to downtown Portland in stages. Most recently completed—in 2003—was a 4-mile connection between the Hawthorne and Sellwood Bridges along the Willamette River through Oaks Bottom, the city's wildlife-rich wetland refuge.

Immediately prior was the Eastbank Esplanade, an embarrassingly expensive ($30 million) 2-mile concrete loop between the Hawthorne and Steel Bridges. It sometimes floats upon the Willamette River on a 1,000-foot-long, 18-foot-wide walkway, buffered

to walk alongside ski tracks in order to avoid obliterating them. Portland has more than a dozen ski clubs, which have banded together to form the Northwest Ski Club Council (503/243-1332).

Bend Ranger District

180 MILES SOUTHEAST OF PORTLAND; 541/383-4000 Fifteen miles west of Bend on the road to **MOUNT BACHELOR**, the Forest Service's Swampy Lakes trail system has warming huts and exquisitely beautiful (if hilly) terrain. Six more miles up Century Drive is the Sno-Park for Dutchman Flat, a trail system that connects back to Swampy Lakes. Together, the systems are the best-planned web of trails in Oregon. The commercial Nordic Center (541/382-1709 or 800/829-2442; www.mtbachelor.com) at Mount Bachelor is the state's best, with its 56 kilometers of groomed trails.

Mount Hood

55 MILES EAST OF PORTLAND It takes more than looking out the window to assess weather conditions at Mount Hood. Miserable rainy weather in Portland sometimes shrouds excellent Nordic conditions on the mountain. Snow reports can be dialed at the mountain's ski areas (the snow is rarely the same at all three): Timberline (503/222-2211), Mount Hood Meadows (503/227-SNOW), and Skibowl (503/222-BOWL). In Portland, call 800/977-6368 for road conditions. Of the three major downhill ski areas, only **MOUNT HOOD MEADOWS** (off Hwy 35, watch for signs; 503/287-5348 [from Portland] or 503/337-2222; www.skihood.com) has a from highway and railroad noise by vegetative screening and sound-barrier walls.

Since opening in 2001, the esplanade has become Downtown's "in" place to jog, bike, and/or gawk. Besides offering a dynamite view of the skyline, urban designers expect it to help rejuvenate Portland's long-neglected Inner Southeast neighborhoods. In addition, the trail and some adjacent public spaces will help alleviate the city's shortage of outdoor event space.

Key links must be completed, however, before Portland's dedicated bicycle/walking trail runs its full length of 21-3/4 miles from downtown to the southeast edge of the city's urban growth boundary. Eventually, the trail will extend into the Mount Hood National Forest, but that will take several more years.

The trail needs better definition east from the Hawthorne Bridge. But most important, it needs three bridges over Johnson Creek, over McLoughlin Boulevard, and over the main north–south rail line. Another $5 million has been earmarked for the bridges, with completion due in 2006.

Until the bridges are built, parts of the trail are fun to use, but only a committed bike commuter will make the effort to decipher its missing links.

—Terry Richard

Nordic center, featuring 15 kilometers of cross-country and snowshoe trails; when the Nordic trails are groomed, the fee is in the $10 range.

The Portland chapter of the **OREGON NORDIC CLUB** (PO Box 3906, Portland OR 97208; 503/246-0616; www.onc.org) operates the popular weekend Nordic center at **TEACUP LAKE**, on the east side of Hwy 35, across from the Mount Hood Meadows parking lot. The 20 kilometers of groomed trails are open to the public for a small donation. The Nordic Club schedules year-round weekend activities, including hiking, backpacking, and cycling. The Barlow Pass Sno-Park nearby has the highest elevation (4,800 feet) of any Nordic ski-trail system at Mount Hood.

South of Hwy 26, just past the Timberline Lodge turnoff (watch for signs), the **TRILLIUM LAKE BASIN** is especially popular. A local resident grooms the two main areas, Trillium Lake Road and Still Creek Campground Loop, as well as six other trails. For trail information and other Sno-Park areas, check with the **MOUNT HOOD INFORMATION CENTER** (503/622-3360) in Welches, about 45 miles east of Portland.

Santiam Pass

136 MILES SOUTHEAST OF SALEM VIA HWY 20; 503/854-3366 (DETROIT RANGER DISTRICT) OR 541/549-7700 (SISTERS RANGER DISTRICT) The Forest Service trail system at Ray Benson Sno-Park near Hoodoo Ski Area is one of the most extensive in the state, with warming huts (and woodstoves) at the trailhead and beyond.

Southwest Washington

76 MILES EAST OF PORTLAND, 26 MILES NORTH OF CARSON WA; 509/427-3200 (WIND RIVER INFO CENTER) OR 360/247-3900 (MOUNT ST. HELENS HEADQUAR-TERS) Oregon winter parking permits are valid for Sno-Parks in Washington. Along the Upper Wind River the terrain is generally rolling, through heavy clear-cuts and forested areas (20 miles of groomed, well-marked trails; be sure to check whether the road has been plowed). Two areas south of Mount St. Helens are both accessible from Forest Service Road 83. Recommended are the Marble Mountain–Muddy River area and the Ape Caves–McBride Lake–Goat Marsh area. Unmarked roads through gentle, wide-open areas offer extensive views of the volcano.

SKIING: DOWNHILL

Mount Bachelor

21 MILES WEST OF BEND, 180 MILES SOUTHEAST OF PORTLAND VIA HWYS 20 OR 97; 503/382-7888 Oregon's premier winter-sports resort is one of the most highly regarded in the country. Bachelor has runs for skiers of all abilities across nearly 3,700 acres of patrolled terrain. Panoramic views from the apex of the 9,065-foot volcanic peak ogle the Three Sisters Wilderness (thus the name "Bachelor") and, on a clear day, the entire range of the Oregon Cascades from Mount Hood to Crater Lake. Ten lifts serve 21,000 skiers per day from mid-November to Memorial Day, and the mountain offers a 3,365-foot vertical drop. The U.S. Olympic team has trained on Bachelor's uppermost slopes in summer. Adult tickets are $44 to $47. *www.mtbachelor.com*

Mount Hood Meadows

68 MILES EAST OF PORTLAND, OFF HWY 35; 503/287-5438 (FROM PORTLAND) OR 503/337-2222 Located 68 miles east of Portland, Meadows offers the most varied terrain of all Mount Hood ski areas, from wide-open slopes for beginners and novices to plenty of moguls and steep, narrow chutes for the experts. This ski area is big: there are 85 runs, including one that goes on for 3 miles. Lift lines can be long on weekends, but four high-speed express lifts and six double chairs get skiers up the mountain in a hurry. The rope tow is free. The vertical drop is 2,777 feet from a 7,300-foot summit. There are two day lodges, and night skiing is offered Wednesday through Sunday. Adult tickets are $44. Meadows also operates Cooper Spur Mountain Resort, a family ski area with a nearby overnight lodge and restaurant, on the northeast side of Mount Hood. *www.skihood.com*

Mount Hood Skibowl

53 MILES EAST OF PORTLAND, OFF HWY 26 AT GOVERNMENT CAMP; 503/222-2695 With 210 acres under lights, Skibowl is one of America's largest night-skiing areas. It also is the state's lowest-elevation ski area (its base elevation is just 3,500 feet), which means it suffers during seasons with light or late snowfall. The lower bowl suits beginners and intermediates, while the upper bowl is challenging enough to host ski races and draws the region's very best skiers for extreme, steep challenges. Also, a snowboard park includes an in-ground half-pipe for the above-ground hardcore. Facilities include four double chairs and five rope tows. Adults tickets are $25 to $31. The ski area stays busy during summer with its Action Park and concerts. *www.skibowl.com*

Timberline

58 MILES EAST OF PORTLAND VIA HWY 26, FOLLOW THE SIGNS 4 MILES FROM GOVERNMENT CAMP; 503/231-7979 (FROM PORTLAND) OR 503/272-3311 North America's only year-round ski area, with four high-speed quad lifts and triple and double chairs, is focused around the historic 1937 Timberline Lodge (see Mount Hood Loop Highway in the Day Trips chapter), situated at the mountain's 6,000-foot level. In summer, one lift carries diehard skiers up to the Palmer Snowfield at 8,500 feet elevation. Limited night skiing is offered here as well. Adult tickets are $39. *www.timberlinelodge.com*

SWIMMING

Water, water everywhere . . . but Portland Parks and Recreation discourages swimmers from plunging into the Willamette River. Though cleaner than it was a half century ago, the Willamette still has sewer system overflows after rainstorms. The Columbia River, however, has two popular wading areas, at Rooster Rock State Park and at Walton Beach on Sauvie Island (see Parks and Beaches in the Exploring chapter). The Sandy River at Troutdale and the Clackamas River at Gladstone draw crowds on hot summer days, but both are fed by chill mountain water and have been the settings for numerous drownings over the years.

The indoor public pools in the city are busy during the winter. Every year, thousands of children take swimming lessons through Portland Parks and Recreation (503/823-SWIM); the Wilson High School pool (1151 SW Vermont St, Multnomah Village; 503/823-3680) and the Sellwood Pool (7951 SE 7th Ave, Sellwood; 503/823-3679)—both outdoor pools—are among the more popular. Ask about the "Dive-In Movie" presentations—in August 2004, *Finding Nemo*—at these pools.

The largest indoor swim spot is **NORTH CLACKAMAS AQUATIC PARK** (7300 SE Harmony Rd, Milwaukie; 503/650-3483 hotline or 503/557-7873; map:LL4), where there are attractions for all ages. Four-foot waves roll into one pool, and older kids can dare the twister and drop slides. There's a heart-shaped whirlpool for adults and an outdoor sand volleyball court. Admission isn't cheap: $9.99 for adults; $6.99 for ages 9–17; $4.99 for ages 3–8; under age 3 free (less for the lap pool only). Lessons and aquatic exercise programs are available.

Most high schools have pools, but public access is usually limited to the summer months. Both the Mount Hood Community College and Tualatin Hills Aquatics Centers can handle many swimmers (see listings). The following are the better public pools in the area.

Columbia Pool

7701 N CHAUTAUQUA BLVD, NORTH PORTLAND; 503/823-3669 One of Portland's largest indoor pools is actually two 25-yard pools side by side. The shallow one ranges from 1½ to 4 feet deep; the deep pool slopes to 7 feet. Adults (18 and over) $3, children (3–17) $1.75. *Map:DD7* &

A MAJOR-LEAGUE PASSION

For a metropolitan area the size of Portland (1.7 million in four counties, 22nd largest in the country), major-league sports fans don't have much to get excited about. Of course, most Portlanders would rather be participating in sports than watching them, but the same could be said about Seattle, which has three major-league franchises (baseball, basketball, football) compared with Portland's one (basketball).

It's great to live in a city where active sports are king, but cheering for more home teams would add a missing element to Portland's status as a major American city.

Since 1970, Portland's only major-league franchise has been the Trail Blazers of the NBA. The team (players, coaches, peanut vendors) has been absolutely adored most of the time, but it's been a rough ride in recent years. After the early '90s, when a class group of players made the league finals twice but came up short of winning a title, the franchise has fielded more persons of interest to local police departments than to collectors of sports memorabilia. Cynics took to calling them the "Jail Blazers" and other equally unkind names.

The boom was lowered after another recent first-round-and-out elimination from

Dishman Pool

77 NE KNOTT ST, IRVINGTON; 503/823-3673 This indoor public pool's best feature is its 10-person whirlpool. Adults (18 and over) $3, children (3 to 17) $1.75. *Map: FF6* &

Harman Swim Center

7300 SW SCHOLLS FERRY RD, BEAVERTON; 503/643-6681 A hot spot in the Tualatin Hills Park and Recreation District's award-winning swim program, the water's 88 degrees—4 degrees higher than most—make it noticeably warmer than the other pools in the district. Swimming instruction is available for all ages. The pool runs the area's largest water therapy program for disabled or physically limited individuals. Out-of-district walk-in rates are $4 for adults, $3 for teens and children. *Map:HH9* &

Metro Family YMCA

2831 SW BARBUR BLVD, LAIR HILL; 503/294-3366 Its location next to the Duniway Park track and running trail makes the Barbur YMCA extremely popular. (Avoid parking headaches and take one of the many buses that stop here.) The pool is available for lap swimming whenever the YMCA is open, except for a brief period on Tuesdays and Saturdays. A $12 day pass entitles visitors to use the entire facility ($6 for 18 and under). Members of the Southeast and Northeast YMCAs are welcome free anytime. Water step-aerobics and swim lessons are available to members. *Map: A1* &

the season-ending 16-team playoff series. Personnel and attitude on the 12-man active players' roster, plus previously unknown office workers, were the targets of front-office ax wielders. Whether the moves make a difference will be determined over time. Club owners hope Portlanders continue to fill the 21,500-seat Rose Garden Arena, where nearly every game is a sellout.

Meanwhile, as this edition went to press, Portland was actively pursuing a major-league baseball franchise. More specifically, the city was immersed in a competition with several other cities to lure the National League's Montreal Expos, a team with long-standing financial problems in a home market more attuned to ice hockey.

The passion for more pro sports led the Oregon Senate, in August 2003, to approve $150 million in funding for a new baseball stadium, with the money to come from state income taxes levied on the salaries of the team's players and executives. Likely increases in Portland city lodging taxes would offset part of the additional cost of the proposed $350 million stadium. A favored location is the east bank of the Willamette River near the Blazers's Rose Quarter arena.

—Terry Richard

Mount Hood Community College

26000 SE STARK ST, GRESHAM; 503/491-7243 The Aquatics Center runs four pools: an outdoor 50-meter pool (Jun–early Oct) with morning, noon, and evening lap swims; an indoor 25-yard six-lane pool; a very warm (90–92 degrees) 4-foot-deep pool for the physically impaired; and an oft-used hydrotherapy pool. Fee is $4 for adults, or $3 for youths, per visit; annual memberships are available for families ($305) and individuals ($230). Summer passes are also available. &

Mount Scott Community Center

5530 SE 72ND AVE, SOUTHEAST; 503/823-3183 A Portland Parks and Recreation facility, the community center has a 25-yard pool with six lanes. Another play pool has a slide, a lazy river, and a water vortex. Walk-in rates are $3.50 for adults (18–59), $2.75 for teens and seniors, $2.25 for children, and free for kids under 4. *Map:*KK4 &

Oregon City Municipal Swimming Pool

1211 JACKSON ST, OREGON CITY; 503/657-8273 Lap swimming, swimming lessons, and water exercise classes are all available in this 25-meter, six-lane indoor pool. Nonresident walk-in rates are $3.50 for adults, $3.25 for youth and children. *Map:*OO4 &

Southwest Community Center

6820 SW 45TH AVE, MULTNOMAH VILLAGE; 503/823-2840 This attractive Portland Parks and Recreation facility in Gabriel Park has a 25-yard pool with six lanes.

Children have their own pool with a slide and fountain structure. Walk-in prices are $5 for adults (18–59), $3.75 for teens and seniors, $2.75 for children, free for tots under the age of 3. *Map:II8* &

Tualatin Hills Park and Recreation Swim Center

15707 SW WALKER RD, BEAVERTON; 503/645-7454 At 50 meters long, this is Portland's largest enclosed public swimming pool. It's part of a large recreation complex in the Sunset Corridor, where the facilities include covered tennis courts, playing fields, and a running trail. $4 per swim for adults; $3 for children. Memberships and lessons are available. The parks district operates an additional five indoor and two outdoor pools in Washington County. &

TENNIS

Portland is well supplied with public tennis courts. Portland Parks and Recreation has 110 outdoor courts at 40 sites. Washington Park, which has six lit courts above the rose garden—and a waiting line on warm weekends—is a favorite. For a nominal fee, one-hour court reservations can be made May through September for individual outdoor courts at Grant, Portland Tennis Center, and Washington Park. Otherwise it's first come, first served . . . and free.

In addition, the city owns two indoor tennis centers. The excellent **PORTLAND TENNIS CENTER** (324 NE 12th Ave, Buckman; 503/823-3189; map:GG5) was the first municipal indoor court in the western states financed by revenue bonds. It has eight free outdoor courts and four indoor courts ($20 for doubles, $16 for singles per 75-minute session). At **ST. JOHN'S RACQUET CENTER** (7519 N Burlington St, Saint Johns; 503/823-3629; map:DD8), everything is under cover: three indoor tennis courts (same costs as Portland Tennis Center) and the city's only parks-department racquetball courts (there are three; $10 per hour).

Other area **INDOOR COURTS** that are open to the public, though some require more than a day's advance notice, include **GLENDOVEER TENNIS CENTER** (NE 140th Ave and Glisan St, Glendoveer; 503/253-7507; map:FF7); **LAKE OSWEGO INDOOR TENNIS CENTER** (2900 SW Diane Dr, Lake Oswego; 503/635-5550; map: KK6); **TUALATIN HILLS PARKS AND RECREATION DISTRICT TENNIS CENTER** (15707 SW Walker Rd, Beaverton; 503/645-7457); and, across the Columbia, **VANCOUVER TENNIS AND RACQUETBALL CENTER** (5300 E 18th St, Vancouver; 360/696-8123; map:BB5). Weekdays are a better deal.

Here are a few of the better courts in the area (call Portland Parks and Recreation for others; 503/823-2223).

West Side

GABRIEL PARK: SW 45th Ave and Vermont St; map:II8
HILLSIDE: 653 NW Culpepper Terrace; map:GG7

Southeast

COLONEL SUMMERS: SE 20th Ave and Belmont St; map:HH5
KENILWORTH: SE 34th Ave and Holgate Blvd; map:HH4

Northeast

ARGAY: NE 141st Ave and Failing St; map:FF1

U.S. GRANT: NE 33rd Ave and Thompson St; map:FF5

WINDSURFING
See Columbia River Gorge in the Day Trips chapter.

Spectator Sports

Multnomah Greyhound Park

NE 223RD AVE AND GLISAN ST, FAIRVIEW; 503/667-7700 You've seen the Kentucky Derby, right? Well, here dogs run instead of horses; the track is smaller (no race is longer than 770 yards); and instead of a jockey urging the animals on, the greyhounds chase a mechanical rabbit. The season runs from May to October. Admission is free. Children under 12 are allowed during the Sunday matinee. *www.ez2winmgp.com*

Portland Beavers

PGE PARK, 1844 SW MORRISON ST, DOWNTOWN; 503/553-5555 Portland rejoined the Triple A Pacific Coast League for the 2001 season by buying and moving the Albuquerque Dukes as the cornerstone of its revitalization plans for long-established (1926) Civic Stadium, now known as PGE Park. The Dukes are now the Beavers, having assumed the name of previous Portland baseball teams, and the Beavs have a polished place to play ball after a $38.5 million refurbishment. Seating capacity is just over 20,000. The 140-game PCL schedule runs April through September. This league provides a last stop before many players move up to the major leagues; the Beavers are the top farm club of the National League's San Diego Padres. *www.pgepark.com/beavers; map:GG7*

Portland Meadows

1001 N SCHMEER RD, NORTH PORTLAND; 503/285-9144 It's possible to catch live horse racing at the Meadows (Oct into May; call for a schedule), but if the timing isn't right, you can always watch simulcasts of greyhound and horse racing. *www.portlandmeadows.com; map:DD6*

Portland International Raceway

WEST DELTA PARK, 1940 N VICTORY BLVD, NORTH PORTLAND; 503/823-7223 The PIR hosts more than 400 events each year, including the Championship Auto Racing Teams (CART) World Series during the Portland Rose Festival in June. *www.portlandraceway.com*

Portland Timbers

PGE PARK, 1844 SW MORRISON ST, DOWNTOWN; 503/553-5555 A partner of the Beavers, Portland's soccer team is also managed by Metropolitan Sports. The Timbers play a 30-game A League schedule from late April into September. The city loves its soccer and routinely hosts world-caliber games and exhibitions. *www.pgepark.com/timbers; map:GG7*

Portland Trail Blazers

ROSE GARDEN ARENA, ROSE QUARTER (NEAR LLOYD CENTER); 503/231-8000 (SEASON TICKETS), 503/224-4400 (SINGLE TICKETS), OR 503/321-3211 (ROSE QUARTER EVENT HOTLINE) Owned by Paul Allen, one of the country's richest men and a self-avowed basketball nut, the Trail Blazers' long run of playoff appearances ended in 2004. They haven't won an NBA championship since Bill Walton starred here in 1977. Since 1995, the team has played the home half of their 82-game regular-season schedule in the beautiful, 21,500-seat Rose Garden Arena. The season runs from mid-October into May . . . later as playoff success permits. *www.nba.com/blazers/; map:*O7

Portland Winter Hawks

MEMORIAL COLISEUM, ROSE QUARTER (NEAR LLOYD CENTER); 503/238-6366 Tomorrow's National Hockey League players play today in the WHL (Western Hockey League). This developmental league grooms young hockey players for the big time, but the Winter Hawks already think their team is the best. The 72-match season runs from September through March. Some matches are held at the Rose Garden Arena. *www.winterhawks.com; Map:*O7

CONFERENCES, MEETINGS, AND RECEPTIONS

CONFERENCES, MEETINGS, AND RECEPTIONS

Most hotels and many restaurants have private meeting rooms for rent. The following is a list of other rental facilities appropriate for business meetings, private parties, and receptions. Private functions can also be held at the Multnomah County Library (call 503/248-5123 or the branch nearest you to reserve a room), most museums, Portland State University (which has numerous halls, auditoriums, and meeting rooms), and other educational facilities. A good resource, too, is the Portland Oregon Visitors Association (503/275-8355; www.pova.com).

Edgefield

2126 SW HALSEY ST, TROUTDALE; 503/669-8610 The former Multnomah County Poor Farm at Edgefield was acquired by the McMenamin brothers (of brewing fame) in the early 1990s, and they've turned it into a multiuse theme park offering everything from art to beer to wine to fine dining to cheap movies to blues concerts. There are also overnight accommodations. Twelve rooms are available for private functions, the largest of which seats 176 people (225 standing). Ask for the conference packet when you inquire. *www.mcmenamins.com* &

Executive Meeting Center

DOUBLETREE HOTEL PORTLAND–LLOYD CENTER, 1000 NE MULTNOMAH ST; 503/281-6111 Open in March 2004, this 9,000-square-foot facility is specially geared to corporate training seminars. Ten separate meeting rooms, with state-of-the-art sound and lighting, high-speed Internet access, and a fully-staffed business center, are part of the draw; an adjacent ballroom accommodates up to 1,100 guests. *www.executivemeetingcenter.com; map:GG5* &

Jenkins Estate

8005 SW GRABHORN RD, ALOHA; 503/642-3855 An Arts and Crafts–style house, stable, and gatehouse sit on 68 idyllic acres, 33 of which are landscaped and crisscrossed with trails. The general public is just as welcome as estate guests to stroll the grounds; trail maps are available. The gatehouse is perfect for small business meetings, and the main house can accommodate varying numbers of people, depending upon room arrangements. The stable can handle even more guests on its two floors. The old stalls make for great breakout sessions during a meeting or can serve as intimate dining alcoves. Catering by the Jenkins Estate staff can provide breakfast, lunch, and snacks for corporate groups in any of these facilities during the week. Business dinners and appetizer events are also available weekday evenings. Weekends are usually reserved for weddings and social events. Make wedding reservations a year in advance. *www.thprd.org/Facilities/* &

Menucha Retreat and Conference Center

38711 E CROWN POINT HWY, CORBETT; 503/695-2243 Nonprofit religious, cultural, educational, and governmental groups are welcome at this center, perched high on a bluff overlooking the Columbia River. Personal spiritual retreats and family reunions are also welcomed. Part of Portland's First Presbyterian Church, it has a kinder, gentler atmosphere than some of the other conference locales. Trails wind through Menucha's 100 wooded acres, and a swimming pool, volleyball court, and tennis court are available. Lodging and Internet access are available. The home-style cooking with freshly baked bread is a draw, but no alcohol is allowed in the dining room. Mailing address: PO Box 8, Corbett, OR 97019. *www.fpcpdx .org/menucha* &

Montgomery Park

2701 NW VAUGHN ST, NORTHWEST; 503/224-6958 A soaring, nine-story-tall atrium is at the heart of this landmark office building, built in the early 1900s as Montgomery Ward's original West Coast warehouse. Huge glass windows invite the sun (or moon) to shine on weddings, proms, and other private parties of up to 800 standing guests. Beneath the atrium, Don Campbell Hall can accommodate as many as 250 for sit-down dinners, and there are also two small conference/meeting rooms. *www.naitoproperties.com/montgomerypark.asp; map:GG7* &

Oregon Convention Center

777 NE MARTIN LUTHER KING JR BLVD, ROSE QUARTER (NEAR LLOYD CENTER); 503/235-7575 Purposefully recognizable by its twin green towers (glowing when lit from within), this facility just across the river from downtown has 255,000 square feet of open exhibit space with numerous reception, banquet, and meeting rooms. The OCC is huge—it has accommodated as many as 100,000 people at one time, although groups as small as 50 are welcomed as well. A covered parking lot has spaces for 850 cars; a MAX light-rail stop at the front door makes a trip into downtown effortless and free. Or it's a pleasant walk across the Steel Bridge. *www.oregoncc.org; map:N9* &

Oregon Museum of Science and Industry

1945 SE WATER AVE, SOUTHEAST; 503/797-4671 After regular museum hours, this science center offers its facilities for private special events. Offering a marvelous view of the downtown Portland skyline from the east bank of the Willamette River, it can accommodate groups of 50 to 2,500. The five large exhibit halls, filled with hands-on, interactive exhibits, are extremely popular event spaces. There's also an outside courtyard, auditorium, dining room, and smaller meeting rooms. Catering is handled by in-house event planners. Groups may rent the 320-seat Omnimax Theater for private screenings; the 200-seat Murdock Planetarium, with its astronomy and laser light shows; and the USS *Blueback*, a submarine permanently docked on the Willamette. *www.omsi.org; map:HH6* & *(except submarine)*

Pittock Mansion

3229 NW PITTOCK DR, PITTOCK ACRES; 503/823-3623 This Portland landmark leases space during the evening to recognized community groups, commercial and nonprofit alike. In its lofty location high above the city, the mansion can host 50 for a sit-down dinner or 250 for a standing reception; you'll need to hire the caterer. It's a popular locale; reserve a year in advance for the holiday season. The mansion is partially wheelchair accessible. *www.pittockmansion.com; map:HH8*

Portland Conference Center

300 NE MULTNOMAH ST, ROSE QUARTER (NEAR LLOYD CENTER); 503/239-9921 This full-service, privately owned facility welcomes parties of 5 to 500. Twelve rooms—ranging in size from boardroom to ballroom—include stage areas and teleconferencing equipment. Located adjacent to the Oregon Convention Center, it's also convenient to downtown. In-house catering is carried out by a large staff. The Conference Center is partially wheelchair accessible. *www.portlandcc.com; map:N9*

Portland's White House

1914 NE 22ND AVE, IRVINGTON; 503/287-7131 OR 800/272-7131 Weddings and private receptions are popular at this elegant inn, an Irvington mansion built in 1911 for timber baron Robert F. Lytle. The White House features a 1,650-square-foot ballroom with room for 90 dancers, and hosts Lanning Blanks and Steve Holden love to entertain. In the spacious parlor, surrounded by a world-class collection of Meissen porcelain, is a baby grand piano. For stayovers, the White House has nine lovely bed-and-breakfast guest rooms with private baths. *www .portlandswhitehouse.com; map:GG5*

Tryon Creek State Park

11321 SW TERWILLIGER BLVD, 1 MILE OFF HWY 43 IN LAKE OSWEGO; 503/636-9886 A meeting room for up to 50 in the Nature Center at picturesque Tryon Creek is available (for a small charge) for retreats, meetings, and occasional receptions. The lovely setting offers limited facilities. *Map:JJ6*

World Forestry Center

4033 SW CANYON RD, WASHINGTON PARK; 503/228-1367 Three facilities and a large outdoor plaza welcome all kinds of parties, from class reunions to academic conferences. Catering may be arranged from a list of preferred providers. The largest building can accommodate 300 guests; the smallest seats up to 60, classroom-style. This is an exceptionally nice and very popular place. Make wedding reservations at least a year in advance. *www.worldforestry.org; map:HH7* &

World Trade Center

121 SW SALMON ST, DOWNTOWN; 503/464-8688 This private conference facility offers 20,000 square feet of flexible meeting space, with 14 reception rooms and a 225-seat, state-of-the-art auditorium that is unique to downtown Portland. A broad, covered outdoor plaza is ideal for summer evening events. Business meetings, wedding receptions, and other events are fully catered; executive chef Allen Faigin supervised corporate hospitality at the Barcelona Olympics. *www.wtcpd .com; map:G5*

Best Places Portland Report Form

Based on my personal experience, I wish to nominate the following restaurant, place of lodging, shop, nightclub, sight, or other as a "Best Place"; or confirm/correct/disagree with the current review.

_____

_____

_____

(Please include address and telephone number of establishment, if convenient.)

REPORT

Please describe food, service, style, comfort, value, date of visit, and other aspects of your experience; continue on another piece of paper if necessary.

_____

_____

_____

_____

_____

_____

_____

I am not associated, directly or indirectly, with the management or ownership of this establishment.

_____

SIGNED

_____

ADDRESS

_____

_____

_____

PHONE   **DATE**

Please address to Best Places Portland and send to:
SASQUATCH BOOKS
119 SOUTH MAIN STREET, SUITE 400
SEATTLE, WA 98104
Feel free to email feedback as well: **CUSTSERV@SASQUATCHBOOKS.COM**

Best Places Portland Report Form

Based on my personal experience, I wish to nominate the following restaurant, place of lodging, shop, nightclub, sight, or other as a "Best Place"; or confirm/correct/disagree with the current review.

_____

_____

_____

_____

(Please include address and telephone number of establishment, if convenient.)

REPORT

Please describe food, service, style, comfort, value, date of visit, and other aspects of your experience; continue on another piece of paper if necessary.

_____

_____

_____

_____

_____

_____

_____

_____

I am not associated, directly or indirectly, with the management or ownership of this establishment.

_____

SIGNED

_____

ADDRESS

_____

_____

_____

PHONE   **DATE**

Please address to Best Places Portland and send to:
SASQUATCH BOOKS
119 SOUTH MAIN STREET, SUITE 400
SEATTLE, WA 98104
Feel free to email feedback as well: **CUSTSERV@SASQUATCHBOOKS.COM**

We Stand By Our Reviews

Sasquatch Books is proud of *Best Places Portland*. Our editors and contributors go to great lengths and expense to see that all of the restaurant and lodging reviews are as accurate, up-to-date, and honest as possible. If we have disappointed you, please accept our apologies; however, if a recommendation in this 6th edition of *Best Places Portland* has seriously misled you, Sasquatch Books would like to refund your purchase price. To receive your refund:

1. Tell us where and when you purchased your book and return the book and the book-purchase receipt to the address below.
2. Enclose the original restaurant or lodging receipt from the establishment in question, including date of visit.
3. Write a full explanation of your stay or meal and how *Best Places Portland* misled you.
4. Include your name, address, and phone number.

Refund is valid only while this 6th edition of *Best Places Portland* is in print. If the ownership, management, or chef has changed since publication, Sasquatch Books cannot be held responsible. Tax and postage on the returned book is your responsibility. Please allow six to eight weeks for processing.

Please address to Satisfaction Guaranteed, *Best Places Portland*, and send to:
Sasquatch Books
119 South Main Street, Suite 400
Seattle, WA 98104

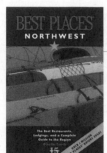